LEGALITY IN EUROPE

LEGALITY IN EUROPE

On the principle *nullum crimen, nulla poena sine lege* in EU law and under the ECHR

Mikhel Timmerman

intersentia
Cambridge – Antwerp – Portland

Intersentia Ltd
Sheraton House | Castle Park
Cambridge | CB3 0AX | United Kingdom
Tel.: +44 1223 370 170 | Fax: +44 1223 370 169
Email: mail@intersentia.co.uk
www.intersentia.com | www.intersentia.co.uk

Distribution for the UK and Ireland:
NBN International
Airport Business Centre, 10 Thornbury Road
Plymouth, PL6 7 PP
United Kingdom
Tel.: +44 1752 202 301 | Fax: +44 1752 202 331
Email: orders@nbninternational.com

Distribution for Europe and all other countries:
Intersentia Publishing nv
Groenstraat 31
2640 Mortsel
Belgium
Tel.: +32 3 680 15 50 | Fax: +32 3 658 71 21
Email: mail@intersentia.be

Distribution for the USA and Canada:
International Specialized Book Services
920 NE 58th Ave. Suite 300
Portland, OR 97213
USA
Tel.: +1 800 944 6190 (toll free) | Fax: +1 503 280 8832
Email: info@isbs.com

Legality in Europe. On the principle *nullum crimen, nulla poena sine lege* in EU law and under the ECH

ISBN 978-1-78068-304-1 (paperback)
ISBN 978-1-78068-682-0 (PDF)
D/2018/7849/54
NUR 828

British Library Cataloguing in Publication Data. A catalogue record for this book is available from the British Library.

ACKNOWLEDGMENTS

Although perhaps the best theses result from a continuous focus on the research, I feel fortunate to describe my Ph.D. experience as one of constant change and distraction. The very commencement of the research project that culminated in this monograph was, in fact, a result of major change. After having worked with great pleasure at the Criminal Law Department of the Radboud University's Law Faculty, I managed to acquire a fulltime research position at the European University Institute. Taking up this position not only meant changing the focus of my research from Dutch criminal law to EU and ECHR law, it also meant moving from Nijmegen in The Netherlands to Florence in Italy. Adapting to life and work in a foreign culture provided not just the aforementioned change, it also brought about many – welcome – distractions from the research that enriched me, both as a person and as a researcher.

I am very grateful to have worked in the great and beautiful international (research) environment of the EUI, where I have met – and lived together with – several kind and interesting people from different nationalities. I am equally thankful to have written my thesis under the supervision of prof. Bruno de Witte. I have especially appreciated Bruno's approach to view every draft in relation to the project as a whole and to ensure that I would not wander too far from the central aim of the research. The thesis has also benefited significantly from Bruno's broad expertise in EU law and his specialist knowledge of the relationship between the law of the ECHR and Union law.

While – among many things – the surroundings and the food culture improved significantly when I moved to Florence in September 2013, several aspects of my life fortunately remained unaltered. Conducting research on the legality principle, for example, meant that the field of criminal law would remain a key research interest for my thesis. By adding the criminal law aspect to the EU and ECHR perspective of the thesis, I was happy to learn that Prof. Piet Hein van Kempen, as an expert in – especially – the interaction between these three legal fields, accepted the invitation to remain involved with my project. I am very grateful to Piet Hein for encouraging me to accept the position at the EUI (or, in other words, for getting rid of me as a staff member). In addition, I am thankful for his willingness to continue to supervise my thesis although it was no longer conducted at 'his' Radboud University, and – perhaps most importantly – for his meticulous comments and feedback on draft chapters that were always merely presented as an encouragement to improve the work.

Another aspect of my life that I was pleased to learn did not suffer from my move to Florence is the relationship with my former colleagues at the Radboud University. Being able to continue to lecture in EU criminal law in Nijmegen meant that I would have regular meetings with my former colleagues, both formally and informally. I have much appreciated being included in discussions about Dutch criminal law over the years, when my focus was more on the supranational law. I hope that we will continue to see each other as regularly as we have set out to, in Nijmegen or elsewhere.

What is true for my former colleagues, is even more true for my friends and family. I am happy to ascertain that we have seen each other regularly over the years, even when I was living abroad. I am especially glad that we have mostly got to share the key celebratory moments, the family holidays and the rest of the regularly returning highlights, such as: Sinterklaas at the Van Rossum's, the weekend or single-day trips with friends and family, the yearly expeditions to Berlin, the summer festivals, but also the more frequent dinners, drinks, runs and bike rides. While my life as a Ph.D. researcher at a foreign institute was not easy to relate to for all of you with 'real' jobs, I have appreciated your continuous interest in the progress of the research. Your involvement is not just evidenced by the fact that you have previously visited me in Florence, but also by the fact that so many of you have made it to my thesis defence.

A special word of thanks goes to my mother. Carla, I am thankful for the many trips to and from Eindhoven airport over the years, for your design of the cover of this book and, most importantly, for giving me the gift of a happy and care-free childhood which – as a single mother – cannot have been an easy task.

Although there is much to be thankful for when looking back at the past few years as a researcher, I am most thankful for having been able to share the whole experience with Marloes. Marloes, you are the only person that both helped me make the decision to move to Florence and provided the incentive to move back to Nijmegen. I am grateful to have traveled all over Italy with you and to have experienced life in Florence together. I have also highly appreciated your much needed feedback and encouragement over the years, especially during the time when I was mainly working from home and was missing the regular discussions with colleagues. Thank you for all your love and support!

After a year in which I completed my thesis while becoming a father to our wonderful Len and starting a new job as judicial assistant at the Supreme Court of The Netherlands, I look forward to more steady times ahead (with a bit more sleep). While I am happy to conclude that my time as a researcher was one of constant change and distraction, I hope that the coming years will be so to a lesser extent. Whether that wish comes true or not, I cannot wait to start the post-thesis chapter in our life together as a family. There are great times ahead!

Mikhel Timmerman

CONTENTS

CHAPTER 1
INTRODUCTION

1.0 A VERY SHORT INTRODUCTION

The establishment of European Union criminal law as a legal field entails the novel situation in which EU actors influence the definition and interpretation of domestic crimes and penalties. Both the EU legislature and the CJEU define and interpret provisions of EU law with relevance for the determination of criminal liability and the prescription of the applicable penalties in the law of the Member States. The influence on definitions and interpretations of substantive criminal law raises questions about the limits to these legislative and interpretive activities. Requirements for the definition, interpretation, and application of substantive criminal law are traditionally provided by the principle *nullum crimen, nulla poena sine lege*. The present thesis examines and compares the actual constructions of the supranational European legality principles; ie the legality principles protected under the ECHR and in EU law. The ultimate aim is to determine whether the present construction of the EU legality principle is appropriate in light of the characteristics of the novel field of EU criminal law in which EU definitions and interpretations interact with domestic definitions and interpretations of crimes and penalties.

1.1 OBJECT OF THE RESEARCH

1.1.1 THE LEGALITY PRINCIPLE

The legality principle in criminal law is commonly referred to as the principle *nullum crimen, nulla poena sine lege*.[1] The principle's Latin formulation indicates its relevance for both offenses (*crimen*) and penalties (*poena*). The *nullum crimen* principle essentially requires that a clear legal basis determines criminal liability for

1 See, eg, Boot 2002, p. 81; Claes 2003, p. 15; Antolisei and Conti 2003, p. 66; Westen 2007, p. 231; Dreyer 2012, p. 170; Ashworth and Horder 2013, p. 57; Pradel 2014, p. 114; Bernardini 2015, p. 167; Peristeridou 2015, p. 79. P.J.A. von Feuerbach is credited for having first used this Latin formulation in his *Lehrbuch des gemeinen in Deutschland gültigen peinlichen Rechts*, see Von Feuerbach 1801, para 20. Cf Schünemann 1978, p. 3; Krey 1983, p. 18–19; Boot 2002, p. 84.

certain behavior prior to the occurrence of that behavior.[2] It places demands on the definition, interpretation, and application of the relevant legal basis. The *nulla poena* principle additionally requires that the applicable penalties for the criminally liable behavior are clearly established at the time of the accused's acts. As with the *nullum crimen* principle, *nulla poena* demands both the clear definition, interpretation, and application of the relevant legal bases that establish the applicable penalties.

The legality principle – as described in a basic manner above – is broadly supported across Europe, and, as some argue, it has even gained worldwide recognition as a rule of customary international law.[3] The principle is, in any event, deemed to have emerged from a rather univocal historical and theoretical background. A broad consensus does, in fact, credit theories formulated by both philosophers in England and on the European continent as the root of legality.[4]

That broad support exists for the legality principle is illustrated by how the principle is presently accepted in European states with divergent legal traditions. The legality principle's relevance and significance is not only recognized in states with a civil law tradition. It is also increasingly recognized in common law states.[5] This latter development is particularly noteworthy in light of how the legality principle's applicability has been traditionally rejected in the common law tradition.[6]

In accordance with European theory on the legality principle, this thesis distinguishes four secondary principles as relevant elements of legality.[7] These elements are: the principle that only legislation can define offenses and penalties (hereinafter also: 'the *lex scripta* principle' or '*lex scripta*'), the principle that offenses and penalties require a clear legal definition (hereinafter also: 'the *lex certa* principle' or '*lex certa*'), the prohibition on the overly extensive interpretation of offenses and penalties (hereinafter also: 'the *lex stricta* principle' or '*lex stricta*'), and the prohibition on the retroactive[8] application of the definitions of offenses and penalties (hereinafter also: 'the *lex praevia* principle' or '*lex praevia*').

---

2 Cf Claes and Krolikowski 2009, p. 89; Pradel 2014, p. 136–139; Peristeridou 2015, p. 6; Pin 2016, p. 20.

3 See Gallant 2009, p. 352, 378, 404. Cf Schabas 2015, p. 328. This is still very much debated, however, see Kadelbach 2006, p. 723.

4 See section 2.2.

5 See Claes and Krolikowski 2009, p. 97–99; Peristeridou 2011, p. 74–75; Peristeridou 2015, p. 65, 79, 126. Some authors remain skeptical about the applicability of the legality principle in common law legal systems, see Jefferson 2015, p. 5–8.

6 See Forster 2008, p. 30; Ashworth and Horder 2013, p. 48, 57; Peristeridou 2015, p. 67, 71. At the same time, however, common law countries generally acknowledged the need for the adoption of a protective principle that offered equivalent protection, see Forster 2008, p. 29; Claes and Krolikowski 2009, p. 89–90; Ashworth and Horder 2013, p. 56–71; Peristeridou 2015, p. 67, 69, 71.

7 See further subsection 2.3.1.

8 This prohibition is sometimes referred to as a prohibition on *retrospective* application, but it is more accurate to exclusively use the term retroactive application for the criminal law that operates at a time prior to its enactment, see Juratowitch 2008, p. 6–9.

The principle of the retroactive application of more lenient offenses and penalties, the so-called *lex mitior* principle, is sometimes related to the legality principle as well.[9] Traditionally, however, *lex mitior* has not been viewed as an element of the principle *nullum crimen, nulla poena sine lege*.[10] Since this thesis takes modern criminal law theory as a point of departure, the *lex mitior* principle will be excluded from the scope of the present research.[11] Hereinafter, the sole focus will be on the four above-mentioned elements in relation to both the *nullum crimen* principle and the *nulla poena* principle.[12]

The four distinct elements indicate that the legality principle sets limits to the definition, interpretation, and application of offenses and penalties. For that reason, the principle is not just relevant for actors who usually define offenses and penalties such as the legislature, but also for actors who generally interpret and apply offenses and penalties such as the judiciary. While the legality principle is clearly relevant for the legislature and judiciary since it unmistakably restricts the available room for definition, interpretation, and application of criminal law, it is not self-evident what these restrictions entail exactly.[13] The exact limits provided by the principle's elements are ultimately dependent on the value(s) they are deemed to protect.

This thesis departs from the historical recognition of legality as a prohibition on arbitrariness. It connects this historical aim to the value of legal certainty and the notion of the rule of law. This first identification of the principle's potential rationale(s) will then be complemented by the examination of two other notions: the doctrine of the separation of powers and the principle of democracy.[14] Further notions, such as the principle of guilt and the value of crime prevention, will not be examined in this thesis. Although these notions have sometimes been deemed to constitute rationales for the legality principle,[15] these views are not

---

9 This is done explicitly in Article 49(1) Charter of Fundamental Rights of the European Union, last sentence and, perhaps consequently, it has been interpreted as enshrined in Article 7 European Convention on Human Rights and Fundamental Freedoms as well by the ECtHR's judgment in *Scoppola v. Italy (No. 2)*, CE:ECHR:2012:0522JUD000012605, para 108.

10 See Peristeridou 2015, p. 16; Altena-Davidsen 2016, p. 2–3, 14, 33. See also partly dissenting opinion of judges Nicolaou, Bratza, Lorentzen, Jočienė, Villiger and Sajó in ECtHR, *Scoppola v. Italy (No. 2)*, CE:ECHR:2012:0522JUD000012605.

11 Peristeridou has also excluded *lex mitior* from the scope of her research, see Peristeridou 2015, p. 16. Conversely, Altena-Davidsen examined *lex mitior*, see p. 303–366.

12 Unlike recent monographs on the EU legality principle, this research will not be limited to the *nullum crimen* principle, see Peristeridou 2015, p. 15; Altena-Davidsen 2016, p. 13–14. It includes an examination of the legality principle's requirements for the definition, interpretation, and application of criminal *penalties* (ie the *nulla poena* principle).

13 The legality principle's potential relevance for the executive branch will not be examined hereinafter, cf Peristeridou 2015, p. 15–16; Altena-Davidsen 2016, p. 12.

14 See subsection 2.4.3.

15 With regard to the principle of guilt, see Schreiber 1976, p. 209–210; Groenhuijsen 1987, p. 26; Westen 2007, p. 303–305; De Hullu 2015, p. 86. With regard to the value of crime prevention, see Beccaria 1764, Ch. 41, p. 104; Von Feuerbach 1801, para 20. Cf Boot 2002, p. 84–85; Lelieur, Pfützner and Volz 2008, p. 41; Gallant 2009, p. 26; Borgers 2011, p. 106; Peristeridou 2015, p. 40–41.

generally accepted.[16] Therefore, and in accordance with recent monographs on the EU legality principle,[17] the present research will not view the principle of guilt and the value of crime prevention as rationales for the legality principle.[18]

Although widely recognized and generally considered significant, the legality principle is not axiomatic and uniform. Its scope, content and rationales have been given distinct interpretations by legal actors within different legal traditions and, of course, in legal theory. Naturally, different interpretations have also occurred at different points in history. In criminal law theory in Europe, there still exist substantially different views on the rationale(s) behind the legality principle, the exact elements it enshrines, and the substantive content of these elements. These differences, which are ultimately attributable to the theoretical distinction between the civil law and the common law conception of legality, are examined in detail in chapter 2. For present purposes, it suffices to underline that, while a large consensus exists about the general relevance of the legality principle and its basic content, the principle's exact substance and rationale(s) remain subject to disagreement.

1.1.2 LEGALITY AS A EUROPEAN FUNDAMENTAL RIGHT

As a supranational fundamental right in Europe, the legality principle is presently protected under the European Convention on Human Rights and Fundamental Freedoms (hereinafter also: 'the ECHR' or 'the Convention') and in European Union law (hereinafter also: 'EU law' or 'Union law').[19] The ECHR legality principle is enshrined in Article 7, which reads:

---

16 Several writers have, for example, argued that the principle of guilt is better viewed as a notion that is closely related to the legality principle rather than as its theoretical foundation, see, eg, Husak and Von Hirsch 1993, p. 166; Ashworth and Horder 2013, p. 56–57; Dubber 2013, p. 384; Peristeridou 2015, p. 62–63. Cf Schünemann 1978, p. 15; Nan 2011, p. 79. Crime prevention is also not recognized at present as a rationale for the legality principle. The relationship between crime prevention and the legality principle rather appears to have resulted from an exaggerated believe in the deterrent function of criminal law by the theorists that first formulated the legality principle, see Schreiber 1976, p. 216; Gallant 2009, p. 26–28; Dubber 2013, p. 381–382; Peristeridou 2015, p. 40–41. Cf Schünemann 1978, p. 11–14. Even if prevention did constitute a sound rationale for legality it would have to be left outside the scope of the present research, because the preventive effect of, for example, clearly formulated and published criminal law would be impossible to measure using legal research methods, cf Altena-Davidsen 2016, p. 39.

17 See Peristeridou 2015, p. 40–41, 62–63; Altena-Davidsen 2016, p. 38–39.

18 The fact that, in two judgments, the ECtHR deemed the principle of guilt to be inherent in Article 7 ECHR is due to the fact that the Convention lacks a self-standing principle of guilt. This characteristic forced the ECtHR to point to notions such as 'guilty' enshrined in Article 7 to protect individuals against, for example, the conviction for acts committed by another person. See *Sud Fondi SRL and Others v. Italy*, CE:ECHR:2009:0120JUD007590901, paras 116–117; *Varvara v. Italy*, CE:ECHR:2013:1029JUD001747509, paras 69, 71. See further subsections 3.4.2; 3.7.5.

19 The term EU law is generally used to refer to European Community law, or, simply, 'Community law' or 'EC law', as well. Specific references to EC law are only made when it is necessary to employ the historical distinction between EU law and EC law, see, for example, section 5.2.

> "1. No one shall be held guilty of any criminal offence on account of any act or omission which did not constitute a criminal offence under national or international law at the time when it was committed. Nor shall a heavier penalty be imposed than the one that was applicable at the time the criminal offence was committed.
> 2. This Article shall not prejudice the trial and punishment of any person for any act or omission which, at the time when it was committed, was criminal according to the general principles of law recognised by civilised nations."

In EU law, the legality principle is, inter alia, enshrined in Article 49 Charter of Fundamental Rights of the European Union (hereinafter: 'the Charter' or 'the CFR'), which contains the following definition:

> "1. No one shall be held guilty of any criminal offence on account of any act or omission which did not constitute a criminal offence under national law or international law at the time when it was committed. Nor shall a heavier penalty be imposed than the one that was applicable at the time the criminal offence was committed. If, subsequent to the commission of a criminal offence, the law provides for a lighter penalty, that penalty shall be applicable.
> 2. This Article shall not prejudice the trial and punishment of any person for any act or omission which, at the time when it was committed, was criminal according to the general principles recognized by the community of nations. (...)".[20]

Article 49 CFR is not the only EU source of the legality principle, however. Before the Charter's entry into force, the principle was, in fact, recognized as an EU fundamental right in the case-law of the Court of Justice of the European Union (hereinafter: 'the CJEU' or 'the Luxembourg Court'). As is generally the case with EU fundamental rights, multiple sources become relevant for the EU legality principle and its interpretation. This is clearly apparent in Article 6 Treaty on European Union (hereinafter: TEU).[21]

The Convention is the obvious point of departure for this research, since it sets a minimum standard that the ECHR signatories have to protect. That minimum standard has not only influenced the legal systems of the individual EU Member States, but it has also been directly relevant for EU law. As Article 6(3) TEU indicates, the ECHR is relevant for (the interpretation of) fundamental rights as general principles of Union law. Moreover, Article 7 ECHR and the case-law of the European Court of Human Rights (hereinafter: 'the ECtHR' or 'the Strasbourg Court') have also been deemed influential for the interpretation of the Charter's

---

20 Article 49(1) and (2) CFR. Article 49(3) Charter enshrines the distinct principle that penalties must not be disproportionate to the criminal offense.

21 As established by the Treaty of Lisbon amending the Treaty on European Union and the Treaty establishing the European Community, [2007] OJ C 306. References to the EU Treaty will hereinafter indicate the provisions in the Consolidated version of the Treaty on European Union, [2012] OJ C 326 (unless expressly indicated that an earlier version of the EU treaty is referred to). About Article 6 TEU see chapter 5, especially subsection 5.7.2.

legality principle.[22] The ECHR's relevance for EU law could increase even further if the Union accedes to the Convention as Article 6(2) TEU stipulates.[23]

The Convention's potential relevance for the EU legality principle has not always been as noticeable as it is today. In fact, the recognition of Article 7 ECHR's relevance, or of a self-standing EU legality principle, did not generally occur until after the Maastricht Treaty.[24] This was because, for a long time, the EU seemed to have nothing to do with the field of criminal law. Due to this generally accepted point of departure, the first limited influence of supranational Union law on national criminal law was heavily contested.[25] The consensus on the desirability of keeping criminal law beyond the reach of EU law shaped the historical development of EU competences in the field of criminal law. This past consensus, in turn, limited the possibility to recognize, explicitly, a criminal law principle such as legality under EU law. The specific characteristics of early EU law arguably provided an incentive for the CJEU to protect elements of the legality principle under distinct, more general, legal principles such as the principle of legal certainty and the principle that penalties must have a proper legal basis. As a result of these historical specificities, this thesis has to examine the aforementioned EU principles of administrative law to explain their relationship with the Union legality principle. To this extent, the present research goes beyond the EU legality principle *sensu stricto*.

The multiplicity of sources relevant for the legality principle, its interpretation in EU law, its specific historical development, and the relevance of related principles of administrative law, make it rather difficult to determine the exact content and rationale(s) of the Union legality principle. The EU legality principle will therefore require detailed examination. However, in light of the Convention's function as a minimum standard for EU Member States and the ECHR's relevance for the interpretation of EU fundamental rights, the analysis of the Convention's legality principle cannot be brief. While the ultimate goal will be to analyze the EU legality principle, an exhaustive examination of the Convention's legality principle constitutes a necessary, and welcome, by-product of this research.

1.1.3 LEGALITY AND ITS ROLE IN MULTILEVEL EU CRIMINAL LAW

The focus on the EU legality principle is not only warranted due to the specificities of how Union law came to influence national criminal law and EU fundamental

---

22 See Article 52(3) CFR and the Explanations on Article 52 CFR, see Explanations relating to the Charter of Fundamental Rights, [2007] OJ C303/02. See further subsection 5.5.4.

23 Accession is nevertheless far away due to *Opinion 2/13 on the Accession of the European Union to the European Convention for the Protection of Human Rights and Fundamental Freedoms*, EU:C:2014:2454.

24 Treaty on European Union (Maastricht Treaty), [1992] OJ C 191. On the historical development of EU criminal law, see chapter 5.

25 This is strictly speaking the influence of supranational EC law, see further section 5.2.

rights protection. It is additionally justified by the specificities of the field that can be labeled as 'EU criminal law'. The most significant specificities among these are immediately visible when we consider the opening remarks of Klip's influential book on European criminal law. Klip introduces the field in the following way:

> "European criminal law deals with a multi-layered patchwork of legislation and case law in which both European and national courts, European and national legislatures, and other authorities and bodies play a role. It is a hybrid system, even though it does possess some common notions and values, which therefore justifies its classification as a separate field of law".[26]

And later, Klip defines European criminal law as:

> "(...) the multilevel field of law in which the European Union has normative influence on either substantive criminal law / criminal procedure, or on the co-operation between the Member States".[27]

Klip's formulations illustrate that EU criminal law constitutes a multilevel and multi-layered field of law in which EU law and its actors influence, inter alia, substantive criminal law. The influence on substantive criminal law includes the obligation to prescribe criminal liability and/or criminal penalties for specific conduct. Most notable in this regard are the competences to harmonize/approximate[28] substantive criminal law enshrined in Article 83 Treaty on the Functioning of the European Union (hereinafter: TFEU).[29] EU law thus allows, encourages and requires the Member States to adopt measures that are detrimental to individuals.

Despite the EU's limited competence to approximate national criminal laws under the conditions enshrined in Article 83(1) and 83(2) TFEU, Member States have prescribed criminal penalties for the violation of EU law in many other situations. For that reason, protective principles of criminal law such as legality acquire an importance that goes beyond the harmonization of substantive criminal law based on Article 83 TFEU. The room for implementation of non-criminal EU law via domestic criminal law makes the potential relevance of the EU legality principle rather extensive. This is aptly illustrated by the fact that

---

26 Klip 2016, p. 1.

27 Klip 2016, p. 2.

28 I will use the terms 'harmonization' and 'approximation' of substantive criminal law interchangeably in order to refer to the EU's competence to require Member States to criminalize conduct, and to prescribe certain criminal penalties, in their national laws. Klip has observed that the terms harmonization and approximation have been used interchangeably in EU legislation, see Klip 2016, p. 34–35. The term approximation is nevertheless used in the Treaties, see Article 83(2) TFEU.

29 References to the Treaty on the Functioning of the European Union will be to the Consolidated version of the Treaty on the Functioning of the European Union, [2012] OJ C 326.

internal market law has indeed given rise to many CJEU considerations on the legality principle.[30]

The large potential relevance of the EU legality principle is a result of the specific way in which Union definitions and interpretations influence the definition and interpretation of implementing criminal law.[31] When an EU definition is implemented via national criminal law, there are two relevant definitions that originate from two different actors: the EU definition enacted by the Union actor(s) and the national definition enacted by the national legislature. A similar situation occurs with regard to interpretation of these definitions. The EU definition is ultimately interpreted by the CJEU, while the national courts are competent to interpret and apply the definitions in implementing criminal law. Unlike the traditional situation where the definition, interpretation, and application of crimes and penalties occur within a single state, in EU law, definitions and interpretations of criminal law are necessarily multilevel. It is this characteristic that led to Klip's definition of EU criminal law as a 'multi-layered patchwork of legislation and case-law'.

That EU criminal law entails the multilevel definition and interpretation of offenses and penalties requires additional reflection on the operation of the legality principle's protective function in such a situation.[32] The present research ultimately aims to determine whether a specific theoretical conception of legality, and/or the ECHR's construction of the legality principle, is appropriate for EU criminal law with its *sui generis* character. The appropriateness of a specific construction of legality will be determined by reflecting on the characteristics of EU criminal law and how they affect the protection of legal certainty.

In addition to the multilevel definition and interpretation of offenses and penalties in EU criminal law, the Union legality principle is also relevant for administrative sanctions imposed by EU institutions. The EU legality principle is presently understood as applicable to measures deemed 'administrative' from the EU perspective. The most notable are fines for competition law infringements and 'restrictive measures' imposed on suspected terrorists.[33] These measures are relevant for the Union legality principle due to their quasi-criminal character.[34]

In light of the relevance of criminal law principles for EU administrative measures, the field of EU criminal law can be defined broadly. Alongside Klip, I will consider EU criminal law to encompass certain administrative measures and thus include EU competition law within the object of the research.[35] The

30 See further chapter 4.

31 See further section 5.6.

32 Cf Peristeridou 2015, p. 10; Altena-Davidsen 2016, p. 3.

33 See further chapter 4.

34 Cf Herlin-Karnell 2016, p. 244.

35 See Klip 2016, p. 2–3. See, conversely, Altena-Davidsen 2016, p. 11. An important reason for bringing competition law within the scope of this research is that CJEU judgments outside the field of competition law do refer to legality(-related) considerations made by the CJEU

present research then does not only go beyond the EU legality principle *sensu stricto*, it also has to go beyond the area of criminal law *sensu stricto*. In addition to the aforementioned need to examine certain administrative principles, this thesis will have to examine certain areas of EU administrative law as well.

1.1.4 THE EUROPEAN LEGALITY PRINCIPLE AS THE OBJECT OF THE RESEARCH

The above overview indicates several reasons for conducting research on the European legality principle. The co-existence of multiple constructions of legality in contemporary European criminal law theory forms the first reason. In order to understand the actual construction of the legality principle as enshrined in the ECHR and EU law, it is helpful to map the differences between theoretical constructions of legality, both with regard to content and rationales. Although the distinction between the civil law legality conception and its common law counterpart is not novel, this thesis aims to add to the existing debate by demonstrating that both conceptions provide different minimum levels of legal certainty.

In addition to the complication of theoretical disagreements on the legality principle's content and rationale(s), the recognition of legality as a European fundamental right forms a second reason for the present research. As a fundamental right, the legality principle is protected as a minimum norm under the ECHR. The legality principle has subsequently been recognized as an EU fundamental right in multiple sources. As a Charter right and as a general principle of Union law, the EU legality principle must be interpreted with reference to the ECHR principle. As a result, a relationship exists – or has to exist – between the two European constructions of legality as a fundamental right. The multiple European sources of, and actors with interpretive authority regarding the construction of, the legality principle justify an extensive comparative examination into the actual construction of the European legality principles. The exhaustive analysis of the ECHR legality principle and comparisons made between the ECHR and EU legality principle add to the existing literature.[36]

---

in judgments on matters of competition law, see, eg, Case C-546/09, *Aurubis Balgaria AD v Nachalnik na Mitnitsa Stolichna*, EU:C:2011:199, para 42; Case C-72/15, *PJSC Rosneft Oil Company v Her Majesty's Treasury and Others*, EU:C:2017:236, para 167.

36 The English literature on Article 7 ECHR is mostly limited to handbooks on the ECHR and generally provides a non-exhaustive overview of the ECtHR's case-law, see, eg, Bleichrodt 2006, p. 651–662; Grabenwarter 2014, p. 171–182; Harris, O'Boyle, Bates and Buckley 2014, p. 493–502; Schabas 2015, p. 328–357; Jacobs, White and Ovey 2017, p. 328–336. Moreover, the existing literature does not generally distinguish between the specific elements of the Convention's legality principle and their particular demands. The two recent monographs on the EU legality principle have not exhaustively examined the ECtHR's case-law and, also for

The third reason for conducting the present research is particular to EU law. As mentioned, the EU legality principle has developed rather specifically due to the contested nature of the Union's (early) influence on the field of criminal law. The apparent relevance of related principles of administrative law and the applicability of the Union legality principle to EU administrative measures is illustrative in this regard. In addition, the multilevel definition and interpretation of offenses and penalties in EU criminal law warrants further examination of the construction of an EU legality principle. This latter particularity of EU criminal law has, in fact, inspired two recent monographs on the EU legality principle.[37] Where appropriate, the insights of these earlier works will be used in the analysis of both ECtHR and CJEU case-law.

1.2 RESEARCH QUESTIONS AND CHAPTER OUTLINE

This thesis describes, explains and, evaluates the scope and substance of the European legality principles. The following question is central to my research:

Is the present scope and substance of the EU legality principle in conformity with the requirements set by Article 7 ECHR and is it appropriate in light of the specific characteristics of EU law?

To answer the central research question, it is first necessary to provide an overview of the distinct conceptions of legality currently recognized in criminal law theory. These theoretical distinctions will be employed to provide an insight into the content and rationale(s) of the actual constructions of both the ECHR and EU legality principle. In order to do so, chapter 2 answers the following research sub-question:

What elements of, and rationale(s) for, the legality principle have historically been recognized and are they discernable in the conceptions of legality recognized in contemporary criminal law theory in Europe?

After the historical and theoretical overview, chapter 3 will analyze the construction of the ECHR legality principle by examining the Strasbourg Court's case-law. Chapter 3 employs the distinctions from criminal law theory to inform analysis of the ECtHR's considerations and to determine the content and rationale(s) of Article 7 ECHR. As mentioned, the exhaustive analysis of the Convention's legality principle has an instrumental value in this thesis: as is

that reason, provide only a limited comparison between the construction of the ECHR and EU legality principles, see Peristeridou 2015, p. 95–103; Altena-Davidsen 2016, p. 93.

37 See Peristeridou 2015; Altena-Davidsen 2016.

apparent from the central research question, the examination of Article 7 ECHR will mainly be used as a comparator for the EU legality principle. Chapter 3 answers the following research sub-question:

What elements of, and rationale(s) for, the legality principle can be identified in the case-law of the ECtHR on Article 7 ECHR?

Chapter 4 analyzes the complicated current construction of the legality principle in EU law. The approach in, and motivation for, this chapter is comparable to that in and for Chapter 3. The goal is to exhaustively examine the CJEU's case-law related to the EU legality principle.

Due to the historical specificities of EU criminal law, chapter 4 requires the examination of different strands of CJEU case-law. As is mentioned in subsections 1.1.2 and 1.1.3, the examination of the EU legality principle requires an investigation of case-law on certain EU principles of 'administrative law' and case-law on measures that are deemed 'administrative' from the EU perspective. Since the relevant CJEU considerations occurred in several contexts, there is potential for inconsistency. For this reason, the focus in chapter 4 is on mapping the relevant CJEU considerations to provide a structure for the EU legality principle that is not immediately visible when the different relevant strands of CJEU case-law are examined in isolation. Unlike chapter 3, however, chapter 4 will not yet contain firm conclusions on the apparent elements of, and rationale(s) for, the EU legality principle. Chapter 4 answers the following research sub-question:

What are the different strands of CJEU case-law with relevance for the legality principle and how do they relate to each other?

Chapter 5 adds to the analysis of the CJEU case-law in chapter 4 by identifying multiple factors that potentially explain the EU principle's current scope and substance. Chapter 5 first describes the specificities of the historical development of EU criminal law and the Union system of fundamental rights protection. After identifying these particularities, it determines whether these characteristics could indeed explain the CJEU's construction of legality. Since several particularities developed historically, chapter 5 will structure the CJEU's legality considerations chronologically. In addition to the particularities that developed historically, the chapter will also examine whether the multilevel character of definitions and interpretations of offenses and penalties in EU criminal law explain the CJEU's approach to legality. Chapter 5 answers the following research sub-question:

Do the (historical) specificities of EU criminal law and EU fundamental rights protection explain the CJEU case-law relating to the legality principle?

Chapter 6 will answer the central research question. It will first determine where to situate the EU legality principle in relation to the theoretical distinctions described in chapter 2. It will then assess whether the current construction of the EU legality principle is in conformity with the minimum requirements set by Article 7 ECHR. Finally, and most tentatively, chapter 6 will examine whether reasons exist to adopt a higher Union standard than that protected by the ECtHR. The final chapter will propose some adaptations to the EU legality principle in order to ensure greater protection of legal certainty in EU law.

1.3 RESEARCH METHODS AND LIMITATIONS

This thesis examines and compares the actual constructions of the European legality principles. Since these constructions have been the work of the ECtHR and the CJEU, the present research focusses on case-law.[38] To find the relevant ECtHR case-law, I examined all judgments on Article 7 ECHR in the HUDOC database.[39] To ensure the research was manageable, I have not consistently reviewed admissibility decisions, although I have examined them when secondary sources indicated their relevance. To find relevant CJEU case-law, I searched the CURIA database by using the following search terms: '7 ECHR', '49 Charter', 'nulla', 'nullum', 'principle of legality', 'the principle that penalties', 'non-retroactivity', 'extensive interpretation'.[40] I have additionally examined judgments when secondary sources indicated their relevance for the present research.

As mentioned, this thesis will use criminal law theory to structure and analyze the actual constructions of legality. Since the European legality principles are the object of the research, *European* criminal law theory constitutes the relevant instrument. The use of criminal law theory in Europe does imply some concessions. The most obvious is the inevitable incompleteness of the historical and theoretical examination. Since this research is unable to describe *all* conceptions of the legality principle in *all* European states over time, interpretive debates about the legality principle's scope, content and function in European criminal law theory are necessarily left out.[41] The theoretical examination in chapter 2 is therefore inevitably incomplete and, to some extent, over-simplified.

---

38 Cf Altena-Davidsen 2016, p. 16. Relevant Council of Europe documents, EU legislation, and EU policy documents are, of course, examined when necessary.

39 The HUDOC database can be accessed via https://hudoc.echr.coe.int.

40 The CURIA database can be accessed via https://curia.europa.eu.

41 Comparative research into all EU and ECHR Member States would be impossible within the framework of a doctoral thesis for obvious reasons, cf Peristeridou 2015, p. 25. I have mainly used textbooks on substantive criminal law and monographs on the (EU) legality principle since they generally provide an overview of the different theoretical positions on the principle within specific countries.

Despite its inevitable incompleteness, the theoretical examination aims to compare views originating from criminal justice systems with a continental tradition that favor statutory law, with those from the common law tradition which has traditionally allowed the judicial definition of crimes and penalties. Chapter 2 incorporates insights from criminal law theory in the civil law legal systems of France, Germany, Italy, and The Netherlands. It contrasts these insights with views that emerge from criminal law theory in the common law traditions of England and Wales. These examinations provide an adequate overview of the theory on the legality principle for the purpose of this thesis.

The focus on European criminal law *theory* implies an additional concession. Chapter 2 will not examine the actual construction and functioning of the legality principle in the practice of individual European states.[42] This research does not, therefore, include comparative legal research *sensu stricto*. The subsequent chapter merely derives distinct conceptions of legality from criminal law theory of different European states. Since the theoretical conceptions of legality are based on a *cumulative* overview of criminal law theory in different states, these conceptions do not necessarily describe the actual construction of the principle in all, or any, of the European states.

The theoretical examination also requires an additional limitation. The aim is to identify specific rationales for the legality principle that have been recognized in criminal law theory in Europe. These rationales entail rather abstract notions which often involve complicated concepts that are the subject of theoretical debate. Different views on concepts such as 'the rule of law', 'democracy', 'separation of powers', and 'legal certainty' unmistakably exist.[43] In addition, theoretical examinations on how the legality principle should be construed raise complicated questions. These include: what does judicial interpretation entail,

---

42 Since EU law has not actually looked at the functioning of the legality principle in the laws of the Member States, an extensive comparative investigation into the construction of the principle in the different Member States is not an obvious point of departure. A theoretical examination is, moreover, appropriate because theoretical insights have informed the development of the legality principle in the positive law of the Member States and continue to form the basis for their actual construction. In this regard, one could even justify the focus on the theoretical background by arguing that the theory provides a purer tool for understanding the legality principle than does actual constructions of that principle in the laws of the Member States. This is because all actual constructions of the principle are, to some extent, based on a comparable theoretical framework and are thus, arguably, derivative. See, conversely, Peristeridou 2015, p. 22–26, 65–95. Peristeridou nevertheless acknowledges that, for the legality principle, the actual influence of comparative analysis of national legal systems has been very limited at best, see Peristeridou 2015, p. 25. Even though Peristeridou examines the constructions of the legality principle in different EU Member States she acknowledges the large significance of a theoretical examination as well by emphasizing 'the strong theoretical nature' of an examination into the functioning of the legality principle (in EU law), see Peristeridou 2015, p. 26.

43 Peristeridou has been more elaborate about these concepts, most likely because her research aims to construct an EU legality principle that legitimizes the European *ius puniendi*, see Peristeridou, 2015, p. 10–13; 33–64.

what is required for language to be sufficiently clear, and is a separation between legislative and judicial functions practically possible. I have tried to keep these broader issues outside the scope of the present research as a far as possible, because their incorporation would lead to infinite regress.[44] Incorporating these questions would, in any event, require the extensive examination of topics of multiple doctoral theses in the field of constitutional law theory, legal theory, political philosophy, and/or theoretical linguistics. Since the present research focusses on the analysis of the actual legal constructions of the European legality principles, the theoretical examination has been kept as limited and straightforward as possible.

The research is up to date as of 1 October 2017. Legislation, case-law, and literature beyond that date has only been incorporated occasionally.

---

[44] This potential for infinite regress and/or circular reasoning can, in my view, be illustrated by the determinations in the report on the rule of law by the The European Commission for Democracy through Law' (hereinafter also: 'the Venice Commission'), which is a Council of Europe independent consultative body on issues of constitutional law. After identifying that legal certainty constitutes a core element of the notion of the rule of law, the Commission provides more details about its understanding of the concept of legal certainty by using other general terms – mainly those used by the ECtHR – such as 'accessibility', 'foreseeability', the need for limited discretionary powers, 'clear and precise rules', and 'non-retroactivity', see Venice Commission, Report on the Rule of Law, CDL-AD(2011)003rev, p. 10–13. This shows how the identification of elements of one notion (ie the rule of law) leads to questions about the substance of the identified elements. These questions are outside the scope of the present research, which means that certain abstract notions will be used in a straightforward, perhaps even intuitive, manner.

CHAPTER 2

THE PRINCIPLE *NULLUM CRIMEN, NULLA POENA SINE LEGE*: A HISTORICAL AND THEORETICAL EXAMINATION

2.1 INTRODUCTION

This chapter provides a theoretical framework for the legality principle by deriving distinguishable conceptions of legality from criminal law theory across European states. Preceding the description of the two different conceptions of legality is a historical examination in section 2.2. That section places the early formulations of the legality principle within the broader framework of the theories of modern political philosophy from which they emerged. It also identifies the theoretical justifications that were historically proposed for upholding rudimentary formulations of the legality principle. The first two substantive sections thus essentially aim to describe the relevant features of the contemporary legality principle in Europe and its historical emergence from, essentially, modern political philosophy.

Section 2.4 takes the preceding description as a point of departure and examines the rationales that are often understood as underlying the legality principle. It will determine the relevance of two theoretical foundations for the legality principle: 'the rule of law rationale' and 'the democracy rationale'. The rule of law rationale forms the foundation for both civil law and common law conceptions of legality. The democracy rationale, on the other hand, is only found in the civil law conception.

Subsections 2.4.2 and 2.4.3 compare the two conceptions of legality and demonstrate that each conception could protect a different level of legal certainty. Whereas the civil law principle appears to require the maximum predictability of criminal responsibility and penalties, the common law view necessarily ensures only a rather general level of legal certainty consisting of a prohibition on arbitrariness. The impact of differing rationales for the legality principle's protective scope will be illustrated by a comparison between the Dutch 'stepchild case' and the English 'marital rape case' (subsection 2.4.4). Subsection 2.4.5

examines the practical relevance of the aforementioned theoretical observations. Section 2.5 contains concluding remarks.

2.2 MODERN POLITICAL PHILOSOPHY AS THE BASIS FOR THE DEVELOPMENT OF THE LEGALITY PRINCIPLE

2.2.1 THE MODERN STATE AND THE PROTECTION OF INDIVIDUAL SECURITY AND LIBERTY THROUGH LAW

There exists a broad consensus about the historical origins of the legality principle.[45] It is generally acknowledged that the contemporary recognition of the legality principle results from theories formulated in the Enlightenment era.[46] The recognition and growth of the principle has therefore essentially emerged from modern political philosophy.[47] Our current conceptions of the relationship between the state and its subjects are deeply influenced by theories formulated in this period.[48] Prominent thinkers such as Thomas Hobbes, John Locke, Montesquieu, and Cesare Beccaria have all played a part in shaping our present views about the organization and exercise of governmental power. It is not, therefore, a coincidence that these theorists all recognize, in some form or another, the legality principle in their political philosophies.[49]

Contrary to pre-modern political philosophy which appealed to the divine to justify the concentration of power in the state, modern philosophy emphasized the

---

45 About this consensus, see Schreiber 1976, p. 32; Gallant 2009, p. 47.

46 See, eg, Hall 1937, p. 165–170; Krey 1983, p. 12; Claes 2003, p. 87; Desportes and LeGunehec 2008, p. 146–147; Hallevy 2010, p. 8; Nan 2011, p. 63; Satzger 2012a, p. 85; Scalia 2012, p. 13; Peristeridou 2015, p. 33–34; Altena-Davidsen 2016, p. 21.

47 Although some elements related to the legality principle can also be found before the period of modern political philosophy. For an overview of pre-modern theories with relevance for the legality principle, see Schreiber 1976, p. 17–31; Krey 1983; Altena-Davidsen 2016, p. 22–24. Cf Peristeridou 2015, p. 34.

48 Modern political philosophy covers the period between the beginning of the sixteenth century and the beginning of the nineteenth century, see Kenny 2006, p. 273–302. Referring to 'the' theories of modern political philosophy as the basis for the legality principle necessarily generalizes specific theories and misrepresents them to some extent. Since my interest is in legal research, and not in political philosophy or legal history, the present chapter nevertheless employs such generalizations. The historical discussion in this chapter will, therefore, be oversimplified to some extent.

49 Cf Nan 2011, p. 63–73. Historians could, of course, question the causal relationship between modern political philosophy and the present recognition of the legality principle. For legal research, such as the present work, the fact that there exists a broad consensus about the historical development of the legality principle sufficiently justifies an examination of the above-mentioned theories of modern political philosophy. Unlike Peristeridou, I will not, therefore, question the broad consensus on the historical origins of the legality principle, cf Peristeridou 2015, p. 34–35.

significance of the rational subject and placed it at the center of the moral world.[50] In modern political philosophy, the state was not justified by an appeal to God, but its legitimacy depended upon its respect for – and protection of – rational persons.[51] Since individuals were viewed as equally[52] endowed with the natural rights[53] to self-preservation and liberty,[54] the protection of these rights became of paramount importance.[55] In this modern view, the state essentially existed for all its individual subjects and this gave rise to the notion that the concentration of power was a means to an end. As a consequence of this instrumental justification, the modern state could be legitimate only if it protected the individual rights to self-preservation and liberty better than in the absence of a concentration of power.

Modern political philosophy argued for state power on the basis of the undesirability of the situation where no concentration of power exists; the so-called state of nature.[56] Hobbes famously qualified the natural condition very negatively as a state of war of every man against every man where there is a continual fear of danger and violent death.[57] Locke, Montesquieu, and Beccaria were, arguably, less pessimistic,[58] but they still made a strong case for a concentration of power.[59] Locke and Beccaria did so because, in their view, state power could remedy the inconveniences of the state of nature such as the irregular and unpredictable exercise of power by every individual.[60] Montesquieu, on the other hand, deemed the concentration of power necessary in order to allow individuals to defend their life and goods against others with whom they were inevitably confronted in a *de facto* society.[61]

---

50 This is largely due to the works of Descartes, see, eg, Schreiber 1976, p. 34; Kenny 2006, p. 36–37. The works of Locke have also been recognized in this regard, see Strauss 1953, p. 248. Cf Foqué and 't Hart 1990, p. 94–95; Boot 2002, p. 84; Claes 2003, p. 88–89; Hilgendorf 2012, p. 17.

51 Cf Claes 2003, p. 90-91

52 See, eg, Locke 1690, Ch. VIII, nr. 95, p. 44, Ch. IX, nr. 123, p. 57, nr. 131, p. 59; Montesquieu 1748, Bk. 8, Ch. 3, p. 114. On the importance of equality for modern political philosophy, see Tamanaha 2004, p. 32.

53 Cf Strauss 1953, p. 182, 227; Schreiber 1976, p. 37.

54 See Hobbes 1651, Ch. XIV, p. 189, Ch. XV, p. 212; Locke 1690, Ch. VII, nr. 87–88, p. 39, Ch. VIII, nr. 95, p. 44, Ch. XVI, nr. 190, p. 87; Beccaria 1764, Ch. 30, p. 77.

55 See Locke 1690, Ch. XI, nr. 142, p. 66, Ch. XIII, nr. 149, p. 69; Montesquieu 1748, Bk. 26, Ch. 23, p. 516; Beccaria 1764, Ch. 8, p. 25, Ch. 16, p. 42. Modern political philosophy was therefore clearly based on a theory of modern natural right, cf Schreiber 1976, p. 34–35. On modern natural right theory and its relationship with classical natural right theory, see Strauss 1953, p. 165–251.

56 See, eg, Hobbes 1651, Ch. XIII, p. 185; Locke 1690, Ch. I-II, p. 2; Montesquieu 1748, Bk. 1, Ch. 2, p. 6.

57 Hobbes 1647, Ch. I, p. 29; Hobbes 1651, Ch. XIII, p. 186, Ch. XV, p. 215–216.

58 See Locke 1690, Ch. III, nr. 19, p. 9; Montesquieu 1748, Bk. 1, Ch. 2, p. 6–7; Beccaria 1764, To the Reader, p. 5, Ch. 40, p. 102.

59 See Locke 1690, Ch. IX, nr. 123, p. 57; Beccaria 1764, Ch. 1, p. 9, Ch. 9, p. 27, Ch. 42, p. 105.

60 See Locke 1690, Ch. II, nr. 13, p. 6, Ch. III, nr. 21, p. 10, Ch. IX, nr. 125, 127, p. 58; Beccaria 1764, Ch. 9, p. 27.

61 See Montesquieu 1748, Bk. 1, Ch. 3, p. 7, Bk. 8, Ch. 3, p. 114, Bk. 26, Ch. 1, p. 494. Cf Foqué and 't Hart 1990, p. 102.

Modern political philosophy thus essentially argued for state power in order to better safeguard the individual rights of self-preservation and liberty than would be possible in the natural state or a *de facto* society.[62] Since the erection of the state served the goal of protecting individual rights, modern theorists deemed it necessary to constitute limits to the exercise of the state's powers.[63] Locke famously derived a theory of limited government from the instrumental justification for the state.[64] In his view, governmental force should only be based on the power given to the authorities on the basis of the law[65] and it should be exercised for the public good alone.[66] As a result, Locke clearly renounced absolute and arbitrary state power.[67]

Like Locke, and Beccaria thereafter,[68] Montesquieu identified the general good of society and the well-being of the people as the end for which power was concentrated in the state.[69] Montesquieu used the instrumental justification for the state to identify the desirable organization of governmental powers. He deemed moderate government[70] most desirable for safeguarding the rights to self-preservation and individual liberty.[71] This was partly because, unlike in a despotic state,[72] the exercise of governmental power is then bound to the law.[73] Limiting the exercise of governmental power through law is therefore an important element of Montesquieu's political theory as well.[74]

---

62 See Hobbes 1651, Ch. XV, p. 202, 205, Ch. XXI, p. 272, Locke 1690, Ch. VII, nr. 87, p. 39, Ch. VIII, nr. 95, p. 44; Montesquieu 1748, Bk. 1, Ch. 3, p. 7, Bk. 11, Ch. 6, p. 157, Bk. 26, Ch. 15, p. 510; Beccaria 1764, Ch. 1, p. 9, Ch. 8, p. 25, Ch. 9, p. 27, Ch. 16, p. 39, Ch. 42, p. 105.

63 Cf Soleil 2013, p. 154.

64 See Locke 1690, Ch. VII, nr. 90, p. 40, Ch. IX, nr. 123–124, p. 57, Ch. XI, nr. 135, p. 62, Ch. XV, nr. 171, p. 79. See also Strauss 1953, p. 231; Simmons 1992, p. 94; Tully 1993, p. 35.

65 See Locke 1690, Ch. XVIII, nr. 202, p. 92. Cf Schreiber 1976, p. 50–51; Ashcraft 1994, p. 229.

66 See Locke 1690, Ch. XI, nr. 135, p. 62, Ch. XVII, nr. 199–200, p. 91–92. See also Schreiber 1976, p. 36–37; Ashcraft 1994, p. 228. Cf Montesquieu 1748, Bk. 26, Ch. 9, p. 502.

67 See Locke 1690, Ch. VII, nr. 91, p. 41, Ch. VII, nr. 94, p. 43, Ch. IX, nr. 123, p. 57, Ch. IX, nr. 131, p. 59, Ch. XI, nr. 135, p. 61–62, Ch. XI, nr. 137–138, p. 63–64, Ch. XIII, nr. 149, p. 68, Ch. XV, nr. 171, p. 79. See further Gough 1973, p. 24, 120, 123; Schreiber 1976, p. 37, 51; Tully 1993, p. 30. Although Hobbes is often perceived as an advocate for absolute state power, he also argued against arbitrary power and found good laws to be those laws made for the good of the people, see Hobbes 1651, Ch. XXX, p. 376, 385, 388.

68 Beccaria 1764, To the Reader, p. 4–5, 7, Ch. 2, p. 11, Ch. 3, p. 13, Ch. 6, p. 19, Ch. 7, p. 22, Ch. 32, p. 84 Ch. 36, p. 94, Ch. 41, p. 103.

69 See Montesquieu 1748, Bk. 26, Ch. 9, p. 502, Bk. 26, Ch. 23, p. 516.

70 See Montesquieu 1748, Bk. 8, Ch. 8, p. 118. As opposed to despotic government, both republican and monarchical government could be moderate according to Montesquieu. On these three types of government, see Montesquieu 1748, Bk. 2, Ch. 1, p. 10.

71 See Montesquieu 1748, Bk. 11, Ch. 6, p. 157. Cf Montesquieu 1748, Bk. 5, Ch. 14, p. 63. See further Krausse 2001, p. 232, 259.

72 See Montesquieu 1748, Bk. 2, Ch. 1, p. 10, Bk. 3, Ch. 8, p. 27, Bk. 5, Ch. 16, p. 66, Bk. 6, Ch. 3, p. 76. Richter even concludes that there cannot be positive law in despotism as a result of Montesquieu's definition of despotic government, see Richter 1977, p. 82.

73 See Montesquieu 1748, Bk. 3, Ch. 3–4, p. 22–24. See further Merry 1970, p. 234–244; Pangle 1973, p. 82–83.

74 See also Richter 1977, p. 57, 66,;Groenhuijsen 1987, p. 30; Foqué and 't Hart 1990, p. 81.

2.2.2 THE TWOFOLD FUNCTION OF POSITIVE LAW AND LEGAL RESTRICTIONS ON THE RIGHT TO PUNISH

The brief overview of modern political philosophy in the preceding subsection warrants the following two statements. First, the concentration of power in the modern state is justified instrumentally. This implies that a legitimate exercise of state power must intend to safeguard the interests of security and liberty for all individuals equally. Secondly, in the modern state, the protection of individual security and liberty can be realized only if the exercise of arbitrary and absolute power is limited by positive law.[75] As a consequence, positive law fulfils two main functions in the modern state.[76] On the one hand, the law intends to protect security and liberty for all by precluding individuals from doing anything they pleased.[77] In this regard, the law is conceived as an instrument for social control and public order.[78] On the other hand, positive law aims to limit the use of governmental powers.[79] Therefore, the instrument of positive law essentially regulates and restricts not only the exercise of power by individual citizens, but also by the state.[80] As a result, modern positive law aims to prevent the arbitrary exercise of power in two distinguishable ways.[81] This subsection further examines these two functions.

In order to limit the exercise of individual power, positive law needs to be able to bind individuals. In the modern view, the binding character of the law follows from the erection of the state, which transforms individuals into legal subjects.[82] This, in turn, introduces a vertical legal relationship between the state and its citizens,[83] which is exemplified by the fact that individuals can be made to comply with the state's positive law through the use of force.[84] This use of force culminates in a right to punish individuals for violating positive law[85] and this constitutes the most invasive legitimate use of governmental powers.[86]

75 Cf Schreiber 1976, p. 49; Foqué and 't Hart 1990, p. 82, 99; Boot 2002, p. 83; Claes 2003, p. 87–90.
76 Cf Groenhuijsen 1987, p. 28–30; Claes 2003, p. 76–78; Hallevy 2010, p. 10; Nan 2011, p. 93.
77 See Montesquieu 1748, Bk. 11, Ch. 3, p. 155, Bk. 11, Ch. 4, p. 155–156, Bk. 26, Ch. 20, p. 514; Beccaria 1764, Ch. 8, p. 25, Ch. 42, p. 105. See further Venturi 1971, p. 100; Maestro 1973, p. 30; Schreiber 1976, p. 53; Reuter 1989, p. 68. Cf Hobbes 1647, Ch. I, p. 28, Ch. II, p. 34; Hobbes 1651, Ch. XIV, p. 189–191, Ch. XV, p. 209, Ch. XVII, p. 227; Schreiber 1976, p. 39.
78 See Hallevy 2010, p. 9; Peristeridou 2015, p. 132.
79 Cf Hallevy 2010, p. 9–10.
80 Cf Foqué and 't Hart 1990, p. 80, 90–91; Nan 2011, p. 93–94. Beccaria underlined this by stating that it is conventional law that marks the limit of the force which man may legitimately use against man, see Beccaria 1764, To the Reader, p. 4, Ch. 7, p. 23, Ch. 8, p. 25, Ch. 29, p. 74, Ch. 39, p. 100.
81 Cf Fernandez Esteban 1999, p. 80.
82 See Hobbes 1651, Ch. XXVI, p. 313, 317, Locke 1690, Ch. VII, nr. 87, p. 39; Montesquieu 1748, Bk. 1, Ch. 3, p. 7–8. Cf Foqué and 't Hart 1990, p. 104–105.
83 See, eg, Locke 1690, Ch. VIII, nr. 107, p. 49. Cf Groenhuijsen 1987, p. 30.
84 See Hobbes 1651, Ch. XIV, p. 200, Ch. XV, p. 202, Ch. XVII, p. 223, Locke 1690, Ch. I, nr. 3, p. 2; Montesquieu 1748, Bk. 26, Ch. 2, p. 495.
85 Cf Foqué and 't Hart 1990, p. 88–89.
86 Cf Packer 1969, p. 5.

As the most far-reaching state power, criminal punishment becomes the ultimate means through which the state limits the arbitrary use of individual power by providing tangible motives not to violate the law.[87] Modern criminal law is therefore clearly considered to be an instrument to guide individual behavior in order to ensure that individuals refrain from violating the rights of others and to punish them if they do.[88] By limiting the use of individual power through criminal law, the state serves the general interests of society and better protects individual security and the right of liberty for all.[89] It is therefore evident that modern criminal law aims to limit the arbitrary exercise of power by individuals and to protect society against it, which is in accordance with the first element of the twofold function of modern positive law.

The second element of positive law's function is perceivable in the requirements that were formulated for the law. Since positive law and its potential enforcement by state power[90] could not only protect, but also infringe, individual rights, state force is subject to legal restrictions. In order to protect, essentially, individual liberty, modern philosophy introduces general requirements for the law.[91]

The need for the promulgation of law is widely recognized for example.[92] In the absence of sufficient publication, individuals would not be obliged to comply with the law because, in Hobbes words, "(…) he who has never come to know to whom he is obligated or what his obligations are cannot obey, and is exactly as if he were not obligated".[93] An additional requirement for positive law is simplicity. Positive law should not be overly detailed or vague.[94] If the law is insufficiently published or incomprehensible, individuals should be able to rely on the excuse of error in law.[95]

Due to the invasive nature of punishment, modern political philosophers have also formulated more specific requirements for the field of criminal law. Hobbes, for example, derives a specific prohibition on the retroactive application of criminal law from the general requirement that the law be published.[96] In conformity with

87 See, eg, Hobbes 1647, Ch. XIII, p. 152 and Beccaria 1764, Ch. 1, p. 9, Ch. 2, p. 10–11, Ch. 9, p. 27.

88 Montesquieu 1748, Bk. 1, Ch. 3, p. 7–8; Beccaria 1764, To the Reader, p. 4, Ch. 2, p. 10, Ch. 4, p. 14. Cf Packer 1969, p. 19, 26–27, 31; Naucke 1989, p. 44 et seq; Foqué and 't Hart 1990, p. 90, 92; Borgers 2011, p. 106; Nan 2011, p. 93; Mayaud 2015, p. 27; Peristeridou 2015, p. 42, 133.

89 See, eg, Beccaria 1764, Ch. 2, p. 11, Ch. 8, p. 25, Ch. 9, p. 27. See further Naucke 1989, p. 44.

90 Cf Schreiber 1976, p. 47; Foqué and 't Hart 1990, p. 98.

91 Cf Packer 1969, p. 78; Foqué and 't Hart 1990, p. 96–97; Peristeridou 2015, p. 38–39, 133–134. Hallevy deems liberty in the form of individual autonomy to be the social concept behind the *supra*-principle of (modern) criminal law theory, see Hallevy 2010, p. 3–4.

92 See, eg, Hobbes 1647, Ch. XIV, p. 160, Hobbes 1651, Ch. XXVI, p. 319; Locke 1690, Ch. II, nr. 9, Ch. VII, nr. 87, p. 39, Ch. IX, nr. 124, 127, p. 57–58, Ch. XI, nr. 136–137, p. 63. See also Dreyer 2012, p. 178–179.

93 Hobbes 1647, Ch. XIV, p. 159. Cf Locke 1690, Ch. VI, nr. 57, p. 25.

94 See, eg, Hobbes 1647, Ch. XIII, p. 151; Hobbes 1681, p. 71; Montesquieu 1748, Bk. 12, Ch. 7, p. 194, Bk. 29, Ch. 16, p. 612–614. Cf Krey 1983, p. 85.

95 See Hobbes 1651, Ch. XXVII, p. 338. Cf Schreiber 1976, p. 42.

96 See Hobbes 1651, Ch. XXVII, p. 339, Ch. XXVIII, p. 354. See further Schreiber 1976, p. 40–41; Hüning 2007, p. 226.

the acknowledgement that vague laws need to be avoided, Beccaria identifies the need for intelligible and clearly formulated criminal laws.[97] In his opinion, clear laws could not only prevent crimes,[98] they could also prevent the arbitrary application of criminal law.[99] Beccaria additionally recognizes the need for criminal law to be framed in general terms in order to bind all individuals equally.[100]

2.2.3 FROM THE CONSTRUCTION OF POSITIVE LAW TO ITS APPLICATION: REGULATING JUDICIAL ACTIVITY

In addition to regulating the use of state force and formulating requirements for positive (criminal) law, modern political philosophers addressed the relationship between the construction and the application of (criminal) law. Most authors recognize the need for positive law to be applied and interpreted by the judiciary. Hobbes, for example, finds the need for legal interpretation to result from the ambiguous character of words.[101] In his view, the judge that interprets the law should take both the spirit of the law into account, as well as the rule's equity.[102] Locke appears to be of a similar opinion. He grants room for judicial interpretation by rejecting the strict and rigid observation of the laws.[103] Montesquieu largely agrees with his predecessors on the inevitability of interpretation, but he prominently argues for limitations on judicial discretion. In his view, it is the text of the law that should guide interpretation to help preclude arbitrariness.[104]

The danger of unrestrained judicial power is also countered by a separation of powers as proposed by Locke[105] and prominently elaborated on by Montesquieu.[106] In order to preclude the concentration of power over the life and liberty of citizens from becoming arbitrary,[107] Montesquieu deems it necessary to separate the different branches of state power and balance them against one another.[108] Montesquieu's famous theory essentially requires the separation

97 See Beccaria 1764, Ch. 14, p. 35, Ch. 34, p. 91, Ch. 42, p. 105.
98 See Beccaria 1764, Ch. 41, p. 104. See further Maestro 1973, p. 22, Deimling 1989, p. 175; Foqué and 't Hart 1990, p. 90.
99 See Beccaria 1764, Ch. 11, p. 29, Ch. 29, p. 73, Ch. 34, p. 90.
100 See Beccaria 1764, Ch. 3, p. 12.
101 See Hobbes 1651, Ch. XXVI, p. 326.
102 See Hobbes 1651, Ch. XXVI, p. 321, 322, 326. Cf Nan 2011, p. 64; Klimchuk 2012, p. 178.
103 See Locke 1690, Ch. XIV, nr. 159, p. 74.
104 See Montesquieu 1748, Bk. 6, Ch. 3, p. 76. See further Schreiber 1976, p. 54–55; Carrithers 2001, p. 296. Cf Schönfeld 1979, p. 6; Christ 2003, p. 200; Nan 2011, p. 68; Altena-Davidsen 2016, p. 30–31.
105 See Locke 1690, Ch. VII, nr. 107, p. 49. See further Gough 1973, p. 104–109; Tamanaha 2004, p. 49; Nan 2011, p. 65–66.
106 See further Möllers 2013, p. 16–26, 40–43.
107 See Montesquieu 1748, Bk. 11, Ch. 6, p. 157. Cf Beccaria 1764, Ch.11, p. 29.
108 See Montesquieu 1748, Bk. 5, Ch. 14, p. 63, Bk. 11, Ch. 4, p. 155. See further, eg, Merry 1970, p. 295,; Pangle 1973, p. 132; Richter 1977, p. 90; Boot 2002, p. 83.

of the judiciary from the executive and legislative powers in order to prevent moderate government from degenerating into despotism.[109] In Montesquieu's view, individual liberty would be sacrificed completely if the judicial powers were not separated from the other two and, in that event, all would be lost.[110]

Beccaria agrees with the above views on the need to limit judicial discretion by separating the legislative and adjudicative powers,[111] but he focusses his theory on criminal law.[112] In fact, Beccaria aims to follow Montesquieu's enlightened footsteps while concentrating his writings on the specific field of criminal justice, which he characterizes as a prominent, yet neglected, field of legislation.[113] Beccaria argues in favor of limiting judicial power in criminal law to an absolute minimum.[114] In his view, judicial interpretation should only take the form of syllogistic reasoning.[115] Judges should not refer to the spirit of the law,[116] but they should only apply general rules to specific factual circumstances in the interest of certainty and public security.[117] In addition, judges should have no discretion with regard to the imposition of punishment.[118] Beccaria thus clearly advocates the largest possible limitation of judicial discretion in the interpretation of criminal law.[119]

2.2.4 TENTATIVE RECOGNITION OF THE LEGALITY PRINCIPLE

While accepting the need for positive criminal law in order to safeguard individual rights, modern political philosophy attempts to prevent the arbitrary exercise of governmental powers since that would jeopardize the individual and his liberty.[120] As a result, modern criminal law is not only used for the criminalization of conduct and the imposition of punishment (the first function of positive law).[121] In conformity with the second function of positive law, criminal law is also used to restrict governmental discretion, both in the construction of crimes and penalties, as well as in its interpretation and application. It is this second function that forms the basis for the recognition of the legality principle in modern criminal law.[122]

---

109 See Montesquieu 1748, Bk. 6, Ch. 5, p. 78, Bk. 11, Ch. 6, p. 156–157. Cf Schreiber 1976, p. 54; Krey 1983, p. 13–14.
110 See Montesquieu 1748, Bk. 11, Ch. 6, p. 157. See further Merry 1970, p. 300; Rahe 2001, p. 82.
111 See Beccaria 1764, Ch. 3, p. 12–13. See further Reuter 1989, p. 62.
112 Cf Boot 2002, p. 83.
113 See Beccaria 1764, Introduction, p. 8.
114 See also Heath 1963, p. 14; Hart 1982, p. 48; Reuter 1989, p. 65; Foqué and 't Hart 1990, p. 96.
115 See Beccaria 1764, Ch. 4, p. 14.
116 See Beccaria 1764, Ch. 4, p. 14–15. See further Maestro 1973, p. 22; Hart 1982, p. 48.
117 See Beccaria 1764, Ch. 4, p. 14, Ch. 14, p. 35, Ch. 29, p. 73.
118 See Beccaria 1764, Ch. 3, p. 12.
119 See Beccaria 1764, Ch. 4, p. 15. Cf Altena-Davidsen 2016, p. 31.
120 Cf Krey 1983, p. 14, 73–74; Rebut 2001, p. 250–251; Boot 2002, p. 83; Peristeridou 2015, p. 36, 40.
121 On this twofold function, see subsections 2.2.1 and 2.2.2 above.
122 Cf Masferrer 2013, p. 267–268.

In conformity with the second function of law, several theorists have formulated legal requirements for the construction of legitimate criminal law. In addition, modern political philosophy identifies the need to limit governmental power in the application and interpretation of crimes and penalties. These requirements and limits already constitute early recognitions of the legality principle. In fact, rudimentary formulations of the legality principle are perceivable in the modern theories described in the preceding subsections.[123]

Hobbes, for example, deems positive law to be the measure of good and evil[124] and he states that "(...) when the Soveraign Power ceaseth, Crime also ceaseth: for where there is no Power, there is no protection to be had from the Law".[125] Since Hobbes requires power to be concentrated in a sovereign for the existence of crimes, he apparently limits crimes to their definition in positive law.[126] The above formulation has, therefore, been qualified as an early, yet incomplete,[127] recognition of the legality principle.[128]

Locke also recognizes the need for crimes and penalties to be enshrined in law.[129] In his view, positive criminal law contributes to both the objective and cognizable criminalization of conduct, as well as to the impartial application of the criminal law by the judiciary.[130] The law, according to Locke, is intended to preclude arbitrariness and to ensure legal certainty so that the state is bound to the law and individuals may know how to act.[131]

Beccaria's views are in conformity with the above. Beccaria deems the absence of arbitrariness and legal certainty highly important in the field of criminal law, because "[u]ncertainty as to one's fate has sacrificed more victims to a hidden tyranny than public and official cruelty ever has".[132] He formulates an early legality principle by stating that "(...) laws alone can decree punishments for crimes, and (...) this authority resides only with the legislature, who represents the whole of society united by the social contract".[133] In Beccaria's view, the law should not only clearly define the prohibited conduct,[134] it should also clearly prescribe the applicable penalty.[135]

---

123 See Schreiber 1976, p. 55; Krey 1983, p. 14, 55.
124 See Hobbes 1651, Ch. XXIX, p. 365. Cf Hobbes 1651, Ch. XXVIII, p. 354.
125 Hobbes 1651, Ch. XXVII, p. 337.
126 Cf Schreiber 1976, p. 43.
127 See Schreiber 1976, p. 47.
128 See Hüning 2007, p. 220; Ristroph 2012, p. 100.
129 Cf Scalia 2012, p. 16–17.
130 See Locke 1690, Ch. VII, nr. 87, p. 39.
131 See, especially, Locke 1690, Ch. XI, nr. 136–137, p. 62–64.
132 Beccaria 1764, Ch. 11, p. 29–30. See also Beccaria 1764, Ch. 19, p. 48. See further Naucke 1989, p. 49–50.
133 Beccaria 1764, Ch. 3, p. 12. See also Beccaria 1764, Ch. 11, p. 29, Ch. 29, p. 73 and, perhaps most significantly, Ch. 47, p. 113. Cf Scalia 2012, p. 22; Altena-Davidsen 2016, p. 25.
134 See Beccaria 1764, Ch. 34, p. 90.
135 See Beccaria 1764, Ch. 3, p. 12.

Despite not being recognized as fully-fledged principles of legality at the time, the above formulations – and the broader theories from which they emerged – contain, in a rudimentary form, the distinguishable requirements that were later to become the four elements of the legality principle.[136] Beccaria's emphasis on the need for legislatively constructed offenses and penalties, for example, can hardly be interpreted other than as an embryonic recognition of the *lex scripta* principle. In addition, the widely recognized need for clear, simple and intelligible criminal laws indicates the relevance of the *lex certa* principle. The *lex stricta* principle is also clearly perceivable, as firm limits on judicial interpretation are established by only allowing syllogistic legal reasoning. Finally, the relevance of the *lex praevia* principle results from, inter alia, Hobbes' explicit recognition of a prohibition on retroactive application of criminal law.[137]

2.3 THE CONTEMPORARY LEGALITY PRINCIPLE AND ITS ELEMENTS

2.3.1 INTRODUCTION

The present section describes the content of the legality principle from the perspective of contemporary criminal law theory in Europe. As described in subsection 2.2.4, modern political philosophy formulated a rudimentary principle of legality that demonstrates four distinguishable elements: the secondary principles *lex scripta*, *lex certa*, *lex stricta* and *lex praevia*. Unsurprisingly, contemporary criminal law theory in Europe generally distinguishes these four elements as well.[138]

The apparent consensus regarding the elements of the legality principle has not, however, resulted in a univocal interpretation of these secondary principles. The specific elements of the legality principle have, in fact, been subject to diverging interpretations. As briefly mentioned in subsection 1.1.1, the most notable historical differences arose between states with a civil law legal tradition and

---

136 On these elements, see subsection 1.1.1 and, in more detail, section 2.3 below. Cf Altena-Davidsen 2016, p. 29–34.

137 See subsection 2.2.2.

138 See, eg, Schreiber 1976, p. 11, 55–61; Schünemann 1978, p. 3; Krey 1983, p. 1–2, 12; Groenhuijsen 1987, p. 15; Di Punzio and Natalini 2006, p. 39–47; Forster 2008, p. 33–37; Lelieur, Pfützner and Volz 2008, p. 42–52; Jarvers 2008, p. 57–64; Claes and Krolikowski 2009, p. 89–93; Gallant 2009, p. 358–367; Eser 2010, Rn 10; Borgers 2011, p. 106; Renout 2012, p. 21–31; Satzger 2012a, p. 86–87; Schohr 2012, p. 260–261; Ashworth and Horder 2013, p. 57–71; Masferrer 2013, p. 281–283; Pradel 2014, p. 136–140; Bernardini 2015, p. 174–176; Cupido 2015, p. 7–8, Peristeridou 2015, p. 6–7, 79; Altena-Davidsen 2016, p. 2; Manes 2017, p. 338. Hall, as well as Westen (who mainly examined the legality principle in the Anglo-American tradition) also acknowledges the relevance of the four specific elements, see Hall 1937, p. 165; Westen 2007, p. 231–232, 235–302.

those with systems based on common law.[139] In the civil law tradition the legality principle underlines the *exclusive* competence of the legislature to create criminal law. On this view, the principle prohibits the judiciary from autonomously creating crimes and penalties. This results in the requirement that a statute forms the basis for the imposition of criminal responsibility and punishment.

Common law countries, on the other hand, have traditionally allowed the judicial creation of offenses and penalties. As a result, the civil law legality principle, with its strong emphasis on the legislative creation of criminal law, has not been deemed relevant within the common law legal tradition for quite some time. Common law states have nevertheless started to recognize the relevance of the principle in recent decades.[140] However, while common law systems have recognized the legality principle, this has not led to the adoption of the civil law interpretation.[141] The emphasis on codification and the prohibition on the judicial creation of criminal law are still not as strong in the common law tradition. The historical differences between the two legal traditions have, therefore, resulted in diverging interpretations of the legality principle's content that continue to exist.

The present section examines the four elements that constitute the legality principle and provides an overview of their sometimes diverging interpretations among European legal traditions. The aim is to set out a straightforward overview of the areas of agreement and dispute in contemporary criminal law theory about the content and scope of the legality principle. Due to this limited aim, section 2.3 only provides an introduction to the differing interpretations of the legality principle. Section 2.4 will subsequently use this introductory description to further examine the distinct conceptions of legality and their rationales.

2.3.2 THE PRINCIPLE THAT ONLY LEGISLATION CAN DEFINE OFFENSES AND PENALTIES *(LEX SCRIPTA)*

Although not (yet) an element of the legality principle under customary international law,[142] the requirement that offenses and penalties be prescribed by *legislation* is often associated with the legality principle.[143] This requirement precludes substantive criminal law that is exclusively based on custom or case-law. Since it prohibits the judicial creation of offenses and penalties, *lex scripta* is merely explicitly recognized in the continental legal tradition with its focus on

139 See Boot 2002, p. 81; Claes and Krolikowski 2009, p. 89; Gallant 2009, p. 13, 48–51; Masferrer 2013, p. 274–275; Peristeridou 2015, p. 65, 67–78.

140 See Forster 2008, p. 30; Ashworth and Horder 2013, p. 48, 57; Masferrer 2013, p. 278; Peristeridou 2015, p. 67, 71.

141 Cf Masferrer 2013, p. 275–276, 280.

142 See Gallant 2009, p. 356.

143 See Claes 2003, p. 15; Masferrer 2013, p. 281–282; Peristeridou 2015, p. 79–80.

statutory codification of criminal law.[144] Due to the historical acceptability of the creation of offenses and penalties through case-law, the *lex scripta* principle is not (yet) generally acknowledged to constitute an element of the legality principle in common law countries.[145]

As a result of the differences between the common law and civil law traditions here, a consensus about the significance of *lex scripta* as an essential element of the legality principle has not yet materialized. Such a consensus is not necessarily far away, however. This is because, in Europe, legislation is increasingly considered to be the primary, if not the sole, instrument for the creation of substantive criminal law. Even states with strong common law backgrounds such as England and Wales have, in fact, started to codify offenses and penalties.[146] English judges have therefore begun to leave the construction of criminal law explicitly to the legislature, though not consistently.[147] That common law states have started to recognize the preeminence of the legislature in the construction of offenses and penalties could, arguably, indicate an emerging European consensus on the need for codified criminal law to the exclusion of customary and judge-made law.[148] At present, however, these developments are not (yet) sufficient to reverse the historical non-recognition of *lex scripta* in the common law tradition. The *lex scripta* principle can therefore merely be identified as an unequivocal element of legality in the continental legal tradition.

To assign the task of defining offenses and penalties exclusively to the legislature establishes a division of labor between, especially, the legislature and the judiciary. This division of labor is deemed desirable for multiple reasons. It is, for example, proposed that only the legislature should enact criminal law because the legislature can best ensure democratic legitimacy.[149] Another reason for the *lex scripta* principle is the doctrine of the separation of powers, which is, arguably, violated if a judge can usurp the 'legislative power' to create substantive

---

144 Cf Boot 2002, p. 85; Gallant 2009, p. 13, 48; Hallevy 2010, p. 36; De Hullu 2015, p. 86; Peristeridou 2015, p. 71–72.

145 See Munday 2001, p. 364; Westen 2007, p. 231–232, 286; Forster 2008, p. 33; Gallant 2009, p. 13; Hallevy 2010, p. 40; Peristeridou 2015, p. 72; Altena-Davidsen 2016, p. 101. This is also exemplified by the fact that Ashworth and Horder identify only three principles that derive from legality and omit *lex scripta*. They did, however, acknowledge the importance of codifying offenses and penalties but this is rather described as a matter of 'constitutional propriety', see Ashworth and Horder 2013, p. 45, 57.

146 See Wilson 1998, p. 20; Westen 2007, p. 286; Ashworth and Horder 2013, p. 8, 45–48; Peristeridou 2015, p. 70. On the clarity and accessibility of English criminal law legislation, see, critically, Stevenson and Harris 2010, p. 519–526.

147 See Wilson 1998, p. 15–16, 19; Ashworth and Horder 2013, p. 60; Peristeridou 2015, p. 70–72, 80–82. Cf Westen 2007, p. 286; Gallant 2009, p. 35.

148 See Hallevy 2010, p. 36, 41; Peristeridou 2015, p. 82. Cf Munday 2001, p. 364; Norrie 2001, p. 19; Simester and Sullivan 2007, p. 23.

149 See Krey 1983, p. 131; Westen 2007, p. 289; Claes and Krolikowski 2009, p. 91–92; Gallant 2009, p. 25; Hallevy 2010, p. 35–36, 40; Peristeridou 2015, p. 45, 72, 80.

criminal law under the guise of interpretation.[150] In light of the general wording of legislation, its democratic legitimation, as well as its public promulgation, it is also argued that *lex scripta* enhances legal certainty and prevents the arbitrary application of criminal law.[151]

2.3.3 THE PRINCIPLE THAT OFFENSES AND PENALTIES REQUIRE A CLEAR LEGAL DEFINITION *(LEX CERTA)*

The *lex certa* principle requires offenses and penalties to be clearly defined.[152] Since the construction of criminal law undeniably constitutes an element of the legislature's competence,[153] *lex certa* addresses the legislature by setting qualitative requirements for definitions of offenses and penalties.[154] If the *lex scripta* principle is not strictly upheld, however, and the judiciary is permitted to (partly) construct offenses and/or penalties, the *lex certa* principle could still apply to judge-made definitions in substantive criminal law.[155] Irrespective of the exact source of criminal law, the *lex certa* principle requires precise definitions of offenses and penalties so that individuals are able to distinguish between permitted and forbidden conduct in order to determine the applicable range of legal consequences for certain behavior.[156] Unsurprisingly, *lex certa* is therefore also safeguarded in common law legal systems, albeit mostly through its functional equivalent of the principle of maximum legal certainty.[157]

Since *lex certa* aims to enable individuals to distinguish between prohibited and permitted behavior, as well as between applicable and inapplicable penalties, an important goal of the principle is to provide legal certainty and to preclude the arbitrary use of criminal law.[158] Several authors from the civil law tradition have additionally identified the use of clear legislative definitions as a means to preclude the judicial creation of substantive criminal law. *Lex certa* is accordingly viewed as a principle that upholds the doctrine of the separation

---

150 See Krey 1983, p. 130–131; Claes and Krolikowski 2009, p. 91; Gallant 2009, p. 24; Hallevy 2010, p. 40. Cf Peristeridou 2015, p. 54.

151 See Krey 1983, p. 41, 130–131; Jarvers 2008, p. 57; Claes and Krolikowski 2009, p. 92; Peristeridou 2015, p. 72, 79–80.

152 See, eg, Wilson 1998, p. 21; Nan 2011, p. 16; Dreyer 2012, p. 179–186; Masferrer 2013, p. 282.

153 Certainly if one upholds the *lex scripta* principle as was traditionally done in civil law systems, see subsection 2.3.2 above.

154 See Desportes and LeGunehec 2008, p. 169; Hallevy 2010, p. 139–140; Borgers 2011, p. 106; Peristeridou 2011, p. 70, 72–73.

155 See Forster 2008, p. Cf Peristeridou 2011, p. 74, 80, 85.

156 Cf Alldridge 2002, p. 103, 119; Peristeridou 2011, p. 71, 74–75; Peristeridou 2015, p. 86–88.

157 See Peristeridou 2011, p. 73–75; Ashworth and Horder 2013, p. 62–65; Peristeridou 2015, p. 86.

158 See Krey 1983, p. 136–137; Jarvers 2008, p. 60; Claes and Krolikowski 2009, p. 91; Nan 2011, p. 16, 79; Ashworth and Horder 2013, p. 64–65; Pradel 2014, p. 136; Peristeridou 2015, p. 90. Cf Packer 1969, p. 94–95; Westen 2007, p. 292–293.

of powers by ensuring a separation between the construction of criminal law by the legislature and its application and interpretation by the judiciary.[159] By aiming to prevent the judicial construction of criminal law, *lex certa* is also understood as protecting the democratic legitimacy of criminal norms and penalties.[160]

2.3.4 THE PROHIBITION ON THE OVERLY EXTENSIVE INTERPRETATION OF OFFENSES AND PENALTIES (*LEX STRICTA*)

As an element of the legality principle, *lex stricta* aims to limit certain expansive interpretations of criminal law and/or their immediate application. It does not absolutely preclude these interpretations and applications, which reduces *lex stricta* to the prohibition on *overly* extensive interpretation of offenses and penalties. This prohibition is obviously addressed to the actor that mainly interprets and applies criminal law: the judiciary.[161]

In civil law legal systems, *lex stricta* was traditionally viewed as binding the judiciary to the wording of the applicable criminal law *legislation*.[162] Conceptually, however, *lex stricta* could be perceived as binding the application and interpretation of crimes and penalties to the pre-existing law, regardless whether that law is democratically legitimated legislation or judge-made case-law.[163] As noted above with regard to *lex certa*, the *lex stricta* principle could still restrict the available room for judicial interpretation even when viewed in isolation from the *lex scripta* principle. This means that a functional equivalent of the *lex stricta* principle is conceivable in common law legal systems and it is not, therefore, surprising that it is noticeable in, for example, the functioning of judicial precedents in common law states.[164]

When *lex stricta* is viewed in isolation from the requirement that offenses and penalties are defined by *statutory* criminal law, it becomes apparent that the principle is primarily intended to preclude arbitrariness in the application

159 Cf Krey 1983, p. 85, 138; Claes 2011, p. 98; Nan 2011, p. 108; Peristeridou 2015, p. 90; Altena-Davidsen 2016, p. 159.

160 See Krey 1983, p. 138; Nan 2011, p. 79; Peristeridou 2015, p. 90.

161 See Peristeridou 2015, p. 91.

162 See Boot 2002, p. 101, 107; Desportes and LeGunehec 2008, p. 150–151; Peristeridou 2015, p. 90–91.

163 Cf Ashworth and Horder 2013, p. 69.

164 See Hall 1937, p. 179–180; Packer 1969, p. 88; Wilson 1998, p. 21; Peristeridou 2015, p. 94–95. The rule of strict construction of penal statutes could also be considered to be a functional equivalent, see Wilson 1998, p. 21; Simester and Sullivan 2007, p. 47–49; Forster 2008, p. 35–36; Ashworth and Horder 2013, p. 67–71; Peristeridou 2015, p. 91–92. For observations about the link between the rule of strict construction and the legality principle in US criminal law, see Packer 1969, p. 95–96; Boot 2002, p. 122–125; Westen 2007, p. 281.

of criminal law and to protect legal certainty.[165] Both continental and common law legal systems require limits on judicial interpretation in order to prevent the judge from employing its powers in a way that results in arbitrary conviction and punishment.[166] If judicial interpretation is unlimited, and the existing law could be expanded and applied without constraints, individuals could never be certain about what conduct falls within the scope of criminal law, nor about the applicable penalties.[167] All could then depend on the subjective opinion of the judge in an individual case. Requiring judicial interpretations to be sufficiently in line with previously established law provides guidance about the scope of criminal law by establishing more or less objective limits to the (use of) interpretive activity in individual cases.[168]

In order to safeguard legal certainty and preclude arbitrariness for individuals, the room for judicial interpretation itself does not necessarily need to be limited. For *lex stricta* to protect the aforementioned values it could be sufficient to establish limits to *the application of* expansive judicial interpretations to the detriment of the accused.[169] Expansive judicial interpretations are, in fact, only unforeseeable or arbitrary from the perspective of the individual when they are directly applied to his/her case (while being sufficiently novel and expansive).

In addition to prohibiting the application of overly expansive interpretations to the detriment of the accused, *lex stricta* could also be interpreted as limiting the room for judicial interpretation *as such*.[170] This is the case in the civil law tradition where *lex stricta* is additionally deemed to safeguard both the doctrine of the separation of powers and the principle of democracy.[171] By only allowing limited room for the judicial interpretation of crimes and penalties, it is argued, *lex stricta* ensures the proper division of labor between the legislature and the judiciary.[172] The principle is then viewed as precluding the judiciary from taking over the legislative task by constructing offenses and penalties under the guise

165 See Krey 1983, p. 136; Claes and Krolikowski 2009, p. 91; Peristeridou 2015, p. 90. Peristeridou interpreted arbitrariness broadly. In her view, illegitimate substantive interpretations by the judiciary violate the *lex stricta* principle, see Peristeridou 2015, p. 114, 128. I will not consider 'substantive illegitimacy' as a factor to indicate judicial arbitrariness.

166 See Desportes and LeGunehec 2008, p. 150; Claes and Krolokowski 2009, p. 90. Cf Boot 2002, p. 107.

167 Cf Boot 2002, p. 101; Gallant 2009, p. 13.

168 Cf Boot 2002, p. 94, 107; Gallant 2009, p. 34.

169 Cf Altena-Davidsen 2016, p. 214–216. The distinction between interpretation and application is based on the distinction between 'interpretation' and 'adjudication' as distinct (judicial) stages in the operation of the law, see Popović 2014, p. 60.

170 Cf Altena-Davidsen 2016, p. 214–216.

171 See Krey 1983, p. 135–136; Altena-Davidsen 2016, p. 32. Ashworth and Horder have deemed the 'constitutional argument' about a proper division of roles between the legislature and judiciary as relevant for the principle of strict construction in English common law, see Ashworth and Horder 2013, p. 69.

172 Cf De Hullu 2015, p. 108.

of interpretation and application.[173] In this view, the principle limits not just the application of overly expansive judicial interpretations to the individual's detriment, but also the interpretive leeway that the judiciary is generally allowed.

2.3.5 THE PROHIBITION ON THE RETROACTIVE APPLICATION OF THE DEFINITIONS OF OFFENSES AND PENALTIES *(LEX PRAEVIA)*

The *lex praevia* principle prohibits the retroactive construction and application of offenses and penalties to the detriment of the accused.[174] The principle is relevant for both the legislature and the judiciary.[175] It precludes the legislature from attaching retroactive force to freshly constructed offenses and penalties.[176] At the same time, it aims to prevent the judiciary from retroactively applying new offenses and penalties.[177]

The principle of non-retroactivity is mainly acknowledged as a tool to prevent arbitrariness and to protect legal certainty in both European legal traditions.[178] A state would be able to arbitrarily target individuals by retroactively prescribing criminal responsibility for acts that were previously permitted. The same is true when the judiciary is given the power to retroactively apply new crimes and penalties.[179] Like the secondary principles described in the preceding subsections, the *lex praevia* principle is sometimes also considered to uphold the doctrine of the separation of powers and to protect democracy.[180]

---

173 The prohibition on overly extensive interpretation is therefore mostly recognized as a prohibition on analogical interpretation, which underlines that the courts should not go beyond the offenses and penalties as constructed by the legislature, see Schünemann 1978, p. 17; Boot 2002, p. 100–102; Desportes and LeGunehec 2008, p. 155–158; Jarvers 2008, p. 61; Gallant 2009, p. 37, 49; Hallevy 2010, p. 147–148; Renout 2012, p. 27; Masferrer 2013, p. 282; De Hullu 2015, p. 100; Peristeridou 2015, p. 93–94. Altena-Davidsen deems the distinction between analogical and (overly) extensive interpretation impure, because analogical interpretation refers to the process and methods of interpretation, while (overly) extensive interpretation refers to the product of interpretation, see Altena-Davidsen 2016, p. 212–213.

174 It does not prevent retroactivity which restricts the scope of previously existing criminal liability or reduces the severity of the applicable penalty, see Peristeridou 2015, p. 82–83. Under the *lex mitior* principle, the state can even be required to retroactively apply more lenient criminal law, see further on this principle ECHR chapter and EU chapter and chapter 1. On the *lex mitior* principle see also Peristeridou 2015, p. 16; Altena-Davidsen 2016, p. 33, 303–315.

175 See Simester and Sullivan 2007, p. 23; Forster 2008, p. 36–37; Ashworth and Horder 2013, p. 67; Peristeridou 2015, p. 82; Altena-Davidsen 2016, p. 291. On the functioning of the *ex post facto* prohibition in US criminal law and the distinguishable requirements for the legislature and the judiciary, see Boot 2002, p. 119; Westen 2007, p. 249–250.

176 Cf Fuller 1969, p. 59; Juratowitch 2008, p. 35.

177 See Juratowitch 2008, p. 225–226; Peristeridou 2015, p. 82–83.

178 See Packer 1969, p. 80; Krey 1983, p. 132–133; Jarvers 2008, p. 63; Ashworth and Horder 2013, p. 58; Atrill 2005, p. 108; Peristeridou 2015, p. 85.

179 See Juratowitch 2008, p. 56. Cf Packer 1969, p. 85–86; Gallant 2009, p. 13, 21.

180 See Schünemann 1978, p. 24; Krey 1983, p. 55–56, 133; Gallant 2009, p. 24–25; Peristeridou 2015, p. 85; Altena-Davidsen 2016, p. 32–33, 291. For critique on this view, see Schreiber 1976, p. 219.

As a limit on judicial activity, the *lex praevia* principle is closely related to the *lex stricta* principle described in the preceding subsection. This is because both secondary principles essentially prohibit interpretations and applications of crimes and penalties that are insufficiently conform the criminal law that existed at the time that the individual conducted himself. Like *lex stricta*, the *lex praevia* principle can therefore be related to the rules on precedent in English law as well.[181] As a limit to judicial interpretation and application, the *lex praevia* principle actually fulfils a function that is very similar to the *lex stricta* principle.[182]

Although both *lex stricta* and *lex praevia* have been invoked to limit (the application of) novel and expansive judicial interpretations, the prohibition on adjudicative retroactivity does not extend the scope of the legality principle beyond the protection provided by *lex stricta*.[183] In the interest of conceptual clarity it is preferable to discard overlapping notions. I will therefore use the *lex praevia* principle only as a prohibition on the most obvious and explicit cases of retroactivity. These are: on the one hand, a legislature that constructs crimes and penalties on date X and requires the judiciary to apply that law to acts committed before date X, and, on the other hand, a judge that actually applies crimes and penalties that entered into force on date X to conduct displayed before date X.

Novel expansive interpretations of crimes and penalties that were formally in force at the time of the individual's conduct will not be considered relevant under the *lex praevia* principle. Even though (the application of) such interpretations could amount to (adjudicative) retroactivity in substance,[184] I will merely consider these judicial interpretations and applications to be potentially problematic under the *lex stricta* principle.

2.3.6 CONCLUDING REMARKS

The preceding subsections illustrated the four different elements of the legality principle. The growing consensus on the legality principle indicates that, in some form or another, the secondary principles *lex scripta*, *lex certa*, *lex stricta* and *lex praevia* are all of value for the review of the legality principles constructed under the ECHR and in EU law. Although the emerging consensus justifies the focus on the aforementioned specific elements, it is important to underline that some of the elements continue to be perceived differently between the main European legal traditions. The legality principle in common law states therefore still remains distinguishable from the legality principle in civil law states.

---

181 See Fuller 1969, p. 57; Juratowitch 2008, p. 42, 125–126; Peristeridou 2015, p. 84–85.

182 See Gallant 2009, p. 35.

183 Peristeridou comes to the same conclusion under the 'relational model of criminal justice', albeit, in her view, because the need to apply *lex praevia* in addition to *lex stricta* would indicate the illegitimacy of the product of judicial interpretation, see Peristeridou 2015, p. 169.

184 See Juratowitch 2008, p. 35–42, 120; Hallevy 2010, p. 41–42, 148, 151–152.

The most obvious difference between the two legal traditions concerns the *lex scripta* principle. Strictly speaking, *lex scripta* is only upheld by European states with a civil law tradition. *Lex scripta* resulted from the continental view that it was highly important to separate the legislative task of creating criminal law from the judicial task of interpreting and applying the law in specific circumstances. By incorporating *lex scripta*, the civil law legality principle is viewed as protecting the doctrine of the separation of powers and the value of democracy.

The relevance of the doctrine of the separation of powers and the value of democracy goes beyond the recognition of the *lex scripta* principle, however. In the civil law tradition, criminal law theory also recognizes *lex certa*, *lex stricta* and *lex praevia* as fostering the doctrine of the separation of powers and the value of democracy. In addition to preventing arbitrariness and ensuring legal certainty, the continental view on legality thus recognizes two further rationales: the doctrine of the separation of powers and the value of democracy.[185]

Since common law countries have traditionally allowed the judicial creation of offenses and penalties, legal theory in that tradition has not required a comparably strict separation of powers between the legislature and the judiciary.[186] When the judiciary is allowed to create new offenses and penalties, the requirement that criminal law be legislatively constructed is not fully protected. Since judges are not generally elected democratically in European states, the requirement to construct criminal law democratically will not be upheld absolutely either. Accordingly, common law views do not generally identify the separation of powers and the value of democracy as rationales for the legality principle. In the common law view, legality is essentially deemed to protect legal certainty by precluding arbitrariness in the use of criminal law.

The historical acceptability of the judicial creation of offenses and penalties in the common law tradition has not only resulted in the understanding that the prohibition on arbitrariness and the value of legal certainty are the principle's sole theoretical foundation. It has also impacted the recognition of the specific elements of the legality principle. Contrary to civil law legality, the common law view does not generally recognize *lex scripta*. Strictly speaking, therefore, the common law legality principle merely contains three elements: the secondary principles *lex certa*, *lex stricta* and *lex praevia*, which are, as described above, mostly protected through the use of functional equivalents.

The differences between the two legal traditions have thus resulted in two distinct conceptions of legality: a civil law conception and a common law conception (see the two figures below). Section 2.4 will further examine these conceptions of legality with a particular focus on their rationales. That section will also illustrate how the distinct rationales affect the substantive content of the secondary elements of each conception.

---

185 Cf Manes 2017, p. 336.

186 Cf Lautenbach 2013, p. 26, 36.

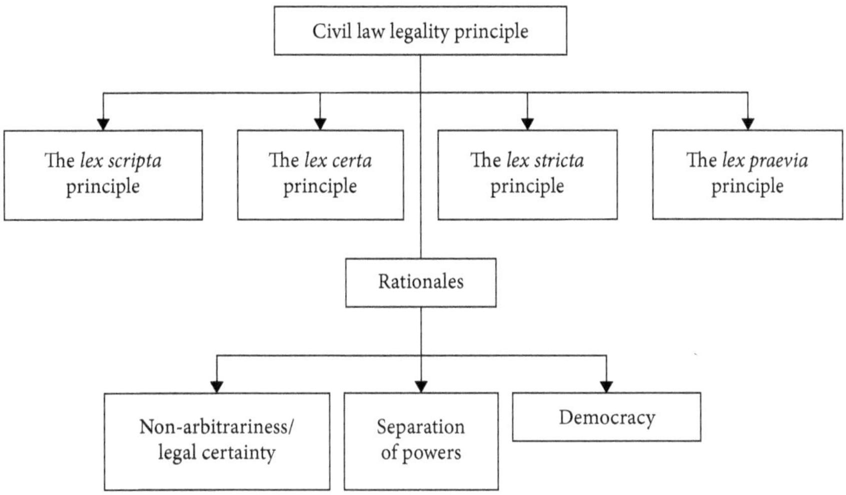

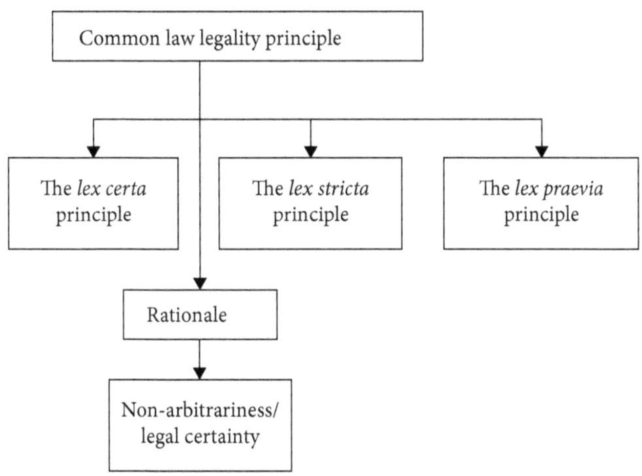

2.4 DISTINCT CONCEPTIONS OF LEGALITY AND THE RATIONALES FOR THE PRINCIPLE

2.4.1 INTRODUCTION

The preceding sections described the legality principle's univocal historical development and its interpretation in contemporary criminal law theory. The overview of contemporary theory shows that, despite a broad consensus on the principle's significance, there continue to exist different conceptions of the legality principle. Since the different conceptions correspond to the differences between the civil law tradition and the common law, I have distinguished between a civil law legality principle and a common law conception of legality.

As briefly described in section 2.3, the two conceptions of legality each have their own substantive content, although overlap exists. The present section examines the two conceptions of legality further by focusing on the distinct rationales that have been recognized in criminal law theory. It examines the following as potential rationales for the legality principle: firstly, the related notions of non-arbitrariness and legal certainty, secondly, the doctrine of the separation of powers and, thirdly, the principle of democracy.[187] Subsection 2.4.3 demonstrates that these notions can actually be reduced to two rationales: 'the rule of law rationale' and 'the democracy rationale'.

The present section determines that the two conceptions of legality protect different levels of legal certainty as a result of their distinct substantive content and rationales. Although both conceptions could protect legal certainty to the same extent, the level of legal certainty that is *necessarily* required is lower under the common law conception. It will be argued that this is mostly due to the recognition of the rule of law as the exclusive rationale for the common law legality principle. The different minimum level of legal certainty that is protected under both conceptions of legality will be illustrated, in subsection 2.4.4, by comparing legality protection in the Dutch 'stepchild case' with that in the English 'marital rape case'. Finally, subsection 2.4.5 will examine some arguments against the practical relevance of the theoretical distinction between the two conceptions.

2.4.2 INDIVIDUAL LIBERTY: THE PROTECTION AGAINST ARBITRARINESS, THE NOTION OF THE RULE OF LAW, AND THE PROTECTION OF LEGAL CERTAINTY

Section 2.3 set out how both the civil law conception of the legality principle and its common law counterpart are based on the importance of prohibiting arbitrariness and safeguarding legal certainty. The consensus that these values underpin the legality principle makes their examination an appropriate point of departure. Since the legality principle was historically developed in order to preclude the arbitrary use of criminal law,[188] this subsection will initially focus on the prohibition on arbitrariness.

The context of the legality principle's first modern formulations illustrates that the principle was mainly intended to protect against the arbitrary exercise

[187] As set out in chapter 1, I will not examine the principle of guilt or the value of crime prevention.
[188] See further section 2.2.

of punitive power by the state.[189] This primary aim was essential for legitimate government, because the arbitrary use of state power would fail to contribute to the better protection of the individual right to liberty.[190] Historically, the legality principle was, therefore, mostly intended to safeguard individual liberty against illegitimate interferences by the state which has the power to use criminal law as a tool for social control and public order.[191] As a prohibition on arbitrariness, the legality principle is unmistakably instrumental to the second function that positive law fulfills in the modern state.[192]

By regulating what is a legitimate interference with individual rights, positive criminal law limits the room for the exercise of invasive state power. The limiting role of positive law is presently recognized under the general notion of 'the rule of law'. Although the concept of restricted governmental power under the rule of law is not necessarily connected to the protection of individual liberty,[193] there exists a close connection between the contemporary (Western) notions of the rule of law and the value of liberty.[194] Unsurprisingly, the limitation of state power via the notion of the rule of law has been considered as safeguarding individual liberty.[195]

Since, in the above view, both the legality principle and the rule of law essentially aim to prevent the arbitrary exercise of state power in order to safeguard individual liberty, a conceptual connection exists between the two notions.[196] This connection is strengthened by the fact that both the legality principle and the rule of law were developed in broadly the same historical period by the same political philosophers.[197] One could therefore argue that the legality principle constitutes a specific expression, in the field of criminal law, of the overarching concept of the rule of law.[198] Whether or not legality is actually viewed as a specific expression of the rule of law, their close connection merits a brief examination of the conceptual background to the rule of law.

---

189 See Packer 1969, p. 80, 85; Krey 1983, p. 12, 129, 137–139; Rebut 2001, p. 250–251; Claes and Krolikowski 2009, p. 90, 92; Gallant 2009, p. 21–23; Nan 2011, p. 108; Borgers 2011, p. 105; Soleil 2013, p. 151; Cupido 2015, p. 5, 7–8; Peristeridou 2015, p. 16, 33, 137.

190 Cf Krey 1983, p. 13, 41; Gallant 2009, p. 21; Pradel 2014, p. 116.

191 See Schreiber 1976, p. 13, 52–55, 217, 219; Cadoppi and Veneziani 2005, p. 47; Peristeridou 2015, p. 33, 40.

192 See subsections 2.2.2, 2.2.4.

193 See Tamanaha 2004, p. 114–115, 137, 139.

194 On the close connection between modern conceptions of the rule of law and liberalism, see: Claes 2003, p. 93; Tamanaha 2004, p. 32–33; MacCormick 2005, p. 25; Westen 2007, p. 231; Ashworth and Horder 2013, p. 57; Lautenbach 2013, p. 22, 57.

195 See Schreiber 1976, p. 50; Krey 1983, p. 12–13, 130, 135, 137–139; Claes 2003, p. 89–91; Lautenbach 2013, p. 5, 15, 22, 54, 67; Himma 2014, p. 22; Peristeridou 2015, p. 56–57.

196 Cf Norrie 2001, p. 8; Rebut 2001, p. 251; Tamanaha 2004, p. 97–98, 139; Gallant 2009, p. 15; Schoep 2010, p. 79; Lautenbach 2013, p. 39–40, 56; Ramacci 2013, p. 68.

197 Tamanaha identifies classical and medieval roots of the rule of law but he deems the Enlightenment decisive for modern conceptions of the notion, see Tamanaha 2004, p. 27–29, 47–54. Cf Fernandez Esteban 1999, p. 68–89.

198 Cf Schreiber 1976, p. 213; Westen 2007, p. 230–231; Gallant 2009, p. 15.

As described, the rule of law is generally considered to safeguard individual liberty. On this understanding, the rule of law essentially provides legal liberty: the freedom for individuals to do whatever is not explicitly proscribed by law and to remain free from consequences that the laws fail to stipulate.[199] Legal restrictions on the state's powers consequently provide individuals with the ability to rely on the law.[200] The legal limitations allow individuals to identify conduct that will not, in principle, be within the scope of the law.[201] Individuals are thereby able to take notice of the scope of the applicable offenses and penalties so that they can adapt their behavior on the basis of the foreseeability of its legal implications.[202] This enables individuals to conduct themselves with the confidence that their behavior falls outside the scope of legal prohibitions and without the fear of being subjected to the exercise of punitive powers.[203] The legal restrictions on the use of the law thus simultaneously provide legal liberty and legal certainty for individuals.[204]

The importance of legal liberty and legal certainty are clearly perceivable in formal conceptions of the rule of law.[205] Formal conceptions of the rule of law are considered dominant.[206] They focus on the source and form of the law and do not require the law to have a specific content.[207] Tamanaha identified several influential formal theories.[208] Despite their internal differences, the formal conceptions of the rule of law formulated by Friedrich Hayek,[209] Joseph Raz,[210] and Lon Fuller[211] all require law to be prospective, general, clear, public, equal, and relatively stable.[212] These requirements illustrate that the law implies legal

---

199 See Raz 1979, p. 220; Claes 2003, p. 62, 93; Tamanaha 2004, p. 34–35, 94; Lautenbach 2013, p. 48.

200 The *ability* to rely on the law is key here, actual reliance on the law is not necessary for a violation of legal certainty under the legality principle. On the distinction between the ability to rely and actual reliance, see Juratowitch 2008, p. 44–48; Hallevy 2010, p. 27–28.

201 Cf Gallant 2009, p. 18–19; Hallevy 2010, p. 5; De Hullu 2015, p. 86–87.

202 See Gallant 2009, p. 20–22; Brink and Nelkin 2013, p. 307.

203 Cf Claes 2003, p. 36–38; Gallant 2009, p. 21; Hallevy 2010, p. 27.

204 Cf Eser 2010, Rn 10. In addition to legal liberty and legal certainty, legal equality and the neutrality of the state have also been considered essential in states which respect the rule of law, see Claes 2003, p. 100–101; Tamanaha 2004, p. 32–33; Claes and Krolikowski 2009, p. 92–93; Lautenbach 2013, p. 43–44; Peristeridou 2015, p. 57–58.

205 See Fuller 1969, p. 53, 59; Raz 1979, p. 213–214, 218; Tamanaha 2004, p. 66, 93, 119, 122, 135; MacCormick 2005, p. 12, 16; Simester and Sullivan 2007, p. 21; Stevenson and Harris 2010, p. 521; Ashworth and Horder 2013, p. 73; Lautenbach 2013, p. 41–42, 47–48; Himma 2014, p. 22; Peristeridou 2015, p. 55.

206 See Tamanaha 2004, p. 92, 93, 111, 119; Celano 2013, p. 123; Lautenbach 2013, p. 21, 37–38, 48; Himma 2014, p. 16–17; Merli 2016, p. 44. Schroeder views the established European rule of law tradition to entail the prohibition on arbitrariness as a material element, see Schroeder 2016, p. 26. In my view, however, the prohibition on arbitrariness is upheld as a result of the formal requirements. It does not, itself, constitute a substantive element.

207 See Fernandez Esteban 1999, p. 91; Tamanaha 2004, p. 92; Peristeridou 2015, p. 55–56.

208 See Tamanaha 2004, p. 93–94. See also Peristeridou 2015, p. 55.

209 See Hayek 1945, p. 57.

210 See Raz 1979, p. 213.

211 See Fuller 1969, p. 46–91.

212 See Tamanaha 2004, p. 65–67, 93–94. Cf Lautenbach 2013, p. 67; Himma 2014, p. 19–20; Merli 2016, p. 42.

limitations on the use of governmental power and that predictability is essential: the law needs to enable individuals to know what conduct is permissible and the limited range of activities the law prohibits.[213]

The unmistakable relevance of legal certainty to the rule of law should be viewed with caution, however.[214] It is important to note that, under the rule of law, the protection of legal certainty results from the need to create legal restrictions on the exercise of punitive state power. Historically, these legal restrictions were deemed necessary to preclude governmental arbitrariness.[215] The level of legal certainty necessarily required by the rule of law could, therefore, be qualified by the aim of precluding arbitrariness by binding state power to the law. The risk of arbitrariness will be diminished when legal restrictions exist for the exercise of state power. In that event, legal liberty will be protected because state power is not then absolute and, as a result, there is a legal distinction between behavior that will prohibited and permitted. In this view, the rule of law unmistakably safeguards individual liberty by establishing a sphere of action beyond the state's reach.

Although the limitation on state power and the distinction between prohibited and permitted behavior offers some certainty about the reach of the law, this does not necessarily provide a meaningful ability to rely on the law.[216] The exercise of state power can still be deemed to be limited and non-arbitrary even if individuals are unaware of the exact limitations on state power. Strictly speaking, therefore, the legal limitations under the rule of law demarcate an area of individual behavior where the state cannot intervene, irrespective of the foreseeability of this demarcation.[217] As a prohibition on arbitrariness, the rule of law requires legal limitations on the exercise of state powers, whether they are widely known or not.

The above interpretation of the rule of law becomes relevant for the legality principle when the rule of law is understood as its rationale. As under this interpretation of the rule of law, the level of legal certainty necessarily protected by the legality principle could be equally limited. It has therefore been argued that, under the rule of law rationale, the legality principle merely aims to generate a climate of trust in the criminal justice system that the most invasive state powers will not be exercised arbitrarily.[218] As a matter of concept, the legality principle's rule of law rationale can thus be viewed

---

213 See Fuller 1969, p. 53, 59; Raz 1979, p. 213–214, 218; Tamanaha 2004, p. 66, 93, 119, 122, 135; MacCormick 2005, p. 12, 16; Simester and Sullivan 2007, p. 21; Stevenson and Harris 2010, p. 521; Ashworth and Horder 2013, p. 73; Lautenbach 2013, p. 41–42, 47–48; Himma 2014, p. 22; Peristeridou 2015, p. 55.

214 Peristeridou also distinguishes protection against arbitrariness from protection against uncertainty, see Peristeridou 2015, p. 134.

215 See Fernandez Esteban 1999, p. 93; Himma 2014, p. 20, 22–23.

216 Cf Himma 2014, p. 22–23.

217 Only a complete lack of foreseeability of prohibited conduct and the applicable penalties would necessarily amount to arbitrariness.

218 See Schreiber 1976, p. 214–217. Cf Claes 2009, p. 106–107; Claes 2011, p. 101–102.

as ensuring only a general certainty about the functioning of the criminal justice system in accordance with the law.[219] On this interpretation, the legality principle only requires the *non-arbitrary* exercise of criminal justice powers.[220] It does not necessarily entail the notion that individuals deserve to know the *exact* consequences of their specific acts and omissions before criminal punishment can be justified.[221] As a result, the legality principle's rule of law rationale does not *necessarily* protect the maximum predictability of the criminal law.

What is inevitably required of criminal law under the rule of law rationale is merely that the law limits the state's punitive power which, in turn, generates a climate of trust and enables individuals to *generally* foresee the consequences of their conduct and plan their actions accordingly.[222] In accordance with the views of several authors, the legality principle would still protect the value of legal certainty under the rule of law rationale.[223] It would, however, necessarily protect only the more general certainty that the law will not be defined and applied arbitrarily. The protection of the ability to rely on the law could thus be rather limited when the legality principle is merely deemed to protect the rule of law.

Subsection 2.4.4 makes these rather abstract considerations more tangible by providing two examples.

2.4.3 THE DOCTRINE OF THE SEPARATION OF POWERS AND THE VALUE OF DEMOCRACY

The overview of contemporary criminal law theory in section 2.3 shows that the legality principle is also understood as safeguarding the doctrine of the separation of powers and protecting the value of democracy. The present subsection will further examine these additional rationales, as well as their potential relevance for the civil law conception of legality and its common law counterpart.

---

219 Cf Schreiber 1976, p. 217–218.

220 Cf Claes 2003, p. 195–196, 200–201, 209–211, 404, 465–466. Packer has argued that the legal certainty rationale is merely a thinly disguised version of the prohibition on arbitrariness which is a more sophisticated rationale for the legality principle, see Packer 1969, p. 85.

221 For critique of this 'conventional' view in which fair notice is the legality principle's central aim, see Packer 1969, p. 80, 85; Westen 2007, p. 264, 279–280, 296. For an overview of the debate about legal certainty as foreseeability of criminal responsibility in German criminal law doctrine, see Peristeridou 2015, p. 68.

222 Cf Schreiber 1976, p. 215.

223 See subsection 2.4.2 and further Schreiber 1976, p. 214–220; Krey 1983, p. 132, 135–136; Groenhuijsen 1987; p. 31; Claes and Krolikowski 2009, p. 92–93; Gallant 2009, p. 21; Borgers 2011, p. 105; De Hullu 2015, p. 86–87; Mayaud 2015, p. 28–31; Peristeridou 2015, p. 55, 58, 61; Altena-Davidsen 2016, p. 41–42. Cf Claes 2003, p. 193; Stevenson and Harris 2010, p. 526.

The doctrine of the separation of powers is often identified as a rationale for the legality principle.[224] As described in subsection 2.2.3, the separation of powers was historically proposed to prevent the abuse of state power by distributing it over different organs.[225] It was deemed necessary to separate the power of constructing criminal law on the one hand, and its interpretation and application on the other. Failure to attribute these powers to distinct institutions would increase the risk of misuses of power and, consequently, the arbitrary deployment of criminal law.

On the above view, the doctrine of the separation of powers evidently constitutes an instrument to preclude the arbitrary use of criminal law.[226] The separation of powers can help ensure the aim behind the legality principle of protecting individual liberty by precluding the arbitrary exercise state power.[227] Since, in this view, the separation of powers aims to protect the exact same values as the rule of law rationale,[228] it merely constitutes a secondary rationale for the legality principle. On this interpretation, the doctrine of the separation of powers is thus best viewed as a subordinate element of the primary rule of law rationale.[229] Like the rule of law rationale, this interpretation of the separation of powers could be equally relevant for the two distinguishable conceptions of legality.[230]

There are, however, different interpretations of the separation of powers. A divergent interpretation of the relationship between the separation of powers and the legality principle does, in fact, exist. This second interpretation essentially considers the separation between the legislative construction and the judicial interpretation of criminal law necessary for the protection of democracy.[231] This is because, unlike the judiciary, the legislature in a democratic state is usually elected on the basis of representative procedures.[232] In order to protect

---

224 See Schreiber 1976, p. 218–219; Schünemann 1978, p. 9; Krey 1983, p. 131–139; Boot 2002, p. 83; Claes and Krolikowski 2009, p. 91; Gallant 2009, p. 24–26; Hallevy 2010, p. 39–42; Renout 2012, p. 20; Masferrer 2013, p. 275; Peristeridou 2015, p. 48–54; Manes 2017, p. 336, 338, 346. Cf Ashworth and Horder 2013, p. 45, 57, 69.

225 For a more elaborate and detailed historical description, see Möllers 2013, p. 16–50.

226 Cf Lautenbach 2013, p. 49–50.

227 See the references to the theories of Locke, Montesquieu and Beccaria in subsection 2.2.3. Cf Schreiber 1976, p. 58; Schünemann 1978, p. 2, 9–11; Peristeridou 2015, p. 49; Altena-Davidsen 2016, p. 26–28.

228 For this rationale, see subsection 2.4.2.

229 This could explain why Krey regards the doctrine of the separation of powers to be an element of the legality principle's rule of law rationale ('*Rechtstaatliche Aspekte*'), see Krey 1983, p. 130–138. Some authors do indeed regard the doctrine of the separation of powers to be inherent in the notion of the rule of law, see Fernandez Esteban 1999, p. 95; Lautenbach 2013, p. 49, 67.

230 Cf Peristeridou 2015, p. 70–71.

231 See Schünemann 1978, p. 11; Claes 2003, p. 103–104, 215–216, 459; Claes and Krolikowski 2009, p. 91; Gallant 2009, p. 25; Hallevy 2010, p. 40; Peristeridou 2015, p. 48.

232 Cf Gallant 2009, p. 25.

the democratic legitimacy of criminal law, the construction of offenses and penalties should be assigned exclusively to the legislature. On this view, it is the value of democracy that provides the argument for upholding the doctrine of the separation of powers.[233]

The second interpretation of the separation of powers doctrine shows how the principle of democracy is a rationale for the principle of legality.[234] Democracy, as a rationale for legality, has been deemed particularly important for securing the legitimacy of criminal law. If substantive criminal law is democratically legitimated, it is argued, the law conforms to the will of the people.[235] This legitimates the exercise of the state's most invasive powers; the people can be viewed as having agreed to be subjected to these powers in certain circumstances.[236] The exercise of punitive state powers would then respect the people's self-determination and, consequently, collective autonomy and political liberty.[237]

If substantive criminal law must be democratically legitimated, this affects the legality principle's protection of both legal liberty and legal certainty. Under the democracy rationale a conviction is traditionally considered legitimate only if it strictly conforms to existing criminal law *legislation*, meaning that the application and interpretation of criminal law should be restrictive. This generally requires a rather reserved judiciary that willingly defers to the democratically legitimated legislature when it is confronted with the possibility of the judicial development of criminal law. Thus, the democracy rationale results in a *strict* separation of powers.[238] This strict separation of powers restricts the scope of application and interpretation of criminal law by the executive and the judiciary, which could consequently provide a broader sphere of action for individuals than is necessarily provided by the rule of law rationale. Legal liberty could thus be enhanced by the acknowledgment of the democracy rationale and the ensuing strict separation of powers.

233 Cf Lautenbach 2013, p. 51.

234 See Schreiber 1976, p. 218–219; Krey 1983, p. 131, 135–139; Groenhuijsen 1987, p. 56; Boot 2002, p. 95; Desportes and LeGunehec 2008, p. 148–149; Claes and Krolikowski 2009, p. 91; Gallant 2009, p. 24–25; Borgers 2011, p. 107; Dreyer 2012, p. 169–170; Peristeridou 2015, p. 43–48.

235 Cf Hallevy 2010, p. 21–22.

236 See Groenhuijsen 1987, p. 56–57; Boot 2002, p. 95; Claes and Krolikowski 2009, p. 91–92; Peristeridou 2015, p. 45.

237 See, eg, Claes 2003, p. 102–103, 426; Tamanaha 2004, p. 105; Claes and Krolikowski 2009, p. 91; Peristeridou 2015, p. 37–38, 43, 47. Cf Fernandez Esteban 1999, p. 83.

238 While a strict separation of powers with limited room for judicial interpretation have been related to democracy, especially in civil law conceptions of legality, this relationship is not conceptually necessary. It is, for example, possible for the democratically legitimated legislature to intentionally draft legislation that provides broad room for judicial interpretation. In that event, it could be argued that the lack of a strict separation of powers would not necessarily be problematic with regard to democracy, because the legislature intentionally deferred to the judiciary.

A consequence of the increased deference to the legislature in the field of criminal law is not only the potentially greater sphere of permitted individual action. The democracy rationale and the strict separation of powers also mean that the legality principle potentially protects a higher amount of legal certainty. Deference to the legislature is further encouraged by the idea that consent to the construction of offenses and penalties increases the foreseeability of the use of the state's criminal law powers.[239] On this understanding, the legality principle requires a legal resolution in the accused's favor if the existing criminal law raises doubts about the exact scope of criminal responsibility or the applicable penalty for the individual's acts. This contrasts with the rule of law rationale, where legal certainty is only violated when criminal law is used in an arbitrary fashion and where there is a lack of foreseeability regarding criminalized conduct and the applicable penalties. The legality principle is therefore deemed to protect not just a general, but rather a specific, legal certainty which provides an actual ability to rely on the law.[240]

Greater protection of legal certainty by the legality principle amounts to what Claes has described as 'maximum predictability'.[241] The maximum predictability of the state's punitive powers has been deemed relevant under classical constructions of the legality principle in civil law. On the classical continental view, a conviction is legitimate only when it is completely and strictly in conformity with existing criminal law *legislation*.[242] The view that the legality principle requires maximum predictability is, therefore, highly compatible with the civil law conception which, in turn, requires a strict separation of powers under the democracy rationale. Essentially, it requires that near absolute certainty about the scope of criminal offenses can be derived from the wording of legislation. It consequently precludes the judicial and executive expansion of crimes and penalties.[243]

The present and preceding subsections illustrate that the three notions underlying the legality principle result in two distinguishable rationales, which in turn, impact the level of legal certainty that is necessarily protected. The figures below provide a brief overview of the two conceptions of legality and can be compared with the figure presented at the end of subsection 2.3.6.

---

239 Cf Merli 2016, p. 43.

240 See Borgers 2011, p. 148; Peristeridou 2015, p. 68.

241 See Claes 2003, p. 19, 22, 25, 38–39, 67, 84, 192–193, 214–215.

242 Cf De Jong 1999, p. 687.

243 See Claes 2003, p. 38–39.

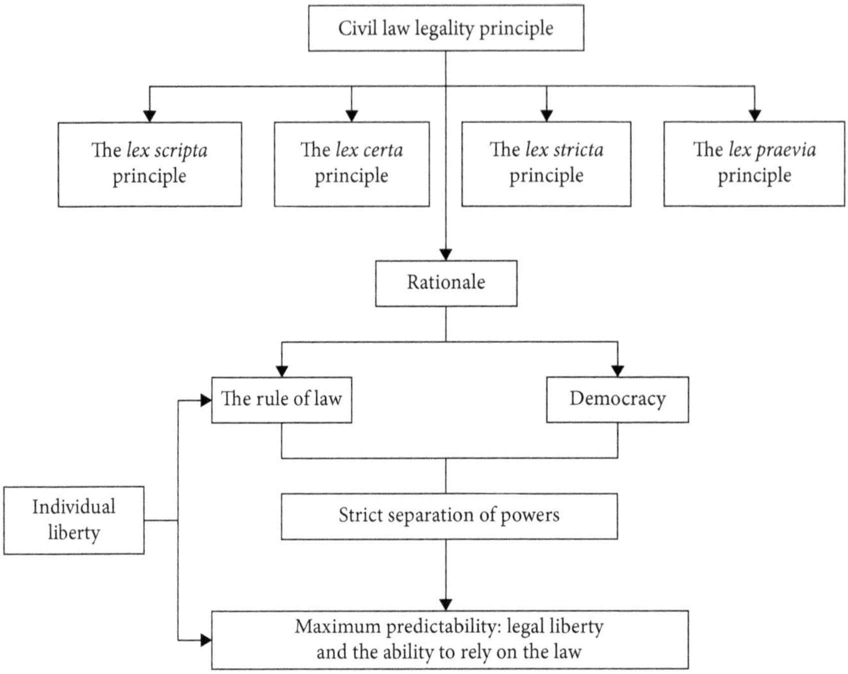
Civil law legality principle
The *lex scripta* principle
The *lex certa* principle
The *lex stricta* principle
The *lex praevia* principle
Rationale
The rule of law
Democracy
Individual liberty
Strict separation of powers
Maximum predictability: legal liberty and the ability to rely on the law

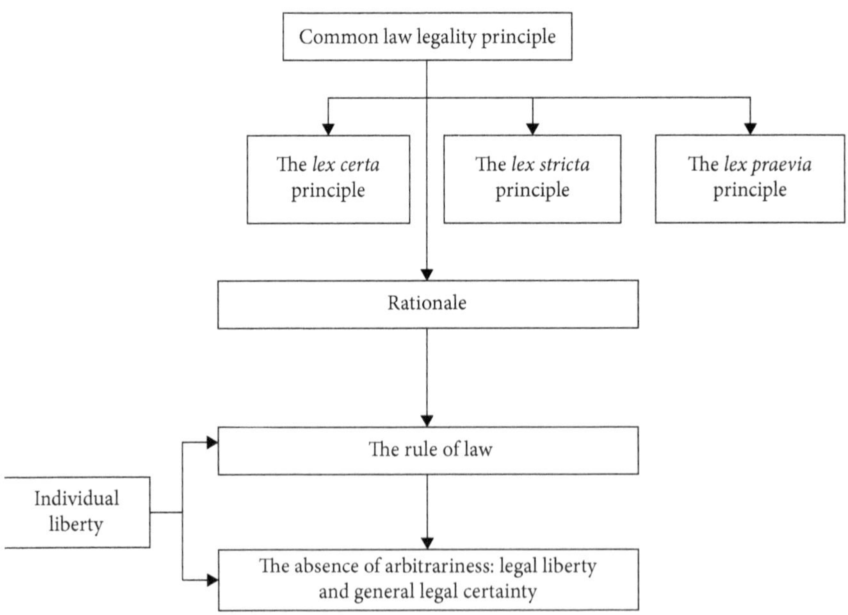
Common law legality principle
The *lex certa* principle
The *lex stricta* principle
The *lex praevia* principle
Rationale
The rule of law
Individual liberty
The absence of arbitrariness: legal liberty and general legal certainty

2.4.4 ILLUSTRATIONS OF THE DISTINCT CONCEPTIONS: SEXUAL ABUSE OF A STEPCHILD AND MARITAL RAPE

This subsection illustrates the practical effects that stem from the recognition that different theoretical foundations underpin the legality principle. By comparing the Dutch 'stepchild case' with the English 'marital rape case' this subsection highlights the differing attitudes towards the expansive judicial interpretation of criminal law in the two legal traditions. This comparison will illustrate how the democracy rationale restricts the potential for judicial interpretation more than under a legality principle that merely protects the rule of law. The comparison between the two approaches exemplifies how the distinct conceptions impact the protection of legal certainty.

The stepchild case

In the stepchild case – decided by the Supreme Court of The Netherlands (*Hoge Raad*) – the defendant was accused of committing sexual indecencies with his partner's seventeen year old daughter.[244] The defendant was prosecuted under (what was then) Article 249 of the Dutch Criminal Code (*Wetboek van Strafrecht*), which criminalized the commission of indecencies with a minor child or a stepchild. At the time of the indecencies, however, the defendant was not married to the victim's mother. This circumstance made it questionable whether the victim could be qualified as the defendant's 'stepchild' as (then) required for a conviction under Article 249 CC.

The Supreme Court deemed the provision's legislative history decisive for the interpretation of the statutory term. According to the *Hoge Raad*, the legislature drafting the provision in 1936 had, by the term stepchild, only intended to criminalize indecencies with the minor child of a partner to whom the suspect was married.[245] Marriage with the parent of the minor child was therefore a necessary element for a conviction for sexual abuse of a stepchild under Article 249 CC. According to the Supreme Court, the legality principle required judicial restraint due to the existence of the historical legislative intention.[246] It precluded an interpretation of the statutory term that would expand criminal liability to those not married to the victim's parent. Although a broader interpretation of the term stepchild would fit better with the contemporary views on living arrangements, the court left it to the legislature to explicitly expand the scope of the provision in accordance with the evidently changed societal views.[247]

---

244 See Hoge Raad, 7 January 1997, ECLI:NL:HR:1997:ZD0608.

245 See para 4.3.1.

246 See para 4.3.2. This interpretation is in line with the description of judicial interpretation of criminal law under the classical continental legality principle, see Claes 2003, p. 29–33, 52–53, 106. Cf Borgers 2011, p. 115; Nan 2011, p. 30, 33–34.

247 See para 4.3.2.

In the stepchild case the legality principle precluded a contemporary interpretation of the statutory term. The Dutch Supreme Court deferred to the legislature to expand the scope of criminal responsibility, even though the court implied that it deemed such an expansion appropriate in light of the purpose of the provision. In order to fully protect minors from sexual abuse by people on whom they depend, it would be necessary to acknowledge that life companions were increasingly living together outside of marriage. That the legislature had not intended for the statutory term 'stepchild' to apply to the unmarried partner of the minor's parent was only because such living arrangements were highly exceptional, if not inconceivable, when the provision was drafted many decades ago.

As the *Hoge Raad* indicated, a broader interpretation could be justified in light of both the purpose of Article 249 CC and the contemporary societal views on living arrangements. The Supreme Court could have invoked both these arguments to contend that an expansive judicial interpretation would not result in the arbitrary use of criminal law and would, therefore, respect general legal certainty. Under these circumstances, an expansive interpretation of the term stepchild could have been in conformity with the rule of law rationale for the legality principle. It could be argued that the Supreme Court would then only have brought the interpretation of Article 249 CC up to date and that it would not have substantively expanded the scope of the offense to the detriment of the accused. Since the *Hoge Raad* nevertheless deemed itself bound by the historical intentions of the legislature, it implicitly invoked the democracy rationale and the ensuing strict separation of powers to conclude that the legality principle precluded an expansive judicial interpretation. Deference to the legislature in the stepchild-case clearly protected the defendant from an expansive judicial interpretation to his detriment.

The marital rape case

The application of the civil law legality principle in Dutch law can be contrasted with the expansive approach to judicial interpretation by the House of Lords (now UK Supreme Court) in the marital rape case.[248] In this well-known English case, the male suspect attempted to have non-consensual sexual intercourse with his wife. At the time of the attempt, the suspect and the victim were legally married, but they were living separately and both had communicated the intention to petition for divorce.[249] After conviction by the trial court, the defendant appealed to the higher English courts arguing that sex within marriage could not amount to rape because the wife had automatically consented to the intercourse by virtue of the marriage.[250] This view had long been deemed correct under the common law and the statutory provision that criminalized

---

248 R. v. R. [1992] 1 AC 599. See further Juratowitch 2008, p. 127–138; Peristeridou 2015, p. 82–83.
249 R. v. R. [1992] 1 AC 599, p. 603 (CA).
250 R. v. R. [1992] 1 AC 599, p. 602 (CA).

rape had, arguably, codified this view by defining rape as 'unlawful sexual intercourse without consent'.[251] It was argued that the term 'unlawful' meant 'outside the bounds of matrimony' because it expressed the marital exception to rape that had been recognized in the common law.

Although the marital exemption had been restricted in case-law leading up to the marital rape case, it had never been abolished completely.[252] At the time the defendant attempted to rape his wife, both the wording of the applicable statutory provision and the common law still indicated the existence of limited criminal responsibility for rape within marriage. However, the English courts still interpreted the existing law on rape expansively to his detriment. As in the stepchild case, such an expansive interpretation was considered appropriate in light of changed societal views. The marital exception to rape was formulated at a time where the position of women was highly unequal to men.[253] Since societal views had changed significantly on these matters, the Court of Appeal did not consider itself limited by either the historical recognition of the marital exception in the common law or its apparent codification in the Sexual Offenses Act. In the appellate court's view "(...) the time has now arrived when the law should declare that a rapist remains a rapist subject to the criminal law, irrespective of his relationship with the victim."[254]

While the Court of Appeal's interpretation unmistakably expanded the scope of the existing offense of rape, such an interpretation was not deemed problematic with regard to the legality principle. In fact, reference to that principle is completely absent in the reasoning of both the Court of Appeal and the House of Lords.[255] The courts did, however, consider whether the expansion of the offense's scope needed to be left to the Parliamentary process. The Court of Appeal found this unnecessary since no new offense was created by judicial interpretation.[256] Instead, judicial interpretation merely removed an offensive and anachronistic common law fiction. The House of Lords confirmed the Court of Appeal's reasoning by concluding that, in modern times, the supposed marital exemption to rape forms no part of the law of England.[257]

Although expansive, the judicial interpretation of rape could be deemed non-arbitrary, because at the time of the suspect's attempt, there existed case-law that limited the scope of the marital exception to rape and societal views on marriage were unmistakably changed. The preceding cases and changed circumstances arguably provide legally relevant reasons for the expansion of the crime of

---

251 See Section 1(1) of the Sexual Offenses Act 1956 which was later copied into Section 1(1) of the Sexual Offenses Act 1976 as referred to in R. v. R. [1992] 1 AC 599, p. 608 (CA).
252 R. v. R. [1992] 1 AC 599, p. 610 (CA).
253 R. v. R. [1992] 1 AC 599, p. 617–618 (HL).
254 R. v. R. [1992] 1 AC 599, p. 611 (CA).
255 Cf Juratowitch 2008, p. 128.
256 R. v. R. [1992] 1 AC 599, p. 611 (CA).
257 R. v. R. [1992] 1 AC 599, p. 623 (HL).

rape to cases of forced sex within marriage. In light of these circumstances, the expansive interpretation to the detriment of the accused was not arbitrary. For that reason, the judicial expansion of rape could be viewed as according with the rule of law rationale for the legality principle.

At the same time, however, both the Court of Appeal and the House of Lords acknowledged the relevance of the statutory terms that could reasonably be viewed as precluding an expansive interpretation of the offense of rape. The same was true for a long line of authority in the common law that indicated the existence of a marital exemption. These circumstances clearly limited the foreseeability of the expansive interpretation of rape for the accused. They were not deemed to require deference to the legislature for the expansion of the scope of the offense, however. The absence of deference to the legislature could be explained by the historical refusal to recognize the democracy rationale for legality in the common law tradition and the ensuing absence of a *lex scripta* principle.

Observations

The comparison between the stepchild case and the marital rape case illustrates how the room for expansive judicial interpretation of criminal law diverges between European legal traditions. The difference can, in my view, be explained by the different theoretical foundations that underlie the distinct conceptions of the legality principle. If the rule of law rationale is understood as the sole foundation of the legality principle, there is room to apply expansive judicial interpretations of criminal law to the detriment of the accused. The criterion that necessarily determines the limits of such interpretations is only non-arbitrariness. In this view, the legality principle (ie *lex stricta*) potentially allows novel and expansive interpretations of crimes and penalties and their immediate application. It could also allow rather broad definitions in criminal law, because, under the rule of law rationale, the legality principle (ie *lex certa*) would merely preclude definitions that could easily result in the arbitrary application of criminal law by the judiciary and the executive.

When the legality principle is merely viewed as protecting the rule of law, the principle does not necessarily protect a high level of legal certainty. As described above, the lack of exact foreseeability of criminal responsibility in the marital rape case was not deemed decisive. Although the existing law had historically included a marital exemption for rape, and that exemption had never been officially abolished, the courts were not precluded from doing so for the first time in the case of the accused. It was not deemed decisive that the applicable law made the existence of criminal responsibility for rape within marriage highly doubtful. In order to be deemed non-arbitrary, it was sufficient that legal arguments existed for the novel and expansive interpretation. In essence, therefore, the rule of law rationale necessarily precludes only unreasonable interpretations and applications of the existing law which would jeopardize the protection of legal liberty. As a consequence, the interpretation by the English courts did not need to ensure specific foreseeability of criminal responsibility as required by maximum predictability. As described, the interpretation merely had to respect, and in fact respected, a more general certainty that is protected by upholding the prohibition on arbitrariness.

If, on the other hand, the democracy rationale is viewed as an additional foundation for the legality principle, the result appears to be a more stringent principle. As illustrated by the approach taken in the stepchild case, the legality principle can require deference to the legislature instead of the judicial expansion of the scope of criminal law. This deference follows from a strict separation of powers between the legislature and judiciary, which is ultimately deemed appropriate in order to safeguard the democratic legitimacy of criminal law. The democracy rationale could thus constitute an additional reason for judicial restraint in the interpretation of existing offenses and penalties. As a limit to judicial interpretation itself, it would obviously prevent the application of expansive judicial interpretations to the detriment of the accused. Conceptually, therefore, the civil law *lex stricta* principle could be more demanding than its common law counterpart.

The democracy rationale could potentially also require greater clarity in how criminal offenses are defined. Instead of merely precluding definitions that pose a high risk of arbitrariness, definitions could be required to be so precise that they ensure that their application remains conform their exact, democratically established, purpose.[258] The democracy rationale requires clearer legislative definitions than what is necessary if the aim is merely to preclude arbitrary application. As well as *lex stricta*, the civil law *lex certa* principle appears to require greater legal certainty than under the common law interpretation.

Deference to the legislature in the stepchild case could also be perceived as protecting an individual's ability to rely on the law. Although the purpose of the Dutch provision and changed societal circumstances provided some foreseeability of criminal responsibility for the accused's acts, the historical meaning of the legislative wording created doubts. By not convicting the accused under the existing law in these circumstances, the Dutch approach protected the defendant's ability to rely on the law. Although a conviction would not have amounted to the arbitrary use of criminal law, it would have violated the requirement of maximum predictability. This is because the application of the law to the accused's behavior was not exactly foreseeable on the basis of the historically communicated meaning of the term 'stepchild' in the existing legislation. The additional rationale of protecting democracy and the ensuing strict separation of powers, means the civil law legality principle necessarily enhances an individual's ability to rely on the law. This greater legal certainty could theoretically be protected under the rule of law rationale as well, but, as subsection 2.4.2 and the marital rape case demonstrated, this is not necessarily the case.

---

258 Cf Altena-Davidsen 2016, p. 139.

2.4.5 PRACTICAL RELEVANCE OF THE THEORETICAL DISTINCTIONS

The distinct conceptions of legality in European criminal law theory indicate divergence in the rationale for the legality principle. Differing rationales, in turn, appear to impact the minimum level of legal certainty required under each conception of legality. The civil law conception necessarily safeguards the ability to rely on the law by additionally recognizing the protection of democracy as a rationale for the principle of legality alongside the rule of law. The common law conception, on the other hand, necessarily ensures only a rather general certainty; the rule of law rationale protects against the arbitrary use of criminal law. Since the civil law legality principle evidently aims to ensure greater legal certainty for the accused, this conception is, at first sight, most protective of the individual that is subjected to the state's punitive powers.

The increased protection of the individual under the civil law legality conception appears to result from the recognition of the democracy rationale and the ensuing strict separation of powers. These characteristics explain why the civil law conception enshrines a *lex scripta* principle and why the principles of *lex certa* and *lex stricta* are generally more demanding than under the common law conception. The comparison between the stepchild case and the marital rape case demonstrated the additional demands of the civil law legality principle. In my view, this comparison illustrates that the civil law legality principle could indeed ensure a higher level of legal certainty than what is necessarily protected under the common law conception's rule of law rationale.

The theoretical distinction between the two conceptions of legality and their distinct rationales is not just an academic matter. It could have tangible consequences, because the two conceptions and/or their rationales regulate the legality principle's substantive content and, as a result, determine the level of legal certainty that is necessarily protected. The practical relevance of the theoretical distinctions set out above should, however, be assessed critically. It is, in fact, increasingly questioned whether the civil law legality principle is actually able to provide protection beyond the common law conception's rule of law rationale.

In essence, it is argued that the civil law legality principle is unable to effectively fulfil its aim as a limit on the exercise of criminal justice powers, because of, inter alia, the vague definitions used in contemporary criminal law and the significant room that is allowed for judicial interpretation of crimes and penalties.[259] These developments have, arguably, jeopardized the attainability

[259] See Schünemann 1978, p. 3–8; Claes 2003, p. 19, 125–166; Claes and Krolikowski 2009, p. 90–91; Borgers 2011, p. 107, 113, 115–116; Nan 2011, p. 18, 30–49; Renout 2012, p. 31–33; Pradel 2014, p. 137–138; Bernardini 2015, p. 174, 180–181; Peristeridou 2015, p. 119.

of a strict division of labor between the legislature and the judiciary.[260] Some observers, therefore, deem it to be "(...) a common experience among lawyers and legal practitioners that legality has encountered important limits with regard to its guarantee-providing role".[261]

Recognizing it as possible, in practice, to distinguish the tasks of constructing and applying the law is said to result from an overly simplistic view of language, as well as an unsophisticated understanding of legal reasoning.[262] With regard to language, criminal law doctrine now seems to accept that language and, consequently, legal norms, inevitably allow for multiple reasonable interpretations.[263] Therefore, it is argued that even sufficiently promulgated crimes and penalties can never be completely clear in themselves. The general, abstract and, sometimes evaluative, terms used in criminal law cannot provide absolute certainty prospectively and they cannot, for that reason, offer complete foreseeability regarding the applicability and scope of the law in all specific circumstances.[264] As a result of the openness and indeterminacy of (legal) language, individuals will have to accept an amount of vagueness and uncertainty.[265] Contrary to what might have been the prevailing view at the time of the first tentative formulations of the legality principle, criminal law is presently deemed to be unable to provide notice on the applicability of crimes and penalties in all specific circumstances.[266]

The law's indeterminacy not only implies that some uncertainty about the meaning and scope of criminal law has to be accepted. It also implies that the meaning of the law can sometimes be discovered only in light of specific factual circumstances.[267] This is especially because the legislature cannot anticipate every factual situation in advance.[268] This means that, now and then, the clarification of the law depends on its interpretation in a specific case, which indicates a significant role for the judiciary.[269] In addition to the contemporary consensus on the limited certainty that language can provide, it is presently acknowledged that

260 See Packer 1969, p. 86–87, 92–93; Schreiber 1976, p. 221, 225; Claes and Krolikowski 2009, p. 104; Borgers 2011, p. 120–12; Cupido 2015, p. 13.

261 Claes and Krolikowski 2009, p. 90. Cf Packer 1969, p. 86; Schreiber 1976, p. 220–221; Groenhuijsen 1987, p. 49; Borgers 2011, p. 117–118, 120; Peristeridou 2015, p. 103.

262 See Schreiber 1976, p. 220–222, 228; Claes and Krolikowski 2009, p. 101–103; Gallant 2009, p. 31–35; Möllers 2013, p. 91.

263 Cf MacCormick 2005, p. 26, 52–53; Ashworth and Horder 2013, p. 65.

264 See Packer 1969, p. 86, 92; Schreiber 1976, p. 224–225; Krey 1983, p. 137; Boot 2002, p. 97; Claes 2003, p. 67; Simester and Sullivan 2007, p. 28; Jarvers 2008, p. 60; Claes and Krolikowski 2009, p. 101; Gallant 2009, p. 31–32, 408; Masferrer 2013, p. 291; Mayaud 2015, p. 32–35; Peristeridou 2015, p. 119–121. Cf Tamanaha 2004, p. 86–90.

265 See Groenhuijsen 1987, p. 22; Claes 2003, p. 18–19, 42–43, 66–67, 199–201; Tamanaha 2004, p. 123; Claes and Krolikowski 2009, p. 101; Gallant 2009, p. 32, 359–360; Borgers 2011, p. 113, 118; Cupido 2015, p. 15; Peristeridou 2015, p. 53. Cf MacCormick 2005, p. 28.

266 Cf Claes and Krolikowski 2009, p. 102.

267 See Schreiber 1976, p. 221–223, 228; Claes 2003, p. 199; Borgers 2011, p. 116–117; Nan 2011, p. 96; Cupido 2015, p. 17; Peristeridou 2015, p. 91.

268 Cf Tamanaha 2004, p. 88.

269 See Claes 2003, p. 18–19; Gallant 2009, p. 33; Peristeridou 2015, p. 105.

the conventional civil law conception of the legality principle relies on an overly simplistic view of legal reasoning.[270] This is because, at the time of the first tentative recognitions of the legality principle, and for some time after that, the adjudicative process was mostly understood in terms of syllogistic reasoning.[271] This entails the idea that the judge should only engage in the neutral and mechanical activity of bringing the facts of the case under the legal rule in order to impose the applicable sanction.[272] This idea relies on the assumption that the application of the law to certain facts would allow for only a single reasonable interpretation.[273]

However, it is presently acknowledged that the meaning of the law is not always straightforward and can permit multiple reasonable interpretations.[274] Adjudication can therefore require more evaluation and interpretive activity than simple and straightforward syllogistic reasoning.[275] Therefore, it has been determined that even analogical reasoning in criminal law is employed in practice,[276] even though that type of reasoning was explicitly prohibited by the conventional civil law conception of the *lex stricta* principle.[277]

The inevitable indeterminacy of legal language and the complex process of judicial interpretation have led to the conclusion that the law itself can only provide limited certainty and notice for individuals. Since the law cannot generally provide absolute certainty about the meaning and scope of criminal law in advance there exists some room for judicial interpretation of offenses and penalties.[278] These observations show that an absolute division of labor between the legislature and the judiciary is not always attainable,[279] contrary to what was generally opined by the theorists that laid the foundations for the legality principle.[280] As a result, contemporary criminal law theorists have questioned

---

270 See Schreiber 1976, p. 221, 228; Borgers 2011, p. 116.

271 See subsection 2.3.3 above. See also Schreiber 1976, p. 221–222; Schünemann 1978, p. 10; Claes 2003, p. 118–125; Desportes and LeGunehec 2008, p. 154; Lelieur, Pfützner and Volz 2008, p. 47; Claes and Krolikowski 2009, p. 102; Popović 2014, p. 59; Cupido 2015, p. 13.

272 Cf Borgers 2011, p. 117; Silva Sánchez 2012, p. 57–59; Peristeridou 2015, p. 91.

273 The proper interpretation of the law is nevertheless arguable and contestable, see MacCormick 2005, p. 27–28. Cf Claes 2003, p. 43, 178.

274 When the law is clarified and a new understanding of the law is determined by a judge this might still be based on syllogistic reasoning. However, the syllogism used to decide the case will be somewhat different from the one that existed before the case at hand. There is a difference between a concluding syllogism which resulted from judicial development and clarification of the law and the starting syllogism which resulted from the law as it stood before it was applied to a specific case by the judge. See further MacCormick 2005, p. 27–28, 42. Cf Claes 2003, p. 179; MacCormick 2005, p. 52–53.

275 See Schreiber 1976, p. 222–223, 229–229; Schünemann 1978, p. 10; Claes 2003, p. 125–166, 216–217; MacCormick 2005, p. 42, 53; Borgers 2011, p. 120; Möllers 2013, p. 83.

276 See Peristeridou 2015, p. 106–109.

277 See subsection 2.3.4 above.

278 See Claes and Krolikowski 2009, p. 103; Renout 2012, p. 26–27; Bernardini 2015, p. 180–181; Mayaud 2015, p. 37–39.

279 Cf Packer 1969, p. 91–92; Möllers 2013, p. 84.

280 See sections 2.2–2.3.

whether the secondary principles *lex certa* and *lex stricta* can fully accomplish their protective function, as these principles especially aimed to preclude the amalgamation of construction and interpretation of criminal law by prohibiting vague legal definitions and limiting the room for judicial interpretation.[281]

These doubts about the ability of the legality principle to ensure a strict separation of powers and, consequently, the ability to rely on the law, illustrate that the practical difference between the two conceptions of legality may be less significant than indicated by criminal law theory for a long time. Objections regarding the practical attainability of the more demanding civil law conception of legality does not deprive the theoretical distinctions of relevance for the present research, however. As the comparison between the stepchild case and the marital rape case illustrates, the two conceptions of legality can still lead to different practical approaches, especially regarding the elements *lex scripta*, *lex certa*, and *lex stricta*.

That the two approaches can practically converge in a number of cases does not make their distinct points of departure irrelevant. For this reason, the present thesis will take an intermediate position between endorsing the theoretical distinctions as practically attainable on the one hand, and the complete dismissal of the civil law conception as being practically unattainable on the other. Even if there are only a few cases where the theoretical distinction will have a practical impact, the distinction is still relevant for the analysis and evaluation of the legality principles enshrined in Article 7 ECHR and in EU law. The practical relevance of the theoretical distinction will most likely not be limited to a few cases, however, because the indeterminacy of language and law is mostly deemed to affect specific hard cases. The indeterminacy thesis is not, in any event, deemed to generally preclude the successful communication of criminal offenses through language and the effective functioning of the legal system.[282]

2.5 CONCLUSION

This chapter described two conceptions of the legality principle: the civil law conception and its common law counterpart. The civil law conception contains more substantive elements than the common law conception. Under the civil law interpretation, the legality principle contains the elements *lex scripta*, *lex certa*, *lex stricta* and *lex praevia*. The notion of the rule of law and the principle of democracy form its theoretical foundations. The democracy rationale means that the civil law legality conception essentially requires a strict separation between the legislative construction and the judicial (and executive) interpretation and

---

281 See subsections 2.3.3–2.3.4. See further Schünemann 1978, p. 8; Claes 2003, p. 16–17, 165–166; Peristeridou 2011, p. 79–85; Peristeridou 2015, p. 89, 104, 115–117, 121.

282 Cf Tamanaha 2004, p. 86–90; Barnett 2014, p. 97–99; Fenwick and Wrbka 2016, p. 2.

application of criminal law. As a consequence, the principle protects the ability of individuals to rely on the law by requiring a precise foreseeability of criminal responsibility and penalties.

The common law legality principle enshrines only three elements: the secondary principles *lex certa*, *lex stricta* and *lex praevia*. Its theoretical foundation is the rule of law. Under the common law conception, the principle essentially aims to preclude the arbitrary use of criminal law. It does not necessarily protect the democratic legitimacy of criminal law to require a strict separation of powers between the legislature and the judiciary. As a consequence, the common law principle of legality necessarily protects only a general legal certainty. It does not, therefore, require that the law establishes specific foreseeability. The common law legality principle appears to be respected so long as criminal law is not applied arbitrarily. While this protects legal liberty, it does not necessarily protect a meaningful ability to rely on the law.

In light of the significant differences between the two conceptions of legality, it is important to establish which conception the legality principles enshrined in Article 7 ECHR and in EU law conform to. Sections 3.8 and 6.2 provide this assessment.

CHAPTER 3

ARTICLE 7 ECHR: THE PRINCIPLE *NULLUM CRIMEN, NULLA POENA SINE LEGE* IN THE ECTHR'S CASE-LAW

3.1 INTRODUCTION

Article 7 of the European Convention on Human Rights and Fundamental Freedoms enshrines the legality principle as a fundamental right. Article 1 ECHR stipulates that the Convention's signatories are required to secure ECHR rights for everyone within their jurisdiction. Article 13 ECHR requires national authorities to provide an effective remedy for violations of the Convention. In light of these binding obligations for parties to the Convention, the ECHR's legality principle is directly relevant for the contracting states.[283] Article 7 ECHR is therefore primarily relevant as a minimum standard for definitions, interpretations, and applications of national criminal law.[284]

While being primarily relevant for domestic legal systems, the ECHR has additionally acquired special significance for EU law, even in the absence of the Union's accession to the Convention.[285] Because all EU Member States are parties to the ECHR, the Convention is relevant for the Member States individually on the one hand,[286] and of special significance for the Union as a whole on the other. This double importance justifies an elaborate examination of the ECHR's legality principle. While the ultimate aim is to determine and evaluate the actual significance of the Convention's legality principle for EU law, the present chapter can be read as a self-standing examination into the scope and substance of Article 7 ECHR.

This chapter intends to provide an exhaustive analysis of the ECtHR's judgments on Article 7 ECHR. It aims to clarify and structure existing case-law by identifying multiple specific principles and distinct criteria that the Strasbourg

283 Cf Zwaak 2006, p. 4–5; Harris, O'Boyle, Bates and Buckley 2014, p. 84.

284 Article 53 ECHR underlines that more extensive protection than under the ECHR may be achieved via, for example, national equivalents of these fundamental rights. The ECHR standard is therefore only a minimum standard.

285 See subsection 1.1.2 and, more elaborately, section 5.5.

286 See also the *Bosphorus* doctrine as described in subsection 6.3.3.

Court[287] recognized. The general structure of this chapter is derived from the wording of Article 7 ECHR as well as the ECtHR's general considerations on the Convention's legality principle. Section 3.2 examines Article 7's wording as a point of departure. Sections 3.3 and 3.4 examine the Court's judgments to determine the principle's scope and provide a first indication about its substance. Section 3.5 will then assess the potential relevance of the subsidiarity principle for the ECtHR's review of complaints under Article 7 ECHR.

A detailed examination of the substance of the Convention's legality principle is undertaken in sections 3.6 and 3.7. Section 3.6 examines the legality requirements for criminal offenses and section 3.7 focuses on the requirements for penalties. Section 3.8 examines the Court's approach to legality in light of the theoretical observations in the preceding chapter. It aims to determine whether Article 7 ECHR conforms to a specific conception of legality and to assess the level of legal certainty that the Convention principle protects.

3.2 THE WORDING OF ARTICLE 7 ECHR

3.2.1 ARTICLE 7(1) ECHR

Article 7 ECHR consists of two paragraphs. Article 7(1) ECHR enshrines the legality principle as a fundamental right; it reads:

> "No one shall be held guilty of any criminal offence on account of any act or omission which did not constitute a criminal offence under national or international law at the time when it was committed. Nor shall a heavier penalty be imposed than the one that was applicable at the time the criminal offence was committed."

Article 7(1)'s first sentence requires the criminalization of acts or omissions as a precondition for finding a person guilty of a criminal offense (hereinafter also: 'a conviction'). As discussed further below, Article 7(1) sets qualitative standards for the legal definition of punishable conduct and for the interpretation and application of these definitions in individual cases. Article 7(1)'s second sentence refers to the imposition of a penalty for a criminal offense and prohibits the imposition of a heavier penalty than the one prescribed at the time of the material acts.[288]

The wording of Article 7(1) shows that the Convention's legality principle applies to both offenses and penalties. In accordance with criminal law theory, the ECHR's legality principle thus reflects the principle that only the law can define a crime and prescribe a penalty, which the preceding chapter has also

---

[287] The present chapter will not just refer to the ECtHR as 'the Strasbourg Court', but also simply as 'the Court'.

[288] Cf Kadelbach 2006, p. 735.

referred to as the principle *nullum crimen, nulla poena sine lege*.[289] While the requirements of legality for offenses and penalties were previously described without distinction, the present chapter requires more precision. This is because the ECtHR distinguishes between the requirements for the definition of an offense in the first sentence of Article 7(1) and the requirements for the prescription of a penalty in the second sentence.[290] Although the Court has not consistently employed an explicit distinction between the requirements of Article 7(1)'s first and second sentences, two distinct protective principles are perceivable in the ECtHR's case-law.[291] The present chapter will, therefore, consider Article 7(1)'s first sentence as an expression of *nullum crimen sine lege* (hereinafter also: 'the *nullum crimen* principle') and the second sentence as expressing *nulla poena sine lege* (hereinafter also: 'the *nulla poena* principle').[292] This distinction will be used to structure the analysis of both the scope and substance of Article 7(1) ECHR (see, particularly, sections 3.3 and 3.6–3.7).

An additional distinction in the wording of Article 7(1) will be used to structure the present chapter: the distinction between two possible sources of offenses and penalties. Since Article 7(1) ECHR acknowledges that offenses and penalties can stem from both *national* law and *international* law[293] this distinction should be employed when classifying the Court's judgments. The present chapter will nevertheless focus on national law, because the vast majority of the ECtHR's case-law examines offenses and penalties defined by domestic law. The exceptional cases concerning international law will mostly be examined as an element of the specific secondary principle that offenses require a clear definition (see subsection 3.6.2 below).

289 See section 2.1 above and cf Schabas 2015, p. 334.

290 See, eg, *Başkaya and Okçuoğlu v. Turkey*, CE:ECHR:1999:0708JUD002353694, paras 40–42; *Ecer and Zeyrek v. Turkey*, CE:ECHR:2001:0227JUD002929595, paras 30–31; *Alimuçaj v. Albania*, CE:ECHR:2012:0207JUD002013405, paras 152, 154; *Rohlena v. The Czech Republic*, CE:ECHR:2015:0127JUD005955208, para 56.

291 An example of a somewhat confusing use of the principles *nullum crimen* and *nulla poena* see *Kasymakhunov and Saybatalov v. Russia*, CE:ECHR:2013:0314JUD002626105. In this case, the Court first established that the imposition of criminal liability lacked foreseeability (see para 93) before concluding that this constituted merely a violation of the *nulla poena* principle (see para 94). This is rather odd because a lack of foreseeability of criminal responsibility indicates a violation of the *nullum crimen* principle.

292 Cf Bleichrodt 2006, p. 651–652.

293 Cf Frowein 2009, p. 275.

The above-mentioned distinctions result in the following figure:

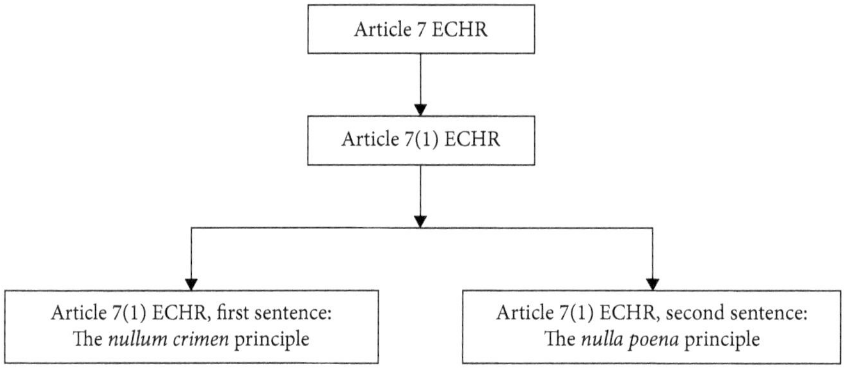

3.2.2 ARTICLE 7(2) ECHR

Unlike Article 7(1), Article 7(2) ECHR does not enshrine the legality principle or a part thereof. Instead, Article 7's second paragraph provides a specific exception to the protection provided in Article 7(1) by stating the following[294]:

> "This Article shall not prejudice the trial and punishment of any person for any act or omission which, at the time when it was committed, was criminal according to the general principles of law recognised by civilised nations."

The exception's wording indicates a potentially-broad possibility for states to escape a violation of Article 7(1) ECHR.[295] It appears that, as long as acts or omissions were, at the time of conduct, 'criminal according to the general principles of law recognized by the civilized nations',[296] domestic conviction and punishment cannot violate the legality principle.[297] Such an interpretation of Article 7(2) essentially implies that the requirements of the legality principle do not apply to certain types of crimes.[298] To accept that Article 7(2) implies such a broad exception to a fundamental Convention right like the legality principle seems problematic in light of the non-derogatory character of Article 7(1) ECHR.[299]

---

294 Cf the concurring opinion of judge Zupančič in *Streletz, Kessler and Krenz v. Germany*, CE:ECHR:2001:0322JUD003404496.

295 Cf Bleichrodt 2006, p. 660; Murphy 2010, p. 205; Valentini 2011, p. 194, note 56.

296 This formulation reflects the recognition of 'general principles of law recognised by civilised nations' as a formal source of international law, see Article 38(c) of the Statute of the International Court of Justice which is annexed to the Charter of the United Nations. See further Boot 2002, p. 158; Bleichrodt 2006, p. 660; Harris, O'Boyle, Bates and Buckley 2014, p. 501; Morre 2015, C.3.

297 Cf Dhont and Cromheecke 2004, p. 697; Bleichrodt 2006, p. 661; Morre 2015, C.3.

298 Cf Dhont and Cromheecke 2004, p. 697–702.

299 See Article 15(2) ECHR and further about the non-derogatory character below in subsection 3.3.1. Cf Beddard 1996, p. 12; Bleichrodt 2006, p. 662; De Hullu 2015, p. 94; Morre 2015, C.3.

Both the European Commission of Human Rights (hereinafter also: 'EComHR' or, in this chapter, 'the Commission') and the Court have avoided ruling on the scope of the exception by restrictively interpreting the wording of Article 7(2). By referring to the Convention's *travaux préparatoires* they established that the purpose of Article 7(2) was "(...) to specify that Article 7 did not affect laws which, in the wholly exceptional circumstances at the end of the Second World War, were passed in order to punish, inter alia, war crimes so that Article 7 does not in any way aim to pass legal or moral judgment on those laws."[300] As a result of this case-law, the exception contained in Article 7(2) appears to have been limited to the specific historical situation in which war criminals of the Second World War were sentenced on the basis of *ex post facto* legal rules.[301]

The restrictive interpretation of Article 7(2) has not settled questions about the scope of the exception, however.[302] There are two reasons for this. Firstly, the broad wording of Article 7(2) clearly provides room to argue that it applies to conduct that took place outside the scope of World War II.[303] And, secondly, the Court has sometimes diminished the significance of the *travaux préparatoires* when interpreting the Convention,[304] which provides an argument against the restrictive interpretation of Article 7(2) ECHR. The doubts surrounding the scope of Article 7(2) ECHR provide room for domestic governments to try and justify domestic convictions by arguing that the committed acts were, in any event, 'criminal according to general principles of law recognized by civilized nations'. In these cases, the Court avoids questions about the applicability of the exception by concluding that either national or international law defined the applicable crimes and penalties in accordance with the Convention requirements.[305]

While we cannot be certain about the scope of the exception contained in Article 7(2), the Court's reluctance to invoke it indicates that it is of limited practical importance.[306] The ECtHR's acceptance of definitions in (customary)

---

300 See, eg, EComHR, *Touvier v. France* (dec.), CE:ECHR:1997:0113DEC002942095, para 7; *Kononov v. Latvia*, CE:ECHR:2010:0517JUD003637604, para 186; *Maktouf and Damjanović v. Bosnia and Herzegovina*, CE:ECHR:2013:0718JUD000231208, para 72; *Vasiliauskas v. Lithuania*, CE:ECHR:2015:1020JUD003534305, para 188–190.

301 Restrictively interpreting the scope of an exception to a Convention right does, moreover, seem in line with the Court's approach to violations of rights other than the legality principle, see, eg, *Witold Litwa v. Poland*, CE:ECHR:2000:0404JUD002662995, para 59.

302 See Schabas 2015, p. 354.

303 Cf Schabas 2015, p. 353.

304 See, outside the context of Article 7 ECHR, eg, *Young, James and Webster v. The United Kingdom*, CE:ECHR:1981:0813JUD000760176, para 52; *Loizidou v. Turkey* (preliminary objections), CE:ECHR:1995:0323JUD001531889, para 71; *Banković and Others v. Belgium* (dec.), CE:ECHR:2001:1212DEC005220799, paras 63–65. See further Letsas 2007, p. 65–68; Gerards 2011, p. 67–70.

305 See, eg, *Kolk and Kislyiy v. Estonia* (dec.), CE:ECHR:2006:0117DEC002305204; *Ould Dah v. France* (dec.), CE:ECHR:2009:0317DEC001311303. Cf Morre 2015, C.3. See further subsection 3.6.2.

306 Cf Boot 2002, p. 158; Harris, O'Boyle, Bates and Buckley 2014, p. 502; Schabas 2015, p. 354.

international criminal law[307] (eg crimes against humanity and war crimes) supports this inference, since the use of international criminal law averts the need to rely on the exception in Article 7(2) ECHR in most cases.[308] Therefore, many cases that could possibly have been considered under Article 7(2) ECHR were actually considered under Article 7(1) as cases concerning a definition of a crime in 'international law'.[309] Due to the limited practical significance of Article 7(2) ECHR, the following sections will not examine this provision further.

After adding Article 7(2) ECHR to the previous figure, it looks as follows:

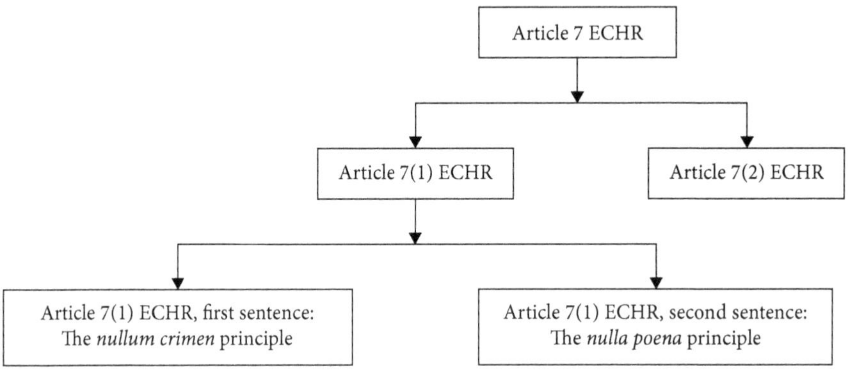

3.3 SCOPE OF APPLICATION

3.3.1 INTRODUCTION

The use of the terms 'criminal offense' and 'penalty' in Article 7(1) ECHR implies that the scope of the provision is limited to *substantive* criminal law. This indicates that rules of criminal *procedure* generally fall outside the scope of the Convention's legality principle. That Article 7 does not generally apply to rules of procedural law has been confirmed by the Court.[310] Examples of procedural rules excluded

---

307 Cf Kadelbach 2006, p. 740–741; Harris, O'Boyle, Bates and Buckley 2014, p. 498–499; Grabenwarter 2014, p. 177; Schabas 2015, p. 343–344.

308 See, eg, *Kononov v. Latvia*, CE:ECHR:2010:0517JUD003637604, paras 237, 246 and further subsection 3.6.2. Cf Corstens and Pradel 2002, p. 362; Dhont and Cromheecke 2004, p. 702; Schabas 2015, p. 353.

309 For this reason several authors argue that the exception of Article 7(2) ECHR is merely a contextual clarification of the term 'international law' in Article 7(1) ECHR, see, eg, Boot 2002, p. 157–161, 170; Grabenwarter 2014, p. 178 and cf Schabas 2015, p. 355. In their view, Article 7(2) does not add anything to the Court's interpretation of the term 'international law' in Article 7(1) ECHR.

310 See *Coëme and Others v. Belgium*, CE:ECHR:2000:0622JUD003249296, paras 149–150; *Previti v. Italy* (dec.), CE:ECHR:2013:0212DEC000184508, paras 78–81; *Khodorkovskiy and Lebedev v. Russia*, CE:ECHR:2013:0725JUD001108206, paras 789–790. Cf Harris, O'Boyle, Bates and Buckley 2014, p. 493; Schabas 2015, p. 335.

from the scope of Article 7 include: time-limits for appeals, rules concerning the assessment of evidence, and rules on statutory limitation of crimes.[311]

To determine Article 7(1)'s applicability, the Court looks beyond the classification of the rules in domestic law. Even when rules are regarded as procedural rules under national law, the ECtHR will determine whether the rules do, in fact, establish criminal offenses and/or penalties. In *Scoppola* the Court examined whether rules of Italian criminal procedure changed the length of the applicable sanctions.[312] Since the ECtHR concluded that the Italian rules did concern the length of the sanctions, and the sanctions amounted to criminal penalties, it considered these rules fell within the scope of Article 7(1) ECHR's second sentence.[313] The Italian rules of 'criminal procedure' were therefore deemed to constitute rules of *substantive* criminal law for the purposes of the legality principle.[314]

While procedural rules are, in principle, outside the scope of Article 7(1) ECHR, the Court has implied that this could be otherwise in exceptional circumstances. In *Coëme* the ECtHR held that procedural rules on statutory limitation could generally be applied immediately, even if this extended the prosecutorial possibilities after the conduct occurred.[315] Strictly speaking, however, the Court explicitly allowed the retroactive application of these rules only for cases where the relevant offenses had never become subject to a statutory limitation. This implies that Article 7(1) ECHR could still preclude the retroactive application of procedural rules in situations where the relevant offenses had previously been subject to a statutory limitation. Even if the Court could exceptionally apply Article 7 to procedural rules, the general rule remains unaltered: the Convention's legality principle is limited to substantive criminal law: ie rules that enshrine criminal offenses and/or penalties.

The Court has used the terms 'criminal offense' and 'penalty' to determine the scope of Article 7(1) ECHR's distinct principles. Both the *nullum crimen* principle enshrined in the first sentence of Article 7(1) and the *nulla poena* principle in the second sentence have, therefore, been given their own scope of application. Subsection 3.3.2 will first describe the Court's criteria for the applicability of the *nullum crimen* principle. This description will be rather brief, because the ECtHR employs the well-known '*Engel*-criteria' which it first developed to determine the scope of Article 6 ECHR. Subsection 3.3.3 then describes the criteria that determine the applicability of Article 7(1) ECHR's second sentence. Since the Court identifies six different criteria to determine the scope of the *nulla poena* principle, it is useful to illustrate their relative weight in individual circumstances. To that end, subsection 3.3.3 will examine a few of the ECtHR's judgments in more detail. Subsection 3.3.4 contains a brief recapitulation.

---

311 See *Scoppola v. Italy (No. 2)*, CE:ECHR:2012:0522JUD000012605, para 110.

312 *Scoppola v. Italy (No. 2)*, CE:ECHR:2012:0522JUD000012605, para 111.

313 See para 112–113. On the applicability of Article 7(1) ECHR's second sentence, see subsection 3.3.3.

314 See para 113.

315 *Coëme and Others v. Belgium*, CE:ECHR:2000:0622JUD003249296, paras 148–150. Cf Schabas 2015, p. 342–343.

3.3.2 ARTICLE 7(1) ECHR, FIRST SENTENCE

Only a finding of guilt for a criminal offense (ie a criminal conviction) triggers the applicability of Article 7(1)'s first sentence. This means that if the domestic criminal case results in an acquittal or a discharge, this will usually result in a complaint being inapplicable under Article 7 ECHR.[316] The same is true for complaints about extradition because a decision to extradite does not amount to a finding of guilt.[317]

In addition to the need for a conviction, the scope of protection provided by Article 7(1) is heavily dependent on the meaning of the words 'criminal offense'. Whether an act amounts to a conviction for a criminal offense is determined by the same criteria used by the Court to establish the applicability of Article 6 ECHR.[318] In Article 6 cases, the Court examines whether acts amount to a 'criminal charge'[319] or whether a person is being 'charged with a criminal offense'.[320] These criteria have been given an autonomous[321] interpretation in well-known case-law, most notably in the judgments in *Engel*[322] and *Öztürk*.[323] The Court uses three criteria to determine whether an act amounts to a criminal offense: first, the classification in domestic law, secondly, the nature of the offense, and finally, the nature and severity of the applicable sanctions.[324] I will only consider these '*Engel* criteria' briefly.

The first criterion merely provides a starting point: Article 7 applies if domestic law classifies an offense as 'criminal'.[325] If domestic law labels an offense as non-criminal, the two other criteria determine the applicability of Article 7. In the Court's view, the second criterion is more important than both the first and the third.[326] Moreover, the second and third criteria are, in general, alternative and not cumulative.[327] However, when the individual criteria do not enable a

316 EComHR, *Lukanov v. Bulgaria* (dec.), CE:ECHR:1997:0320JUD002191593, para 6. Cf Kadelbach 2006, p. 727; Grabenwarter 2014, p. 173; Harris, O'Boyle, Bates and Buckley 2014, p. 494; Morre 2015, C.2.3.

317 EComHR, *X. v. The Netherlands* (dec.), CE:ECHR:1976:0706DEC000751276. Cf Morre 2015, C.2.3.

318 See, eg, *Engel and Others v. The Netherlands*, CE:ECHR:1976:0608JUD000510071, para 81; *Öztürk v. Germany*, CE:ECHR:1984:0221JUD000854479, para 49; *Paksas v. Lithuania*, CE:ECHR:2011:0106JUD003493204, para 68; *Žaja v. Croatia*, CE:ECHR:2016:1004JUD003746209, para 86. See further Boot 2002, p. 145; Dhont and Cromheecke 2004, p. 667; Bleichrodt 2006, p. 652–653; Kadelbach 2006, p. 726; Jacobs, White and Ovey 2017, p. 329; Morre 2015, C.2.1.1.

319 See Article 6(1) ECHR.

320 See Articles 6(2) and 6(3) ECHR.

321 See *Engel and Others v. The Netherlands*, para 81; *Öztürk v. Germany*, para 50. See further Van Dijk and Viering 2006, p. 539; Kadelbach 2006, p. 726; Letsas 2007, p. 40–57; Jacobs, White and Ovey 2017, p. 275; Gerards 2011, p. 49–58.

322 *Engel and Others v. The Netherlands*, CE:ECHR:1976:0608JUD000510071.

323 *Öztürk v. Germany*, CE:ECHR:1984:0221JUD000854479.

324 See *Engel*, para 82–83 and *Öztürk*, para 50. Cf Kadelbach 2006, p. 727; Jacobs, White and Ovey 2017, p. 276; Leanza 2014, p. 20.

325 See *Žaja v. Croatia*, CE:ECHR:2016:1004JUD003746209, para 86. Cf Van Dijk and Viering 2006, p. 543–544; Jacobs, White and Ovey 2017, p. 276; Leanza 2014, p. 22; Morre 2015, C.2.

326 See, eg, *Engel*, para 82; *Öztürk*, para 54; *Jussila v. Finland*, CE:ECHR:2006:1123JUD007305301, para 38.

327 See, with references to ECtHR case-law, Van Dijk and Viering 2006, p. 548; Leanza 2014, p. 27.

clear conclusion about the 'criminal' character of an offense, the Court has been willing to adopt a cumulative approach with regard to the latter two criteria.[328]

The Court examines the second criterion, ie the nature of the offense, by considering several features, which include: whether the offense applies to a restricted group of people, whether the proceedings are brought by a public body under statutory powers of enforcement, whether an offense is classified as a part of the criminal law in the vast majority of Convention States, and whether the accompanying penalty has a deterrent or compensatory purpose.[329] Factors indicating the applicability of Article 7(1) ECHR are: when an offense applies to all individuals equally, when proceedings are brought by a public body, when an offense is classified as criminal in most Convention states, or when the penalty has a deterrent purpose. When a prohibition has a general character and the purpose of the accompanying penalty is both deterrent and punitive, the Court will consider the domestic offense to be a 'criminal offense' for the purpose of the Convention.[330]

The Court uses the third criterion, ie the nature and severity of the penalty, to apply the Convention to offenses for which penalties with appreciably detrimental effects are prescribed.[331] Measures depriving a person of his liberty will, in principle, fall within this category, except when they are not, by their nature, duration or manner of execution, appreciably detrimental.[332] In general, a penalty consisting of a short period of imprisonment is insufficient to deem an offense 'criminal' on the basis of the severity of the penalty.[333] At the same time, larger fines, which go significantly beyond the mere reparation of the damage, can trigger the applicability of Article 7(1) via the third criterion.[334]

3.3.3 ARTICLE 7(1) ECHR, SECOND SENTENCE

Multiple factors

As with the term 'criminal offense', the Court treats the concept of a 'penalty' in Article 7(1) as autonomous.[335] To render Article 7's protection effective, the

328 See, eg, *Ezeh and Connors v. The United Kingdom*, CE:ECHR:2003:1009JUD003966598, para 86. See further Leanza 2014, p. 27.

329 See *Žaja v. Croatia*, CE:ECHR:2016:1004JUD003746209, para 88. Cf, with further references to ECtHR case-law, Van Dijk and Viering 2006, p. 544–547; Leanza 2014, p. 22–26.

330 See *Öztürk*, para 53; *Žaja v. Croatia*, CE:ECHR:2016:1004JUD003746209, para 88. Cf Van Dijk and Viering 2006, p. 546.

331 What is relevant is the legally prescribed penalty, not the penalty actually imposed, see, eg, *Engel*, para 85.

332 See *Engel*, para 82. Cf Van Dijk and Viering 2006, p. 549.

333 See, eg, *Engel*, para 85. Cf Jacobs, White and Ovey 2017, p. 276.

334 See Van Dijk and Viering 2006, p. 554.

335 See, eg, *Welch v. The United Kingdom*, CE:ECHR:1995:0209JUD001744090, para 27; *Del Río Prada v. Spain*, CE:ECHR:2013:1021JUD004275009, para 81. Cf Dhont and Cromheecke 2004, p. 685–687; Schabas 2015, p. 345.

Court must be able to go beyond appearances and assess whether a specific measure amounts to a penalty in substance.[336] As the wording of Article 7(1)'s second sentence indicates, the general starting-point for examining whether a measure constitutes a penalty is 'whether it is imposed following a conviction for a criminal offense' (factor 1).[337] According to the Court, other factors can also be taken into account. These are: (2) the characterization of the measure under domestic law; (3) its nature; (4) its purpose; (5) the procedures involved in the making and implementation of the measure, and; (6) its severity.[338] The severity of the measure is not, however, a decisive factor in this assessment; many preventive measures are quite severe, but are not necessarily a penalty for the purpose of the Convention.[339]

While preventive measures are not generally penalties, they can still fall within the scope of the Convention's *nulla poena* principle. The use of preventive detention in Germany is illustrative here, since it has given rise to multiple judgments regarding the applicability of Article 7(1) ECHR. This case-law warrants examination as it illustrates the ECtHR's use of the six aforementioned criteria. It shows, in particular, that the applicability criteria enable a case-by-case assessment of whether a measure constitutes a penalty.

Over the course of several related judgments since 2009, the ECtHR has deemed that German preventive detention constitutes a penalty for the purposes of the second sentence of Article 7(1) ECHR.[340] Although the Court acknowledged that preventive detention is not a penalty under German law,[341] the domestic characterization of preventive detention is only one relevant factor.[342] An important[343] reason for considering preventive detention a penalty was its imposition following a conviction of a criminal offense (factor 1).[344] Another factor pointing in the direction of a penalty was the nature of preventive detention (factor 3). In the Court's view, there was no substantial difference between the execution of preventive detention and the execution of an evident penalty such as a prison

336 See *Scoppola* set out in subsection 3.3.1. See also, eg, *Welch*, para 27; *Del Río Prada*, para 81.

337 See, eg, *Welch*, para 28; *Del Río Prada*, para 82.

338 See *M. v. Germany*, CE:ECHR:2009:1217JUD001935904, para 120. Cf *Welch*, para 28; *Del Río Prada*, para 82.

339 See, eg, *Welch*, para 32; *Del Río Prada*, para 82. For examples of a preventive measure outside the scope of Article 7(1) ECHR, see *Gardel v. France*, CE:ECHR:2009:1217JUD001642805, paras 41–46; *Berland v. France*, CE:ECHR:2015:0903JUD004287510, paras 38–47 and cf the early judgment in *Lawless v. Ireland (No. 3)*, CE:ECHR:1960:1114JUD000033257, para 19. See further, eg, Atrill 2005, p. 112–124; Murphy 2010, p. 195–199; Baumbach 2011, p. 131–133; Harris, O'Boyle, Bates and Buckley 2014, p. 499–500; Grabenwarter 2014, p. 173.

340 See, eg, *M. v. Germany*, CE:ECHR:2009:1217JUD001935904; *Jendrowiak v. Germany*, CE:ECHR:2011:0414JUD003006004; *Glien v. Germany*, CE:ECHR:2013:1128JUD000734512. Cf Sanz-Caballero 2017, p. 799–802.

341 *M. v. Germany*, paras 125–126.

342 *M. v. Germany*, para 124.

343 *M. v. Germany*, para 121.

344 *M. v. Germany*, para 124; *Jendrowiak v. Germany*, para 47; *Glien v. Germany*, para 121.

sentence.[345] Especially striking in this regard was the lack of specific measures aiming to diminish the danger of the persons held in preventive detention.[346] Preventive detention was generally executed in the same institution where people serve prison sentences with no mental health care being offered in some cases.

The fourth factor, the purpose of the preventive detention, did not alter the assessment on the basis of factors 1 and 3. Although the main purpose of preventive detention is not punitive, in the Court's view, a long-term of deprivation of liberty entails a deterrent element and can nevertheless be understood as additional punishment for an offense. As a consequence, the ECtHR found that the aims of preventive detention were largely similar to those of imprisonment.[347] The two final factors, the procedure for preventive detention (factor 5) and the severity of the measure (factor 6), indicated that preventive detention also constituted a penalty. Detention was exclusively ordered by the criminal courts and constituted one of the most severe measures under German criminal law as it entailed the deprivation of liberty without a maximum duration.[348] Since five out of the six factors indicated that German preventive detention constituted a penalty, the Court applied Article 7(1) ECHR, second sentence, to the German measure.

The applicability of the *nulla poena* principle resulted in multiple violations of Article 7(1) ECHR by Germany.[349] In response to these violations, Germany introduced a new federal law which aimed to remove preventive detention from the scope of the Convention's legality principle.[350] In *Bergmann*, the Court assessed the new legal regime.[351] The Court concluded that, *as a rule*, the German preventive detention still constitutes a penalty, because it is still ordered by the criminal courts (factor 5) following a criminal conviction (factor 1) and it entails a severe deprivation of liberty (factor 6).[352]

This could nevertheless be otherwise if certain conditions were met. If the detainee is offered actual treatment in detention, both the purpose (factor 4) and the nature (factor 3) of the detention would be substantially changed into a preventive measure.[353] In such circumstances, preventive detention no longer constitutes a penalty within the meaning of Article 7(1) ECHR and the

---

345 *M. v. Germany*, para 127; *Glien v. Germany*, para 125.

346 *M. v. Germany*, paras 128–129.

347 *M. v. Germany*, para 130.

348 *M. v. Germany*, paras 131–132; *Glien v. Germany*, paras 128–129.

349 The retroactive extension of preventive detention violated the principle of non-retroactivity of heavier penalties enshrined in Article 7(1) ECHR, see *M. v. Germany*, paras 133, 137; *Jendrowiak v. Germany*, para. 48; *Glien v. Germany*, paras 130–131. On the *lex praevia* principle for penalties, see subsection 3.7.4.

350 See Gesetz zur bundesrechtlichen Umsetzung des Abstandsgebots im Recht der Sicherungsverwahrung of 05 December 2012, BGBl I S. 2425. Cf *Bergmann v. Germany*, CE:ECHR:2016:0107JUD002327914, para 43.

351 *Bergmann v. Germany*, CE:ECHR:2016:0107JUD002327914.

352 *Bergmann v. Germany*, para 181.

353 *Bergmann v. Germany*, para 182.

prohibition of non-retroactivity of heavier penalties would not apply to any extension of detention.[354] As long as the courts assess the detainee's continued dangerousness on the basis of an existing mental order, and the applicant is offered treatment for his disorder, the preventive detention will fall outside the scope of the Convention's legality principle.

The distinction between substantive penalties and execution measures

The case-by-case assessment of the scope of the *nulla poena* principle is not limited to preventive measures. The Court's case-law on execution measures forms another illustrative example. Like the Commission, the Court distinguishes between 'substantive penalties' and measures concerning the execution or enforcement of a penalty.[355] Measures concerning changes in the regime for early release or the remission of a sentence are not, therefore, a part of a penalty.[356] As a rule, therefore, measures concerning the execution and enforcement of a penalty are outside the scope of the Convention's legality principle.

The Court nevertheless recognizes that the distinction between penalties and execution measures is not always clear-cut[357]:

> "In order to determine whether a measure taken during the execution of a sentence concerns only the manner of execution of the sentence or, on the contrary, affects its scope, the Court must examine in each case what the 'penalty' imposed actually entailed under the domestic law in force at the material time, or in other words, what its intrinsic nature was. In doing so it must have regard to the domestic law as a whole and the way it was applied at the material time".[358]

Even measures that are introduced after the pronouncement of the sentence can therefore be 'imposed' in the sense of Article 7(1)'s second sentence.[359] These types of measures are thus not *fully* outside the scope of the *nulla poena* principle.[360] To argue otherwise would, in the Court's view, deprive Article 7 of any useful effect for convicted persons whose sentences have been changed *ex post facto* to their disadvantage.[361]

---

354 *Bergmann v. Germany*, para 183. Cf *W.P. v. Germany*, CE:ECHR:2016:1006JUD005559413, paras 75–80; *Ilnseher v. Germany*, CE:ECHR:2017:0202JUD001021112, paras 78–84.

355 See *Del Río Prada*, para 83. For examples of execution measures, see eg, *Grava v. Italy*, CE:ECHR:2003:0710JUD004352298, paras 50–51; *Kafkaris v. Cyprus*, CE:ECHR:2008:0212 JUD002190604, para 151.

356 See *Del Río Prada*, para 83. For other examples of measures that fall outside the scope of Article 7(1) ECHR, see Dhont and Cromheecke 2004, p. 691–697.

357 See *Del Río Prada*, para 85. See further Harris, O'Boyle, Bates and Buckley 2014, p. 500–501.

358 See *Del Río Prada*, para 90.

359 See *Del Río Prada*, para 88.

360 See *Del Río Prada*, para 89.

361 See *Del Río Prada*, para 89.

The Court's willingness to incorporate measures impacting a penalty after its pronouncement, shows how the scope of the *nulla poena* principle could be quite broad. The judgment in *Del Río Prada* illustrates this aptly.[362] At the time of Del Río Prada's offense, the Spanish Criminal Code of 1973 limited the maximum term of imprisonment to thirty years in the event of multiple sentences.[363] The 1973 Criminal Code entitled the detainee to a remission of one day for every two days of work.[364] The Criminal Code did not, however, establish how to apply remissions of sentences when multiple sentences had been imposed but they were, at the same time, limited to a cumulative statutory maximum of thirty years.[365] This issue was only clarified after the introduction of a new provision in the Criminal Code of 1995. That provision stated, "(...) with regard to the application of sentence adjustments, that in exceptional cases the total duration of the sentences imposed could be taken into account, rather than the maximum term provided for by law."[366]

In addition to the statutory law, the Court also considered the case-law and practice relating to the Criminal Code of 1973.[367] It noted that the domestic courts had always applied the remissions for work done in detention to the maximum term of thirty years for multiple offenses.[368] It was therefore clearly the practice of the Spanish prison and judicial authorities to treat the maximum term of thirty years as the sentence to which remissions apply.[369] While the applicant was serving the sentence, she had every reason to believe that remissions for work done were applied to the sentence of thirty years.[370] As a result, at the time the applicant committed the offenses, Spanish law, taken as a whole, including the case-law, was formulated with sufficient precision to enable the applicant to discern the scope of the penalty imposed on her. Therefore, the penalty consisted of a thirty year sentence and the remissions for work done would be deducted from that maximum penalty.[371]

A judgment from the Spanish Supreme Court in 2006 nevertheless changed the law on the remissions of a sentence in case of multiple sentences. In the 2006 judgment, the Supreme Court considered that

> "(...) the new rule by which remissions of sentence for work done in detention were to be applied to each of the individual sentences – rather than to the thirty-year maximum term as previously – was more in conformity with the actual wording of the provisions of the 1973 Criminal Code, which distinguished between the 'sentence' (*pena*) and the 'term to be served' (*condena*)".[372]

---

362 *Del Río Prada v. Spain*, CE:ECHR:2013:1021JUD004275009.
363 See paras 97, 24.
364 See paras 97, 24.
365 See para 97.
366 Para 97.
367 See para 98.
368 See para 98.
369 See para 99.
370 See para 100.
371 See para 103.
372 Para 104.

Following the Supreme Court's judgment, the domestic court refused to apply the remission for work done to the applicant's thirty-year sentence.[373]

The ECtHR had to determine whether the domestic court's refusal to apply the remission for work to the statutory maximum affected the scope of the penalty or merely related to its execution.[374] The Court noted that the way the domestic court applied the Supreme Court decision meant the remission of the applicant's sentence for work done had little useful effect.[375] The applicant's combined sentences amounted to such a long prison sentence that any remissions would not actually reduce the length of incarceration. In effect, "(…) the maximum term of thirty years' imprisonment ceased to be an independent sentence to which remissions of sentence for work done in detention were applied, and instead became a thirty-year sentence to which no such remissions would effectively be applied".[376] In these circumstances, the application of the new interpretation on applying remissions for work done led to a redefinition of the scope of the penalty.[377] For that reason, the case came within the scope of Article 7(1) ECHR's second sentence.[378]

3.3.4 RECAPITULATION

Both the '*Engel* criteria', and the six criteria relevant under Article 7(1) ECHR's second sentence, provide room for a case-by-case assessment of the scope of applicability of the legality principle. While generally procedural rules, preventive measures, and execution measures fall outside the scope of Article 7(1), the above analysis illustrates that the Court's approach is flexible. It can be concluded, therefore, that the scope of applicability of the legality principle is not necessarily interpreted restrictively.[379]

3.4 SUBSTANCE OF ARTICLE 7(1) ECHR: A BRIEF OVERVIEW

3.4.1 INTRODUCTION

The current section precedes the more elaborate examination of the Court's substantive approach to legality in sections 3.6 and 3.7. It describes the general

---

373 See para 104.
374 See para 104. Cf *Koprivnikar v. Slovenia*, CE:ECHR:2017:0124JUD006750313, para 52.
375 See para 107.
376 See para 109.
377 See paras 107, 110.
378 The ECtHR's considerations on the substance of legality principle in this judgment will be examined in subsection 3.7.3.
379 Cf Sanz-Caballero 2017, p. 791, 810.

principles of Article 7 ECHR as reiterated in recent judgments of the ECtHR's Grand Chamber.[380] The initial focus on the Court's general principles is useful, because these principles establish a relatively clear and concise framework.[381] This framework provides an overview of the substance of Article 7 ECHR which will be used to structure the more detailed analysis of the Court's substantive considerations in the following sections. The straightforward framework also enables us to classify the ECHR's legality principle in light of the theoretical distinctions described in chapter 2.

While the initial focus on general principles entails advantages, there is a drawback. In order to capitalize on the advantage of relative simplicity, the present section has to leave out a lot of detail and context. Since the ECtHR usually reiterates the applicable general principles before considering the factual and legal circumstances of a specific case, the present section follows suit. This section will therefore focus exclusively on abstract considerations rather than the individual circumstances of a specific case. The context for the Court's considerations is provided later in sections 3.6 and 3.7.

Subsection 3.4.2 first examines the general considerations regarding the object and purpose of Article 7. Subsection 3.4.3 distinguishes the three specific principles that are inherent in Article 7(1) ECHR. Subsection 3.4.4 describes the implications of the Court's general principles for the structure of this chapter and offers some first observations on the Convention's legality principle in light of criminal law theory.

3.4.2 OBJECT AND PURPOSE

The importance of the legality principle as a fundamental right is hard to overstate. The Court has underlined the principle's significance by recalling that

---

380 I have focused on the Court's Grand Chamber judgments on Article 7 ECHR published in or after the year 2010, with special emphasis on the judgments in *Del Río Prada v. Spain*, CE:ECHR:2013:1021JUD004275009; *Kononov v. Latvia*, CE:ECHR:2010:0517JUD003637604; *Rohlena v. The Czech Republic*, CE:ECHR: 2015:0127JUD005955208; *Vasiliauskas v. Lithuania*, CE:ECHR:2015:1020JUD003534305. This is because only these judgments contain self-standing considerations on the general principles of Article 7. Although these judgments reiterated principles established in preceding case-law, they did so by employing separate, and elaborate, formulations of these principles. Other recent Grand Chamber judgments are not discussed here. The judgment in *Maktouf* is irrelevant in this regard because it merely cited the general principles as formulated in *Kononov*, see *Maktouf and Damjanović v. Bosnia and Herzegovina*, CE:ECHR:2013:0718JUD000231208, para 66. The judgment in *Paksas* did not reiterate general principles because it deemed Article 7 inapplicable, see *Paksas v. Lithuania*, CE:ECHR:2011:0106JUD003493204, para 68.

381 The Court will not depart from its earlier case-law lightly, especially when the precedents have been widely accepted, see, eg, *Cossey v. The United Kingdom*, CE:ECHR:1990:0927JUD 001084384, para 35; *Goodwin v. The United Kingdom*, CE:ECHR:2002:0711JUD002895795, para 74. See further Gerards 2011, p. 24–29.

Article 15(2) ECHR does not allow derogation from Article 7, not even in times of war or other public emergency threatening the life of the nation.[382] In addition, the Court affirms the fundamental nature of the legality principle by considering the guarantee enshrined in Article 7 an essential element of the rule of law.[383] As an essential component of the rule of law, Article 7 aims to provide effective safeguards against arbitrary prosecution, conviction and punishment.[384] This purpose is clearly linked to one of the six core elements recognized by the so-called Venice Commission: ie 'prohibition of arbitrariness'.[385]

Interestingly, the formulation of Article 7's object and purpose set out above was first proposed by judge Martens in his partly dissenting opinion in the early case of *Kokkinakis*.[386] In *Kokkinakis*, the Court merely established that Article 7's function was to ensure that an individual is able to know in advance, and on the basis of law, what acts and omissions will make him criminally liable.[387] Judge Martens found this formulation insufficient and he argued that Article 7 is additionally, and primarily, intended – in accordance with its historical origin[388] – to secure protection against arbitrary prosecution and conviction.[389] He considered that this was a consequence of the need for criminal law to be compatible with the rule of law.[390] In the related cases of *C.R. v. The United Kingdom* and *S.W. v. The United Kingdom*, which were published within three years of *Kokkinakis*, the Court adopted Martens' view on the object and purpose of Article 7.[391] As exemplified by its consistent reiteration in recent Grand Chamber judgments, this has become the generally accepted formulation of Article 7's object and purpose.[392]

382 See *Kononov*, para 185; *Del Río Prada*, para 77; *Vasiliauskas*, para 153. Cf Kadelbach 2006, p. 725; Bleichrodt 2006, p. 652; Morre 2015, C.1.

383 See *Kononov*, para 185; *Del Río Prada*, para 77; *Vasiliauskas*, para 153. Cf Sudre 2001, p. 347; Bleichrodt 2006, p. 651–652; Harris, O'Boyle, Bates and Buckley 2014, p. 493. About the relevance of the rule of law for other Convention provisions, see Steiner 2016, p. 135–154.

384 See *Kononov*, para 185; *Del Río Prada*, para 77; *Vasiliauskas*, para 153. Cf Kadelbach 2006, p. 724–725.

385 The Venice Commission is a Council of Europe independent consultative body on issues of constitutional law and is officially named 'The European Commission for Democracy through Law'. For the six core elements, see Venice Commission, Report on the Rule of Law, CDL-AD(2011)003rev, p. 10–13.

386 *Kokkinakis v. Greece*, CE:ECHR:1993:0525JUD001430788. See further subsection 3.6.2.

387 See para 52. Cf Boot 2002, p. 144.

388 Cf subsection 2.4.2.

389 See para 4 partly dissenting opinion judge Martens in *Kokkinakis*.

390 See para 4 partly dissenting opinion judge Martens in *Kokkinakis*.

391 See *C.R. v. The United Kingdom*, CE:ECHR:1995:1122JUD002019092, para 32; *S.W. v. The United Kingdom*, CE:ECHR:1995:1122JUD002016692, para 34.

392 See also, notably, *Streletz, Kessler and Krenz v. Germany*, CE:ECHR:2001:0322JUD003404496, para 88. In one case the Court nevertheless considered an additional element of relevance for Article 7 ECHR. In *Sud Fondi SRL*, the ECtHR concluded that the imposition of a penalty on the basis of a definition of an offense that failed to meet the standards required by Article 7 regarding the quality of law would violate the principle of criminal law that requires a 'guilty

The safeguards against the arbitrary use of criminal law are provided by the principle that only law can define a crime and prescribe a penalty (*nullum crimen, nulla poena sine lege*), which the Court considers to be the most general principle enshrined in Article 7 ECHR.[393] In addition to this general formulation of the guarantee enshrined in Article 7, the Court has identified several specific principles and prohibitions.[394] Since the ECtHR deems the principle of *nullum crimen, nulla poena sine lege* to be the most general principle, these specific principles and prohibitions can be viewed as derived from this general principle.[395]

It should be kept in mind that Article 7's protective principles are, in the Court's view, to be construed and applied in accordance with the ECtHR's understanding of the object and purpose of the legality principle.[396] In other words, the specific prohibitions and requirements enshrined in Article 7 should only offer protection from *arbitrary* prosecution, conviction and punishment. The focus on non-arbitrariness is also in line with the Court's review on the basis of the general 'quality of law' standards which it employs to evaluate whether interferences with Convention rights are in accordance with the law.[397]

The recognition of the rule of law rationale for Article 7, together with the emphasis on the aim of precluding arbitrariness, indicates the principle's conformity to the common law legality conception.

---

individual' as a precondition for punishing that person (ie the principle of *nulla poena sine culpa*), *Sud Fondi SRL and Others v. Italy*, CE:ECHR:2009:0120JUD007590901, paras 116–117. The Court apparently deemed the principle *nulla poena sine culpa* to be included in Article 7 ECHR, but there is no additional support for this consideration in other judgments on Article 7 ECRH. See further about this judgment subsection 3.7.5.

393 See *Kononov*, para 185; *Del Río Prada*, para 78; *Vasiliauskas*, para 154. This also follows from the title of the Court's reiteration of the general principles in *Del Río Prada*. In that judgment, the ECtHR started its reiteration of the general principles under the heading of *nullum crimen, nulla poena sine lege*, see principle 1(a), just above para 77.

394 They are: the principle that offenses and penalties require a clear legal definition, the prohibition on the overly extensive interpretation of criminal law, and the prohibition on the retroactive application of criminal law. See further subsection 3.4.3.

395 The formulation of the general principles in the following judgments confirms this interpretation as well: *Achour v. France*, CE:ECHR:2006:0329JUD006733501, para 41; *Custers, Deveaux and Turk v. Denmark*, CE:ECHR:2007:0503JUD001184303, para 76; *Kafkaris v. Cyprus*, CE:ECHR:2008:0212JUD002190604, para 138; *Liivik v. Estonia*, CE:ECHR:2009:0625JUD001215705, para 92; *Varvara v. Italy*, CE:ECHR:2013:1029JUD001747509, para 52. In these cases, the Court considered that Article 7 embodies the *nullum crimen, nulla poena sine lege* principle in general terms. Only after this did it refer to several particular prohibitions and principles. Cf Murphy 2010, p. 202–203.

396 See *Kononov*, para 185; *Del Río Prada*, para 77; *Vasiliauskas*, para 153.

397 The Court has, for example, considered that the Convention's quality of law standards require "(...) foreseeability and, generally, an absence of arbitrariness (...)", see *Rekvényi v. Hungary*, CE:ECHR:1999:0520JUD002539094, para 59. On the general quality of law requirements and their relationship with the review of complaints about Article 7 ECHR, see subsection 3.6.2.

3.4.3 SPECIFIC PRINCIPLES

From Article 7 follow three specific principles which the Court has formulated as prohibitions or requirements.[398] From the general requirement that only the law can define a crime and prescribe a penalty follows, logically, a principle requiring certain standards in the legal definition of offenses and penalties. This requirement fits well with the previously mentioned general quality of law standards that the Convention sets for domestic law under several provisions.[399]

The first distinguishable principle is that offenses and penalties require a clear legal definition. The requirement of a clear legal basis in criminal law is unmistakably a *lex certa* requirement.[400] For that reason, this ECHR requirement will also be referred to as the Convention's '*lex certa* principle' hereinafter. The second specific principle inherent in Article 7(1) ECHR is that the law must not be extensively construed to the accused's detriment. This principle is obviously a reflection of the *lex stricta* principle.[401] It will therefore also be referred to as 'the *lex stricta* principle' or 'the prohibition on overly extensive interpretation'.[402] The third, and final, specific principle this subsection examines is the so-called prohibition on the retroactive application of criminal law. This prohibition is in line with the *lex praevia* principle.[403] It will be subsequently referred to as 'the *lex praevia* principle' or 'the principle of non-retroactivity'.[404]

Before elaborating on the implications of these specific principles for the more detailed examination in sections 3.6 and 3.7, the remainder of this subsection examines the Court's general considerations on the three above-mentioned principles.

The principle that offenses and penalties require a clear legal definition ('lex certa')

The Court's recent Grand Chamber judgments emphasize that the *lex certa* principle follows from, inter alia,[405] the general principle of *nullum crimen, nulla*

398 Many authors have distinguished between multiple specific principles, see, eg, Corstens and Pradel 2002, p. 357–361; Kadelbach 2006, p. 725; Murphy 2010, p. 193; Jacobs, White and Ovey 2017, p. 328; Valentini 2011, p. 193–198; Van Kempen and Fedorova 2015, p. 14; Schabas 2015, p. 334–335.

399 See *Sunday Times v. The United Kingdom*, CE:ECHR:1979:0426JUD000653874, para 47–49.

400 See subsection 2.3.3.

401 See subsection 2.3.4.

402 Cf *Dragotoniu and Militaru-Pidhorni v. Romania*, CE:ECHR:2007:0524JUD007719301, para 40.

403 See subsection 2.3.5.

404 Although the Strasbourg Court identifies this specific principle as the prohibition on *retrospective* application, I will continue to use the more appropriate term *retroactive* application, see Juratowitch 2008, p. 6–9 and chapter 2 above.

405 The Court has stated on multiple occasions that the *lex certa* principle follows from other, previously identified, principles which included the general principle of *nullum crimen, nulla poena sine lege*. However, it has never referred to the general principle of *nullum crimen, nulla poena sine lege* exclusively. Strictly speaking, the Court thus views the *lex certa* principle as a

poena sine lege.[406] By acknowledging the need for a clear legal definition, the Court calls for criminal law to be of a certain clarity and it, consequently, sets qualitative standards for the law. Therefore, the Convention definitely contains a principle that requires offenses to be clearly defined.[407] The Court regards this requirement of clarity to be satisfied:

> "(...) where the individual can know from the wording of the relevant provision, if need be with the assistance of the courts' interpretation of it and after taking appropriate legal advice, what acts and omissions will make him criminally liable and what penalty he faces on that account (...)".[408]

The reference to the need for interpretive assistance from the courts shows how the ECtHR considers the task of defining offenses and penalties to be accomplished by both the domestic legislature and the domestic courts.[409] This is because the term 'law' in Article 7 alludes to the very same concept to which the Convention refers elsewhere, notably in the limitation clauses of the second paragraphs of the Articles 8–11 ECHR.[410] This means that both written and unwritten law will be considered 'law' for the purpose of Article 7 ECHR.[411] More specifically, the Convention's concept of law comprises statutes, bylaws[412] and case-law.[413] As a result, the definition of offenses and penalties does not have to be the exclusive task of the domestic legislature; courts can define crimes and penalties through case-law as well.[414] The Court does not, however, recognize as law a state practice which consistently applies written rules in a way that flagrantly violates human rights.[415]

Although the ECHR's concept of law is quite broad, the Court has established that the law always needs to satisfy certain qualitative requirements.

---

consequence of all previously mentioned principles, and thus of the principles *lex praevia*, *lex stricta* and *nullum crimen, nulla poena sine lege*. See *Kononov*, para 185; *Del Río Prada*, para 79. Cf *Cantoni v. France*, CE:ECHR:1996:1115JUD001786291, para 29; *Veeber v. Estonia (No. 2)*, CE:ECHR:2003:0121JUD004577199, para 31.

406 See *Kononov*, para 185; *Del Río Prada*, para 79; *Vasiliauskas*, para 154. *Cf* Kadelbach 2006, p. 733.

407 Cf Kadelbach 2006, p. 732; Morre 2015, C.2.1.2; Van Kempen and Fedorova 2015, p. 18–19.

408 *Del Río Prada*, para 79. Cf *Kononov*, para 185; *Vasiliauskas*, para 154.

409 Cf Valentini 2011, p. 193; Van Kempen and Fedorova 2015, p. 21.

410 See *Sunday Times v. The United Kingdom*, CE:ECHR:1979:0426JUD000653874, para 47–49. Cf Sudre 2001, p. 344; Boot 2002, p. 146–147; Dhont and Cromheecke 2004, p. 668–669.

411 See *Kononov*, para 185. Cf *Sunday Times v. The United Kingdom*, para 47.

412 See *Khodorkovskiy and Lebedev v. Russia*, CE:ECHR:2013:0725JUD001108206, para 779.

413 See *Del Río Prada*, para 91. Cf Sudre 2001, p. 345; Kadelbach 2006, p. 724, 730; Schabas 2015, p. 337.

414 See *Contrada v. Italy (No. 3)*, CE:ECHR:2015:0414JUD006665513, paras 64, 74–75; *Dallas v. The United Kingdom*, CE:ECHR:2016:0211JUD003839512, paras 72–78.

415 See *Streletz, Kessler and Krenz v. Germany*, CE:ECHR:2001:0322JUD003404496, para 87; *K.-H. W. v. Germany*, CE:ECHR:2001:0322JUD003720197, para 90. See further Murphy 2010, p. 195–196.

Regardless of whether statutory law, a regulation, or case-law defines offenses and penalties, they always need to comply with both the requirement that the law is sufficiently accessible (hereinafter also: 'the accessibility requirement') and with the requirement that the law is sufficiently foreseeable (hereinafter also: 'the foreseeability requirement').[416] The Court has explicitly added that the qualitative requirements must be satisfied as regards to both the definition of an offense and of a penalty.[417] As a result, the first specific requirement of Article 7 applies to rules that define offenses and rules that prescribe penalties.[418]

The requirements of accessibility and foreseeability are often generally referred to as 'the quality of law requirements'. As mentioned above, these requirements were previously developed with regard to other Convention provisions that also contain the term 'law'.[419] In fact, the Court's first judgments on the need to clearly define offenses and penalties did not actually consider complaints about the lack of a clear definition separately under Article 7 ECHR. Instead, the early judgments examined these claims as an element of the question whether an interference with other Convention rights was 'prescribed by law'.[420] According to the Court, the standards a domestic interference needs to satisfy as a result of the 'prescribed by law requirement' are largely the same as the standards a definition of an offense or penalty has to conform to under Article 7 ECHR.[421]

Since the Court deems the clear definition of offenses and penalties to be a task of both the domestic legislature and the courts, it includes considerations about the functioning of both actors in the definition of offenses and penalties.[422] These considerations are particularly relevant for how much clarity the Court requires from a legal definition in light of the foreseeability requirement.[423] The Court has accepted that, since legal rules are of general

416 See *Kononov*, para 185; *Del Río Prada*, para 91; *Vasiliauskas*, para 154. Cf *Sunday Times v. The United Kingdom*, para 49. See further Jacobs, White and Ovey 2017, p. 343–347.

417 See *Del Río Prada*, para 91. Cf *Achour v. France*, CE:ECHR:2006:0329JUD006733501, para 41; *Kafkaris v. Cyprus*, CE:ECHR:2008:0212JUD002190604, para 141.

418 Cf Kadelbach 2006, p. 733.

419 See *Sunday Times v. The United Kingdom*, para 48–49. See further, eg, Harris, O'Boyle, Bates and Buckley 2014, p. 506–509.

420 See *Kokkinakis v. Greece*, CE:ECHR:1993:0525JUD001430788; *Grigoriades v. Greece*, CE:ECHR:1997:1125JUD002434894; *Erdoğdu and İnce v. Turkey*, CE:ECHR:1999:0708JUD 002506794; *Polat v. Turkey*, CE:ECHR:1999:0708JUD002350094. In more recent cases the Court took this approach as well, see, eg, *Kalin v. Turkey*, CE:ECHR:2004:1110JUD003123696, para 35; *Flinkkilä and Others v. Finland*, CE:ECHR:2010:0406JUD002557604, paras 94, 68. The Court can nevertheless choose to exclusively consider a complaint about the 'prescribed by law-requirement' as a potential violation of Article 7 ECHR, see, eg, *K.A. and A.D. v. Belgium*, CE:ECHR:2005:0217JUD004275898, para 46. It can also take a cumulative approach and consider both related complaints separately, see, eg, *Vyerentsov v. Ukraine*, CE:ECHR: 2013:0411JUD002037211, paras 67, 55. See further subsection 3.6.2.

421 See *Başkaya and Okçuoğlu v. Turkey*, CE:ECHR:1999:0708JUD002353694, para 49. Cf Kadelbach 2006, p. 730.

422 See *Del Río Prada*, para 92.

423 See *Kononov*, para 185; *Del Río Prada*, para 92.

application, many provisions include broad characterizations which mean they are inevitably couched in terms which are to some extent vague and whose interpretation and application are questions of practice. Therefore, however clearly drafted a provision of criminal law may be, there will always be the need for judicial interpretation.[424] The general wording of legal rules will always lead to doubts.[425] The role of adjudication vested in the courts is precisely to dissipate any remaining interpretational doubts.[426]

In addition, the Court identifies another reason why the judicial interpretation of rules establishing offenses and prescribing penalties is inevitable. In the ECtHR's view, judicial interpretation is also inevitable because of the need to adapt legal rules to changing circumstances.[427] In the drafting and application of rules of criminal law, legal certainty is apparently not the only value worth adhering to. Although certainty is highly desirable, it should not, according to the Court, regress into excessive rigidity as the law should be able to keep pace with changing circumstances.[428] Consequently, the law's ability to keep pace with changing circumstances is evidently a separate value worth protecting, even if this sometimes obscures legal certainty.[429] In addition to doubts that arise because of the general wording of legal rules, the domestic courts will also be called upon to interpret legal rules in order to adapt them to changing circumstances.[430] Such judicial interpretation will not necessarily violate the foreseeability requirement of criminal law.[431]

Another element in the Court's reiteration of Article 7's general principles is that the ECtHR leaves domestic courts room to develop legal rules. The Court consistently reiterates that the progressive development of the criminal law through judicial law-making is a well-entrenched and necessary part of legal tradition in the Convention States.[432] Domestic courts are thus allowed to *progressively* develop rules of criminal law through judicial interpretation, which implies that domestic courts can, for example, change the scope of a legal rule by offering a novel interpretation of the content of that rule.[433] The Court has

424 Cf *Camilleri v. Malta*, CE:ECHR:2013:0122JUD004293110, para 37.

425 See *Kononov*, para 185; *Del Río Prada*, para 92.

426 See *Del Río Prada*, para 93.

427 See *Kononov*, para 185; *Del Río Prada*, para 92; *Vasiliauskas*, para 155.

428 See *Del Río Prada*, para 92. Cf Altena-Davidsen 2016, p. 160.

429 Cf *Kokkinakis v. Greece*, CE:ECHR:1993:0525JUD001430788, para 40; *Cantoni v. France*, CE:ECHR:1996:1115JUD001786291, paras 28, 31–33. See further about these judgments subsection 3.6.2.

430 Cf Beddard 1996, p. 8.

431 See *Kononov*, para 185; *Del Río Prada*, paras 91–93.

432 See *Kononov*, para 185; *Del Río Prada*, para 93; *Vasiliauskas*, para 155. The Court has deemed this form of law-making to be a well-entrenched part of the legal tradition in *certain* or *most* Convention States. For a reference to certain Convention States, see *Kononov*, para 185; *Alimuçaj v. Albania*, CE:ECHR:2012:0207JUD002013405, para 151. For a reference to most Convention States, see *Khodorkovskiy and Lebedev v. Russia*, para 780.

433 Cf *Khodorkovskiy and Lebedev v. Russia*, CE:ECHR:2013:0725JUD001108206, para 780.

nevertheless limited the room for developing definitions of offenses and penalties via judicial interpretation, but mostly by virtue of the *lex stricta* principle.[434]

The prohibition on the overly extensive interpretation of criminal law ('lex stricta')

In addition to the *lex certa* requirement, Article 7 enshrines the principle that criminal law must not be extensively construed to the accused's detriment.[435] Contrary to what the wording indicates, the principle does not absolutely preclude interpretations that increase the scope of the existing criminal law. It protects against *overly* extending the scope of existing offenses, for example by analogy.[436] Since the Court deems analogical application of criminal law to be an example of extensive construction, the use of analogy by domestic courts is certainly suspect in light of the *lex stricta* principle.[437] In addition to prohibiting the extensive construction of an offense, Article 7 also prohibits the extensive interpretation of a rule prescribing a penalty.[438] The Court's general formulation of the *lex stricta* principle as precluding the extensive interpretation of 'criminal law' confirms that the principle applies to rules that establish criminal offenses and to rules that prescribe penalties.[439]

Limits to interpretation and application of previously defined offenses and penalties are essential to safeguarding the right enshrined in Article 7, especially in light of the Court's acceptance of the inevitability of judicial interpretation.[440] Although the *lex stricta* principle requires strict interpretation,[441] it does not require domestic courts to give the most restrictive interpretation of offenses and penalties.[442]

That there is not an absolute prohibition on extensive interpretation is exemplified by the fact that the Court allows the progressive judicial development of rules of criminal law. The progressive judicial development of

434 Especially with regard to judicial definitions of offenses and penalties, the principles of *lex certa* and *lex stricta* are sometimes hard to distinguish, cf subsection 2.3.3. Some authors regard the limits to judicial interpretation as an element of the *lex certa* principle, see Kadelbach 2006, p. 732–735; Morre 2015, C.2.1.2.

435 See *Kononov*, para 185; *Del Río Prada*, para 78.

436 See *Kononov*, para 185; *Del Río Prada*, para 78. See further Valentini 2011, p. 197–198.

437 See, eg, *Radio France and Others v. France*, CE:ECHR:2004:0330JUD005398400, para 20; *Dragotoniu and Militaru-Pidhorni v. Romania*, CE:ECHR:2007:0524JUD007719301, para 39. Cf Altena-Davidsen 2016, p. 230.

438 See *Del Río Prada*, para 78.

439 Cf Kadelbach 2006, p. 733.

440 See the examination of the *lex certa* principle above. The Court has explicitly underlined the supreme importance of the *lex stricta* principle as an element of Article 7, by considering the prohibition of extensive interpretation to be the 'first consequence' ('une premiere consequence') of the requirement that an offense and a penalty are to be provided by law, see *Varvara v. Italy*, CE:ECHR:2013:1029JUD001747509, para 62.

441 See *Dragotoniu and Militaru-Pidhorni v. Romania*, CE:ECHR:2007:0524JUD007719301, para 40.

442 See Kadelbach 2006, p. 733; Valentini 2011, p. 197–198.

criminal law is nevertheless only allowed conditionally. It is only in accordance with Article 7 if judicial interpretation results in a *gradual* clarification of the rules of criminal liability. The judicial development needs to be consistent with the essence of the offense and its immediate application needs to be reasonably foreseeable.[443] The first requirement limits the room for judicial interpretation, as it prevents the judiciary changing the essence of the offense as previously established by statutory provisions and case-law.[444] The second requirement, that of reasonable foreseeability, essentially limits the room for immediate application of the expansive interpretation to the detriment of the accused. Such applications are only allowed on the condition that the interpretations were reasonably foreseeable at the time of the accused's conduct.

The *lex stricta* principle simultaneously limits the room for judicial interpretation and the possibility for the immediate application of certain interpretations. The Court deems these restrictions necessary to safeguard the object and purpose of Article 7, which is to prevent individuals being subjected to arbitrary prosecution, conviction or punishment.[445]

The prohibition on the retroactive application of criminal law ('lex praevia')

In line with the explicit wording of Article 7(1) ECHR, the Court clearly prohibits the retroactive application of criminal law to an accused's disadvantage. The Strasbourg Court has consistently underlined that Article 7 is not confined to this prohibition,[446] thereby implying that Article 7 definitely bans the retroactive application of criminal law.[447] The Court prohibits the retroactive application of an offense and a penalty by referring to the non-retroactivity of 'criminal law'.[448] Therefore, and fully in line with the scope of the principles of *lex certa* and *lex stricta*, the prohibition on the retroactive application of criminal law precludes the retroactive application of a rule establishing an offense and a rule imposing a penalty to the detriment of the accused. In addition, the *lex praevia* principle prohibits the application of a provision that, although in force at the time of the material conduct, is not in force at the time the case is prosecuted.[449]

It is important to note that there seems to be some theoretical overlap between the principles of *lex praevia* and *lex stricta*.[450] In fact, when a domestic

443 See *Kononov*, para 185; *Del Río Prada*, para 93; *Vasiliauskas*, para 154. Cf Boot 2002, p. 154; Kadelbach 2006, p. 733; Van Kempen and Fedorova 2015, p. 19.

444 See also EComHR, *G. v. Germany* (dec.), CE:ECHR:1989:0306DEC001307987.

445 See *Del Río Prada*, para 93.

446 As mentioned above, the Court refers to Article 7 as prohibiting the *retrospective* application of criminal law.

447 See *Kononov*, para 185; *Del Río Prada*, para 78.

448 See *Del Río Prada*, para 78.

449 See EComHR, *X. v. Germany* (dec.), CE:ECHR:1963:0924DEC000116961. Cf Kadelbach 2006, p. 734; Morre 2015, C.2.1.2.

450 For observations on the theoretical overlap between the principles outside the context of the ECHR, see subsection 2.3.5.

court applies an extensive construction of criminal law for the first time, this will amount to a retroactive application of a new judicial interpretation of the offense or penalty. Although the Court has occasionally indicated that it views the prohibition of 'extending the scope of existing offenses to acts which previously were not criminal offenses' as an element of the *lex praevia* principle,[451] it has generally examined these situations as potential violations of the *lex stricta* principle.[452] In addition, in *Del Río Prada* the Court's wording indicated that the prohibition on extending the scope of existing offenses is more closely related to the *lex stricta* principle than to the *lex praevia* principle.[453] I will not, therefore, treat the retroactive application of a new judicial interpretation of an existing provision as falling within the scope of the *lex praevia* principle.[454]

As a final observation it should be noted that retroactive application is only prohibited when the accused is worse off as result.[455] When retroactive application benefits the accused, it is required by Article 7. Ever since its judgment in *Scoppola*, the Court considers that Article 7 implicitly enshrines the principle of retroactive application of the more lenient criminal law (ie the *lex mitior* principle).[456] An important reason for considering the *lex mitior* principle as inherent in Article 7 was the emergence of a European and international consensus around treating *lex mitior* as a fundamental principle of criminal law. In the ECtHR's view, both Article 49(1) of the Charter and the CJEU's judgment in *Berlusconi*[457] played an important role in evidencing this emerging consensus.[458] As a result, Article 7 requires that

> "(...) where there are differences between the criminal law in force at the time of the commission of the offence and subsequent criminal laws enacted before a final judgment is rendered, the courts must apply the law whose provisions are most favourable to the defendant".[459]

Since *lex mitior* is not generally considered to constitute an element of the legality principle in criminal law theory, I will not examine judgments on this principle.[460]

---

451 See *M. v. Germany*, CE:ECHR:2009:1217JUD001935904, para 118.

452 This approach has also been adopted by the EComHR, see, eg, EComHR, *X. Ltd and Y. v. United Kingdom* (dec.), CE:ECHR:1982:0507DEC000871079, para 8–9.

453 See par 78. Cf *Achour v. France*, CE:ECHR:2006:0329JUD006733501, para 41.

454 This approach is, moreover, in line with the approach taken in subsection 2.3.5. See, conversely, Valentini 2011, p. 194.

455 See, eg, *G. v. France*, CE:ECHR:1995:0927JUD001531289, para 26; *Moiseyev v. Russia*, CE:ECHR:2008:1009JUD006293600, paras 237–238; *Maktouf and Damjanović v. Bosnia and Herzegovina*, CE:ECHR:2013:0718JUD000231208, para 65.

456 *Scoppola v. Italy (No. 2)*, CE:ECHR:2012:0522JUD000012605, para 108–109. See further Baumbach 2011, p. 125–142; Schabas 2015, p. 350–351.

457 See *Criminal Proceedings against Silvio Berlusconi, Sergio Adelchi, Marcello Dell'Utri and Others*, EU:C:2005:270.

458 See para 105.

459 *Scoppola*, para 109.

460 Cf the partly dissenting opinion of judges Nicolaou, Bratza, Lorentzen, Jočienė, Villiger and Sajó in *Scoppola*. See also the considerations about the scope of this thesis in chapter 1.

3.4.4 STRUCTURE AND HYPOTHESIS

Article 7's wording and the aforementioned general principles result in several substantive distinctions. The updated figure provides an overview:

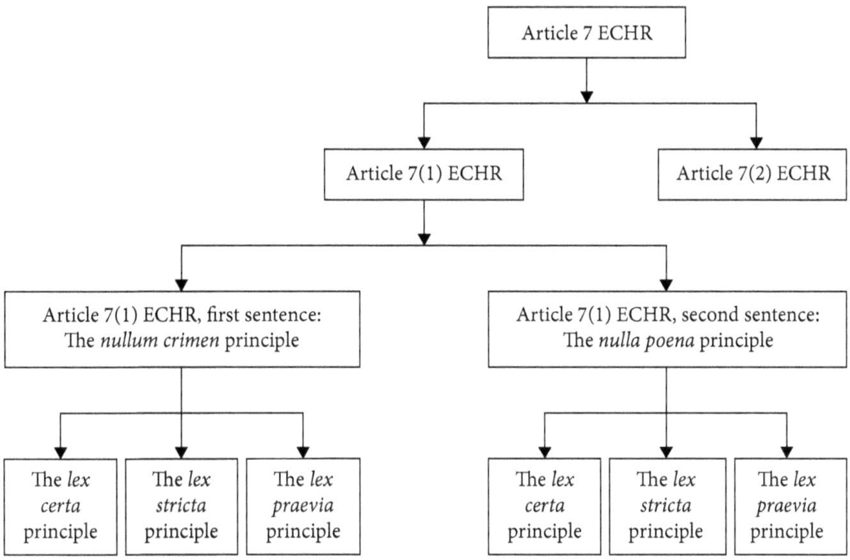

These distinctions will be used to structure the more detailed analysis of the substance of Article 7(1) ECHR as established by the Strasbourg Court's case-law. While it is far too early to draw conclusions about the ECHR's legality principle, the general considerations of the ECtHR do justify a hypothesis. In light of the explicit recognition of the rule of law rationale and the focus on precluding arbitrariness, as well as the absence of an explicit recognition of a *lex scripta* requirement, Article 7 ECHR appears to protect only a common law legality principle. Subsection 3.8 revisits this hypothesis and determines whether it can be validated after the detailed analysis of the Court's considerations on the substance of the legality principle.

3.5 THE SCOPE AND INTENSITY OF THE COURT'S REVIEW: THE INFLUENCE OF THE SUBSIDIARITY PRINCIPLE

3.5.1 SUBSIDIARITY AS THE POINT OF DEPARTURE

Before turning to analyze the substance of the legality principle in-depth, it is important to describe the scope and intensity of the ECtHR's review under Article 7(1) ECHR. Because Article 7(1) ECHR protects against overly extensive interpretations and retroactive applications of criminal law, complaints under the Convention's legality principle often concern the interpretation and application of national law by the domestic authorities.[461] In these situations, the ECtHR is required to evaluate domestic legal interpretations and factual assessments in light of their compatibility with Article 7's legality principle. The Court is not completely free in this evaluation, however, because of the subsidiary role of the Convention system of fundamental rights protection.[462]

It is well-known that the ECtHR's review is inherently restricted by its special position as an international court, which obstructs a sufficiently thorough and contextual appreciation of both the facts of the case and the applicable domestic law.[463] In line with the subsidiarity principle, the Court has, therefore, stressed that the domestic authorities are, in principle, better placed to establish the relevant facts and interpret the domestic law before them.[464] As a result, it will not easily substitute its own views on the facts and the interpretation of domestic law for that of the domestic authorities.[465] Ultimately, however, it is for the Court to determine whether the domestic factual assessments and legal interpretations are in conformity with the ECHR, as the ECtHR provides supervision.[466]

3.5.2 THE COURT'S REVIEW I: JUDICIAL RESTRAINT WITH ROOM FOR MORE INTENSE SCRUTINY

The subsidiarity principle is understood as diminishing the intensity of the Court's review of complaints about factual determinations and the application and interpretation of national law by the domestic authorities. In general, the Court will only conduct a marginal review of domestic law and its interpretation by national authorities, as well as factual assessments by domestic

---

461 Cf Harris, O'Boyle, Bates and Buckley 2014, p. 493; Grabenwarter 2014, p. 175.

462 The legal bases of the principle of subsidiarity are, according to the Court, Articles 1, 13, 19, and 35(1) ECHR, see *Kudła v. Poland*, CE:ECHR:2000:1026JUD003021096, para 152; *Austin and Others v. The United Kingdom*, CE:ECHR:2012:0315JUD003969209, para 61. See further Mowbray 2015, p. 319–320. Cf Gerards 2011a, p. 104.

463 Cf Brems 1996, p. 302–303; Christoffersen 2009, p. 229, 276, 291; Gerards 2011, p. 185, 209; Mowbray 2015, p. 320, 323.

464 See, eg, *Winterwerp v. The Netherlands*, CE:ECHR:1979:1024JUD000630173, para 46. Cf Christoffersen 2009, p. 3, 229, 276–296; Gerards 2011, p. 209–2011; Gerards 2011a, p. 111; Van de Heyning 2011, p. 69.

465 The Convention States stressed the need for the Court to acknowledge its subsidiary position with regard to domestic factual assessments and legal interpretations, see High Level Conference on the Future of the European Court of Human Rights, Interlaken Declaration, 19 February 2010, under E, 9a and 9b. See further Spano 2014, p. 490–491; Mowbray 2015, p. 329–330.

466 See *Handyside v. The United Kingdom*, CE:ECHR:1976:1207JUD000549372, para 49; *Austin and Others v. The United Kingdom*, para 61. Cf Beddard 1996, p. 7; Brems 1996, p. 303–304; Kadelbach 2006, p. 733; Christoffersen 2009, p. 251–253; Van de Heyning 2011, p. 86–87.

institutions.[467] The Strasbourg Court has often stressed this general approach in judgments that concerned complaints about a violation of Article 7 ECHR. In the *Rohlena* judgment, for example, the Grand Chamber reiterated that the interpretation and application of domestic law is primarily for the national authorities, notably the courts.[468] And in *Kononov*, the Court underlined that it does not deal with errors of fact or law committed by the national courts unless this has led to a violation of a Convention right or when the domestic assessment has been manifestly arbitrary.[469] This means, for example, that domestic courts are allowed to draw common-sense inferences from established facts.[470]

Because it is for the domestic courts to construe and apply domestic law and assess the facts,[471] the ECtHR, in principle, leaves it to the national courts to rule on individual criminal responsibility.[472] Under Article 7 ECHR, the Court will merely evaluate whether the applicant's acts were, at the time of conduct, legally defined as offenses that satisfied the requirements of accessibility and foreseeability.[473] The Court's task in this regard is to "(...) verify that at the time when an accused person performed the act which led to his being prosecuted and convicted there was in force a legal provision which made that act punishable, and that the punishment imposed did not exceed the limits fixed by that provision (...)".[474]

In order to determine whether the alleged acts were indeed performed by the accused, and whether these acts fell within the scope of the applicable national provision, the ECtHR cannot avoid assessing both the factual evidence and the domestic criminal law. The object of review in Article 7 cases will thus inevitably

---

467 The same approach is taken when domestic law refers to rules of international law, see *Kolk and Kislyiy v. Estonia* (dec.), CE:ECHR:2006:0117DEC002305204; *Korbely v. Hungary*, CE:ECHR:2008:0919JUD000917402, para 72. Cf Christoffersen 2009, p. 292–293.

468 See *Rohlena*, para 51 and further about that judgment Timmerman 2015. Other examples include: *Streletz, Kessler and Krenz v. Germany*, CE:ECHR:2001:0322JUD003404496, para 49; *K.A. and A.D. v. Belgium*, CE:ECHR:2005:0217JUD004275898, para 52; *Jorgic v. Germany*, CE:ECHR:2007:0712JUD007461301, para 102; *Korbely v. Hungary*, CE:ECHR:2008:0919JUD000917402, para 72.

469 See *Kononov*, para 189 and further, eg, *Streletz Kessler and Krenz v. Germany*, para 49; *Jorgic v. Germany*, CE:ECHR:2007:0712JUD007461301, para 102; *Vasiliauskas*, para 160; *Poletan and Azirovik v. the former Yugoslav Republic of Macedonia*, CE:ECHR:2016:0512JUD002671107, para 109. In exceptional circumstances the Court will nevertheless engage in fact-finding when the domestic authorities have failed to do so, see Mowbray 2015, p. 340.

470 See *Poletan and Azirovik v. the former Yugoslav Republic of Macedonia*, CE:ECHR:2016:0512JUD002671107, para 111.

471 See, outside the specific context of Article 7, *Pla and Puncernau v. Andorra*, CE:ECHR:2004:1110JUD003123696, para 46 and, with regard to Article 7 ECHR, *Vasiliauskas*, para 164. Cf Mowbray 2015, p. 321 and 340–341.

472 See *Kononov*, para 187. See also *Streletz Kessler and Krenz v. Germany*, para 51; *Vasiliauskas*, para 164. Cf Schabas 2015, p. 337.

473 See *Kononov*, para 187. See also *Streletz Kessler and Krenz v. Germany*, para 51; *Veeber v. Estonia (No. 2)*, CE:ECHR:2003:0121JUD004577199, para 33; *K.A. and A.D. v. Belgium*, para 52.

474 See *Del Río Prada*, para 80. See for subsequent reiterations of this consideration: *Rohlena*, para 50; *Contrada v. Italy (No. 3)*, CE:ECHR:2015:0414JUD006665513, para 60; *Vasiliauskas*, para 161.

require the Court to review domestic factual assessments and legal interpretations. Since factual assessments and legal interpretations by national authorities constitute the object of review, the subsidiarity principle could influence the standard of protection of the Convention's legality principle. The more marginal the review of the domestic assessments and interpretations due to the subsidiarity principle, the lower the practical protection that is provided by Article 7 ECHR.

The Court has acknowledged the potential impact of the subsidiarity principle on the protection provided by the Convention's legality principle. In *Kononov*, the Court explicitly considered that the powers of review of domestic interpretations need to be greater under Article 7 ECHR. In the words of the ECtHR:

> "Article 7 §1 requires the Court to examine whether there was a contemporaneous legal basis for the applicant's conviction and, in particular, it must satisfy itself that the result reached by the relevant domestic courts was compatible with Article 7 of the Convention. To accord a lesser power of review to this Court would render Article 7 devoid of purpose (…)".[475]

With regard to Article 7 ECHR, the Court is thus apparently willing to scrutinize domestic judicial interpretations that lead to the imposition of a criminal penalty. This would imply that both the factual assessments and the legal interpretation by the domestic authorities could be reviewed more intensely if necessary in order to determine the conformity with the legality principle.[476] The absence of subsidiarity considerations in the above formulation appears to indicate the applicability of a more than marginal review of the domestic conviction under Article 7.

3.5.3 THE COURT'S REVIEW II: APPARENT PREVALENCE OF JUDICIAL RETICENCE

It is nevertheless hard to determine whether the ECtHR actually conducts intense reviews of the domestic authorities' activities under Article 7 ECHR. The case-law does, in fact, contain examples to the contrary, because the Court has also applied its general, more marginal, standard of review in Article 7 cases. In *Alimuçaj*, for example, the ECtHR accepted that the facts amounted to the relevant domestic criminal offense because the domestic courts' findings and interpretations did not seem unreasonable or arbitrary.[477] This was sufficient

475 See *Kononov*, para 198. This consideration was recently reiterated in *Rohlena*, para 52; *Contrada v. Italy (No. 3)*, para 62; *Vasiliauskas*, para 161; *Poletan and Azirovik v. the former Yugoslav Republic of Macedonia*, CE:ECHR:2016:0512JUD002671107, para 110. Cf *Žaja v. Croatia*, CE:ECHR:2016:1004JUD003746209, paras 91–92.

476 Cf Gerards 2011, p. 210–211; Schabas 2015, p. 337–338.

477 *Alimuçaj v. Albania*, CE:ECHR:2012:0207JUD002013405, para 152. This fits well with the view judge Zupančič expressed in his concurring opinion in the judgment in *Streletz Kessler and Krenz v. Germany*. Zupančič argued that as long as the national courts had applied national law

to approve the domestic judicial approach and to conclude that the authorities had remained within the generally acceptable rules of interpretation of criminal statutes. In *Huhtamäki* the Court reiterated its general approach of only marginally reviewing the application and interpretation of national law by national courts as an argument for finding that there had been no violation of Article 7 ECHR.[478] The ECtHR has observed that it would only reject a domestic interpretation if there was a flagrant non-observance or arbitrariness in the application of national law.[479] In *Khodorkovskiy* the ECtHR employed a similar reasoning. It stated that, according to existing case-law, its supervisory function

> "(...) consists in considering whether the national court, in reaching its decision, has not unreasonably interpreted, and applied to the applicant, the law concerned. In other words, the Court applies a relaxed standard in such matters, which allows the States to develop their case-law and adjust it to the changing condition of modern society (...)".[480]

The above judgments show that the subsidiarity principle has also impacted the Court's review of domestic factual and legal assessments under Article 7 ECHR. For that reason, the Court's review of the activities of national authorities in the field of criminal law has, at times, only been marginal.[481] Since the intensity of the Court's review influences the level of protection under the Convention, Article 7 ECHR has not always provided substantial effective protection. Although, at present, the ECtHR appears to require more than a marginal review under Article 7,[482] it does not indicate what exactly this higher degree of scrutiny entails. It will continue, in any event, to allow some margin to the national authorities, because, in Article 7 cases, the Court continues to reiterate that it is generally for the domestic authorities to assess the facts, determine their legal classification, and interpret and apply national law.[483] It is, therefore, fair to consider the subsidiarity principle relevant for the intensity of the Court's reviews under the ECHR's legality principle and, as a consequence, for its standard of protection.

The apparent relevance of the subsidiarity principle could explain the actual construction of the substantive protection in the ECtHR's case-law. It is useful to keep this in mind when we examine the principle's substantive protection in the subsequent sections.

---

in way that was legally consistent, Article 7(1) ECHR could not be violated by their interpretation. The emphasis on legal consistency is, in my view, easily connected to the absence of arbitrariness in legal reasoning. See also Murphy 2010, p. 205 and, with regard to the legal reasoning employed by domestic courts outside the context of Article 7, Van de Heyning 2011, p. 91–94.

478 *Huhtamäki v. Finland*, CE:ECHR:2012:0306JUD005446809, para 52.

479 See, similarly, Custers, Deveaux and Turk v. Denmark, CE:ECHR:2007:0503JUD001184303, para 84.

480 *Khodorkovskiy and Lebedev v. Russia*, para 781.

481 Cf Christoffersen 2009, p. 294–295.

482 Due to the reiterations of the above-cited *Kononov* consideration, see *Kononov*, para 198 and, recently, *Rohlena*, para 52; *Contrada v. Italy (No. 3)*, para 62.

483 See *Rohlena*, para 51.

3.6 THE *NULLUM CRIMEN* PRINCIPLE

3.6.1 INTRODUCTION

This section examines the relevance of the principles of *lex certa*, *lex stricta* and *lex praevia* for the *nullum crimen* principle. In other words: it examines the content of the three previously distinguished specific principles with regard to *offenses*. Subsection 3.6.2 first examines the principle that the law needs to clearly define offenses. Subsection 3.6.3 subsequently examines the prohibition on overly extensive interpretation of offenses. The principle that offenses should not be retroactively established is then the focus of subsection 3.6.4.

3.6.2 THE PRINCIPLE THAT OFFENSES REQUIRE A CLEAR LEGAL DEFINITION (*LEX CERTA*)

The Court reviews the domestic definition of an offense in light of the general quality of law requirements of accessibility and foreseeability. This is the case under Article 7 ECHR, but the same is true when the Court examines whether an interference with other Convention rights is prescribed by law.[484] Although the substantive criteria regarding the clarity of an offense under Article 7 and the prescribed by law requirement in, notably,[485] Articles 8–11 ECHR are the same,[486] there is one difference that impacts the Court's review.[487] This is the point in time that the law has to satisfy the Convention's demands regarding clarity.

The present subsection commences by remarking on the difference between the two reviewing options. Thereafter, the role of the requirements of accessibility and foreseeability when reviewing the clarity of definitions of offenses is addressed. The actual substance of these criteria is subsequently considered by examining several judgments with relevance for the *lex certa* principle. A general picture of the ECHR's requirements for an acceptable definition of an offense will then emerge.

Reviewing the clarity of an offense: the relevance of other Convention provisions

In several judgments the Court merely referred to its considerations about the 'prescribed by law requirement' to substantiate its conclusions with regard to the *lex certa* principle. In *Kokkinakis*, for example, the ECtHR found that

484 See subsection 3.3.2 above. For an overview of the ECtHR's case-law about the Convention's 'prescribed by law requirement', see Viljanen 2003, p. 185–208.

485 Several authors have observed that the Court generally requires interferences with almost all Convention rights to be prescribed by law, see, eg, Viljanen 2003, p. 200; Gerards 2011, p. 112.

486 Cf Jacobs, White and Ovey 2017, p. 334–335.

487 For an examination of the meaning of the quality of law standards for provisions other than Article 7 ECHR, see Gerards 2011, p. 112–132.

although a conviction for the relatively vaguely worded offense of proselytism interfered with the freedom of religion, it was nevertheless prescribed by law as required by Article 9(2) ECHR.[488] In the Court's view, that conclusion sufficed to subsequently dismiss the complaint about violations of Article 7 ECHR.[489]

The Court adopted the same approach in *Grigoriades*.[490] In that case the applicant claimed that his conviction for the broadly worded offense of insulting the military was both a violation of his right to freedom of expression protected by Article 10 ECHR[491] and a violation of Article 7 ECHR.[492] Again, the Court only examined whether the interference with the other Convention right, ie Article 10 ECHR, was prescribed by law. Since the ECtHR concluded that the interference with the freedom of expression was indeed prescribed by law as required by Article 10(2) ECHR, it held that there was no violation of Article 7 ECHR either.[493]

The more recent judgment in *Flinkkilä* confirmed the relationship between the review under Article 7 ECHR and the prescribed by law requirement.[494] The applicants in *Flinkkilä* were held criminally liable for printing the names of convicted persons in a newspaper. This amounted to the offense of publicly disseminating information depicting the private life of another.[495] Although the applicants complained that – at the time of conduct – their acts did not fall clearly within the scope of the applicable criminal law,[496] the Court first considered the complaint under Article 10 ECHR. It examined whether the absence of a sufficiently clear legal basis made the interference with the freedom of expression fall short of the prescribed by law requirement.[497] Since the ECtHR found the interference with the freedom of expression to be prescribed by law, it determined that the definition of the offense was, consequently, in accordance with Article 7 ECHR.[498]

This short survey of the judgments in *Kokkinakis*, *Grigoriades*, and *Flinkkilä* indicates that the Court's review of whether an interference with a Convention right is prescribed by law is, in substantive terms, similar to the review of the

---

488 See *Kokkinakis v. Greece*, CE:ECHR:1993:0525JUD001430788, para 40–41.

489 See para 52–53. For the opposite approach in similar factual circumstances, see *Larissis and Others v. Greece*, CE:ECHR:1998:0224JUD002337294, paras 34, 41. For another example of a case in which the Court first considered the complaint under Article 7 and only then looked at the question whether an interference with another Convention right was 'prescribed by law', see *Başkaya and Okçuoğlu v. Turkey*, CE:ECHR:1999:0708JUD002353694, paras 49, 39–40.

490 *Grigoriades v. Greece*, CE:ECHR:1997:1125JUD002434894.

491 See para 34. Cf *Erdoğdu and İnce v. Turkey*, CE:ECHR:1999:0708JUD002506794, paras 36–39.

492 See para 49. Cf *Erdoğdu and İnce v. Turkey*, CE:ECHR:1999:0708JUD002506794, paras 57–59.

493 See para 50.

494 *Flinkkilä and Others v. Finland*, CE:ECHR:2010:0406JUD002557604. Cf the identical approaches in the related cases in *Tuomela and Others v. Finland*, CE:ECHR:2010:0406JUD002571104; *Jokitaipale and Others v. Finland*, CE:ECHR:2010:0406JUD004334905, and the later, but substantively identical, *Reinboth and Others v. Finland*, CE:ECHR:2011:0125JUD003086508.

495 See para 8 and 24.

496 See para 63.

497 See para 63–68 and 94.

498 See para 68 and 94.

lex certa principle under Article 7 ECHR.[499] Despite the correspondence between how the Court reviews of the clarity of offenses under Article 7 on the one hand, and Articles 8–11, second paragraph, on the other, the Court has underlined one difference.[500] This difference concerns the point in time that the offense has to satisfy the Convention's clarity requirements. Under Article 7, the definition of the offense needs to satisfy the clarity requirements at the time the offense is committed.[501] However, interferences with other Convention rights only need to satisfy the prescribed by law requirement at the time of the interference.[502] Interference with other Convention rights will occur only at the time of the conviction or, at best, with the prosecution for the conduct protected by Articles 8–11 ECHR. Article 7 ECHR requires, therefore, a definition of an offense to comply with the clarity standards at an earlier point in time than the Convention's other provisions.[503]

Since the Convention's other provisions only require an offense to comply with the clarity standards at the time of conviction, it is remarkable that the Court has merely referred to its conclusions on the prescribed by law requirement in the three above-mentioned cases. The prescribed by law requirement could, in fact, indicate a lower amount of protection from the *lex certa* principle. This is because an interference can satisfy the prescribed by law requirement when a domestic definition of an offense is insufficiently clear at the time of the applicant's acts so long as it complies with the clarity requirement at the time of conviction. The absence of a separate *lex certa* review in these cases seems to lower the standard of protection provided by Article 7 ECHR. Therefore, it is doubtful whether the Court conducted a sufficiently thorough review of the clarity of the definition of the offense at the time of the material conduct in the cases *Kokkinakis*, *Grigoriades*, and *Flinkkilä*.

'Kokkinakis' as a point of departure for assessing the requirements of accessibility and foreseeability

As mentioned above, Article 7 ECHR demands that the legal definition of an offense complies with the requirements of accessibility and foreseeability.[504] The importance of the accessibility and foreseeability requirements for the legal

499 Cf *Sunday Times v. The United Kingdom*, CE:ECHR:1979:0426JUD000653874, para 49; *Başkaya and Okçuoğlu v. Turkey*, CE:ECHR:1999:0708JUD002353694, para 49.

500 See *Başkaya and Okçuoğlu v. Turkey*, CE:ECHR:1999:0708JUD002353694, para 50–51.

501 See *Başkaya and Okçuoğlu v. Turkey*, para 50.

502 See *Başkaya and Okçuoğlu v. Turkey*, para 50.

503 Cf Murphy 2010, p. 198.

504 For explicit statements about these requirements in the context of Article 7 ECHR, see, eg, *Streletz, Kessler and Krenz v. Germany*, CE:ECHR:2001:0322JUD003404496, para 51; *Custers, Deveaux and Turk v. Denmark*, CE:ECHR:2007:0503JUD001184303, paras 81–83, 89; *Kuolelis, Bartoševičius and Burokevičius v. Lithuania*, CE:ECHR:2008:0219JUD007435701, para 116; *Kasymakhunov and Saybatalov v. Russia*, CE:ECHR:2013:0314JUD002626105, para 79.

definition of an offense was already apparent in the early case of *Kokkinakis*, although mostly implicitly.[505] As mentioned, in *Kokkinakis* the Court reviewed the quality of the statutory offense of proselytism in light of a potential violation of Article 9 ECHR.[506] It first underlined that the wording of statutory provisions will often not be absolutely precise and that some vagueness is permitted.[507] The Court then stated that, for this reason, the interpretation and application of the offense of proselytism depended on practice.[508] Importantly, the Court determined that, at the time of the applicant's acts, there existed a body of settled domestic case-law which was published and, for that reason, accessible.[509] The domestic courts' case-law interpreting the – relatively vaguely worded – statutory offense of proselytism enabled the applicant to regulate his conduct.[510] Although the conviction for the offense of proselytism interfered with the freedom of religion, it was prescribed by law as required by Article 9(2) ECHR.[511] Consequently, the definition of the offense was in accordance with the requirement that an offense needs to be clearly defined by law.[512]

Kokkinakis implies that the Court deems the accessibility requirement to be satisfied by publication of the law. Since both the statutory definition of the offense and case-law interpreting it were published at the time of the applicant's conduct, that law was apparently sufficiently accessible. The Court then established that the applicant was enabled to regulate his conduct because domestic case-law had interpreted the applicable statutory definition before his acts. The mere existence of accessible case-law was apparently sufficient to conclude that the applicant was able to regulate his conduct. The domestic case-law had thus, arguably, made the criminal responsibility for the applicant's acts foreseeable. As a result, the Court implicitly found that the cumulative legal definition of proselytism in statutory law and case-law satisfied the foreseeability requirement.

In addition to the foreseeability requirement being mostly implicit,[513] the Court's review of that requirement seems to have been rather undemanding. The

505 *Kokkinakis v. Greece*, CE:ECHR:1993:0525JUD001430788.

506 See para 37.

507 See para 40. Cf Dhont and Cromheecke 2004, p. 669–672.

508 See para 40.

509 See para 40. Cf Boot 2002, p. 148.

510 See para 40. See, critically, judge Martens in his partly dissenting opinion in *Kokkinakis*, para 5.

511 See para 41.

512 See para 52. For a full confirmation of this ruling in similar factual circumstances, see *Larissis and Others v. Greece*, CE:ECHR:1998:0224JUD002337294, para 34.

513 As we will see below, the Court has been more explicit about the foreseeability requirement in its subsequent case-law. One exception is several judgments against Turkey that were published on the same day. In these cases the Court merely regarded the existence of a statutory definition of an offense to be sufficient in light of Article 7's requirements. See, eg, *Erdoğdu and İnce v. Turkey*, CE:ECHR:1999:0708JUD002506794, paras 59, 39; *Polat v. Turkey*, CE:ECHR:1999:0708JUD002350094, paras 35–36. In these cases the Court refrained from conducting independent reviews of the statutory wording and interpretive case-law. As a result, the Court seemed to have only reviewed the definition of an offense in light of the requirement of accessibility. In one of the related cases, however, the Court

ECtHR attached a lot of weight to the mere existence of accessible domestic case-law interpreting the statutory definition of an offense. Essentially, the existence of interpretive case-law was sufficient for a finding that the legal definition of an offense was compatible with Article 7. As a result, the Court did not conduct an intensive review of the wording of the statutory provision,[514] nor of the interpretation of that wording by the domestic courts.[515] This is evident because the Court did not examine whether, *taken together*, the statutory definition and the domestic courts' interpretive case-law enabled the applicant to foresee what conduct made him criminally liable.[516] As a result, an intensive review of the foreseeability of criminal responsibility was absent.

The accessibility requirement

Kokkinakis indicates that the accessibility requirement will not generally be hard to satisfy. This requirement merely calls for the official publication of the statutory provisions and/or the applicable case-law at the time of the material conduct.[517] The official publication of the text in a separate brochure can already satisfy the accessibility requirement, certainly when this is accompanied by a publication of the synopsis of the official text in other publications that target the rules' intended audience.[518] For this reason, the accessibility requirement does not require the publication of the full text in an official journal.

As a result of the relatively low demands of the accessibility requirement, this test is only taken as a first step in determining whether a legal definition is sufficiently clear. Therefore, the foreseeability requirement, discussed hereafter, has been the most distinctive criterion when examining compatibility with the *lex certa* principle.[519] The lesser importance of the accessibility requirement is exemplified by several judgments about the *lex certa* principle. This is because the Court only examined whether the legal definition complied with the foreseeability requirement

---

did consider the clarity of the wording specifically, see *Başkaya and Okçuoğlu v. Turkey*, CE:ECHR:1999:0708JUD002353694, para 39.

514 Judge Martens was very critical about this aspect of the Court's judgment, see his partly dissenting opinion in *Kokkinakis*, para 5.

515 Since the vague statutory wording was considered to be 'cured' by domestic case-law, Martens considered the ECtHR's review of the domestic courts' interpretations to be of supreme importance in light of the legality principle, see his partly dissenting opinion in *Kokkinakis*, para 6. Martens found that the Court's review has failed in this regard as well, see para 7–12 of his dissent.

516 For an example of a judgment where the Court did review both the statutory wording and the case law of the domestic courts in light of the *lex certa* principle, see *Plechkov v. Romania*, CE:ECHR:2014:0916JUD000166003, paras 69–76.

517 See, eg, *G. v. France*, CE:ECHR:1995:0927JUD001531289, para 25; *Custers, Deveaux and Turk v. Denmark*, CE:ECHR:2007:0503JUD001184303, paras 82–83; *Korbely v. Hungary*, CE:ECHR:2008:0919JUD000917402, para 75. Cf Gerards 2011, p. 110; Van Kempen and Fedorova 2015, p. 21.

518 See *Korbely v. Hungary*, CE:ECHR:2008:0919JUD000917402, para 75.

519 The exception is *Kokkinakis*, discussed above.

in many of these judgments. In several cases the ECtHR justified this focus review on the grounds that the essence of the dispute concerned the foreseeability of criminal responsibility.[520] In these cases, the Court omitted to examine the accessibility requirement due to a lack of complaints about inaccessibility.

Although the 'essence of the dispute formulation' is the most commonly cited reason for not considering the accessibility requirement, at times, the Court has focused on the foreseeability requirement for other reasons. In *Vyerentsov*, for example, the Court found that it had no reason to doubt the accessibility of the applicable offense because it had a basis in domestic law.[521] Thus, the Court essentially presumed the accessibility of provisions enshrined in a criminal code.[522] This presumption indicates that the Court will not thoroughly examine the domestic definition in light of the accessibility requirement in the absence of clear signs that the law was inaccessible.[523]

The same 'hands off approach' with regard to the accessibility requirement is apparent in *Contrada*.[524] There the Court merely reviewed a judicially created offense in light of the foreseeability requirement,[525] although the first judgment defining that offense was only handed down in the final two years of the applicant's acts.[526] Therefore, during the majority of the applicant's acts in the years 1979–1988, the judicial definition of the offense was not at all accessible to him as it did not yet exist before the year 1987.[527] Without giving reasons for not reviewing the judicial definition in light of the accessibility requirement, the Court only examined that definition in light of the foreseeability requirement. In the subsequent *Dallas* judgment, the Court also reviewed the acceptability of a judicially defined offense, in this instance a common law offense, exclusively on the basis of the foreseeability requirement.[528]

520 See *Grigoriades v. Greece*, CE:ECHR:1997:1125JUD002434894, paras 34, 37–38; *Cantoni v. France*, CE:ECHR:1996:1115JUD001786291, para 29; *Flinkkilä and Others v. Finland*, CE:ECHR:2010:0406JUD002557604, para 64; *Kasymakhunov and Saybatalov v. Russia*, CE:ECHR:2013:0314JUD002626105, para 80; *Ashlarba v. Georgia*, CE:ECHR:2014:0715 JUD004555408, para 35. All these cases are discussed below with regard to the foreseeability requirement. For examples of cases that do not contain the 'essence of the dispute formulation', but in which the absence of complaints about accessibility have probably influenced the Court's focus on foreseeability, see *Liivik v. Estonia*, CE:ECHR:2009:0625JUD001215705, paras 97, 101; *Kononov v. Latvia*, CE:ECHR:2010:0517JUD003637604, paras 234–235.

521 *Vyerentsov v. Ukraine*, CE:ECHR:2013:0411JUD002037211, para 53. This case will be discussed in the subsequent section.

522 Cf *Flinkkilä and Others v. Finland*, CE:ECHR:2010:0406JUD002557604, para 64.

523 Cf *K.-H. W. v. Germany*, CE:ECHR:2001:0322JUD003720197, para 73.

524 *Contrada v. Italy (No. 3)*, CE:ECHR:2015:0414JUD006665513. This case will be discussed below in the context of the foreseeability requirement.

525 See para 74–75.

526 See para 67.

527 Cf para 68 and 74.

528 See *Dallas v. The United Kingdom*, CE:ECHR:2016:0211JUD003839512, paras 74–75, 77. See further Timmerman 2016a.

This survey of the Court's case-law on the accessibility requirement warrants two conclusions. First, the accessibility requirement is not hard to satisfy as it merely demands *some* official publication of the applicable legal definition contained in statute and/or case-law. Second, the Court will not generally conduct an in-depth review of the accessibility requirement. Instead, it relies heavily on the applicant's arguments about the inaccessibility of the applicable offense.[529] In the absence of clear complaints about inaccessibility, the Court will not generally conduct an autonomous review of the accessibility requirement. Even when a case, like *Contrada*, indicates a potential problem with accessibility, the Court prefers to review the legal definition of an offense exclusively in light of the foreseeability requirement.

The foreseeability requirement I: statutory wording within its context

Given the Court's light-touch review of the accessibility requirement, it is safe to say that the *lex certa* principle's protective function will be provided mostly by reviewing a definition in light of the foreseeability requirement. When a provision is available,[530] the offense's statutory wording constitutes the starting point for the Court's examination and a factor in determining the compatibility with the foreseeability requirement.[531] In *Cantoni* the Court recalled that:

> "(...) the scope of the notion of foreseeability depends to a considerable degree on the content of the text in issue, the field it is designed to cover and the number and status of those to whom it is addressed (...). A law may still satisfy the requirement of foreseeability even if the person concerned has to take appropriate legal advice to assess, to a degree that is reasonable in the circumstances, the consequences which a given action may entail (...)".[532]

The above citation exemplifies how the Court takes a contextual approach to the statutory offense by considering the content of the text, the field it is designed to cover, and its addressees.[533] This contextual approach provides some flexibility when reviewing the clarity of the wording of an offense. Further leeway is

529 For an example of a dispute about the accessibility requirement between the parties and the Court's explicit response, see *Korbely v. Hungary*, CE:ECHR:2008:0919JUD000917402, paras 60, 63, 75.

530 See below for judgments that accept judicial definitions as sufficient in light of the foreseeability requirement.

531 See, eg, *Custers, Deveaux and Turk v. Denmark*, CE:ECHR:2007:0503JUD001184303, para 81; *Flinkkilä and Others v. Finland*, CE:ECHR:2010:0406JUD002557604, para 67. Cf *Soros v. France*, CE:ECHR:2011:1006JUD005042506, paras 57–58.

532 See *Cantoni*, para 35.

533 Cf Dhont and Cromheecke 2004, p. 669; Grabenwarter 2014, p. 180–181. For a general examination of these requirements under the 'prescribed by law requirement' outside the context of Article 7 ECHR, see Viljanen 2003, p. 192–195.

provided by making the foreseeability of criminal responsibility dependent on legal advice.[534] As a consequence, the level of clarity the Court demands from the wording of offenses does not seem very high under the foreseeability requirement.

That the ECtHR is not very demanding in this regard can be illustrated by several judgments where it approved relatively vaguely worded offenses. Some of these judgments are especially striking, because the Court accepted the foreseeability of criminal responsibility based on additional grounds that are deemed to contribute to the foreseeability, such as existing interpretive case-law or a professional legal subject. In *Grigoriades,*[535] for example, the Court found the domestic definition of insulting the military to be in accordance with the Convention's foreseeability requirement, although it recognized that the definition was couched in very broad terms.[536] In the Court's view, it ought to have been clear to the applicant that he risked incurring a criminal sanction for his acts on the basis of the ordinary meaning of the word 'insult'.[537] The Court thereby essentially invoked the apparently obvious meaning of the domestic offense as the reason why a *very* broad legal definition satisfied the foreseeability requirement.[538]

Other judgments provide additional examples of an undemanding approach to the clarity of the wording of an offense. In *Flinkkilä,*[539] a case described above, the Court held the foreseeability requirement was satisfied by considerations in the preparatory works of the statutory offense which indicated criminal responsibility for the applicants' conduct.[540] In light of the preparatory works of the offense of publicly disseminating information depicting another's private life,[541] the applicants, who were professional journalists, should have either

534 In one case the Court even considered the predictability of criminal responsibility as a matter of 'common sense' to be an additional reason for conformity with the foreseeability requirement of Article 7(1) ECHR, see *Kuolelis, Bartoševičius and Burokevičius v. Lithuania*, CE:ECHR:2008:0219JUD007435701, para 121.

535 *Grigoriades v. Greece*, CE:ECHR:1997:1125JUD002434894.

536 See para 37–38.

537 See para 38. A relevant aspect for this reasoning seems to have been the fact that the word 'insult' is akin to the expression 'offend' that was contained in other statutory offenses which had, in fact, been interpreted by domestic courts at the time of the applicant's acts, see also para 34–35. The ECtHR had not, however, explicitly used this aspect as a part of its legal reasoning. The conclusion must therefore be that the Court found the ordinary meaning of legal term to provide a sufficient amount of foreseeability of criminal responsibility, even in the absence of a clear statutory definition or interpretive case-law.

538 This approach was more recently confirmed in *Ashlarba v. Georgia*, CE:ECHR:2014:0715JUD004555408. In this case the Court considered relevant for the foreseeability of criminal responsibility that the legal concepts in the wording of the offense 'were matters of common knowledge and widely understood', see para 37, 40.

539 *Flinkkilä and Others v. Finland*, CE:ECHR:2010:0406JUD002557604. Cf the identical approaches in the related cases in *Tuomela and Others v. Finland*, CE:ECHR:2010:0406JUD002571104; *Jokitaipale and Others v. Finland*, CE:ECHR:2010:0406JUD004334905, and the later, but substantively identical, *Reinboth and Others v. Finland*, CE:ECHR:2011:0125JUD003086508.

540 See para 67 and 25. Cf Van Kempen and Fedorova 2015, p. 20.

541 See para 24.

sought advice about the exact scope of the penal provision or refrained from publishing the information.[542] Since the ECtHR found the applicants were under the obligation to either seek advice or refrain from publishing, it apparently considered it sufficiently foreseeable for the applicants that their publication would give rise to criminal responsibility.[543]

In addition to the preparatory works of an offense, the Court has found that other legislative acts contribute to the foreseeability of criminal responsibility as well. In *Kasymakhunov* the ECtHR noted that the offense for which the applicant was convicted, ie incitement to participate in the activities of a terrorist organization, did not define what is a terrorist organization.[544] At the same time, however, it underlined that the statutory provisions preceding the applicable offense and another piece of legislation contained such a definition.[545] Therefore, when read in conjunction with other provisions and legislation, the applicable offense had, in the Court's view, defined the prohibited conduct with sufficient foreseeability.[546] It follows that the foreseeability requirement can also be satisfied if the definition of the applicable offense is sufficiently clear after consulting the offense in conjunction with other provisions and legislative acts.[547] In such a case, the Court will nevertheless have to review the clarity of the wording of the provisions and any acts to which the applicable offense refers. If the other pieces of legislation are themselves insufficiently clearly worded, they cannot contribute to the foreseeability of the applicable offense.[548] In those circumstances the ECtHR will have no choice but to find a violation of the foreseeability requirement under Article 7 ECHR.[549]

The foreseeability requirement II: (interpretive) case-law and the applicant's professional capacity

In the Court's view, criminal responsibility can also be sufficiently foreseeable for reasons other than statutory clarity. As *Kokkinakis* indicated, the existence of accessible case-law interpreting the wording of the offense can mean a domestic definition satisfies the foreseeability requirement even in the absence of a clear statutory definition.[550] That interpretive case-law provides a ground

---

542 Cf *Cantoni v. France*, CE:ECHR:1996:1115JUD001786291, para 35.
543 See para 67–68 and 94.
544 See *Kasymakhunov and Saybatalov v. Russia*, CE:ECHR:2013:0314JUD002626105, para 82.
545 See para 82.
546 See para 82.
547 Cf para 83. For a similar use of other legislation in order to satisfy the requirements of clear definition of an offense, see *Ashlarba v. Georgia*, CE:ECHR:2014:0715JUD004555408, paras 36, 39–40.
548 See *Vyerentsov v. Ukraine*, CE:ECHR:2013:0411JUD002037211, paras 54–55, 67. See further Van Kempen and Fedorova 2015, p. 20.
549 See *Vyerentsov v. Ukraine*, para 67.
550 Cf Sudre 2001, p. 346.

for compatibility with the foreseeability requirement is confirmed by *Cantoni*.[551] This judgment deserves some further attention because it also includes elaborate considerations about the acceptability of vague terms in the statutory wording of offenses. Supermarket owner Cantoni was convicted for selling medicinal products, which constituted a criminal offense under French law if carried out by non-pharmacists.[552] Cantoni complained that the clarity of the offense's definition was impaired by uncertainties about the meaning of the term 'medicinal product'.[553]

The Court reiterated, first, that the use of general characterizations in statutory rules is a standard technique of regulation and that this may, inevitably, lead to the inclusion of statutory terms that are more or less vague.[554] When a general definition like 'medicinal product' is used, there will often be grey areas at the fringes of the definition.[555] The fact that doubts arise about the applicability of the definition in borderline cases will not, in itself, make the definition incompatible with Article 7.[556] As long as the definition is sufficiently clear in the majority of cases, it will be in accordance with Article 7's requirement of a clear legal definition.

The Court found it inconclusive that case-law from lower courts had previously ruled differently on the issue of whether the sale of the applicant's products constituted the prohibited sale of medicinal products.[557] This was because the questions before the lower courts were principally questions of fact and the divergent decisions could therefore have resulted from differences in factual circumstances. Conversely, on questions of law, the French Court of Cassation had consistently classified as medicinal products goods that were similar to the ones the applicant sold.[558] "Thus, well before the events in the present case, the Court of Cassation had adopted a clear position on this matter, which with the passing of time became even more firmly established."[559]

In view of the consistent case-law of the Court of Cassation, the applicant should have appreciated that, at the time he sold his products, he ran the real risk of prosecution for the unlawful sale of medicinal products.[560] This was more the case since the applicant was a professional who could be expected to take special care in assessing the risks his activity entails.[561] As a result of both the case-law of the Court of Cassation and the fact that the applicant carried out the

551 *Cantoni v. France*, CE:ECHR:1996:1115JUD001786291.
552 See para 11.
553 See para 11, 22 and 26.
554 See para 31.
555 See para 32. Cf *Soros v. France*, CE:ECHR:2011:1006JUD005042506, para 54.
556 See para 32.
557 See para 34.
558 See para 34.
559 Para 34. This shows that rulings of higher courts are more important with regard to foreseeability of judicial interpretations.
560 See para 35.
561 See para 35. Cf *Vasiliauskas*, para 157.

prohibited conduct as a professional, the legal definition of the offense satisfied the requirement of foreseeability. Accordingly, there was no breach of Article 7.[562]

Cantoni underlined how the existence of interpretive case-law at the time of the material conduct can make a relatively vaguely worded statutory definition of an offense satisfy the foreseeability requirement.[563] This obviously places demands on the clarity of the domestic courts' case-law and it is reasonable to assume that vaguer statutory definitions place higher demands on the domestic case-law. With regard to foreseeability under the *lex certa* principle, statutory definitions and interpretive case-law are communicating vessels. The judgment in *Liivik*[564] illustrates this observation aptly.

The applicant in *Liivik* was convicted of misuse of an official position. In order to determine whether the legal definition was in conformity with Article 7, the Court considered both the wording of the penal provision and the interpretive case-law that existed at the time of the applicant's acts.[565] With regard to the provision's wording, the ECtHR observed that it established the 'causing of significant damage' as a necessary element of the offense.[566] That element was not clarified by the text of the provision or accompanying documents. It was nevertheless interpreted by the Estonian Supreme Court. That court had attached importance to the creation of danger as damage under the applicable provision, but it had not developed criteria for assessing such a risk.[567] The ECtHR found that the case-law interpreting the relevant offense had used such broad notions and vague criteria that the legal definition of the offense was of insufficient quality in terms of its clarity and the foreseeability of its effects.[568] As a result, the domestic definition lacked foreseeability due to the insufficient clarity of the domestic case-law that interpreted the indeterminate wording of the statutory definition.[569]

In addition to the emphasis on clear interpretive case-law, the judgment in *Cantoni* made clear that an individual's professional capacity contributes to the foreseeability of criminal responsibility. For this reason, it potentially lowers the level of clarity required of the domestic definition.[570] Professionals are expected

---

562 See para 36.

563 For a comparable conclusion in the context of other Convention rights than Article 7's legality principle, see Viljanen 2003, p. 202.

564 *Liivik v. Estonia*, CE:ECHR:2009:0625JUD001215705.

565 For a similar approach, see *Soros v. France*, CE:ECHR:2011:1006JUD005042506, para 54.

566 See para 99.

567 See para 99.

568 See para 100–101. The emphasis on previously established legal criteria for the exercise of invasive government powers is also perceivable in judgments about potential violations of other Convention rights. A good example is the case about a broad power stop-and-search police power which gave rise to a clear risk of arbitrary interferences with Article 8 ECHR, see *Gillan and Quinton v. The United Kingdom*, CE:ECHR:2010:0112JUD000415805, para 85.

569 Another clear example of insufficient clarity in both the statutory provisions and the interpretive case-law can be found in *Sud Fondi SRL and Others v. Italy*, CE:ECHR:2009:0120 JUD007590901, paras 111–114.

570 See for similar approaches, eg, *Kuolelis, Bartoševičius and Burokevičius v. Lithuania*, CE: ECHR:2008:0219JUD007435701, para 120; *Flinkkilä and Others v. Finland*, CE:ECHR:

to take special care in assessing the risk that their activity entails.[571] Moreover, they are sometimes required to abide by non-binding professional guidelines before they can claim that criminal responsibility was unforeseeable for them.[572] As a result, the ECtHR identifies two potential grounds for satisfying the foreseeability requirement: interpretive case-law on the one hand, and an individual's professional capacity on the other.[573]

Case-law is not just relevant *in addition to* statutory provisions. Judicial definitions of offenses can satisfy the foreseeability requirement even in the absence of statutory definitions. This is clearly apparent from the judgment in *Contrada*.[574] The Court accepts the foreseeability of offenses on the condition that consistent case-law defined the criminalized conduct in a non-contradictory manner before the applicant acted.[575] This means that the sole judicial definition of an offense can sufficiently enable an applicant to foresee criminal responsibility and regulate his conduct accordingly. This is, moreover, in line with the above-mentioned *Dallas* judgment, where the Court accepted the foreseeability of the judicially established common law offense of contempt of court.[576]

Although case-law can be sufficient for foreseeability even in the complete absence of statutory definitions, the judicial interpretations and/or definitions need to have a certain quality. As mentioned above, the consistency of case-law has been deemed relevant, both for interpretive case-law as well as for case-law that exclusively constitutes the definition of an offense. The consistency requirement in relation to interpretive case-law was recently emphasized in *Žaja*.[577]

In *Žaja*, the applicant was fined for having imported goods without paying customs duties.[578] The crucial question for the applicant's liability was whether he was a resident of Croatia or the Czech Republic.[579] The term 'person resident' in Croatian law was based on the Istanbul Convention. That term was nevertheless

---

2010:0406JUD002557604, para 67; *Soros v. France*, CE:ECHR:2011:1006JUD005042506, para 59. For an early case about professional parties and foreseeability in the context of the prescribed by law requirement, see *Groppera Radio AG and Others v. Switzerland*, CE:ECHR:1990:0328JUD001089084, para 68.

571 See *Cantoni*, para 35; *Khodorkovskiy and Lebedev v. Russia*, CE:ECHR:2013:0725JUD001108206, para 781; *Varvara v. Italy*, CE:ECHR:2013:1029JUD001747509, para 56. The Court also stresses the assumption of foreseeability for professionals outside the scope of Article 7 ECHR, see, eg, *Amihalachioaie v. Moldova*, CE:ECHR:2004:0420JUD006011500, para 33.

572 See *Flinkkilä and Others v. Finland*, CE:ECHR:2010:0406JUD002557604, para 67.

573 For a similar approach, see *Soros v. France*, CE:ECHR:2011:1006JUD005042506, paras 57–62.

574 *Contrada v. Italy (No. 3)*, CE:ECHR:2015:0414JUD006665513.

575 See *Contrada*, para 66–70, 74–75. For a similar determination within the context of the prescribed by law requirement under Article 10 ECHR, see *Sunday Times v. The United Kingdom*, CE:ECHR:1979:0426JUD000653874, para 47, 50, 52.

576 See *Dallas v. The United Kingdom*, CE:ECHR:2016:0211JUD003839512, paras 72–78.

577 *Žaja v. Croatia*, CE:ECHR:2016:1004JUD003746209.

578 See para 94.

579 See paras 95–96.

inconsistently translated in the Croatian version of that document.[580] This inconsistency gave rise to legal uncertainty and ambiguity as to who may benefit from an exemption from the prohibition on importation of goods without paying custom duties.[581] In light of this uncertainty, the ECtHR examined the interpretation of the international convention by the domestic authorities.

The Strasbourg Court determined that the meaning of the term was not consistently established by domestic case-law at the time when the applicant imported his goods. For that reason, the domestic case-law could not be used to rectify the uncertainty arising from the legislative texts. In the words of the ECtHR:

> "In this connection the Court finds it evident that an interpretation capable of clarifying the meaning of an otherwise insufficiently clear provision which serves as the legal basis for an offence must, in order to comply with the requirements of Article 7, result from a practice (case-law) of the domestic authorities which is consistent. That is so because an inconsistent case-law lacks the required precision to avoid all risk of arbitrariness and enable individuals to foresee the consequences of their actions (...)".[582]

Although the requirement of consistent case-law was established in the context of complaints under Article 1 of Protocol No. 1 to the ECHR, it also applies under Article 7 ECHR.[583] According to the Court,

> "No person should be forced to speculate, at peril of conviction, whether his or her conduct is prohibited or not, or to be exposed to unduly broad discretion of the authorities, in particular if it was possible, either by drafting legislation in more precise terms or through judicial interpretation, to specify the relevant provision in a way that would dispel uncertainty".[584]

Since the Croatian translation of the relevant international convention gave rise to uncertainty, and that provision was not consistently interpreted by the domestic authorities, the offense was not defined with sufficient foreseeability. The combination of an ambiguous legal text and inconsistent case-law violated Article 7 ECHR as it left too much room for arbitrary prosecution and punishment.[585]

International law as the legal source defining crimes

As subsection 3.2.1 indicates, Article 7(1) ECHR identifies international law as an additional source defining crimes and penalties. This implies that a

580 See para 97.
581 See para 97.
582 Para 103.
583 See paras 104–105. About this requirement outside the context of Article 7 ECHR, see Gamper 2016, p. 88–91.
584 Para 41.
585 See para 106.

criminal conviction can comply with the Convention even in cases where the national legal definition, or its application or interpretation, would violate the Convention's legality principle. In other words, as long as international law defines an offense in accordance with the requirements of accessibility and foreseeability, that definition forms an acceptable legal basis for a criminal conviction in accordance with Article 7(1) ECHR.[586] As with national definitions of crimes, the application and interpretation of crimes defined by international law will obviously need to conform with the principles of *lex stricta* and *lex praevia* (see further subsections 3.6.3 and 3.6.4).

The Court's case-law contains a few important examples of international law as the source of offenses. These cases are the judgments about the East-German border-policing regime, ie the related judgments in *Streletz*[587] and *K.-H.W.*,[588] and the later cases of *Korbely*,[589] *Kononov*[590] and *Vasiliauskas*.[591] All these Grand Chamber judgments focused on the question whether a sufficient legal basis existed at the time of the applicants' acts to uphold a conviction that was only imposed many years after the applicants' conduct.[592]

In *Streletz* and *K.-H.W.*, the ECtHR examined both the domestic legal definitions and the definitions contained in international law.[593] This cumulative examination is quite remarkable, because the Court concluded that the domestic legal definitions already satisfied the Convention's standards of accessibility and foreseeability. Since domestic law provided a sufficient legal definition of the applicants' crimes at the time of their acts, the examination of international law seems superfluous.[594] The ECtHR nevertheless felt obliged to examine the case from the standpoint of the principles of international law because the domestic courts had also referred to international law to substantiate their convictions.[595]

---

586 See *Vasiliauskas v. Lithuania*, CE:ECHR:2015:1020JUD003534305, para 166. Cf Dhont and Cromheecke 2004, p. 680; Harris, O'Boyle, Bates and Buckley 2014, p. 498; Schabas 2015, p. 343.

587 *Streletz, Kessler and Krenz v. Germany*, CE:ECHR:2001:0322JUD003404496. See further, eg, Boot 2002, p. 161–170.

588 *K.-H. W. v. Germany*, CE:ECHR:2001:0322JUD003720197. See further, eg, Boot 2002, p. 161–170.

589 *Korbely v. Hungary*, CE:ECHR:2008:0919JUD000917402, para 74.

590 *Kononov v. Latvia*, CE:ECHR:2010:0517JUD003637604.

591 *Vasiliauskas v. Lithuania*, CE:ECHR:2015:1020JUD003534305.

592 See *Streletz*, para 51; *K.-H. W.*, para 46; *Korbely*, para 73; *Kononov*, para 199; *Vasiliauskas*, paras 165–166.

593 Cf *Streletz*, para 55–89 with para 90–106; *K.-H. W.*, para 48–91 with para 92–106.

594 The Court itself seems to imply this by underlining that it needs to determine whether domestic law *or* international law defined the applicants' crimes with sufficient accessibility and foreseeability, see *Streletz*, para 51. See also the partly dissenting opinion of judge Pellonpää in *K.-H. W.* and, rather clearly on this view, *Kuolelis, Bartoševičius and Burokevičius v. Lithuania*, para 122.

595 See *Streletz*, para 90; *K.-H. W.*, para 92. Cf *Jorgic v. Germany*, CE:ECHR:2007:0712JUD 007461301, paras 106, 114.

In the more recent cases of *Korbely*, *Kononov*, and *Vasiliauskas* the Court focused its examination on the definition of the crimes in international law. Contrary to *Streletz* and *K.-H.W.*, these cases concerned whether international law defined the applicants' acts in accordance with the requirements of accessibility and foreseeability. In *Korbely*, the Court was able to focus on international law because the Hungarian courts had relied on Article 3 of the Geneva Convention to qualify the multiple homicide committed by the applicant as a crime against humanity.[596] For this reason, the ECtHR found the applicant's conviction to be exclusively based on international law.[597] The focus on international law was possible in *Kononov* because the Latvian criminal code had introduced criminal responsibility for war crimes by referring to the definitions contained in other 'relevant legal conventions'.[598] The Court consequently examined whether, at the time of the applicant's acts in 1944, international law defined criminal responsibility for these acts with sufficient accessibility and foreseeability.[599] In *Vasiliauskas* the ECtHR examined whether genocide was sufficiently defined as a crime under international law at the time of the applicant's acts in 1953, although his conviction was based on the subsequently introduced Lithuanian criminal code which criminalized genocide.[600]

Although the approaches differed, the aforementioned cases clearly examined whether international law defined the applicants' acts as crimes with sufficient accessibility and foreseeability. To be more precise: all judgments identified the criteria of accessibility and foreseeability.[601] However, as with examinations of the definitions of crimes in national law, the Court focused on the foreseeability requirement.[602] In *Streletz* and *K.-H.W.*, the Court concluded that the former German Democratic Republic's (hereinafter also: 'GDR') border-policing regime clearly disregarded the right to life and the right to free movement.[603] At the time of the East-German border-policing regime, several international human rights documents had already codified those rights.[604] Therefore, criminal responsibility for violations of the right to life could either be based on those international instruments directly or in connection with the GDR's provision

596 See para 38, 74. Cf *Streletz*, para 90; *K.-H. W.*, para 92 in which the ECtHR finds it necessary to review international law because the domestic courts had used international law as an argument to determine criminal responsibility.
597 See paras 74, 76.
598 See paras 196, 48.
599 See para 199.
600 See paras 165–166.
601 See *Streletz*, para 91; *K.-H. W.*, para 93; *Korbely*, para 73; *Kononov*, para 235, 244; *Vasiliauskas*, paras 167, 169.
602 See *Streletz*, para 103; *K.-H. W.*, para 104; *Korbely*, para 76–95; *Kononov*, para 235–239, 243; *Vasiliauskas*, paras 167–186.
603 See *Streletz*, para 102; *K.-H. W.*, para 102.
604 See *Streletz*, para 92–101; *K.-H. W.*, para 94–101.

that criminalized a violation of international obligations.[605] According to the Court, the international human rights documents, certainly when read together with the GDR's criminal code, defined criminal responsibility for violations of the right to life with sufficient accessibility and foreseeability.[606] How the codification of human rights documents affirming the right to life specifically contributed to either the accessibility or foreseeability of (international) criminal responsibility was not, however, substantiated.[607]

Contrary to the judgments on the East-German border-policing regime, the judgment in *Korbely* made an explicit distinction between the requirements of accessibility and foreseeability.[608] *Korbely* concerned a military officer who was convicted of a multiple homicide committed in 1956 which was deemed to constitute a crime against humanity by virtue of the Geneva Convention. The Court deemed the Geneva Convention accessible to the applicant because it was proclaimed by a Hungarian Law-Decree in 1954, the text of the Convention was published in a brochure in 1955, and a synopsis of the Convention was published in the Military Gazette in 1956.[609]

In order to subsequently determine whether it was foreseeable that the act the applicant was convicted for would be qualified as a crime against humanity, the Court first examined the concept of 'crime against humanity' at the time of the applicant's conduct.[610] The ECtHR found that the domestic courts had not considered whether the applicant's acts satisfied all the legal elements necessary to determine whether the crime of murder constituted a crime against humanity.[611] "[I]t is thus open to question whether the constituent elements of a crime against humanity were satisfied in the present case."[612] In addition, the Court was unconvinced by the domestic courts' conclusion that the murder victim fell within one of the categories of non-combatants protected by Article 3 of the Geneva Convention.[613] In light of the doubts about the applicability of Article 3 of the Geneva Convention, it had not been shown that

605 See *Streletz*, para 103–104; *K.-H. W.*, para 103–104. When domestic provisions are necessary to establish individual criminal responsibility for violations of international obligations, the criminal conduct will be defined by national law and not international law, see concurring opinion of judge Loucaides in *Streletz*.

606 See *Streletz*, para 105; *K.-H. W.*, para 105.

607 See further para 3 of the partly dissenting opinion of judge Cabral Barreto and the partly dissenting opinion of judge Pellonpää. Moreover, the implicit conclusion that international human rights documents provide a sufficient legal basis for criminal responsibility for violations of these rights seems to stretch the meaning of 'international law' beyond the field of international *criminal* law, see Kadelbach 2006, p. 740; Grabenwarter 2014, p. 177. Cf Harris, O'Boyle, Bates and Buckley 2014, p. 498–499.

608 See para 74–96.

609 See para 75.

610 See para 76, 78.

611 See para 84–85.

612 Para 85.

613 See para 94.

it was foreseeable that the applicant's acts constituted a crime against humanity under international law.[614] Accordingly, Article 7(1) ECHR was violated.

Kononov provides an additional example of international law defining a crime. In this case the applicant was convicted for committing war crimes in 1944. His conviction was based on a provision of the Latvian criminal code that defined war crimes by referring to the definitions contained in other 'relevant legal conventions'.[615] Since the domestic provisions made an explicit reference to other legal documents for the precise definition of the criminalized acts, the Court found the applicant's conviction to be based on international rather than domestic law.[616] The Court thus examined whether, at the time of the applicant's acts in 1944, international law defined criminal responsibility for these acts with sufficient accessibility and foreseeability.[617] Contrary to the approach in *Korbely*, and more in accordance with the approach in *Streletz* and *K.-H.W*, the Court stated that the two quality of law requirements needed to be considered together.[618] This statement was apparently made to justify the focus on the review of the foreseeability requirement.[619]

The Strasbourg Court first determined that, in 1944, the prevailing definition of a war crime was that of an offense contrary to the laws and customs of war and that international law had, at that time, defined an extensive range of acts constituting those crimes.[620] Already in 1944 war crimes defined by international law could give rise to individual criminal responsibility. Accordingly, domestic courts and, in exceptional cases, international tribunals could convict individuals on the basis of war crimes as defined by international law.[621] The acts for which Kononov was convicted were included in the category of war crimes that could give rise to criminal responsibility under international law in 1944.[622]

Since the Court found that Kononov's acts gave rise to individual criminal responsibility on the basis of international law in 1944, it had to determine whether international law defined criminal responsibility in accordance with the requirements of accessibility and foreseeability.[623] The Court deemed it inconclusive that the applicable criminal code failed to refer to international law and customs of war or that the international rules and customs of war were not formally published in Latvia.[624] According to the ECtHR, the state of international law had developed the concepts of war crimes in such a clear way

614 See para 95.
615 See para 196, 48.
616 See para 196. For an opposite conclusion in comparable circumstances, see *Jorgic v. Germany*, CE:ECHR:2007:0712JUD007461301, para 106 and further about that judgment subsection 3.6.3.
617 See para 199.
618 See para 235.
619 See para 235–239, 243.
620 See para 205, 213.
621 See para 208.
622 See para 216–222, 227.
623 See para 235.
624 See para 237.

that it constituted a sufficient legal basis for individual criminal responsibility. Because the laws and customs of wars addressed the armed forces, the applicant, who was a commanding military officer, should have assessed the legal risks of his behavior. In the Court's view:

> "(...) even the most cursory reflection by the applicant would have indicated that, at the very least, the impugned acts risked being counter to the laws and customs of war as understood at that time and, notably, risked constituting war crimes for which, as commander, he could be held individually and criminally accountable."[625]

In light of the applicant's professional capacity it was reasonable to find that he could have foreseen in 1944 that his acts could be qualified as war crimes.[626] In conclusion, the Court found the applicant's acts were defined with sufficient accessibility and foreseeability by the laws and customs of war.[627]

Vasiliauskas provides the most recent example of the Court's approach to international law as a source of criminal prohibitions. As in *Korbely*, the Court separated the requirements of accessibility and foreseeability. The ECtHR first deemed the international law instruments prohibiting genocide to have been sufficiently accessible to the applicant in 1953. This is mainly because the Soviet Union signed the Genocide Convention in 1949 and that document entered into force in 1951.[628] In light of its accessibility, the Strasbourg Court subsequently focused on the foreseeability of the criminalization of genocide of political groups under international law. In the Court's view, neither the Genocide Convention, nor customary international law criminalized the genocide of political groups.[629] As a result, the Lithuanian courts violated Article 7 ECHR by having convicted the applicant for genocide on the basis of the domestic offense that was enacted after the alleged acts.[630] The retroactive application of *domestic* law to the accused's detriment was contrary to the Convention, because *international* law had not foreseeably defined the applicant's acts as genocide in 1953.[631]

Recapitulation

The Court's review of the definitions of crimes in light of the *lex certa* principle has not set very strict standards. The first criterion for review, the accessibility requirement, will not generally be hard to satisfy. This requirement merely calls for *some* official publication of the statutory provisions and/or the applicable

---

625 Para 238.
626 See para 239.
627 See para 244.
628 See paras 167–168.
629 See paras 170–175.
630 See para 191.
631 See para 181. On the prohibition of the retroactive application of offenses, see subsection 3.6.4.

case-law defining offenses at the time of the material conduct.[632] What is more, the Court will not generally conduct an in-depth review of accessibility in the absence of clear complaints about inaccessibility. Therefore, the *lex certa* principle's protective function is provided mostly by the Court's review of domestic offenses in light of the foreseeability requirement.[633]

In the ECtHR's view, criminal responsibility can be sufficiently foreseeable for multiple reasons. The first, and most obvious, being the wording of a statutory provision. Clear wording of offenses and penalties is thus a first way to comply with the foreseeability requirement.[634] The level of clarity definitions have to meet, however, is not very high. This is partly because the Court has sometimes failed to conduct an intensive review of the statutory and judicial wording of offenses.[635] In addition, the Court explicitly accepts that the statutory wording of offenses and penalties may include terms that are more or less vague.[636] The fact that doubts will arise about the applicability of the definition in borderline cases will not, in itself, make the definition incompatible with Article 7.[637] As a consequence, the wording of domestic definitions of crimes will not easily violate Article 7's *lex certa* principle.

A violation of *lex certa* is even harder to establish as a result of the ECtHR's contextual approach to the clarity of statutory definitions. In order to determine if a definition meets the foreseeability requirement, the Court looks at more than just the text of the offenses and penalties. It also considers the field the text is designed to cover and the number and status of those to whom it is addressed.[638] This means that the context of a vaguely worded offense can nevertheless make criminal responsibility foreseeable. Reasons for the Court to find relatively vaguely worded offenses sufficiently foreseeable include: the fact that an individual acted in a professional capacity,[639] that the scope of an element of an offense was unambiguous in light of its ordinary meaning,[640] that considerations in the preparatory works of a provision indicated criminal liability,[641] the fact that the wording was clear when read together with other legislative provisions,[642] and, apparently as a secondary factor, common sense.[643]

---

632 See, eg, *Kokkinakis*, para 40; *Custers*, para 82–83; *Korbely*, para 75. For a different interpretation of the accessibility requirement, see Murphy 2010, p. 199.

633 See, eg, *Grigoriades*, para 34, 37–38; *Cantoni*, para 29; *Flinkkilä*, para 64; *Kasymakhunov and Saybatalov v. Russia*, para 80; *Ashlarba v. Georgia*, para 35; *Contrada*, para 74–75.

634 See, eg, *Custers*, para 81; *Flinkkilä*, para 67. Cf *Soros v. France*, para 57–58.

635 See, eg, *Kokkinakis*.

636 *Cantoni*, para 31.

637 See *Cantoni*, para 32.

638 *Cantoni*, para 35.

639 See *Cantoni*, para 35–36; *Kuolelis, Bartoševičius and Burokevičius v. Lithuania*, para 120; *Flinkkilä*, para 67; *Soros v. France*, para 59. Cf Schabas 2015, p. 341.

640 See *Grigoriades*, para 38.

641 See *Flinkkilä*, para 67, 25.

642 See *Kasymakhunov and Saybatalov v. Russia*, para 82–83; *Ashlarba v. Georgia*, para 36, 39–40.

643 *Kuolelis, Bartoševičius and Burokevičius v. Lithuania*, para 121.

Another important factor for the foreseeability of criminal liability is interpretive case-law. The Court accepts that, however clearly drafted a provision of criminal law may be, it will always require judicial interpretation.[644] One reason for this is the fact that the general wording of legal rules will always raise doubtful points.[645] The role of adjudication vested in the courts is precisely to dissipate any remaining interpretational doubts.[646] Therefore, the ECtHR will accept relatively vague statutory definitions of offenses as long as there is, at the time of the material conduct, consistent interpretive case-law that enables the applicant to regulate his conduct.[647] The quality of the interpretive case-law is not generally scrutinized. The existence of consistent case-law appears to be sufficient for conformity with *lex certa*.

In addition to the above factors that add to the foreseeability of – even rather vague – statutory offenses, criminal offenses can be sufficiently foreseeable on the sole basis of case-law. The Court does not necessarily require a statutory definition for compliance with the *lex certa* principle of Article 7 ECHR. If consistent case-law has defined the conduct giving rise to criminal responsibility in a non-contradictory manner before the applicant's acts, that definition can meet the foreseeability requirement as well.[648] With regard to definitions of criminal responsibility in international law, the Court does not require a clear statutory definition either. In that event, the ECtHR merely requires that the state of international law had reached a certain stage of development wherein individual criminal responsibility had become foreseeable.[649]

In conclusion, criminal liability and the applicable penalties can be sufficiently foreseeable for three reasons: first, because statutory provisions (when read within their context) provide clarity, secondly, because statutory provisions provide clarity when read together with interpretive case-law, or, thirdly, in the absence of domestic statutory provisions, when either consistent case-law or international law enables an individual to know to which offenses his conduct gives rise. With regard to all three reasons it is, moreover, important to note that the perspective from which the Court's examines the foreseeability of crimes is that of the individual who *took legal advice*.[650] The Court will not look at foreseeability from the perspective of a layperson, but from the perspective of a layperson that benefited from legal advice. The Court's reference to the objective ability to know criminal responsibility after taking legal advice certainly diminishes the strictness of the foreseeability requirement. It consequently moderates the demands that are put on the legal definition of offenses.

---

644 Cf *Camilleri v. Malta*, CE:ECHR:2013:0122JUD004293110, para 37.

645 See *Kononov*, para 185; *Del Río Prada*, para 92.

646 See *Del Río Prada*, para 93.

647 *Kokkinakis*, para 40; *Cantoni*, para 35; *Žaja*, para 103. See, critically, judge Martens in his partly dissenting opinion in *Kokkinakis*, para 5.

648 See *Contrada*, para 66–70, 74–75; *Dallas*, paras 72–78.

649 See, eg, *Kononov*, paras 238–239, 244.

650 *Cantoni*, para 35.

3.6.3 THE PROHIBITION ON THE OVERLY EXTENSIVE INTERPRETATION OF AN OFFENSE (*LEX STRICTA*)

Relationship with the lex certa principle and criteria for review

Since the Court understandably allows room for the judicial interpretation of offenses, limits to interpretation are necessary for the protection of the legality principle's object and purpose. If domestic courts were allowed to interpret and apply previously established offenses in any way they pleased, arbitrary prosecution, conviction and punishment could certainly be the result.[651] Limits to judicial interpretation are therefore provided by the prohibition on the overly extensive interpretation of an offense. Since the *lex stricta* principle provides protection from the interpretation of offenses and their immediate application, the ECtHR will only consider whether an offense meets this standard when the definition of the offense itself complies with the *lex certa* principle.[652] The review of domestic law in light of the *lex certa* principle therefore precedes the review of the *lex stricta* principle.[653] In this sense, the *lex stricta* principle complements the *lex certa* principle and provides *supplementary* protection.

In addition to a differing order of review against the principles of *lex certa* and *lex stricta*, the principles' objects of review differ as well. Instead of a review of the offense's definition, *lex stricta* merely calls for the evaluation of the interpretation and application of criminal law by domestic courts. As is mentioned in section 3.5, the nature of the Convention system means that domestic interpretations and applications of law are generally subject to more limited review. That the ECHR's *lex stricta* principle requires the evaluation of interpretations and applications of domestic law could, for that reason, be a relevant characteristic for the practical protection provided by the Court.

A final significant distinction between the principles of *lex certa* and *lex stricta* lies in the criteria the Court uses for assessing the compatibility of domestic law with these principles. As described, the Court uses the Convention's general qualitative requirements of accessibility and foreseeability to assess the clarity of the definition of the offense. In order to assess compliance with the *lex stricta* principle, however, the Court tests judicial interpretations in light of the requirements of 'essence of the offense' (hereinafter also: 'the essence

651 Cf *Dragotoniu and Militaru-Pidhorni v. Romania*, CE:ECHR:2007:0524JUD007719301, para 43.

652 See, eg, *Custers, Deveaux and Turk v. Denmark*, CE:ECHR:2007:0503JUD001184303, paras 89–90.

653 Although it is sometimes hard to separate the two types of review. For cases that reviewed domestic law and its interpretation by the domestic courts against the *lex certa* criteria, see *Streletz, Kessler and Krenz v. Germany*, CE:ECHR:2001:0322JUD003404496, paras 85, 89; *K.-H. W. v. Germany*, CE:ECHR:2001:0322JUD003720197, paras 88, 91; *Vasiliauskas v. Lithuania*, CE:ECHR:2015:1020JUD003534305, paras 181–186. See further subsection 3.6.2.

of the offense requirement') and 'reasonable foreseeability' (hereinafter also: 'the reasonable foreseeability requirement').[654]

The essence of the offense requirement

The requirement that judicial interpretations remain consistent with the essence of the offense, prevents judicial interpretation from establishing a new offense. This was already apparent from the early case of *M.C. v. Germany*, where the EComHR underlined that domestic courts are only allowed to adapt existing constituent elements of an offense to new circumstances if the new interpretation can reasonably be brought under the original concept of the offense.[655] Domestic courts cannot, therefore, change the elements of an offense through case-law to the detriment of the accused. The essence of the offense requirement thus provides a firm, yet abstract, limit to judicial interpretation.[656]

The exact limits to judicial interpretation are quite hard to extract from the Court's case-law. This is mainly because the ECtHR has not always separated its review of domestic interpretations in light of the essence of the offense requirement from that of the reasonable foreseeability requirement.[657] In several cases the Court merely ruled on the compatibility with the *lex stricta* principle on the basis of the *joint* requirements of essence of the offense and reasonable foreseeability.[658]

There are, nevertheless, cases that shed light on the individual content of the essence of the offense requirement. An example is *Jorgic*.[659] This judgment concerned an applicant who had been convicted in Germany for acts of genocide committed in Bosnia.[660] These acts were punishable under German law even in the absence of a relation to Germany.[661] The German criminal code had adopted

654 See, eg, *C.R. v. The United Kingdom*, CE:ECHR:1995:1122JUD002019092, para 34, 41; *S.W. v. The United Kingdom*, CE:ECHR:1995:1122JUD002016692, para 36, 43; *Dragotoniu and Militaru-Pidhorni v. Romania*, CE:ECHR:2007:0524JUD007719301, paras 37–38; *Radio France and Others v. France*, CE:ECHR:2004:0330JUD005398400, para 20; *Moiseyev v. Russia*, CE:ECHR:2008:1009JUD006293600, paras 240–241; *Jorgic v. Germany*, CE:ECHR:2007:0712 JUD007461301, paras 103, 114; *Huhtamäki v. Finland*, CE:ECHR:2012:0306JUD005446809, para 51; *Martirosyan v. Armenia*, CE:ECHR:2013:0205JUD002334106, para 61.

655 See EComHR, G. *v. Germany* (dec.), CE:ECHR:1989:0306DEC001307987, para 1.

656 Cf De Hullu 2015, p. 101.

657 See, eg, *Savvas Kyriakides v. Cyprus* (dec.), CE:ECHR:2001:1211DEC005305999. In this case the Court first reviewed the case at hand in light of reasonable foreseeability. In order to subsequently assess whether the domestic courts changed the essence of the offense the ECtHR again used the criterion of foreseeability.

658 See, eg, *C.R. v. The United Kingdom*, CE:ECHR:1995:1122JUD002019092, para 41; *S.W. v. The United Kingdom*, CE:ECHR:1995:1122JUD002016692, para 43; *Radio France and Others v. France*, CE:ECHR:2004:0330JUD005398400, para 20; *Khodorkovskiy and Lebedev v. Russia*, CE: ECHR:2013:0725JUD001108206, para 821. In *Dragotoniu* the Court even omitted to explicitly review the judicial interpretation against the essence of the offense requirement, see *Dragotoniu and Militaru-Pidhorni v. Romania*, CE:ECHR:2007:0524JUD007719301, paras 39–48.

659 *Jorgic v. Germany*, CE:ECHR:2007:0712JUD007461301.

660 See para 15, 23.

661 See para 34–35.

the statutory offense of genocide as a result of its accession to the Genocide Convention.[662] The applicant complained that the domestic courts had employed a wide interpretation of the statutory wording 'genocidal intent to destroy a group' and had, thereby, violated Article 7.[663] He argued that he had not aimed to destroy the physical existence of the Muslims, but that he had only expelled that group from the region by using force.[664]

The ECtHR started its examination by considering the essence of the offense.[665] It noted that the domestic courts had not construed the scope of the offense narrowly by determining that 'intent to destroy' did not require the destruction of a group in the physical or biological sense.[666] The interpretation of the domestic courts meant that it was sufficient that the perpetrator aimed to destroy the group as a social unit. In the ECtHR's view, the interpretation of the domestic courts was based on a systematic interpretation of the statutory provision as a whole.[667] For this reason, the Court found the wide interpretation to be covered by the provision's wording when read in its broader context.[668] In addition, the Court underlined that, at the time of the commission of the crime, this wide interpretation had been advocated by a considerable minority[669] of national and international scholars, as well as the United Nations General Assembly.[670] In light of the systematic interpretation by the German courts and the fact that the interpretation converged with other (scholarly) interpretations, the applicant's acts could be reasonably regarded as falling within the scope of genocide.[671]

Since the offense of genocide was enshrined in the German criminal code in order to incorporate Article II of the Genocide Convention, the Court found it necessary to also examine the wording of that Convention in order to determine the essence of the offense of genocide.[672] The consideration of international law was based on the apparent need for the German definition of genocide to be construed in light of the prohibition of genocide as codified in the Genocide Convention. As the Convention's definition of genocide corresponded with that in the German provision, the Court found no reason to alter its conclusion that the domestic interpretation was both covered by the wording and not unreasonable.[673] The domestic courts' wide interpretation of genocidal intent was not, therefore, contrary to the essence of the offense.

---

662 See para 35.
663 See para 89,
664 See para 92.
665 See para 104–108.
666 See para 104.
667 See para 105.
668 See para 105.
669 That a majority of national and international legal scholars explicitly regarded genocidal intent to require the aim of a group's physical destruction (see para 36, 47), was apparently not problematic for the reasonability of the domestic courts' interpretation.
670 See para 105, 107.
671 See para 105, 108.
672 See para 106.
673 See para 106.

Jorgic indicates that an examination of the statutory definition of an offense constitutes an element of the Court's review of the essence of the offense requirement.[674] The acceptability of the domestic court's interpretation of the offense is, thus, dependent on the previously established definition of that offense. In order to determine whether that previously established definition precludes the domestic court's interpretation, the Court has been willing to look beyond the wording of the offense. To establish that the domestic court's interpretation remained consistent with the essence of the offense, the ECtHR looked at both the context of the statutory offense[675] and the function of individual terms in the offense.[676] In addition, the Court has also looked at preceding domestic case-law in order to identify the essence of the previously established offense.[677]

The ECtHR's focus on the offense's statutory wording and interpretive case-law shows that the essence of the offense requirement precludes a judicial interpretation that extends the notion of the offense to conduct that manifestly falls outside of its scope.[678] The essence of the offense component thus chiefly requires that a judicial interpretation is not explicitly precluded by the previously established definition of the offense.[679] This appears to leave considerable room for judicial interpretation by the domestic courts as it essentially merely rules out *unreasonable* interpretations.[680] The emphasis on reasonableness implies that the ECtHR will be inclined to accept an interpretation of an offense if national courts have carefully explained in detail why they found that interpretation possible.[681] The Court's review of domestic interpretations is therefore quite limited and this approach to the essence of the offense requirement could have very well been influenced by the subsidiarity principle.[682]

---

674 See *Jorgic*, para 105. Cf *Radio France and Others v. France*, CE:ECHR:2004:0330JUD005398400, para 20; *Moiseyev v. Russia*, CE:ECHR:2008:1009JUD006293600, paras 239–240.

675 See *Jorgic*, para 105.

676 See *Radio France and Others v. France*, CE:ECHR:2004:0330JUD005398400, para 20.

677 See eg, *Martirosyan v. Armenia*, CE:ECHR:2013:0205JUD002334106, paras 37–38, 60–61.

678 See *Martirosyan v. Armenia*, CE:ECHR:2013:0205JUD002334106, para 61. Cf *Jorgic*, para 108.

679 *C.R. v. The United Kingdom*, CE:ECHR:1995:1122JUD002019092, para 40; *S.W. v. The United Kingdom*, CE:ECHR:1995:1122JUD002016692, para 42.

680 See *Jorgic*, para 105, 108. Cf EComHR, *X. Ltd and Y. v. United Kingdom* (dec.), CE:ECHR:1982:0507DEC000871079, para 8–10; *Martirosyan v. Armenia*, CE:ECHR:2013:0205JUD002334106, para 61. The Court's focus on reasonableness is also underlined by its willingness to accept judicial interpretations as long other authorities have adopted a similar interpretation, see *Jorgic*, para 105, 107. Apparently, the ECtHR finds that the convergence with other interpretations indicates that such an interpretation is not unreasonable. Cf Corstens and Pradel 2002, p. 359.

681 See, eg, *C.R. v. The United Kingdom*, CE:ECHR:1995:1122JUD002019092, para 40; *S.W. v. The United Kingdom*, CE:ECHR:1995:1122JUD002016692, para 42; *K.A. and A.D. v. Belgium*, CE:ECHR:2005:0217JUD004275898, para 60; *Alimuçaj v. Albania*, CE:ECHR:2012:0207JUD002013405, para 152; *Martirosyan v. Armenia*, CE:ECHR:2013:0205JUD002334106, para 61.

682 See section 3.5.

The reasonable foreseeability requirement

Since the essence of the offense requirement approves *reasonable* interpretations of offenses, this requirement is related to the second precondition for compliance with the *lex stricta* principle: the *reasonable* foreseeability requirement. Reasonable foreseeability does, however, seem stricter than the essence of the offense requirement. In fact, it adds the requirement of foreseeability to the requirement of reasonableness. It therefore restricts the possibility for *applying*, to the detriment of the accused, expansive interpretations that are themselves deemed consistent with the essence of the offense. As the essence of the offense requirement mostly rules out interpretations that obviously conflict with the previously established definition of an offense, it does not provide strict limits to expansive judicial interpretation. The protective core of the *lex stricta* requirement is therefore mostly provided by the requirement that an expansive interpretation of an offense must be reasonably foreseeable before it can be applied to the applicant.

The requirement of reasonable foreseeability seems to be satisfied when an individual could determine that certain acts and omissions may give rise to criminal responsibility at the material time. This requirement is therefore closely related to the foreseeability requirement that the Court uses to evaluate offenses in light of the *lex certa* principle. It essentially requires that the law enables the individual, after taking legal advice, to suspect that certain acts and omissions were punishable at the time he intended to commit them.[683] Applying a judicial interpretation will only violate the requirement of reasonable foreseeability when indications pointing towards that interpretation are absent from both the wording of the offense and the preceding case-law.[684] Like with the foreseeability requirement of the *lex certa* principle, the Court will also use an individual's professional capacity as a factor in favor of concluding that an expansive interpretation complies with the *lex stricta* principle.[685]

The judgment in *Dragotoniu*[686] illustrates how both the offense's statutory wording and the preceding interpretive case-law determine whether a judicial interpretation complies with the reasonable foreseeability requirement. In the *Dragotoniu* case, the domestic courts had, for the first time, applied the offense of passive bribery to the applicants (employees of commercial organizations such

683 See, eg, *Radio France and Others v. France*, CE:ECHR:2004:0330JUD005398400, para 20; *Pessino v. France*, CE:ECHR:2006:1010JUD004040302, paras 35–36; *Dragotoniu and Militaru-Pidhorni v. Romania*, CE:ECHR:2007:0524JUD007719301, para 44.

684 See *C.R. v. The United Kingdom*, para 41; *S.W. v. The United Kingdom*, CE:ECHR:1995:1122JUD002016692, para 43; *Radio France and Others v. France*, CE:ECHR:2004:0330JUD005398400, para 20; *Pessino v. France*, CE:ECHR:2006:1010JUD004040302, para 35; *X and Y v. France*, CE:ECHR:2016:0901JUD004815811, para 56.

685 See *Radio France and Others v. France*, CE:ECHR:2004:0330JUD005398400, para 20; *X and Y v. France*, CE:ECHR:2016:0901JUD004815811, para 57.

686 *Dragotoniu and Militaru-Pidhorni v. Romania*, CE:ECHR:2007:0524JUD007719301.

as private banks).[687] According to the Court, indications about the applicability of the offense to the applicants' acts were absent in the wording of the statutory offense.[688] It found that the wording of the law failed to show that banks could constitute organizations of which employees could commit passive bribery.[689] In fact, a new law had amended the relevant statutory provision after the applicants' actions. This amendment intended to extend the scope of conduct covered by that provision as a legislative response to the changing economic and political system of the respondent State.[690] The new law had therefore equated passive bribery by employees of commercial organizations with that of, previously punishable, bribery by employees of collective (ie public) organizations. As a result, and also in light of the title of the statutory provision, the Court found that the Criminal Code in force at the time did not criminalize passive bribery by persons in a private commercial company.[691]

Since the wording of the offense did not indicate the new judicial interpretation,[692] the Court compared the new interpretation with previous judicial interpretations of that offense. The ECtHR determined that the alleged acts had previously only been interpreted as giving rise to criminal liability when they were perpetrated by employees of *public* organizations. The domestic court had thus, in fact, given a new interpretation to the terms 'employees' and 'other employees' of 'collective organizations'.[693] The Court underlined that the application of the new interpretation was contrary to Article 7 ECHR in the absence of preceding and accessible case-law indicating such an interpretation.[694] Without indications about the new expansive interpretation of the offense in either the text of the offense or preceding case-law,[695] the Court was forced to establish a violation of Article 7 ECHR.[696] Under these conditions, it was difficult or impossible to foresee the judicial interpretation of the offense even after legal advice.[697]

As *Dragotoniu* implies, new and expansive judicial interpretations of offenses could be acceptable even in the absence of any indication in the wording of the offense. The Court finds these interpretations acceptable when they are based on preceding case-law indicating that an expansive interpretation will be applied.

687 See para 42.
688 See para 46–47. See also *Pessino v. France*, CE:ECHR:2006:1010JUD004040302, para 35.
689 See para 46.
690 See para 46.
691 See para 47.
692 See, conversely, *Başkaya and Okçuoğlu v. Turkey*, CE:ECHR:1999:0708JUD002353694, paras 39–40; *Radio France and Others v. France*, CE:ECHR:2004:0330JUD005398400, para 20.
693 See para 43, 45.
694 Cf *Pessino v. France*, CE:ECHR:2006:1010JUD004040302, paras 34–36.
695 Clear indications in the preceding case-law could have sufficed with regard to the *lex stricta* principle, see *Dragotoniu*, para 43. Cf *Martirosyan v. Armenia*, CE:ECHR:2013:0205JUD002334106, paras 60, 62; *Dallas v. The United Kingdom*, CE:ECHR:2016:0211JUD003839512, paras 47, 74, 77.
696 See para 48.
697 See para 44. Cf *Pessino v. France*, CE:ECHR:2006:1010JUD004040302, para 36.

The demands regarding the necessary indications are not very high however. An interpretation can be reasonably foreseeable when lower court judgments had previously established criminal responsibility for acts in factual circumstances related to that in the applicant's case.[698] As a consequence, the preceding case-law need not have considered acts identical to those the applicant is accused of. It is only necessary that the existing case-law interpreted those concepts and constituent elements at the heart of the applicant's case.[699] Within the context of Article 6(1) ECHR the Court has already made clear that the requirement of judicial certainty and the protection of legitimate expectations do not involve the right to settled case-law.[700] New judicial interpretations are in accordance with Article 7 as long as they can still be qualified as a *gradual* development of the scope of an offense.[701] Or, in other words, judicial interpretation is acceptable as long as "(…) the law-making function of the [domestic] courts remained within reasonable limits (…)".[702]

That the *gradual* expansion of the scope of an offense generally satisfies the reasonable foreseeability requirement is clearly illustrated by the landmark judgment in *C.R. v. The United Kingdom*.[703] C.R. was convicted of attempting to rape his wife.[704] At the time of the conduct, statute defined rape as, essentially, unlawful sexual intercourse without consent.[705] At the material time, the domestic courts had generally considered the term 'unlawful' to constitute some form of marital immunity for rape and they had done so for quite some time.[706] At the same time, however, the domestic courts had formulated exceptions to marital immunity on a case by case basis. In the years leading up to the attempt by C.R., the scope of martial immunity was limited by several exceptions. At the time of the applicant's conduct, no exception was, however, formulated that completely revoked marital immunity for rape. Nor did the circumstances of the case result in the applicability of a previously formulated limit of marital

698 See, *Soros v. France*, CE:ECHR:2011:1006JUD005042506, paras 57–58. See also the reiteration of this consideration as a general principle in *Khodorkovskiy and Lebedev v. Russia*, CE:ECHR:2013:0725JUD001108206, para 785.

699 See, conversely, *Khodorkovskiy and Lebedev v. Russia*, CE:ECHR:2013:0725JUD001108206, paras 793–794.

700 See *Boumaraf v. France* (dec.), CE:ECHR:2011:0830DEC003282008; *Lupeni Greek Catholic Parish and Others v. Romania*, CE:ECHR:2016:1129JUD007694311, para 116.

701 See *Soros v. France*, CE:ECHR:2011:1006JUD005042506, para 58. This view was, however, criticized as amounting to an extensive interpretation prohibited by Article 7 in the common dissenting opinion of judges Villiger, Yudkivska and Nussberger in *Soros*.

702 *Dallas v. The United Kingdom*, CE:ECHR:2016:0211JUD003839512, para 77.

703 *C.R. v. The United Kingdom*, CE:ECHR:1995:1122JUD002019092. See also the related judgment *S.W. v. The United Kingdom*, CE:ECHR:1995:1122JUD002016692. As both judgments are almost identical, I will just examine *C.R.* v. *The United Kingdom*. I will only refer to *S.W. v. The United Kingdom* where there are notable dissimilarities.

704 See para 26. Instead, S.W. was convicted of the completed offense of rape, see *S.W. v. The United Kingdom*, para 28.

705 See para 17.

706 See para 19.

immunity. The domestic courts nevertheless convicted the applicant for attempting to rape his wife.[707] In these circumstances, the applicant's conviction required the immediate application of a judicial extension of the scope of the previously existing offense.

The ECtHR concluded that this application of the broadened offense was reasonably foreseeable at the time of the material acts. It did so for two reasons. First, because it was well-established that several exceptions existed to marital immunity for rape at the time of the material acts.[708] Secondly, because there was an evident evolution of the criminal law through judicial interpretation towards treating rape within marriage as within the scope of the offense of rape.[709] As a result, the Court considered the judicial interpretation in the case at hand to have continued a perceptible line of case-law dismantling marital immunity.[710] Since the evolution of the law had reached a stage where the judicial removal of immunity had become a reasonably foreseeable development of law, and the evolution was consistent with the essence of the offense, the application of the expansive judicial interpretation was acceptable under Article 7 ECHR.[711]

The exceptional primacy of the essence of the offense requirement

Although the reasonable foreseeability requirement limits the room for applying expansive judicial interpretations in addition to the restrictions of the essence of the offense requirement,[712] the latter is sometimes the only applicable constraint on domestic courts. Such a situation arises when domestic courts have never had the opportunity to interpret the applicable offense before the applicant's case. In *Jorgic,* the Court considered that the first judicial interpretation of an offense must, as a rule, be considered foreseeable when it is in accordance with the essence of the offense.[713] In these circumstances the Court will essentially only review the interpretation of the domestic court in light of whether it respects the essence of the offense. In exceptional cases, however, the applicant can rely, by virtue of the requirement of reasonable foreseeability, on an assumption

707 This was 'the marital rape case' described in the previous chapter, see subsection 2.4.4. See, critically, Harris, O'Boyle, Bates and Buckley 2014, p. 498.
708 Para 41.
709 Para 41.
710 Para 41.
711 Para 41, 44.
712 See above under 'the reasonable foreseeability requirement'.
713 See para 109. In *Moiseyev* the Court interpreted this consideration very generally as meaning that an interpretation of the scope of an offense which was consistent with the essence of the offense must, as a rule, be considered as foreseeable, see *Moiseyev v. Russia*, CE:ECHR:2008:1009JUD006293600, para 241. However, this interpretation of the consideration in *Jorgic* disregards the Court's qualification that this rule applies in case of the *first* judicial interpretation of the statutory offense.

regarding what the first judicial interpretation of the provision will be.[714] This is the case, for example, when accessible authoritative interpretations by other legal authorities or scholars have consistently indicated a specific interpretation at the time of the applicant's conduct.[715] When the case concerns a provision that corresponds to a provision of international law, the authoritative interpretations of international law become relevant for the foreseeability of what the first judicial interpretation of the domestic law will be.[716]

In addition to cases involving the first judicial interpretation of the offense, domestic courts are sometimes faced with situations that are sufficiently distinguishable from earlier cases. In these situations, the previously established definition of the offense does not necessarily indicate a particular interpretation of the offense. Like in cases involving the first judicial interpretation of the offense, the reasonable foreseeability of the judicial interpretation seems to be complicated. Although the ECtHR has not explicitly stated that the requirement of reasonable foreseeability is less important than the essence of the offense requirement in these situations, it has not reviewed the immediate application of judicial interpretations strictly in light of reasonable foreseeability either. In *Radio France*, for example, the Court established that the facts of the case fell somewhere in-between cases that were clearly within, and cases that were clearly outside, the scope of the previously established offense.[717] After assessing the reasons behind the domestic courts' interpretation in the applicant's case, the Court merely concluded that the judicial interpretation was consistent with the essence of the offense and reasonably foreseeable.[718] This undifferentiated conclusion indicates that the reasonability of the domestic interpretation made it acceptable in light of the *lex stricta* principle. This implies that, when the domestic courts are faced with a situation that is underdetermined by the previously-established definition of the offense, *reasonable* interpretations are not only consistent with the essence of the offense, but their immediate application will generally be deemed reasonably foreseeable as well. *Radio France*'s approach to judicial interpretations in unprecedented cases is therefore in line with the Court's explicit considerations in *Jorgic*. Moreover, the approach in *Radio France* has been subsequently confirmed.[719] The Court's focus on the reasonability of the domestic courts' interpretation is perhaps influenced by the subsidiarity principle.[720]

---

714 See para 109.

715 See *Jorgic*, para 110–113.

716 See *Jorgic*, para 110, 112.

717 *Radio France and Others v. France*, CE:ECHR:2004:0330JUD005398400, para 20.

718 See para 20.

719 See *Huhtamäki v. Finland*, CE:ECHR:2012:0306JUD005446809, paras 50–51; *Khodorkovskiy and Lebedev v. Russia*, CE:ECHR:2013:0725JUD001108206, para 821; *X and Y v. France*, CE: ECHR:2016:0901JUD004815811, paras 61–65.

720 See subsection 3.5.

The relevance of the severe nature of the offense

In addition to the requirements of essence of the offense and reasonable foreseeability, the Court has sometimes used a further consideration to determine the acceptability of the immediate application of the domestic courts' judicial interpretation. This occurred already in the early judgment of *C.R. v. The United Kingdom*. There, the ECtHR stated that the manifestly debasing character of rape meant that the domestic courts' interpretation was not contrary to the object and purpose of Article 7, since it did not result in arbitrary prosecution, conviction or punishment.[721]

In *C.R. v. The United Kingdom*, the Court seems to have found the severity of the crime as contributing to the foreseeability of criminal responsibility. On this view of the legal reasoning, expansive judicial interpretations are more acceptable in light of Article 7 when the nature of the crime is more severe. This view could be justified by regarding conduct that potentially constitutes a severe crime as evidently punishable. Therefore, if a person conducts himself in such an evidently punishable way, the determination that his conduct was indeed punishable, even when this determination is based on an extensive judicial interpretation, cannot easily imply an *arbitrary* conviction.

Although the above-mentioned justification for the Court's reference to the severity of the crime is not a priori unacceptable, it is doubtful that the Strasbourg Court intended its reference to the severity of the crime that way. In fact, a subsequent consideration in *C.R. v. The United Kingdom* points to a different reason for why the Court referred to the debasing character of rape. The Court referred to the 'unacceptable idea' of marital immunity for rape in light of the civilized concept of marriage and the fundamental objectives of the Convention, the very essence of which is respect for human dignity and freedom.[722] In effect, the ECtHR thus deemed the application of the domestic courts' judicial interpretation to be acceptable because it was in accordance with the substantive values the Court endorses.[723] As a consequence of this determination, the Court seems to actually regard the severe nature of the crime as a *self-standing* reason behind allowing the application of the domestic courts' interpretation under Article 7 ECHR.[724]

In the later judgment in *Pessino*,[725] the Court revisited its considerations on the debasing character of rape. It stated that the debasing character of rape had

---

721 Para 42.

722 Para 42. See for comparable considerations about the 'essence of the Convention' outside the context of Article 7, eg, *Pretty v. The United Kingdom*, CE:ECHR:2002:0429JUD000234602, para 65. See further Gerards 2011a, p. 112–113.

723 Cf Kadelbach 2006, p. 737; Bleichrodt 2006, p. 655; Valentini 2011, p. 196–197. A comparable approach was taken in the judgments about the East-German border-policing regime, see *Streletz*, para 87; *K.-H.W.*, para 90 and further about these cases subsection 3.6.2. See also Atrill 2005, p. 124–126; Murphy 2010, p. 201.

724 Cf Boot 2002, p. 156–157; Altena-Davidsen 2016, p. 231.

725 *Pessino v. France*, CE:ECHR:2006:1010JUD004040302, para 36.

made the criminalization of the act so obvious that the judicial interpretation was sufficiently foreseeable. Here, the Court seems to have explicitly taken the position that the detrimental nature of the offense adds to the foreseeability of the punishability of the conduct, which allows more room for expansive judicial interpretation.[726] The Court then, however, considered the judicial interpretation to be in accordance with the Convention because it was in conformity with its fundamental objectives. Like in *C.R. v. The United Kingdom*, the Court again seems to indicate that application of the domestic judicial interpretation was acceptable *because* it safeguards the substantive values the Convention endorses. In *Dragotoniu*, however, the Court explicitly rejected this view by underlining that the principles enshrined in Article 7 should apply in the same manner in all criminal proceedings no matter how detrimental the alleged crimes by the applicant.[727]

The Court's diverging indications about the relevance of the severity of the offense prevents a clear conclusion on its relevance for limits to judicial interpretation and its immediate application. As a consequence, it is presently unclear whether the severe nature of the offense is only a factor that strengthens the foreseeability of criminal responsibility, or, instead, constitutes a self-standing factor justifying an expansive interpretation because it leads to the conviction of individuals who violated the fundamental freedoms of the victims. If the latter is true, the absolute requirements of Article 7 would be relinquished and the legality principle would become a right that could be restricted when the rights of the alleged victim were violated in a sufficiently significant matter.[728] That interpretation finds some support in the Court's judgment in *Coëme*, where the ECtHR underlined that the interpretation of Article 7 could also imply a balancing act between the general interest and fundamental rights of individuals.[729]

More importantly, in *Rohlena* the Grand Chamber recently reiterated the relevant considerations in *C.R. v. The United Kingdom* as an additional reason why the domestic courts had not violated Article 7 ECHR.[730] In *Rohlena* the Court stated that

> "(...) by reinforcing the national legal protection against domestic violence – such violence perpetrated against women being still a matter of grave concern in contemporary European societies (...) – it also conforms to the fundamental objectives of the Convention, the very essence of which is respect for human dignity and freedom (...)".[731]

726 In *Jorgic*, the Court also considered the severity of the offense as a relevant factor for judicial interpretation, but it did not clearly state how it used this consideration in its review of the domestic courts' interpretation, see *Jorgic v. Germany*, CE:ECHR:2007:0712JUD007461301, para 113.

727 *Dragotoniu and Militaru-Pidhorni v. Romania*, CE:ECHR:2007:0524JUD007719301, para 41.

728 Cf Murphy 2010, p. 206; Valentini 2011, p. 198.

729 *Coëme and Others v. Belgium*, CE:ECHR:2000:0622JUD003249296, para 145. Cf Atrill 2005, p. 124–125.

730 *Rohlena v. The Czech Republic*, CE:ECHR:2015:0127JUD005955208, para 71.

731 *Rohlena*, para 71.

Although the Strasbourg case-law is not completely consistent on the issue of balancing the rights of victims with that of the accused under Article 7, there is certainly case-law that indicates the relevance of a balancing act. Such an approach could, moreover, be supported by Article 17 ECHR, which precludes the invocation of a Convention right to justify the 'destruction' of other Convention rights.[732] Therefore, the severe nature of the applicable offense seems to constitute a relevant factor in determining the room the ECtHR allows domestic courts to interpret and apply offenses to the accused's detriment.

Recapitulation

The requirements of essence of the offense and reasonable foreseeability set limits to judicial interpretation and the immediate application of judgments. The essence of the offense requirement demands that judicial interpretation does not stray too far from the previously established definition of the offense. It basically rules out unreasonable interpretations of existing offenses. This implies that judges are not allowed to convict individuals for conduct that was not criminalized at the time of conduct, even though, in the domestic court's view, it should have been.

In order to determine the previously established definition of a crime, the Court's starting point is the offense's statutory wording.[733] In addition, the ECtHR has been willing to consider the context of the offense[734] and, sometimes, the function of individual legal terms enshrined therein to establish the essence of the offense.[735] Since the Court has accepted the inevitability of judicial interpretation of offenses, it also examines existing interpretive case-law in order to determine the essence of the offense at the time of the applicant's acts.[736] In light of the multiple factors used to determine the essence of the offense, and the preclusion of unreasonable interpretations, there is quite some room for domestic courts to interpret crimes progressively and expansively.

As with the foreseeability requirement of the *lex certa* principle, the requirement of reasonable foreseeability generally forms the protective core of the *lex stricta* principle.[737] Reasonable foreseeability essentially requires that the law enables the individual, after taking legal advice, to suspect the potential punishability of certain acts and omissions at the time he intended to commit

---

732 Cf Murphy 2010, p. 206; Valentini 2011, p. 198–199. The Court has nevertheless rejected the idea that Article 17 prevents an individual from relying on Article 7 ECHR, see *Ould Dah v. France* (dec.), CE:ECHR:2009:0317DEC001311303.

733 See *Jorgic*, para 105. Cf *Radio France and Others*, para 20; *Moiseyev v. Russia*, para 239–240.

734 See *Jorgic*, para 105.

735 See *Radio France and Others*, para 20.

736 See, eg, *Martirosyan v. Armenia*, CE:ECHR:2013:0205JUD002334106, paras 37–38; 60–61.

737 An important exception is when the domestic courts are faced with a situation that is undetermined or underdetermined by the existing law. In such circumstances the essence of the offense requirement has primacy and requires reasonable judicial interpretations, see *Radio France*, para 20; *Jorgic*, para 109.

them.[738] Like with *lex certa*, the starting point for the assessment of foreseeability is the offense's statutory wording.[739] The Court also considers the statutory context of the provision to determine the foreseeability of punishability[740] and an individual's professional capacity.[741] In addition, existing interpretive case-law can contribute to the reasonable foreseeability of criminal responsibility.[742] Accessible case-law preceding a novel and expansive judicial interpretation can mean that interpretation is acceptable in light of *lex stricta*, even in the absence of indications about such an expansive interpretation in the offense's wording. The preceding case-law does not have to indicate a novel expansive interpretation very clearly.[743] It is sufficient that the new interpretation can be qualified as a gradual development of the scope of an offense.[744] One example of this is if the new interpretation continues a perceptible line of case-law demonstrating an evident evolution in the interpretation of the offense.[745]

That the judicial development of criminal law is acceptable means that the *lex stricta* principle allows the judicial expansion of existing offenses and their immediate application to the detriment of the accused. The addition of 'reasonable' to the foreseeability requirement apparently confirms the limited protection that Article 7 provides in this regard. It is not unthinkable that the Court's recognition of its subsidiary position has contributed to the formulation of the rather undemanding requirements of essence of the offense and reasonable foreseeability.[746] The deferential approach towards domestic judicial interpretations of criminal law is, in any event, in line with the subsidiarity principle.

An important characteristic of the Convention's *lex stricta* principle is the potential relevance of the severe nature of the applicant's offense. Since the Court has deemed the severe nature of the offenses to allow more room for extensive judicial interpretation under Article 7,[747] the Court arguably weighs the importance of the predictability of criminal law against the importance of protecting the rights of the victim.[748] With severe crimes like rape and domestic violence against women, the ECtHR is evidently willing to allow more room for judicial interpretation under Article 7 than it otherwise might. To provide the domestic courts room to punish

---

738 See, eg, *Radio France*, para 20; *Pessino v. France*, para 35–36; *Dragotoniu*, para 44.
739 See *Dragotoniu*, para 46–47. See also, *Pessino v. France*, para 35.
740 See *Dragotoniu*, para 47.
741 See *Radio France*, para 20.
742 See *Dragotoniu*, para 43. Cf *Martirosyan v. Armenia*, para 60, 62.
743 Cf Valentini 2011, p. 195.
744 See *C.R. v. The United Kingdom*, para 41–44. Cf *Soros v. France*, para 58.
745 See *C.R. v. The United Kingdom*, para 41, 44.
746 On the impact of the Court's review on the development of the Convention's protective standards outside Article 7 ECHR, see Christofferen 2009, 268–274.
747 Cf Valentini 2011, p. 198. A comparable approach was taken in the cases about the East-German border-policing regime, see *Streletz, Kessler and Krenz v. Germany*, para 87; *K.-H.W. v. Germany*, para 90 and further about these cases subsection 3.6.2. See further Juratowitch 2008, p. 133–134; Murphy 2010, p. 201.
748 Cf Murphy 2010, p. 200.

severe crimes against, for example, women, is clearly the result of allowing some precedence to crime control interests. This precedence is granted because the crime control interests coincide with the Convention's fundamental objectives that are apparently allowed to trump legal certainty provided by the legality principle.[749]

Although the willingness to provide less protection of *lex stricta* in order to safeguard the rights of the victim is only perceivable in a few cases,[750] it is a significant cause of concern for the level of protection provided by Article 7.[751] If the extent of legality protection depends on the severity of the offense and the rights of the victim, the Court would certainly make the level of legality protection case-dependent. The Court should instead require absolute conformity with the existing minimum standards for the definition, interpretation, and application of offenses and penalties. The Court's references to respect for human dignity, human freedom and the notions of self-determination and personal autonomy as 'the very essence of the Convention'[752] should not, within the context of Article 7, be considered relevant for interpreting the minimum protection provided by the legality principle.[753] As Murphy concluded, "[w]hile [the Court] might be reluctant to allow a charter grounded in human dignity to be used by those who have willfully disregarded it, such use is the essence of the rule of law protected by art. 7."[754]

3.6.4 THE PROHIBITION ON THE RETROACTIVE APPLICATION OF THE DEFINITION OF AN OFFENSE (*LEX PRAEVIA*)

The scope of the 'lex praevia' principle and its relationship with 'lex stricta'

Like the *lex stricta* principle, the principle *lex praevia* prohibits certain forms of application of domestic criminal law. In this sense, both principles are interrelated and their relevance for the application of domestic criminal law distinguishes them from the *lex certa* principle. Moreover, both the

---

749 Cf Murphy 2010, p. 206.

750 In *Coëme* the Court also underlined that Article 7 could imply a balancing act between the general interest and fundamental rights of individuals and, outside the context of Article 7, the *Soering* judgment underlined that the interpretation of Convention rights should be consistent with the general spirit of the Convention which aims to promote the ideals and values of a democratic society, see ECtHR (22 June 2000), Appl. nos. 32492/96, 32547/96, 32548/96, 33209/96 and 33210/96, *Coëme and Others v. Belgium*, para 145; *Soering v. The United Kingdom*, CE:ECHR:1989:0707JUD001403888, para 87. See further subsection 3.6.3 above.

751 Cf Murphy 2010, p. 196.

752 See for this reference outside the context of Article 7, eg, *Jehovah's Witnesses of Moscow and Others v. Russia*, CE:ECHR:2010:0610JUD000030202, para 135.

753 Cf Valentini 2011, p. 196; De Hullu 2015, p. 108.

754 Murphy 2010, p. 206.

principle of non-retroactivity of an offense and the *lex stricta* principle provide substantive protection that is quite similar. This is because the extensive judicial interpretation of an offense under the applicable law could, in fact, amount to enacting a new judicial definition of an offense. The immediate application of an extensive interpretation of a previously established definition could therefore amount to retroactively applying a new offense to the applicant's conduct. The ECtHR has given the *lex praevia* principle a limited scope and so complaints about the immediate application of extensive interpretations are examined solely in light of the *lex stricta* principle.[755]

The limited scope of the *lex praevia* principle is, for example, apparent in *Dragotoniu*.[756] In that case, a new statutory provision amended the definition of an offense *after* the applicants' conduct. The applicants argued that the domestic courts had in fact interpreted the old law as prohibiting the conduct criminalized by the new law.[757] Since the domestic court had *formally* only used the provision in force at the material time, the ECtHR concluded that the domestic court could not be accused of having carried out a retroactive application of criminal law.[758] Instead, the Court examined the applicants' complaints with regard to the prohibition on the overly extensive interpretation of an offense.

The approach taken in *Dragotoniu* illustrates that the ECtHR's examination of domestic law in light of the *lex praevia* principle is dependent on the *formal* qualification under domestic law.[759] If the statutory provisions themselves do not stipulate their retroactive application and the domestic court does not formally use statutes or judgments that were established after the material conduct, there will not be a violation of the principle of non-retroactivity of an offense.

The substantive review: the reappearance of the requirements of accessibility and foreseeability

The Court's approach to *lex praevia* indicates that it will only review the application of national law when it is not convinced that the domestic courts have *exclusively* applied the law in force at the material time. In order to determine whether the domestic courts have also used subsequent definitions of offenses to convict the applicant, it will assess whether the applicant's acts fell within the scope of the applicable offenses. A violation of *lex praevia* is

---

755 See also subsections 3.4.3 and 3.6.3.

756 *Dragotoniu and Militaru-Pidhorni v. Romania*, CE:ECHR:2007:0524JUD007719301. See for further discussion of this case subsection 3.6.3.

757 See para 29–30.

758 See para 39. For a similar approach, see, eg, *Grigoriades v. Greece*, CE:ECHR:1997:1125JUD002434894, para 34; *Liivik v. Estonia*, CE:ECHR:2009:0625JUD001215705, para 96; *Alimuçaj v. Albania*, CE:ECHR:2012:0207JUD002013405, para 152.

759 See also, eg, *Streletz, Kessler and Krenz v. Germany*, CE:ECHR:2001:0322JUD003404496, para 55.

ruled out if the applicable law defined the applicant's acts as a criminal offense in accordance with the requirements of accessibility and foreseeability. This is clearly illustrated by the early case in *G. v. France*.[760]

In *G. v. France*, the applicant was convicted of forcing a woman into sexual acts which allegedly constituted the offense of 'indecent assault' under the French Criminal Code.[761] At the time of the applicant's acts, the wording of the relevant provisions only criminalized an indecent assault when committed with violence.[762] A subsequent amendment of the Criminal Code had, however, expanded the statutory definition of indecent assault by explicitly criminalizing indecent assaults involving coercion in addition to violent assaults.[763] Since G. had not used violence and was nevertheless convicted of an indecent assault under the old law, he claimed that the new, broader, definition of indecent assault was retroactively used as the basis for his conviction.

In the Court's view, however, the applicable law had already criminalized indecent assaults committed by coercion. The reason was that accessible case-law from the French Court of Cassation had consistently interpreted the notion of violence in relation to an indecent assault as including coercion or non-physical violence.[764] Since the combination of the statutory definition and the domestic court's case-law satisfied the qualitative requirements of foreseeability and accessibility *at the time of the material conduct*, the applicant's acts were clearly punishable as an indecent assault under the applicable law.[765] With regard to the definition of the offense, a retroactive application of a new definition was therefore neither necessary nor present. In the ECtHR's view, the new statutory definition had merely confirmed what was already the applicable legal definition of the offense as a result of consistent case-law.[766]

As with the *lex certa* principle, the ECtHR will look at both statutory law and case-law in order to determine whether an offense is *sufficiently* established by law at the time of the material acts. The Court will only find a violation of the principle of non-retroactivity if the *combination* of statutory and case-law has failed to define the offense with sufficient accessibility and foreseeability at the time of the applicant's acts. When the law *only* satisfied the quality of law requirements after the applicant's acts, the Court has found a violation of the *lex praevia* principle. This is illustrated by the related[767] cases *Veeber*[768] and *Puhk*.[769]

760 *G. v. France*, CE:ECHR:1995:0927JUD001531289.
761 See para 7. Cf Boot 2002, p. 149–150.
762 See para 13.
763 See para 14.
764 See para 25 and 13.
765 See para 25. Cf *Rohlena v. The Czech Republic*, CE:ECHR:2015:0127JUD005955208, paras 63–64.
766 See para 25.
767 See *Puhk*, para 26.
768 *Veeber v. Estonia (No. 2)*, CE:ECHR:2003:0121JUD004577199.
769 *Puhk v. Estonia*, CE:ECHR:2004:0210JUD005510300.

In *Veeber* and *Puhk* a new statutory provision on tax evasion broadened the scope of the conduct previously criminalized. The new law defined tax evasion as a criminal offense when it was *either* committed after an administrative penalty, *or* when it was committed with intent.[770] Conversely, the old statutory provision had *exclusively* required the existence of a previously-imposed administrative penalty as a prerequisite for criminal responsibility.[771] In both *Veeber* and *Puhk*, the applicants were convicted for violating the *new* definition of tax evasion, although a large part of their conduct had been committed before the entry into force of that new definition.[772] The domestic courts had nevertheless upheld these convictions, since the acts of tax evasion were a continuing criminal activity which lasted beyond the entry into force of the new statutory definition.

The ECtHR concluded that the domestic courts had retroactively applied the amended legal definition to acts which did not previously constitute a criminal offense.[773] It did so because it found it problematic in light of the foreseeability requirement that the new definition of tax evasion was applied to acts that were both committed before and after the entry into force of the new provision.[774] At the time when most of the applicant's acts were committed, the statutory definition of tax evasion required the previous imposition of an administrative penalty as a prerequisite for criminal responsibility. At that time, the wording of the applicable law did not, therefore, make it foreseeable that the intentional commission of tax evasion would be a self-standing ground for criminal responsibility.[775]

This conclusion was not altered by the fact that case-law of the Estonian Supreme Court had introduced the possibility of retroactively applying the new provision in cases of intentional and continuing acts of tax evasion.[776] This was because the judgments of the Supreme Court were only handed down after the applicants actions.[777] The new judicial interpretation resulting in criminalizing intentional and continued tax evasion in the absence of a preceding administrative penalty was, therefore, not foreseeable for the applicants at the time of their actions. As a result, the domestic courts had partly applied a legal definition of an offense to acts which had not, with sufficient accessibility and foreseeability,[778] criminalized these acts at the time they were committed. For

---

770 See *Veeber*, para 25; *Puhk*, para 18.

771 See *Veeber*, para 24; *Puhk*, para 17, 31.

772 See *Veeber*, para 36; *Puhk*, para 29.

773 See *Veeber*, para 38; *Puhk*, para 33. See, conversely, *Rohlena v. The Czech Republic*, CE:ECHR:2015:0127JUD005955208, para 62.

774 See *Veeber*, para 37 and *Puhk*, para 32.

775 Cf *Puhk*, para 31.

776 See *Veeber*, para 29; *Puhk*, para 23. See, conversely, *Rohlena v. The Czech Republic*, CE:ECHR:2015:0127JUD005955208, paras 59–64.

777 See *Veeber*, para 37; *Puhk*, para 32. See, conversely, *Rohlena v. The Czech Republic*, CE:ECHR:2015:0127JUD005955208, para 60.

778 Cf *Veeber*, para 33; *Puhk*, para 28.

this reason, this constituted retroactive application of criminal law[779] and, consequently, a violation of Article 7 ECHR.[780]

Veeber and *Puhk* illustrate that the retroactive application of an offense causes problems with regard to the foreseeability of criminal responsibility. Retroactive application can, therefore, amount to a problem with the foreseeability of the offense applied by the domestic courts.[781] Domestic conviction on the basis of a retroactive offense can, then, be viewed as a problem with the legal definition of the offense that the domestic court used for the conviction. In this line of reasoning, the Court can review the offense that the domestic courts actually employed with regard to accessibility and foreseeability under the *lex certa* principle. If the offense is applied retroactively, the offense relied upon to convict the applicant will fail to satisfy the *lex certa* requirements at the time of the applicant's conduct. The Court can then use the apparent retroactive application as the reason to conclude that the offense used to convict the applicant failed to satisfy the *lex certa* requirement of, for example, foreseeability. This shows that, in addition to a potential overlap between the requirements of *lex praevia* and *lex stricta*, there is also a close relationship between the requirements of *lex praevia* and *lex certa*.

That the Court has, in fact, employed the above reasoning is illustrated by the judgment in *Contrada*.[782] That case concerned an applicant who was convicted for actions that took place between 1979 and 1988 on the basis of a judicial definition of an offense that was only clearly enacted in 1994. Therefore, the domestic court of appeal had explicitly used the 1994 judicial definition established by domestic case-law as the basis for upholding the conviction in first instance.[783] Although this indicates that the domestic courts applied the 1994 judicial definition retroactively to the acts in the period 1979–88, the ECtHR concluded that the definition of the offense lacked foreseeability at the time of the acts.[784] As a result, the ECtHR viewed this as a problem with the foreseeability of the definition of the offense instead of as a problem with the application of the definition of an offense that, in itself, satisfied the *lex certa* requirements. It deemed the retroactive application of the 1994 offense, therefore, as indicating an insufficient legal definition at the time of the applicant's acts. Instead of finding a violation of the *lex praevia* principle, the Court concluded that Article 7 was violated because the legal definition itself failed to satisfy the *lex certa* requirements.

---

779 See *Veeber*, para 38; *Puhk*, para 33.

780 See *Veeber*, para 39; *Puhk*, para 34.

781 Cf Murphy 2010, p. 202–203.

782 *Contrada v. Italy (No. 3)*, CE:ECHR:2015:0414JUD006665513. On this judgment see subsection 3.6.2.

783 See para 18, 72.

784 See para 75.

Recapitulation

The case-law examined in this subsection indicates a close relationship between the principles *lex praevia* and *lex certa*. In order to determine whether the domestic courts applied offenses retroactively, the Court examines the offenses used by the domestic courts to convict the applicant. If the domestic courts formally only used offenses that were non-existent at the time of the material acts, the Court will easily find a violation of the *lex praevia* principle.

Matters are more difficult, however, when domestic courts formally base their conviction on offenses that were applicable at the time of the material acts. In that situation, the ECtHR will be required to evaluate the applicable offenses in order to determine whether they criminalized the applicant's acts at the material time. In order to do so, the Court examines whether the applicable offense satisfied, at the time of the material acts, the requirements of accessibility and foreseeability (ie the *lex certa* requirements). If the applicable offense satisfies the *lex certa* principle, the domestic courts are able to apply it to the applicant's acts and use it as the basis for their conviction. Conformity with the *lex certa* principle will, in that situation, automatically satisfy the *lex praevia* principle. In these circumstances, the Court would actually use only the *lex certa* principle to determine conformity with Article 7 ECHR and *lex praevia* provides no additional protection.

To determine whether an offense is sufficiently established by law at the time of the material acts, the Court looks at statutory law and case-law. The substance of the *lex certa* review, then, remains unaltered by the context of complaints that the principle of *lex praevia* has been violated. *G. v. France* shows that interpretive case-law can provide a sufficient legal basis for criminal liability in the absence of a statutory provision that explicitly establishes criminal responsibility at the time of the acts.[785] If the combination of statutory law and case-law does not, however, provide a sufficient legal basis at the time of the material conduct, and this is only introduced by subsequent law, the Court will establish a violation of the principle of non-retroactivity. In fact, *Veeber* and *Puhk* indicate that the *lex praevia* principle prohibits even the application of a new provision to acts which were not, during the whole period in which they were committed, criminalized with sufficient foreseeability by either statutory and/or case-law. The non-retroactivity principle provides its protection even when the domestic court has classified the applicant's acts as a single, continuing, offense.[786]

---

785 See *G. v. France*, para 25.

786 On the difference between 'continuing' and 'continuous' offenses, see *Rohlena v. The Czech Republic*, CE:ECHR:2015:0127JUD005955208, para 28.

3.7 THE *NULLA POENA* PRINCIPLE

3.7.1 INTRODUCTION

This section examines the relevance of the elements *lex certa*, *lex stricta*, and *lex praevia* for the *nulla poena* principle. The approach is the same as in the preceding section, only the subject of examination differs: the section focuses on rules prescribing a penalty. Subsection 3.7.2 examines the principle that the law needs to clearly define penalties. Subsection 3.7.3 focusses on the prohibition on the overly extensive interpretation of penalties. The principle that rules prescribing penalties should not be retroactively applied forms the subject of subsection 3.7.4. Some other grounds for violation of the *nulla poena* principle are examined thereafter in subsection 3.7.5. Subsection 3.7.6 contains a recapitulation.

3.7.2 THE PRINCIPLE THAT PENALTIES REQUIRE A CLEAR LEGAL DEFINITION (*LEX CERTA*)

Article 7(1) requires that domestic law prescribes penalties with sufficient clarity. Like all other legal provisions, and notably offenses, the prescription of a penalty needs to satisfy the general requirements of accessibility and foreseeability. How the Court employs these requirements with regard to the clarity of a penalty, will be illustrated by a brief description of the judgments in *Achour,*[787] *Kafkaris,*[788] and *Camilleri.*[789]

In *Achour,* the Court examined the compatibility of an increased penalty for a second conviction with Article 7 ECHR. The applicant disputed whether recidivism could be an aggravating factor in relation to the second offense. In his view, the first offense could not be considered an aggravating factor when determining the penalty for the second offense, because the statutory period had expired in which the first offense could be considered to be the first component of recidivism.[790] Only after the statutory period expired did a new provision enter into force extending that statutory period and only this new provision enabled the domestic court to use the first offense as a factor to impose a harsher sentence for the second offense. In the applicant's view, relying on the new provision to impose an increased penalty amounted to the retroactive imposition of a harsher sentence.[791] In any case, according to the applicant, the use of the new provision to impose a harsher sentence had obscured the foreseeability of the penalty and thus legal certainty.[792]

787 *Achour v. France*, CE:ECHR:2006:0329JUD006733501.
788 *Kafkaris v. Cyprus*, CE:ECHR:2008:0212JUD002190604.
789 *Camilleri v. Malta*, CE:ECHR:2013:0122JUD004293110.
790 See para 40.
791 See para 38.
792 See para 39.

The ECtHR dismissed the complaint about retroactivity as it found that the instant case only concerned the successive application of statutes each designed to exclusively apply prospectively.[793] In any event, the Court made it clear that taking into account past convictions should be distinguished from retroactive application of law *stricto sensu*.[794] For this reason, the Court only examined the complaint about the foreseeability of the effects of the sentencing provisions. It stated that it had to examine whether the text of the statutory rule, read in the light of the interpretative case-law, satisfied the requirements of accessibility and foreseeability at the material time.[795]

The Court noted that the new rules on recidivism were applicable at the time the applicant committed the second offense.[796] Since his first conviction remained on his criminal record, a new law extending the statutory period during which that offense could be considered as the first component of recidivism was in principle acceptable.[797] This was especially the case because the French Court of Cassation had long established that new rules on recidivism apply immediately when the second offense is committed after the entry into force of the new rules.[798] This consistent case-law on the effects of new rules on recidivism was manifestly capable of enabling the applicant to regulate his conduct.[799] In these circumstances, the applicant could have foreseen that he ran the risk of being convicted as a re-offender when he committed a second comparable offense in the given period.[800] Since the applicant could have foreseen the increase in the applicable penalty,[801] the statutory provisions and case-law satisfied the qualitative requirements of accessibility and foreseeability and were therefore compatible with Article 7 ECHR.[802]

In *Kafkaris*, the applicant was convicted for murder, which was, at the time of the conviction, punishable by mandatory life imprisonment under the Criminal Code.[803] The applicant complained that the statutory wording 'life imprisonment' meant a prison sentence of twenty years at the time of the material conduct.[804] The Court observed that, although the Criminal Code explicitly prescribed a penalty of life imprisonment for murder, the executive and administrative authorities interpreted this sentence as being tantamount to twenty years imprisonment.[805] This was the case because the Prison Regulations

793 See para 58.
794 See para 59. See about retroactive application of penalties subsection 3.7.4 below.
795 See para 47.
796 See para 49.
797 See para 51.
798 See para 52.
799 See para 52.
800 See para 53.
801 See para 53.
802 See paras 55, 60–61.
803 See para 143.
804 See para 144.
805 See para 146.

in force at the time of the offense defined life imprisonment as twenty years and the prison authorities consistently applied this definition in practice.[806]

The Court found that the application of the Prison Regulations went beyond the mere execution of the penalty and had an effect on its actual scope.[807] As a result, at the time of the applicant's conduct, there were opposite indications in the law as to the exact meaning of 'life imprisonment'. The formulation in the Criminal Code indicated that life imprisonment would amount to a prison sentence for the remainder of a convicted person's biological life, while the Prison Regulations – as consistently applied – indicated a maximum term of imprisonment of twenty years. The possibility of opposite interpretations was only removed subsequent to the applicant's conduct.[808] At the time of the material conduct, the law as a whole was not, therefore, formulated with sufficient precision to enable the applicant to discern the scope of the penalty of life imprisonment.[809] Since the combination of the Criminal Code and the Prison Regulations failed to satisfy the foreseeability requirement, the law was of insufficient quality.[810]

Camilleri also concerned the clarity of the prescribed penalty.[811] Although the applicable provisions provided for the imposed penalty, it remained for the Court to determine whether these provisions prescribed these penalties with sufficient foreseeability.[812] The foreseeability of the penalties for the applicant's conduct was questionable because the applicable sentencing regime was determined by the choice of jurisdiction. The choice of jurisdiction for prosecuting the applicant depended on the public prosecutor. Since the prosecutor's decision was not limited by legal criteria,[813] the applicable maximum penalty was, in effect, subject to the unfettered discretion of the public prosecutor.[814] As a result, the law had not made it possible to foresee which sentencing regime, and, notably, which mandatory minimum sentence[815] applied to the applicant's acts.[816] In light of the unfettered discretion of the prosecutor, the domestic provision providing for two sentencing regimes failed to satisfy the foreseeability requirement and, hence, violated Article 7 ECHR.[817]

---

806 See para 146.

807 See para 148. On the scope of Article 7(1) ECHR, second sentence, see subsection 3.3.3.

808 See para 148.

809 See para 150.

810 See para 150, 152. Cf Schabas 2015, p. 336–337 and see, critically, Murphy 2010, p. 202; Sanz-Caballero 2017, p. 794–796.

811 See para 39.

812 See para 40.

813 See para 43. According to Judge Quintano, however, the domestic case-law enabled the applicant to foresee the applicable penalty for his acts, see para 11 of the partly dissenting opinion of judge Quintano in *Camilleri v. Malta*.

814 See para 42.

815 See para 43.

816 See para 41, 44.

817 See para 44–45. This approach is in line with case-law on other Convention rights, because the Court has often required the establishment of legal criteria that limit the

3.7.3 THE PROHIBITION ON THE OVERLY EXTENSIVE INTERPRETATION OF A PENALTY (*LEX STRICTA*)

Recent case-law identified the judgment in *Başkaya*[818] as a prominent example of the application of a penalty by analogy.[819] In *Başkaya*, the domestic courts had sentenced a book publisher to a term of imprisonment for propaganda undermining the territorial integrity of Turkey. However, at the time of the offense, the relevant statutory provision defining the penalty for this offense had only prescribed the possibility of a prison sentence in case of offenses committed by an editor. If the offense was committed by a publisher, the provision only prescribed a pecuniary penalty.[820] The Court observed that, by nevertheless sentencing a publisher to a term of imprisonment, the domestic courts used a sentencing rule that only applied to editors to impose a penalty on a publisher.[821] This amounted to the application by analogy of a rule prescribing a penalty which, as a form of prohibited overly extensive interpretation of a penalty, was contrary to the *nulla poena* principle.[822]

Another example of the *lex stricta* principle with regard to penalties is *Alimuçaj*.[823] In this case the domestic court sentenced the applicant to twenty years imprisonment for violating a provision with a maximum penalty of five years.[824] Although the penalty imposed clearly exceeded the statutory limit,[825] the ECtHR examined whether interpretive case-law had made the application of a maximum sentence of twenty years foreseeable.[826] According to the Court, there was no domestic case-law providing for the multiplication of the applicable penalties to a term superior to five years, not even where the offense of deception had given rise to several injured parties as in the case at hand.[827] In order to justify the imposition of the twenty year sentence the domestic courts relied on a sentencing provision providing for a cumulative sentence in the case of multiple offenses.[828] However, at the time of the material acts, that provision stipulated that conviction of multiple offenses under two or more

---

discretion of the executive, see, eg, *Margareta and Roger Andersson v. Sweden*, CE:ECHR:1992:0225JUD001296387, para 75; *P.G. and J.H. v. The United Kingdom*, CE:ECHR:2001:0925JUD004478798, para 63.

818 *Başkaya and Okçuoğlu v. Turkey*, CE:ECHR:1999:0708JUD002353694.

819 See *Del Río Prada*, para 78.

820 See para 27.

821 See para 42.

822 See para 42–43.

823 *Alimuçaj v. Albania*, CE:ECHR:2012:0207JUD002013405.

824 See para 155.

825 A provision that entered into force after the applicant's conduct had provided for a maximum penalty of twenty years, but this provision was not formally used by the domestic courts so that a violation of the *lex praevia* principle was excluded, see paras 112, 152.

826 See para 156.

827 See para 155–156.

828 See para 158.

distinct provisions was a precondition for its application.[829] The case at hand did not satisfy this condition because Alimuçaj was only sentenced for multiple violations of the same offense (ie 57 923 counts of deception).[830] That the domestic courts nevertheless applied the provision on cumulative sentences in order to multiply the applicable maximum penalty amounted to an extensive and unforeseeable interpretation of the sentencing rules and, consequently, violated Article 7 ECHR.[831]

As is mentioned in subsection 3.3.3, the judgment in *Del Río Prada* is an example of an examination in light of the *lex stricta* principle regarding penalties. In this case, the Court examined whether a reversal of a judicial interpretation regarding the scope of a penalty to the accused's detriment was contrary to Article 7.[832] The Court noted that it needed to determine whether the new interpretation of the provisions on the remission of prison terms in the case of multiple offenses, was reasonably foreseeable to the applicant. Thus, the ECtHR used one of the two requirements it uses to assess a judicial interpretation in light of the *lex stricta* principle regarding *offenses*. With regard to the prohibition on overly extensive interpretations of a *penalty*, the Court omitted the essence of the offense requirement.[833] It probably did so because, with regard to rules prescribing penalties, the domestic courts are not altering the scope of the prohibited conduct, but only the scope of the penalty for unaltered conduct. This type of judicial interpretation will not, therefore, amount *de facto* to establishing a new offense and, for that reason, review in light of the essence of the offense criterion will not be necessary.

In order to determine whether the immediate application of the new judicial interpretation was reasonably foreseeable at the time of conviction, the Court reiterated that this would be the case if the new interpretation reflected a perceptible line of case-law.[834] This could have been the case when the judicial and administrative practice had consistently indicated that the statutory penalties would be interpreted extensively. Since judicial and administrative practice at the time of the applicant's conviction had consistently taken the opposite approach to that of the new judicial interpretation, a departure from this practice was not foreseeable.[835] Therefore, both at the time of conviction and when combining her sentences into a maximum term of thirty years, there was no indication of any perceptible line of case-law pointing towards to the new judicial interpretation.[836] The modification of the scope of the penalty to the

---

829 See para 159.
830 See para 155.
831 See para 160–162.
832 See para 112.
833 On that requirement, see subsection 3.6.3.
834 See para 112.
835 See para 112–115.
836 See para 117.

detriment of the accused did not, therefore, satisfy the requirement of reasonable foreseeability and was, consequently, contrary to Article 7.[837]

More recently, the ECtHR underlined the need to restrictively interpret a provision establishing a penalty. In *Koprivnikar* the Court assessed the permissibility of an interpretation of the statutory term 'twenty-year imprisonment' as allowing a prison sentence of thirty years by the domestic courts.[838] The interpretation – going beyond the explicit statutory limit of twenty years – was necessary, according to the domestic courts, because the legislature had made an evident mistake in establishing the twenty-year maximum for situations such as that of the applicant.[839] Even if the legislature had mistakenly enacted a twenty year maximum term of imprisonment for the applicant's acts, the domestic courts are not completely free to resolve this apparent deficiency. In the ECtHR's view, "(...) the only way for the courts to have ensured the observance of [the legality principle] and to mitigate the effect of the law's unpredictability in the present case would have been to interpret the deficient provision restrictively, that is to say to the advantage of the applicant".[840] The domestic courts should not have attempted to fill the legislative lacuna by immediately applying an overly extensive interpretation of the provision, they should have respected the apparently deficient statutory upper limit of twenty-years imprisonment.[841] By having imposed a prison sentence beyond the statutory upper limit, the domestic courts violated Article 7(1) ECHR.[842]

3.7.4 THE PROHIBITION ON THE RETROACTIVE APPLICATION OF A PENALTY (*LEX PRAEVIA*)

As with the prohibition on the retroactive application of an *offense*,[843] the test for retroactivity of a penalty is quite formalistic. In *Fruni* the Court found the complaint under Article 7 to be manifestly ill-founded, because the applicant was sentenced to a penalty under the applicable sentencing rules and the penalty remained within the statutory limit of those rules.[844] The fact that the applicant was sentenced close to the maximum of the statutory limit, and that new penalty rules provided for harsher sentences, did not mean that a harsher penalty was actually applied. If the penalty is formally based on the applicable rules, and remains within the limits set thereby, there can be no retroactive application of a penalty in the view of the Court. The possibility that the entry into force of new sentencing rules

837 See para 117.
838 See *Koprivnikar v. Slovenia*, CE:ECHR:2017:0124JUD006750313, para 53.
839 See para 55.
840 Para 56.
841 See para 57.
842 See paras 59–60.
843 See subsection 3.6.4.
844 *Fruni v. Slovakia*, CE:ECHR:2011:0621JUD000801407, paras 216–217.

might have motivated the domestic court to impose a higher penalty *under the old rules* is apparently not problematic in light of the *lex praevia* principle.

The same approach is also clearly apparent in *Del Río Prada*, because there the Court ruled out a violation of the *lex praevia* principle by determining that the domestic courts had formally applied only the law in force.[845] As noted with regard to the principle of non-retroactivity of an offense, a new judicial interpretation to the detriment of the accused can nevertheless amount to retroactivity in substance. Although the Court shared this observation in *Del Río Prada*, it only examined the judicial interpretation of the penalty's scope in light of the *lex stricta* principle.[846] Once again, this warrants the conclusion that the room for violating the ECHR's *lex praevia* principle is rather limited.

The protective scope of the *lex praevia* principle is, moreover, limited in cases where the description of the penalty is unclear. This follows from *Kafkaris* where the Court concluded that the domestic court had not violated the principle of non-retroactivity since the actual legal definition of the maximum sentence was not clear.[847] As a consequence, it could not be determined that the imposed sentence was clearly harsher than the one prescribed by law at that time. Therefore, the Court exclusively examined whether the definition of the penalty satisfied the quality of law requirements in light of Article 7 ECHR (ie the *lex certa* principle).[848]

Matters are different, however, when new sentencing rules are explicitly applied retroactively. In these circumstances, there is a *formal* case of retroactive application of new sentencing rules and the Court needs to determine whether the new rules are, in fact, harsher than the old rules. There are clear examples of this in the Strasbourg case-law. The ECtHR's reiteration of the general principles in *Del Río Prada* already refers to multiple cases.[849] In the first of these cases, *Welch*,[850] a confiscation order was imposed when, at the time of the offense, the law did not provide for confiscation after conviction for the applicant's actions.[851] Since confiscation amounted to a penalty in substance,[852] the law providing for the imposition of the confiscation order was retroactively applied to the applicant, and was, therefore, in violation of Article 7(1)'s second sentence.[853]

In *Jamil*,[854] the Court determined that imprisonment in default, ie imprisonment in order to compel the debtor to pay his debts to the State,[855]

---

845 See *Del Río Prada*, para 116. *Kafkaris v. Cyprus*, CE:ECHR:2008:0212JUD002190604, para 143.
846 See para 116–117.
847 *Kafkaris v. Cyprus*, CE:ECHR:2008:0212JUD002190604, para 149. Cf *M. v. Germany*, CE:ECHR:2009:1217JUD001935904, para 136.
848 See para 150.
849 See para 78.
850 *Welch v. The United Kingdom*, CE:ECHR:1995:0209JUD001744090.
851 See para 11, 26.
852 See para 27–35.
853 See para 26, 35.
854 *Jamil v. France*, CE:ECHR:1995:0608JUD001591789.
855 See para 32.

amounted to a penalty in substance.[856] At the time of the applicant's offense the law limited the time of imprisonment in default to four months.[857] The domestic court nevertheless applied a new law providing for a maximum term of imprisonment of two years.[858] That law had entered into force after the material conduct.[859] Since it clearly increased the term of the prison sentence, the domestic court had retroactively applied a harsher penalty to the applicant.[860] As a result, the domestic court had violated Article 7.[861]

In *Ecer*[862] the domestic courts used a provision prescribing a penalty that entered into force in 1991 to sentence the applicants for acts committed between 1988 and 1989. The 1991 provision increased the sentence compared with the rules in force before 1991.[863] The government argued that the use of the 1991 provision did not actually amount to retroactive application, because the applicants' acts were a part of an ongoing criminal activity which continued after the entry into force of the new law.[864] The ECtHR rejected the government's argument, since neither the prosecution nor the domestic court had explicitly considered the period between 1988 and 1989 to be the mere commencement of the applicants' offenses. The government's view that the applicants had actually been convicted for an offense that continued after the entry into force of the new penalty therefore lacked factual support.[865] As a consequence, the Court concluded that the 1991 provision had been used to impose a penalty on acts committed between 1988 and 1989. Since the 1991 law carried a heavier sentence than the preceding law, the applicants' sentence was contrary to the *lex praevia* principle.[866]

In *Mihai Toma*,[867] the last of the cases referred to in light of the *lex praevia* principle in *Del Río Prada*, a new law deprived the authorities of the choice whether to annul a driving license after a conviction for road offenses.[868] Under the law in force at the time of the applicant's conduct it was up to the discretion

---

856 See para 32.
857 See para 34.
858 See para 34.
859 See para 11.
860 See para 35. In *M. v. Germany*, the Court concluded similarly, because the domestic courts had retroactively applied a new law that abolished the previously applicable maximum duration of preventive detention. As the Court established that preventive detention amounted to a penalty in substance, the domestic courts had violated Article 7(1) ECHR by retroactively applying the new sentencing provision, see *M. v. Germany*, CE:ECHR:2009:1217JUD001935904, paras 123, 133, 135, 137. Cf *Glien v. Germany*, CE:ECHR:2013:1128JUD000734512, paras 119, 127–131. See about these judgments also subsection 3.3.3.
861 See para 36.
862 *Ecer and Zeyrek v. Turkey*, CE:ECHR:2001:0227JUD002929595.
863 Cf para 36.
864 See para 33. See about the potential relevance of a continuing offense in light of the *lex praevia* principle subsection 3.6.4.
865 See para 34–35.
866 See para 36–37.
867 *Mihai Toma v. Romania*, CE:ECHR:2012:0124JUD000105106.
868 See para 16.

of the police to annul a driving license and it was not an automatic result of a conviction for a road offense.[869] The Court examined whether the automatic annulment of the applicant's driving license after a conviction constituted the retroactive application of heavier penalty.[870] It first observed that, by applying the new law, the domestic authorities deprived the applicant of the possibility that his driving license might not be annulled, when that was possible under the law applicable at the time of his offense.[871] Replacing a non-mandatory penalty with an exact same mandatory one apparently constituted a harsher penalty. Since the new law did not provide for retroactive application, the applicant could not have foreseen that the new law might be applied to him.[872] The Court concluded that, the applicant's driving license was annulled ten years after the facts by virtue of a new law which lacked foreseeability, the authorities retroactively applied a new provision prescribing a penalty to the detriment of the accused.[873]

The emphasis on the foreseeability of the retroactive application of the new provision in *Mihai Toma* seems to imply that foreseeability can justify the retroactive application of a new penalty. If this were the case, the prohibition on the retroactive application of penalties would not be absolute. Other case-law does, however, treat the *lex praevia* principle as precluding the retroactive imposition of *all* harsher penalties. In *Jendrowiak*, for example, the Court underlined that a State's positive obligation to protect potential victims from inhuman or degrading treatment does not oblige the imposition of measures in breach of Article 7(1) ECHR.[874]

Although the above cases quite clearly concerned retroactive application of a penalty to the detriment of the accused, there are cases in which it has been tougher to determine whether the application of a new penalty disadvantaged the accused. The question about the accused's detriment depends on whether it is possible to determine that the new penalty constituted a 'heavier' penalty.[875] In *Maktouf* the ECtHR found a violation of the *lex praevia* rule even though the penalties imposed based on the new sentencing rules remained within the latitude of the old sentencing rules.[876] Since the new sentencing rules carried

869 See para 15, 27.

870 *Gurhuchiani v. Spain* also concerned a new provision removing the discretion whether to impose a penalty. In this case, a new sentencing provision was retroactively applied which amounted to the almost automatic expulsion of the applicant. In addition, the retroactive application of the new provision enabled the imposition of a longer term of expulsion. In the Court's view, the applicant's expulsion under the new law amounted to the retroactive imposition of a harsher sentence, see *Gurhuchiani v. Spain*, CE:ECHR:2009:1215JUD001601206, paras 43–44.

871 See para 28.

872 See para 30.

873 See para 31.

874 *Jendrowiak v. Germany*, CE:ECHR:2011:0414JUD003006004, para 48.

875 Cf Bleichrodt 2006, p. 656. For examples of case-law on this particular matter, see Schabas 2015, p. 349–350.

876 *Maktouf and Damjanović v. Bosnia and Herzegovina*, CE:ECHR:2013:0718JUD000231208, paras 69–70.

a higher mandatory minimum sentence than the old rules, it could not be excluded that the new sentencing rules increased the applicants' penalties. Although the Court could not be sure that the application of the new rules led to the imposition of a heavier penalty, the mere 'real possibility' that it did, constituted a violation of the *lex praevia* principle.[877] The Grand Chamber has since reiterated this 'real possibility criterion'.[878] As a result, the Strasbourg Court seems to have increased the protection provided by the *nulla poena* principle to cover *potential* harsher penalties based on new sentencing rules.

3.7.5 OTHER GROUNDS FOR VIOLATION OF THE *NULLA POENA* PRINCIPLE

In addition to the categories of violations mentioned in the previous subsections, there are examples of more straightforward violations of the *nulla poena* principle in the Court's case-law. In *Gabarri Moreno,*[879] the domestic court had erroneously convicted the applicant to eight years and one day in prison while the statutory maximum for the offense was eight years.[880] Since the applicant's sentence exceeded the applicable maximum prescribed by the Spanish Penal Code, the penalty imposed on the applicant breached Article 7 ECHR.[881] According to the Court, the principle of legal certainty that is inherent in the legality principle required – at a minimum – that the higher domestic courts corrected the imposed sentence so that it fell within statutory limits.[882]

Varvara[883] also concerned a violation of the *nulla poena* principle that can be distinguished from the ones described in the previous subsections. In this case, the applicant had not been convicted of an offense but his goods were nevertheless confiscated. The domestic courts deemed the confiscation possible in the absence of a criminal conviction, since they regarded the measure as merely constituting an administrative sanction.[884] The ECtHR nevertheless found confiscation to amount to a penalty for the purpose of Article 7(1) ECHR.[885] For this reason, the Court determined that a penalty was imposed without previously establishing the applicant's criminal responsibility by a criminal conviction. In effect, there was thus a penalty without a crime and,

877 See para 70. Cf Grabenwarter 2014, p. 182.
878 *Rohlena v. The Czech Republic*, CE:ECHR:2015:0127JUD005955208, para 56.
879 *Gabarri Moreno v. Spain*, CE:ECHR:2003:0722JUD006806601.
880 See para 27.
881 See para 31–32. Morre classifies this case as a violation of the *lex certa* principle, see Morre 2015, C.2.2.2.
882 See para 33.
883 *Varvara v. Italy*, CE:ECHR:2013:1029JUD001747509.
884 See para 60.
885 See para 51, 59.

according to the Court, punishing an individual without first convicting him is incompatible with the principle of legality in criminal law.[886] In the Court's view, Article 7(1) ECHR both prohibits punishing an individual for acts that did not lead to a conviction or acts committed by another individual.[887] Like in *Sud Fondi SRL,*[888] the Court reiterated that no penalty can be imposed unless personal liability has been established.[889] Since the penalty in the case at hand was imposed in the absence of the applicant's conviction, that penalty was not prescribed by law as required by Article 7(1) ECHR.[890] Consequently, the applicant's punishment was arbitrary and violated the Convention.[891]

3.7.6 RECAPITULATION

The scope of Article 7(1)'s second sentence is quite broad. The Court's autonomous interpretation of the concept of a penalty allows it to go beyond appearances and assess whether a measure amounts to a penalty in substance. Even though execution measures are outside the scope of Article 7(1), the ECtHR has sometimes deemed measures that mainly concern the execution of a sentence to constitute a penalty as well.[892]

The Court uses the requirements of accessibility and foreseeability to examine the clarity of the definition of a penalty. The protective core of the *lex certa* principle is once again provided by the foreseeability requirement and, as with the definition of an offense, the ECtHR reviews both the statutory definition and interpretive case-law in light thereof. Even when the statutory wording clearly prescribes the (maximum) penalty, the law as a whole can still fail to be sufficiently foreseeable. This will be the case when administrative practice or interpretive case-law has consistently applied the statutory provision in a more limited manner than the wording of the penalty allows. In those circumstances the applicable law as a whole (ie statutory law and case-law) will not have defined the applicability of the harsher penalty with sufficient clarity.[893] The same is true when the applicability of differing penalties is made dependent on the unfettered discretion of an official.[894] Even the unforeseeable application of penalties that

---

886 See para 61, 66–67.

887 See para 63–67.

888 *Sud Fondi SRL and others v. Italy*, CE:ECHR:2009:0120JUD007590901, paras 116–117. See further subsection 3.4.2 and, about the difference between *Varvara* and *Sud Fondi SRL and others v. Italy*, Bemelmans 2018, p. 214–215.

889 See para 69, 71.

890 See para 72.

891 See para 73.

892 See *Del Río Prada*, para 107, 110.

893 See *Kafkaris*, para 150, 152 and, conversely, *Achour*, para 52–55, 60–61.

894 See *Camilleri*, paras 44–45.

are, in themselves, defined with sufficient clarity, could make the definition of the applicable penalties fall foul of the Convention's *lex certa* principle.[895]

The criteria the Court uses to review penalties in light of the *lex stricta* principle differs from the *lex stricta* review of offenses. Instead of using both the requirements of 'essence of the offense' and 'reasonable foreseeability', the ECtHR only uses the reasonable foreseeability requirement. The obvious explanation for this is that when reviewing the judicial construction of penalties the Court does not need to consider the essence of the *offense*. It could be argued that since the essence of the offense merely precludes unreasonable interpretation of existing offenses, a functional equivalent with regard to penalties could certainly be constructed. It could, in fact, have been possible to determine whether a new judicial interpretation of a penalty had the effect of enacting a new penalty that did not exist prior to that interpretation.

The protective function of *lex stricta* with regard to penalties is exclusively provided by the reasonable foreseeability requirement. Like with the extensive interpretation of offenses, the Court looks at both statutory wording and case-law to establish the applicable definition of the penalty.[896] As long as judicial interpretations only gradually broaden the scope of a penalty they will not violate the *lex stricta* principle. As with the scope of offenses, the scope of penalties can therefore certainly be expanded if new judicial interpretations are deemed to continue a perceptible line of case-law.[897] The Convention's prohibition on extensive interpretation is, thus, not absolute with regard to penalties either and it, once again, enshrines only a prohibition of *overly* extensive interpretation.

With regard to the room for *lex praevia* violations by applications of penalties, the Court has been equally restrictive as with regard to offenses. As long as the domestic courts have formally applied the penalties in force at the time of conduct, a violation of the non-retroactivity principle is ruled out.[898] A violation of *lex praevia* is equally impossible if the description of the applicable penalties is not sufficiently clear at the time of conduct, because it will be hard to establish that the imposed penalties exceeded the existing limit.[899] The recent judgment in *Maktouf*, and its reiteration in *Rohlena*, nevertheless indicates a more protective approach to the *lex praevia* principle. In *Maktouf* the Court considered the *lex praevia* principle to protect against situations in which the application of new sentencing rules merely amounted to a real possibility of a heavier penalty.[900] It is not yet clear whether the ECtHR will, in all future cases, provide protection against the real possibility of a heavier penalty under the *lex praevia* principle.

---

895 Unfettered discretion for officials applying rules that limit the rights enshrined in Articles 8–11 ECHR could also fall foul of the Convention's prescribed by law requirement, see, eg, *Moiseyev v. Russia*, CE:ECHR:2008:1009JUD006293600, paras 246–251.

896 See, eg, *Alimuçaj*, paras 156, 160–162; *Del Río Prada*, paras 112–115.

897 See *Del Río Prada*, paras 112, 117.

898 See *Fruni*, paras 216–217; *Del Río Prada*, para 116.

899 See *Kafkaris*, para 149.

900 See para 70.

Things are more obvious when the domestic courts have formally applied *ex post facto* rules. When there has, in fact, been an explicit retroactive application of penalties the Court examines whether the new penalties are 'heavier' than the old ones. In the Court's view, a heavier penalty will, for example, have been imposed when the length of imprisonment is increased,[901] or when the domestic courts have applied a new, and previously inapplicable, type of penalty to the applicant.[902] Retroactively turning a discretionary penalty into a mandatory one also amounts to heavier penalty in the sense of Article 7(1) ECHR.[903] These cases are certainly precluded by Article 7's *lex praevia* principle with regard to penalties.

There are also more straightforward violations of the *nulla poena* principle. A clear example is when the domestic court exceeds the statutory limit without the retroactive application of new sentencing rules.[904] Another clear way to violate the *nulla poena* principle is by imposing a penalty without first establishing individual criminal responsibility. If a penalty is imposed without first determining that an individual committed a crime, the imposed penalty is not prescribed by law.[905]

3.8 THE ECHR'S LEGALITY PRINCIPLE: OBSERVATIONS IN LIGHT OF THEORETICAL DISTINCTIONS

3.8.1 THE ABSENCE OF *LEX SCRIPTA* AND THE EMPHASIS ON THE RULE OF LAW: A COMMON LAW LEGALITY CONCEPTION

In accordance with criminal law theory the Court recognizes the relevance of the Latin formulation *nullum crimen, nulla poena sine lege* for the Convention's legality principle.[906] The Court additionally identifies several specific requirements and prohibitions under Article 7 ECHR. Since the ECtHR referred to 'the principle that offenses and penalties require a clear legal definition', 'the principle that the law must not be extensively construed to the accused's detriment', and 'the prohibition of retroactive application of criminal law',[907] the Convention enshrines the principles of *lex certa*, *lex stricta* and *lex praevia* as

901 See *Jamil*, paras 34–35.
902 See *Welch*, paras 11, 26, 35.
903 See *Mihai Toma*, para 31.
904 See *Gabarri Moreno*, paras 31–32.
905 See *Varvara*, paras 72–73.
906 Cf section 2.1 and subsection 3.4.3.
907 See subsection 3.4.3.

elements of the legality principle.[908] The Convention does not, however, require that offenses and penalties are exclusively defined by *legislation*. Due to the broad meaning of the term 'law' in Article 7(1) ECHR,[909] the *lex scripta* principle does not constitute an element of the Convention's legality principle.[910]

The recognition of merely the elements *lex certa*, *lex stricta*, and *lex praevia* provides a first indication that, rather than a civil law conception, the Convention actually enshrines a common law legality principle.[911] By interpreting the substance of the legality principle in line with the common law conception,[912] the Court has limited the principle's protective elements to three instead of four. The exclusion of *lex scripta* was apparently deemed necessary in order not to dismiss, as a matter of principle, the judicial creation of offenses and penalties in, for example, the United Kingdom.[913] Although understandable from that perspective, the Court's broad interpretation of the term 'law' has undeniably narrowed the substantive scope of the legality principle from the viewpoint of the civil law conception. Article 7's substance has not been expanded since then, even though common law states are increasingly recognizing the need for legislative definitions of crimes and penalties.[914] As a result, the ECHR's legality principle continues to enshrine only three elements and the principle's substance is, consequently, in accordance with the common law conception.

The Court's general considerations on Article 7's object and purpose provide a further indication that the Strasbourg interpretation is more limited than the civil conception. This is because, contrary to the civil law legality conception,[915] the Convention's legality principle is not explicitly deemed to protect the principle of democracy or the doctrine of the separation of powers.[916] For that reason, Article 7 ECHR does not require the democratically legitimated construction of offenses and penalties. Perhaps consequently, the Convention's legality principle does not explicitly require a strict division of competences between the legislature and the judiciary either. Instead, the ECtHR merely reiterates that the legality principle forms an essential element of the rule of law and that it aims to effectively protect against arbitrary prosecution, conviction and punishment.[917]

---

908 For general considerations on these elements on the basis of criminal law theory, see section 2.3.

909 See subsection 3.4.3.

910 On *lex scripta* in criminal law theory, see subsection 2.3.2.

911 For an overview of the substantive differences between the civil law legality principle and its common law counterpart, see subsection 2.3.6.

912 Cf De Jong 1999, p. 689; Sudre 2001, p. 356.

913 The Court has explicitly aimed to accommodate the common law states by adopting a broad interpretation of the Convention's term 'law', see *Sunday Times v. The United Kingdom*, CE:ECHR:1979:0426JUD000653874, para 47. This approach has evidently influenced the Court's interpretation of the legality principle as well. Cf Sudre 2001, p. 346.

914 See subsections 2.3.1–2.3.2.

915 See, particularly, subsections 2.3.6; 2.4.3.

916 Cf Atrill 2005, p. 109.

917 See subsection 3.4.2.

By viewing legality as an element of the rule of law that aims to preclude the arbitrary use of crimes and penalties, the Strasbourg Court emphasizes the need for limited criminal law powers. It therefore evidently protects legal liberty. As determined in section 2.4, the exclusive recognition of the rule of law rationale does not necessarily protect a high level of legal certainty.[918] In fact, by precluding the arbitrary use of criminal law, it only provides certainty about the general functioning of criminal justice powers in accordance with the law. Contrary to the civil law approach which, through the additional recognition of the democracy rationale, aims to ensure the maximum predictability of criminal law,[919] Article 7 is apparently only committed to protecting legal liberty and the ensuing general legal certainty. As a result, and in conformity with the common law conception described in the preceding chapter, the Convention's legality principle does not protect the exact foreseeability of criminal responsibility and the applicable penalties.

3.8.2 THE SUBSTANTIVE PROTECTION OF THE CONVENTION'S LEGALITY PRINCIPLE

Subsection 3.8.1 illustrates Article 7 ECHR's proximity to the common law legality conception, both on substance and with regard to the legality principle's object and purpose. The apparent adoption of the common law conception provides a protective scope for the legality principle that is narrower than in the civil law conception. This is clearly perceivable, because the Convention's legality principle enshrines only three out of the possible four substantive elements and it recognizes only one of the two rationales that are recognized in the civil law conception.[920] As described in section 2.4, the proximity to the common law conception could very well affect the minimum level of legal certainty that is theoretically[921] protected under the ECHR legality principle. The present subsection will describe how the Strasbourg Court's approach to legality actually impacts the protection of legal certainty by successively revisiting the protection of the principles *lex certa*, *lex stricta*, and *lex praevia*.

The protection provided by the 'lex certa' principle

The Convention's *lex certa* principle requires offenses and penalties to be of a certain clarity.[922] The Court uses the requirements of accessibility and

918 See subsection 3.4.2. About the connection between the rule of law and the value of legal certainty outside the context of Article 7 ECHR, see, eg, *Lupeni Greek Catholic Parish and Others v. Romania*, CE:ECHR:2016:1129JUD007694311, para 116.

919 See subsections 2.4.3–2.4.4.

920 See subsection 2.3.6 and section 2.4.

921 On the practical attainability of the potential advantages of the civil law conception, see subsection 2.4.5.

922 See further subsections 3.4.3; 3.6.2; 3.7.2.

foreseeability to review whether criminal law satisfies this principle. The level of protection that the ECtHR has afforded this specific principle, and the ensuing legal certainty, has not been very high, however. There are several reasons for this.

In line with the common law conception of *lex certa*, the Court accepts offenses and penalties that are exclusively defined by case-law as long as they are sufficiently clear.[923] When statutory definitions do exist, the ECtHR will still consider case-law that interprets the legislative definitions. For that reason, the Court undoubtedly deems it the task of both the legislature and the courts to clearly define offenses and penalties. As a result, the ECtHR accepts both statutory and judicial definitions of substantive criminal law as long as they satisfy, at the time of the applicant's acts, the requirements of accessibility and foreseeability.

The Court has not always required conformity with these requirements at the time of the applicant's acts, however. In several cases, the ECtHR merely examined whether interferences with other Convention rights (eg Articles 8–11 ECHR) satisfied the 'prescribed by law requirement' which it found comparable to the requirements set by Article 7. If the Court merely points to whether the interference was prescribed by law to establish conformity with the *lex certa* principle, the protection will be diminished. This is because the Court will then, in fact, relinquish the requirement that the offenses and penalties need to satisfy the *lex certa* principle at the time of the material conduct. Instead, it will, in that case, only examine whether the offenses and penalties were sufficiently clear at the time of the applicant's conviction.[924]

By requiring conformity with the requirements of accessibility and foreseeability at the time of conviction the Court does limit the potential use of criminal law. By requiring a legal basis of a certain quality as the basis for a conviction, the ECtHR precludes the arbitrary use of criminal law. Merely requiring conformity with Article 7 ECHR's requirements at the time of conviction could, therefore, still be deemed to protect the rule of law. This approach cannot, however, be deemed to protect a high level of legal certainty. By not requiring conformity with the foreseeability requirement at the time of the individual's material conduct, the ECtHR does not ensure any, let alone the maximum, predictability of the criminal law. Merely reviewing whether interferences with other Convention rights satisfied the 'prescribed by law requirement', therefore, provides only a very limited protection of legal certainty.

However, reviewing whether offenses and penalties conformed with Article 7 at the time of the material conduct does not necessarily establish a high level of protection for individuals either. This is because the *lex certa* principle's requirements have not provided very demanding standards. It follows from the

923 See *Contrada*, para 66–70, 74–75; *Dallas*, paras 72–78. The Court's approach to *lex certa* is, inter alia, in line with the common law conception due to the absence of a *lex scripta* principle in the Convention, see subsection 2.3.3.

924 See subsection 3.6.2.

ECtHR's case-law that the first criterion for review, the accessibility requirement, will not generally be hard to satisfy. This requirement merely calls for *some* official publication of the statutory provisions and/or the applicable case-law defining offenses and penalties at the time of the material conduct. What is more, the Court will not generally conduct an in-depth review of the accessibility requirement in the absence of obvious complaints about inaccessibility.

The second criterion, the foreseeability requirement, does not set a particularly high bar for the definition of offenses and penalties either. This is partly due to the fact that the Court deems both statutory provisions and case-law as relevant factors for foreseeability. Therefore, the ECtHR accepts relatively vague statutory definitions of offenses and penalties as long as there is, at the time of the material conduct, interpretive case-law that enables the applicant to regulate his conduct. By accepting that a *combination* of statutory provisions and case-law potentially satisfies the *lex certa* principle, the Court does not provide an incentive to enact the clearest possible definition of offenses and penalties in *either* legislation *or* case-law. By allowing definition by a combination of legal sources, the ECtHR has arguably lowered the clarity demands for the distinct sources of crimes and penalties. The ECHR's broad concept of 'law' could thus have the effect of accepting a rather vague definition enshrined in one legal source so long as this is compensated by more clarity in another source. For that reason, the demands regarding clarity for each individual source is not, in principle, very strict.

That the Court allows offenses and penalties to be defined by multiple, complimentary, sources could diminish legal certainty. As a result of the ECtHR's approach, individuals are in fact required to consult multiple legal sources in order to gain insight into the potential legal consequences of their acts. The need to consult multiple sources to determine the applicable definition could complicate the predictability of potential criminal consequences for an individual. In this regard, the ECtHR does not ensure the maximum predictability of criminal law. It should be noted, however, that the diminished predictability will not easily result in the ECtHR accepting arbitrary definitions of criminal law. Even when several distinct legal sources define offenses and penalties, the Court will require the cumulative definitions to abide by certain standards. The cumulative definitions will continue to be reviewed against the requirements of accessibility and foreseeability. Through this review, the Court ensures the general certainty that definitions remain within certain legal limits and this approach is therefore compatible with the rule of law rationale.

That the *lex certa* approach essentially ensures only a general certainty by providing legal limits for definitions is also visible in the Court's interpretation of the foreseeability requirement. This is because the Court readily finds that the applicable legal definitions satisfy the foreseeability requirement. One reason for this is the fact that the ECtHR considers not only the wording of the definition itself, but also the field the text is designed to cover and the number and status of those to whom it is addressed.[925] This means that the context of an in itself vaguely worded offense can nevertheless make criminal responsibility foreseeable.[926] An important factor in this regard is whether the applicant acted in a professional capacity. If this was the case, the foreseeability of criminal responsibility will be accepted even more swiftly.

Another reason why foreseeability does not demand a lot from the relevant legal definitions is the fact that the Court examines the foreseeability of crimes and penalties from the perspective of an individual who took legal advice. The Court's reference to the ability to foresee criminal responsibility after taking legal advice diminishes the strictness of the foreseeability requirement compared with what would be required if the relevant perspective was that of a layperson.

The emphasis on the context of the definitions of crimes and penalties, together with the evaluation of foreseeability from the perspective of an individual who took legal advice, certainly moderate how clear the relevant definitions are required to be. Together with the acceptance of definitions via a combination of legal sources, the *lex certa* approach shows how the Court does not accept claims that offenses and penalties had been unforeseeable easily. Apparently, definitions of crimes and penalties do not need to enable regular applicants to foresee the exact consequences of their actions. It is sufficient that the applicable definitions, even if only in combination with other sources or within their broader context, provide notice that conviction and punishment *might* occur if the applicant continues to act in that way.[927] The law as a whole must generally be able to guide the applicant's behavior and prevent arbitrariness.[928] This shows that the Court deems a broad category of definitions acceptable. It does not require definitions to specify that certain forms of behavior will incur criminal consequences. Instead, it only requires a connection between the risk of criminal consequences and the applicable definitions. The ability to rely on the law is, therefore, protected only in a minimal fashion.

Taken together, the above-mentioned factors illustrate that the ECHR's *lex certa* principle provides a rather limited protection for individual legal certainty.[929] This limited protection of legal certainty is sometimes explained by 'the thin ice principle' which the Court has arguably incorporated.[930] Citing Lord Morris, Murphy described this principle as the idea that those who skate on thin ice,

---

925 *Cantoni*, para 35.

926 See further subsection 3.6.2.

927 See, eg, the references to the 'real risk of prosecution' in *Cantoni*, para 35, to 'the risk of being convicted' in *Achour v. France*, CE:ECHR:2006:0329JUD006733501, para 53 and to the predictability of the risk of being sentenced in *Custers, Deveaux and Turk v. Denmark*, CE:ECHR:2007:0503JUD001184303, para 81.

928 See *Žaja v. Croatia*, CE:ECHR:2016:1004JUD003746209, para 93.

929 Cf Sudre 2001, p. 352.

930 Murphy 2010, p. 200.

can hardly expect to find a sign that shows the exact spot where he will fall in.[931] Since the ECtHR requires the law to enable the foreseeability that certain acts constitute *a risk* of incurring criminal responsibility from the perspective of the individual that benefited from legal advice, the thin ice principle fits well with the *lex certa* approach. In line with the common law legality conception, the ECHR's *lex certa* principle is more about providing general legal certainty by precluding arbitrariness than about securing the exact foreseeability of crimes and penalties in specific circumstances. In effect, the Convention's *lex certa* principle merely requires a non-arbitrary use of the applicable definitions, which illustrates, once again, Article 7's rule of law rationale. Maximum predictability is not required.

The protection provided by the 'lex stricta' principle

The *lex stricta* principle precludes certain interpretations and applications of criminal law.[932] *Lex stricta* protection complements the protection provided by the *lex certa* principle. Instead of using the requirements of accessibility and foreseeability, the Court uses the requirement of reasonable foreseeability and, with regard to the interpretation of offenses, also the essence of the offense requirement.

The essence of the offense requirement does not offer much protection, because it merely appears to rule out interpretations of offenses that are unreasonable. Judicial interpretations of existing offenses can therefore certainly be expansive. As long as they remain reasonable, they will not be viewed as the judicial enactment of a new crime contrary to the essence of the offense requirement. The essence of the offense requirement, therefore, allows expansive judicial interpretations and the Court will not easily conclude that such an interpretation is prohibited as it amounted to an overly extensive interpretation to the detriment of the accused.

In order to determine the previously established definition of a crime, the Court's starting point is the offense's statutory wording. In addition, the ECtHR has been willing to consider the context of the offense and, sometimes, the function of individual legal terms enshrined therein. Since the Court accepts the inevitability of judicial interpretation of offenses, it also examines existing interpretive case-law in order to determine the essence of the offense at the time of the applicant's acts. In light of the multiple factors used to determine the essence of the offense, and the preclusion of unreasonable interpretations, there is considerable room for domestic courts to interpret crimes progressively and expansively. The room for expansive interpretation shows that the essence of the offense requirement does not protect the maximum predictability of criminal law.

Due to the undemanding essence of the offense requirement, and the absence of a functional equivalent with regard to penalties,[933] the substantive protection

---

931 Murphy 2010, p. 199–200.

932 See further subsections 3.4.3; 3.6.3; 3.7.3.

933 See subsections 3.6.3; 3.7.3.

against overly extensive interpretations is provided by the requirement of reasonable foreseeability. Reasonable foreseeability essentially requires that the law enables the individual, after taking legal advice, to suspect the potential imposition of specific penalties for certain acts and omissions at the time he intended to commit them. In order to determine this, the Court looks at the statutory wording, its context, an individual's professional capacity and accessible interpretive case-law. The ECtHR has accepted that judicial interpretations sometimes need to be expansive in order to progressively develop the existing law and to adapt the existing law to changing circumstances.

The Court's acceptance of the progressive development and judicial adaptation of the applicable law shows that the Convention's *lex stricta* principle does not protect maximum predictability. By allowing the judicial development of pre-existing definitions and their immediate application, the ECtHR does not ensure the exact foreseeability of the applicable law's content and scope. The Court could have protected the maximum predictability of criminal law by requiring that the law is developed and adapted outside the context of pending disputes. In that event, novel judicial interpretations could only be applied to acts occurring after the adaptation of the law took place. Although the ECtHR allows expansive interpretations to be applied to acts that preceded them, it has set limits to the judicial development and adaptation of the criminal law. This is because, judicial interpretations of criminal law always need to conform to, in any event, the requirement of reasonable foreseeability. The acceptance of the need for the law to limit potential interpretations illustrates, once again, that the Court does protect the rule of law under Article 7 ECHR.

As a result of the above characteristics, a novel and expansive judicial interpretation can be acceptable in the absence of indications pointing towards such an interpretation in the statutory wording of offenses and penalties. It is sufficient for conformity with *lex stricta* if accessible case-law indicates the possibility of the novel and expansive interpretation. The preceding case-law does not have to indicate the expansive interpretation very clearly, nor does the preceding case-law have to be univocal. It is sufficient that the new interpretation could be qualified as a gradual development of the scope of the offense and applicable penalties. One example of this is if the new interpretation continues a perceptible line of case-law that amounts to an evident evolution in the interpretation of criminal law.

The above remarks show how the requirement of reasonable foreseeability is closely related to the foreseeability requirement under the *lex certa* principle. As observed with regard to *lex certa*, the Convention's *lex stricta* requirement does not necessarily protect a high level of legal certainty. Although the foreseeability requirement itself already seems to protect only a low level of legal certainty, the level of certainty could be lowered under the *lex stricta* principle. This is due to the addition of 'reasonable' to the requirement of 'foreseeability'.[934] In fact, the emphasis

---

934 Cf Sudre 2001, p. 354–355; Viljanen 2003, p. 199.

on 'reasonability' seems to confirm that what is essentially excluded by the *lex stricta* principle is an *unreasonable* judicial interpretation of an offense or penalty.

By essentially precluding unreasonable interpretations, the *lex stricta* principle does not offer a high level of protection against extensive interpretations of offenses and penalties. It merely affords protection against *overly* extensive judicial constructions of crimes and penalties. By solely precluding overly extensive interpretations and their immediate application, the Court does not ensure the maximum predictability of criminal law. That the ECtHR does not (always) aim protect maximum legal certainty is also apparent in the case-law wherein the Court deemed the severe nature of the applicant's offense relevant for – arguably – lowering the level of *lex stricta* protection with regard to offenses.[935]

In conclusion, the legal certainty that is protected under the *lex stricta* principle is, once again, only the rather general certainty that the law is not interpreted in an arbitrary fashion. In this regard, the ECtHR's approach is, yet again, close to the common law conception with its exclusive recognition of the rule of law rationale.

The protection provided by the 'lex praevia' principle

The *lex praevia* principle precludes the application of offenses and penalties that were not established at the time of the applicant's conduct.[936] As long as statutory provisions have not been enacted retroactively, and domestic courts have merely applied the law in force at the time of the applicant's acts, there will be no violation of the *lex praevia* principle. In other words, as long as the conviction and penalty are *formally* based on the rules that were applicable at the time of conduct, there is no violation of Article 7's non-retroactivity principle.

The Court's formalistic *lex praevia* approach indicates that it offers straightforward protection from the retroactive application of criminal law. The ECtHR will only review the application of national law when it is not convinced that the domestic courts have *exclusively* applied the law in force at the material time. In order to determine whether the domestic courts have also used subsequent definitions of criminal law, it will assess whether the applicant's acts fell within the scope of the applicable law. To determine whether offenses and penalties were established by law at the time of the material acts, the Court looks at statutory law and case-law.

Although the ECtHR's formalistic approach limits the scope of the *lex praevia* principle, it has not, generally, diminished the intensity of the Court's review.[937] The ECtHR is, in fact, rather strict in upholding the prohibition on retroactive application. It prohibits, for example, the application of a new

935 See subsection 3.6.4.

936 See subsections 3.4.3; 3.6.4; 3.7.4.

937 Although *Mihai Toma* indicated that non-retroactivity would depend on a lack of foreseeability, other judgments treated the non-retroactivity principle as an absolute prohibition, see subsections 3.6.4; 3.7.4; 3.7.6. Cf Murphy 2010, p. 202–203.

provision to acts which were not criminalized – with sufficient accessibility and foreseeability – by statute and/or case-law during *the whole period* in which they were committed. As a result, Article 7 prohibits even the application of a provision that was, strictly speaking, only *partly* retroactive.

With regard to penalties, the protection provided by the *lex praevia* principle depends on the notion of a 'heavier penalty' enshrined in the second sentence of Article 7(1). The autonomous interpretation of the term 'penalty' enables the Court to potentially offer broad protection of the *nulla poena* principle.[938] The same could be true for the notion 'heavier'. Although most cases involved *ex post facto* criminal sanctions that were obviously harsher, the Court has quite recently used a new, relatively broad, criterion. Even the mere 'real possibility' that the retroactive imposition of a penalty amounted to a heavier sentence was sufficient for a violation of the *lex praevia* principle. By apparently precluding even the 'real possibility' of imposing a heavier penalty, the Court comes close to safeguarding the maximum predictability of penalties. Such an approach implies the protection of a high level of individual legal certainty, which fits well with the protection of legal certainty theoretically provided under the civil law conception of legality.

Despite the potential for a highly protective *lex praevia* principle with regard to penalties, the Court's general approach to the principle of non-retroactivity is largely in conformity with that under the principles *lex certa* and *lex stricta*. Since the ECtHR uses, inter alia, the foreseeability requirement to evaluate whether there existed – at the time of the applicant's acts – an applicable offense and penalty, it will not generally protect maximum predictability. The observations concerning the protection of legal certainty on the basis of the foreseeability requirement under *lex certa* and *lex stricta* are, therefore, largely transferable to the *lex praevia* principle. For that reason, the Convention's non-retroactivity principle commonly protects only a rather limited legal certainty instead of the maximum predictability of criminal law. The principle of non-retroactivity of penalties could be the noteworthy exception.

3.8.3 THE PROTECTION OF LEGAL CERTAINTY: A MINIMUM STANDARD

The apparent incorporation of the common law conception is not only visible in Article 7's elements and rationale,[939] but also in the Convention's protection of legal certainty. Instead of aiming to ensure the maximum predictability of substantive criminal law, the Court merely protects a rather general certainty by precluding the arbitrary use of criminal law. The ECtHR ensures that criminal

938 Cf De Hullu 2015, p. 90.

939 See subsection 3.8.1 and cf sections 2.3–2.5.

law powers are only exercised within legal limits, which is clearly in accordance with the legality principle's rule of law rationale. It could therefore be concluded that the exclusive recognition of the rule of law rationale under the Convention has influenced the protection of legal certainty in Article 7 ECHR.

The rather limited protection of legal certainty by the Convention's legality principle is not inevitable, however. Although the Court allows the judicial construction of offenses due to the absence of *lex scripta*, the extent to which it accepts this could have been restricted. While continuing to recognize, as a point of departure, that legislation can never be absolutely clear and some vagueness has to be permitted,[940] the ECtHR could have been more critical about the application of unclear statutory provisions in individual cases. It could have easily established the requirement that statutory definitions need to be sufficiently clear in the majority of cases as a precondition for conformity with *lex certa*. Such a requirement was never recognized, however, even though it does seem to be inherent in *Cantoni*. In that case the Court accepted definitions which gave rise to doubts about their applicability but only if those doubts were confined to borderline cases.[941] The reference to doubts about applicability in borderline cases shows how the ECtHR implicitly requires definitions to be clearly applicable in the large majority of cases.

Had the Court been more explicit about the need for clarity in the majority of cases, the ECtHR could have regularly reviewed the clarity of the applicable definitions as a first step. It could have then indicated, to the domestic lawmaker(s), whether the definitions generally provided sufficient clarity for individuals. By first reviewing the clarity of offenses and penalties outside of the broader context, the Court could help improve the quality of domestic law in light of the *lex certa* principle. The approach to legality would then come closer to the civil law conception by recognizing, to some extent, the need to ensure maximum predictability from the applicable (statutory or judicial) definitions alone.

However, instead of requiring a high amount of predictability from the applicable definitions, the Court has mostly looked at the broader legal context to ensure conformity with *lex certa*. This approach illustrates that the Convention's legality principle is about precluding arbitrariness rather than ensuring a high level of legal certainty. The *Grigoriadis* judgment illustrates this observation. In *Grigoriadis* the Court accepted a statutory definition that was couched in very broad terms because the ordinary meaning of the statutory term made criminal consequences for the applicant's acts foreseeable.[942] Since the domestic courts had apparently applied the definition in line with the ordinary meaning of the wording, the use of the criminal law could not qualify as arbitrary. However, conformity with the ordinary meaning of a legal term does not, in itself, make

940 See *Kokkinakis*, para 40; *Cantoni*, para 31.
941 *Cantoni*, para 32.
942 See *Grigoriades*, paras 37–38.

that term in the definition more clear, especially when that term is, as was the case, already very broad.

Grigoriadis illustrates that the ECHR's *lex certa* is about conformity with the rule of law and precluding arbitrariness. The Court does not place high demands on the clarity of individual legal definitions by requiring something closer to the maximum predictability of the criminal law. It merely requires that all legal sources together lead to consequences that are deemed to be non-arbitrary from the perspective of an individual that took legal advice.

As with *lex certa*, a more protective approach to the *lex stricta* principle could have also been possible without relinquishing the general characteristics of the present approach to legality. The Court's acceptance of the judicial construction of criminal law, for example, does not necessarily preclude the adoption of stricter limits to extensive interpretation in individual cases. This can be illustrated by revisiting the Court's evaluation of the marital rape case in *C.R. v. The United Kingdom*. Instead of accepting the expansive interpretations by the domestic courts, the ECtHR could have emphasized that, at the time of the applicant's acts, the law had not unequivocally and explicitly criminalized marital rape. By having recognized that some form of immunity existed for rape within marriage in the United Kingdom at the time of the applicant's acts, the Court could have precluded the complete abolition of this immunity to the detriment of the applicant. It could have concluded that, while it accepts the domestic court's decision to expand the scope of rape to forced intercourse within marriage, it cannot accept the immediate application of such an expansion in the case of the applicant. It could have pointed to the absence of legal sources criminalizing the applicant's behavior *unequivocally*. Instead of prioritizing the need to give room for the progressive development of criminal law, even in changed circumstances, the ECtHR could have attached more weight to the interests of legal certainty. It could then have then required a higher amount of notice from the existing law than the mere possibility that the existing law could be judicially expanded and applied as long as this is, essentially, reasonable and non-arbitrary. Requiring a pre-existing legal basis to unequivocally indicate that a certain act falls within the scope of an offense would come closer to ensuring the maximum predictability of substantive criminal law.

The above observations indicate that the Court could have protected a higher level of legal certainty under Article 7 ECHR, especially with regard to the principles *lex certa* and *lex stricta*. The absence of a *lex scripta* principle, and the ensuing recognition of room for judicial construction of offense and penalties, does not necessarily preclude such an approach. What does appear to have limited the protection of legal certainty is the exclusive recognition of the rule of law rationale. As a result of this rationale, the Convention's legality principle allows considerable room for the application of vague legal definitions and expansive interpretations as long as they do not result in arbitrary prosecution, conviction and punishment. For that reason, the Convention does not ensure the maximum predictability of criminal law. As a result, and in accordance with Article 53 ECHR, the Strasbourg legality principle could be deemed to provide only a minimum standard of protection.[943]

The specific elements protected by Article 7 ECHR, its object and purpose, and the level of legal certainty it practically protects all indicate the provision's conformity to the common law legality conception. At this point we can therefore confirm the hypothesis formulated in subsection 3.4.4: the Convention's legality principle reflects a common law legality conception.

943 Cf Brems 1996, p. 302; Christoffersen 2009, p. 275.

CHAPTER 4

THE PRINCIPLE *NULLUM CRIMEN, NULLA POENA SINE LEGE* IN EU CASE-LAW

4.1 INTRODUCTION

At present, the EU legality principle is codified in Article 49 Charter.[944] Before the Charter's entry into force, the legality principle was already recognized as fundamental right in the case-law of the CJEU.[945, 946] The judicial definition of the EU legality principle in *Advocaten voor de Wereld* has been especially influential.[947] In *Advocaten voor de Wereld*, the Luxembourg Court stipulated that the legality principle

> "(…) implies that legislation must define clearly offences and the penalties which they attract. That condition is met in the case where the individual concerned is in a position, on the basis of the wording of the relevant provision and with the help of the interpretative assistance given by the courts, to know which acts or omissions will make him criminally liable (…)".[948]

While Article 49 CFR and the *Advocaten voor de Wereld* provide explicit points of reference, they have not been employed consistently. Both before and after the recognition and definition of the legality principle as an EU fundamental right, the CJEU's case-law provides diverging indications about the relevance of the specific criminal law principle. As a whole, the Court's case-law is not presently consistent and clear about the EU legality principle's sources, scope, and substance. The aim of the present chapter is to survey the different strands of

---

944 See subsection 1.1.2 for the provision's wording.

945 The CJEU will be used as the general term for the Court of Justice. When referring to individual judgments, however, I will refer to the specific EU court that authored it; ie the European Court of Justice (ECJ), the General Court, or the former Court of First Instance (CFI). The present chapter will not just refer to the CJEU as 'the Luxembourg Court', but also simply as 'the Court'.

946 On the judicial development of EU fundamental rights as general principles, see section 5.5.

947 See Case C-303/05, *Advocaten voor de Wereld v Leden van de Ministerraad*, EU:C:2007:261. On this judgment, see subsection 4.5.4.

948 Para 50.

case-law and structuralize the CJEU's considerations to provide insight into the EU principle.

Before we examine the CJEU's judgments, it is helpful to say a word or two about the types of judgments that have been relevant for the development of the Union legality principle. When we consider that legality constitutes a criminal law principle it is perhaps unexpected that the relevant CJEU judgments are not limited to cases concerning criminal law *sensu stricto*.[949] Internal market law, for example, has been an important area for the development of the EU legality principle for quite some time. This is a result of the early influence of European Community law (hereinafter also: 'EC law' or 'Community law') on national criminal law. The reason behind this influence was, inter alia, because the EC Member States implemented non-criminal EC law (presently and hereinafter: EU law)[950] via national criminal law. For that reason, the Court was confronted with criminal matters when interpreting EU law, essentially on the internal market, even while the EC Treaty lacked provisions indicating a Community competence in criminal matters.[951]

Despite being controversial and contested, EU law's early influence on national criminal law resulted in a solid amount of case-law where the Court considered, sometimes implicitly, criminal law principles such as legality. This influence continues today under the Lisbon Treaty which, inter alia, replaced the EC Treaty with the presently applicable TEU and the Treaty on the Functioning of the European Union (hereinafter: TFEU).[952] In order for implementation via national criminal law to trigger the development of the EU legality principle, however, that principle needs to be applicable to Member States' acts. The recognized applicability of EU fundamental rights to the Member States' implementing provisions has therefore been indispensable for the legality principle's development as well.[953]

EU measures of a non-criminal character were not just relevant for the development of EU criminal law and the EU legality principle due to their implementation via national criminal law. EU criminal law was also shaped by punitive administrative sanctions: those that were directly imposed by EU institutions and those imposed by Member State authorities on the basis of EU

949 Cf Mitsilegas 2014a, p. 1359.

950 Although the pre-Lisbon judgments resulting from this influence concerned EC law, in the interest of uniformity and simplicity I will generally use only the term EU law. Chapter 5 will nevertheless employ the historical distinction between EC law and EU law in order to accurately describe the historical development of EU criminal law.

951 See section 5.2.

952 See Treaty of Lisbon amending the Treaty on European Union and the Treaty establishing the European Community, [2007] OJ C 306. References to the EU Treaty will hereinafter indicate the provisions in the Consolidated version of the Treaty on European Union, [2012] OJ C 326 (unless expressly indicated that an earlier version of the EU treaty is referred to). References to the Treaty on the Functioning of the European Union will also be to the Consolidated version of the Treaty on the Functioning of the European Union, [2012] OJ C 326.

953 See section 5.5.

law.[954] Sanctions imposed by EU institutions were especially significant, because they required an assessment of the direct conformity of EU acts with criminal law's protective principles such as legality.[955] An important category of these 'administrative' sanctions are fines for competition law infringements. These sanctions have resulted in a large number of CJEU judgments recognizing the legality principle.[956] Another relevant category of administrative sanctions are the so-called 'restrictive measures' imposed on suspected terrorists.[957] While not formally concerning criminal law, EU administrative sanctions have played an important role in the judicial recognition and development of the EU legality principle due to their quasi-criminal character.[958]

Paradoxically, EU legislation explicitly concerning criminal matters has not resulted in a large number cases on the EU legality principle. The Court has, in fact, only considered the legality principle's relevance in two judgments.[959] Although the Lisbon Treaty arguably increased the potential for the CJEU to test the conformity of EU criminal law with the legality principle, the post-Lisbon period has yet to see a judgment concerning the legality principle in the 'Area of Freedom, Security and Justice' (hereinafter also: 'the AFSJ').[960, 961] Due to the limited relevance of EU criminal law legislation for the development of the legality principle, the present chapter will mostly examine CJEU case-law on matters that are deemed non-criminal from an EU perspective. This particularity characterizing how the EU legality principle has developed will be examined in the subsequent chapter (ie sections 5.2–5.4) and invoked as a factor explaining the CJEU's approach to legality. Other explanatory factors, such as the particularities of EU fundamental rights protection, will be examined in chapter 5 as well.

As mentioned, the aim here is to survey the recognition and development of the principle *nullum crimen, nulla poena sine lege* in EU law. Since considerations with relevance for the legality principle have been made in very different contexts and using diverging formulations, the present chapter provides some structure by distinguishing different strands of CJEU case-law. This chapter employs a general distinction between judgments concerning implementation via national (criminal) law or domestic administrative sanctions on the one hand, and those that concern administrative sanctions imposed by EU institutions on the other. Sections 4.2–4.5 examine relevant case-law resulting from national implementation measures, while judgments on EU administrative sanctions form the subject of section 4.6. Section 4.7 contains concluding remarks.

954 Cf Dougan 2012, p. 87–88; Herlin-Karnell 2016, p. 233–234.
955 See Miettinen 2013, p. 2; Craig and De Búrca 2015, p. 406–407.
956 Cf Satzger 2012, p. 50; Harding 2016, p. 250; Herlin-Karnell 2016, p. 233; Klip 2016, p. 2–3.
957 Cf Cameron 2016, p. 545; Herlin-Karnell 2016, p. 238.
958 Cf Herlin-Karnell 2016, p. 244.
959 See section 5.3.
960 See TFEU, Part Three, Title V.
961 See subsection 5.4.4.

4.2 LIMITS TO THE DUTY TO GIVE FULL EFFECT TO EU LAW

4.2.1 INTRODUCTION

Early on, the CJEU established limits to the duty to give full effect to EU law. The direct effect of directives and the duty of consistent interpretation have both been limited in light of their potential effect on national criminal proceedings. The present section examines whether, and if so to what extent, the legality principle is at the foundation of the limits to EU law's effect in criminal matters. Subsection 4.2.2 examines the limits to direct effect and subsection 4.2.3 focusses on the limits to consistent interpretation. Subsection 4.2.4 contains concluding remarks.

4.2.2 LIMITS TO DIRECT EFFECT OF DIRECTIVES IN CRIMINAL MATTERS

Ever since *Van Gend en Loos* it is well-established that EU law is capable of having direct effect.[962] As a result, national courts can apply EU provisions, and individuals can rely on them, provided that they are sufficiently clear, precise, and unconditional.[963] It is not just Treaty Articles that are capable of direct effect, but also provisions of secondary Union law. The Court ruled that regulations,[964] directives,[965] and decisions[966] all contain the potential for direct effect.[967] With regard to directives, however, the ECJ has explicitly established a limit to direct effect. Even when a directive's provision is sufficiently clear, precise and unconditional, and the deadline for implementation has passed, it cannot be invoked *against an individual.* In *Marshall* the Court unequivocally considered that "(…) a directive may not of itself impose obligations on an individual and that a provision of a directive may not be relied upon as such against such a person"[968] (hereinafter also: 'the *Marshall* limitation').[969]

---

962 See Case 26/62, *NV Algemene Transport- en Expeditie Onderneming van Gend & Loos v Netherlands Inland Revenue Administration*, EU:C:1963:1.

963 See Craig and De Búrca 2015, p. 192.

964 See, eg, Case C-253/00, *Antonio Muñoz y Cia SA and Superior Fruiticola SA v Frumar Ltd and Redbridge Produce Marketing Ltd*, EU:C:2002:497, para 27.

965 See, eg, Case 41/74, *Yvonne van Duyn v Home Office*, EU:C:1974:133, paras 12, 15.

966 See, eg, Case 9/70, *Franz Grad v Finanzamt Traunstein*, EU:C:1970:78, paras 5–6, 10.

967 Framework decisions are not capable of having direct effect, see eg, Case C-554/14, *Criminal proceedings against Atanas Ognyanov*, EU:C:2016:835, paras 56–57.

968 Case 152/84, *M.H. Marshall* v *Southampton and South-West Hampshire Area Health Authority (Teaching)*, EU:C:1986:84, para 48.

969 The refusal of a benefit as a result of fraud on the basis of a directive is not, in the Court's view, the imposition of an obligation, see Joined Cases C-131/13, C-163/13 and C-164/13,

The *Marshall* limitation, which arguably amounts to the exclusion of 'horizontal direct effect',[970] has subsequently been reiterated in criminal matters. In *Pretore di Salò* the Court invoked the *Marshall* limitation in order to formulate a specific rule concerning the effect of directives on national substantive criminal law.[971] The ECJ concluded that, as a consequence of the *Marshall* limitation, a directive "(...) cannot, of itself and independently of a national law adopted by a Member State for its implementation, have the effect of determining or aggravating the liability in criminal law of persons who act in contravention of the provisions of that directive".[972]

Although the Court could have exclusively used the *Marshall* limitation to preclude direct effect in the main proceedings, it formulated the aforecited prohibition on determining or aggravating criminal liability on the basis of a directive (hereinafter also: 'the *Pretore di Salò* rule'). This additional formulation apparently resulted from the need to unequivocally prohibit using the directive in the manner intended by the referring court. In its order for reference, the domestic court had, in fact, mentioned the directive's 'undeniable possibilities' for broadening the application of national criminal law and its 'decisive importance' for criminal responsibility.[973] In light of this intention the ECJ evidently deemed it necessary to add a specific limitation to the general exclusion of horizontal direct effect. By protecting individuals from (aggravated) criminal liability on the basis of a directive, the Court, in effect, underlined the need for a domestic legal basis for criminal liability. Due to the demands it sets for the legal basis of offenses, the *Pretore di Salò* rule could be related to the legality principle.[974]

The *Pretore di Salò* rule has subsequently been reiterated in order to establish limits to the direct effect of directives in criminal proceedings, most prominently in *Arcaro*[975] and *Berlusconi*.[976] In *Arcaro,* the accused in the main proceedings was suspected of having discharged cadmium into the water without having obtained prior authorization.[977] This appeared to violate national criminal law, because provisions prohibiting the unauthorized discharge of certain dangerous substances had been introduced in Italy to implement a directive on water pollution.[978] Italian criminal law had, however, only expressly prohibited the

---

Staatssecretaris van Financiën v Schoenimport 'Italmoda' Mariano Previti vof, EU:C:2014:2455, paras 55–57. For further discussion of this judgment, see subsection 4.5.3.

970 Cf Craig and De Búrca 2015, p. 204.

971 Case 14/86, *Pretore di Salò v X*, EU:C:1987:275, paras 19–20.

972 Para 20.

973 Paras 17–18.

974 For some tentative considerations in this regard, see Joined Cases C-304/94, C-330/94, C-342/94 and C-224/95, *Criminal proceedings against Euro Tombesi and Others*, EU:C:1997:314, paras 42–43; Case C-457/02, *Criminal proceedings against Antonio Niselli*, EU:C:2004:707, paras 29–30.

975 Case C-168/95, *Criminal proceedings against Luciano Arcaro*, EU:C:1996:363.

976 Joined Cases C-387/02, C-391/02 and C-403/02, *Criminal Proceedings against Silvio Berlusconi and Others*, EU:C:2005:270.

977 See paras 2–3.

978 See para 8.

unauthorized discharge of cadmium by *new* industrial plants. *Existing* industrial plants, such as Mr Arcaro's, were exempt from obtaining an authorization.[979] Since the directive stated that *all* discharges required prior authorization by the Member State's competent authority,[980] the national court doubted whether the legal distinction between new and existing plants was in conformity with the applicable directive.[981] Therefore, the national court asked the ECJ whether, if Italian law was indeed contrary to the directive, it would be possible to give direct effect to the directive's provisions.[982]

After the ECJ determined that the directive did require the prior authorization of all cadmium discharges,[983] it examined whether the national court could rely on the directive's provisions in the criminal proceedings against Mr Arcaro. The Court considered it unnecessary to examine whether the relevant provision satisfied the criteria for direct effect,[984] because, due to the *Marshall* limitation, that provision could not be invoked against an individual.[985] The Court subsequently considered that the rule that a directive cannot independently determine or aggravate criminal liability was laid down in the 'same line of authority' as the *Marshall* limitation.[986] In the Court's view, the *Pretore di Salò* rule apparently entails a specific formulation of the *Marshall* limitation. According to this reasoning, the rationale for the *Marshall* limitation arguably applies for the *Pretore di Salò* rule. Instead of protecting the legality principle, the *Pretore di Salò* rule could then be viewed as protecting the rationale of the *Marshall* limitation which "(…) seeks to prevent a Member State from taking advantage of its own failure to comply with [Union] law".[987]

Additional doubts about the legality principle's relevance for the *Pretore di Salò* rule arise out of the *Berlusconi* judgment. In *Berlusconi* the ECJ interpreted several company law directives to determine whether the Italian penalties for, essentially, false accounting were 'appropriate' in light of EU law.[988] The referring courts doubted the effectiveness of the penalties, because, after the defendants' acts,[989] Italian legislation significantly reduced the potential sentences.[990] As in the later *Taricco* judgment,[991] the Court was essentially asked to assess the

979 See paras 10, 13.
980 See para 3.
981 See para 18.
982 See para 19.
983 See para 32.
984 See para 35.
985 See para 36.
986 See para 37.
987 See Case C-91/92, *Paola Faccini Dori v Recreb Srl*, EU:C:1994:292, para 22; *Arcaro*, para 36.
988 See paras 36, 52.
989 See para 26.
990 Cf paras 20–21.
991 Case C-105/14, *Criminal proceedings against Ivo Taricco and Others*, EU:C:2015:555. For further discussion on this judgment, see subsection 4.5.4.

effectiveness of Italian criminal penalties for the violation of a prohibition originating in EU law.[992]

In the ECJ's view, its assessment could not lead to the disapplication of the new Italian penalties, not even if these penalties violated the Union duty to impose appropriate penalties.[993] According to the Court, the duty to provide appropriate penalties for false accounting could not be relied on against Mr Berlusconi and others, because that duty was based on a directive.[994] It would be contrary to the *Marshall* limitation, the *Pretore di Salò* rule, and 'the essential nature of any directive' if national courts could invoke a directive against an individual with the result of applying harsher criminal penalties than would have been possible without the reference to the directive.[995]

Although the disapplication of the new Italian rules would indeed result in the applicability of the old rules which carried more severe penalties, that would not necessarily violate either the *Marshall* limitation or the *Pretore di Salò* rule. This is because the old Italian provisions on false accounting were fully, even *exclusively*, applicable at the time of the defendants' acts. The directive would not, therefore, impose an obligation on Mr Berlusconi *et al* that did not, at the time of the relevant acts, exist under domestic law.[996] Nor would the use of the directive determine or aggravate liability *of itself and independently* of national implementing law. In these circumstances,

> "[a]rguably the only consequence of setting aside the new rules as not compatible with [Union] principles concerning the adequacy of sanctions would have been the application of the former rules, any direct application of the directive provisions to the detriment of the individual being excluded".[997]

It cannot, therefore, be concluded that the existing case-law on limits to a directive's direct effect dictated the outcome of the *Berlusconi* judgment.[998]

---

992 On the duty to provide effective sanctions in the ECJ's case-law, see Timmerman 2016, p. 787–790.

993 See paras 75–76.

994 See, critically, Biondi and Mastroianni 2006, p. 564–566.

995 See paras 73–74, 77–78.

996 Cf Opinion of AG Kokott, para 151.

997 Biondi and Mastroianni 2006, p. 561.

998 Before *Berlusconi*, the Court explicitly dismissed the applicability of *Marshall* limitation and the *Pretore di Salò* rule to situations in which subsequent, more lenient, domestic criminal law would need to be disapplied on the basis of EU law. In those circumstances, according to the ECJ, the effect of EU law would be unproblematic, because national courts would merely need to apply the old domestic criminal law which was fully applicable at the time of the defendants acts, see Joined Cases C-304/94, C-330/94, C-342/94 and C-224/95, *Criminal proceedings against Euro Tombesi and Others*, EU:C:1997:314, paras 42–43; Case C-235/02, *Criminal proceedings against Marco Antonio Saetti and Andrea Frediani*, EU:C:2004:26, paras 25–26; Case C-457/02, *Criminal proceedings against Antonio Niselli*, EU:C:2004:707, paras 28–30. Cf Biondi and Mastroianni 2006, p. 563.

Since a domestic legal basis for the harsher penalties existed at the time of the defendants' conduct, the directive would not require the national court to look beyond the applicable domestic law to determine criminal liability or to impose penalties. For that reason, the use of a directive would not violate the principle *nullum crimen, nulla poena sine lege.*[999] Since *Berlusconi* nevertheless precluded the use of a directive, the rationale for the *Marshall* limitation and the *Pretore di Salò* rule appears to lie beyond the legality principle. As the ECJ recognized the principle of the retroactive application of the more lenient penalty as a fundamental EU right,[1000] that principle is the most obvious explanation for the Court's reasoning.

Formally, however, the Court did not invoke the *lex mitior* principle as a limit to direct effect in *Berlusconi.*[1001] The ECJ avoided the issue whether *lex mitior* applies if a new, more lenient, penalty violates EU law by considering the *Marshall* limitation and the *Pretore di Salò* rule to preclude the potential disapplication of the new rules.[1002] As a result, the Court took its existing case-law on limits to the direct effect of directives further than before and beyond what would be required by the principle *nullum crimen, nulla poena sine lege.*

With regard to limits to direct effect, the rationale of the *Pretore di Salò* rule remains obscure for two reasons. Firstly, because the rule has not been consistently reiterated in preliminary rulings on matters of substantive criminal law. In fact, in multiple preliminary rulings the Court has merely invoked the *Marshall* limitation to establish limits to direct effect with relevance for national criminal liability.[1003] This raises doubts about the intrinsic value of the *Pretore di Salò* rule for the limits to direct effect in criminal matters.

Doubts about the rationale of the *Pretore di Salò* rule arise, in the second place, from judgments where the ECJ explicitly recognized that rule. In these judgments the ECJ only reiterated the *Pretore di Salò* rule after first citing the *Marshall* limitation.[1004] It could, therefore, be argued that the Court considers the *Pretore di Salò* rule to merely constitute a specific additional formulation of the general *Marshall* limitation. When viewed as a non-

---

[999] Cf Opinion of AG Kokott, paras 145, 147–148, 153; Biondi and Mastroianni 2006, p. 562.

[1000] See paras 66–69.

[1001] Contrary to AG Kokott, who did examine whether *lex mitior* would preclude direct effect, see Opinion of AG Kokott, paras 158, 162–167.

[1002] See paras 70–71, 77–78. Cf Case C-574/15, *Proceedings against Mauro Scialdone*, Opinion of AG Bobek, EU:C:2017:553, para 167.

[1003] See Case 80/86, *Criminal proceedings against Kolpinghuis Nijmegen*, EU:C:1987:431, paras 9–10; Joined Cases C-74/95 and C-129/95, *Criminal proceedings against X*, EU:C:1996:491, para 23; Joined Cases C-304/94, C-330/94, C-342/94 and C-224/95, *Criminal proceedings against Euro Tombesi and Others*, EU:C:1997:314, paras 42–43; Case C-224/09, *Criminal proceedings against Martha Nussbaumer*, EU:C:2010:594, para 30.

[1004] See *Pretore di Salò*, paras 19–20; *Arcaro*, paras 36–37; Case C-235/02, *Criminal proceedings against Marco Antonio Saetti and Andrea Frediani*, EU:C:2004:26, paras 25–26; Case C-457/02, *Criminal proceedings against Antonio Niselli*, EU:C:2004:707, paras 29–30; *Berlusconi*, paras 73–74.

essential secondary formulation of the *Marshall* limitation, the *Pretore di Salò* rule is more closely connected to the exclusion of horizontal direct effect than to the legality principle. In that event, the limited effect of an unimplemented directive in criminal matters is best explained by the rationales of the *Marshall* limitation.[1005] Instead of protecting the legality principle, the *Pretore di Salò* rule then, arguably, intends to prevent Member States from taking advantage of their lack of implementation in criminal proceedings.[1006] As a result, and in contrast with the clear views of multiple Advocates General on this matter,[1007] it remains uncertain whether the legality principle actually corresponds with the *Pretore di Salò* rule.[1008]

4.2.3 LIMITS TO THE DUTY OF CONSISTENT INTERPRETATION IN CRIMINAL MATTERS

The effectiveness of secondary EU law is encouraged by the duty to interpret national law in conformity with provisions of Union law.[1009] This duty, which is deemed to result in the 'indirect effect' of, inter alia, directives and framework decisions,[1010] will be referred to as 'the duty of consistent interpretation'.[1011] The duty obliges national courts to try and give effect to Union law by interpreting national law in conformity with the EU provisions. This could require lower domestic courts to alter settled case-law of courts of last instance.[1012] National

---

1005 On the rationales for excluding horizontal direct, see, critically, Craig and De Búrca 2015, p. 204–205.

1006 Cf Groussot 2006, p. 192.

1007 See Joined Cases C-74/95 and C-129/95, *Criminal proceedings against X*, Opinion of AG Ruiz-Jarabo Colomer, EU:C:1996:239, para 54; Joined Cases C-304/94, C-330/94, C-342/94 and C-224/95, *Criminal proceedings against Euro Tombesi and Others*, Opinion of AG Jacobs, EU:C:1996:399, para 37; Case C-457/02, *Criminal proceedings against Antonio Niselli*, Opinion of AG Kokott, EU:C:2004:365, paras 53–55; Joined Cases C-387/02, C-391/02 and C-403/02, *Criminal Proceedings against Silvio Berlusconi and Others*, Opinion of AG Kokott, EU:C:2004:624, paras 141–142; Case C-303/05, *Advocaten voor de Wereld VZW v Leden van de Ministerraad*, Opinion of AG Ruiz-Jarabo Colomer, EU:C:2006:552, para 73.

1008 Cf Dougan 2012, p. 115–116. See, conversely, Peristeridou 2015, p. 213. The judgment in Joined Cases C-189/02 P, C-202/02 P, C-205/02 P to C-208/02 P and C-213/02 P, *Danske Rørindustri and Others v Commission of the European Communities*, EU:C:2005:408 could be viewed as recognizing a link between the *Pretore di Salò* rule and the legality principle, see further subsection 4.6.5.

1009 See, eg, Case 14/83, *Sabine Von Colson and Elisabeth Kamann v Land Nordrhein-Westfalen*, EU:C:1984:153, paras 26, 28; Case C-60/02, *Criminal proceedings against X*, EU:C:2004:10, paras 59–60; Case C-105/03, *Criminal proceedings against Maria Pupino*, EU:C:2005:386, para 43.

1010 See, eg, Craig and De Búrca 2015, p. 210.

1011 For a short overview of the (very different) other formulations for this duty, see Prechal 2005, p. 181.

1012 See, recently, Case C-441/14, *Dansk Industri (DI) v Estate of Karsten Eigil Rasmussen*, EU:C:2016:278, paras 33–34; Case C-554/14, *Criminal proceedings against Atanas Ognyanov*, EU:C:2016:835, para 67.

courts cannot, however, be required to interpret national law *contra legem*,[1013] or in violation of a fundamental principle of domestic law.[1014] In addition, and in conformity with the limits to direct effect in criminal matters, national courts cannot interpret domestic law in conformity with EU law when this would result in the determination or aggravation of criminal liability.[1015]

The limitation of the duty of consistent interpretation in matters of substantive criminal law was first formulated in *Kolpinghuis*.[1016] In this preliminary ruling, the defendant in the main proceedings was charged with violating a domestic regulation by selling goods of 'unsound composition'.[1017] The prosecution charged the defending undertaking with that offense, because it had sold tap-water with added carbon dioxide as 'mineral water'.[1018] To establish that these acts amounted to the criminal offense of selling goods of unsound composition, the prosecution referred to the provisions of Directive 80/777/EEC, which, at that time, ought to have been implemented in The Netherlands, but had not been.[1019]

This raised the question whether the national court would be required to interpret national law in light of the directive's wording and purpose.[1020] The Court answered affirmatively, but limited the national court's obligation by inter alia reiterating the *Pretore di Salò* rule. The Court stated that the

> "(...) obligation on the national court to refer to the content of the directive when interpreting the relevant rules of its national law is limited by the general principles of law which form part of [Union] law and in particular the principles of legal certainty and non-retroactivity. Thus the Court ruled in [*Pretore di Salò*] that a directive cannot, of itself and independently of a national law adopted by a Member State for its implementation, have the effect of determining or aggravating the liability in criminal law of persons who act in contravention of the provisions of that directive".[1021]

By the above consideration the ECJ expressly acknowledged the need for the protection of legal certainty and non-retroactivity in the criminal sphere. The Court apparently recognized that these general principles would be jeopardized

---

1013 See, eg, Case C-105/03, *Criminal proceedings against Maria Pupino*, EU:C:2005:386, para 47; Case C-441/14, *Dansk Industri (DI) v Estate of Karsten Eigil Rasmussen*, EU:C:2016:278, para 31; Case C-554/14, *Criminal proceedings against Atanas Ognyanov*, EU:C:2016:835, para 66.

1014 Cf Craig and De Búrca 2015, p. 213; Peristeridou 2015, p. 216; Altena-Davidsen 2016, p. 252. Prechal is less certain about the firmness of these limits, see Prechal 2005, p. 193–210.

1015 Interestingly, AG Elmer found it unnecessary and inappropriate to *additionally* limit consistent interpretation in criminal matters, see Case C-168/95, *Criminal proceedings against Luciano Arcaro*, Opinion of AG Elmer, EU:C:1996:107, paras 39–43. On the debated relationship between the general limitation of *contra legem* and the specific limitation in the field of criminal law, see Peristeridou 2015, p. 215–219; Altena-Davidsen 2016, p. 252–253; Klip 2016, p. 161–172.

1016 Case 80/86, *Criminal proceedings against Kolpinghuis Nijmegen*, EU:C:1987:431.

1017 See para 2.

1018 See para 2.

1019 See para 3.

1020 See para 12.

1021 Para 13.

when a national court used an unimplemented directive as an interpretive tool to determine or aggravate criminal liability independently from national law. In order to preclude such use of a directive, the Court employed the *Pretore di Salò* rule which it originally formulated to limit the direct effect of directives.[1022] By incorporating the *Pretore di Salò* rule in its considerations in *Kolpinghuis*,[1023] the ECJ confirmed that substantive criminal law forms a specific legal field which sometimes requires the limitation of a directive's effect.[1024]

The Court has relied upon the aforecited ruling in *Kolpinghuis* to set limits to the duty to interpret national substantive criminal law in conformity with other instruments of secondary law, such as regulations[1025] and framework decisions.[1026] Unlike with regard to limits to direct effect in criminal matters and the *Pretore di Salò* rule, the ECJ has explicitly linked the *Kolpinghuis* consideration to the legality principle. In accordance with the views of Advocates General Jacobs, Kokott, and Ruiz-Jarabo Colomer,[1027] the Court considered the legality principle relevant for limits to the indirect effect of EU law in the judgments *X 1996*,[1028] *X 2004*,[1029] and *Caronna*.[1030] In the pre-Lisbon rulings in *X 1996* and *X 2004*, for example, the Court related the *Kolpinghuis*-consideration to Article 7 ECHR.[1031] In these judgments the ECJ considered that consistent interpretation in criminal matters could violate either 'the principle that a provision of the criminal law may not be applied extensively to the detriment of the defendant, which is the corollary of the principle of legality'[1032] or 'the principle of non-retroactivity of penalties'.[1033] In the post-Lisbon *Caronna* judgment the Court related the *Kolpinghuis*-consideration to Article 49(1)

1022 See subsection 4.2.2.

1023 After *Kolpinghuis*, the Court has sometimes only used the *Pretore di Salò* rule to set limits to consistent interpretation and it has thus omitted a reference to the principles of legal certainty and non-retroactivity, see *Arcaro*, para 42; Joined Cases C-74/95 and C-129/95, *Criminal proceedings against X*, EU:C:1996:491, para 24; Case C-384/02, *Criminal proceedings against Knud Grøngaard and Allan Bang*, EU:C:2005:708, para 30.

1024 Cf Prechal 2005, p. 205.

1025 See Case C-60/02, *Criminal proceedings against X*, EU:C:2004:10, paras 61–62.

1026 See Case C-105/03, *Criminal proceedings against Maria Pupino*, EU:C:2005:386, paras 43–45 and, recently, Case C-554/14, *Criminal proceedings against Atanas Ognyanov*, EU:C:2016:835, paras 63–64.

1027 See Joined Cases C-206/88 and C-207/88, *Criminal proceedings against G. Vessoso and G. Zanetti*, Opinion of AG Jacobs, EUC:1989:644, paras 25–26; Joined Cases C-304/94, C-330/94, C-342/94 and C-224/95, *Criminal proceedings against Euro Tombesi and Others*, Opinion of AG Jacobs, EU:C:1996:399, para 37; Case C-457/02, *Criminal proceedings against Antonio Niselli*, Opinion of AG Kokott, EU:C:2004:365, paras 54; Case C-303/05, *Advocaten voor de Wereld VZW v Leden van de Ministerraad*, Opinion of AG Ruiz-Jarabo Colomer, EU:C:2006:552, para 73.

1028 Joined Cases C-74/95 and C-129/95, *Criminal proceedings against X*, EU:C:1996:491.

1029 Case C-60/02, *Criminal proceedings against X*, EU:C:2004:10.

1030 Case C-7/11, *Criminal proceedings against Fabio Caronna*, EU:C:2012:396.

1031 *X 1996*, paras 24–25; *X 2004*, paras 61–63.

1032 *X 1996*, para 25.

1033 *X 2004*, para 63.

Charter and 'the principle that criminal penalties must have a proper legal basis'.[1034]

The aforementioned case-law restricts consistent interpretation in order to prevent EU law being relied upon in the determination or aggravation of criminal liability or in the alteration of the applicable penalty to the accused's disadvantage.[1035] EU law thus establishes limits to the interpretation of *substantive* criminal law. Although limits to the judicial interpretation of substantive criminal law could be related to the principle of non-retroactivity, as explained in subsection 2.3.5, it is more appropriate to view these limits arising out of the prohibition of overly extensive interpretation (*lex stricta*).[1036] In accordance with the views of Advocates General Jabobs, Kokott, and Ruiz-Jarabo Colomer, the limits to the duty of consistent interpretation in criminal matters are therefore best regarded as an expression of the *lex stricta* principle.[1037]

The relevance of *lex stricta* for the *Kolpinghuis*-consideration becomes perceivable when we examine the preliminary rulings that linked consistent interpretation and its limits to the legality principle. In *X 1996*, for example, the ECJ was asked to interpret a directive so that the national court could determine whether the implementing provisions complied with EU law. The Italian implementing provisions imposed criminal liability for employers who failed to respect certain requirements of a directive on health and safety requirements for work with display screen equipment.[1038] The criminal responsibility of the defendants in the main proceedings hinged on the scope of certain terms in Italian law, which were arguably defined more narrowly than in the applicable directive.[1039]

Since the national court suspected that the directive required the broad construction of the definitions in the Italian law, it asked the Court for confirmation. In light of the intended use of the directive for the interpretation of domestic offenses, the ECJ felt obliged to first restate the limits to interpretation of implementing offenses. The Court referred to Article 7 ECHR and the ECtHR's case-law[1040] and considered the *lex stricta* principle, as a corollary of the legality

1034 Paras 55–56.

1035 See, more recently, Case C-554/14, *Criminal proceedings against Atanas Ognyanov*, EU:C:2016:835, para 65. Cf Case C-79/11, *Criminal proceedings against Maurizio Giovanardi and Others*, Opinion of AG Sharpston, EU:C:2012:297, para 69.

1036 The ECtHR has also taken that approach to *lex stricta*, see subsections 3.4.3, 3.6.3–3.6.4.

1037 See Joined Cases C-206/88 and C-207/88, *Criminal proceedings against G. Vessoso and G. Zanetti*, Opinion of AG Jacobs, EU:C:1989:644, paras 25–26; *X 1996*, Opinion of AG Ruiz-Jarabo Colomer, EU:C:1996:239, paras 57–63; *X 2004*, Opinion of AG Ruiz-Jarabo Colomer, EU:C:2003:326, paras 43–46; Case C-457/02, *Criminal proceedings against Antonio Niselli*, Opinion of AG Kokott, EU:C:2004:365, para 53–54, 60; *Berlusconi*, Opinion of AG Kokott, EU:C:2004:624, paras 141, 150.

1038 See para 5.

1039 See para 22. Cf *X 1996*, Opinion of AG Ruiz-Jarabo Colomer, paras 22–34.

1040 The Court referred, inter alia, to the related judgments *S.W. v. The United Kingdom* and *C.R. v. The United Kingdom*, which are relevant for the interpretation of the Convention's *lex stricta* requirement, see ECtHR, *S.W. v. The United Kingdom*, CE:ECHR:1995:1122JUD002016692;

principle, to constitute a general principle of Union law.[1041] It subsequently determined, unequivocally, that the national court is required to respect *lex stricta* when it interprets criminal law that implements a directive.[1042] In the ECJ's view, the *lex stricta* principle precludes "(...) bringing criminal proceedings in respect of conduct not clearly defined as culpable by law".[1043] Later in the judgment the Court added that the legality principle "(...) precludes any reference by the competent national authorities to the relevant provisions of the Directive when contemplating the institution of criminal prosecutions in the field covered by the Directive".[1044]

The Court's formulations imply rather extensive protection via the *lex stricta* principle.[1045] In the ECJ's view, that principle precluded *any* reference by the national court to the directive because that would jeopardize the clear domestic definition of the culpable conduct.[1046] This apparently broad protection of *lex stricta* is also perceivable in the later *Caronna* judgment. In this preliminary ruling, the Italian *Tribunale di Palermo* asked the ECJ whether Directive 2009/120/EC obliged pharmacists, such as Mr Caronna, to obtain an authorization prior to the sale of medicinal products.[1047] If that were the case, Italian law, which appeared to exclude criminal responsibility for the unauthorized sale of medication by pharmacists,[1048] would, in principle, have to be interpreted in conformity with the directive. As a result, the unauthorized sale of medication by pharmacists could become subject to criminal liability due to EU law's effect on Italian law.

The Court concluded that Directive 2009/120/EC indeed required pharmacists to obtain a prior authorization, even when they were authorized by national law to operate as a wholesaler for medicinal products.[1049] The ECJ then reiterated the full *Kolpinghuis*-consideration to limit the duty of consistent interpretation in criminal matters.[1050] It subsequently related the limits to consistent interpretation to the Charter's legality principle. In the Court's view, Article 49(1) Charter prohibits the use of a directive which determines or aggravates criminal liability that is not expressly provided for by a provision of domestic law.[1051] A directive would evidently have that prohibited effect if the applicable Italian law was interpreted in conformity with Directive 2009/120/

ECtHR, *C.R. v. The United Kingdom*, CE:ECHR:1995:1122JUD002019092. For further discussion of these judgments, see subsection 3.6.3.

1041 See para 25.

1042 See para 26.

1043 Para 25.

1044 Para 31.

1045 The Court has apparently offered broad protection for *lex stricta* as proposed by AG Ruiz-Jarabo Colomer, see *X 1996*, Opinion of AG, paras 40–41, 45, 58, 63, 74.

1046 Cf Altena-Davidsen 2016, p. 250–251.

1047 Paras 26–27.

1048 Para 19.

1049 Para 41.

1050 See paras 51–52. For a recent reiteration of the full *Kolpinghuis*-consideration, see Case C-554/14, *Criminal proceedings against Atanas Ognyanov*, EU:C:2016:835, paras 63–64.

1051 See paras 53, 55.

EC when domestic law excluded pharmacists from liability at the time of Mr Caronna's acts.

The ECJ's noteworthy formulation of the Charter's legality principle contains clues about the protection established against extensive interpretation. Instead of 'the principle of legality of criminal offenses and penalties', the Court considered Article 49(1) Charter to enshrine 'the principle that criminal penalties must have a proper legal basis'. The use of the broad terms 'proper legal basis' appears to allow definitions of prohibited conduct by either legislation or case-law. Other formulations in *Caronna* make it highly questionable whether the ECJ would actually allow the imposition of criminal penalties on the sole basis of judicial definitions of offenses. By establishing limits to EU law's effect on the basis of Article 49(1) Charter, the Court stated that the use of a directive would be prohibited if it would lead to the imposition of criminal penalties for conduct that was not within the scope of an *express provision* of applicable Italian law. The use of the term 'provision' implies that Article 49(1) Charter prohibits the determination of criminal liability in the absence of applicable *statutory* domestic law.[1052] The Court's formulation could therefore be considered a recognition of a *lex scripta* principle.[1053]

This interpretation is confirmed by the apparent need for an 'express provision' of domestic law to prohibit the relevant conduct. This wording implies that, if the conduct is not prohibited on the basis of the explicit wording of the applicable domestic law, a directive cannot be used as the basis for criminal responsibility and penal sanctions. By this formulation the ECJ thus seems to exclude any expansive interpretation of the wording of domestic criminal law on the basis of Union law. On this view, the Court would *absolutely* prohibit extensive judicial interpretation of offenses.[1054] The apparent absolute prohibition on extensive interpretation formulated in *X 1996* is therefore supported by the formulations in *Caronna*. It could thus still be maintained that the ECJ absolutely precludes national courts from expansively interpreting substantive criminal law.

It should be noted, however, that the need for limits to consistent interpretation in criminal matters have not been explicitly recognized without exception. In fact, just a year before *Caronna*, and equally concerning a directive on medicinal products, the Court failed to recognize the relevance of the limits to consistent interpretation or the legality principle. This occurred in

1052 The need for a domestic *statutory* legal basis for the determination or aggravation of criminal liability is arguably perceivable in the *Kolpinghuis*-consideration. The term 'national law' indicates legislation in other language versions as well, see, for example, *nationale wet* (Dutch), *innerstaatlichen Rechtsvorschriften* (German), *loi interne* (French), *legge interna* (Italian). Cf Altena-Davidsen 2016, p. 106.

1053 This appears to be the view of Advocate General Bobek as well, see Case C-574/15, *Proceedings against Mauro Scialdone*, Opinion of AG Bobek, EU:C:2017:553, para 148.

1054 Cf *X 1996*, para 31.

Damgaard,[1055] a preliminary ruling that arose out of criminal proceedings for the advertisement of unlawful medicinal products. Damgaard was prosecuted because he had provided information on the supposed positive effects of an unlawful medicinal product on his website, although he had no commercial interest in the sale thereof.[1056] Since the Danish provision on advertising unlawful medicinal products implemented the prohibition on advertising in Directive 2001/83, the ECJ was asked to determine the scope of the term 'advertisement' in the directive.[1057]

The ECJ did not construe the term narrowly. Since the directive's wording did not specify the people disseminating information on medicinal products, even information provided by an independent third party such as Damgaard could constitute advertisement. This interpretation was clearly purposive, as the Court determined that the goal of the prohibition – the protection of public health – was liable to be harmed not only when information on unlawful medicinal products is provided by commercial parties, but also when this information is disseminated by independent third parties.[1058]

Since the interpretation of the term advertisement in the directive, in effect, determined the scope of criminal liability in the main proceedings, the Court could have acknowledged the impact of its interpretation for the judicial interpretation of national criminal law implementing the directive. As in *Caronna*, it could have underlined that its interpretation of the directive could not have the effect of determining or aggravating criminal liability in the main proceedings.[1059] By, instead, merely interpreting the directive, the ECJ disregarded the potential effect of its purposive interpretation on the interpretation of term advertisement under Danish criminal law.[1060] Since the Court did not construe the term in the directive narrowly, the Court's interpretation could result in an extensive judicial interpretation by the referring court.[1061] Given this possibility following the interpretation of the directive, the ECJ could have been expected to underline the need for the referring court's interpretation to respect the EU legality principle.

4.2.4 CONCLUDING REMARKS

The judicially established limits to the effect of EU law in criminal matters can be related to the legality principle. With regard to limits to the direct effect of

1055 Case C-421/07, *Criminal Proceedings against Frede Damgaard*, EU:C:2009:222. Cf. Peristeridou 2015, p. 213–214.
1056 See paras 11–12.
1057 See para 15.
1058 See paras 16–17, 22.
1059 Cf Case C-224/09, *Criminal proceedings against Martha Nussbaumer*, EU:C:2010:594, paras 29–30.
1060 Cf Dougan 2012, p. 117.
1061 Cf Klip 2016, p. 197.

directives, however, the rationale of the *Pretore di Salò* rule remains open to diverging interpretations. Partly due to the Court's reasoning in *Arcaro* and *Berlusconi*, it is not clear whether the effect of directives is indeed limited on the basis of the legality principle.

Matters are different with regard to limits to consistent interpretation. The ECJ related limits to EU law's indirect effect to the protection of the legality principle in *X 1996*, *X 2004* and *Caronna*. The legality principle has thus been invoked to limit the influence of Union law on the interpretation of domestic substantive criminal law.[1062] As mentioned, these limits to judicial interpretation are best regarded as an expression of the legality principle's *lex stricta* element. As *Damgaard* illustrates, however, the Court does not always recognize the relevance of these limits.

The ECJ's considerations on limits to consistent interpretation imply a high level of protection of the *lex stricta* element. The Luxembourg Court, indeed, appeared to prohibit any expansive interpretation of the statutory wording of criminal law. By requiring the existence of a statutory legal basis for the determination of criminal liability as *Caronna* indicates, and by apparently precluding all expansive interpretations of that provision, the ECJ arguably protects the element *lex scripta* in addition to *lex stricta*. It is, moreover, noteworthy that – unlike the ECtHR – the Luxembourg Court appears to preclude certain interpretations by the domestic courts and not just the possibility, for these courts, to immediately apply certain interpretations to the detriment of the accused.[1063]

4.3 THE PRINCIPLE THAT PENALTIES MUST HAVE A PROPER LEGAL BASIS

4.3.1 INTRODUCTION

In addition to the Charter's legality principle and the general EU principle based on references to Article 7 ECHR,[1064] the Court has recognized the principle that penalties must have proper legal basis. For this principle to apply, it is not necessary to determine that provisions constitute a 'criminal offense' or prescribe a 'penalty' within the meaning of Article 49 Charter or Article 7 ECHR. This is because, in the ECJ's view, "(…) a penalty, even of a non-criminal nature, cannot be imposed unless it rests on a clear and unambiguous legal basis (…)".[1065]Although the requirement of a clear legal basis thus appears

1062 See also subsection 4.6.5 about the relevance, in this regard, of Joined Cases C-189/02 P, C-202/02 P, C-205/02 P TO C-208/02 P and C-213/02 P, *Danske Rørindustri and Others v Commission of the European Communities*, EU:C:2005:408.

1063 See Altena-Davidsen 2016, p. 255.

1064 See, eg, *X 1996*; *X 2004*; *Caronna* as described in subsection 4.2.3.

1065 Case 117/83, *Karl Könecke GmbH & Co. KG, Fleischwarenfabrik v Bundesanstalt für landwirtschaftliche Marktordnung*, EU:C:1984:288, para 11.

to constitute a self-standing principle, the judgment in *Caronna* illustrates that a relationship exists between this requirement and the legality principle.[1066]

The present section examines the Luxembourg Court's case-law on the principle that penalties must have a proper legal basis. Subsection 4.3.2 determines the scope and substance of this principle and subsection 4.3.3 aims to clarify the relationship of the requirement of a proper legal basis with the legality principle. Subsection 4.3.4 contains concluding observations.

4.3.2 THE REQUIREMENT OF A PROPER LEGAL BASIS FOR PENALTIES AS A SELF-STANDING PRINCIPLE

The Court first established the need for penalties to rest on a clear and unambiguous legal basis in *Könecke*.[1067] The main proceedings in this preliminary ruling concerned agricultural aid for the storage of beef and veal. After having determined that the undertaking Könecke had falsely applied for aid, the German Federal Office for the Organization of Agricultural Markets demanded repayment. At the same time, it declared Könecke's deposit to the Federal Office forfeit as a result of the fraud.[1068] At that time, however, the deposit had erroneously been released back to the German undertaking.

The opportunity to require the repayment of a wrongly released deposit was not expressly provided for by the applicable EU regulation.[1069] Such an obligation would, in the Court's view, constitute a penalty for failing to store the products in accordance with EU law.[1070] Although the absence of a penalty to store beef and veal in accordance with Union law may represent a lacuna in the deposit system, this determination could at most provide an argument to interpret existing provisions as including a legal basis for a penalty.[1071] It could not, however, provide a clear and unambiguous basis for the imposition of a penalty.[1072] Since provisions imposing penalties need to satisfy certain requirements as a matter of Union law, the domestic authorities could not impose a penalty in the absence of a sufficient legal basis.[1073] As a result, the ECJ apparently prioritized the need for an unambiguous legal basis over the effective penalization of violations of EU law.[1074]

1066 See subsection 4.2.3.

1067 Case 117/83, *Karl Könecke GmbH & Co. KG, Fleischwarenfabrik v Bundesanstalt für landwirtschaftliche Marktordnung*, EU:C:1984:288, para 11.

1068 See para 3.

1069 See para 13.

1070 See para 15.

1071 See para 16.

1072 See para 16.

1073 See paras 16–17.

1074 Cf Altena-Davidsen 2016, p. 102.

The preliminary ruling in *Milchwerke Köln* confirmed *Könecke*.[1075] Milchwerke Köln, a purchaser of cow milk, was held liable to pay additional levies for having purchased milk in excess of the maximum quantity determined by EU law.[1076] On the basis of the applicable regulation, Member States were given two, mutually exclusive, possibilities to establish responsibility for the payment of additional levies. The Member States could establish liability for either the milk producers or, alternatively, for the purchasers.[1077] Since Germany had provided liability for producers, Milchwerke Köln, as a purchaser of milk, could not be liable to pay an additional levy.[1078] In the view of the German collection authority it should be possible to oblige the purchaser to pay an additional levy if that entity committed fraud.[1079] While underlining the need to combat fraudulent transactions, the ECJ precluded the imposition of a penalty consisting in the substitution of the purchaser's liability for that of the producer. In the Court's view, such a penalty "(…) presupposes the existence of a legal basis laying down the conditions for, and the scope of, that penalty".[1080] The imposition of a penalty was thus again precluded by EU law due to the absence of a sufficient legal basis.

In *SGS Belgium*, another preliminary ruling concerning EU fraud, the Court examined elaborately whether sufficient legal bases existed for the imposition of a penalty.[1081] SGS Belgium challenged the penalty that the Belgian authority imposed on it for having enabled another undertaking to obtain a refund for the export of beef to which it was not entitled.[1082] It was contested whether EU law provided a legal basis for the imposition of a penalty for irregularities regarding export refunds committed by those other than the exporter.[1083] In the ECJ's view, the provisions of Regulation 2988/95 did not provide a sufficient basis for the imposition of administrative penalties. The Court determined that

> "(…) those provisions merely lay down general rules for supervision and penalties for the purpose of safeguarding the EU's financial interests (…). In particular, those provisions do not specify which of the penalties listed in Article 5 of Regulation No 2988/95 should be applied in the case of an irregularity detrimental to the EU's financial interests nor the category of operators on whom such penalties are to be imposed in such cases".[1084]

1075 Case C-352/92, *Milchwerke Köln/Wuppertal eG v Hauptzollamt Köln-Rheinau*, EU:C:1994:294.
1076 See paras 3–4.
1077 See paras 14–15.
1078 See para 15.
1079 See para 19.
1080 Para 22.
1081 Case C-367/09, *Belgische Interventie- en Restitutiebureau v SGS Belgium NV and Others*, EU:C:2010:648.
1082 See paras 2, 16–23.
1083 See para 25.
1084 Para 36.

Although neither Regulation 2988/95 nor specific EU sectoral rules contained provisions that could directly form the basis for penalties,[1085] domestic legal bases potentially could.[1086] In fact, Article 325 TFEU and the 'principle of sincere cooperation'[1087] enshrined in Article 4(3) TEU, entitle Member States to impose penalties on undertakings such as SGS Belgium.[1088] In the ECJ's view, the requirement of effective penalization of EU fraud should even prevail over a literal interpretation of the regulation's 'legality principle'. The Court considered the penalization of SGS Belgium possible on the sole basis of domestic law,[1089] despite the wording of Article 2(2) of Regulation 2988/95, which "(...) provides, in keeping with the principle of legality of criminal offenses and penalties, that no administrative penalty may be imposed unless an EU act prior to the irregularity has made provision for it".[1090]

Although Article 2(2)'s 'legality principle' literally requires a Union legal basis for the imposition of administrative penalties, the Court concluded that domestic law could provide a sufficient legal basis in the absence of employable EU provisions. The domestic law would have to meet certain standards, however, because EU law only allows penalties to be imposed when they rest on a clear and unambiguous legal basis.[1091] As a result of this requirement, the referring court should determine whether the domestic legal bases for the imposition of the penalty were sufficiently clear and unambiguous.

On the basis of the judgments discussed above, the principle that penalties must have a proper legal basis evidently constitutes a self-standing principle.[1092] It appears to have a wider scope than the legality principle, as it unequivocally applies to non-criminal penalties. The above judgments nevertheless indicate substantive overlap between the legality principle and the requirement for a proper legal basis. In fact, the need for a clear and unambiguous legal basis for penalties is clearly comparable to the *lex certa* requirement of the legality principle. It could therefore be concluded that the principle that penalties must have a proper legal basis establishes a *lex certa* requirement for all EU and implementing provisions

---

1085 Cf para 37.

1086 See para 43. See, conversely, *SGS Belgium*, Opinion of Advocate General Kokott, EU:C:2010:440, para 76.

1087 A variety of terminology is used to refer to this principle, eg, 'the duty of loyal cooperation', 'the duty of loyalty', 'the principle of (Community/Union) loyalty'. I will use the terminology employed in recent CJEU case-law, see, eg, *Opinion 2/13 on the Accession of the European Union to the European Convention for the Protection of Human Rights and Fundamental Freedoms*, EU:C:2014:2454, para 173; Case C-243/15, *Lesoochranárske zoskupenie VLK v Obvodný úrad Trenčín*, EU:C:2016:838, para 50.

1088 See paras 40–42. Cf Case C-105/14, *Criminal proceedings against Ivo Taricco and Others*, EU:C:2015:555, paras 36–37, 47 and see further subsection 4.5.4.

1089 See paras 43, 46, 52–53, 60, 63.

1090 Para 39. Cf Case T-199/99, *Sgaravatti Mediterranea Srl v Commission of the European Communities*, EU:T:2002:228, paras 126–127.

1091 See para 61.

1092 Cf Case T-76/11, *Kingdom of Spain v European Commission*, EU:T:2012:613, para 66.

imposing penalties. For that reason, the requirement of a proper legal basis is more widely applicable than the legality principle's *lex certa* element.

4.3.3 THE REQUIREMENT OF A PROPER LEGAL BASIS IN RELATION TO THE LEGALITY PRINCIPLE

As observed above, a substantive overlap exists between the requirement of a proper legal basis and the legality principle, especially with regard to *lex certa*. The close relationship between the two principles is sometimes confirmed expressly. In her Opinion in *SGS Belgium*, for example, Advocate General Kokott explicitly related the requirement that penalties rest on a proper legal basis to the principles of legality and legal certainty.[1093] In her view, "(...) there is nothing to prevent the substance of the principle of the legality of criminal offenses and penalties being used for guidance (...)" for the interpretation of the principle that penalties must rest on a proper legal basis.[1094]

The relationship between the principle that penalties must have a proper legal basis and the legality principle is also perceivable in *Caronna*.[1095] In this preliminary ruling the ECJ related the requirement of a proper legal basis to *criminal* penalties.[1096] The Court subsequently linked that principle to Article 49(1) Charter.[1097] With regard to criminal penalties, the ECJ thus explicitly related the requirement of a proper legal basis to the Charter's legality principle.

The judgment in *Aurubis Balgaria*, a preliminary ruling on EU customs rules, is also relevant for linking the aforementioned principles.[1098] As in *SGS Belgium*, the ECJ was asked about the need for a domestic legal basis as a requirement for the imposition of a penalty. In *Aurubis Balgaria* the domestic court inquired specifically about the possibility under Union law to impose a penalty in the absence of national provisions that expressly provided for such a penalty.[1099] In line with the ECJ's conclusion in *SGS Belgium*, the Court required a clear legal basis for the imposition of a penalty. The Court confirmed that, if EU law itself does not provide a legal basis due to the absence of harmonization, domestic law still could. It added, however, that the Member States' competence to penalize violations of EU rules should be exercised in accordance with the general principles of Union law,[1100] such as the principle of the legality of criminal offenses and penalties.[1101] Accordingly, the Court concluded that the EU legality principle

1093 See Opinion of Advocate General Kokott, para 36.
1094 See para 37 and cf para 71.
1095 As described in subsection 4.2.3.
1096 See *Caronna*, para 55.
1097 See para 55.
1098 Case C-546/09, *Aurubis Balgaria AD v Nachalnik na Mitnitsa Stolichna*, EU:C:2011:199.
1099 See para 21.
1100 Cf *SGS Belgium*, para 40.
1101 See paras 41–42.

precluded "(...) national authorities from applying, to a customs offense, a penalty for which no express provision is made under the national legislation".[1102]

Since the domestic penalties for the customs offense were not criminal penalties under Bulgarian law,[1103] and the ECJ did not dispute this, the Court could have exclusively employed the principle that penalties must have a proper legal basis to substantiate its conclusion. In fact, exclusively referring to that principle could have been expected in light of the ECJ's approach in the case-law described in subsection 4.3.2. In these circumstances, the ECJ's reference to the EU legality principle confirms the substantive overlap between the principle that penalties must have a proper legal basis and the legality principle. It is clear, therefore, that both principles require a clear and unambiguous legal basis for the imposition of a penalty.

4.3.4 CONCLUDING REMARKS

The requirement of a proper legal basis for penalties is unmistakably related to the legality principle. There is a substantive overlap between both principles. The principle that penalties must have a proper legal basis could, in fact, be viewed as an expression of the legality principle's *lex certa* element.[1104] In addition to the apparent substantive overlap, a close relationship between the aforementioned principles can be perceived in some of the Court's case-law.

Despite their evident relationship, both principles can still be distinguished. Whereas the requirement of a clear and unambiguous legal basis is only one element of the legality principle, it appears to be the sole requirement of the principle that penalties must have a proper legal basis. The last-mentioned principle could, therefore, be qualified as a distinct formulation of the legality principle's *lex certa* element.

This distinct formulation contains added value since the principle that penalties must have a proper legal basis has a broader scope. Unlike the legality principle, which is essentially limited to criminal matters, the principle that penalties must have a proper legal basis apparently applies to all penalties, criminal or otherwise. The applicability of the requirement of a proper legal basis beyond the criminal sphere even allows it to be invoked by Member States when the EU imposes penalties for their non-compliance with EU law.[1105]

Since the legality principle provides protection beyond *lex certa*, the legality principle should be exclusively invoked when it applies. In criminal matters within the scope of EU law it would be best to apply only the legality principle and to reserve the application of the general requirement of a proper legal basis

1102 Para 43.

1103 See paras 10–11, 18–19.

1104 On *lex certa*, cf subsections 2.3.3; 3.4.3; 3.6.2; 3.7.2.

1105 See Case T-76/11, *Kingdom of Spain v European Commission*, EU:T:2012:613, paras 36, 66, 69, 71–72, 75, 78–79. On this judgment, see subsection 4.6.3.

to circumstances that clearly involve non-criminal penalties. With regard to the requirement of a proper legal basis for *criminal* penalties, the legality principle should constitute a *lex specialis*. To determine the applicability of the *lex specialis*, the CJEU could employ the terms 'criminal offense' and 'penalty' enshrined in Articles 49 CFR and 7 ECHR.[1106]

The Luxembourg Court has not determined that, in criminal matters, only the legality principle may be applicable, however. In fact, in *Grøngaard and Bang*, the Court explicitly deemed the principle that penalties must have a proper legal basis relevant for domestic criminal proceedings.[1107] Due to the absence of a clear and explicit distinction between the two principles in the Court's case-law, the requirement of a proper legal basis could still be applied to implementing criminal law in addition to, or instead of, the legality principle.[1108]

The lack of a clear distinction between the two principles could also broaden the scope of the EU legality principle. This potential follows from *Aurubis Balgaria*, where the ECJ referred to the legality principle in relation to penalties that were not explicitly deemed to be 'criminal'.[1109] Apparently, the EU legality principle could also be applied to non-criminal penalties, which could imply that it applies to situations beyond those covered by the terms 'criminal offense' and 'penalty'. In light of these uncertainties, the relationship between the principle that penalties must have a proper legal basis and the legality principle remains open to interpretation. It can be concluded, however, that the legality principle is not consistently viewed as a *lex specialis* of the general principle that penalties require a proper legal basis.

4.4 THE LEGALITY PRINCIPLE IN RELATION TO OTHER GENERAL PRINCIPLES OF EU LAW

4.4.1 INTRODUCTION

As *Kolpinghuis* illustrated, the Court apparently considers the principles of legal certainty and non-retroactivity to be related to the legality principle.[1110] The present section examines the relationship between the aforementioned general principles of Union law and the legality principle. Subsection 4.4.2 focusses on the relationship between legal certainty and legality. Subsection 4.4.3 examines the principle of non-retroactivity. Concluding remarks are made in subsection 4.4.4.

1106 For further discussion on the applicability requirements for these provisions, see section 3.3 and subsection 4.5.3.

1107 Case C-384/02, *Criminal proceedings against Knud Grøngaard and Allan Bang*, EU:C:2005:708, para 28. On this judgment, see subsection 4.5.5.

1108 Cf *Caronna* as described in subsection 4.2.3.

1109 See *Aurubis Balgaria*.

1110 See subsection 4.2.3.

4.4.2 THE PRINCIPLE OF LEGAL CERTAINTY AND THE LEGALITY PRINCIPLE

As pointed out above, the ECJ has drawn links between the principle of legal certainty and the legality principle or elements thereof.[1111] The most relevant judgments in this regard have not yet been examined. The ECJ's Grand Chamber judgment in *Intertanko* constitutes the obvious point of departure.[1112] In *Intertanko* the national court questioned the permissibility of using the terms 'serious negligence' in a directive's provision.[1113] The claimants in the main proceedings contended that the unclear terms breached the principle of legal certainty.[1114] Since the directive obliged Member States to punish certain conduct as an infringement, the ECJ did not limit its examination to the principle of legal certainty.[1115] The Court considered that the contested provision *must also* observe the requirements of the principle of legality of criminal offenses and penalties.[1116] It thus examined the permissibility of the use of 'serious negligence' successively in light of the principles of legal certainty and legality.

The ECJ first reiterated that, as a general principle of Union law, legal certainty "(...) requires, in particular, that rules should be clear and precise, so that individuals may ascertain unequivocally what their rights and obligations are and may take steps accordingly (...)".[1117]The Court acknowledged that the terms serious negligence could be potentially problematic for legal certainty, because the applicable directive included these terms without defining them.[1118] The ECJ nevertheless deemed the directive's definition in accordance with the principle of legal certainty.[1119] One of the reasons for this seems to be the consideration that it is impossible for legislation to lay down terms that are always absolutely clear. Since the concept of serious negligence must apply to an indeterminate number of situations it is impossible to envisage the test for incurring liability in advance in a legislative measure of Union or of national law.[1120]

In addition to the lack of clarity, which was deemed inevitable, the Court determined that the concept of negligence was fully integrated into Member State legal systems.[1121] Without explicit comparative research, the ECJ concluded that

1111 See subsection 4.2.3. Cf AG Kokott in her Opinion in *SGS Belgium*, described in subsection 4.3.3.
1112 Case C-308/06, *The Queen, on the application of International Association of Independent Tanker Owners (Intertanko) and Others v Secretary of State for Transport*, EU:C:2008:312.
1113 See paras 29, 67.
1114 See para 68.
1115 See para 70.
1116 See para 70.
1117 Para 69.
1118 See para 72.
1119 See para 79.
1120 See para 73.
1121 See para 74.

all legal systems use negligence to refer to an unintentional act or omission by which a responsible person breaches his duty of care.[1122] In that light, the concept of serious negligence can only refer to a patent breach of the duty of care.[1123] By apparently extracting the above definition from Member State legal systems, the Court defined the directive's terms using the aforementioned elements.[1124]

The apparent conformity of the Court's interpretation of serious negligence with Member State legal systems was thus used to infer the non-violation of the principle of legal certainty. The Court essentially deemed the apparent consensus on the substance of the concept serious negligence sufficient for conformity with the principle of legal certainty. Both the directive's use of the terms serious negligence without defining it, as well as its first judicial definition in *Intertanko*, were, in the ECJ's view, sufficiently clear and precise so that individuals could unequivocally ascertain their rights and obligations.[1125] That conclusion is, however, unconvincing without further substantiation of the Member States' consensus on the substance and use of the concept serious negligence.

Although the ECJ formulated its answer to the national court's question exclusively on the basis of the principle of legal certainty, as mentioned, it did recognize the EU legality principle. In fact, in the Court's view, the legality principle constitutes a specific expression of the general principle of legal certainty.[1126] The Court largely reiterated the legality definition first laid down by the ECJ's Grand Chamber in *Advocaten voor de Wereld*, which stipulated that the legality principle

> "(...) implies that legislation must define clearly offences and the penalties which they attract. That condition is met in the case where the individual concerned is in a position, on the basis of the wording of the relevant provision and with the help of

1122 See para 75.

1123 See para 76.

1124 See para 77.

1125 Cf Peristeridou 2015, p. 202.

1126 See para 70. Cf *X 1996*, para 25; Case T-43/02, *Jungbunzlauer AG v Commission of the European Communities*, EU:T:2006:270, para 71; Case T-69/04, Schunk GmbH and Schunk Kohlenstoff-Technik GmbH v Commission of the European Communities, EU:T:2008:415, para 28; Case C-266/06 P, *Evonik Degussa GmbH v Commission of the European Communities*, EU:C:2008:295, para 43; Case T-446/05, *Amann & Söhne GmbH & Co. KG and Cousin Filterie SAS v European Commission*, EU:T:2010:165, para 124; Case C-584/15, *Glencore Céréales France v Etablissement national des produits de l'agriculture et de la mer (FranceAgriMer)*, EU:C:2017:160, para 73. For other expressions of the close connection between the principles of legality and legal certainty, see, eg, Case 85/76, *Hoffman-La Roche & Co. AG v. Commission of the European Communities*, Opinion of AG Reischl, EU:C:1978:162, p. 594; Case C-63/00, *Land Baden-Württemberg v Günther Schilling and Bezirksregierung Lüneburg v Hans-Otto Nehring*, Opinion of AG Léger, EU:C:2001:497, para 36; Case C-198/01, *Consorzio Industrie Fiammiferi (CIF) v Autorità Garante della Concorrenza e del Mercato*, Opinion of AG Jacobs, EU:C:2003:58, para 48; Case C-303/05, *Advocaten voor de Wereld VZW v Leden van de Ministerraad*, Opinion of AG Ruiz-Jarabo Colomer, EU:C:2006:552, para 102; Case C- 76/06 P, *Britannia Alloys & Chemicals Ltd v Commission of the European Communities*, Opinion of AG Bot, EU:C:2007:128, para 123; *SGS Belgium*, Opinion of Advocate General Kokott, para 36; Case C-102/16, *Vaditrans BVBA v Belgische Staat*, Opinion of AG Tanchev, EU:C:2017:82, para 72.

the interpretative assistance given by the courts, to know which acts or omissions will make him criminally liable (...)."[1127]

The reiteration of *Advocaten voor de Wereld* is noteworthy, because that definition was established in order to assess the validity of EU legislation *on criminal matters*, ie the Framework Decision on the European arrest warrant.[1128] Since *Intertanko* concerned *non-criminal* Union law, the reiteration of the existing definition of legality underlines that the EU legality principle additionally applies when Union law is implemented via national criminal law or punitive domestic sanctions. That the EU legality principle applies in these situations has been consistently confirmed since *Intertanko*.[1129]

Intertanko's reiteration of the definition of legality is additionally significant, because the ECJ modified the definition by adding that EU legislation must clearly define offenses and penalties.[1130] This modification arguably implies that the applicable directive *itself* must comply with the EU legality principle. The applicability of the EU legality principle to the directive's definitions was not accepted in *Interanko*, however. Instead, the ECJ underlined that the prohibited conduct is actually defined by national criminal law, even when a directive requires Member States to sanction that conduct.[1131] This consideration implies that the requirements of the EU legality principle apply only to the actual definitions of offenses and penalties. In other words, the legality principle only applies to the national penal provisions implementing EU law. Since an EU directive does not formally define the applicable offenses and penalties, Union law merely needs to comply with the principle of legal certainty and not, apparently, with the legality principle 'as a specific expression thereof'.[1132] As *Intertanko* illustrated, the principle of legal certainty does not necessarily set strict requirements for definitions in EU legislation.

The close relationship between the principles of legal certainty and legality is also perceivable in *M and Others*, a preliminary ruling that concerned the interpretation of Regulation No 881/2002 imposing restrictive measures on persons and entities associated with Bin Laden, Al-Qaeda and the Taliban.[1133] The appellants in the main proceedings were married to persons designated

1127 See Case C-303/05, *Advocaten voor de Wereld v Leden van de Ministerraad*, EU:C:2007:261, para 50. Further about this judgment, see subsection 4.5.4.

1128 See paras 44, 49. The framework decision: Council Framework Decision 2002/584/JHA of 13 June 2002 on the European arrest warrant and the surrender procedures between Member States [2002] OJ L 190.

1129 See, eg, *Aurub is Balgaria*; *Caronna* as described in, subsections 4.2.3; 4.3.3.

1130 See para 71.

1131 See para 78. Cf Altena-Davidsen 2016, p. 153.

1132 Cf *Intertanko*, Opinion of AG Kokott, EU:C:2007:689, para 144; Cases C-403/08 and C-429/08, *Football Association Premier League Ltd and Others v. QC Leisure and Others and Karen Murphy v Media Protection Services Ltd*, Opinion of AG Kokott, EU:C:2011:43, para 56.

1133 See Case C-340/08, *The Queen, on the application of M and Others v Her Majesty's Treasury*, EU:C:2010:232, para 1.

as being associated with Bin Laden *et al.* As a result of their marriage to such designated persons, the Treasury of the United Kingdom (hereinafter: 'the Treasury') considered the spouses' financial benefits were caught by the prohibition in Article 2(2) of the Regulation.[1134]

According to the Treasury, paying the appellants their income support and child benefits would amount to indirectly making available of funds for the benefit of designated persons as prohibited by the regulation.[1135] Paying those benefits would consequently constitute a criminal offense under national law, because the UK criminalized the violation of Article 2(2) of the regulation.[1136] As a result of the national implementation of the regulation via criminal law, the ECJ's interpretation of the regulation became relevant for criminal liability under UK legislation.

When hearing an appeal to the unsuccessful challenge to the Treasury's decisions, the House of Lords (as it was then) asked the ECJ about the scope of the prohibition in Article 2(2). The national court essentially wanted to know whether the payments to the spouses of designated persons was prohibited because the spouses may use the money to buy goods and services which benefit the household and, hence, the designated persons.[1137] The ECJ determined that the objective of the prohibition was to stop designated persons from accessing economic or financial resources of any nature to prevent them from supporting terrorist activities.[1138] According to the Court, this meant that the prohibition only applied to funds that were capable of being used to support terrorist activities.[1139]

By determining that Article 2(2) implicitly contained the qualification 'capable of being used to support terrorist activities', the Court essentially added an element to the definition of the prohibited conduct. The Court's interpretation thereby clearly restricted the scope of the prohibited conduct.[1140] In order to violate Article 2(2) it was no longer sufficient to make certain funds indirectly available to designated persons. It now needed to be established that funds were made available to the designated persons in a way that enabled them to support terrorist activities.

As a result of this restricted scope, the Court determined that the prohibition did not apply to the payment of the social security benefits such as those in the main proceedings.[1141] Those benefits were, in the Court's view, designed to meet only the essential needs of the household. They could not, therefore, compromise the regulation's objective, because the payments were incapable of being used to support terrorism.[1142]

1134 See paras 23–24.
1135 See para 25.
1136 See paras 17–22.
1137 See para 32.
1138 See para 54.
1139 See para 56.
1140 See para 57.
1141 See para 63.
1142 See paras 61–62.

Although the Court justified its restrictive interpretation by referring to the regulation's objective,[1143] it provided further considerations on this matter. The ECJ explicitly acknowledged the additional relevance of the principle of legal certainty.[1144] In the Court's view, that principle requires legislation

> "(...) such as Regulation No 881/2002, which imposes restrictive measures having considerable impact on the rights and freedoms of the designated persons (*Kadi and Al Bakaraat International Foundation v Council and Commission*, para 375) and which, as provided in Article 10 of that regulation, in domestic law involves penalties, in this instance criminal penalties, for infringement of those measures, to be clear and precise so that the persons concerned, including third parties such as the social security bodies involved in the main proceedings, may know unambiguously their rights and duties and take measures accordingly".[1145]

By expressly recognizing that the infringement of the regulation could lead to criminal penalties, the ECJ evidently considered the context of the prohibited conduct a relevant factor for its interpretation. In fact, in light of the need for rules leading to penalties to be clear and precise, the Court considered that a non-restrictive construction would pose the danger of engendering legal uncertainty.[1146] In the absence of a clear judicial limitation of the prohibition's wording, that prohibition could, according to the ECJ, even apply to large categories of conduct.[1147]

As in *Intertanko*, the judgment in *M and Others* lacked a clear distinction between the requirements of the EU legality principle and the general Union principle of legal certainty. *M and Others*, in fact, referred only to the principle of legal certainty. The Court deemed only that principle relevant for the interpretation of EU legislation even if this resulted in the imposition of domestic criminal penalties. As in *Intertanko*, the Court apparently found its interpretation of the wording of EU legislation sufficiently clear and precise to require the imposition of criminal penalties.

The close relationship between the principles of legal certainty and legality is also apparent in the more recent *Karelia* judgment.[1148] In this preliminary ruling, the ECJ again used only the principle of legal certainty to examine the clarity of EU and national law leading to criminal penalties. The Greek Council of State inquired about the permissibility of the imposition of criminal liability on a warehousekeeper when the excise duties on products under his care remained unpaid.[1149] The ECJ established that the applicable directive merely required

---

[1143] See para 63.
[1144] See para 64.
[1145] Para 65.
[1146] See para 66.
[1147] See paras 66–67. Cf *M and Others*, Opinion of AG Menogzzi, EU:C:2010:13, para 91.
[1148] Case C-81/15, *Kapnoviomichania Karelia AE v Ypourgos Oikonomikon*, EU:C:2016:398.
[1149] See para 30.

the imposition of liability on the warehousekeeper for *the payment* of the excise duties.[1150] It did not, however, explicitly require that the warehousekeeper was additionally liable to pay financial penalties for his initial failure to pay the excise duties.[1151] The general requirement to take the necessary measures to deal with any offense or irregularity under the directive and to impose effective penalties was not, according to the Court, sufficient to establish a duty to impose criminal responsibility on the warehousekeeper.[1152]

Although the directive did not require the imposition of criminal responsibility on the warehousekeeper, it did not preclude it either.[1153] The imposition of criminal liability in national law must nevertheless respect general principles of Union law, such as the principles of proportionality and legal certainty.[1154] Remarkably, however, the Court did not refer to Article 49 Charter here as the source of the apparently relevant legality principle and the explicitly recognized relevance of the principle of proportionality.[1155] Unlike Advocate General Bot,[1156] the ECJ merely recognized the principle of legal certainty with regard to the clarity of the legal basis of penalties. It explicitly deemed that principle applicable when Member States exercise their power to choose the appropriate penalties in the transposition of a directive.[1157]

At the start of its examination of the implementing law's conformity with legal certainty, the ECJ formulated the requirements of the EU principle. The principle of legal certainty requires that

> "EU legislation must be certain and its application foreseeable by those subject to it and that requirement of legal certainty must be observed all the more strictly in the case of rules liable to entail financial consequences, in order that those concerned may know precisely the extent of the obligations which those rules impose on them (...)".[1158]

By this formulation the ECJ recognized a foreseeability requirement for EU legislation. By requiring that individuals may the precise extent of the relevant obligations, the Court apparently demanded a high level of foreseeability.[1159] The ECJ considered that the required level of foreseeability was probably not provided by the applicable legislation. This was most likely because the additional liability for the warehousekeeper was not expressly provided for in

1150 See paras 32–33.
1151 See paras 39–40.
1152 See paras 35–41.
1153 See paras 41–43.
1154 See para 44.
1155 The principle of proportionality is enshrined in Article 49(3) Charter.
1156 See *Karelia*, Opinion of AG Bot, EU:C:2016:66, paras 48–40.
1157 See para 45.
1158 Para 45.
1159 See, conversely, Case C-63/00, *Land Baden-Württemberg v Günther Schilling and Bezirksregierung Lüneburg v Hans-Otto Nehring*, EU:C:2002:296, para 41.

the applicable directive or in the domestic implementing provisions.[1160] In the absence of legislative provisions that formed a clear and express basis for the warehousekeeper's liability, the applicable penalties did not appear sufficiently certain and foreseeable to meet the requirements of the principle of legal certainty.[1161] In light of the division of competences in preliminary rulings, the ECJ left the verification of its conditional determination to the referring court.[1162]

As mentioned, Advocate General Bot did consider the legality principle relevant.[1163] In his view, that principle would be violated if the Court allowed the imposition of liability on the warehousekeeper. Bot deemed the absence of an express legislative provision as the reason for this.[1164] In the absence of an express provision providing for liability, he pointed out, the Greek courts would need to resort to an extensive interpretation of the applicable directive or the domestic legislation.[1165] The Advocate General thus clearly considered such an extensive interpretation to constitute a violation of the EU legality principle.

The above judgments illustrate the relevance of the principle of legal certainty for EU prohibitions implemented via national criminal law. Both the clarity of the wording of EU legislation and its interpretation by the Court are apparently required only to conform with the general Union principle.[1166] The more specific legality principle did not provide additional protection in these situations. The EU principle of legal certainty could also apply to national provisions implementing EU legislation. In line with the *lex certa* principle, it could then preclude the imposition of criminal liability in the absence of a clear and express legal basis. The Court's emphasis on the need for a *clear* and *express* legal basis for liability in implementing *legislation* could even be viewed as a recognition of a *lex scripta* requirement under the EU principle of legal certainty.[1167]

4.4.3 THE PRINCIPLE OF NON-RETROACTIVITY AND THE LEGALITY PRINCIPLE

The CJEU has explicitly referred to the principle of non-retroactivity of criminal law.[1168] That specific element of the Convention's legality principle was, in fact,

---

1160 See para 46.
1161 See paras 47, 53.
1162 On this division of competences, see further subsection 4.5.6.
1163 See *Karelia*, Opinion of AG Bot, para 61.
1164 See para 67. The need to use legislative implementing measures for conformity with the EU legality principle is also stressed in Case C-119/15, *Biuro podróży 'Partner' Sp. z o.o, Sp. komandytowa w Dąbrowie Górniczej v Prezes Urzędu Ochrony Konkurencji i Konsumentów*, Opinion of AG Saugmandsgaard Øe, EU:C:2016:387, paras 54–57.
1165 See para 61.
1166 See *Intertanko* and *M and Others*.
1167 See further subsection 6.2.3. On the *lex scripta* principle in general, see subsection 2.3.2.
1168 See, eg, *X 2004* as mentioned in subsection 4.2.3 and several judgments on EU competition law which will be examined in subsection 4.6.5.

recognized early on in *Kent Kirk*.[1169] In this preliminary reference the Newcastle Crown Court asked whether a UK prohibition on foreign vessels fishing in the UK coastal zone was compatible with EU law.[1170] The question was asked to determine whether Union law allowed the imposition of a fine for fishing with a Danish vessel in UK waters.[1171]

The ECJ determined that, at the time of Kent Kirk's acts, the UK prohibition was contrary to the Union principle of non-discrimination on grounds of nationality.[1172] By violating EU law at the time of the material conduct, the UK provision establishing criminal responsibility did not *validly* establish that responsibility.[1173] The fact that Union legislation subsequently removed the basis for finding national criminal law invalid,[1174] and arguably did so retroactively,[1175] could not lead to individual criminal responsibility.[1176] In the Court's view, the retroactive validation of the national provision would lead to a penalty for an act that was not in fact punishable at the time of individual conduct. Therefore, the ECJ found that the establishment of criminal responsibility for the suspect's conduct would violate 'the principle that penal provisions may not have retroactive effect'.[1177] The Court thus essentially stated that the principle of non-retroactivity of criminal law precluded the *ex post facto* validation of national criminal law in the case at hand.[1178]

Like *Kent Kirk*, the judgment in *Fedesa* concerned the potential effect of retroactive Union law on national penal legislation.[1179] The applicable directive in *Fedesa* required Member States to prohibit the use of certain hormones in livestock farming via national legislation by 1 January 1988 even though the directive itself was only adopted on 7 March 1988.[1180] Since the directive's obligation apparently allowed the establishment of national criminal offenses for the use of the indicated hormones in livestock farming,[1181] the ECJ explicitly distinguished two aspects of retroactivity: "(…) the retroactive effect of penal provisions and retroactive effect outside the criminal sphere".[1182]

1169 Case 63/83, *Regina v Kent Kirk*, EU:C:1984:255. Cf Herlin-Karnell 2012, p. 19; Peristeridou 2015, p. 187.

1170 See para 3.

1171 See paras 1–2.

1172 See para 16.

1173 Cf para 21.

1174 See para 13.

1175 The ECJ did not examine the 'general legality of the retroactivity' of the provision removing the basis for the invalidity of the provision of United Kingdom criminal law, see para 21.

1176 See para 23.

1177 See paras 22–24.

1178 See paras 22–23.

1179 Case C-331/88, *The Queen v Minister of Agriculture, Fisheries and Food and Secretary of State for Health, ex parte: Fedesa and others*, EU:C:1990:391.

1180 See para 41.

1181 See para 44.

1182 Para 41.

The Court began its examination of the directive's retroactive effect by confirming that the principle that penal provisions may not have retroactive effect constitutes a general principle of EU law.[1183] It then reiterated the *Pretore di Salò* rule[1184] and determined that this rule was not violated because none of the directive's provisions sought to produce the precluded effect of determining or aggravating criminal liability under national law.[1185] The ECJ subsequently determined that the contested provision was not contrary to EU law on other grounds either. In the Court's view the directive could not "(...) be interpreted as imposing on Member States the obligation to adopt measures which conflict with [EU] law, in particular with the principle that penal provisions may not have retroactive effect".[1186]

Even when EU law could retroactively oblige Member States to have penal provisions in force, the principle of non-retroactivity of criminal law would still preclude the retroactive *application* of the implementing penal provisions.[1187] Although Union law could legally oblige the retroactive enactment of national penal provisions, the application of these provisions needed to be limited to acts that occurred after their official enactment. Since EU law did not itself impose criminal responsibility,[1188] and it did not require the retroactive application of national criminal law,[1189] the principle of non-retroactivity of penal provisions was not violated.

The above approach to non-retroactivity of penal provisions was largely confirmed in *E and F*, a post-Lisbon preliminary ruling concerning restrictive measures combatting terrorism.[1190] Giving rise to this judgment were questions about the validity of an EU measure listing DHKP-C as an entity subject to restrictive measures.[1191] E and F were prosecuted for raising funds for that organization, because violating the restrictive measures against, inter alia, DHKP-C constituted a criminal offense under German law.[1192] Together with the prohibition of 'making available' funds to listed entities in Regulation No 2580/2001, the actual listing of DHKP-C in the Council decision formed the basis for national criminal responsibility.[1193]

The ECJ's Grand Chamber determined that the initial listing of DHKP-C was illegal due to the lack of a statement of reasons provided by the Council in its

1183 See para 42.
1184 See section 4.3.
1185 See para 43.
1186 Para 44.
1187 Cf Peristeridou 2015, p. 192.
1188 Cf *Fedesa*, Opinion of AG Mischo, EU:C:1990:109, para 65.
1189 Cf *Fedesa*, Opinion of AG Mischo, para 80.
1190 See Case C-550/09, *Criminal proceedings against E and F*, EU:C:2010:382.
1191 See paras 27–30.
1192 See para 26.
1193 See para 47. Cf *E and F*, View of AG Mengozzi, EU:C:2010:272, paras 49–54.

earlier decisions.[1194] The question then arose whether a newly established valid Council decision listing DHKP-C could form the basis for criminal liability in the period when the previous illegal listing applied.[1195] The ECJ underlined that, even if the new Council decision listing DHKP-C could retroactively validate that listing in the previous period, it could not be used as the basis for criminal liability for acts that occurred in the earlier period. The new Council decision would then "(...) in reality form part of the basis for a criminal conviction in respect of acts committed during [the previous] period, notwithstanding the fact that, throughout that period, that decision did not exist".[1196] Such an effect would infringe, in the words of the Court, 'the principle of non-retroactivity of provisions which may form the basis for a criminal conviction'.[1197]

By referring to *Kent Kirk* and *Fedesa*, the Court clearly limited the effect that the potential retroactive validation of EU legislation could have on national criminal proceedings. As in the earlier rulings, the retroactive effect of EU law could not result in the determination of national criminal responsibility which was not, at the time of the defendants' conduct, based on *valid* EU legislation. Unlike in *Kent Kirk* and *Fedesa*, however, the Court did not refer to Article 7 ECHR as the basis for the principle of non-retroactivity, nor did it refer to Article 49 Charter.[1198] The ECJ apparently employed the principle of non-retroactivity of criminal law as a general principle of Union law.

The above judgments illustrate that the Court has afforded broad protection against retroactivity in the criminal sphere.[1199] Comparably broad protection is not necessarily provided outside the criminal sphere. As mentioned, in *Fedesa*, the Court additionally examined the acceptability of retroactivity of non-criminal legislation. The ECJ reiterated that although the principle of legal certainty would generally preclude a substantive measure of EU law from taking effect before its publication, this may exceptionally be otherwise.[1200] Outside the criminal sphere, Union law could have retroactive effect if the purpose of the measure so demanded and as long as the legitimate expectations of those concerned were duly respected.[1201] Since both conditions were satisfied in *Fedesa*, the Court concluded that the directive did not violate the principle that legislation should not be retroactive.[1202]

1194 See paras 55–57, 62.

1195 See para 58.

1196 Para 60.

1197 See para 59.

1198 Unlike Advocate General Mengozzi in his View in *E and F*, see para 116.

1199 Cf Altena-Davidsen 2016, p. 296.

1200 See para 45. Cf Case C-17/10, *Toshiba Corporation and Others v Úřad pro ochranu hospodářské soutěže*, EU:C:2012:72, para 47.

1201 See para 45. According to Advocate General Bot, the principle of non-retroactivity of substantive rules is derived from the legality principle enshrined in Article 49(1) Charter and Article 7(1) ECHR, see Case C-352/99, *ThyssenKrupp Nirosta GmbH v European Commission*, Opinion of AG Bot, EU:C:2010:635, paras 89–90.

1202 See paras 46–48.

The distinction in *Fedesa* between non-retroactivity in the criminal sphere and non-retroactivity as a general principle is confirmed in *Gerekens*.[1203] In this preliminary ruling the Luxembourg Court of Cassation asked whether EU law allowed the retroactive penalization of the production of milk in excess of production quotas.[1204] The ECJ dismissed the applicability of the principle of non-retroactivity of penal provisions because the imposition of an additional levy did not, according to the Court, constitute a penalty.[1205] The Court, therefore, exclusively examined the permissibility of the retroactive application of implementing provisions in light of the general principles of legal certainty and non-retroactivity.

The ECJ reiterated that the principle of legal certainty generally precludes EU law from taking effect before its publication, but that this may be allowed due to the purpose of the measure and as long as legitimate expectations are respected.[1206] Therefore, both EU legislation and national implementing provisions can be applied retroactively as long as the aforementioned conditions are satisfied.[1207] Since the Grand Duchy of Luxembourg replaced implementing provisions that were incompatible with EU law with compatible provisions, the effectiveness of EU law required the retroactive application of the compatible implementing rules.[1208] The milk producers had not, moreover, acquired a legitimate expectation that the new implementing provisions would not be applied retroactively.[1209] As a consequence, when the applicable EU regulations entered into force, the individuals concerned could have expected to be subject to additional levies on milk produced in excess of the allocated quotas.[1210] The Court therefore found the retroactive application of the non-criminal implementing provisions to be in conformity with the general principles of legal certainty and non-retroactivity.[1211]

Gerekens does not just deserve attention as a judgment confirming the *Fedesa* distinction. The Court's dismissal of the applicability of the principle of non-retroactivity of penal provisions requires some scrutiny. As mentioned, the Court used the term 'penalty' to determine the applicability of the principle of non-retroactivity of penal provisions. It, moreover, referred to that principle as enshrined in Article 7 ECHR. In light of these considerations, the ECJ could have been expected to determine the applicability of the EU principle of non-retroactivity of penal provisions on the basis of the Strasbourg criteria

1203 Case C-459/02, *Willy Gerekens and Association agricole pour la promotion de la commercialisation laitière Procola v État du grand-duché de Luxembourg*, EU:C:2004:454.
1204 See para 20.
1205 See paras 35–36.
1206 See paras 22–23.
1207 See para 24.
1208 See paras 25–27.
1209 See paras 28–32.
1210 See para 33.
1211 See para 38.

for determining whether a measure constitutes a 'penalty' for the purpose of Article 7 ECHR.[1212]

Instead of employing the Strasbourg criteria, however, the Court merely referred to its own case-law to conclude that an additional levy did not constitute a penalty.[1213] In the Court's view, the additional levy is used to stabilize the milk sector and to provide the EU with the necessary funds for the disposal of the excess milk.[1214] In light of this, the measure aims to re-establish the balance between supply and demand in the milk market. It does not aim to punish those who have exceeded milk quotas and is not, therefore, a penalty.

The above case-law illustrates the evident relationship between the principle of non-retroactivity of criminal law and the general principles of Union law of non-retroactivity and legal certainty. The aforementioned judgments indicate that, as a principle of criminal law, the principle of non-retroactivity provides more protection than the general principles of non-retroactivity and legal certainty. Whereas the retroactivity of non-criminal substantive rules is allowed under certain conditions, the above case-law does not appear to allow the retroactive application of offenses and penalties in the criminal sphere.[1215] As a result, the CJEU appears to have recognized the legality principle's *lex praevia* element as a self-standing general principle of Union Law.[1216] Since the Court deemed the principle to be enshrined in Article 7 ECHR,[1217] it has linked the principle of non-retroactivity to the Convention's legality principle,[1218] although not without exception.[1219] It has not, in any event, used the Strasbourg criteria for the application of Article 7 ECHR in order to determine the scope of the EU principle of non-retroactivity of penal provisions. Nor has it referred to Article 49(1) Charter as the legal basis for this principle after the Charter's entry into force.[1220]

4.4.4 CONCLUDING REMARKS

The preceding sections examined the relationship between the EU legality principle and the general principles of, respectively, legal certainty and non-retroactivity. The judgments described in subsection 4.4.2 confirm the close relationship between the EU legality principle and the general principle of legal certainty. Despite the apparent relevance of the legality principle, the Court applied

1212 On these criteria, see subsection 3.3.3.
1213 See paras 35–38.
1214 See para 37 and Joined Cases C-231/00, C-303/00 and C-451/00 *Cooperativa Lattepiù and Others*, EU:C:2004:178, paras 73–75.
1215 Cf Peristeridou 2015, p. 188.
1216 On the *lex praevia* requirement in general, see subsection 2.3.5.
1217 See *Kent Kirk*, para 22; *Fedesa*, para 42; *Gerekens*, para 35.
1218 Cf Altena-Davidsen 2016, p. 300.
1219 See *E and F*.
1220 See *E and F*.

only the principle of legal certainty in the judgments in *Intertanko*, *M and Others*, and *Karelia*. *Intertanko* illustrates that the principle of legal certainty does not, by definition, impose demanding clarity standards. *Karelia*, on other hand, indicates that the EU principle of legal certainty could require implementing criminal law to abide by, essentially, the requirements of *lex scripta* and *lex certa*.[1221]

Although the Court could provide protection that is comparable to the legality principle via the principle of legal certainty, this is not always the case. Especially where the clarity of EU legislation is contested, the Court appears to be hesitant to impose strict demands regarding clarity. For that reason, the principles of legal certainty and legality should not be viewed as fully-fledged alternatives. Since the legality principle is deemed to provide additional protection for legal certainty in criminal matters,[1222] the EU principles of legality and legal certainty should rather be viewed as *lex specialis* and *lex generalis*.[1223] Thus, the principle of legal certainty should only be applied when the legality principle is clearly inapplicable. Such a distinction presupposes the recognition of clear and consistent applicability criteria, however, which are absent from the above judgments. As observed in subsection 4.3.4, to determine the applicability of the *lex specialis*, the CJEU should employ the terms 'criminal offense' and 'penalty' as enshrined in Articles 49 CFR and 7 ECHR.[1224]

Regarding the non-retroactivity of criminal law, *Kent Kirk*, *Fedesa*, *Gerekens*, and *E and F* indicate that EU law protects the *lex praevia* element of the legality principle.[1225] Some of these judgments additionally underlined the relationship between the principle of non-retroactivity of substantive rules on the one hand, and the principle of non-retroactivity of criminal laws on the other. The retroactive application of substantive rules is explicitly allowed under the conditions described in subsection 4.4.3. In light of this exception to the prohibition on retroactivity, the principle of non-retroactivity of substantive rules evidently entails a lower level of protection than the specific criminal law principle does.[1226]

The protection of the principle of non-retroactivity of substantive rules is not without purpose, however. This principle could, in fact, be the only relevant protection against retroactivity in EU law if the rules that are applied retroactively are not deemed 'criminal' and do not lead to the imposition of

1221 On these requirements in general, cf subsections 2.3.2–2.3.3.

1222 On the higher level of legality protection required in criminal matters, see Cases C-403/08 and C-429/08, *Football Association Premier League Ltd and Others v. QC Leisure and Others and Karen Murphy v Media Protection Services Ltd*, Opinion of AG Kokott, EU:C:2011:43, para 56; Case C-111/16, *Criminal proceedings against Giorgio Fidenato and Others*, Opinion of AG Bobek, EU:C:2017:248, para 70.

1223 The Court has recently done so in Case C-72/15, *PJSC Rosneft Oil Company v Her Majesty's Treasury and Others*, EU:C:2017:236. See subsection 4.5.7.

1224 For further discussion on these applicability requirements for these provisions, see section 3.3 and subsection 4.5.3.

1225 On the *lex praevia* principle in general, see subsection 2.3.5.

1226 Cf Groussot 2006, p. 201.

'penalties' for the purpose of the EU legality principle. As with the relationship between, for example, *lex certa* and the principle that penalties must have a proper legal basis,[1227] the principle of non-retroactivity of penal provisions and the principle of non-retroactivity of substantive rules should be considered *lex specialis* and *lex generalis*. In order to clarify that EU law protects the specific criminal law principle, the CJEU could have been expected to employ the terms 'criminal offense' and 'penalty' as enshrined in Articles 49 CFR and 7 ECHR.[1228] By not referring to Article 49(1) Charter as the source of the principle of non-retroactivity of criminal law in *E and F*, however, the Court circumvents an assessment of applicability on the basis of these terms. Where it did employ the term 'penalty', the Court focused on its own case-law to determine whether a measure constitutes a penalty for the purpose of the *lex praevia* principle.

4.5 CONSIDERATIONS ON LEGALITY AS A SELF-STANDING EU PRINCIPLE

4.5.1 INTRODUCTION

The preceding sections illustrate that multiple strands of EU case-law have not generally recognized and applied the legality principle as a self-standing principle of Union law. Although some of the earlier CJEU considerations were subsequently related to the EU legality principle, they were not generally developed to set out the specific protection provided by the legality principle in criminal matters. One exception is the case-law on the principle of non-retroactivity of penal provisions, because that element of the legality principle was recognized as a protective principle of criminal law early on. The CJEU has thereby explicitly acknowledged the need to protect this criminal law safeguard as a principle of Union law.[1229]

The entry into force of the Charter altered the above point of departure. Instead of merely having to examine its own considerations with apparent relevance for the legality principle, the CJEU could now be confronted with the principle of legality of crimes and penalties as a codified fundamental right in EU law. For that reason, the Court is actually required to interpret the definition of the legality principle as enshrined in Article 49 CFR.[1230] That formulation is modeled on Article 7 ECHR, which indicates the relevance of the Convention

[1227] See subsection 4.3.4.

[1228] For futher discussion on these applicability requirements for these provisions, see section 3.3 and subsection 4.5.3.

[1229] The prime importance of this element of the legality principle was recently underlined in Case C-574/15, *Proceedings against Mauro Scialdone*, Opinion of AG Bobek, EU:C:2017:553, paras 146–149.

[1230] For the wording of Article 49 CFR, see subsection 1.1.2.

for the interpretation of the Charter's legality principle.[1231] The Charter's entry into force with the Lisbon Treaty could, therefore, be expected to result in more explicit consideration by the CJEU of the EU legality principle.

The present section examines the CJEU's explicit consideration of the EU legality principle. In light of the significance of the codified legality principle, most considerations concern the Charter's legality principle. Subsection 4.5.2 first addresses the Court's considerations regarding the distinct EU sources of the legality principle post-Lisbon and their relationship with Article 7 ECHR. Subsections 4.5.3–4.5.6 subsequently examine the principle's applicability and its application, with special emphasis on the interplay between EU law and its implementation via domestic criminal law. Subsection 4.5.7 focusses on the *lex certa* principle as a specific element that was recently identified by the ECJ. Some concluding remarks are made in subsection 4.5.8.

4.5.2 DISTINCT EU SOURCES AND THE RELEVANCE OF ARTICLE 7 ECHR

With the addition of Article 49 Charter, the EU legality principle is no longer just protected as a general principle of Union law.[1232] As with most other EU fundamental rights, the legality principle presently has two sources in EU law: the Charter and the general principles of Union law. With regard to the EU legality principle, the ECJ implicitly considered the relationship between these two sources in *Paoletti*.[1233]

In *Paoletti*, a preliminary ruling that concerned alleged labor trafficking from Romania into Italy, the ECJ established that the Charter's legality principle could be applied to national proceedings that took place before the entry into force of the Charter in 2009.[1234] In the Court's view, Article 49 Charter could be applied to domestic proceedings before 2009, because, at the time of the main proceedings, the EU legality principle was already applicable.[1235] Since the legality principle applied as a general principle of Union law before 2009, the use of a provision that subsequently codified that unwritten right would not, according to the Court's implicit reasoning, be problematic. By deeming the Charter's legality principle applicable to national proceedings before 2009, the ECJ apparently considered the unwritten EU legality principle to

1231 The ECHR's relevance is explicitly recognized in Articles 52(3) and 53 Charter. See further section 5.5.

1232 For judgments recognizing legality as a general principle, see, eg, *Advocaten voor de Wereld*, para 49; *Intertanko*, para 70. See for further discussion of these judgments subsections 4.4.2; 4.5.4.

1233 Case C-218/15, *Criminal proceedings against Gianpaolo Paoletti and Others*, EU:C:2016:748.

1234 Para 26.

1235 Para 25.

be integrally codified in Article 49 Charter.[1236] As a result, the Court appears to consider that the Charter's legality principle has completely absorbed the legality principle that was initially developed as a general principle of Union law.

In addition to its considerations on the relationship between the two sources of the EU legality principle, *Paoletti* provides an insight into the Court's current appreciation of the relevance of the ECHR for EU fundamental rights. Since the ECHR was generally deemed to have 'special significance' for the interpretation of EU rights,[1237] Article 7 ECHR has, in fact, been referred to when interpreting the EU legality principle.[1238] In *Paoletti*, however, the ECJ found it necessary to underline the formal status of the ECHR in EU law. The Court reiterated that, as long as the Union has not acceded to the ECHR, the Convention is not an instrument that is formally incorporated into EU law.[1239] The ECJ used this general consideration to conclude that, with regard to the EU legality principle, reference should only be made to Article 6 TEU and Article 49 Charter.[1240] Unlike the referring court, which had mentioned Article 7 ECHR first,[1241] the two EU sources that formally contain the legality principle are to be considered exclusively or, at least, primarily.

The formal focus on the EU sources of the legality principle has not precluded the Court from referring to Article 7 ECHR and the Strasbourg Court's case-law, however. It did so before *Paoletti*, in *Taricco*, but also more recently in *Rosneft*. In both judgments the ECJ explicitly deemed the Convention's legality principle, and its interpretation by the ECtHR, relevant for the EU legality principle.[1242]

Due to the focus on the EU sources of fundamental rights in *Paoletti* it is not completely clear, however, to what extent Article 7 ECHR and the Strasbourg Court's case-law will be used for interpretation of the EU legality principle.

1236 This position was already adopted by the General Court in competition matters, see Joined Cases T-373/10, T-374/10, T-382/10, T-402/10, *Villeroy & Boch Austria GmbH and Villeroy & Boch AG v European Commission*, EU:T:2013:455, para 163.

1237 1669 – Legality in Europe.

1238 See, for example, the aforementioned judgments *Kent Kirk*, *Fedesa*, *X 1996*, *X 2004*, *Gerekens*, see further subsections 4.2.3, 4.4.3.

1239 *Paoletti*, para 21. Cf Case C-617/10, *Åklagaren v Hans Åkerberg Fransson*, EU:C:2013:105, para 44.

1240 Para 22. By this consideration, the ECJ adopted the Grand Chamber's approach in *Otis and Others*, see Case C-199/11, *Europese Gemeenschap v Otis NV and Others*, EU:C:2012:684, para 47. See further subsection 5.5.4.

1241 Para 11.

1242 See C-105/14, *Criminal proceedings against Ivo Taricco and Others*, EU:C:2015:555, para 57; Case C-72/15, *PJSC Rosneft Oil Company v Her Majesty's Treasury and Others*, EU:C:2017:236, paras 164–167. See further about these judgments, respectively, subsections 4.5.4; 4.5.7. Even more recently the Court has continued this approach, see Case C-42–17, *Criminal proceedings against M.A.S. and M.B. (Taricco II)*, EU:C:2017:936, paras 53, 55.
taken the same approach as in Taricco and Rosneft in Taricco

4.5.3 SCOPE OF APPLICATION I: THE TERMS 'CRIMINAL OFFENSE' AND 'PENALTY'

Article 49(1) Charter employs the terms 'criminal offense' and 'penalty' in its first two sentences. These sentences enshrine a legality principle with the same meaning and scope as Article 7(1) ECHR.[1243] For this reason, at least with regard to Article 49(1) Charter, the criteria that determine the applicability of the Strasbourg legality principle become relevant. As described in section 3.3, the ECtHR employs distinct criteria to determine whether a person was found guilty of a 'criminal offense' for the purpose of Article 7(1)'s first sentence, or whether a measure constituted a 'penalty' within the meaning of Article 7(1)'s second sentence. The distinction between the terms 'criminal offense' and 'penalty' correspond to the distinction between the principles *nullum crimen* and *nulla poena*. The present subsection takes the ECtHR's distinction as a point of departure and examines how the CJEU has interpreted the aforementioned terms.

Criminal offense

Although the CJEU has never determined the applicability of the EU legality principle on the basis of the term 'criminal offense', the Court has interpreted the notions 'criminal' or 'criminal proceedings' within the meaning of the Convention. In *Spector Photo*, for example, the ECJ explicitly used the ECtHR's *Engel* criteria[1244] to determine whether infringements of Directive 2003/6, which required the imposition of *administrative* sanctions, should nevertheless be labeled as criminal for the purposes of the Convention.[1245] After ruling affirmatively on this matter, the Court examined whether legal or factual assumptions in the directive would violate the principle of the presumption of innocence enshrined in Article 6(2) ECHR.[1246]

The ECJ's Grand Chamber took a similar approach in *Bonda*. In this preliminary ruling the Court examined whether sanctions imposed on the basis of a regulation were imposed in criminal proceedings within the meaning of the Convention's *ne bis in idem* principle.[1247] Following Advocate General Kokott,[1248] the ECJ explicitly employed the *Engel* criteria to conclude

1243 Only a *lex mitior* principle is added in Article 49(1)'s third sentence, see Explanation on Article 49 in Explanations relating to the Charter of Fundamental Rights, [2007] OJ C 303/02.

1244 On these criteria, see subsection 3.3.2.

1245 Case C-45/08, *Spector Photo Group NV and Others v Commissie voor het Bank-, Financie- en Assurantiewezen (CBFA)*, EU:C:2009:806, para 42.

1246 See para 43.

1247 Case C-489/10, *Criminal proceedings against Łukasz Marcin Bonda*, EU:C:2012:319, para 36.

1248 See *Bonda*, Opinion of AG Kokott, EU:C:2011:845, paras 42–71.

that the sanctions on the basis of EU law were not criminal and could not, consequently, be contrary to protective principles of criminal law such as *ne bis in idem*.[1249]

The judgments in *Spector Photo* and *Bonda* thus clearly indicate the ECJ's willingness to refer to the *Engel* criteria for the interpretation of the term 'criminal'.[1250] As observed in subsection 3.3.2, the Strasbourg Court interprets the terms 'criminal' or 'criminal proceedings' on the basis of the *Engel* criteria, irrespective of which Convention provision is subject to interpretation. Based on *Spector Photo* and *Bonda* it is therefore reasonable to assume that the ECJ will use the *Engel* criteria to determine the applicability of Article 49(1) Charter with regard to the term 'criminal offense'.[1251]

The *Bonda* judgment contains further clues about the future approach of the Luxembourg Court on this matter. In line with the focus on EU fundamental rights in *Paoletti*,[1252] the Grand Chamber first examined whether EU law considered the prohibited behavior as criminal.[1253] Only after this examination did the Court determine that the EU qualification of the provision as non-criminal was not called into question by the ECtHR case-law on the matter.[1254] This implies that the Court will primarily employ its own case-law in order to interpret the term 'criminal offense'.

Support for this view can also be derived from the *Taricco* judgment.[1255] In this judgment the ECJ has, in fact, used the above approach to consider the applicability of the EU legality principle to procedural rules, although not on the basis of the term 'criminal offense'. In line with the approach in *Bonda*, the Grand Chamber first examined the interpretation of the EU legality principle on the basis of EU case-law and only subsequently, and apparently as a secondary matter, on the basis of ECtHR case-law.[1256]

In conclusion, in order to determine the applicability of the Charter's legality principle, the CJEU will probably refer to the Strasbourg case-law on the terms 'criminal offense' as a secondary instrument and a source of inspiration. The *Engel* criteria will thus be relevant for the applicability of the *nullum crimen* principle enshrined in the first sentence of Article 49(1) Charter.

1249 See paras 36–45.

1250 This is confirmed in Case C-617/10, *Åklagaren v Hans Åkerberg Fransson*, EU:C:2013:105, para 35.

1251 This is also the approach proposed by Advocate General Bot, see C-81/15, *Kapnoviomichania Karelia AE v Ypourgos Oikonomikon*, Opinion of AG Bot, EU:C:2016:66, paras 44–50.

1252 See subsection 4.5.2.

1253 See paras 28–35.

1254 See paras 36–45.

1255 Case C-105/14, *Criminal proceedings against Ivo Taricco and Others*, EU:C:2015:555. Further about this judgment, see subsection 4.5.4.

1256 The ECJ considered that the ECtHR case-law on Article 7 ECHR supported its conclusion on the scope of the EU legality principle, see paras 56–57.

Penalty

In order to determine the applicability of Article 49(1) Charter, the CJEU has not employed the term 'penalty' in judgments concerning national implementation of Union law via criminal law or punitive sanctions.[1257] The Court has mainly dismissed the applicability of the legality principle because the measure did not constitute a penalty according to the CJEU's own, pre-Lisbon, case-law. This approach is in line with the Court's focus on its own case-law for the interpretation of EU fundamental rights in, for example, the aforementioned judgments in *Bonda* and *Taricco*.[1258]

The preliminary ruling in *Italmoda* is a clear example of the Court's EU-centered approach.[1259] In this judgment the Supreme Court of the Netherlands (*Hoge Raad*) asked whether it could refuse the benefit of, inter alia, the right to deduct VAT in cases of fraud. More specifically, the *Hoge Raad* wanted to know whether it could refuse the benefit of the rights deriving from the Sixth Directive in the absence of an explicit domestic legal basis for the refusal.[1260] Apparently on the basis of a principle of good faith that underlies the common VAT system,[1261] the Court required national authorities to refuse the benefit of certain VAT system rights when they were claimed fraudulently or abusively.[1262] Although the applicable directive did not explicitly provide for a possibility to refuse the benefits,[1263] in the Court's view, the ability to refuse those benefits must be regarded as inherent in the system.[1264] Since the possibility to refuse the benefits is inherent in the common VAT system, national courts and authorities are even required to refuse to grant the benefits when national provisions do not contain an explicit legal basis for the refusal.[1265]

In its observations during the preliminary ruling procedure, Italmoda contended that the refusal to grant the rights of the VAT system required an applicable legal basis under Article 7 ECHR and Article 49 Charter since it constituted 'a penalty in the substantive sense'.[1266] The Court rejected this argument by considering that the refusal of a benefit in the case of fraud merely constitutes a consequence of a failure to satisfy the conditions for benefiting from

---

1257 It has done so with regard to administrative sanctions imposed by EU institutions, however, see subsection 4.6.4.

1258 See further section 5.5.

1259 Joined Cases C-131/13, C-163/13 and C-164/13, *Staatssecretaris van Financiën v Schoenimport 'Italmoda' Mariano Previti vof*, EU:C:2014:2455.

1260 See para 41.

1261 See para 46 and, more explicitly and in greater detail, *Italmoda*, Opinion of AG Szpunar, EU:C:2014:2217, paras 44–50.

1262 See paras 42–50.

1263 Cf Opinion of AG Szpunar, para 57.

1264 See paras 59, 62.

1265 See paras 54, 59.

1266 See Opinion of AG Szpunar, para 60.

the rights of the VAT system. It is not, therefore, a penalty within the meaning of Article 7 ECHR or Article 49 Charter.[1267] As a result, the refusal of the benefit of the rights of the VAT system does not require an explicit legal basis in either EU legislation or in domestic legislation.

Had the legality principle applied to the refusal to grant the rights, it could certainly have precluded the refusal in the case at hand. The imposition of a penalty for behavior that was not clearly punishable on the basis of explicit provisions in either EU law or domestic law, would likely violate the *lex certa* principle.[1268] In light of the potential violation of the *lex certa* element the Court could have been more elaborate about the inapplicability of the EU legality principle in *Italmoda*. This could have been expected in light of the ECJ's explicit references to Article 7 ECHR and Article 49 Charter. In these circumstances, the Court could have reasonably been expected to examine the factors used by the ECtHR when determining the applicability of the Convention's legality principle.

Instead of using the ECtHR's criteria to interpret the terms 'criminal offense' and 'penalty', the ECJ substantiated the inapplicability of the EU legality principle on the basis of its own pre-Lisbon case-law. The ECJ referred primarily to its judgment in *Emsland-Stärke* to determine that the obligation to repay EU funds that were awarded wrongly due to the abuse of rights did not constitute a penalty.[1269] In *Emsland-Stärke*, a case that concerned an alleged abuse of rights when obtaining export refunds for agricultural products, the Court substantiated this decision by considering that the obligation to repay undue EU funds was merely the consequence of artificially creating the conditions required to obtain the funding.[1270] In *Italmoda*, the Court evidently used these considerations as the sole basis for the inapplicability of the EU legality principle to the refusal to grant the benefit of rights under EU law.

Italmoda illustrates that the Court continues to use its pre-Lisbon considerations relating to the principle that penalties require a proper legal basis to determine the applicability of the EU legality principle.[1271] This approach is not just conceptually flawed as it amalgamates the requirement of a proper legal basis with the legality principle, but it could also lead to a divergence between the scope of Article 7(1) ECHR and Article 49(1) Charter. Potential for such a divergence is also present in the Court's approach in the recent judgment in *BB construct*.[1272] In this judgment the Court determined that an obligation to

1267 See para 61. Cf Opinion of AG Szpunar, para 60.

1268 On *lex certa*, see subsections 2.3.3; 3.4.3; 3.6.3; 4.3.3.

1269 See *Italmoda*, para 61 and Case C-110/99, *Emsland-Stärke GmbH v Hauptzollamt Hamburg-Jonas*, EU:C:2000:695, para 56. For a comparable recent approach, see Case C-607/13, *Ministero dell'Economia e delle Finanze and Others v Francesco Cimmino and Others*, EU:C:2015:448, paras 73–75.

1270 See para 56.

1271 See section 4.3.

1272 Case C-534/16, *Finančné riaditeľstvo Slovenskej republiky v BB construct s. r. o.*, EU:C:2017:820.

provide a guarantee of up to 500 000 Euro in order to prevent VAT fraud did not constitute a penalty for the purpose of Article 49(1) CFR.[1273] It did not substantiate that determination, however, by referring to either the ECtHR's definition of the term 'penalty' or by referring to its own case-law. To dismiss the applicability of the EU legality principle, the Luxembourg Court essentially focused on how the aim of an obligation to provide a guarantee is not enforcement.[1274] That determination is not sufficient in light of the Strasbourg criteria, however, since the purpose of a measure is only one of six relevant criteria for the applicability of the ECHR's legality principle.[1275]

The approach in *Italmoda* and *BB construct* is therefore unclear about the exact scope of Article 49(1) CFR and, in addition, about the convergence of the scope of that provision with that of Article 7(1), second sentence, ECHR.

4.5.4 SCOPE OF APPLICATION II: THE DISTINCTION BETWEEN PROCEDURAL AND SUBSTANTIVE RULES

In addition to the possible limitation of the scope of Article 49(1) Charter to criminal offenses and penalties, the Charter's legality principle also appears to apply exclusively to rules of substantive criminal law. In *Taricco* the ECJ's Grand Chamber ruled that Italian courts could be required to disapply national statutory limitation periods for serious cases of VAT fraud in order to comply with the duty to provide effective and dissuasive criminal penalties for that conduct.[1276] The disapplication of strict limitation periods would extend the period after which the prosecution of a criminal offense becomes time-barred.[1277] Such an effect would obviously have a negative impact on the position of the accused in the main proceedings.[1278] Suspects of serious forms of VAT fraud could, in fact, be convicted on the basis of EU law's effect on national law, although that would have been impossible on the basis of the applicable Italian rules alone.[1279]

After potentially broadening the possibilities for a criminal conviction, the ECJ examined EU law's effect on national criminal proceedings in light of the legality principle.[1280] The Court referred to Article 49 Charter and established that this

1273 See paras 6, 8, 19, 31–33.
1274 See paras 32–33.
1275 On the other criteria, see subsection 3.3.3.
1276 See Case C-105/14, *Criminal proceedings against Ivo Taricco and Others*, EU:C:2015:555, paras 49, 52–53. Further about this judgment, see Timmerman 2016, p. 779–796.
1277 See paras 47–49.
1278 The ECtHR has acknowledged this impact by deeming that an extension of a limitation period has a detrimental effect on the situation of the accused, in particular by frustrating their expectations, see ECtHR, *Coëme and Others v. Belgium*, CE:ECHR:2000:0622JUD003249296, para 149.
1279 See para 53.
1280 See para 54.

provision enshrines the principle of legality of criminal offenses and penalties "(...) according to which, inter alia, no one is to be held guilty of any criminal offense on account of any act or omission which did not constitute a criminal offense under national law or international law at the time when it was committed."[1281] The ECJ thereby cited the first sentence of Article 49(1) Charter and used the provision's wording to determine that the extension of national limitation periods would not require the use of a *criminal offense* that was not already applicable in Italian law, nor would it require the introduction of a previously inapplicable domestic *penalty*.[1282] By focusing on the terms 'criminal offense' and 'penalty' the ECJ determined that the scope of the EU legality principle is limited to rules of *substantive* criminal law.[1283] In the Court's view, EU law's effect on national law would only provide additional time for prosecuting before national courts offenses and penalties that were fully applicable under Italian law.[1284] Union law would not, therefore, affect substantive criminal law in the main proceedings, which, according to the Court, ruled out a violation of the Charter's legality principle.[1285]

A distinction between substantive and procedural rules for the applicability of the EU legality principle is also perceivable in earlier judgments by the ECJ's Grand Chamber, for example in *Pupino*.[1286] In this judgment the ECJ famously applied the duty of consistent interpretation to framework decisions.[1287] It simultaneously applied 'legality principle-related'[1288] limits to that duty for acts under the former third pillar.[1289] In the Court's view, however, these limits did not necessarily apply when national rules of criminal *procedure* required consistent interpretation.[1290] Contrary to substantive rules, procedural rules would not, generally,[1291] alter domestic substantive criminal law by determining or aggravating criminal liability.[1292] By limiting the scope of the legality principle

---

1281 Para 54.

1282 See para 56.

1283 More explicitly on the limitation of the legality principle's scope to substantive rules, see *Taricco*, Opinion of AG Kokott, ECLI:EU:C:2015:293, paras 115–119. Cf Case C-296/08 PPU, *Ignacio Pedro Santesteban Goicoechea*, View of AG Kokott, EU:C:2008:455, para 45; Case C-79/11, *Criminal proceedings against Maurizio Giovanardi and Others*, Opinion of AG Sharpston, EU:C:2012:297, para 69. Cf Case C-42-17, *Criminal proceedings against M.A.S. and M.B. (Taricco II)*, EU:C:2017:936, para 42.

1284 See para 55.

1285 In *Taricco II* the Court nevertheless found decisive the fact that in Italy rules on statutory limitation formed part of the substantive criminal law, see Case C-42-17, *Criminal proceedings against M.A.S. and M.B. (Taricco II)*, EU:C:2017:936, paras 45, 59–61.

1286 Case C-105/03, *Criminal proceedings against Maria Pupino*, EU:C:2005:386. Cf Miettinen 2013, p. 90, 99.

1287 See para 43. For further discussion of this judgment, see subsection 5.3.3.

1288 On these limits, see subsection 4.2.3.

1289 Paras 44–45. Cf *Pupino*, Opinion of AG Kokott, EU:C:2004:712, paras 41–42.

1290 Para 46.

1291 In one judgment the ECtHR nevertheless found Italian 'procedural rules' to affect the scope of a criminal penalty, see subsection 3.3.3.

1292 Cf *Pupino*, Opinion of AG Kokott, EU:C:2004:712, paras 41–42; Lenaerts and Corthaut 2006, p. 296–297. Regarding the distinction between substantive and procedural rules in *Pupino*

to substantive rules, procedural provisions, such as the rules on taking evidence in *Pupino*, and the rules of statutory limitation in *Taricco*, can apparently be altered to the detriment of the accused after the alleged criminal behavior occurred.[1293]

That the legality principle's scope is limited to substantive criminal law is also perceivable in another well-known judgment: *Advocaten voor de Wereld*.[1294] In this preliminary ruling, the Grand Chamber assessed the validity of the Framework Decision on the European arrest warrant.[1295] The Court examined the framework decision's conformity with the legality principle, even though the EU measure exclusively harmonized *procedural* rules on extradition between Member States.[1296] The ECJ quickly dismissed the claims concerning a violation of the legality principle, however. It concluded that the principle of the legality of criminal offenses and penalties was not violated by the abolition of the requirement of double criminality for listed offenses, because the actual definition of the offenses and penalties continued to be a matter of the criminal law of the Member States.[1297] The Court essentially rejected a violation of the legality principle because EU law did not itself define offenses and penalties, nor did it require the alteration of offenses and penalties in national law via harmonization.[1298] As in *Pupino*, the Court implied that the EU legality principle would not be violated by Union law that merely affects rules on criminal procedure.[1299]

Although the framework decision itself did not violate the legality principle, the domestic definitions of offenses and penalties still could. According to the Court,

> "(...) while Article 2(2) of the Framework Decision dispenses with verification of double criminality for the categories of offences mentioned therein, the definition of those offences and of the penalties applicable continue to be matters determined by the law of the issuing Member State, which, as is, moreover, stated in Article 1(3) of the Framework Decision, must respect fundamental rights and fundamental legal principles as enshrined in Article 6 EU, and, consequently, the principle of the legality of criminal offences and penalties."[1300]

---

and the inapplicability of 'legality principle-related' limits to consistent interpretation, see, critically, Spaventa 2007, p. 13–14; Mitsilegas 2009, p. 30–31; Dougan 2012, p. 122. Mitsilegas is also critical about the distinction in *Taricco*, see Mitsilegas 2016, p. 79–80.

1293 Cf Case C-42-17, *Criminal proceedings against M.A.S. and M.B. (Taricco II)*, EU:C:2017:936, para 42.

1294 Case C-303/05, *Advocaten voor de Wereld v Leden van de Ministerraad*, EU:C:2007:261.

1295 See para 44. The framework decision: Council Framework Decision 2002/584/JHA of 13 June 2002 on the European arrest warrant and the surrender procedures between Member States [2002] OJ L 190.

1296 See paras 48–54.

1297 See para 53.

1298 See para 52.

1299 For more detail on this matter, see *Advocaten voor de Wereld*, Opinion of AG Ruiz-Jarabo Colomer, EU:C:2006:552, paras 100–107 and cf Case C-296/08 PPU, *Ignacio Pedro Santesteban Goicoechea*, View of AG Kokott, EU:C:2008:455, para 45. See, critically, Herlin-Karnell 2012, p. 27.

1300 Para 53.

By this consideration the Court essentially deems the EU legality principle applicable to the definition of the offenses and penalties mentioned in Article 2(2) of the framework decision. The Member States are thereby obliged to ensure that the national definitions of these offenses and penalties satisfy the demands of the EU legality principle, because these definitions could trigger mutual recognition on the basis of the framework decision. As a consequence, a framework decision that exclusively harmonized rules of criminal procedure resulted in the potential applicability of the EU legality principle to a large area of domestic substantive criminal law.[1301]

Despite significant differences in substance, the judgments in *Taricco*, *Pupino* and *Advocaten voor de Wereld* have all upheld the distinction between rules of substantive criminal law and rules of criminal procedure. For that reason, the Charter's legality principle, which, moreover, employs the terms 'criminal offense' and 'penalty', can be understood as applying exclusively to rules of substantive criminal law.[1302] However, as *Advocaten voor de Wereld* illustrates, that limited scope does not preclude the Charter's legality principle from applying to domestic substantive criminal law on the basis of EU instruments that exclusively intend to impact rules of criminal procedure.

4.5.5 SCOPE OF APPLICATION III: THE SIGNIFICANCE OF IMPLEMENTATION VIA CRIMINAL LAW OR PUNITIVE SANCTIONS

As subsection 4.4.2 determined, in *Intertanko* the Court deemed *Advocaten voor de Wereld*'s definition of legality relevant for non-criminal EU law implemented via national criminal law or domestic punitive sanctions. This consideration was subsequently reiterated with regard to Article 49(1) Charter, which underlines the applicability of the legality principle in these situations.[1303] At the same time, however, implementation via national criminal law has been considered as a limit on the applicability of the legality principle. When interpreting non-criminal EU law with relevance for national criminal law, the Court has, in fact, deemed itself unconstrained by the requirements of the EU legality principle. In other words, the EU legality principle is not considered applicable to the

1301 Cf Mitsilegas 2009, p. 142.

1302 See also Case C-574/15, *Proceedings against Mauro Scialdone*, Opinion of AG Bobek, EU:C:2017:553, paras 147, 149. This is, moreover, in line with settled EU case-law in which substantive rules, unlike procedural rules, are generally not applied to situations existing before their entry into force, see, with references, Case C-17/10, *Toshiba Corporation and Others v Úřad pro ochranu hospodářské soutěže*, EU:C:2012:72, para 47. Advocate General Ruiz-Jarabo Colomer nevertheless deemed the legality principle relevant for the CJEU's interpretation of rules of criminal procedure, see Case C-297/07, *Criminal proceedings against Klaus Bourquain*, Opinion of AG Ruiz-Jarabo Colomer, EU:C:2008:206, para 70.

1303 See, eg, *Aurubis Balgaria*; *Caronna* as described in, subsections 4.2.3; 4.3.3.

interpretation of non-criminal EU law by the CJEU even if this interpretation is directly relevant for the interpretation of national criminal law.

The above-mentioned consequences are essentially a result of the pre-Lisbon judgment in *Grøngaard and Bang*.[1304] In this preliminary ruling, the Court explicitly established that the interpretation of a prohibition in EU legislation "(...) cannot be dependent upon the civil, administrative or criminal nature of the proceedings in which it is invoked".[1305] In the Court's view, an exception to a general Union prohibition needs to be construed strictly, even when that prohibition is implemented via national criminal law.[1306] Although the Court's interpretation could affect the interpretation of implementing criminal law, the prohibited conduct in EU law should nevertheless be interpreted broadly. Since it is for the referring court to ensure that its interpretation of implementing legislation conforms with the legality principle, the ECJ is not, in these situations, limited by legality considerations such as the prohibition on overly extensive interpretation.[1307] This is not just the case with regard to directives, the Court also took this position early on with regard to the interpretation of regulations.[1308]

Grøngaard and Bang has not been reversed following the entry into force of the Charter and it appears to apply today. That the Court's interpretation of non-criminal EU legislation is unconstrained by the legality principle is perceivable in *A and B*.[1309] This preliminary ruling concerned the alleged participation of A and B in the evasion of VAT on trading in greenhouse gas emission allowances.[1310] The domestic criminal responsibility of A and B depended on the interpretation of the term 'similar right' in the VAT Directive,[1311] which had been transposed into German law.[1312] Although the interpretation of the term in the directive determined the criminal responsibility of the accused persons in the main proceedings, the Court did not let this influence its interpretation. The ECJ essentially referred only to the wording and purpose of the VAT Directive to interpret the term 'similar right'.[1313] While the accused in the main proceedings submitted that the Court's interpretation should be guided by the legality principle,[1314] the Court evidently followed Advocate General Wathelet. The Advocate General essentially reiterated the decision in *Grøngaard and Bang* by stating that

1304 Case C-384/02, *Criminal proceedings against Knud Grøngaard and Allan Bang*, EU:C:2005:708.
1305 Para 28.
1306 See para 27.
1307 Cf paras 29–30.
1308 See Case 238/84, *Criminal proceedings against Hans Röser*, EU:C:1986:88, paras 13–15, 24–26. Cf Altena-Davidsen 2016, p. 235–237.
1309 Case C-453/15, *Criminal proceedings against A and B*, EU:C:2016:933.
1310 See para 8.
1311 Directive 2006/112/EC.
1312 See paras 13–14.
1313 See paras 21–30.
1314 See *A and B*, Opinion of AG Wathelet, EU:C:2016:639, para 23.

"[f]irst and foremost, I should make clear that the Court's answer must concern only the interpretation of the VAT Directive and not the criminal law consequences that it may have in the main proceedings, since they fall within the exclusive jurisdiction of the referring court, which does not ask the Court about this".[1315]

Not all Advocates General are as convinced of the appropriateness of *Grøngaard and Bang* as Advocate General Wathelet, however. Advocate General Bot, for example, appears to reject the *Grøngaard and Bang* consideration in his Opinion in the preliminary ruling in *Afrasiabi*.[1316] Giving rise to this preliminary ruling were criminal proceedings against Afrasiabi and others for allegedly having violated restrictive measures imposed by Regulation No 423/2007.[1317] The national court requested the ECJ's guidance to resolve whether the defendants had infringed the regulation's prohibition by having participated in the supply and installation of a ceramic sintering furnace in Iran.[1318] The Court's interpretation was directly relevant for the scope of national criminal liability, because German law criminalized the violation of Regulation No 423/2007.[1319]

Advocate General Bot explicitly acknowledged the relevance of the legality principle for the interpretation of the regulation. He stated that

"(...) the search for the meaning and effect of the concepts to be defined must, first and foremost, take into account the penal context of which they form part. With regard to the criminal sphere, the provisions in which these notions appear must be specific and clear enough to ensure observance of the general principles of the law of the Union and, in particular, the principle of legal certainty and the principle *nullum crimen, nulla poena sine praevia lege poenali* [no crime and no penalty without a previous penal law]".[1320]

After recognizing the relevance of the legality principle, the Advocate General identified the limits it would provide. In Bot's view,

"(...) the necessary interpretation must be purposive in order to seek and express the *ratio legis* of the provision whose effectiveness Article 7(4) of the Regulation is intended to ensure. This method of interpretation is traditionally accepted, interpretation by analogy being, in contrast, strictly prohibited here because by its imprecision it infringes the principle that there must be a basis in law for all crimes and punishments".[1321]

By recognizing the prohibition on analogical interpretation, the Advocate General evidently deemed the legality principle relevant for the interpretation of EU legislation. Although Bot failed to recognize that analogical interpretation

1315 Opinion of AG Wathelet, para 36.
1316 Case C-72/11, *Criminal proceedings against Mohsen Afrasiabi and Others*, EU:C:2011:874.
1317 See paras 1, 18.
1318 See para 2.
1319 See para 18.
1320 *Afrasiabi*, Opinion of AG Bot, EU:C:2011:737, para 45.
1321 Para 46.

is only one form of overly extensive interpretation that could be prohibited,[1322] he apparently deemed a *lex stricta* principle applicable to judicial interpretations in preliminary rulings. The Court did not, however, recognize the legality principle or the principle of legal certainty as relevant for the interpretation of the regulation's 'broad' terms in its preliminary ruling.[1323] It thereby followed the *Grøngaard and Bang* approach, although not explicitly.

Advocate General Bobek has recently argued for the applicability of the principles of legality and legal certainty to the interpretation of EU legislation in preliminary rulings. In his Opinion in *Cosmetic Ingredients*, a preliminary ruling that concerned the interpretation of Regulation No 1223/2009 on cosmetic products,[1324] Bobek deemed it relevant that infringement of the regulation required sanctions under national law. In his view, the requirement of sanctions results in the applicability of the principles of legal certainty and legality and, more specifically, *lex certa*, "(...) which commands a very careful and a rather restrictive interpretative approach in cases where sanctions or fines are envisaged for violations of provisions with unclear scope or meaning".[1325] When the national court asks guidance on the interpretation of a regulation, the violation of which entails criminal sanctions under national law, the principles of legal certainty and legality must, according to the Advocate General, play a role in the interpretation of the regulation.[1326] As in *Afrasiabi*, however, the Court did not refer to the principles of legal certainty and legality when interpreting the regulation.[1327]

Although several Advocates General consider it appropriate to apply the legality principle to judicial interpretation by the Court in preliminary rulings, the *Grøngaard and Bang* approach is still upheld. This means that the EU legality principle is not applicable to the Court's interpretation in preliminary rulings, at least when the EU provisions themselves are not deemed to have a criminal character. As *Grøngaard and Bang* indicates, it is only for the referring court to use the CJEU's interpretation of EU law in a manner that is compatible with the EU legality principle.

4.5.6 FROM APPLICABILITY TO APPLICATION: THE DIVISION OF COMPETENCES IN PRELIMINARY RULINGS

As described in the preceding subsection, that the legality principle applies to definitions and interpretations of implementing law does not appear to limit the CJEU's interpretation of EU law. The judgment in *Grøngaard and Bang*

1322 See, eg, subsections 2.3.3; 3.4.3.
1323 See paras 37–57.
1324 See Case C-592/14, *European Federation for Cosmetic Ingredients v Secretary of State for Business, Innovation and Skills and Attorney General*, EU:C:2016:703, para 1.
1325 *Cosmetic Ingredients*, Opinion of AG Bobek, EU:C:2016:179, para 23.
1326 See paras 25, 27.
1327 See paras 28–45.

implies that, in these situations, it is only the domestic implementation via national criminal law or punitive sanctions that has to conform with the EU legality principle. Despite the applicability of the Charter's legality principle to implementing provisions and their interpretations, however, the Court has not itself examined these provisions and interpretations in light of Article 49(1) CFR. As will be illustrated, the Court has not actually applied the EU legality principle to national criminal law or punitive sanctions or their interpretation and application. Nor has it generally provided guidance to the national courts regarding the legality principle's application to these provisions and interpretations.

This lack of application and guidance by the CJEU can be illustrated by the *Garenfeld* judgment.[1328] Giving rise to the preliminary ruling in this case were criminal proceedings against Garenfeld for having allegedly exported old car parts to Lebanon.[1329] This conduct could give rise to criminal responsibility under German law if that export was prohibited by an EU regulation. Since German law criminalized the export of waste contrary to Regulation No 1418/2007, the national court asked the ECJ whether Garenfeld's conduct was prohibited by the regulation. Both the prohibition in the regulation and the interpretation given to it by the Court thereby became directly relevant for the scope of the criminal offense under German law.[1330]

After concluding that the accused's conduct was indeed prohibited by the regulation,[1331] which had the effect of criminalizing Garenfeld's conduct, the ECJ reiterated that the legality principle constituted a general principle of Union law which is, inter alia, enshrined in Article 49(1) Charter.[1332] As in *Intertanko*, and subsequently in *Rosneft*, the Court essentially reiterated the definition of legality first laid down in *Advocaten voor de Wereld*.[1333] The Court added, however, that the Member States are, in particular, required to observe this principle when they prescribe a penalty to punish a failure to comply with provisions of Union law.

Despite the explicit recognition of the EU legality principle's relevance for the Member States when they implement EU law via criminal law, the Court did not provide any guidance for the referring court's assessment other than the mere reiteration of the definition laid down in *Advocaten voor de Wereld*. The ECJ stated that

> "[a]s for the question whether, in this context, the provisions of EU law are sufficiently clear as to yield the constituent elements of the national law definition of an offence, in accordance with the principle of the legality of criminal offences and penalties, this falls (…) to be assessed by the referring court".[1334]

1328 Case C-405/10, *Criminal proceedings against Özlem Garenfeld*, EU:C:2011:722.
1329 See para 25.
1330 See paras 22–23.
1331 See paras 39–47.
1332 See para 48.
1333 See subsections 4.4.2; 4.5.7.
1334 Para 48.

Although the EU legality principle was evidently applicable to implementing criminal law, the Court left the assessment of whether the national law conformed with the EU legality principle entirely up to the referring court.[1335]

In the absence of specific interpretive guidelines for the German court, the ECJ essentially deferred the responsibility to protect the legality principle to the national court. This deference is indeed the standard in preliminary rulings concerning national implementing criminal law or punitive sanctions. In *SGS Belgium*, for example, the Court concluded that it was for the referring court to determine whether the application of a domestic penalty imposed for irregularities as defined by a regulation rested on a clear and unambiguous legal basis.[1336] The same approach was essentially taken in *Caronna*, where the Court left it to the domestic court to determine whether the appropriate domestic interpretation of implementing criminal law would be possible in light of the Charter's legality principle.[1337] The conformity of national legislation with, especially, the *lex certa* element of the EU legality principle and the conformity of domestic judicial interpretations with, in particular, the *lex stricta* element are therefore essentially matters for the referring courts.

The Court has only been less deferential in one judgment concerning the *lex praevia* element of the legality principle. In *E and F*, examined above in subsection 4.4.3, the Court determined the consequences of the EU principle of non-retroactivity for determinations of national criminal liability. The ECJ essentially dictated the outcome of the main proceedings by stating that

> "[i]n those circumstances, it is for the national court to decline to apply, in the proceedings before it, the [relevant EU provisions], which consequently cannot form any part of the basis for criminal proceedings against the defendants in respect of the period prior to 29 June 2007".[1338]

In contrast with the *Garenfeld* approach, the Court acknowledged the direct relevance of EU provisions for domestic criminal liability in light of (an element of) the legality principle. It consequently precluded the national court's use of the EU provisions in the main proceedings in order to protect the *lex praevia* principle.

The general deference to the national courts regarding protection of *lex certa* and *lex stricta* could have a procedural explanation. The relevant considerations relating to legality as described in sections 4.2–4.5 were all laid down in preliminary rulings. This is because all of these judgments concerned

---

1335 See paras 48–49.

1336 See para 62. On this judgment, see subsection 4.3.2.

1337 See paras 54–55 and for further discussion of this judgment, see subsection 4.2.3. For similar considerations, see, eg, *X 1996*, para 26; *Grøngaard and Bang*, para 29 as described in, respectively, subsections 4.2.3; 4.3.4; 4.5.5. See also Joined Cases C-206/88 and C-207/88, *Criminal proceedings against G. Vessoso and G. Zanetti*, Opinion of AG Jacobs, EUC:1989:644, para 26.

1338 *E and F*, para 61.

national criminal law or domestic punitive sanctions that raised questions about the protection of the EU legality principle or related principles. That national implementing law was the reason for most CJEU judgments on the legality principle evidently resulted in a limitation to a certain procedure.

The limitation to using the preliminary ruling procedure could explain the discernible deference of questions concerning legality protection to the national courts. This is because preliminary rulings entail a division of competence between the CJEU and Member State courts and tribunals. On the basis of Article 267 TFEU, the Luxembourg Court is only competent to interpret EU law, while it is a matter for the national courts alone to apply the CJEU's interpretation in the main proceedings and to interpret and apply domestic law.[1339] In theory, therefore, both the interpretation and application of national law, as well as the application of EU law to the facts in the main proceedings, are outside of the CJEU's jurisdiction. This characteristic explains why the Court has not itself applied the EU legality principle to the facts in the main proceedings to assess whether implementing provisions or their proposed interpretation conform with that principle.

The division of competence between the CJEU and national courts does not, however, fully explain the Court's approach to legality in preliminary rulings. As described above, the Court does not just leave the application of the EU legality principle to the referring courts. It does so in the absence of any guidance on the application of that principle, at least with regard to the elements *lex certa* and *lex stricta*. The absence of guidance for national courts on the protection of these elements of EU legality principle is not a necessary result of the preliminary reference procedure, however.

Regarding the conformity of implementing legislation with the principle of legal certainty, for example, the ECJ has provided more guidance to national courts. In *Karelia*, a judgment examined in subsection 4.4.2, the Court indicated that, in its view, the domestic penalties resulting from implementing legislation did not appear to be in line with the requirements of legal certainty. By indicating the reasons why domestic legislation would fall short of the EU requirements of legal certainty, the ECJ clearly limited the discretion of the referring court in its actual assessment of national law in light of the general principle of Union law. Due to the jurisdictional limitations in preliminary procedures, the Court left it up to the national court to verify and apply its considerations on the principle of legal certainty.

The approach in *Karelia* illustrates that the absence of guidance on the application of the *lex certa* element of the EU legality principle is not dictated by the division of competences in preliminary rulings. That it is possible to provide more guidance on whether interpretations of national law conform with EU fundamental rights, is perceivable in the previously examined judgment in *Damgaard*.[1340] After establishing how EU law requires the implementing

---

1339 See, eg, Lenaerts, Arts, Maselis and Bray 2006, p. 186–189; De la Mare and Donelly 2011, p. 367–368; Tridimas 2011, p. 738; Borberg and Fenger 2014, p. 1, 428; Tridimas 2015, p. 407.

1340 See subsection 4.2.3.

criminal law to be interpreted, the Court assessed whether the domestic criminal conviction would infringe the right to freedom of expression under EU law.[1341] The ECJ provided guidance to the referring court by considering that a criminal conviction as required by Union law would not necessarily infringe the right to freedom of expression as it "(...) could be considered reasonable and proportionate, in the light of the legitimate aim pursued, namely the protection of public health".[1342] While again stopping short of applying the EU right to national criminal law, the Court indicated that the right would not be infringed if the referring court interpreted national law in conformity with Union law. Such an approach could also have been taken with regard to the *lex stricta* element in cases where the interpretation of EU law affected domestic criminal responsibility.

Although the division of competences in preliminary rulings can explain the CJEU's non-application of the EU legality principle to implementing provisions and their interpretation, it does not convincingly explain the Court's lack of guidance to national courts on the protection of, particularly, the elements *lex certa* and *lex stricta*. As *Karelia* and *Damgaard* illustrate, the Court could have provided stronger guidance on the requirements of the EU legality principle for the interpretation and application of domestic implementing provisions.[1343]

4.5.7 SUBSTANCE: THE EXPLICIT RECOGNITION OF THE *LEX CERTA* PRINCIPLE

After the Charter's entry into force, the CJEU laid down explicit considerations on the substance of the legality principle by referring to Article 49(1) CFR. The recent *Rosneft* judgment is a clear example of this approach.[1344] This Grand Chamber preliminary ruling concerned EU restrictive measures on Russian undertakings, which applied to Rosneft. These measures gave rise to a preliminary ruling because Rosneft contested the validity of the EU restrictive measures and their implementation domestically before the High Court of Justice of England and Wales.[1345] Rosneft claimed that EU law violated the Union principles of legal certainty and *nulla poena sine lege certa* by, apparently,[1346] requiring the prescription of criminal penalties in national law for conduct that was unclearly

---

1341 See para 25.

1342 Para 28.

1343 On the potential for the CJEU to provide guidance on how to solve the dispute in the main proceedings, or even to determine the outcome of the dispute at the heart of the prelimary reference, see Tridimas 2011, p. 739–745; Tridimas 2015, p. 408–411.

1344 Case C-72/15, *PJSC Rosneft Oil Company v Her Majesty's Treasury and Others*, EU:C:2017:236.

1345 See paras 32–33.

1346 The applicable regulation does not expressly require 'criminal' penalties, see Article 8(1) Council Regulation (EU) No 833/2014 of 31 July 2014 concerning restrictive measures in view of Russia's actions destabilising the situation in Ukraine, [2014] OJ L 229. The Court apparently understands the requirement to adopt 'effective, proportionate and dissuasive' penalties for infringements of the regulation as a duty to criminalize infringements.

defined by an EU regulation.[1347] The applicant in the main proceedings contended that the Member States were, in any event, precluded from imposing criminal penalties for conduct defined by EU measures as long as the Court had not clarified the scope of the conduct prohibited by the EU provisions.[1348]

As in the earlier *Intertanko* ruling,[1349] the Court first recognized and defined the principle of legal certainty and then reiterated the legality principle.[1350] By referring to *Intertanko*, the Court, moreover, reiterated that the EU legality principle constitutes a specific expression of the principle of legal certainty.[1351] Unlike in *Intertanko*, however, the Court explicitly recognized the principle *nulla poena sine lege certa,* ie the *lex certa* principle, as an element of the Charter's legality principle.[1352] The ECJ, in fact, used only the *lex certa* principle to assess the acceptability of the use of general terms in the applicable regulation.[1353] The Court apparently viewed the *lex certa* principle in Article 49 Charter as a *lex specialis* of the general EU principle of legal certainty.[1354] Whereas the principles of legal certainty and legality were not strictly distinguished in *Intertanko* and *Karelia,*[1355] *Rosneft* was undeniably more clear-cut in this regard.

In *Rosneft*, the Court defined the legality principle by referring to the definition in *Intertanko*, which, as mentioned, largely reiterated the definition first laid down in *Advocaten voor de Wereld.* The ECJ considered that the principle "(...) implies, inter alia, that legislation must clearly define offenses and the penalties which they attract".[1356] By using the terms 'inter alia' the ECJ evidently acknowledged that the legality principle entails other requirements in addition to the need to provide clear definitions of crimes and penalties. This implicit acknowledgment is noteworthy, because it was omitted in the earlier definitions in *Advocaten voor de Wereld* and *Intertanko.*[1357] For that reason, earlier definitions arguably implied that the EU legality principle merely entailed a *lex certa* principle.

As in *Intertanko*, the ECJ commenced its examination by acknowledging that the contested EU measure contained general terms, in this instance: 'financial assistance', 'waters deeper than 150 meters', 'shale' and 'transferrable securities'. In the Court's view, however, general expressions are not by definition unclear.[1358] The use of general expressions in EU legislation does not, in any event, constitute a violation of the *lex certa* requirement in and of itself.[1359] The ECJ substantiated this determination by referring to the Strasbourg Court's

1347 See paras 35, 158.
1348 See paras 152, 160.
1349 See subsection 4.4.2.
1350 See paras 161–162.
1351 See para 162.
1352 See para 162.
1353 See paras 163–170.
1354 Cf subsections 4.4.2; 4.4.4.
1355 See subsection 4.4.2.
1356 Para 162.
1357 See subsection 4.4.2.
1358 See paras 159, 163.
1359 See para 165.

judgment in *Cantoni*, which underlines that the Convention's legality principle does not require the wording of legislation to be absolutely precise.[1360] In the Court's view, those considerations are equally valid for the *lex certa* principle in Article 49 Charter due to Article 52(3) Charter.[1361]

The *prima facie* acceptability of general terms in EU legislation requiring criminal penalties is, according to the Court, additionally supported by the ECtHR's foreseeability requirement.[1362] Since under Article 7 ECHR persons could be required to obtain legal advice in order to assess the consequences of certain conduct, the regulation's general terms, while not perfectly precise, did not make it impossible for an individual to know which acts and omissions he may be criminally liable for.[1363]

Finally, and again on the basis of ECtHR case-law,[1364] the Court established that the *lex certa* principle does not prohibit the gradual clarification of rules of criminal liability in case-law by means of reasonably foreseeable interpretations.[1365] The fact that the general terms used in EU legislation may be clarified by the Court does not, therefore, prevent a Member State from prescribing criminal penalties for the violation of the Union measure.[1366] On the basis of the Strasbourg Court's considerations, the ECJ concluded that the *lex certa* principle does not preclude a Member State from imposing criminal penalties for conduct prohibited by general expressions in the regulation.[1367]

By concluding that there had not been a violation of the *lex certa* principle, the Court clearly deemed that principle applicable to EU legislation requiring the imposition of domestic criminal penalties. This appears to be in contrast with the approach in *Intertanko*, where the ECJ dismissed the applicability of the EU legality principle to definitions in the applicable directive.[1368] It is also in apparent contrast with *Garenfeld*, where the Court did not apply the EU legality principle to a regulation, even though that instrument prohibited behavior that was criminalized by domestic law.[1369]

The applicability of the EU legality principle to non-criminal Union legislation in *Rosneft* apparently results from the Court's view that infringement of the regulation *required* the imposition of criminal penalties.[1370] In that situation, the Court could no longer deem the legality principle inapplicable to

1360 See para 164.
1361 See para 165.
1362 See para 166.
1363 See para 166.
1364 The Court referred to its judgment in *Danske Rørindustri*, but that judgment reiterated rather extensively ECtHR considerations on Article 7 ECHR, see, particularly, subsections 4.6.2; 4.6.5.
1365 See para 167.
1366 See para 168.
1367 See paras 169–170.
1368 See subsection 4.4.2.
1369 See subsection 4.5.6.
1370 See para 169.

non-criminal EU legislation by arguing that EU law left the type of sanctions up to the Member States. The Court's view that the violation of the regulation in *Rosneft* would require criminal penalties could thus explain why the Court, for the first time, applied the *lex certa* principle directly to EU legislation.

In addition to the explicit recognition of the *lex certa* element, *Rosneft* contains relevant considerations for the *lex stricta* principle. This results from the Court's acceptance of the gradual clarification of rules of criminal liability via reasonably foreseeable judicial interpretations.[1371] From this consideration the ECJ inferred that the scope of criminal responsibility for the infringement of EU provisions need not be clarified before they are imposed.[1372] The Court thereby essentially accepts uncertainty regarding the scope of EU law and associated provisions of national criminal law so long as this does not amount to the imposition of criminal liability which is not reasonably foreseeable. This underlines that the level of certainty provided by the elements *lex certa* and *lex stricta* is not necessarily very high.

The *lex certa* and *lex stricta* protection in *Rosneft* has, in any event, failed to address the particularities of the definition and interpretation of offenses and penalties in EU criminal law.[1373] Since the conduct prohibited by the regulation required implementation via the prescription of national criminal penalties, the Court could have acknowledged that the conduct in the case at hand is prohibited on the basis of a combination of EU legislation and national law. The ECJ could have then reflected on the potential implications of this special way of defining and prohibiting conduct for the protection of the *lex certa* principle. With regard to the *lex stricta* principle, the Court could have examined the significance of the characteristic that the interpretation of both EU law and national criminal law are relevant for the scope of criminal liability. Instead, however, the Court merely assessed whether this rather particular situation satisfied the ECtHR's minimum criteria developed to apply to the situation where conduct is generally defined and penalized on the basis of domestic legislation alone. The ECJ referred to Article 52(3) Charter as a justification for this. This reasoning is clearly unconvincing, however, because – as long as the ECHR standard is respected – that provision explicitly allows the Luxembourg Court to adopt a level of protection for the legality principle that is more appropriate for the specific situation of EU criminal law.

4.5.8 CONCLUDING REMARKS

The CJEU judgments described above merit several observations about the EU legality principle's sources, scope, and substance. As a point of departure, it is interesting to note the central position of the Charter's legality principle in *Paoletti*. Although Article 6(3) TEU recognizes that fundamental rights

1371 See para 167.
1372 See para 170.
1373 See further sections 5.6 and 6.4.

constitute general principles of EU law, *Paoletti* implies that, when the Charter applies,[1374] Article 49(1) Charter will replace legality as a general principle of Union law. The ECJ nevertheless continues to refer to legality as a general principle of EU law in post-Lisbon case-law.[1375]

In addition to the apparently diminished relevance of legality as a general principle, the ECJ appears to have weakened the importance of Article 7 ECHR for the EU legality principle. Despite the explicit reference to the Convention in Article 6(3) TEU, and the ECHR's relevance for the interpretation of the Charter's legality principle,[1376] the ECJ downplayed the Convention's significance in *Paoletti*. The Court thus evidently considers the legality principle in the Charter to be the primary source of the EU legality principle. At the same time, however, the ECJ continues to refer to both Article 7 ECHR and the Strasbourg Court's case-law when interpreting the legality principle in the Charter.[1377]

The emphasis on Article 49(1) Charter in *Paoletti* has not precluded references to legality as a general principle of Union law and to Article 7 ECHR and the Strasbourg Court's case-law. It is, therefore, questionable whether *Paoletti*'s apparent 'Charter-centrism' will persist in subsequent judgments on the legality principle. As a result of these doubts, the exact relationship between the CFR's legality principle, legality as an unwritten Union principle, and Article 7 ECHR remains underdetermined.[1378]

As a primary, and perhaps even exclusive, source of the EU legality principle, the Charter's scope merits consideration. Article 49(1) CFR's close textual proximity to Article 7 ECHR warrants a comparison between the CJEU's and the ECtHR's approach to the legality principle's applicability. As mentioned, the CJEU has yet to employ the term 'criminal offense' and the ECtHR's *Engel*-criteria to determine the applicability of the first sentence of Article 49(1) Charter. On the basis of judgments described in subsection 4.5.3 it is nevertheless reasonable to assume that the Luxembourg Court will use the *Engel* criteria to determine the applicability of the Charter's legality principle. The Court will not, in all likelihood, apply the Strasbourg Court's criteria exclusively, however. The CJEU will first look to its own case-law for indications on the interpretation of the term 'criminal offense' and the scope of the Charter's legality principle.

With regard to EU law implemented via national criminal law or punitive provisions, the Court has not employed the term 'penalty' either. As *Italmoda* illustrates, the Court has sometimes determined the applicability of the legality principle exclusively on the basis of its own case-law on the interpretation of

1374 For the applicability of the Charter, see further subsection 5.5.4.

1375 See *Aurubis Balgaria*, paras 41–42; *Garenfeld*, para 48. For further discussion of these judgments, see, respectively subsections 4.3.3; 4.5.6. On the relationship between the Charter and the general principles of Union law in post-Lisbon judgments, see subsection 5.5.5.

1376 See Article 52(3) Charter. See further subsection 5.5.4.

1377 See, eg, *Taricco*, para 57; *Rosneft*, paras 164–167.

1378 See further section 5.5.

penalties outside the specific context of Article 49(1) CFR.[1379] Due to the absence of an explicit assessment of the Strasbourg applicability criteria, the CJEU risks interpreting the scope of the legality principle more narrowly than required by the Convention.[1380] The EU-centered approach could therefore fail to respect Article 52(3) Charter.

The terms 'criminal offense' and 'penalty' indicate the applicability of Article 49(1) Charter to *substantive* criminal law. The general inapplicability of the Charter's legality principle to procedural rules is clearly perceivable in *Taricco*. The ECJ's distinction between substantive and procedural rules is, moreover, in accordance with the Court's approach to the applicability of legality as a general principle of Union law in its pre-Charter case-law.

The Charter's legality principle has, moreover, been deemed inapplicable to interpretations by the CJEU, at least when the CJEU is interpreting non-criminal Union law that is implemented via criminal law or punitive sanctions. Although several Advocates General considered the principle applicable, the Court still appears to uphold its considerations in *Grøngaard and Bang*. The fact that EU legislation is implemented via national criminal or punitive sanctions is not, for that reason, sufficient to apply the CFR's legality principle to the interpretation of EU legislation. This reasoning implies that the EU legality principle is also inapplicable to the definitions used in non-criminal Union law which are implemented via national criminal law or punitive sanctions. Although that approach is perceivable in *Intertanko* and *Garenfeld*, the Court has recently deemed the EU *lex certa* principle applicable to non-criminal Union legislation in *Rosneft*. The *Rosneft* approach followed from the Court's determination that the EU regulation *required* criminal penalties. Since EU legislation generally leaves the exact means of implementation up to the Member States, the Charter's legality principle will essentially apply only to the domestic definitions and interpretations of implementing law.

The applicability of the Charter's legality principle to implementing criminal law or punitive sanctions does not lead to a self-evident application of that principle, however. As described in subsection 4.5.6, the CJEU has not itself applied the legality principle to implementing provisions due to its limited jurisdiction in preliminary rulings. It has not, moreover, generally provided guidance to the national courts on the application of the EU legality principle. The protection of the *lex certa* and *lex stricta* elements of Article 49(1) CFR are therefore left completely to the domestic courts in these situations, which leaves the national courts guessing about the requirements of these elements in Union law. Such an approach is not a necessary result of the division of competences in preliminary rulings.

[1379] This approach fits well with earlier observations in the present subsection and with the approach in *Bonda* and *Taricco*, see subsection 4.5.3.

[1380] Cf *BB construct* as described in subsection 4.5.3.

4.6 ADMINISTRATIVE SANCTIONS IMPOSED BY EU INSTITUTIONS

4.6.1 INTRODUCTION

The EU legality principle has not just been relevant in preliminary rulings concerning the implementation of Union law via national criminal law or punitive sanctions. Many relevant considerations in the CJEU's case-law are laid down in judgments concerning administrative sanctions imposed by EU institutions. In quantitative terms, fines imposed by the Commission for the infringement of EU competition law have been most important for the development of the EU legality principle. More recently, challenges to restrictive measures imposed for, essentially, terrorism, have also given rise to considerations on the legality principle. The present section examines the CJEU's considerations on the legality principle in these judgments. In line with the quantitative significance of judgments concerning competition law, legality considerations laid down in that context will figure most prominently hereinafter.

Subsection 4.6.2 examines the applicability of the legality principle to fines imposed for infringements of competition law. Thereafter, subsection 4.6.3 considers the applicability of a closely related principle: the principle that penalties must have a proper legal basis. The applicability of the legality principle to administrative sanctions outside the field of competition law will be examined in subsection 4.6.4. Subsections 4.6.5–4.6.7 focus on substance by examining the CJEU's considerations which, as we will soon see, have generally referred to the Strasbourg Court's case-law on Article 7 ECHR. Subsection 4.6.5 examines the acceptability of the retroactive use of fining guidelines for the calculation of penalties for competition law infringements. Subsections 4.6.6–4.6.7 essentially examine the CJEU's use of the foreseeability requirement in the field of competition law. Concluding observations are made in subsection 4.6.8.

4.6.2 APPLICABILITY OF THE LEGALITY PRINCIPLE TO PENALTIES IN EU COMPETITION LAW

The applicability of the legality principle in EU competition law has been deemed appropriate since the early case of *Bertoli*.[1381] In *Bertoli* the applicant appealed against a fine for failing to comply with Article 60 of the ECSC Treaty. The Commission had imposed the fine because Bertoli had reduced prices without publishing them.[1382] Since Bertoli had reduced prices by more than ten percent,

1381 Case 8/83, *Officine Fratelli Bertoli SpA v Commission of the European Communities*, EU:C:1984:129.

1382 See para 3.

the standard fine equal to the unpublished price reductions was increased by ten percent.[1383] Bertoli claimed that the Commission had acted unlawfully because it had not used calculation criteria in force at the time of the reductions in price. The fine, the applicant pointed out, would have been significantly lower had the Commission applied the correct calculation criteria.[1384] Bertoli therefore contended that the Commission "(...) was under an obligation, by virtue of the principle *nullum crimen, nulla poena sine lege,* whatever the date on which the penalty was imposed, to refer to the criteria in force at the time of the infringement".[1385]

Despite the Commission's objections,[1386] the ECJ examined the applicant's claim regarding the principle *nulla poena sine lege*. At the same time, the Court avoided ruling on the general applicability of that principle to EU administrative penalties.[1387] Although the applicability of the principle *nulla poena sine lege* to administrative penalties was intentionally left unresolved, the Court examined the applicant's argument based on that principle. The ECJ did not accept that there had been any infringement of the legality principle, however, because the rate of the imposed fine was not in excess of the limits laid down in Article 64 of the ECSC Treaty.[1388]

The applicability of the legality principle in competition law was also acknowledged by the ECJ's Grand Chamber in *Danske Rørindustri*.[1389] In this judgment, which will be examined in more detail below,[1390] the ECJ considered that

> "(...) the principle of non-retroactivity of criminal laws, enshrined in Article 7 of the ECHR as a fundamental right (...) must be observed when fines are imposed for infringement of the competition rules and that that principle requires that the penalties imposed correspond with those fixed at the time when the infringement was committed".[1391]

By requiring that penalties remain within the limits that were legally in place at the time of the infringement, the Court essentially applied the principle *nulla poena sine lege* to EU competition law.[1392] *Danske Rørindustri* thus confirmed the early approach in *Bertoli*.

1383 See para 8.
1384 See para 24.
1385 Para 24.
1386 See para 25.
1387 See para 27.
1388 See para 27. On this reasoning, see further subsection 4.6.5.
1389 Joined Cases C-189/02 P, C-202/02 P, C-205/02 P TO C-208/02 P and C-213/02 P, *Danske Rørindustri and Others v Commission of the European Communities*, EU:C:2005:408.
1390 See Subsection 4.6.5.
1391 Para 202.
1392 Cf Case T-99/04, *AC-Treuhand AG v Commission of the European Communities*, EU:T:2008:256, para 139; Case T-446/05, *Amann & Söhne GmbH & Co. KG and Cousin Filterie SAS v European Commission*, EU:T:2010:165, paras 151–152.

The CJEU has subsequently deemed the legality principle applicable to penalties for infringements of competition law. In *AC-Treuhand 2008*, for example, the Court of First Instance (hereinafter also: 'the CFI') recognized the principle *nullum crimen, nulla poena sine lege* as a general principle of EU law and deemed it applicable to EU competition law.[1393] However, due to the administrative nature of competition law, the general principles of Union law "(...) need not necessarily have the same scope as when they apply to a situation covered by criminal law in the strict sense".[1394] While confirming the applicability of the legality principle, the CFI simultaneously identified competition law as a factor that could restrict the scope of the principle when it is applied beyond criminal law *sensu stricto*.[1395]

The General Court adopted a comparable reasoning in *Sasol*.[1396] While recognizing that the applicants relied on the principle of legality of criminal offenses and penalties, the Court underlined the difference between competition law and criminal law. In the Court's view

> "(...) it should be noted that while competition law is indeed similar to criminal law, it is not at the 'heart' of criminal law. Outside the 'hard core' of criminal law, the guarantees in matters of criminal law laid down in Article 6 of the ECHR will not necessarily apply with their full stringency (see European Court of Human Rights, *Jussila v. Finland* [GC], no. 73053/01, §43, ECHR 2006-XIV)".[1397]

With regard to the interpretation of the Charter's legality principle in EU competition law, the General Court ruled that the ECtHR case-law on, essentially, the right to a fair trial should be extended, by analogy, to Article 7 ECHR.[1398] One reason for this is the fact that "(...) in the area of competition law, unlike criminal law, both the benefits and the penalties for unlawful activities are purely pecuniary (...)".[1399]If the fines for violations of competition law were

> "(...) to be more or less predictable, this would have highly damaging consequences for EU competition policy, since the undertakings committing the infringements could directly compare the costs and benefits of their unlawful activities, and also take into account the chances of being discovered, and thus attempt to ensure that those activities are profitable (...)".[1400]

1393 See *AC-Treuhand AG v Commission of the European Communities*, EU:T:2008:256, para 113.

1394 Para 113.

1395 Cf Van Bael 2011, p. 220–222.

1396 Case T-541/08, *Sasol and Others v European Commission*, EU:T:2014:628.

1397 Para 206. With respect to the intensity of the application of the requirements of Article 6 ECHR, the ECtHR has also acknowledged the difference between competition law and criminal law in *A. Menarini Diagnostics S.R.L. v. Italy*, CE:ECHR:2011:0927JUD004350908, para 62.

1398 See para 213. Cf Altena-Davidsen 2016, p. 91. About the applicability of the right to a fair trial to competition law, see, eg, Giannakopoulos 2011, p. 23–27.

1399 Para 207. See, critically, Altena-Davidsen 2016, p. 92.

1400 Para 207.

In order to ensure the effectiveness of EU competition rules,[1401] the General Court apparently required a lower level of foreseeability of the potential penalties for violations of competition law than it would if the violations concerned the 'hard core' of criminal law.[1402]

While *AC-Treuhand 2008* and *Sasol* indicated a special, potentially more limited, protection of legality in EU competition law, both judgments acknowledged the relevance of the legality principle. In other judgments, however, the CJEU recognized the legality principle, or specific elements thereof, without the aforementioned reservations. In *Jungbunzlauer*, for example, the CFI reiterated that 'the principle of legality', as a general principle of EU law, requires that rules that impose or permit penalties are so clear and precise that the persons concerned may be able to unequivocally ascertain their rights and obligations.[1403] In the Court's view, it is settled case-law that this principle must also be observed in relation to specific administrative instruments imposing or permitting the imposition of administrative penalties and that it applies to rules establishing the elements of an offense and rules specifying the consequences that arise from an offense.[1404]

In *Denki* the General Court recognized the relevance of Article 7 ECHR and especially, as an apparent element thereof, the principle that penal provisions may not have retroactive effect.[1405] In conformity with *Danske Rørindustri* the Court considered the principle of non-retroactivity of criminal law applicable to fines under the Treaty rules on competition.[1406] In the General Court's view, the non-criminal nature of fines for infringements of competition law did not preclude the applicability of the principle that penal provisions may not have retroactive effect.[1407] In *Saint-Gobain Glass* the General Court even considered it a matter of settled case-law that the principle of non-retroactivity of criminal

1401 See para 214.

1402 Cf Case T-279/02, Degussa AG v Commission of the European Communities, EU:T:2006:103, para 83; Case T-43/02, *Jungbunzlauer AG v Commission of the European Communities*, EU:T:2006:270, para 84; *Saint-Gobain Glass*, paras 276–277; Cases T-426/10 to T-429/10 and T-438/12 to T-441/12, *Moreda-Riviere Trefilerías, SA and Others v European Commission*, EU:T:2016:33, paras 424–426.

1403 See Case T-43/02, *Jungbunzlauer AG v Commission of the European Communities*, EU:T:2006:270, para 71. See also *AC-Treuhand 2008*, para 139; C-352/09, *ThyssenKrupp Nirosta GmbH v European Commission*, EU:C:2011:191, para 80; Case C-501/11 P, *Schindler Holding Ltd and Others v European Commission*, EU:C:2013:522, para 57.

1404 See para 72. Cf Case C-266/06 P, *Evonik Degussa GmbH v Commission of the European Communities*, EU:C:2008:295, paras 38–39; Case T-704/14, *Marine Harvest ASA v European Commission*, EU:T:2017:753, para 378.

1405 See Case T-83/08, *Denki Kagaku Kogyo Kabushiki Kaisha and Denka Chemicals GmbH v European Commission*, EU:T:2012:48, para 120. See also Case T-92/13, *Koninklijke Philips Electronics NV v European Commission*, EU:T:2015:605, para 136.

1406 See paras 120, 122. See also Case T-92/13, *Koninklijke Philips Electronics NV v European Commission*, EU:T:2015:605, paras 136–137.

1407 See para 122. See also Case T-92/13, *Koninklijke Philips Electronics NV v European Commission*, EU:T:2015:605, para 137.

laws applies to competition law.[1408] In this judgment, the Court reiterated the aforecited consideration in *Danske Rørindustri* while recognizing Article 49(1) Charter as a relevant source of the principle of non-retroactivity in addition to Article 7 ECHR.[1409] The General Court recently confirmed the relevance of Article 49(1) Charter for competition law in *Moreda-Riviere*.[1410] It underlined that, by virtue of Article 52(3) Charter, the Charter's legality principle should provide protection equivalent to that under Article 7 ECHR.

Although the above case-law is inconsistent in terms of how the legality principle is formulated and its protective scope in competition law, all judgments unequivocally deem the legality principle applicable to administrative sanctions imposed for violations of EU competition law. The principle's applicability to competition law is not surprising as certain competition infringements have also been criminalized by several EU Member States.[1411]

4.6.3 APPLICABILITY CONTINUED: REAPPEARANCE OF THE PRINCIPLE THAT PENALTIES MUST HAVE A PROPER LEGAL BASIS

The apparent relationship between the principle that penalties must have a proper legal basis and the legality principle is also perceivable in EU competition law.[1412] In *Degussa*, for example, the CFI deemed the principle that penalties must have a proper legal basis to be enshrined in Article 7 ECHR.[1413] Despite the Council's objections regarding the relevance of Article 7 ECHR for non-criminal competition law,[1414] the CFI reiterated some of the ECtHR's considerations on Article 7 of the Convention.[1415] As in the early judgment of *Bertoli*,[1416] however, the Court circumvented the general issue of the Convention's applicability. Since, in the CFI's view, Article 7 ECHR did not preclude the sanctions imposed on the applicants, it was not necessary "(…) to rule on the question whether, by reason

1408 See Cases T-56/09 and T-73/09, *Saint-Gobain Glass France SA and Others v European Commission*, EU:T:2014:160, para 267.

1409 See para 267. In *Philips* the Court additionally referred to Article 49 Charter as well, while fully confirming the earlier approach in *Denki*, see Case T-92/13, *Koninklijke Philips Electronics NV v European Commission*, EU:T:2015:605, para 136.

1410 Cases T-426/10 to T-429/10 and T-438/12 to T-441/12, *Moreda-Riviere Trefilerías, SA and Others v European Commission*, EU:T:2016:335, para 417.

1411 Cf Whelan 2012, p. 678; Whelan 2014, p. 183–190.

1412 On the relationship between these principles with regard to judgments concerning implementing criminal law or punitive sanctions, see section 4.3.

1413 Case T-279/02, Degussa AG v Commission of the European Communities, EU:T:2006:103, paras 66–68. See also Case T-69/04, Schunk GmbH and Schunk Kohlenstoff-Technik GmbH v Commission of the European Communities, EU:T:2008:415, paras 28–29.

1414 See para 70.

1415 See paras 69, 72. See also *Jungbunzlauer*, paras 76–80.

1416 See subsection 4.6.2.

inter alia of the nature and severity of the fines imposed by the Commission pursuant to Article 15(2) of Regulation No 17, Article 7(1) of the ECHR has authority to apply to such sanctions (…)".[1417] By reiterating several general considerations on Article 7 ECHR, the CFI essentially deemed the Convention's legality principle applicable in EU competition law by referring to the Union principle that penalties must have proper legal basis.[1418]

The General Court took a comparable approach in *Dornbracht*.[1419] Here the Court again recognized the relevance of the principle that penalties must have a proper legal basis, but now it added a reference to Article 49 Charter in addition to Article 7 ECHR.[1420] In the Court's view, the principle enshrined in these provisions "(…) is a corollary of the principle of legal certainty, which requires that EU rules define offenses and penalties clearly (…)".[1421] The use of the terms 'offenses' and 'penalties' confirms the view that, in competition law, the Court has, in fact, deemed the legality principle applicable by referring to it as the principle that penalties must have proper legal basis.

The General Court recently confirmed this approach in *Lundbeck*.[1422] As in *Dornbracht*, the Court understood the principle that penalties must have a proper legal basis as enshrined in Article 49 Charter and Article 7 ECHR.[1423] In the Court's view, this principle may preclude the retroactive application of a new interpretation of a rule establishing an offense.[1424] By referring to the requirements for an 'offense' the Court essentially deems these requirements applicable in EU competition law on the basis of the principle that penalties must have a proper legal basis. That last-mentioned principle was apparently related to the legality principle, because it was deemed to be enshrined in Article 49 Charter and Article 7 ECHR.

1417 Para 71. See also *Jungbunzlauer*, paras 79.

1418 See also Case T-69/04, *Schunk GmbH and Schunk Kohlenstoff-Technik GmbH v Commission of the European Communities*, EU:T:2008:415, para 29; Case T-446/05, *Amann & Söhne GmbH & Co. KG and Cousin Filterie SAS v European Commission*, EU:T:2010:165, paras 124–125.

1419 Case T-386/10, *Aloys F. Dornbracht GmbH & Co. KG v European Commission*, EU:T:2013:450. The appeal against this judgment was dismissed in Case C-604/13 P, *Aloys F. Dornbracht GmbH & Co. KG v European Commission*, EU:C:2017:45.

1420 See paras 59–60.

1421 Para 60. Cf Case T-69/04, *Schunk GmbH and Schunk Kohlenstoff-Technik GmbH v Commission of the European Communities*, EU:T:2008:415, para 29; Case T-446/05, *Amann & Söhne GmbH & Co. KG and Cousin Filterie SAS v European Commission*, EU:T:2010:165, para 124; C-352/09, *ThyssenKrupp Nirosta GmbH v European Commission*, EU:C:2011:191, para 80; Case T-240/07, *Heineken Nederland BV and Heineken NV v European Commission*, EU:T:2011:284, paras 383–384.

1422 Case T-472/13, *H. Lundbeck A/S and Lundbeck Ltd v European Commission*, EU:T:2016:449.

1423 See para 763.

1424 See para 763. See also the related judgment in Case T-470/13, *Merck KGaA v European Commission*, EU:T:2016:452, para 509. Cf Case T-467/13, *Arrow Group ApS and Arrow Generics Ltd v European Commission*, EU:T:2016:450, para 369; Case T-460/13, *Sun Pharmaceutical Industries Ltd, formerly Ranbaxy Laboratories Ltd and Ranbaxy (UK) Ltd v European Commission*, EU:T:2016:453, para 304.

Although the aforementioned judgments confirm the relevance of the legality principle, it should be noted that the requirement of a proper legal basis is not only related to the legality principle. In both *Degussa* and *Dornbracht*, as well as in *Heineken*,[1425] the CJEU considered the principle that penalties must have a proper legal basis as a corollary of the principle of legal certainty.[1426] The close relationship between the two principles in the CJEU's considerations makes it hard to determine which requirements follow from which principle. Although the Court distinguished the requirements of both principles in *Heineken* and *Dornbracht*, in *Degussa* the CFI formulated the requirements of the principle of legal certainty on the basis of the principle that penalties must have a proper legal basis.[1427] Moreover, in *Heineken* and *Dornbracht*, as well as subsequently in *Lundbeck*, the General Court *jointly* examined the applicants' claims about a violation of the principle that penalties must have a proper legal basis and the principle of legal certainty.[1428] This joint examination further complicates the distinction between the requirements that follow from each individual principle with regard to penalties.

It could be concluded that, despite some potential overlap with the principle of legal certainty, the CJEU has often used the principle that penalties must have a proper legal basis to establish the applicability of the legality principle in EU competition law. This indicates that the legality principle is applicable to *non-criminal* penalties by virtue of the general requirement that penalties must rest on a proper legal basis. Although the penalties do not have to be criminal to trigger the substantive protection of the legality principle under the requirement of a proper legal basis, they surely do have to be *penalties*.

This rather obvious limitation of the scope of the requirement of a proper legal basis is illustrated by the judgment *Spain v Commission*, which concerns measures imposed by EU institutions outside the field of competition law.[1429] In this judgment, the Kingdom of Spain objected to the alleged retroactive application of new harsher EU rules on deductions from fishing quotas on the basis of, inter alia, the principle that penalties must have a proper legal basis.[1430] The General Court nevertheless deemed the requirement of a proper legal basis inapplicable, because it rejected the view that deductions from fishing quotas

1425 See Case T-240/07, *Heineken Nederland BV and Heineken NV v European Commission*, EU:T:2011:284, paras 383–384.

1426 See *Degussa*, para 66; *Dornbracht*, para 60. On the relationship between legality and legal certainty in EU case-law, see subsection 4.4.2.

1427 See para 66.

1428 See *Heineken*, paras 383–384, 388; *Dornbracht*, paras 62–64; *Lundbeck*, paras 763–778. See also the related judgments in Case T-467/13, *Arrow Group ApS and Arrow Generics Ltd v European Commission*, EU:T:2016:450, paras 369–377; Case T-460/13, *Sun Pharmaceutical Industries Ltd, formerly Ranbaxy Laboratories Ltd and Ranbaxy (UK) Ltd v European Commission*, EU:T:2016:453, paras 304–313. In the aforementioned judgment in *Arrow* the General Court referred to 'the principle that penalties must be provided for by law' instead of the requirement of a proper legal basis, see para 369.

1429 Case T-76/11, *Kingdom of Spain v European Commission*, EU:T:2012:613.

1430 See paras 36–37.

constitute a penalty.[1431] It can therefore be concluded that, while the principle that penalties must have a proper legal basis can extend the protection of the legality principle to EU administrative sanctions, it cannot extend that protection to EU measures that are not penalties.

4.6.4 APPLICABILITY TO ADMINISTRATIVE SANCTIONS OUTSIDE THE FIELD OF COMPETITION LAW?

The relevance of the legality principle for EU administrative sanctions is not necessarily limited to penalties imposed for infringements of competition law. In fact, the General Court explicitly examined the applicability of the EU legality principle in judgments concerning the freezing of assets based on EU law. In *Ezz and Others*, for example, the Court employed the ECtHR's criteria to determine whether freezing the applicants' assets amounted to a penalty for the purpose of Article 49(1) Charter.[1432] In order to determine whether the 'broad interpretation'[1433] of the legal criteria to be satisfied before the imposition of freezing measures complied with the Charter, the Court referred to the first sentence of Article 7(1) ECHR and the Strasbourg Court's case-law on the term 'penalty'.[1434]

By determining that EU law does not understand the freezing of assets on the basis of Council Decision 2011/172/CFSP as being of a criminal law nature,[1435] the General Court apparently concluded that the freezing measure was not imposed following a criminal conviction. This is important because the ECtHR's starting-point for examining a measure is whether it is 'imposed following a conviction for a criminal offense'.[1436] The absence of aspects relating to criminal law could also have been relevant for finding that the measure was not a criminal penalty under the applicable law, which the ECtHR deems to be one of the other relevant factors for Article 7(1) ECHR. Although it is unclear exactly how the General Court intended its consideration that asset freezing is not of a criminal law nature, it unmistakably used it as an argument for rejecting asset freezing as a penalty.

The Court additionally determined that the purpose of asset freezing is non-punitive, because it merely intends to preserve assets and does not seek to prevent the repetition of conduct or strive to punish individuals for their acts.[1437] The General Court apparently inferred from this that the measure's purpose, which is another factor identified as relevant by the ECtHR, did not require it to label

---

[1431] See paras 66, 69, 71–72, 75, 78–79.

[1432] Case T-256/11, *Ahmed Abdelaziz Ezz and Others v Council of* the European Union, EU:T:2014:93. The appeal against this judgment was dismissed by the ECJ, see Case C-220/14 P, Ahmed Abdelaziz Ezz and Others v Council of the European Union, EU:C:2015:147.

[1433] See paras 67, 69.

[1434] See paras 75–76.

[1435] See para 77.

[1436] See subsection 3.3.3.

[1437] See para 78.

the freezing measure as a penalty. As a final argument, the Court underlined the temporary and reversible effects of the measure.[1438] In so doing, the CJEU arguably employed the ECtHR's case-law concerning the relevance of 'nature of the measure' as a reason for dismissing the freezing as a penalty. As a result, the General Court used three arguments to conclude that the freezing of assets did not come within the scope of Article 49(1) Charter.[1439]

Although the General Court interpreted the scope of the Charter's legality principle on the basis of the Strasbourg case-law, that interpretation remains somewhat obscure. This is because, firstly, the CJEU did not explicitly link its considerations on the freezing measure to the six *individual* criteria established by the ECtHR.[1440] This leads to speculation about how the General Court used the criteria, as set out above. Why the Court only employed the aforementioned three criteria also remains unclear. The Court did not clarify its approach with regard to asset freezing and the legality principle in the subsequent *Al Matri* judgment.[1441] In fact, instead of the three arguments employed in *Ezz and Others*, the General Court only relied upon a single explicit argument. The CJEU excluded asset freezing from the scope of, inter alia, the Charter's legality principle in view of its 'purely precautionary nature'.[1442] It thus considered the 'nature of the measure' an especially significant factor for finding that asset freezing is not a penalty, although it did not consider the ECtHR's other factors. Instead of clarifying the approach in *Ezz and Others*, the Court merely referred to its considerations in that judgment.

A second characteristic that obscures the CJEU's approach to the applicability of the legality principle is the Court's reference to provisions enshrining the EU and ECHR legality principles. In *Ezz and Others* and *Al Matri* the General Court consistently referred to the *first sentence* of both Article 49(1) Charter and Article 7(1) ECHR.[1443] The first sentence of both provisions does not, however, contain the term penalty which the Court used to determine whether freezing measures fall within the scope of the legality principle. That term is only enshrined in the *second sentence* of these provisions. Under the ECHR the term penalty is therefore used to determine the scope of the *nulla poena* principle enshrined in Article 7(1)'s second sentence.[1444] As mentioned in subsections 3.3.3 and 4.5.3, the Strasbourg Court uses the *Engel* criteria with regard to the applicability of the *nullum crimen* principle set out in the first sentence of Article 7(1). As a consequence

---

1438 See para 79. The ECJ had also used the temporary nature of a measure as an argument for why it was non-punitive in *Bonda*, see Case C-489/10, *Criminal proceedings against Łukasz Marcin Bonda*, EU:C:2012:319, para 40.

1439 See *Ezz and Others*, para 80.

1440 See subsection 3.3.3.

1441 Case T-545/13, *Fahed Mohamed Sakher Al Matri v Council of the European Union*, ECLI:EU:T:2016:376.

1442 *Al Matri*, para 85.

1443 See *Ezz and Others*, paras 70, 73, 75, 80; *Al Matri*, para 85.

1444 See section 3.3.

of the consistent reference to the first sentence of Article 49(1) Charter, it is not entirely clear whether the CJEU wanted to use the overlapping, yet distinguishable, Strasbourg criteria to interpret the term penalty or the term 'criminal offense'. It has not, in any event, distinguished both sets of criteria sufficiently.

Although the General Court dismissed the applicability of the legality principle in *Ezz and Others* and *Al Matri*, the Court's reasoning affirms that sanctions that are non-criminal from the EU perspective, could nevertheless come within the scope of the Charter's legality principle. This is a direct result of the General Court's use of the ECtHR's criteria for the determination of the contested measure. By focusing on the substance of the measure instead of the non-criminal label provided for the freezing measures, the EU legality principle could certainly apply to EU administrative sanctions outside the field of competition law.[1445]

4.6.5 SUBSTANCE I: RETROACTIVE USE OF NEW FINING GUIDELINES

A significant share of the CJEU's considerations on the legality principle in competition law address the permissibility of the retroactive use of sanctioning criteria that result in harsher fines. The leading case in this regard is the above-mentioned Grand Chamber judgment in *Danske Rørindustri*.[1446] In an appeal following a judgment of the CFI, the ECJ examined whether the Commission's use of new guidelines for calculating fines for anti-competitive conduct violated the principle of non-retroactivity of criminal laws.[1447] Contrary to the CFI, the ECJ considered that violation of that principle was possible on the basis of a retroactive application of the guidelines. In the Court's view,

> "(...) a change in an enforcement policy, in this instance the Commission's general competition policy in the matter of fines, especially where it comes about as a result of the adoption of rules of conduct such as the Guidelines, may have an impact from the aspect of the principle of non-retroactivity".[1448]

1445 Cf Klip 2016, p. 194.

1446 See subsection 4.6.2. The reasoning in this judgment has been consistently confirmed, see Case C-397/03 P, *Archer Daniels Midland Co. and Archer Daniels Midland Ingredients Ltd v Commission of the European Communities*, EU:C:2006:328, paras 15–26; Case C-3/06 P, *Groupe Danone v Commission of the European Communities*, EU:C:2007:88, paras 87–93; Case C-510/06 P, *Archer Daniels Midland Co. v Commission of the European Communities*, EU:C:2009:166, paras 56–59, 66; *Denki*, paras 120–126; *Saint-Gobain Glass*, paras 267–283; Case T-286/09, *Intel Corp. v European Commission*, EU:T:2014:547, para 1598; *Moreda-Riviere*, paras 415–437; Case C-604/13 P, *Aloys F. Dornbracht GmbH & Co. KG v European Commission*, EU:C:2017:45, paras 42–43.

1447 See Guidelines on the method of setting fines imposed pursuant to Article 15(2) of Regulation No 17 and Article 65(5) of the ECSC Treaty, [1998] OJ C 9.

1448 Para 222.

Since the guidelines constituted, in part, the legal framework for the imposition of penalties,[1449] the ECJ assessed whether the Commission's use of the guidelines violated the principle of non-retroactivity of criminal laws. The Court used Article 7 ECHR and the Strasbourg Court's case-law to identify the limits set by the aforementioned principle. The Court, in fact, used five consecutive paragraphs to paraphrase some considerations of the ECtHR on the Convention's legality principle.[1450]

The ECJ's paraphrasing of the Strasbourg case-law failed to adequately capture all the ECtHR's elaborate general considerations on the legality principle. In fact, the ECJ focused on one element of the ECtHR's case-law: the permissibility of the retroactive application of a rule establishing an offense. Although, when paraphrasing Strasbourg case-law, the ECJ did commence with the general observation that Article 7 ECHR "(...) enshrines in particular the principle that offenses and punishments are to be strictly defined by law (*nullum crimen, nulla poena sine lege*) (...)",[1451] it swiftly returned to the permissibility of the retroactive application of an offense. The Court underlined that an interpretation of a rule establishing an offense may be precluded when "(...) a judicial interpretation (...) produces a result which was not reasonably foreseeable at the time when the offense was committed, especially in the light of the interpretation put on the provision in the case-law at the material time".[1452]

After focusing on the retroactive application of a new interpretation of an offense, the ECJ explicitly stated that its case-law was in line with the ECtHR's on this matter. While referring to the Strasbourg Court's general considerations, the ECJ considered that

> "[t]hose principles are also consistently reflected in the case-law of the Court to the effect that the obligation on the national court to refer to the content of the directive when interpreting the relevant rules of its national law is limited by the general principles of law which form part of [EU] law and in particular the principles of legal certainty and non-retroactivity (see Case 80/86 *Kolpinghuis Nijmegen* [1987] ECR 3969, paragraph 13)."[1453]

To link its case-law on consistent interpretation in criminal matters to the ECtHR's judgments on Article 7 ECHR, the ECJ subsequently cited both the *Marshall* limitation and the *Pretore di Salò* rule.[1454] The ECJ concluded its discussion of this matter by referring to its own judgments and those of the

1449 See paras 214, 222–223.

1450 See paras 215–219. The Court confirmed its earlier references, in *X 1996*, to the ECtHR judgments in *S.W. v. The United Kingdom* and *C.R. v. The United Kingdom*. On *X 1996* and its references to the Strasbourg Court's judgments, see subsection 4.2.3.

1451 Para 217.

1452 Para 218.

1453 Para 220.

1454 See para 221. The Court referred to the judgments in *Kolpinghuis* and *Arcaro*. On the judgments in *Marshall, Pretore di Salò, Kolpinghuis*, and *Arcaro*, see subsections 4.2.2–4.2.3.

Strasbourg Court as the 'case-law on new developments in case-law'.[1455] In this regard, *Danske Rørindustri* provides an additional argument for why Article 7 ECHR's legality principle should be related to the Luxembourg Court's case-law on the limits of EU law's effects in criminal matters.[1456]

When reviewing the permissibility of the Commission's retroactive use of the guidelines, the ECJ placed the criterion of foreseeability at the center.[1457] The ECJ reiterated the Strasbourg interpretation of that criterion in *Cantoni*,[1458] where the ECtHR established that foreseeability depends on the text at issue, the field it is designed to cover and the persons to whom it is addressed.[1459] It simultaneously reiterated the Strasbourg jurisprudence on how foreseeability should be assessed from the viewpoint of an individual who took legal advice and that the consequences of certain acts may be more easily foreseeable for professionals. The ECJ concluded that it needed to assess whether the change in the Commission's enforcement policy was reasonably foreseeable at the time when the infringements were committed.[1460]

In the Court's view, undertakings must take into account the possibility that the Commission may, at any time, decide to raise the level of the fines.[1461] This is not only possible in individual cases, but also if the Commission changes the fine on the basis of new guidelines.[1462] In light of the fact that the Commission is entitled to change its sentencing policy at any time, the use of a new method for calculating fines was reasonably foreseeable for undertakings at the time of the infringements.[1463] "Accordingly, in applying the Guidelines in the contested decision to infringements committed before they were adopted, the Commission did not breach the principle of non-retroactivity".[1464]

The ECJ's approach to the principle of non-retroactivity is remarkable for three reasons. First due to the Court's elaborate paraphrasing of ECtHR case-law on the retroactive application of a rule establishing *an offense*.[1465] While the application of a new enforcement policy could potentially be understood as

---

1455 See para 222.

1456 For an examination of this relationship, see section 4.2.

1457 Foreseeability and non-retroactivity have also been linked in other areas of EU law, see Groussot 2006, p. 199–200.

1458 On this judgment, see subsections 3.4.3; 3.6.2.

1459 See *Danske Rørindustri*, para 219.

1460 See para 224. See also *AC-Treuhand 2008*, para 142.

1461 See para 229.

1462 See para 230.

1463 See para 231.

1464 Para 232. The entry into force of the Charter does not alter this conclusion. In *Intel Corp* the General Court considered that the above conclusion holds true with respect to Article 49(1) Charter, see Case T-286/09, *Intel Corp. v European Commission*, EU:T:2014:547, para 1598.

1465 Instead of 'offense' the General Court has also used the term 'infringement' to paraphrase the ECtHR's considerations on this matter, see *Saint-Gobain Glass*, para 270.

violating the principle of non-retroactivity of *penalties,*[1466] it is not clear how this relates to a new interpretation of a rule establishing an offense. After all, a change in an enforcement policy does not (necessarily) alter the definition of the offense to which that enforcement policy applies. In light of the facts of the cases on appeal, the ECJ's focus on the permissibility of a retroactive application of a new judicial interpretation of an offense is thus not self-evident. The reference to limits to the judicial interpretation of offenses raises doubts about the earlier observation that the Court applied the principle *nulla poena sine lege* to fines in EU competition law.[1467]

The second remarkable element of the reasoning in *Danske Rørindustri* is the ECJ's apparent view that an unforeseeable judicial interpretation of an offense is precluded by the principle of non-retroactivity of criminal laws.[1468] As described in subsection 2.3.5, it is preferable from a conceptual point of view to exclusively consider new judicial interpretations of offenses and penalties under the *lex stricta* principle. As a result, in *Danske Rørindustri* the ECJ failed to distinguish the principles *lex praevia* and *lex stricta* clearly.

The third reason why the ECJ's approach is so remarkable is its apparent inconsistency with other judgments. While the considerations in *Danske Rørindustri* are frequently reiterated, other judgments have followed the seemingly contrary approach first adopted in the *Bertoli* judgment (as mentioned previously).[1469] In *Bertoli,*[1470] and subsequently in *Degussa,*[1471] *Schunk,*[1472] *Heineken,*[1473] *Saint-Gobain Glass,*[1474] and *Sasol,*[1475] the CJEU indicates that it is (almost) impossible to violate the legality principle when the penalties imposed remain within the limits set by the legislative framework.[1476] This implies that, as long as the imposed penalties do not go beyond the maximum limit established by EU law, the imposition of a harsher penalty on the basis of new fining guidelines cannot constitute the retroactive imposition of a harsher penalty prohibited by the EU legality principle.[1477] At present, it is not clear how the *Danske Rørindustri* requirement concerning the reasonably foreseeable use of new fining guidelines relates to the decision in *Bertoli* and the above-mentioned judgments with a comparable reasoning.

1466 The Advocate General examined the applicants' pleas alleging breaches of non-retroactivity solely in light of the principle of non-retroactivity of *penalties*, see Opinion of Advocate General Tizzano in *Danske Rørindustri*, EU:C:2004:415, paras 156, 160, 165.

1467 For that observation, see subsection 4.6.2.

1468 See paras 214–218.

1469 See subsection 4.6.1.

1470 See para 27.

1471 See para 81. On this judgment, see subsection 4.6.3.

1472 Case T-69/04, Schunk GmbH and Schunk Kohlenstoff-Technik GmbH v Commission of the European Communities, EU:T:2008:415, para 43.

1473 See para 386. On the judgment, see subsection 4.6.3.

1474 See para 280. On the judgment, see subsection 4.6.2.

1475 See para 213. On the judgment, see subsection 4.6.2.

1476 Cf Frese 2014, p. 75.

1477 This view is explicitly rejected in *Danske Rørindustri*, see paras 206–208.

4.6.6 SUBSTANCE II: FORESEEABILITY AND THE RELEVANCE OF CASE-LAW

Danske Rørindustri illustrates that the CJEU reiterated several elements of the ECtHR's general considerations on Article 7 ECHR to determine the substance of the legality principle in EU competition law. This approach has been adopted in subsequent cases. This subsection examines the CJEU's approach to the foreseeability requirement in the context of fines imposed for the violation of competition law.

The ECJ's judgment in *Evonik Degussa*[1478] confirmed the adoption of the ECtHR's approach to foreseeability in *Danske Rørindustri*.[1479] In its interpretation of the EU legality principle the Court immediately referred to Article 7 ECHR.[1480] It subsequently reiterated the formulation of the EU legality principle in *Advocaten voor de Wereld*, which emphasized the need for clear definitions in criminal law.[1481] In order to determine whether the CFI judgment under appeal violated the legality principle, the ECJ subsequently referred to the Strasbourg case-law on the level of clarity required of offenses and penalties.[1482] The Court considered how the ECtHR looks at both the legislative wording of criminal law and its interpretation in case-law and how both these sources constitute 'law' for the purpose of Article 7(1) ECHR.[1483] Since the CFI had respected these considerations of the Strasbourg Court on Article 7 of the Convention, it had not, in the ECJ's view, violated the EU legality principle.[1484]

In examining whether the fine imposed by the Commission breached the legality principle, the CFI was correct to establish that absolute certainty and foreseeability of any criminal law consequences are not required by the ECtHR.[1485] In order to determine the clarity and foreseeability of the penalties for violations of competition law, the CFI – rightly – looked beyond the wording of the applicable regulation.[1486] The CFI took into account the criteria for the calculation of fines

1478 Case C-266/06 P, *Evonik Degussa GmbH v Commission of the European Communities*, EU:C:2008:295. This judgment resulted from the appeal to the CFI judgment in *Degussa*. On the earlier judgment, see subsection 4.6.3.

1479 See subsection 4.6.5. See also *AC-Treuhand 2008*, paras 139, 142; Case C-194/14 P, *AC-Treuhand AG v European Commission*, EU:C:2015:717, para 42; *Moreda-Riviere*, para 423; *Lundbeck*, para 767.

1480 See *Evonik Degussa*, para 38. Cf *AC-Treuhand 2008*, paras 139–142.

1481 See *Evonik Degussa*, para 39. On *Advocaten voor de Wereld* and the definition of legality therein, see subsections 4.4.2; 4.5.4. Cf Case T-69/04, *Schunk GmbH and Schunk Kohlenstoff-Technik GmbH v Commission of the European Communities*, EU:T:2008:415, para 32; Case C-194/14 P, *AC-Treuhand AG v European Commission*, EU:C:2015:717, para 40.

1482 See para 41.

1483 See para 40. Cf *Danske Rørindustri*, para 216 and see, with extensive references to the ECtHR's judgments, *AC-Treuhand 2008*, paras 140–141.

1484 See paras 42, 44–45, 63.

1485 See para 44. Cf Case T-69/04, *Schunk GmbH and Schunk Kohlenstoff-Technik GmbH v Commission of the European Communities*, EU:T:2008:415, para 33; *Dornbracht*, para 62.

1486 See paras 46–47, 57–58. Cf Case T-69/04, *Schunk GmbH and Schunk Kohlenstoff-Technik GmbH v Commission of the European Communities*, EU:T:2008:415, para 33; *Dornbracht*, para 63.

in EU competition law set out in previous CJEU case-law. In the ECJ's view, the availability of this case-law contributed to the foreseeability of the consequences of infringing Union law in this area.[1487] For these reasons, the Court rejected the plea that the imposition of the fine violated the legality principle.[1488]

The CFI adopted a comparable approach in *AC-Treuhand 2008*.[1489] In this judgment the applicants argued that the terms of Article 81(1) EC Treaty were insufficiently clear in light of the legality principle. In the Court's view, however, the full implications of the terms 'agreement' and 'undertaking' "(...) must have been sufficiently foreseeable, at the time of the perpetration of the alleged misconducts, in the light of the wording of that provision, as interpreted by the case-law".[1490] According to the CFI, the terms 'agreements between undertakings' had been previously interpreted in settled case-law and, consequently, constituted a sufficiently precise expression of the notions of cartel and perpetrator of the infringement.[1491] In light of the existing case-law on the Treaty prohibition, which stated clearly the conditions for liability, it was reasonably foreseeable that the applicant's conduct would violate EU competition law.[1492] In a related judgment, the ECJ added that the applicant could have certainly expected the imposition of a penalty "(...) in light of the broad scope of the terms 'agreement' and 'concerted practice' established by the [CJEU's] case-law".[1493]

While the CJEU includes interpretive case-law in its assessment of the clarity of prohibitions and the applicable fines,[1494] the legislative formulation of infringements remains relevant. In *Lundbeck*, for example, the General Court determined the foreseeability of the consequences of the applicant's conduct on the basis of the wording of Union law.[1495] The consequences were not unforeseeable, because "(...) a literal reading of Article 101(1) TFEU made it clear that agreements between competitors for the exclusion of some of them from the market were illegal".[1496] These types of agreements, the Court pointed out, are

---

1487 See para 61. Cf *Dornbracht*, para 63; *Sasol*, para 205.

1488 See para 63.

1489 On this judgment, see subsection 4.6.2.

1490 Para 143. Cf Case T-446/05, *Amann & Söhne GmbH & Co. KG and Cousin Filterie SAS v European Commission*, EU:T:2010:165, paras 133; C-352/09, *ThyssenKrupp Nirosta GmbH v European Commission*, EU:C:2011:191, paras 82–83, 86.

1491 See para 145.

1492 See paras 146–147, 150. This reasoning was fully confirmed in T-27/10, *AC-Treuhand AG v European Commission*, EU:T:2014:59, paras 43–45.

1493 Case C-194/14 P, *AC-Treuhand AG v European Commission*, EU:C:2015:717, para 43. Advocate General Wahl is skeptical about the foreseeability of competition law infringements on the basis of a combination of legislation and case-law, see Case C-194/14 P, *AC-Treuhand AG v European Commission*, Opinion of AG Wahl, ECLI:EU:C:2015:350, para 87.

1494 Before the existence of settled EU case-law the CJEU apparently deemed the Member States' practice on competition law concepts relevant, see Case 85/76, *Hoffman-La Roche & Co. AG v Commission of the European Communities*, EU:C:1979:36, paras 128–133.

1495 See paras 764–765. On this judgment, see subsection 4.6.3.

1496 Para 765. Cf Case T-758/14, *Infineon Technologies AG v European Commission*, ECLI:EU:T:2016:737, paras 241–243.

in fact expressly referred to in the aforementioned provision. After employing the wording of the applicable prohibition, the Court examined whether existing CJEU case-law indicated an exemption from liability for the applicant. Since it did not, the General Court dismissed the applicant's plea regarding a lack of foreseeability and clarity.[1497]

A similar emphasis on the clarity of the legislative wording is apparent in the recent judgment in *Marine Harvest*.[1498] Here the Court determined, without further substantiation, that the relevant provisions for imposing a fine on the applicant did not contain broad notions or vague criteria.[1499] For that reason, the wording of the relevant provisions enabled the applicant to foresee that his conduct was punishable by a fine.[1500] Since the wording alone allowed for foreseeability, it was not necessary to look at interpretive case-law. In the General Court's view, the assessment of case-law is only necessary when the legislative wording is not clear due to, for example, the inclusion of indeterminate concepts that require definition.[1501]

The above judgments illustrate that the CJEU intended to adopt the approach of the Strasbourg Court regarding *lex certa*. The Luxembourg Court employed the Strasbourg foreseeability interpretation both with regard to the foreseeability of liability, as well as with regard to the specific penalties imposed for infringements of competition law.[1502] Moreover, the CJEU unequivocally examined the clarity of prohibitions and penalties on the basis of both the statutory wording and the interpretive case-law.[1503] In EU competition law, the CJEU has explicitly confirmed that the legality principle cannot be interpreted as prohibiting the gradual, case-by-case, clarification of the rules on criminal liability by judicial interpretation, provided that the result was reasonably foreseeable at the time of the offense, especially in light of the interpretation of that provision in case-law at the material time.[1504] These characteristics mean that liability for infringements of competition law could be deemed sufficiently foreseeable when the wording of the applicable legislation does not prohibit certain anti-competitive acts explicitly.[1505]

1497 See paras 769–770, 777–778.

1498 See Case T-704/14, *Marine Harvest ASA v European Commission*, EU:T:2017:753.

1499 See para 379.

1500 See para 382.

1501 See paras 383–385.

1502 See, eg, *Degussa*, para 67; *Marine Harvest*, para 378. Cf Peristeridou 2015, p. 183–187; Altena-Davidsen 2016, p. 102–103.

1503 Cf Case C-625/13 P, *Villeroy & Boch AG v European Commission*, EU:C:2017:52, paras 145–149.

1504 Cf *Danske Rørindustri*, paras 217–218; *AC-Treuhand* 2008, para 142; C-194/14 P, *AC-Treuhand AG v European Commission*, EU:C:2015:717, para 41; *Moreda-Riviere*, para 420; *Lundbeck*, para 763.

1505 For critical remarks on this consequence of the CJEU's approach, see Opinion of Advocate General Wahl in Case C-194/14 P, *AC-Treuhand AG v European Commission*, ECLI:EU:C:2015:350, paras 31–89.

4.6.7 SUBSTANCE III: COMMISSION DISCRETION AND FORESEEABILITY

Applicants have also invoked the legality principle to challenge the amount of discretion for the Commission to impose fines for infringements of competition law. The CJEU has consistently dismissed these arguments. In *Degussa*, for example, the CFI acknowledged that the applicable regulation left the Commission with a wide discretion to determine fines, but noted that this discretion was nevertheless limited.[1506] In the Court's view, the applicable provision sets a ceiling to the fines based on the turnover of the undertakings concerned, which is an objective criterion.[1507] For that reason, the absolute ceiling of the fine could be calculated by each undertaking in advance by reference to their turnover.

The Commission's discretion is further restricted by the requirement set out in the applicable provision to have regard to both the gravity and the duration of the infringement when setting fines. Although these criteria again allow for wide discretion, they require the Commission to take the degree of illegality into account when determining the fines.[1508] Since the calculation of the fine is also limited by the principles of equal treatment and proportionality, the Commission is additionally required to respect these principles when determining sanctions.[1509] As a consequence, previous sanctions imposed by the Commission become relevant and provide a potential limit to the Commission's discretion when calculating new fines.[1510] A final limitation is potentially established by the published guidelines that enshrine the applicable sentencing criteria in a general and abstract manner.[1511]

In addition to the limits that follow from the applicable legislation, the general principles of EU law, and the published guidelines, the CFI considered the possibility for judicial review of the Commission's fines relevant.[1512] Judicial review of the imposition of fines is enabled by the requirement to state the

---

1506 See para 74. The reasoning in this judgment was generally confirmed by the ECJ on appeal, see *Evonik Degussa*, paras 50–63. It was also confirmed by the several other judgments, see, eg, *Jungbunzlauer*, paras 85–91; Case T-69/04, *Schunk GmbH and Schunk Kohlenstoff-Technik GmbH v Commission of the European Communities*, EU:T:2008:415, paras 36, 41–46; Case T-446/05, *Amann & Söhne GmbH & Co. KG and Cousin Filterie SAS v European Commission*, EU:T:2010:165, paras 136, 141–147; Case T-240/07, *Heineken Nederland BV and Heineken NV v European Commission*, EU:T:2011:284, paras 385–388; Case C-501/11 P, *Schindler Holding Ltd and Others v European Commission*, EU:C:2013:522, para 57–59; *Sasol*, paras 203–205; Case C-90/15 P, *Hansen & Rosenthal KG and H&R Wax Company Vertrieb GmbH v European Commission*, EU:C:2017:123, paras 78–85.

1507 See para 75.

1508 See para 76.

1509 See para 77.

1510 See para 80.

1511 See para 82. Cf *Dornbracht*, paras 68–79.

1512 See para 79.

reasons for the fine imposed.[1513] This requirement enables undertakings to challenge, before the EU courts, the Commission's calculation of the penalty.[1514] According to the CFI, the judicial review of fines has allowed the clarification of indeterminate concepts enshrined in the applicable regulation. This clarification through judicial interpretation has, in the CFI's apparent view, contributed to the limits on the Commission's discretion.[1515]

In light of the above-mentioned limitations on the Commission's discretion, undertakings are able to foresee, by obtaining legal advice, the magnitude of fines incurred for certain conduct.[1516] The Court essentially deemed the Commission's discretion to be in accordance with the legality principle because, due to the limitations placed on it, the applicable fines are not unforeseeable. By this reasoning the CFI linked the existence of discretion to the legality principle's foreseeability requirement.[1517]

The CJEU has confirmed the relationship between discretion and foreseeability in subsequent judgments. In accordance with *Degussa*,[1518] it determined that

> "[a]ccording to the case-law of the European Court of Human Rights, the existence of vague terms in the provision does not necessarily entail an infringement of Article 7 of the ECHR, and the fact that a law confers a discretion is not in itself inconsistent with the requirement of foreseeability, provided that the scope of the discretion and the manner of its exercise are indicated with sufficient clarity, regard being had to the legitimate aim in question, to give the individual adequate protection against arbitrary interference (see Eur. Court H. R., *Margareta and Roger Andersson v. Sweden*, judgment of 25 February 1992, Series A no. 226, §75)".[1519]

By this consideration the CJEU shows that limited discretion is ultimately necessary in order to offer the individual adequate protection against arbitrary interference. It could therefore be concluded that limits to discretion are not merely required to ensure foreseeability for the sake of legal certainty. In the

1513 See para 84.

1514 Cf Case T-69/04, *Schunk GmbH and Schunk Kohlenstoff-Technik GmbH v Commission of the European Communities*, EU:T:2008:415, para 46.

1515 Cf Case T-446/05, *Amann & Söhne GmbH & Co. KG and Cousin Filterie SAS v European Commission*, EU:T:2010:165, para 136; *Dornbracht*, para 63.

1516 See *Degussa*, paras 72, 74, 83. Cf *Jungbunzlauer*, para 91; Case T-69/04, *Schunk GmbH and Schunk Kohlenstoff-Technik GmbH v Commission of the European Communities*, EU:T:2008:415, para 45; Case T-446/05, *Amann & Söhne GmbH & Co. KG and Cousin Filterie SAS v European Commission*, EU:T:2010:165, para 147; Case T-240/07, *Heineken Nederland BV and Heineken NV v European Commission*, EU:T:2011:284, para 388.

1517 See *Degussa*, para 72.

1518 See para 72.

1519 See Case T-69/04, *Schunk GmbH and Schunk Kohlenstoff-Technik GmbH v Commission of the European Communities*, EU:T:2008:415, para 33; Case T-446/05, *Amann & Söhne GmbH & Co. KG and Cousin Filterie SAS v European Commission*, EU:T:2010:165, para 149. The ECJ confirmed this consideration in Case C-501/11 P, *Schindler Holding Ltd and Others v European Commission*, EU:C:2013:522, para 57.

apparent view of the CJEU, the limits are required to ensure foreseeability in order to preclude the arbitrary exercise of the discretionary powers.

Support for this observation can also be found in *Heineken*. In this judgment the General Court dismissed the complaint about, inter alia, a violation of the principle that penalties must have a proper legal basis by considering that

> "(...) even if the applicants could not know in advance precisely the level of fines which the Commission would impose in the present case, (...) the Commission exercised its discretion in accordance with both the regulatory framework (...) as clarified by the case-law of the [EU courts], and the rules of conduct which it imposed on itself in the Guidelines".[1520]

The emphasis on the legal limits of discretion over the need to ensure a high level of foreseeability arguably confirms that limits to discretion and foreseeability are ultimately deemed necessary to preclude arbitrariness.

The apparent recognition of the legality principle as a prohibition of arbitrariness is in line with the Strasbourg Court's interpretation of the object and purpose of the legality principle. The CJEU deemed the object and purpose of Article 7(1) ECHR relevant in *Saint-Gobain Glass*. After recognizing the relevance of Article 7(1) ECHR, the General Court reiterated that Article 7(1) ECHR "(...) must be interpreted and applied in such a way as to ensure effective protection against arbitrary prosecution, convictions and penalties (...)".[1521]In the earlier judgment of *Evonik Degussa* the ECJ confirmed the relevance of the rule of law for the legality principle. The Court considered the foreseeability requirement for offenses and penalties to be instrumental for the rule of law.[1522]

4.6.8 CONCLUDING REMARKS

Judgments concerning administrative sanctions imposed by EU institutions resulted in a significant body of case-law on both the applicability and substance of the EU legality principle. Most important in this regard were penalties imposed for violations of competition law, as the CJEU deemed (elements of) the legality principle applicable, both explicitly and by referring to the principle that penalties must have a proper legal basis. It remains to be seen, however, whether the Court affords the same substantive protection for administrative sanctions as it does for EU measures that are implemented via criminal law. The CJEU's case-law is not consistent in this regard. Whereas some judgments indicate the applicability of the principle of legality in full, others explicitly lower the

---

1520 Para 388.
1521 *Saint-Gobain Glass*, para 268. On this judgment, see subsection 4.6.2.
1522 See para 58.

protection in light of the specific features of EU competition rules and the need to ensure their effectiveness.[1523]

The Court has examined the applicability of the legality principle regarding EU administrative sanctions imposed for terrorism. These restrictive measures were not deemed to constitute a penalty for the purpose of Article 49(1) Charter, however, which led to the inapplicability of the EU legality principle. The CJEU's use of the ECtHR's applicability criteria illustrates, nonetheless, the potential applicability of the CFR to EU administrative sanctions.

Considerations on the substance of the legality principle were only laid down in judgments concerning competition law. With regard to the foreseeability of liability and the applicable penalties, the CJEU clearly intended to adopt the Strasbourg approach. The Luxembourg Court has often employed interpretation of foreseeability employed by the Strasbourg Court in *Cantoni*.[1524] In line with the ECtHR, the CJEU has, moreover, recognized the relevance of both legislation and case-law for the clarity and foreseeability of liability and its potential consequences.[1525] In EU competition law the CJEU has evidently sought to adopt the main elements of the ECtHR's interpretation of *lex certa*.

The CJEU has additionally referred to the Strasbourg case-law on the acceptability of discretion in light of the foreseeability requirement. It has considered limits to discretion necessary in order to preclude the arbitrary exercise of discretionary powers. It is not required that discretionary powers in EU competition law are used in an absolutely foreseeable manner, however. It is merely necessary that the Commission's power to impose penalties for competition law infringements is exercised in accordance with legal limits. By this interpretation the CJEU affirms its acceptance of the approach to foreseeability in Strasbourg case-law. It, moreover, appears to confirm that, like the ECtHR, the CJEU considers that the legality principle essentially protects against the arbitrary use of punitive powers.[1526]

Regarding administrative sanctions imposed for infringements of competition law, the CJEU has also sought to conform with the ECtHR's approach regarding the permissibility of judicial interpretation. Like the Strasbourg Court, the CJEU underlined that it accepts the judicial development of rules on liability as long as the interpretation is reasonably foreseeable at the time of the infringements. The recognition of reasonable foreseeability as a requirement for the permissibility of judicial interpretation is evidently based on the ECtHR's interpretation of Article 7 ECHR's *lex stricta* principle.

The Court has also recognized the principle of non-retroactivity of criminal law. In line with the early judgments recognizing this principle in cases concerning implementing provisions,[1527] the ECJ in *Danske Rørindustri* acknowledged the

1523 See subsection 4.6.2.
1524 See subsection 4.6.5.
1525 Cf Frese 2014, p. 73.
1526 See subsection 4.6.7.
1527 See subsection 4.4.3.

significance of this principle for fines imposed in competition proceedings. Substantively, however, the Court understood the principle as precluding unforeseeable judicial interpretations of offenses and penalties. In that regard, the Luxembourg Court apparently deemed the EU *lex praevia* principle as protecting of the ECHR's *lex stricta* principle. The extent to which the EU principle precludes the retroactive use of fining guidelines is not clear, however, as the reasoning in *Danske Rørindustri* is in apparent contrast with that in other judgments.[1528]

4.7 CONCLUDING REMARKS

4.7.1 THE OBSCURE RELATIONSHIP BETWEEN EARLY STRANDS OF CASE-LAW AND THE EU LEGALITY PRINCIPLE

Despite the early recognition of the need to limit the effect of EU law in judgments concerning implementation via criminal law, the Court has not consistently and explicitly related these limits to the EU legality principle. While the CJEU recognizes the legality principle in some of its later case-law, this does not occur without exception. The fact that the judicially established limits to EU law were initially developed independently of the legality principle continues to affect the Court's approach. The exact relationship between the limits of EU law in criminal matters and the legality principle is therefore unresolved. It is unclear, for that reason, whether the limits to the effects of EU law in criminal matters apply because of the EU legality principle or, instead, constitute *leges speciales* with a (partly) similar protective substance. Since the above case-law does not allow for a clear conclusion on the relevance of the legality principle, it consequently precludes firm determinations about the scope and substance of the EU principle. It is unascertainable, therefore, whether the EU legality principle *actually* enshrines a *lex stricta* principle, and, if it does, what it would protect exactly and in which situations it would apply.[1529]

Questions about the scope and substance of the EU legality principle emerge from other strands of case-law as well. As with the case-law on limits to the effect of EU law, the Court has sometimes linked its early judgments on other EU principles to the legality principle.[1530] This is the case, for example, with judgments on the requirement of a proper legal basis for penalties. The relationship between these principles has never been clearly established, however. The principles have apparently been viewed as fully-fledged alternatives, because the CJEU has deemed the requirement of a proper legal basis as relevant for

1528 See subsection 4.6.5.
1529 Although *X 1996* did recognize the relevance of *lex stricta*, see subsection 4.2.3.
1530 See section 4.3.

criminal proceedings on the one hand, and the legality principle as relevant for *non-criminal* penalties on the other. The legality principle is not, in any event, regarded as a *lex specialis* of the general requirement of a proper legal basis.

By invoking the general Union requirement in relation to criminal penalties, the Court nevertheless fails to recognize the relevance of the specific criminal law principle. This has apparently precluded an assessment of the applicability of the legality principle, which the CJEU could have, for example, conducted with reference to the terms 'criminal offense' and 'penalty' as enshrined in Article 7(1) ECHR.[1531] It, moreover, makes it hard to determine the exact content of the EU legality principle for those legal bases that come within its scope. Although the requirement of a proper legal basis could impose demands comparable to the *lex certa* element, and it could even require a written legal basis in accordance with *lex scripta*, it is not clear if these demands would be imposed by virtue of the EU legality principle. The lack of a clear-cut distinction between the two principles has, therefore, obscured both the applicability and the substance of the EU legality principle.

The relationship between the general principle of legal certainty and the legality principle is another source of obscurity.[1532] While the Court has often recognized that the legality principle constitutes a specific expression of the general principle of legal certainty, it has not consistently employed the legality principle as a *lex specialis*. In judgments concerning implementation via national criminal law, the CJEU has not consistently applied the legality principle to examine the clarity of EU legislation. By sometimes relying on the general principle of legal certainty, the Court has, once again, failed to provide an insight into the scope of applicability of the legality principle and its substance with regard to definitions in Union law. Although substantively comparable protection to that under the principles of *lex certa* and *lex scripta* could be provided by the principle of legal certainty, in the absence of clear guidelines the applicability and substance of the legality principle this remains within the Court's discretion.

The early judgments on the principle of non-retroactivity of penal provisions are less problematic than the aforementioned strands of case-law. Early on, the Court has clearly protected non-retroactivity as a *specific* principle of criminal law. As described in subsection 4.4.3, the CJEU has actually distinguished the non-retroactivity of criminal laws from the general Union principle of non-retroactivity of substantive rules. By recognizing the need for a more protective standard with regard to criminal matters, the Court evidently regarded the principle of non-retroactivity of criminal laws as a *lex specialis*.

While the Court has clearly recognized non-retroactivity as a specific principle of criminal law, it has not explicitly related this requirement to the EU legality principle. The Court has only referred to Article 7 ECHR as the source of

---

1531 See subsection 3.3.3. As described in subsection 4.5.3, these terms are now also enshrined in Article 49(1) CFR.

1532 See subsections 4.4.2; 4.4.4.

inspiration for the non-retroactivity requirement. It has not, however, linked the principle to either Article 49(1) Charter or legality as a general principle of Union law. It is not beyond dispute, therefore, that the EU legality principle protects the *lex praevia* element. Although that element is undeniably protected under Union law, it is not necessarily protected as an element of the legality principle.

The absence of a clear link between the principle of non-retroactivity and the legality principle entails two consequences. Firstly, it prevents further insight into the substance of the EU legality principle as the principle of non-retroactivity is not unequivocally protected as an element thereof. Secondly, it obscures the scope of the Union principle of non-retroactivity of criminal laws, as its applicability is not necessarily determined with reference to relevant terms such as 'criminal offense' or 'penalty' as enshrined in Article 7(1) ECHR. In the absence of clear applicability criteria, the CJEU arguably fails to clearly distinguish the scope of the non-retroactivity of criminal laws from the general Union principle of non-retroactivity of substantive rules.

Due to inconsistencies and the general lack of explicit considerations on the legality principle, the above-mentioned strands of CJEU case-law prevent clear conclusions on the scope and substance of the EU legality principle. As the older considerations are sometimes referred to in more recent judgments, they continue to obscure the present scope and content of the EU legality principle. While the above judgments contain indications that EU law provides protection that is substantively comparable to the elements *lex scripta*, *lex certa*, *lex stricta* and *lex praevia*, it cannot be ascertained whether, and if so to what extent and in which situations, these elements are protected under the Union legality principle. These obscurities consequently preclude determinations about the relevant rationale(s) of the EU legality principle.

4.7.2 CONSIDERATIONS ON LEGALITY AS A SELF-STANDING EU PRINCIPLE

In addition to judgments that establish a relationship between earlier strands of case-law and the EU legality principle, many judgments – mostly relating to Article 49(1) Charter – discuss legality as a self-standing principle of Union law. These judgments generally provide more insight into the sources, scope, and substance of the EU principle. The CJEU judgments have not completely resolved the above-mentioned lack of clarity about the EU legality principle, however. As will be described below, one reason for this is the absence of consistency in the Court's approach to legality.

With regard to the distinct EU sources of the legality principle, the Court's considerations in *Paoletti* imply that Article 49 CFR absorbed legality as a general principle of Union law.[1533] At the same time, the CJEU occasionally refers

[1533] See subsection 4.5.2.

exclusively to the general principle instead of the legally binding Charter.[1534] It is not completely clear, therefore, whether the legality principle enshrined in the Charter is now to be regarded as the exclusive source of the EU legality principle. This could be important if the scope of the general Union principle is wider, and/or its substance more protective, than the codified legality principle in the Charter. In the absence of more explicit and consistent considerations in this regard, the relationship between the two formal EU sources remains open to speculation.

The exact relevance of Article 7 ECHR and the Strasbourg Court's case-law for the EU legality principle is also unclear. In *Paoletti* the Court underlines that Article 7 ECHR should not be referred to as the Convention is not a formal source of the EU legality principle. The CJEU has not let this apparent point of departure preclude its references to both Article 7 ECHR and the ECtHR's case-law in other judgments, however. The diverging implications of the Luxembourg Court's case-law means the exact relevance of Strasbourg case-law on the legality principle for EU law is not clear.

The lack of a clear stand on the relevance of Article 7 ECHR and the Strasbourg Court's case-law actually results in different judgments on the scope and substance of the legality principle by the CJEU. In some judgments the Court recognizes the relevance of the Convention system and employs several of the ECtHR's general considerations.[1535] In other judgments, however, the Luxembourg Court determines the Union principle's scope and substance without taking account of Strasbourg case-law.[1536] As the judgments in *Bonda* and *Taricco* illustrate, the CJEU is also likely to combine both of these approaches by first determining the scope and substance of the EU principle on the basis of EU law and then subsequently considering, apparently as a secondary matter, the conformity of the EU approach with that of the Strasbourg Court.[1537] The co-existence of these three approaches in the CJEU's case-law provides the potential for inconsistencies which could continue to prevent an insight into the exact scope and substance of the EU legality principle.

Further insight into the scope and substance of the Union legality principle is, moreover, hampered by three additional factors. The first of these factors is the principle's inapplicability to the definition and interpretation of non-criminal EU legislation that is implemented via national criminal law or punitive provisions.[1538] The general inapplicability of the principle to EU legislation and its interpretation has precluded an explicit assessment of the scope of the legality principle on the basis of, for example, the terms 'criminal offense' or 'penalty'. Instead, the Court has generally deemed the principle inapplicable on the basis of the need for implementing provisions or based on the *Grøngaard*

1534 See subsection 4.5.8.

1535 See, eg, subsections 4.5.7; 4.6.4.

1536 See, eg, subsections 4.5.3; 4.6.2; 4.6.3.

1537 See subsections 4.5.3; 4.5.4.

1538 See subsections 4.4.2; 4.5.5. The exception is *Rosneft*, where the Court did apply the EU legality principle to definitions in non-criminal EU legislation, see subsection 4.5.7.

and Bang consideration. While these considerations mean the principle is inapplicable, they only concern the applicability of the EU legality principle in the specific situation of the definition and interpretation of non-criminal EU legislation. These considerations do not, therefore, provide general insight into the scope of application of the legality principle. That the principle does not apply has obviously precluded the CJEU from considering the substance of the Union principle in these situations as well. As a result, the Court has not been able to determine the scope and substance of the EU legality principle in the aforementioned situations concerning implementing criminal law.

The second relevant factor is how the Court does not actually apply the EU legality principle in preliminary rulings and the general absence of guidance to national courts on how to safeguard that principle.[1539] As a result of this approach, which is only partly justified by the division of competences in preliminary rulings, the Court has not generally laid down considerations on the scope and substance of the EU legality principle. It has, therefore, deferred the assessment of whether implementing criminal law conforms with the Union principle to the national courts without any guidance on the principle's requirements.

The third factor that has prevented a clear and consistent CJEU approach is the principle's evident relevance for administrative sanctions imposed by EU institutions.[1540] While the applicability of a criminal law principle to administrative sanctions could have resulted in explicit considerations on the scope of the EU principle, this has not generally been the case. The CJEU has only recognized general criteria for the principle's applicability in asset freezing cases.[1541] It has not done so in the field of competition law.[1542] Where there are the most judgments relating to EU administrative sanctions then the CJEU has been silent on the principle's scope of applicability.

The Court's considerations on the substance of the legality principle in the field of competition law also continue to raise questions. This is especially because the CJEU, at times, indicates the need to lower the general protection of the EU legality principle with regard to administrative sanctions for infringements of competition law.[1543] The Luxembourg Court's considerations on the substance of the legality principle could therefore have been affected by the specific administrative context in which they were laid down.[1544] Since the CJEU has not generally qualified its substantive considerations on the legality principle in the field of competition law, it is not clear whether the substance of the legality principle would differ in criminal matters. While the Court has certainly provided indications about the substance of the EU legality principle, the fact that this was done in the field of

1539 See subsection 4.5.6.
1540 See section 4.6.
1541 See subsection 4.6.4.
1542 See subsections 4.6.2; 4.6.3.
1543 See subsections 4.6.2; 4.6.3.
1544 Cf Altena-Davidsen 2016, p. 92–93.

competition law requires caution concerning the relevance of these considerations in a different context. At the same time, the Court has referred to considerations on the legality principle laid down in the context of competition law in judgments not involving competition law.[1545] It is therefore hard to determine the relevance of the considerations laid down in the context of competition law for the interpretation of the legality principle across Union law as a whole.

The considerations about legality as a self-standing Union principle have not yet allowed a clear view of the EU principle's scope and substance. While the terms 'criminal offense' and 'penalty' enshrined in Article 49(1) CFR and Article 7(1) ECHR are the most plausible candidates for determining the scope of the legality principle, the exact use of these criteria is not insightful. This is because the CJEU has not explicitly used the term 'criminal offense' to define the scope of the legality principle. It has, moreover, failed to use the term 'penalty' consistently and clearly. At the same time, however, the Court has apparently used the aforementioned terms to limit the principle's scope to matters of substantive criminal law. With regard to the EU legality principle the CJEU has recognized the elements *lex certa*, *lex stricta*, and *lex praevia*.[1546] The status of the *lex scripta* principle remains questionable. Since the CJEU's approach lacks detail and explicit clarification, as well as being fairly new, it is too early for clear conclusions. For now, the conclusion suffices that it cannot be unequivocally stated which elements the Union legality principle protects exactly, or what their substantive protection entails. An effort to say more on this will be made in section 6.2 of the final chapter.

4.7.3 POTENTIAL EXPLANATIONS FOR THE CJEU'S LEGALITY APPROACH

Due to the above-mentioned uncertainties, it should be concluded that the Luxembourg Court's case-law makes it hard to determine the exact scope and substance of the EU legality principle at present. It also precludes reaching a clear conclusion on the rationale for the principle and on which conception of legality the EU principle reflects. In order to provide more clarity, the CJEU's case-law should start to adopt a more consistent, explicit, and in-depth approach to the sources, scope, substance, and rationale(s) of the EU legality principle. I will return to these matters in chapter 6.

Undesirable as the present lack of clarity may be, the CJEU's approach to legality could be a result of general characteristics of EU law that the Court

1545 See, eg, Case C-546/09, *Aurubis Balgaria AD v Nachalnik na Mitnitsa Stolichna*, EU:C:2011:199, para 42; Case C-72/15, *PJSC Rosneft Oil Company v Her Majesty's Treasury and Others*, EU:C:2017:236, para 167.

1546 On *lex certa*, see subsections 4.5.7; 4.6.6. On *lex stricta*, see *Ezz and Others*, para 70 as described in subsection 4.6.4. On other (implicit) indications concerning the relevance of *lex stricta*, see subsections 4.5.5–4.5.7; 4.6.5. On the relevance of *lex praevia*, see subsection 4.6.5.

had to work with. The first of these general characteristics is the fact that cases concerning the legality principle have arisen in very different areas of EU law. As described throughout this chapter, the legality principle has not only been relied upon in national criminal proceedings, but also in domestic administrative proceedings on, for example, EU fraud and in proceedings against administrative sanctions imposed by EU institutions.

A second characteristic that could have precluded a clear and consistent approach to the legality principle is the longstanding controversy over the potential impact of Union law on the field of criminal law. As a result, the Court's early case-law on the influence of EU law on criminal matters could have been affected by the need to avoid a clear recognition of criminal law principles under Union law.

In addition to these two circumstances, the specific characteristics of EU fundamental rights protection may have contributed to the CJEU's approach. Like many EU fundamental rights, the legality principle was initially developed by the Court of Justice and is now also enshrined in the Charter. The fact that distinct sources are used in the development of the EU legality principle perhaps influenced the consistency of its interpretation. The inconsistent use of Article 7 ECHR and the Strasbourg Court's case-law on the legality principle has only enhanced the potential for inconsistencies.

Chapter 5 examines these above-mentioned characteristics in greater detail.

CHAPTER 5
THE SPECIFICITY OF THE EU LEGALITY PRINCIPLE

5.1 INTRODUCTION

Chapter 4 examined the CJEU's approach to the legality principle and concluded that the sources, scope, and substance of the EU principle have not been clearly and consistently established. The present chapter discusses general characteristics of EU law that could explain the Court's approach to the EU legality principle. The choice to only identify potential explanatory factors for the Court's approach after the analysis of the CJEU case-law on the legality principle in chapter 4 is deliberate. The goal of structuring the thesis in this manner is to facilitate the comparison between the different constructions of the legality principle under the ECHR and in EU law (cf chapters 3 and 4), while still being able to subsequently provide more context for the construction of the EU legality principle. The consequence of this order of examination is that – perhaps unusually – the general characteristics of EU (criminal) law are only discussed after the analysis of the legality principle as a specific element of Union law.

A first factor that may have influenced the Court's approach to legality – especially early on – is the historical development of EU criminal law into a specific legal field. Sections 5.2–5.3 explore the historical distinction between EC law/the former first pillar of the EU and the Union's former third pillar to determine whether this could explain the CJEU's early approach to legality.[1547] Section 5.4 examines EU criminal law post-Lisbon and identifies the potential implications of the new legal framework for the EU legality principle. The competences to approximate substantive criminal law form a significant element of this discussion. The section will ultimately determine whether the Luxembourg Court's post-Lisbon approach to legality could be explained by the particularities of the present reality of EU criminal law.

Section 5.5 focusses on the particularities of EU fundamental rights protection. That section includes a description of the historical development of EU fundamental rights which resulted in the two distinct EU sources of rights that exist in Union law today. The judicial development of EU rights has also led to the relevance of the ECHR and, arguably, the Strasbourg Court's case-law for

---

[1547] The three pillar structure was established by the Maastricht Treaty, see subsection 5.2.1.

the interpretation of fundamental rights in Union law. Section 5.5 will ultimately assess whether, and if so to what extent, the particularities of EU fundamental rights protection explain the development of the EU legality principle. Section 5.6 looks into multilevel definitions and interpretations of crimes and penalties as an explanatory factor. Section 5.7 contains concluding remarks.

5.2 THE CONTESTED DEVELOPMENT OF SUPRANATIONAL CRIMINAL LAW PRE-LISBON: COMMUNITY LAW

5.2.1 INTRODUCTION

The development of the legality principle in the CJEU's case-law could be explained in part by the historical particularities of EU criminal law. It is well-known that the influence of supranational EC law on domestic criminal law was highly controversial and contested.[1548] The contested nature of supranational EC criminal law in fact contributed to the conclusion of the Maastricht Treaty, which introduced a three-pillar structure and established the European Union.[1549] The Maastricht Treaty introduced Union competences in the field of criminal law, yet only under the third pillar. Since third pillar cooperation was much more intergovernmental than under EC law,[1550] the framework of the Maastricht Treaty indicated that the influence of supranational EC law on criminal matters should not be increased.[1551] It is quite remarkable, therefore, that CJEU case-law resulting from first pillar cooperation contained relevant considerations for the legality principle. In order to explain this case-law, subsection 5.2.2 briefly describes how supranational EC law influenced national criminal law in the absence of criminal law competences in the EC Treaty. Subsection 5.2.3 will then determine whether the historical development of EC criminal law explains the Court's pre-Lisbon case-law on the legality principle.

5.2.2 THE EC AND CRIMINAL LAW

The EC Treaty lacked provisions indicating a Community competence in criminal matters.[1552] Criminal law was in fact considered to be outside the scope

1548 Cf Asp 2012, p. 32; Miettinen 2013, p. 8. The contested nature of EU criminal law is not, according to some, fully settled by the entry into force of the Lisbon Treaty, see Mitsilegas 2016, p. 53.

1549 See Article A Treaty on European Union (Maastricht Treaty), [1992] OJ C 191.

1550 See, eg, Mitsilegas 2009, p. 9; Dougan 2012, p. 93–94; Satzger 2012, p. 6; Miettinen 2013, p. 23–24; Panzavolta 2013, p. 312; Summers, Schwarzenegger, Ege and Young 2014, p. 1, 5; Craig and De Búrca 2015, p. 965–967; Peers 2016b, p. 4, 9.

1551 See Dougan 2012, p. 94; Miettinen 2013, p. 33; Rijpma 2013, p. 271.

1552 See, eg, Mitsilegas 2009; p. 60; Dougan 2012, p. 74; Herlin-Karnell 2012, p. 12; Satzger 2012, p. 54–55; Miettinen 2013, p. 7, 9; Summers, Schwarzenegger, Ege and Young 2014, p. 1, 5, 18; Sicurella 2016, p. 49.

of supranational EC law because crime and punishment were deemed central to national sovereignty.[1553] Initial cooperation in the field of criminal law by the EC Member States had therefore taken place on an intergovernmental level.[1554] At the same time, supranational internal market law exerted influence on national criminal law. This 'spill-over effect' of, especially, the law on free movement, meant that EC law influenced legal areas beyond merely economic and market law.[1555] Due to EC law's primacy and direct effect, Community law impacted national criminal law as well.[1556] In this regard, criminal law was just another area of law being influenced by EC law.[1557] This impact has been described as the 'Europeanization' of national criminal law.[1558]

The impact of EC law on domestic criminal law is perceivable in early judgments. Two types of effects can be distinguished. The first is EC law's 'negative effect' on national criminal law.[1559] EC law had a negative effect when it required domestic provisions of criminal law to be set aside or, at least, limited their application.[1560] This effect was most clearly visible when national criminal law prohibited an activity that was permitted or encouraged by Community law.[1561] An obvious example is a domestic provision that criminalizes the import of goods from another Member State without obtaining an authorization to do so.[1562] In a case like this, EC law's primacy and direct effect preclude the application of the national penal provision.[1563] In addition to the preclusion of national criminal law, EC law could also limit its application. The ECJ has, for example, established limits to the imposition of national criminal penalties by invoking

1553 See Dougan 2012, p. 91–92; Satzger 2012, p. 61, 63–64; Miettinen 2013, p. 9; Summers, Schwarzenegger, Ege and Young 2014, p. 27.

1554 First, in the so-called 'TREVI-group', see, eg, Kostakopoulou 2007, p. 156–157; Mitsilegas 2009, p. 6; Craig 2010, p. 332; Miettinen 2013, p. 20. Later, EC conventions were concluded that were intergovernmental due to their process of negotiation and the need for ratification, see Miettinen 2013, p. 19.

1555 See Mitsilegas 2009, p. 6; Peristeridou 2015, p. 229, 234. This spill-over effect is a result of EC law's goal-oriented competence structure, see Satzger 2012, p. 62. Herlin-Karnell concludes that 'competence boundaries have been easily blurred' in the pursuit of Community policies, see Herlin-Karnell 2012, p. 16.

1556 Cf Sicurella 2016, p. 49–50.

1557 See Asp 2012, p. 28; Miettinen 2013, p. 7.

1558 See Satzger 2012, p. 61.

1559 In addition to 'negative effect' the same (or a similar) influence on national criminal law is referred to by the terms 'negative integration', 'negative influence', 'decriminalisation', 'passive limits', 'neutralization', see Herlin-Karnell 2012, p. 16 (footnote 30); Keiler and Klip 2013, p. 294; Miettinen 2013, p. 10, 122; Altena-Davidsen 2016, p. 69–70; Lenaerts and Gutiérrez-Fons 2016, p. 7–8; Mitsilegas 2016, p. 73–74; Sicurella 2016, p. 50.

1560 See, eg, Corstens and Pradel 2002, p. 492. Cf Summers, Schwarzenegger, Ege and Young 2014, p. 29.

1561 Cf Miettinen 2013, p. 124.

1562 This would be contrary to Article 34 TFEU.

1563 Not only primary EC law can preclude the application of national criminal law. Directly effective secondary law as well, see, eg, Case 8/77, *Criminal proceedings against Concetta Sagulo, Gennaro Brenca and Addelmadjid Bakhouche*, EU:C:1977:131, para 6; Case 148/78, *Criminal proceedings against Tullio Ratti*, EU:C:1979:110, paras 23–24.

the proportionality between the infringement and penalty.[1564] The Court has, moreover, understood EC law's prohibition on discrimination as establishing a limit to the imposition of criminal penalties in the Member States.[1565]

The second perceivable effect on domestic criminal law is the so-called positive effect.[1566] Through this effect EC law allowed, encouraged, or required the use of domestic criminal law by the Member States to ensure the effectiveness of Community law. This effect was already perceivable in *Amsterdam Bulb*, where the Court stated that the principle of sincere cooperation[1567] (now enshrined in Article 4(3) TEU) obliged Member States to take all appropriate measures to ensure the fulfilment of Community obligations.[1568] This judgment underlined the Member States' ability to impose criminal penalties for conduct prohibited by Community law.[1569] Although Community legislation avoided the prescription of criminal penalties by merely calling for, sometimes punitive,[1570] administrative or civil sanctions,[1571] Member States were explicitly given the option of criminalizing violations of EC law.

While the Court left Member States free to impose criminal sanctions for infringements of Community law in *Amsterdam Bulb*, it went significantly further in the so-called *Greek maize* judgment.[1572] In *Greek maize* the ECJ determined that infringements of Community law needed to be treated in the same way as similar breaches of domestic law.[1573] If particular domestic breaches were criminalized, similar infringements of Community law also needed to be sanctioned by criminal penalties.[1574] This rationale for criminalization is better known as 'the assimilation principle'.[1575] The obligation to criminalize violations of EC law under the assimilation principle followed directly from the way domestic law treated similar rules.[1576]

1564 Case 203/80, *Criminal Proceedings against Guerrino Casati*, EU:C:1981:261, para 27.

1565 See Case 186/87, *Ian William Cowan v Le Trésor public*, EU:C:1989:47, para 19. For other examples, see, eg, Corstens and Pradel 2002, p. 507–509; Mitsilegas 2009, p. 61–62; Satzger 2012, p. 66–69, Keiler and Klip 2013, p. 294; Miettinen 2013, p. 11, 123–132, Summers, Schwarzenegger, Ege and Young 2014, p. 30–34; Klip 2016, p. 84 (footnote 256), Peers 2016b, p. 182–183.

1566 Cf Corstens and Pradel 2002, p. 463, 506, 512–516; Herlin-Karnell 2012, p. 16–18.

1567 For other formulations of this principle, see subsection 4.3.2.

1568 See Case 50/76, *Amsterdam Bulb BV v Produktschap voor Siergewassen*, EU:C:1977:13, para 32.

1569 Cf Miettinen 2013, p. 15.

1570 See Case C-240/90, *Federal Republic of Germany v Commission of the European Communities*, EU:C:1992:408, paras 20, 25–29. See further Corstens and Pradel 2002, p. 552–556; Miettinen 2013, p. 17–18. Cf Herlin-Karnell 2012, p. 14.

1571 See Miettinen 2013, p. 13, 18, 133; Summers, Schwarzenegger, Ege and Young 2014, p. 34–37.

1572 Case 68/88, *Commission of the European Communities v Hellenic Republic (Greek maize)*, EU:C:1989:339.

1573 Further on this judgment, see, eg, Mitsilegas 2009, p. 63; Dougan 2012, p. 78–87; Satzger 2012, p. 71; Miettinen 2013, p. 13; Summers, Schwarzenegger, Ege and Young 2014, p. 33.

1574 See para 24.

1575 This principle is also referred to as 'the principle of equivalence' and 'the equality of sanctions principle', cf Dougan 2012, p. 79–80; Peers 2016b, p. 175.

1576 See Miettinen 2013, p. 3, 133; Klip 2016, p. 75–76. It, in fact, depended on the domestic treatment of similar infringements rather than on the type of sanctions EC legislation called

In addition to the assimilation principle, *Greek maize* required Member States to ensure that domestic penalties were, in any event, effective, proportionate and dissuasive.[1577] Independent of the assimilation principle, the requirement of effective and dissuasive penalties could indicate the appropriateness of national criminal penalties for infringements of Community law.[1578] *Greek maize* thus introduced two potential reasons for criminalizing infringements of Community law: first, because comparable infringements of domestic law had been criminalized, and, second, because only criminal penalties would be sufficiently effective, proportionate and dissuasive.[1579]

Since EC law allowed, encouraged and, following *Greek Maize*, sometimes required, the criminalization of conduct first defined at Community level, the interpretation of EC law was already relevant for national criminal liability in the pre-Maastricht era. The positive effect of EC law was essentially responsible for the Court's early confrontations with domestic criminal law implementing Community law.[1580] In preliminary rulings concerning these types of implementing measures the ECJ was therefore requested to interpret EC law with direct relevance for domestic criminal law. As a result, the Court deemed it appropriate to consider this specific (and special) domestic context by implicitly recognizing protective rights and principles of criminal law.[1581] EC law's positive effect was therefore the main reason for the Court's early tentative recognition of criminal law principles such as legality.

Two landmark judgments on Community competence in criminal matters increased the potential for positive effect on national criminal law towards the end of the pre-Lisbon period. In the so-called *Environmental Crime* judgment, the Court explicitly deemed the Community competent to adopt legislation harmonizing Member State substantive criminal law.[1582] The ECJ ruled that, although the rules of criminal law and criminal procedure are generally outside the Community's competence,[1583] this

> "(…) does not prevent the Community legislature, when the application of effective, proportionate and dissuasive criminal penalties by the competent national

---

for. Even if EC legislation called for civil sanctions, Member States could be obliged to impose criminal sanctions due to the of the assimilation principle, see Case C-186/98, *Criminal Proceedings against Maria Amélia Nunes and Evangelina de Matos*, EU:C:1999:376, paras 7, 14.

1577 See para 24. Cf Klip 2016, p. 76–81.

1578 This reading of *Greek maize* is confirmed by *Taricco*, paras 37, 43 and, more recently, in the Opinion of Advocate General Bobek in Case C-574/15, *Proceedings against Mauro Scialdone*, Opinion of AG Bobek, EU:C:2017:553, para 121. Cf Dougan 2012, p. 80–82; Klip 2016, p. 84. Further about *Taricco*, see subsection 5.2.5 and Timmerman 2016, p. 788.

1579 Cf Satzger 2012, p. 70–71; Hecker 2015, p. 248–251. This case-law is now reflected in Article 325(1) and (2) TFEU, cf Timmerman 2016, p. 788–789.

1580 Cf Dougan 2012, p. 84–85.

1581 Cf Corstens and Pradel 2002, p. 516–522, 572–573; Mitsilegas 2009, p. 63–64.

1582 Case C-176/03, *Commission v Council (Environmental Crime)*, EU:C:2005:542.

1583 See para 47.

> authorities is an essential measure for combating serious environmental offences, from taking measures which relate to the criminal law of the Member States which it considers necessary in order to ensure that the rules which it lays down on environmental protection are fully effective".[1584]

The Court thus deemed the Community competent to criminalize behavior when it is essential for the attainment of a Community aim and necessary for the full effectiveness of EC law.[1585] In line with the tendency in earlier judgments, but significantly more explicit and far-reaching, the Court regarded criminal law as just another field of law under the influence of Community law.[1586] The ECJ essentially confirmed the *Environmental Crime* reasoning in the *Ship-Source Pollution* judgment.[1587] At the same time, however, the Court laid down an important limitation on the Community's criminal law competence. It deemed the determination of the types and levels of criminal penalties to be beyond the EC's competence.[1588]

The judgments in *Environmental Crime* and *Ship-Source Pollution* essentially established an EC competence to harmonize criminal law. Before the entry into force of the Lisbon Treaty, the Community could therefore explicitly require the adoption or adaptation of domestic substantive criminal law. This competence could create direct obligations for the Member States to criminalize behavior in addition to the *Greek maize* duty. The recognition of an EC competence for the harmonization of substantive criminal law was therefore an important addition to the pre-existing possibilities for EC law to influence criminal law.

5.2.3 THE CJEU'S APPROACH TO LEGALITY: IN LINE WITH THE DEVELOPMENT OF EC CRIMINAL LAW?

In the pre-Maastricht era, the CJEU (then ECJ) was mostly confronted with the apparent relevance of the legality principle because Member States implemented EC law via national criminal law. Asked about the interpretation of EC law and its potential effect in the domestic legal order, the Court recognized that the field of criminal law required special protective arrangements. As described in section 4.2, the ECJ established 'legality principle-related' limits to both direct effect and consistent interpretation.[1589] Interestingly, the Court did not relate any of those limits to the legality principle in the pre-Maastricht era.

1584 Para 48. See, critically, Satzger 2012, p. 77–78; Klip 2016, p. 188–190.
1585 Cf Mitsilegas 2016, p. 56–57.
1586 Cf Mitsilegas 2009, p. 24, 73, 110.
1587 Case C-440/05, *Commission v Council (Ship-Source Pollution)*, EU:C:2007:625, para 66.
1588 See paras 70–71.
1589 See *Marshall*, *Pretore di Salò* and *Kolpinghuis* as described in subsections 4.2.2–4.2.3.

Explicit discussion of the legality principle is also absent in early rulings recognizing the principle that penalties must have a proper legal basis. While recognizing that penalties for violations of EC law require a proper legal basis, the Court did not, at that time, link this principle to either Article 7 ECHR or a legality principle based on common constitutional traditions.[1590] The Court, moreover, circumvented the question about the legality principle's applicability in judgments on administrative sanctions for violations of competition law.[1591]

An exception to this evasive approach pre-Maastricht is constituted by two early judgments concerning the principle of non-retroactivity.[1592] Both these rulings recognize the principle of non-retroactivity as a specific principle of criminal law and link this principle to the ECHR's legality principle. The potential retroactive effect of EC law on national criminal law was apparently deemed so reprehensible that the ECJ explicitly recognized a principle of criminal law early on in Community law.[1593]

The above judgments with relevance for the legality principle are aptly explained by the spill-over effect of Community law. Questions about conformity with the legality principle were only raised in the aforementioned judgments because Community law allowed, encouraged, or obligated, Member States to implement EC legislation via national criminal law. It was therefore the implementation via national criminal law, ie EC law's positive effect, that resulted in the principle's apparent relevance for EC law. Despite the apparent relevance, none of the pre-Maastricht judgments explicitly recognized an EC legality principle. This could be explained by the controversial and contested influence of supranational EC law on national criminal law.[1594] The combination of positive effect and the contested nature of EC criminal law explains the Court's initial reluctance to expressly recognize criminal law principles.

The pre-Maastricht effects of EC law on national criminal law continued in the Union's first pillar after the entry into force of the Maastricht Treaty. Once again, most relevant judgments in the post-Maastricht era concerned EC measures implemented via national criminal law. A prominent example is *Intertanko*, where the Court explicitly deemed the legality principle relevant for conduct prohibited by first pillar EU legislation.[1595] The explicit recognition of the legality principle in this judgment illustrates how the evasive pre-Maastricht approach changed significantly towards the end of the pre-Lisbon era. It did

1590 See *Könecke* as described in subsection 4.3.2.
1591 See *Bertoli* as described in subsection 4.6.2.
1592 See *Kent Kirk* and *Fedesa* as described in subsection 4.4.3.
1593 Cf Miettinen 2013, p. 105. It is perhaps for this reason that Advocate General Bobek has recently identified the principle of non-retroactivity as the core of the EU legality principle, see Case C-574/15, *Proceedings against Mauro Scialdone*, Opinion of AG Bobek, EU:C:2017:553, paras 146–149.
1594 Cf Asp 2012, p. 32; Miettinen 2013, p. 8.
1595 See further subsection 4.4.2.

not change completely, however, as the clarity of EU legislation was ultimately assessed only on the basis of the general principle of legal certainty.

A more explicit approach to the legality principle was also taken in judgments on limits to consistent interpretation. Post-Maastricht, the Court explicitly recognized the legality principle, the prohibition on the extensive interpretation of criminal law, and the principle of non-retroactivity of crimes and penalties as relevant for limits to consistent interpretation.[1596] In rulings on limits to the direct effect of directives, the Court nevertheless referred to its pre-Maastricht considerations and omitted a reference to the legality principle or elements thereof.[1597]

A development towards a more explicit recognition of criminal law's protective principles is also perceivable with regard to the principle that penalties must have a proper legal basis. Despite continuing its pre-Maastricht approach,[1598] the Court also deemed the requirement of a proper legal basis relevant for national criminal proceedings.[1599] The Court did not yet relate the need for a proper legal basis for criminal penalties to either the legality principle or Article 7 ECHR, however.

As in the pre-Maastricht era, the principle of non-retroactivity continued to be linked to Article 7 ECHR and was consistently recognized as a general principle of Community law. This was not only the case with regard to implementing law,[1600] but also in judgments on direct actions against administrative fines in the field of competition law.[1601] Administrative sanctions did, in fact, become fertile ground for the legality principle. Towards the end of the pre-Lisbon period, the Court generally acknowledged the legality principle's relevance for the validity of sanctions in the field of competition law.[1602]

The judgments in the period between Maastricht and Lisbon illustrate that the Court continued to be confronted with the legality principle due to EC law's positive effect and because the principle was deemed relevant in the field of administrative sanctions for competition law infringements. What did change significantly, however, was the Court's discussion of the legality principle. Instead of the generally evasive pre-Maastricht approach, the Court increasingly recognized the legality principle as a fundamental right in EC law, especially towards the end of the pre-Lisbon era.

The increased recognition towards the end of the pre-Lisbon era could, first of all, be explained by the recognition of an EC competence in the field of

1596 See *X 1996*, *X 2004* as described in subsection 4.2.3.
1597 See *Arcaro*, *Berlusconi* as described in subsection 4.2.2.
1598 See *Milchwerke Köln* as described in subsection 4.3.2.
1599 See *Grøngaard and Bang* as examined in subsections 4.3.4, 4.5.5.
1600 See *Gerekens* as described in subsections 4.4.3.
1601 See, eg, *Danske Rørindustri* as described in subsection 4.6.2. For additional judgments, see subsection 4.6.5.
1602 See, eg, *Danske Rørindustri*; *Jungbunzlauer*; *Evonik Degussa*; *AC-Treuhand 2008* as described in subsection 4.6.2.

substantive criminal law in the *Environmental Crime* and *Ship-Source Pollution* judgments. This recognition arguably removed any of the Court's potential reservations about the recognition of principles of criminal law as fundamental rights of Community law. A second reason for the increased recognition of the legality principle in the Union's first pillar could be the fact that the Court had recognized the legality principle when interpreting third pillar legislation.[1603] The existence of judgments recognizing the legality principle under third pillar Union law allowed the Court to refer to its own case-law when assessing compatibility with the legality principle in the Union's first pillar. The rather uncontroversial relevance of criminal law principles in the Union's third pillar arguably facilitated the recognition of the legality principle under first pillar EC law.

5.3 THE DEVELOPMENT OF CRIMINAL LAW PRE-LISBON: THE UNION'S THIRD PILLAR

5.3.1 INTRODUCTION

The Union's third pillar enlarged the EU law's potential to influence domestic criminal law. This section examines whether the relevant characteristics of criminal law cooperation in the Union's third pillar explain the development of the legality principle in the Court's case-law in the period between Maastricht and Lisbon. Subsection 5.3.2 first describes the general characteristics of third pillar Union law and, more specifically, the Union competence to approximate substantive criminal law. Subsection 5.3.3 examines the two CJEU judgments in which third pillar Union legislation resulted in considerations relevant for the EU legality principle.

5.3.2 APPROXIMATION OF SUBSTANTIVE CRIMINAL LAW

The Maastricht Treaty assigned criminal law competences to the Union in the third pillar. By establishing the pillar structure, the Maastricht Treaty recognized that criminal law constituted a particularly sensitive legal field under the influence of European law. This sensitivity is clearly visible in the Treaty framework which established that the adoption of third pillar instruments required unanimity in the Council and/or ratification by domestic legislatures.[1604] As mentioned in subsection 5.2.1, criminal law cooperation in the Union's third pillar was therefore essentially intergovernmental in nature.

[1603] See subsection 5.3.2.
[1604] See Articles K4(3) and K3(2)(c) Maastricht Treaty.

Although the intergovernmental nature was somewhat weakened by the subsequent amending treaties,[1605] the formal structure of the Treaties of Amsterdam[1606] and Nice[1607] indicated a continued reluctance towards supranational EU criminal law.[1608] At least until the Lisbon Treaty, criminal law cooperation on the basis of explicit treaty competences continued to be subject to special arrangements.[1609] Notwithstanding its intergovernmental nature, the Union competence under the third pillar to harmonize substantive criminal law increased the influence of European law on the definition and interpretation of domestic crimes and penalties.

Article 31(1)(e) TEU 2002, introduced by the Treaty of Amsterdam, conferred the competence to approximate criminal laws in the fields of organized crime, terrorism and illicit drug trafficking.[1610] Although the Union's competence appeared to be limited to the fields specifically mentioned, in practice, EU criminal law legislation was proposed and adopted in several other fields.[1611] This broadened competence to approximate criminal law was based on a joint reading of Articles 31(1)(e) and 29(2) TEU 2002. The combination of both legal bases made it possible to regard the list of crimes enumerated in Article 31(1)(e) TEU 2002 as non-exhaustive. It is, therefore, fair to state that the Union's legislative competences in the field of third pillar criminal law were not interpreted strictly.[1612]

The introduction of an explicit competence to approximate the substantive criminal law of the Member States increased the Union's potential influence on domestic criminal matters. The provision added the possibility of requiring the adoption or amendment of national offenses and penalties to the existing influence on national criminal law under the first pillar. The influence on domestic criminal matters under the third pillar was not limited to legislation

---

1605 Cf Kostakopoulou 2007, p. 164–168; Miettinen 2013, p. 30; Peers 2016b, p. 15.

1606 Treaty of Amsterdam amending the Treaty on European Union, the Treaties establishing the European Communities and certain related acts, [1997] OJ C 340.

1607 Treaty of Nice amending the Treaty on European Union, the Treaties establishing the European Communities and certain related acts, [2001] OJ C 80.

1608 Where I do not indicate a specific historical version of the Treaty on European Union, references are to provisions of the EU treaty in the latest pre-Lisbon version (ie after the amendment by the Treaty of Nice): see consolidated version of the Treaty on European union, [2002] OJ C 325 (hereinafter: 'TEU 2002').

1609 The contested nature of EU criminal law is not, according to some, settled completely by the entry into force of the Lisbon Treaty, see Mitsilegas 2016, p. 53.

1610 Cf Miettinen 2013, p. 33–34; Craig and De Búrca 2015, p. 979–980.

1611 See Mitsilegas 2009, p. 85–87; Mitsilegas 2014, p. 112; Summers, Schwarzenegger, Ege and Young 2014, p. 14–18; Sicurella 2016, p. 62.

1612 Cf Klip 2012, p. 176; Asp 2014, p. 55; Mitsilegas 2016, p. 55. According to Satzger, this was not only the prevailing interpretation of the third pillar competence, but also the correct interpretation of Article 31(1)(e) TEU 2002 when read together with Article 29(2) TEU 2002, see Satzger 2012, p. 74. Peers also finds this interpretation of the third pillar competence correct, he notes that Article 31(1)(e) TEU 2002 contained a non-exhaustive list of crimes, see Peers 2016b, p. 163.

approximating substantive criminal law, however. National rules of criminal procedure could also be affected and this has – perhaps unexpectedly – resulted in the ECJ being confronted with the EU legality principle.

5.3.3 THE CJEU'S APPROACH TO LEGALITY: IN LINE WITH THE DEVELOPMENT OF CRIMINAL LAW IN THE UNION'S THIRD PILLAR?

Only two judgments with relevance for the legality principle resulted from third pillar Union law in the period between the Maastricht Treaty and the Lisbon Treaty. In *Pupino,*[1613] to begin with, the referring Italian Court asked the ECJ about the interpretation of the Framework Decision on the standing of victims.[1614] At the time of the preliminary reference, Italian law allowed young victims to testify under a special procedure in case of sexual offenses only. According to the ECJ, however, the Italian referring court was required to ensure the full effect of the framework decision by extending, as far as possible, the option of testifying under a special procedure to young victims irrespective of the nature of the offense.[1615] In Mitsilegas' view,

> "[t]he Luxembourg Court has in reality re-written the Italian Code of Criminal Procedure. Following the Court's guidance the domestic judge has little choice but to allow minors in this case to take advantage of the Code's protective provisions, although they were not covered by the legislation".[1616]

Third pillar legislation could not just require the adoption or amendment of national rules on criminal matters. It could apparently require a particular judicial interpretation of existing national rules as well. It is not surprising, therefore, that the potential impact of third pillar legislation, which was granted primacy,[1617] has led to the recognition of criminal law principles in the Union's third pillar. In fact, in *Pupino* the Court examined the acceptability of consistent interpretation in light of 'legality principle-related' limits on that duty.[1618] In the later preliminary ruling in *Advocaten voor de Wereld* the Court examined

1613 See Case C-105/03, *Criminal proceedings against Maria Pupino*, EU:C:2005:386. See also subsection 4.5.4.

1614 Council Framework Decision 2001/220/JHA of 15 March 2001 on the standing of victims in criminal proceedings [2001] OJ 2001 L 82.

1615 See para 43.

1616 Mitsilegas 2009, p. 29.

1617 The Court's judgment in *Melloni* arguably confirmed the primacy of framework decisions, see paras 56–58 and cf Besselink 2014, p. 542–545; Peers 2016b, p. 20. For further discussion of the judgment, see subsection 5.5.4. For a short overview of the scholarly debate on the primacy of framework decisions prior to *Melloni*, see Brkan 2013, p. 91 and cf Dougan 2007, p. 936–937.

1618 See paras 44–46. See subsection 4.5.4.

more explicitly whether a third pillar instrument could violate the EU legality principle.[1619]

In light of the above it is safe to say that, like EC law, third pillar Union law clearly affected national criminal law and, consequently, fostered the CJEU's recognition of criminal law principles protected by EU law. Remarkably, however, only the above-mentioned judgments in *Pupino* and *Advocaten voor de Wereld* examined the relevance of the legality principle for third pillar measures. Both judgments concerned the interpretation of EU measures influencing national criminal *procedure*. Rather unexpectedly, third pillar legislation on substantive criminal law has not resulted in judgments on their conformity with the EU legality principle. The legality definition in *Advocaten voor de Wereld* was nevertheless influential, as the Court employed that definition under the former first pillar as well.[1620]

The limited relevance of third pillar legislation for the legality principle could be explained by the characteristics of the third pillar. To begin with, the CJEU only had a limited role in the interpretation of third pillar legislation. It did not have a general competence to interpret third pillar instruments in preliminary rulings.[1621] The CJEU only gained such a competence after the Member States accepted the Court's jurisdiction by 'opting-in'.[1622] Infringement proceedings concerning non-compliance with third pillar legislation were precluded as well.[1623] The lack of a Commission competence to initiate infringement proceedings further restricted the possibilities of the Court to interpret third pillar measures harmonizing substantive criminal law.[1624] As a likely result, the Court has not been granted the opportunity to interpret third pillar legislation on substantive criminal law in the period between Maastricht and Lisbon.[1625]

Notwithstanding the significance of the definition of legality in *Advocaten voor de Wereld*, the addition of the third pillar to first pillar EC law was not a significant factor in the development of the EU legality principle in the era between Maastricht and Lisbon. Although the introduction of the competence to harmonize substantive criminal law held great potential for the judicial development of the legality principle, the Court's limited jurisdiction apparently precluded it from doing so. Despite the addition of the third pillar competence, most judgments recognizing the legality principle still resulted from EC law's

---

1619 In this case: Council Framework Decision 2002/584/JHA of 13 June 2002 on the European arrest warrant and the surrender procedures between Member States [2002] OJ L 190. For further discussion of *Advocaten voor de Wereld*, see subsection 4.5.4.

1620 See *Intertanko* as described in subsection 4.4.2. The *Advocaten voor de Wereld* definition was also reiterated in the field of competition law, see subsection 4.6.6.

1621 See Article 35(2) TEU 2002.

1622 See Article 46(b) and 35(2) TEU 2002. Cf Peers 2016b, p. 13, 20–22.

1623 Cf Mitsilegas 2009, p. 18; Spencer 2014, p. 756; Craig and De Búrca 2015, p. 976.

1624 Cf Klip 2016, p. 41.

1625 See Peers 2016b, p. 165.

positive effect on national criminal law together with a growing body of case-law on administrative sanctions imposed by EU institutions.[1626]

5.4 EU CRIMINAL LAW POST-LISBON

5.4.1 INTRODUCTION

The pillar structure characterized EU criminal law since the Maastricht Treaty. This structure is now mostly of historical importance, however, as the Lisbon Treaty dismantled the distinction between cooperation within the three former Union pillars.[1627] Cooperation on criminal law has now been 'communitarized' and has thereby become largely supranational.[1628] Post-Lisbon, legislation in criminal matters is generally adopted by majority voting in the Council with a veto for the European Parliament,[1629] the legal instruments for adopting criminal law legislation are not precluded from having direct effect,[1630] the Commission may institute infringement proceedings in criminal matters,[1631] and the CJEU's jurisdiction is no longer limited.[1632] In line with pre-existing tendencies in the Court's case-law, criminal law is now treated similarly to other fields of law under the influence of *supranational* EU law.[1633]

As under the former third pillar, criminal law cooperation under the Lisbon Treaty takes place within the broader framework of the 'Area of Freedom, Security and Justice',[1634] a competence which the Union shares with its Member States.[1635] An important element thereof is the EU's ability to harmonize substantive criminal law as explicitly provided by Article 83 TFEU. Although its exact scope remains contested,[1636] supranational EU law approximating national criminal law is a current reality. This explicit competence in the field of substantive criminal law has replaced the third pillar competence in Article 31(1)(e) TEU

1626 See subsection 5.2.3.

1627 Cf, eg, Panzavolta 2013, p. 315; Craig and De Búrca 2015, p. 973.

1628 Cf Mitsilegas 2009, p. 39–41; Satzger 2012, p. 72; Peers 2016b, p. 4; Lenaerts and Gutiérrez-Fons 2016, p. 8; Mitsilegas 2016, p. 4, 14–19; Sicurella 2016, p. 55–56.

1629 Cf Peers 2016b, p. 23. Exceptions where unanimity is still required include Articles 86(1), 87(3) and 89 TFEU.

1630 See Article 288 TFEU which does not exclude the possibility of direct effect of directives like Article 34(2)(b) TEU 2002 did for framework decisions.

1631 See Article 258 TFEU, see further below in the present subsection.

1632 Cf Article 267 TFEU with Article 35 TEU 2002, see further below in the present subsection.

1633 Several intergovernmental elements nevertheless continue to characterize EU criminal law cooperation, see, eg, Articles 67(1), 69, 82(3), 83(3), 86(1), 86(4), 87(3) TFEU. Cf Mitsilegas 2009, p. 37, 41–56, Miettinen 2013, p. 43–44, Rijpma 2013, p. 281; Peers 2016b, p. 34–40.

1634 See Articles 3(2) TEU and 67(1) and (3) TFEU. Cf Miettinen 2013, p. 41, Herlin-Karnell 2014a, p. 22.

1635 See Article 4(2)(j) TFEU. Cf Sicurella 2016, p. 53.

1636 Cf Mitsilegas 2016, p. 53.

2002 and, to a large extent, the EC's harmonization competence confirmed in the *Environmental Crime* and *Ship-Source Pollution* judgments. The influence on national criminal law through so-called negative and positive effects under the former first pillar, however, remains unaffected by the new Treaty framework.[1637]

Since the Lisbon Treaty replaced the previous harmonization competences, subsection 5.4.2 examines the current Union competences for the approximation of crimes and penalties. These competences are highly significant, because they limit the autonomous exercise of national legislative competence in the field of substantive criminal law.[1638] The competence to define substantive criminal law is also relevant for the judiciary at the domestic level. Domestic judges could, in fact, be required to take the CJEU's interpretation of EU legislation into account when interpreting and applying crimes and penalties that implement Union law. As will be described further below, the Lisbon Treaty has thereby confirmed and extended the influence that EC law and pre-Lisbon Union law already had on domestic criminal law.

It should be noted, however, that existing Union competences are significant *in theory* as they provide the *possibility* for the Union to influence domestic criminal law. As the examination of competences under the former third pillar illustrates,[1639] the ability to require the adoption and amendment of national crimes and penalties does not necessarily result in more CJEU case-law on the EU legality principle. That the post-Lisbon competences have nevertheless increased the potential relevance of the EU legality principle will be assessed in subsection 5.4.3. Subsection 5.4.4 will then examine the existing post-Lisbon case-law in order to determine whether the Lisbon Treaty's innovations explain the Court's approach to legality in recent years.

5.4.2 APPROXIMATION OF SUBSTANTIVE CRIMINAL LAW

Article 83(1) TFEU

Article 83(1) TFEU provides the competence to adopt directives establishing minimum rules on the definition of crimes and sanctions. To begin with, Article 83(1) TFEU establishes the competence to criminalize behavior.[1640] The Union legislature can thereby determine the conduct that Member States need to criminalize. Since the definition takes place via a directive, it can only be a *first* definition.[1641] The definition of prohibited conduct that will actually be applied is a second definition. This *second* definition will be a domestic penal provision that was adopted or amended in order to implement the directive's definition.[1642]

1637 On these effects, see section 5.2.
1638 Cf Asp 2014, p. 54; Mitsilegas 2016, p. 62.
1639 See section 5.3.
1640 Cf Klip 2016, p. 180–181.
1641 Cf Mitsilegas 2016, p. 15, 21.
1642 Cf Klip 2016, p. 181.

A directive can additionally require the Member States to prescribe certain domestic criminal sanctions for conduct defined at EU level.[1643] A directive can thus establish the minimum penalty that Member States need to attach to conduct (first) prohibited by EU law. It can certainly require that Member State legislatures ensure a minimum level for maximum penalties (ie 'minimum-maximum penalties').[1644] Whether a directive could also require Member State judiciaries to impose an actual minimum penalty in individual cases is uncertain and highly controversial.[1645] Article 83(1) TFEU does, however, leave room for the prescription of minimum penalties[1646] and the Commission has been a strong proponent of their inclusion in directives on substantive criminal law.[1647]

The competence to harmonize national measures under Article 83(1) TFEU's only applies to areas of particularly serious crime with a cross-border dimension resulting from the nature or impact of such offenses or from a special need to combat them on a common basis.[1648] The provision indicates, exhaustively, the areas of crime for which a legislative competence exists: terrorism, trafficking in human beings and sexual exploitation of women and children, illicit drug trafficking, illicit arms trafficking, money laundering, corruption, counterfeiting of means of payment, computer crime and organized crime.[1649] On the basis of these conditions, the EU appears to be competent only to define offenses and prescribe penalties for 'particularly serious crime with a cross-border dimension'.[1650]

The relationship between particularly serious cross-border crime and the enumeration of areas of crime in Article 83(1) TFEU is nevertheless unclear. Although the English wording certainly implies that the Union is *always* competent to legislate for the enumerated areas of crime,[1651] some authors have argued that the 'serious and cross-border dimension' constitutes an additional condition.[1652] If this interpretation is upheld, the Union would first need to establish that a legislative

1643 Cf Miettinen 2013, p. 140; Klip 2016, p. 181.

1644 Cf Satzger 2012, p. 79; Miettinen 2013, p. 139.

1645 See the European Parliament's amendments 27 and 28 in Report on the proposal for a Directive of the European Parliament and of the Council on the fight against fraud to the Union's financial interest by means of criminal law, A7-0251/2014.

1646 Cf Summers, Schwarzenegger, Ege and Young 2014, p. 48.

1647 See Article 8(1)(a) of Proposal for a Directive of the European Parliament and of the Council on the fight against fraud to the Union's financial interest by means of criminal law, COM(2012) 363 final.

1648 Mitsilegas has labelled this 'securitized criminalization', see Mitsilegas 2014, p. 115–117; Mitsilegas 2016, p. 58–60.

1649 See, eg, Satzger 2012, p. 74–75; Mitsilegas 2014, p. 114; Summers, Schwarzenegger, Ege and Young 2014, p. 48; Peers 2016b, p. 168. It has been noted that these areas of crime largely correspond to areas which were the subject of third pillar legislation, see Summers, Schwarzenegger, Ege and Young 2014, p. 48, 56–57.

1650 Cf Satzger 2012, p. 75.

1651 This follows from a literal interpretation of Article 83(1) TFEU as it states that the areas of crime for which a competence exists 'are the following'.

1652 See Satzger 2012, p. 76; Asp 2014, p. 56.

measure covers an enumerated area of crime[1653] and it would then be required to determine that the conduct satisfies the conditions of 'particular seriousness' and 'cross-border dimension'.[1654] In addition to the uncertainty surrounding the exact conditions for the exercise of the competence set out in Article 83(1) TFEU, it is also unclear what the term 'minimum rules' entails exactly.[1655] The recent proposal for a directive on EU fraud suggests that 'minimum' harmonization allows, and perhaps encourages, Member States to criminalize conduct more extensively and more severely than required by EU law.[1656]

Article 83(1)'s preconditions indicate that it establishes a more limited competence than the one reflected in the legislative practice based on Article 31(1)(e) TEU 2002.[1657] The competence in Article 83(1) TFEU has nevertheless been characterized as broad.[1658] Satzger, for example, finds the enumeration of areas of crime problematic. In his view, due to its vagueness, "(…) it is hardly foreseeable to what extent domestic criminal law may be approximated (…)".[1659] In any event, like the competence under the former third pillar, Article 83(1) TFEU's wording provides room for extensive interpretation.[1660] Article 83(1) TFEU's last sentence indicates that this should not be done lightly, however. The provision requires a unanimous decision by the Council with the consent of the European Parliament for the expansion of the types of crimes on which the Union can legislate.

Whether a specific interpretation of the provision's wording would amount to an expansion of the approximation competence is, of course, open to debate. The Union could, for example, propose that a competence exists to harmonize certain specific crimes not enumerated in Article 83(1) TFEU on the basis of the broad area of 'organized crime'. The provision's wording might therefore lead to CJEU judgments on the extent of the EU's substantive criminal law competence.[1661]

Until legislative practice and/or jurisprudence have clarified the scope of the competence, the interpretation of Article 83(1) TFEU remains somewhat

---

1653 Article 83(1) TFEU enumerates the following areas of crime: terrorism, trafficking in human beings and sexual exploitation of women and children, illicit drug trafficking, illicit arms trafficking, money laundering, corruption, counterfeiting of means of payment, computer crime and organized crime.

1654 Despite being at odds with the English version of Article 83(1) TFEU, the order in which the conditions of the provision's competence are placed, and its wording in other language versions, nevertheless enable such an interpretation.

1655 For an indication of potentially problematic aspects of the use of 'minimum rules' with regard to the definition of the elements of criminal offenses, see Mitsilegas 2014, p. 122–123; Klip 2016, p. 181–183; Mitsilegas 2016, p. 62–63. Cf Altena-Davidsen 2016, p. 72–74.

1656 See Position No 4/2017 of the Council at first reading with a view to the adoption of a Directive of the European Parliament and of the Council on the fight against fraud to the Union's financial interests by means of criminal law adopted by the Council on 25 April 2017, [2017] OJ C 184, Preamble, para 16, which provides that Member States 'are free to adopt or maintain more stringent rules for criminal offenses affecting the Union's financial interests'.

1657 See Satzger 2012, p. 74; Craig and De Búrca 2015, p. 982; Mitsilegas 2016, p. 59.

1658 See Miettinen 2013, p. 42; Mitsilegas 2014, p. 116; Klip 2016, p. 181; Mitsilegas 2016, p. 59.

1659 Satzger 2012, p. 75.

1660 Cf Mitsilegas 2016, p. 59.

1661 Cf Miettinen 2013, p. 44.

uncertain.[1662] Despite the provision's explicit preconditions it is fair to expect Article 83(1) TFEU to be employed rather easily in harmonizing aspects of the Member States' substantive criminal law. The post-Lisbon Union competence in any event contains great potential to influence domestic offenses and penalties.[1663]

Article 83(2) TFEU

Like Article 83(1), Article 83(2) TFEU confers the competence to approximate Member State criminal laws by way of directives establishing minimum rules. Article 83(2) TFEU thus contains an additional Union competence to approximate Member State offenses and penalties.[1664] The difference between both provisions lies in the requirements they set for the exercise of the competence. Article 83's second paragraph grants a competence if the approximation of criminal law proves essential for the effective implementation of a Union policy in an area which has already been subject to harmonization measures.[1665] Unlike the self-standing competence of Article 83's first paragraph, the second paragraph's criminal law competence is clearly derivative. This ancillary competence depends on the pre-existence of harmonization measures enacted in order to implement one of the Union's policies.[1666]

Article 83(2) TFEU is closely related to the EC's criminal law competence which was essentially established by the judgments in *Environmental Crime* and *Ship-Source Pollution*.[1667] As in these judgments, effectiveness is used as the justification for a criminal law competence.[1668] Contrary to the *Ship-Source Pollution* judgment,[1669] however, Article 83(2) TFEU explicitly grants the EU the competence to require Member States to adopt certain penal sanctions. At least in this respect, Article 83(2) TFEU has repealed the CJEU's pre-Lisbon case-law.[1670] Whether Article 83(2) TFEU has integrally replaced the Court's case-law is still subject to debate, however.[1671]

1662 Asp considers the actual delimitation of this competence an important question for the future, see Asp 2014, p. 55.

1663 Cf Sicurella 2016, p. 69–72.

1664 Cf Peers 2016b, p. 169.

1665 Mitsilegas has labelled this 'functional criminalisation', see Mitsilegas 2014, p. 117–118; Mitsilegas 2016, p. 60–62.

1666 Miettinen calls this a classic example of the spill-over effect of EU law, see Miettinen 2013, p. 57 and, for further discussion on this effect, subsection 5.2.2. Cf Satzger 2012, p. 76; Peristeridou 2015, p. 236; Sicurella 2016, p. 62.

1667 Cf Miettinen 2013, p. 56; Miglietti 2014, p. 7; Mitsilegas 2014, p. 115, 117; Summers, Schwarzenegger, Ege and Young 2014, p. 48; Craig and De Búrca 2015, p. 982; Peers 2016b, p. 179–182. Herlin-Karnell even deemed Article 83(2) TFEU to be the codification of the Court's case-law, see Herlin-Karnell 2012, p. 65.

1668 Cf Mitsilegas 2016, p. 60–61.

1669 See para 70.

1670 Cf Miettinen 2013, p. 57, 140; Peers 2016b, p. 169; Sicurella 2016, p. 65.

1671 According to Klip and Keiler, it remains to be seen whether Article 83(2) TFEU is the exclusive competence in this regard, see Keiler and Klip 2013, p. 303; Klip 2016, p. 185. Satzger

Mitsilegas noted that the wording of Article 83(2) TFEU makes it a prime candidate for litigation.[1672] This follows in particular from the condition that approximation of criminal law is possible when it 'proves essential' for the effective implementation of EU policies.[1673] Both Peers and Klip observed that it will be difficult to prove that criminal law is essential.[1674] This will especially be the case given that different institutional actors might very well appreciate the need to use criminal law differently.[1675]

In addition to problems of determining and proving that criminal law is essential, it is also hard to establish when implementing measures will be sufficiently effective.[1676] Uncertainties surround the requirement of preceding harmonization as well. It is not clear, for example, how much harmonization is actually required before a criminal law competence can come into being.[1677] Questions about the meaning of 'minimum rules' in the field of substantive criminal law will also arise with regard to Article 83's second paragraph.[1678]

Due to the above-mentioned uncertainties, the extent of the competence in Article 83(2) remains unclear.[1679] It has been observed, however, that the competence can be construed rather broadly.[1680] As with Article 83(1) TFEU, and perhaps even more so, the competence in the second paragraph contains a rather large potential for the approximation of domestic offenses and penalties.[1681]

Additional legislative competences?

Adding to the uncertainty about the scope of the Union competences to legislate on substantive criminal law are provisions in the TFEU's other Titles that could be viewed as a basis for the approximation of national criminal law.[1682] In particular, Articles 33 and 325(4) TFEU appear to imply a competence to legislate in the field of criminal law.[1683] These provisions grant the competence to take legislative measures in the fields of, respectively, customs cooperation and the

---

is nevertheless quite certain that Article 83(2) TFEU leaves no room for application of the Court's case-law, see Satzger 2012, p. 78.

1672 See Mitsilegas 2009, p. 108; Mitsilegas 2014, p. 117; Mitsilegas 2016, p. 21, 61–62.

1673 Cf Satzger 2012, p. 78; Miglietti 2014, p. 8; Mitsilegas 2014, p. 117.

1674 Cf Klip 2016, p. 184; Peers 2016b, p. 179.

1675 Cf Mitsilegas 2009, p. 108.

1676 See Summers, Schwarzenegger, Ege and Young 2014, p. 49.

1677 Cf Satzger 2012, p. 78; Asp 2014, p. 56; Mitsilegas 2014, p. 118; Summers, Schwarzenegger, Ege and Young 2014, p. 49; Craig and De Búrca 2015, p. 982; Peers 2016b, p. 179–181.

1678 See the references to literature problematizing the definition of minimum rules in Article 83(1) TFEU above.

1679 Cf Summers, Schwarzenegger, Ege and Young 2014, p. 49.

1680 Cf Miglietti 2014, p. 8.

1681 Cf Sicurella 2016, p. 64.

1682 Cf Mitsilegas 2009, p. 109; Asp 2014, p. 56; Klip 2016, p. 185–190; Mitsilegas 2016, p. 65–68.

1683 See Satzger 2012, p. 81; Miettinen 2013, p. 52, 86–87; Klip 2016, p. 185–190; Sicurella 2016, p. 66–67. Articles 75, 79(2)(c) and (d), 86(2) and 86(4) TFEU, 114 TFEU, and 352(1) TFEU have also been suggested to imply a criminal law competence, cf Herlin-Karnell 2012, p. 65–109;

fight against EU fraud. The apparent competence to approximate criminal law on the basis of these provisions results from the deletion of an explicit exclusion of such a competence in the predecessors of Articles 33 and 325(4) TFEU.[1684] The Commission has, in fact, interpreted Article 325(4) TFEU as a sufficient legal basis to propose a measure approximating national criminal law.[1685] The legal basis of this proposal has, however, been changed to Article 83(2) TFEU as a result of the European Parliament[1686] and the Council.[1687] This shows that institutional disagreements over the Union's legislative competences in the field of criminal law exist already.

The acknowledgement of Articles 33 and 325(4) TFEU as appropriate legal bases for the approximation of criminal law would have significant effects. It would not just increase the Union's ability to influence substantive criminal law. It would also grant the possibility to harmonize domestic criminal law via a regulation and allow for maximum harmonization instead of minimum rules based on Article 83 TFEU.[1688] These consequences show that the acknowledgment of Articles 33 and 325(4) TFEU as additional legal bases would change the quality of the Union's competence to approximate substantive criminal law. The fact that the competence to approximate criminal law in Article 83 has been made subject to special arrangements like the 'emergency brake' in Article 83(3) TFEU,[1689] provides a strong argument against legislative criminal law competences outside the framework of Title V TFEU.[1690] In light of the Court's earlier expansive approach

---

Satzger 2012, p. 56; Miettinen 2013, p. 52–53; Asp 2014, p. 57; Mitsilegas 2014, p. 120; Summers, Schwarzenegger, Ege and Young 2014, p. 50; Sicurella 2016, p. 68.

1684 The predecessors of Articles 33 and 325(4) TFEU, Articles 135 and 280 EC Treaty, expressly excluded criminal law from their scope by stating that measures adopted on those provisions 'shall not concern the application of national criminal law or the national administration of justice'.

1685 See Proposal for a Directive of the European Parliament and of the Council on the fight against fraud to the Union's financial interest by means of criminal law, COM(2012) 363 final, p. 6–8, 12. Cf Miettinen 2013, p. 52; Summers, Schwarzenegger, Ege and Young 2014, p. 50–51. See, critically, Peers 2016b, p. 171.

1686 See Report on the proposal for a Directive of the European Parliament and of the Council on the fight against fraud to the Union's financial interest by means of criminal law, A7-0251/2014, Amendment 1. See further the opinion of the European Parliament's legal affairs committee on the legal basis for the proposal for a Directive of the European Parliament and of the Council on the fight against fraud to the Union's financial interests by means of criminal law (COM(2012)0363 – C7-0192/2012 – 2012/0193(COD)) which is annexed to the report on the proposal.

1687 See Position No 4/2017 of the Council at first reading with a view to the adoption of a Directive of the European Parliament and of the Council on the fight against fraud to the Union's financial interests by means of criminal law adopted by the Council on 25 April 2017, [2017] OJ C 184.

1688 Cf Altena-Davidsen 2016, p. 76–77; Mitsilegas 2016, p. 65.

1689 In addition to special arrangements, the proper legislative procedure and legal instruments also constitute potential reasons for disagreeing about legal bases for the approximation of criminal law, cf Miettinen 2013, p. 57–58; Mitsilegas 2014, p. 118.

1690 See also the European Parliament's Report on the proposal for a Directive of the European Parliament and of the Council on the fight against fraud to the Union's financial interest by

to harmonization competences it is not unthinkable, however, that other legal bases such as Articles 33 and 325(4) TFEU would be acknowledged as appropriate for the approximation of criminal law.[1691] Such an acknowledgment would certainly enlarge the Union's opportunities to influence domestic offenses and penalties.

5.4.3 IMPLICATIONS FOR THE EU LEGALITY PRINCIPLE: INCREASED POTENTIAL POST-LISBON

The competences in the Treaty of Lisbon to approximate substantive criminal law create great potential for EU law to require the adoption or amendment of national crimes and penalties.[1692] The Treaty of Lisbon was, in fact, perceived by the Council and the Commission as increasing the Union's involvement with matters of substantive criminal law.[1693] This increase could certainly enhance the relevance of the EU legality principle for the legislature, both at the Union and national level.[1694] It is not surprising, therefore, that the three main Union institutions in the legislative process (ie the Council,[1695] the Commission[1696] and the European Parliament[1697]) have recognized the importance of certain elements of the legality principle for the definition of crimes at the EU level.[1698]

The Council, for example, recognized the need for criminal provisions to clearly address 'defined and delimited conduct'.[1699] It considered that in order to ensure the predictability of the application, scope and meaning of criminal

---

means of criminal law, A7–0251/2014, p. 33–34. Cf Asp 2012, p. 153; Peers 2016b, p. 170–171; Sicurella 2016, p. 67.

1691 See Altena-Davidsen 2016, p. 76–77; Klip 2016, p. 186; Mitsilegas 2016, p. 24–25, 68.

1692 These legislative competences have been used fairly modestly in the early post-Lisbon period, however, see Peers 2016b, p. 211.

1693 In the words of the Council: "The Lisbon Treaty is likely to have the effect that criminal law provisions will be discussed within the Council to an even greater extent than at present", Draft Council conclusions on model provisions, guiding the Council's criminal law deliberations, Council doc 16542/1/09, p. 3. According to the Commission "[t]he legal framework under the Lisbon Treaty provides fresh opportunities to develop EU criminal law legislation", Communication from the Commission to the European Parliament, the Council, the European Economic and Social Committee and the Committee of the Regions, Towards an EU Criminal Policy: Ensuring the effective implementation of EU policies through criminal law, COM(2011) 573 final, p. 3. Mitsilegas has nevertheless observed that criminal law harmonization remained in line with the pre-Lisbon practice, see Mitsilegas 2016, p. 72.

1694 See Mitsilegas 2016, p. 72.

1695 Draft Council conclusions on model provisions, guiding the Council's criminal law deliberations, Council doc 16542/1/0.

1696 Communication from the Commission to the European Parliament, the Council, the European Economic and Social Committee and the Committee of the Regions, Towards an EU Criminal Policy: Ensuring the effective implementation of EU policies through criminal law, COM(2011) 573 final.

1697 European Parliament Resolution of 22 May 2012 on an EU approach to criminal law, (2010/2310 (INI)).

1698 This is also apparent in the Manifesto on European Criminal Policy 2011, p. 87.

1699 See under 2, p. 4.

provisions, the description of criminal conduct 'must be worded precisely'.[1700] The Council thus appeared to acknowledge the importance of *lex certa* when legislating in the field of criminal law. The importance of these determinations were confirmed by the European Parliament. The Parliament's Resolution first reiterated the Council's determinations on the need for clear and precise rules and subsequently added an explicit reference to '*lex certa* requirements'.[1701]

Relevant statements for the legality principle were also made in the Commission's Communication. The Commission stated that the Charter provides important limits for EU action in the field of criminal law, because that legal field comprises particularly intrusive rules.[1702] For that reason, the Commission underlined that EU criminal law legislation demands particular attention from the legislature which, by virtue of the principle of legal certainty, is required to clearly define criminal conduct.[1703] By requiring clearly defined conduct on the basis of the principle of legal certainty, the Commission arguably affirmed the relevance of *lex certa*.

The apparent connection between *lex certa* and legal certainty was recognized explicitly by the European Parliament. The Parliament considered that 'the principle of legal certainty (*lex certa*)' requires that "(...) the description of the elements of a criminal offense must be worded precisely to the effect that an individual shall be able to predict actions that will make him/her criminally liable".[1704] The Parliament's Resolution additionally recognized the importance of the principle of non-retroactivity as a general principle governing criminal law.[1705] Particularly in the Parliament's view, the EU legality principle becomes highly relevant due to the EU competence to define crimes and penalties.

The Lisbon Treaty also enhanced the potential for the CJEU to recognize and develop criminal law principles such as the legality principle.[1706] An important development in this regard is the abolition of the restrictions under the former third pillar on the Court's jurisdiction.[1707] EU criminal law legislation adopted post-Lisbon can therefore be interpreted by the CJEU in preliminary rulings[1708] and in infringement proceedings initiated by the Commission for non-compliance with EU criminal law.[1709] Since the post-Lisbon jurisdiction no longer restricts the possibilities for the Court to interpret EU substantive

---

1700 See under 4, p. 5.

1701 European Parliament Resolution on an EU approach to criminal law, under I and K.

1702 See Communication, p. 4.

1703 See Communication, p. 7.

1704 European Parliament Resolution on an EU approach to criminal law, under 4.

1705 See under 4.

1706 Cf Mitsilegas 2009, p. 112; Craig 2010, p. 378; Hinarejos 2011, p. 429; Keiler and Klip 2013, p. 307. Douglas-Scott is less optimistic about the potential impact of the Lisbon Treaty for the Court's case-law on fundamental rights, see Douglas-Scott 2011, p. 276–294.

1707 On the limited jurisdiction in the former third pillar, see section 5.3.3.

1708 Cf Article 267 TFEU and Article 35 TEU 2002. See also, eg, Mitsilegas 2009, p. 40; Herlin-Karnell 2012, p. 36, 227; Summers, Schwarzenegger, Ege and Young 2014, p. 53; Peers 2016b, p. 24.

1709 See Article 258 TFEU. Cf Mitsilegas 2009, p. 40; Miettinen 2013, p. 70; Summers, Schwarzenegger, Ege and Young 2014, p. 53.

criminal law,[1710] it will be easier for the Court to assess the compatibility of criminal law legislation with the EU legality principle.[1711] The same conclusion presently applies for third pillar legislation, because on 1 December 2014 the Court acquired the (regular) jurisdiction to interpret pre-Lisbon criminal law legislation in both preliminary rulings and infringement proceedings.[1712] The increased potential for the Court to interpret criminal law legislation post-Lisbon has not, however, led to a surge in the number of cases on EU criminal law.[1713]

5.4.4 THE CJEU'S APPROACH TO LEGALITY: IN LINE WITH THE DEVELOPMENT OF EU CRIMINAL LAW POST-LISBON?

The development towards a more explicit recognition of the legality principle at the end of the pre-Lisbon era generally continued post-Lisbon. In the high profile Grand Chamber rulings in *Taricco* and *Rosneft*, for example, the ECJ explicitly recognized the importance of safeguarding the EU legality principle when Union law resulted in, or required, implementation via national criminal law.[1714] Both judgments used Article 49 Charter as the basis for the EU legality principle and this approach has been adopted in other judgments as well.[1715] In *Rosneft*, moreover, the Court explicitly recognized the *lex certa* principle as a specific element of the Charter's legality principle.

The explicit connection between the legality principle and the case-law on the limits to consistent interpretation in criminal matters continued post-Lisbon. In fact, in *Caronna* the Court linked the limits to consistent interpretation to Article 49 Charter.[1716] Instead of referring to the legality principle, however, the Court recognized the principle that penalties must have a proper legal basis as enshrined in Article 49 Charter. This direct connection between the requirement of a proper legal basis and the EU legality principle is not exceptional in the post-Lisbon period.[1717] Unlike in the pre-Lisbon era, the Court referred to the legality

1710 See Mitsilegas 2009, p. 112, Peers 2014, p. 25. Brkan determined that 'freedom, security and justice' as a whole constituted a significantly larger part of the CJEU's case-law in 2012 than before, see Brkan 2013, p. 78.

1711 Cf Bazzocchi 2011, p. 195.

1712 See Article 10(3) of the Protocol on Transitional Provisions annexed to the Lisbon Treaty. Cf Miettinen 2013, p. 67; Craig and De Búrca 2015, p. 977; Klip 2016, p. 56; Peers 2016b, p. 22, 32–34.

1713 See Peers 2016b, p. 24, 167.

1714 See *Taricco*, para 54; *Rosneft*, paras 158, 162. On these judgments, see subsections 4.5.4, 4.5.7.

1715 See *Garenfeld*, para 48. On that judgment, see subsection 4.5.6. See also, more recently, Case C-42-17, *Criminal proceedings against M.A.S. and M.B. (Taricco II)*, EU:C:2017:936, para 52.

1716 See subsection 4.3.3 on the limits to consistent interpretation.

1717 See *Aurubis Balgaria* described in subsection 4.3.3.

principle to substantiate the requirement of a proper legal basis for penalties in judgments concerning domestic implementing law.[1718]

The explicit recognition of the relevance of the legality principle continued in the CJEU's post-Lisbon case-law on administrative sanctions for violations of competition law.[1719] Due to the Charter's entry into force, the Court has explicitly applied Article 49 Charter to these administrative sanctions.[1720] EU administrative sanctions were also required to conform with the principle of non-retroactivity of penal provisions.[1721] The post-Lisbon case-law on the legality principle is therefore largely in line with the Court's reasoning in competition law judgments towards the end of the pre-Lisbon period. It is, moreover, in general accordance with the approach adopted in the above-mentioned post-Lisbon judgments on former first pillar Union law.

The aforementioned judgments illustrate that former first pillar Union law continues to form an important source for the judicial development of the EU legality principle. The Court, first of all, continues to be confronted with the legality principle because Member States have penalized violations of EU law via national criminal law.[1722] Another reason is the evident applicability of the legality principle to EU administrative sanctions for violations of competition law.

Other EU administrative sanctions have also been regarded as potentially relevant for the EU legality principle in the post-Lisbon era. EU secondary law, ie decisions concerning asset freezing measures raised the issue of the applicability of the legality principle. In *Ezz and Others* and *Al Matri* the General Court rejected the applicability of Article 49 Charter,[1723] but this is not necessarily the definitive answer.[1724] As Mitsilegas observed, EU administrative economic sanctions for persons related to terrorism could constitute criminal sanctions for the purpose of the ECHR and the Charter.[1725] The issue will, in all likelihood, give rise to further litigation before the CJEU.[1726]

As in the post-Maastricht era, explicit Union competences in the field of criminal law have not given rise to a large amount of case-law on the legality

---

1718 It has not done so consistently, however. The Court continued its pre-Lisbon approach in *SGS Belgium*, see subsection 4.3.2. In its post-Lisbon judgments in the field of competition law, the CJEU has also connected the principle that penalties require a proper legal basis to the principle of legal certainty, see *Dornbracht*; *Heineken*; *Lundbeck* as described in subsection 4.6.3.

1719 See, eg, *Sasol* as described in subsection 4.6.2.

1720 See, eg, *Dornbracht*; *Moreda-Riviere*; *Lundbeck*; *Marine Harvest* as described in subsections 4.6.2–4.6.3, 4.6.6.

1721 See, eg, *Denki*; *Saint-Gobain Glass* as described in subsection 4.6.2. See further the judgments referred to in subsection 4.6.5.

1722 See, eg, *Garenfeld*; *Caronna*; *Taricco*; *Paoletti*; *Rosneft* described in subsections 4.2.3; 4.5.2; 4.5.4; 4.5.6–4.5.7. Another reason was the apparently punitive nature of non-criminal penalties for the violations of former first pillar EU law, see *Aurubis Balgaria* as described in subsection 4.3.3.

1723 See subsection 4.6.4.

1724 Cf Case T-85/09, *Yassin Abdullah Kadi v European Commission*, EU:T:2010:418, para 150.

1725 See Mitsilegas 2016, p. 262. Cf Cameron 2016, p. 566.

1726 See Mitsilegas 2016, p. 262.

principle. In fact, the post-Lisbon era has yet to see a judgment recognizing the legality principle within the framework of the AFSJ. The complete absence of case-law on the legality principle could partly be explained by the fact that we are only a few years into the post-Lisbon era. Another explanation is the rather modest number of cases on EU criminal law legislation that reached the Court in the early post-Lisbon period.[1727] As in the pre-Lisbon era where the explicit criminal law competences resulted in a small number of relevant judgments,[1728] the Union's criminal law competences have not had a great impact post-Lisbon. As the present section illustrated, however, these competences have the potential to increase the EU legality principle's relevance in the future.

Generally speaking, the CJEU's approach post-Lisbon has continued the development of the EU legality principle in judgments towards the end of the pre-Lisbon era. The most important novelty in the approach post-Lisbon is the rather general recognition of Article 49 Charter as the source of the EU legality principle, which is obviously the result of the Charter acquiring binding effect. While a more explicit approach post-Lisbon is increasingly perceivable, the Court has not consistently recognized the CFR's legality principle post-Lisbon. The principle of non-retroactivity of criminal law, for example, has been exclusively referred to as a general principle of Union law.[1729] Instead of appropriate references to Article 49 CFR, post-Lisbon judgments have also referred exclusively to principles such as legal certainty and the principle that penalties must have a proper legal basis.[1730]

It should be concluded, therefore, that the Charter's entry into force has not fully remedied the lack of consistency in the Court's pre-Lisbon approach to legality.

5.5 EU FUNDAMENTAL RIGHTS PROTECTION: CHARACTERISTICS

5.5.1 INTRODUCTION

The (historical) particularities of EU fundamental rights protection could potentially explain some of the inconsistencies in the CJEU's approach to legality. The present section will eventually revisit the judgments on the legality principle

1727 See Peers 2016b, p. 24, 167.

1728 See section 5.3.3.

1729 See *E and F* as examined in subsection 4.4.3. That the principle of non-retroactivity constitutes an element of the EU legality principle is nevertheless implicit in the recent judgment in Case C-42–17, *Criminal proceedings against M.A.S. and M.B. (Taricco II)*, EU:C:2017:936, para 53.

1730 With regard to legal certainty: see *M and Others* and *Karelia* as examined in subsection 4.4.2. With regard to the principle that penalties must have a proper legal basis: see *SGS Belgium* as examined in subsection 4.3.2.

(subsection 5.5.5). The focus here will be on the Court's treatment of the different sources of the EU legality principle and the references to the Strasbourg Court's case-law. In order to explain the Court's approach, subsections 5.5.2–5.5.4 first assess the characteristics of EU fundamental rights protection.

5.5.2 FUNDAMENTAL RIGHTS AS GENERAL PRINCIPLES I: THE ECHR'S 'SPECIAL SIGNIFICANCE'

The original Treaties lacked express provisions on fundamental rights due to their focus on economic integration.[1731] It is well-known that the CJEU filled this gap by protecting fundamental rights as general principles of Union (then: Community) law.[1732] Although the Court emphasized the autonomous nature of fundamental rights in EU law, it simultaneously recognized the relevance of external sources for the interpretation of 'autonomous' EU fundamental rights.[1733] In *Nold*, for instance, the ECJ considered the Member States' common constitutional traditions relevant for the interpretation of fundamental rights as general principles of Union law.[1734] The Court additionally acknowledged the relevance of international human rights treaties for the construction of fundamental rights in Community law.[1735] The Court consolidated this approach in *Hauer*, while simultaneously identifying the ECHR as an important international human rights treaty.[1736] The early recognition of the Convention's significance was still tentative, however, since the Court merely referred to a joint

1731 See, eg, De Witte 1999, p. 863; Torres Pérez 2009, p. 14; Craig 2010, p. 193–195; Dauses 2010, p. 22; De Búrca 2011, p. 475–476; Raulus 2011, p. 213, 215; Van Bockel and Wattel 2014, p. 873; Craig and De Búrca 2015, p. 382. For interesting comments on the political intentions about human rights protection in Europe before the EEC Treaty, see De Búrca 2011, p. 467–475.

1732 See Case 29/69, *Erich Stauder v City of Ulm, Sozialamt*, EU:C:1969:57, para 7, Case 11/70, *Internationale Handelsgesellschaft v Einfuhr- und Vorratsstelle für Getreide und Futtermittel*, EU:C:1970:114, para 4, Case 4/73, *J. Nold, Kohlen- und Baustoffgrosshandlung v Commission of the European Communities*, para 13. Cf Torres Pérez 2009, p. 9–10, 35; Dauses 2010, p. 25–26; De Búrca 2011, p. 477–478; Sarmiento 2013, p. 1269; De Hert 2016, p. 106–108.

1733 Cf Torres Pérez 2009, p. 35; Di Federico 2011, p. 18; Raulus 2011, p. 219–220; De Búrca 2011, p. 478–479. Von Bogdandy nevertheless characterized the ECJ's human rights jurisprudence as 'the least autonomous part of the supranational legal order', see Von Bogdandy 2000, p. 1333 and cf Senden 2011, p. 381–382.

1734 Case 4/73, *J. Nold, Kohlen- und Baustoffgrosshandlung v Commission of the European Communities*, para 13. The Court previously recognized the common constitutional traditions as a source of inspiration in Case 11/70, *Internationale Handelsgesellschaft v Einfuhr- und Vorratsstelle für Getreide und Futtermittel*, EU:C:1970:114, para 4.

1735 See *Nold*, para 13.

1736 Case 44/79, *Liselotte Hauer v Land Rheinland-Pfalz*, EU:C:1979:290, paras 14–15. The ECJ had already referred to the ECHR in Case 36/75, *Roland Rutili v Ministre de l'intérieur*, EU:C:1975:137, para 32. Cf De Witte 2011, p. 17; Douglas-Scott 2013, p. 157.

declaration of the European Parliament, the Council, and the Commission[1737] which emphasized the ECHR's importance.[1738]

After the CJEU's first reference to the ECHR in 1975, the Court routinely characterized the Convention as having 'special significance'.[1739] The ECHR's privileged position was subsequently confirmed by the Maastricht Treaty[1740] and is presently enshrined in Article 6(3) TEU,[1741] which sets out:

> "Fundamental rights, as guaranteed by the European Convention for the Protection of Human Rights and Fundamental Freedoms and as they result from the constitutional traditions common to the Member States, shall constitute general principles of the Union's law."

The codification[1742] of the Court's case-law in Article 6(3) TEU is noteworthy since a reference to international human rights treaties is omitted. The exclusive reference to the ECHR in Article 6(3) TEU appears to signify that the ECHR is not just *one* specifically important international human rights treaty. It arguably implies that the ECHR is the *only* human rights treaty that acts as an inspirational source for general principles of EU law.

Although the CJEU has used other international human rights treaties far less frequently than the ECHR, it seems rather inconceivable that Article 6(3) TEU actually intended to limit the available inspirational international instruments to the Convention.[1743] Since the ECHR still[1744] appears to have the same

1737 Joint Declaration by the European Parliament, the Council and the Commission, [1977] OJ C103/1. This declaration arguably cloaked the ECJ's fundamental rights approach with legitimacy, see Craig 2010, p. 195. Cf De Witte 1999, p. 866; Raulus 2011, p. 216; De Búrca 2011, p. 479; Senden 2011, p. 323.

1738 See *Hauer*, para 15. It is noteworthy that the Court referred to this declaration, because the declaration arguably intended only to indicate the acceptance of the other institutions of the ECJ's derivation of rights from, inter alia, the ECHR.

1739 The ECJ apparently considered paragraph 18 of its judgment in Case C-222/84, *Marguerite Johnston v Chief Constable of the Royal Ulster Constabulary*, EU:C:1986:206 especially relevant for the ECHR's special significance, see, eg, Joined Cases 46/87 and 227/88, *Hoechst AG v Commission of the European Communities*, EU:C:1989:337, para 13; Case C-260/89, *Elliniki Radiophonia Tiléorassi AE and Panellinia Omospondia Syllogon Prossopikou v Dimotiki Etairia Pliroforissis and Sotirios Kouvelas and Nicolaos Avdellas and others (ERT)*, EU:C:1991:254, para 41.

1740 Article F(2) Treaty on European Union (Maastricht Treaty), [1992] OJ C191.

1741 Senden observes that the fact that all Member States had ratified the ECHR formed an important justification for treating this treaty as particularly significant, see Senden 2011, p. 354, 361. Cf Dauses 2010, p. 31.

1742 See, eg, Case C-571/10, *Servet Kamberaj v Istituto per l'Edilizia Sociale della Provincia autonoma di Bolzano (IPES) and Others*, EU:C:2012:233, para 61.

1743 See Craig and De Búrca 2015, p. 385–388; Peers 2016a, p. 43.

1744 Until the EU eventually accedes to the ECHR as required by Article 6(2) TEU. The actual accession is nevertheless far away due to *Opinion 2/13 on the Accession of the European Union to the European Convention for the Protection of Human Rights and Fundamental Freedoms*, EU:C:2014:2454.

inspirational status as other international instruments, De Witte has deemed the ECHR's special position remarkable.[1745] The notability of the ECHR's position would, however, be diminished if the Convention was viewed as constituting more than a source of inspiration for EU fundamental rights as general principles. De Witte observed that Article 6(3) TEU could, in fact, be interpreted as assigning the ECHR a stronger role than as an inspirational source.[1746] The CJEU has not generally accepted De Witte's reading of Article 6(3) TEU, however.[1747] In fact, after the entry into force of the Lisbon Treaty the Court has explicitly invoked the fact that the Union has not acceded to the ECHR to underline that the ECHR does not constitute a formal source of fundamental rights in EU law.[1748]

The CJEU's use of ECtHR judgments is noteworthy in light of the ECHR's special significance as a source of inspiration for the general principles. The Court only made its first explicit reference to an ECtHR judgment relatively late, in 1996.[1749] Since then, however, references to ECtHR judgments have become quite frequent[1750] and, as De Witte concluded in 2011, the CJEU "(...) hardly ever departs from the Strasbourg case law and never openly contradicts it."[1751] In 2013, Douglas-Scott determined that the CJEU was engaging more with Strasbourg jurisprudence and that judgments in the early post-Lisbon years tended to be more reliant on the ECtHR case-law as a ground for justification.[1752]

De Búrca nevertheless demonstrated that the Court's use of the ECtHR's case-law had actually decreased in the three years after the Charter became legally binding.[1753] De Búrca's observations were subsequently confirmed by Krommendijk. By examining CJEU case-law and interviewing CJEU officials, he concluded that the CJEU has indeed reduced its references to the ECHR and to Strasbourg judgments post-Lisbon.[1754] The need to underline the autonomy of EU fundamental rights forms an obvious explanation for the Luxembourg

---

1745 See De Witte 2011, p. 20.

1746 See De Witte 2011, p. 21–22. See also Senden 2011, p. 360; Krommendijk 2015, p. 815.

1747 See De Witte 2011, p. 23; Douglas-Scott 2013, p. 157; Craig and De Búrca 2015, p. 385.

1748 See, eg, Case C-571/10, *Servet Kamberaj v Istituto per l'Edilizia Sociale della Provincia autonoma di Bolzano (IPES) and Others*, EU:C:2012:233, para 62; Case C-617/10, *Åklagaren v Hans Åkerberg Fransson*, EU:C:2013:105, para 44. Peers still considers the ECHR to be a basic source of human rights protection in the EU legal order, see Peers 2016a, p. 42, 45.

1749 In Case C-13/94, *P v S and Cornwall County Council*, EU:C:1996:170, para 16. See De Witte 1999, p. 878; De Witte 2011, p. 24; Douglas-Scott 2013, p. 158.

1750 See Senden 2011, p. 353; Douglas-Scott 2013, p. 157 (both with further references).

1751 De Witte 2011, p. 25. Cf De Búrca 2011, p. 487; Senden 2011, p. 362; Glas and Krommendijk 2017, p. 569.

1752 See Douglas-Scott 2013, p. 158. The author mentions Joined Cases C-402/05 P and C-415/05 P, *Yassin Abdullah Kadi and Al Barakaat International Foundation v Council of the European Union and Commission of the European Communities*, EU:C:2008:461 as an example of this approach.

1753 See De Búrca 2013, p. 174–175.

1754 See Krommendijk 2015, p. 823–824, 833.

Court's post-Lisbon approach.[1755] This is arguably exemplified by the CJEU's so-called 'Charter-centrism'.[1756]

Despite the perceivable tendency to diminish the explicit use of the Convention and ECtHR judgments, the CJEU does occasionally refer to Strasbourg case-law in post-Lisbon judgments.[1757] There is not, however, a general CJEU approach to the use of the Convention and the ECtHR's jurisprudence, nor has there ever been one.[1758] The lack of a general approach jeopardizes the consistency and predictability of the interpretation of EU fundamental rights that correspond to ECHR rights.[1759] Critical early observations about the CJEU's use of the ECtHR's case-law are therefore fully applicable to recent post-Lisbon judgments. As a consequence, the Court's use of the Strasbourg jurisprudence can still be qualified as 'eclectic and unsystematic',[1760] as well as 'increasingly selective'.[1761]

5.5.3 FUNDAMENTAL RIGHTS AS GENERAL PRINCIPLES II: THE COMMON CONSTITUTIONAL TRADITIONS

As described above, the Court acknowledged the common constitutional traditions of the Member States as an inspirational source for fundamental rights as general principles of Community/Union law.[1762] The CJEU's case-law and Article 6(3) TEU both place the common constitutional traditions of the Member States on equal footing with the ECHR as an inspirational source for EU fundamental rights as general principles.[1763] The relevance of common constitutional traditions as an *actual* source of inspiration is nevertheless open to question. This is because the Court has not made systematic use of national provisions and domestic case-law to determine and interpret EU fundamental rights.[1764]

In the absence of frequent and thorough comparative examinations, the general reference to common constitutional traditions appears to be mostly rhetorical.[1765] This merely symbolic relevance of Member State constitutional traditions results from several difficulties in actually using common

1755 See Krommendijk 2015, p. 831–833.

1756 See Krommendijk 2015, p. 832; Glas and Krommendijk 2017, p. 573–576. See further subsection 5.5.4.

1757 See Krommendijk 2015, p. 833; Krommendijk 2016, p. 358–360; Glas and Krommendijk 2017, p. 573–576, 586–587.

1758 See Krommendijk 2015, p. 817.

1759 On 'corresponding rights' in the Charter and the ECHR, see subsection 5.5.4.

1760 De Witte 2011, p. 25–32.

1761 De Búrca 2013, p. 173–174.

1762 See Case 11/70, *Internationale Handelsgesellschaft v Einfuhr- und Vorratsstelle für Getreide und Futtermittel*, EU:C:1970:114, para 4; *Nold*, para 13.

1763 Cf Dauses 2010, p. 31.

1764 See, eg, De Witte 1999, p. 878; Senden 2011, p. 329–331; Craig and De Búrca 2015, p. 388.

1765 See Senden 2011, p. 331, 340–341.

constitutional traditions as an inspirational source. Obviously, difficulties in genuinely determining the scope and content of *all* national constitutional rights are a first important factor.[1766] A related difficulty lies in deriving a *common* constitutional tradition from (differing) national constitutional standards.[1767] In addition, a more fundamental problem arises when common constitutional traditions need to be 'translated' to autonomous EU fundamental rights.[1768]

The above-mentioned difficulties for using common constitutional traditions as an inspirational source appear to have furthered the ECHR's importance for EU fundamental rights.[1769] It could be argued that the ECHR already reflects the constitutional standards that all Member States (are obliged to) uphold.[1770] In that regard the ECHR clearly expresses a minimum common constitutional standard for the protection of certain fundamental rights.[1771] The existence of the ECHR as a common standard could, moreover, explain the limited practical importance of the Member States' constitutional traditions as inspirational sources.[1772] With the binding Charter as an additional common fundamental rights standard in EU law, the practical importance of the common constitutional traditions is unlikely to increase.

From the perspective of the CJEU, national constitutional traditions should be used solely as inspiration for rights not contained in the ECHR and/or the Charter, or as interpretational tools for the scope of rights enshrined in those documents.[1773] Outside these functions the Court does not recognize the relevance of national constitutional rights in EU law.[1774] It should be noted, however, that several Member State (constitutional) courts have reserved the competence to use domestic constitutional rights to scrutinize EU law. In doing so they would reject the CJEU's conception of primacy,[1775] which makes it reasonable to assume that such a position will not be resorted to on a whim. In exceptional circumstances, however, a protective function for national constitutional rights continues to exist from the perspective of several Member States.[1776]

1766 Cf Dauses 2010, p. 32–33; Senden 2011, p. 329.

1767 Cf Dauses 2010, p. 32; Raulus 2011, p. 220–221, Senden 2011, p. 344–347, Craig and De Búrca 2015, p. 388.

1768 See Craig and De Búrca 2015, p. 390.

1769 This observation seems supported by Senden's finding that in cases where the ECJ has referred to Member States' constitutional traditions it also referred to the ECHR and the ECtHR's case-law, see Senden 2011, p. 343.

1770 Cf Senden 2011, p. 330.

1771 Cf Dauses 2010, p. 31; Craig and De Búrca 2015, p. 388.

1772 See Senden 2011, p. 330, 384.

1773 See Senden 2011, p. 330, 342. Cf Article 52(4) Charter which is examined in subsection 5.5.4.

1774 See, eg, Case C-399/11, *Stefano Melloni v Ministerio Fiscal*, EU:C:2013:107, paras 58–59.

1775 See, eg, De Witte 2014, p. 1529–1530; Claes 2015, p. 180–187; Craig and De Búrca 2015, p. 266–278.

1776 See Claes 2015, p. 187–199; Craig and De Búrca 2015, p. 278–309. This is exemplified by the order for a preliminary ruling from the Italian Constitutional Court following the *Taricco* judgment, see further subsection 5.5.5.

5.5.4 CODIFIED FUNDAMENTAL RIGHTS: THE CHARTER OF FUNDAMENTAL RIGHTS OF THE EUROPEAN UNION

The existence of a binding written catalogue of fundamental rights is a recent development in Union law as the Charter entered into force with the Lisbon Treaty on December 1st 2009. Article 6(1) TEU determines that the Charter's legal value is the same as the Treaties. Like the judicially developed general principles of EU law, the Charter constitutes primary Union law.[1777] The Charter is moreover understood as an expression of Member State common constitutional traditions.[1778]

The distinct process of development and adoption afford the Charter legitimacy as an instrument of fundamental rights protection.[1779] It is not surprising, therefore, that it is regarded as the primary reference point for EU fundamental rights.[1780] Whether – as expected – the Charter's entry into force increased the CJEU's case-law on fundamental rights,[1781] the Court, in any event, referred increasingly to the Charter as the source of EU fundamental rights. De Búrca, for example, determined that the CJEU's references to the Charter have "(...) arisen very significantly since the Charter acquired legal effect."[1782] In Sarmiento's view, the Court has even put the Charter at the forefront of European integration in a series of groundbreaking judgments.[1783] In line with these developments, Krommendijk recently observed an increasing 'Charter-centrism'.[1784]

Examples of Charter-centrism can be found in the judgments in *Chalkor*, *Inuit*, *J.N.*, and *Orsi and Baldetti* in which the CJEU considered that it only needs to refer to the Charter as the source of EU fundamental rights even when these rights are also enshrined in the ECHR.[1785] In several (other) judgments the

---

1777 Cf De Witte 2011, p. 20; Sarmiento 2013, p. 1269; Craig and De Búrca 2015, p. 390.

1778 Cf Von Bogdandy 2000, p. 1329; Senden 2011, p. 384. This observation is strengthened by the fact that Member States' representatives played a role in both the drafting of the Charter and the process of incorporating the Charter in the (rejected) Constitutional Treaty, see, eg, Walter 2007, p. 15–16; Zetterquist 2011, p. 6–7. It moreover appears to follow from the Charter's Preamble which states that "[t]his Charter reaffirms (...) the rights as they result, in particular, from the constitutional traditions and international obligations common to the Member States (...)".

1779 Cf Craig 2010, p. 196.

1780 See Douglas-Scott 2013, p. 161; Krommendijk 2015, p. 817, 832. The Charter's significance as the reference text for fundamental rights in EU law was already underlined in the Joint communication from ECtHR and ECJ Presidents Costa and Skouris of 17 January 2011, see p. 1. The primary importance of the Charter as the source of EU fundamental rights is arguably expressed by Article 6 TEU as well, cf Krommendijk 2015, p. 834.

1781 See Craig 2010, p. 243; Di Federico 2011, p. 52; Douglas-Scott 2013, p. 158.

1782 De Búrca 2013, p. 169. Cf Craig and De Búrca 2015, p. 427.

1783 Sarmiento 2013, p. 1267–1268. The author mentions, inter alia, Case C-617/10, *Åklagaren v Hans Åkerberg Fransson*, EU:C:2013:105; Case C-399/11, *Stefano Melloni v Ministerio Fiscal*, EU:C:2013:107.

1784 See Krommendijk 2015, p. 832; Glas and Krommendijk 2017, p. 573–576. See also subsection 5.5.2.

1785 See Case C-386/10 P, *Chalkor AE Epexergasias Metallon v European Commission*, EU:C:2011:815, para 51; Case C-398/13 P, *Inuit Tapiriit Kanatami and Others v European*

Court stressed the primacy of the Charter by merely referring to the Strasbourg case-law on a corresponding Charter right as an 'afterthought'.[1786] In *J.N.* and *Orsi and Baldetti*, for example, the Court first examined the compatibility with the fundamental rights in light of EU legislation and case-law to subsequently determine, as an apparent secondary matter, that the Strasbourg case-law did not call its own conclusion into question.[1787]

The CJEU has nevertheless produced several post-Charter judgments that have been more focused on the Strasbourg case-law.[1788] In *Deutsche Bahn*, for example, the CJEU concluded that certain inspections by the Commission in the field of competition law were in conformity with Article 8 ECHR and that, "[a]ccordingly it must also be concluded that no infringement of Article 7 of the Charter has been established".[1789] A similar approach was taken in *WebMindLicenses*, where the Court additionally referred to multiple ECtHR judgments to examine the compatibility with Article 8 ECHR and, as a consequence, Article 7 Charter.[1790]

These apparently diverging approaches mean the Court has not taken an absolute turn from the ECHR towards the Charter in the context of corresponding rights.[1791] Charter centrism is nevertheless an evident trend in the CJEU's post-Charter case-law, especially in the judgments delivered post *Opinion 2/13*.[1792] In light of the Charter's importance as a reference text for EU fundamental rights, the remainder of this subsection briefly examines the scope of its provisions, their relationship with national fundamental rights, and the guidelines for the interpretation of Charter rights.

Scope: Article 51(1) CFR

Article 51(1) Charter states that it is addressed to the EU institutions, bodies, offices and agencies. Charter rights are thus fully applicable at the EU level; both EU administrative acts and EU legislation have to respect the rights enshrined in the CFR.[1793] The Charter additionally applies to Member States on the condition

Commission, EU:C:2015:535, para 46; Case C-601/15 PPU, *J. N. v Staatssecretaris van Veiligheid en Justitie*, EU:C:2016:84, para 46; Joined Cases C-217/15 and C-350/15, *Criminal proceedings against Massimo Orsi and Luciano Baldetti*, EU:C:2017:264, para 15.

1786 See Glas and Krommendijk 2017, p. 573–576. Cf Krommendijk 2015, p. 832–833; Krommendijk 2016, p. 359.

1787 *J. N.*, paras 50–82; *Orsi and Baldetti*, paras 16–25.

1788 See Krommendijk 2016, p. 357–358.

1789 Case C-583/13 P, *Deutsche Bahn AG and Others v European Commission*, EU:C:2015:404, para 36.

1790 Case C-419/14, *WebMindLicenses kft v Nemzeti Adó- és Vámhivatal Kiemelt Adó- és Vám Főigazgatóság*, EU:C:2015:832, paras 70–71.

1791 See below on the guidelines for the interpretation of Charter rights that correspond to the ECHR.

1792 *Opinion 2/13 on the Accession of the European Union to the European Convention for the Protection of Human Rights and Fundamental Freedoms*, EU:C:2014:2454.

1793 See, eg, Case C-199/11, *Europese Gemeenschap v Otis NV and Others*, EU:C:2012:684, paras 37–77; Case C-293/12, *Digital Rights Ireland Ltd v Minister for Communications*,

that their acts are implementing EU law.[1794] Despite initial debate about a potentially restricted scope of applicability to Member State actions,[1795] the CJEU determined that Charter rights apply in line with the judicially developed scope of EU fundamental rights as general principles.[1796] By concluding that Article 51(1) Charter does not restrict the pre-Charter application of EU fundamental rights protection, the Court essentially aligned the applicability of the two sources of fundamental rights in EU law.[1797]

Before the Charter's entry into force, legal scholarship had already firmly identified distinct situations in which the CJEU deemed EU fundamental rights applicable to Member State actions. The first of these situations is where Member States are explicitly implementing and applying EU law. In this situation, Member States can be viewed as agents of the Union, which requires them to respect the rights that EU acts and institutions are obliged to conform with.[1798] A second situation concerns the derogation from, or restriction of, EU rules by Member States.[1799]

The seminal post-Charter judgment in *Åkerberg Fransson* indicated that the category 'national implementing measures' would not be defined strictly.[1800] In this judgment the CJEU deemed national criminal penalties and proceedings to be within the scope of EU fundamental rights protection because EU directives and Article 325 TFEU required the effective penalization of VAT fraud.[1801] Although the Swedish legislation on tax fraud was not intended to implement EU law, the Court nevertheless deemed it to constitute an implementing measure for the sake of Article 51(1) CFR.[1802] Since the Swedish provisions penalizing VAT

EU:C:2014:238, paras 29, 69–71. This is in line with the applicability of EU fundamental rights as general principles, cf *Nold*, paras 13–15; Joined cases C-402/05 P and C-415/05 P, *Yassin Abdullah Kadi and Al Barakaat International Foundation v Council of the European Union and Commission of the European Communities*, EU:C:2008:461, paras 326, 352–353.

1794 See Article 51(1) Charter.

1795 Cf Torres Pérez 2009, p. 23–24; Sarmiento 2013, p. 1275; Ward 2014, p. 1425; Dougan 2015, p. 1204–1206.

1796 See Case C-617/10, *Åklagaren v Hans Åkerberg Fransson*, EU:C:2013:105, paras 18–22; Case C-390/12, *Proceedings brought by Robert Pfleger and Others*, EU:C:2014:281, paras 35–36; Case C-198/13, *Víctor Manuel Julian Hernández and Others v Reino de España (Subdelegación del Gobierno de España en Alicante) and Others*, EU:C:2014:2055, para 33. Cf Sarmiento 2013, p. 1277; Ward 2014, p. 1451; Craig and De Búrca 2015, p. 415–416.

1797 Cf Bockel and Wattel 2014, p. 871, 877; Dougan 2015, p. 1206–1207.

1798 See Case 5/88, *Hubert Wachauf v Bundesamt für Ernährung und Forstwirtschaft*, EU:C:1989:321, para 19. See further, eg, Sarmiento 2013, p. 1274–1275. Bockel and Wattel 2014, p. 873–874; Craig and De Búrca 2015, p. 411; Dougan 2015, p. 1211–1215; Lenaerts and Gutiérrez-Fons 2016, p. 10.

1799 See Case C-260/89, *Elliniki Radiophonia Tiléorassi AE and Panellinia Omospondia Syllogon Prossopikou v Dimotiki Etairia Pliroforissis and Sotirios Kouvelas and Nicolaos Avdellas and others (ERT)*, EU:C:1991:254, para 43. See further, eg, Sarmiento 2013, p. 1274–1275; Bockel and Wattel 2014, p. 874–877; Dougan 2015, p. 1211, 1215–1217; Lenaerts and Gutiérrez-Fons 2016, p. 10.

1800 Case C-617/10, *Åklagaren v Hans Åkerberg Fransson*, EU:C:2013:105.

1801 See paras 24–27.

1802 See paras 27–28.

fraud were therefore 'within the scope of EU law',[1803] the EU fundamental rights (enshrined in the Charter) applied as well.[1804] Some observers argued that the Court had hereby expanded the applicability of EU fundamental rights beyond the two generally distinguished applicability situations mentioned above.[1805]

After *Åkerberg Fransson* several judgments attempted to provide guidance for determining which domestic measures would be 'within the scope of EU law'. In order to establish criteria for the apparently broad applicability of EU fundamental rights to domestic legislation, the CJEU considered relevant

> "(...) whether that legislation is intended to implement a provision of EU law; the nature of that legislation and whether it pursues objectives other than those covered by EU law, even if it is capable of indirectly affecting EU law; and also whether there are specific rules of EU law on the matter or capable of affecting it (...)".[1806]

Since the judicially established criteria are general, and the post-*Åkerberg Fransson* case-law has only just started to develop, it is hard to determine the exact scope of applicability of EU fundamental rights to Member State actions.[1807] Despite the uncertainties surrounding the Court's case-law, it is assumed that *Åkerberg Fransson* and subsequent judgments have not made the two applicability situations distinguished in earlier scholarship redundant.[1808] For present purposes it is therefore sufficient to determine that EU fundamental rights will in any event apply when Member States are explicitly implementing Union law or derogating from it.

Charter interpretation: Article 52 CFR and the Explanations relating to the Charter

Several provisions contain rules about the interpretation of Charter rights. Article 6(1) TEU specifies two sources of interpretive tools: the provisions of Title VII of the Charter[1809] and the Explanations relating to the Charter.[1810]

1803 See paras 19–22.

1804 See paras 21, 27.

1805 See Bockel and Wattel 2014, p. 877–878; Craig and De Búrca 2015, p. 415–418. Dougan, however, deemed the approach in *Åkerberg Fransson* to fall within the first situation of 'implementing EU law', see Dougan 2015, p. 1214–1215, cf Hancox 2013, p. 1419.

1806 Case C-206/13, *Cruciano Siragusa v Regione Sicilia – Soprintendenza Beni Culturali e Ambientali di Palermo*, EU:C:2014:126, para 25; Case C-198/13, *Víctor Manuel Julian Hernández and Others v Reino de España (Subdelegación del Gobierno de España en Alicante) and Others*, EU:C:2014:2055, para 37. See further Dougan 2015, p. 1233–1235.

1807 This is exemplified by the opposite conclusions reached by the ECJ's Grand Chamber and the Advocate General regarding the Charter's applicability in Case C-638/16 PPU, *X and X v État belge*, EU:C:2017:173. Cf the judgment, paras 44–45, 51 with the Opinion of Advocate General Mengozzi, EU:C:2017:93, paras 80, 84.

1808 See Dougan 2015, p. 1232.

1809 Which encompasses Articles 51–54 Charter.

1810 Explanations relating to the Charter of Fundamental Rights, [2007] OJ C303/02.

The importance of the official explanations as an interpretive instrument is underlined by the Charter itself in both Article 52(7) and in the Preamble.

Article 52 Charter is the most relevant provision regarding guidelines for the interpretation of the CFR. Article 52(3) stipulates that Charter rights that correspond to Convention rights have the same meaning and scope as under the ECHR.[1811] At the same time, this provision emphasizes that Union law can provide more extensive protection than the ECHR.[1812] This underlines that the ECHR provides the minimum standard of protection for EU fundamental rights.

The reference to the Convention standard arguably affirms the significance of ECtHR judgments on Convention rights.[1813] This can be inferred from the Explanation on Article 52(3) Charter as well, which states that "[t]he meaning and the scope of the [ECHR] rights are determined not only by the text of those instruments, but also by the case law of the European Court of Human Rights (…)".[1814] Despite the evident relevance of the Convention and the ECtHR judgments for Charter interpretation, the CJEU is not, however, legally bound by the Strasbourg case-law.[1815]

In line with Article 6(3) TEU, Article 52(4) CFR recognizes the importance of Member States' common constitutional traditions for the interpretation of Charter rights. According to the official explanations, the reference to the Member States' traditions intends to preclude that Charter rights contain 'a lowest common denominator'.[1816] Charter rights should instead offer a high standard of protection that is adequate for EU law and in harmony with the common constitutional traditions. Article 52(4) thus contains a duty of harmonious interpretation.[1817]

This only seems to be a limited and negative duty, however. It appears to signal the need to avoid unacceptable interpretations in light of the Member States' constitutional traditions rather than a duty to actively conform Charter rights to the standards of the common constitutional traditions. Article 52(4) Charter does not, in any event, take a maximalist approach to the rights set out in national constitutions.[1818] Charter rights are not, therefore, required to reflect the highest standard of protection that is provided in any of the Member States.

1811 Those articles are listed in the Explanations on Article 52 Charter. Article 49(1) and (2) Charter correspond to article 7 ECHR, except for the *lex mitior* principle enshrined in the last sentence of Article 49(1) Charter. Cf Schabas 2015, p. 330.

1812 It is not clear whether this enables the CJEU to provide a more generous interpretation of a corresponding right than under the ECHR or whether more extensive protection can only be offered by the EU legislature, see Peers and Prechal 2014, p. 1501–1503.

1813 See, eg, Craig 2010, p. 233, Douglas-Scott 2013, p. 161–162; Craig and De Búrca 2015, p. 398; Krommendijk 2015, p. 814–816.

1814 Cf Case C-489/10, *Criminal proceedings against Łukasz Marcin Bonda*, Opinion of AG Kokott, EU:C:2011:845, para 43.

1815 See Douglas-Scott 2013, p. 162–163; Krommendijk 2015, p. 815–816.

1816 See Explanation on Article 52 Charter.

1817 See Craig 2010, p. 234.

1818 See Peers and Prechal 2014, p. 1504. This is exemplified by the *Taricco* judgment, see subsection 5.2.6.

Relationship with national fundamental rights: Article 53 CFR

In light of the rather broad scope of EU fundamental rights,[1819] national law can be obliged to conform with different sets of fundamental rights standards. Since Union rights apply to domestic measures even when they are only partly within the scope of Union law, national implementing measures generally need to conform with both EU fundamental rights and their domestic equivalents.[1820] The judgment in *Åkerberg Fransson* confirmed that Member States are entitled to apply domestic fundamental rights standards to national implementing measures on the condition that EU law leaves the Member States some discretion in the implementation of Union law.[1821] EU law granted discretion to the Member States in *Åkerberg Fransson* because it merely required the effective penalization of VAT fraud. Since Union law did not prescribe the precise means and level of the applicable penalties, the Swedish court was, in principle, allowed to examine the domestic penalties within the scope of Union law in light of the domestic constitutional standard of *ne bis in idem*.[1822]

As famously illustrated by *Melloni*,[1823] matters are different when Union law does not allow discretion in the implementation of Union law. In *Melloni*, the Court confirmed that the Framework Decision on the European arrest warrant required Member States to recognize and execute a request for surrender of convicted persons when they were convicted by a trial in which only their lawyer was present.[1824] In Spain, however, the right to a fair trial precluded the surrender of a person who had been tried in his absence, even when his lawyer had been present at the trial.[1825] According to Spanish law, surrender could, in these circumstances, be allowed only on the condition that the surrendered person would be given a fresh trial in the issuing state (which he could attend).

Confronted with the conflict between an EU requirement to surrender Mr Melloni and the Spanish right to a fair trial, the CJEU established that the Spanish executing authorities only needed to comply with the Union right to a fair trial enshrined in the Charter. Since the EU right was not violated by the requirement to recognize and execute an arrest warrant after proceedings *in absentia*,[1826] Member States could, from the point of view of EU law, be obliged

1819 See the above-mentioned judgment in *Åkerberg Fransson*.
1820 Cf Besselink 2014, p. 545; De Witte 2014, p. 1525.
1821 See paras 29, 36.
1822 See paras 25–26. Cf De Witte 2014, p. 1534.
1823 Case C-399/11, *Stefano Melloni v Ministerio Fiscal*, EU:C:2013:107. Cf Sarmiento 2013, p. 1289; Bockel and Wattel 2014, p. 879.
1824 See paras 35–46, 61–63. The framework decision: Council Framework Decision 2002/584/JHA of 13 June 2002 on the European arrest warrant and the surrender procedures between Member States [2002] OJ L 190.
1825 See paras 20–22. Cf Besselink 2014, p. 533–544.
1826 See paras 47–55.

to surrender persons tried in their absence if their lawyer had been present.[1827] That such a surrender violated the greater protection from trials *in absentia* provided by the Spanish constitutional standard was deemed necessary in order not to compromise the unity, primacy and effectiveness of EU law.[1828]

Melloni implies that, in the absence of discretion regarding implementation, EU fundamental rights become the exclusive standard for assessing national implementing law.[1829] In this situation, domestic fundamental rights cannot provide an additional protective standard that national implementing law has to comply with.[1830] Apparently, EU law's unity, primacy and effectiveness are *automatically* violated when national courts rely on a more protective national standard in cases where Union law does not confer discretion over implementation.[1831] Although unity, primacy and effectiveness are not *necessarily* compromised when EU law does confer discretion, this could still be the case. In that event, Union fundamental rights would equally displace more protective national rights.[1832]

Since EU fundamental rights are allowed to replace more protective domestic standards, Union law could negatively affect the level of fundamental rights protection where national measures fall within the scope of Union law.[1833] Article 53 Charter, which states that "[n]othing in this Charter shall be interpreted as restricting or adversely affecting human rights and fundamental freedoms as recognised, in their respective fields of application, (…) by the Member States' constitutions" does not, therefore, imply that more protective domestic standards are *necessarily* given precedence. Instead of allowing the application of the highest fundamental rights standard, the Court, perhaps unsurprisingly, prioritized the absolute primacy of EU law over all national law.[1834]

5.5.5 THE CJEU'S APPROACH TO LEGALITY: IN LINE WITH THE GENERAL CHARACTERISTICS OF EU FUNDAMENTAL RIGHTS?

As described in chapter 4, the CJEU has used different formulations to provide protection related to the legality principle. Several judgments explicitly

1827 See para 64.

1828 See *Melloni*, para 60. Cf *Åkerberg Fransson*, para 29; *Opinion 2/13*, para 188.

1829 Cf Sarmiento 2013, p. 1289–1294.

1830 See *Melloni*, para 64. Cf De Witte 2014, p. 1533–1537.

1831 Cf Lenaerts and Gutiérrez-Fons 2016, p. 22.

1832 See *Åkerberg Fransson*, para 29; Case C-42/17, *Criminal proceedings against M.A.S. and M.B. (Taricco II)*, Opinion of AG Bot, EU:C:2017:564, paras 161–168. Less protective domestic rights are always replaced by EU fundamental rights, see, again, *Åkerberg Fransson*, para 29.

1833 Cf Bockel and Wattel 2014, p. 879; Besselink 2014, p. 546, 552; De Witte 2014, p. 1536; Craig and De Búrca 2015, p. 399; De Hert 2016, p. 112.

1834 See *Melloni*, paras 58–59. Cf De Boer 2013, p. 1092–1094; Besselink 2014, p. 544.

recognized the legality principle or elements thereof. The present subsection revisits these judgments to determine whether the CJEU's approach to legality conforms with the general features of EU fundamental rights protection described in subsections 5.5.2–5.5.4.

Pre-Lisbon I: legality as a general principle in judgments concerning implementation via domestic criminal law or punitive sanctions

Before the Charter's entry into force, the CJEU recognized the legality principle, or elements thereof, as general principles of Union law. In early judgments on alleged retroactive effects of EU law, the ECJ identified the principle that penal provisions may not have retroactive effect as a general principle of Union law because it is common to the Member States' legal orders and enshrined in Article 7 ECHR.[1835] By first referring to the Member States' common constitutional traditions, the Court arguably indicated the prime importance of these traditions as a source of the general principle of non-retroactivity.

In judgments establishing limits to consistent interpretation the ECJ subsequently recognized the principle of legality as a general principle of EU law. In *X 1996* the ECJ again referred to common constitutional traditions as the primary source and considered that the legality principle was *also* enshrined in various international treaties, particularly the ECHR. At the same time, however, the Court did refer to ECtHR judgments on the Convention's legality principle.[1836] These references to ECtHR case-law came shortly after the first ever ECJ reference to the Strasbourg Court's judgments in *P v S and Cornwall County Council*.[1837]

In *X 2004*, a later judgment on limits to consistent interpretation, the Court acknowledged the relevance of Article 7 ECHR and subsequently established that the principle of non-retroactivity of penalties constitutes a general principle of EU law common to the Member States' constitutional traditions.[1838] Although the Court did not refer to Strasbourg case-law in *X 2004*, it arguably found the Convention to be the primary source for the EU principle of non-retroactivity of penalties.

The approach taken in *X 1996* was confirmed by *Advocaten voor de Wereld*. In this Grand Chamber judgment the Court reiterated that the legality principle is protected in EU law because it is found in the common constitutional traditions of the Member States as well as being enshrined in various international treaties, particularly, in Article 7(1) ECHR.[1839] As in *X 1996*, the Court subsequently

[1835] See *Kent Kirk*, para 22; *Fedesa*, para 42. See also the later judgment in *Gerekens*, para 35. On these judgments, see subsection 4.4.3.

[1836] See para 25. On the judgment, see subsection 4.2.3.

[1837] See subsection 5.5.2.

[1838] See para 63. On the judgment, see subsection 4.2.3.

[1839] See para 49. On the judgment, see subsection 4.5.4.

referred to case-law of the ECtHR, in this instance, the judgment in *Coëme*.[1840] Before essentially confirming the approach in *X 1996*, the Court considered it to be 'common ground' that the principle of the legality of crimes and penalties constitutes a general principle of Union law.[1841] The ECJ did not refer to existing EU case-law to substantiate this determination, however. Instead, it referred to the, then, non-binding Charter which in the Court's view 'reaffirmed' the protection of the legality principle in the EU legal order.[1842]

The Court did not repeat its reference to the Charter in subsequent pre-Lisbon judgments. The Grand Chamber judgment in *Intertanko*, for example, merely stated that EU legislation must observe the legality principle because it is one of the general principles found in the constitutional traditions common to the Member States.[1843] At the same time, the Court affirmed the definition of legality in *Advocaten voor de Wereld* and the reference to the Strasbourg Court's *Coëme* judgment as its source of inspiration.[1844]

The pre-Lisbon preliminary rulings on the legality principle warrant several observations. It is, first of all, noteworthy that the CJEU has deemed Article 7 ECHR relevant for the EU legality principle and elements thereof in all but one judgment.[1845] In most judgments the Court moreover referred to ECtHR case-law for the interpretation of the EU legality principle.[1846] In line with the general approach described in subsection 5.5.2, the Court evidently considered the Convention and Strasbourg case-law of special significance for the EU legality principle in the pre-Lisbon era.

At the same time, however, the Court has also referred to common constitutional traditions as the source of the EU legality principle. In line with the previously-described tendency to use common constitutional traditions symbolically, the Court never substantiated its claim that legality is a principle underlying the Member States' legal systems. The CJEU has not, moreover, employed common constitutional traditions to define or interpret the EU legality principle. Although the Court has sometimes referred to common constitutional traditions as the primary,[1847] or even exclusive,[1848] source of inspiration for legality as a general principle, the practical importance of the ECHR was evidently greater.[1849] In the pre-Lisbon era, the

1840 ECtHR, *Coëme and Others v. Belgium*, CE:ECHR:2000:0622JUD003249296. The Court referred to this judgment in *Advocaten voor de Wereld*, para 50.

1841 See paras 45–46.

1842 Cf Mitsilegas 2009, p. 140.

1843 See para 70. On the judgment, see subsection 4.4.2.

1844 See para 71. That the Charter 'reaffirms' rights as general principles of Union law was previously established in Case C-432/05, *Unibet (London) Ltd and Unibet (International) Ltd v Justitiekanslern*, EU:C:2007:163, para 37.

1845 The exception is *Intertanko*.

1846 See *X 1996*; *Advocaten voor de Wereld*; *Intertanko*.

1847 See *Kent Kirk*; *Fedesa*; *X 1996*; *Advocaten voor de Wereld*. See, conversely, *X 2004*.

1848 See *Intertanko*.

1849 This is also in line with Article 6(3) TEU which denominates the ECHR first.

Charter did not yet play a large role. It was merely deemed to reaffirm the CJEU's recognition of legality as a general principle of Union law on one occasion.[1850]

Pre-Lisbon II: legality as a general principle in judgments concerning administrative sanctions imposed by EU institutions

In addition to the above judgments on implementing criminal law, the CJEU recognized the legality principle, or elements thereof, in judgments on administrative sanctions in the field of competition law. In *Danske Rørindustri* the ECJ's Grand Chamber considered the principle of non-retroactivity of criminal laws to be a general principle of EU law apparently because it is enshrined in Article 7 ECHR.[1851] For that reason, and because it was cited by multiple applicants, the Court deemed it 'appropriate' to refer to the case-law of the ECtHR.[1852] The ECJ paraphrased several of the Strasbourg Court's general considerations on Article 7 of the Convention and concluded that the same principles are consistently reflected in the CJEU's case-law.[1853]

Several subsequent judgments in the field of competition law confirmed the relevance of the Convention for the EU legality principle. In *Jungbunzlauer*, for example, the Court of First Instance reiterated that the principle of legality constitutes a general principle found in the common constitutional traditions of the Member States and that it has been enshrined in, especially, Article 7 ECHR.[1854] Although the CFI referred to *X 1996* for this definition, the wording in *Jungbunzlauer* indicates that both common constitutional traditions and the ECHR are *equally important* for the recognition of legality as a general principle. As observed above, the wording in *X 1996* arguably indicated that common constitutional traditions were of more (symbolic) significance than the ECHR.

As in the later judgment in *Advocaten voor de Wereld*, in *Jungbunzlauer* the Court moreover referred to the ECtHR judgment in *Coëme* to define the legality principle.[1855] The Court additionally paraphrased the ECtHR case-law on Article 7 ECHR in a single paragraph with references to six different Strasbourg judgments.[1856] Interestingly, the CFI then turned to the common constitutional traditions. In the Court's view, these traditions did not justify a different interpretation of the legality principle from that of the Strasbourg Court.[1857] The Court underlined that the situation in one Member State is not, in any event,

1850 See *Advocaten voor de Wereld*.

1851 See para 202. On the judgment, see, especially, subsection 4.6.5.

1852 See para 215.

1853 See paras 216–222.

1854 See para 73. On the judgment, see subsection 4.6.2.

1855 See para 76. Cf Case T-69/04, Schunk GmbH and Schunk Kohlenstoff-Technik GmbH v Commission of the European Communities, EU:T:2008:415, para 32.

1856 See para 80.

1857 See para 81. See also Case T-69/04, Schunk GmbH and Schunk Kohlenstoff-Technik GmbH v Commission of the European Communities, EU:T:2008:415, para 34.

sufficient to substantiate the existence of a common constitutional tradition.[1858] Before the entry into force of the Charter, the CFI had thus already rejected the maximalist approach, which would require EU rights to reflect the highest protective standard of a single Member State.[1859]

In *Evonik Degussa* the ECJ referred to the definition of legality in *Advocaten voor de Wereld* which was itself evidently inspired by the CFI judgment in *Jungbunzlauer*.[1860] The Court, moreover, referred to *Advocaten voor de Wereld* and *X 1996* to underline that the principle of legality constitutes a general principle underlying the common constitutional traditions of the Member States and that it has been enshrined in, especially, Article 7 ECHR.[1861] In line with *Jungbunzlauer*,[1862] the Court's wording indicated that both sources informing the EU general principle were equally relevant. That the Court actually considered Article 7 ECHR to be at least as relevant as common constitutional traditions, follows from the reference to ECtHR case-law in *Evonik Degussa*. The ECJ essentially used Strasbourg case-law to establish the framework for examining conformity with the EU legality principle.[1863] The CFI repeated this approach in *AC-Treuhand 2008*, where it referred extensively to the Strasbourg Court's general considerations on Article 7 ECHR in order to establish the requirements of the EU legality principle.[1864]

In the above pre-Lisbon judgments on administrative sanctions imposed by EU institutions, the CJEU was more deferential to the Strasbourg system than in judgments concerning national criminal law laid down in the same period. To begin with, the Court has generally indicated that Article 7 ECHR is at least equally important for the EU legality principle as the common constitutional traditions of the Member States. The CJEU, moreover, referred to the Strasbourg Court's case-law in *all* judgments recognizing the relevance of the legality principle or the principle of non-retroactivity of criminal law as a specific element thereof.[1865]

In line with the perceived tendency not to use common constitutional traditions as an actual source for EU fundamental rights, the CJEU appeared dismissive of providing a different standard of legality protection than that under the ECHR. In the above judgments on administrative sanctions, the CJEU rejected pleas for greater protection under the EU legality principle either because they only referred to a single Member State's constitutional tradition or because

1858 See para 81.
1859 On the maximalist approach, see subsection 5.5.4.
1860 See para 39. On the judgment, see subsection 4.6.6.
1861 See para 38.
1862 Yet arguably contrary to the wording in *Advocaten voor de Wereld* and *X 1996*, see further above.
1863 See para 41.
1864 See *AC-Treuhand 2008*, paras 139–142. On the judgment, see subsection 4.6.2.
1865 As observed above, references to the ECtHR's judgments were not made in all pre-Lisbon preliminary rulings.

they were not sufficiently substantiated.[1866] As in the above pre-Lisbon judgments on implementing measures, the CJEU thus clearly deemed the ECHR of special significance for the EU legality principle. Unlike in *Advocaten voor de Wereld*, the Charter was not referred to in judgments on administrative sanctions.

Post-Lisbon I: the EU legality principle in judgments concerning implementation via domestic criminal law or punitive sanctions

Two early post-Lisbon judgments indicated the continued relevance of legality as a general principle of Union law. In *E and F*, for example, the Court merely recognized the principle of non-retroactivity of criminal law by referring to its own case-law.[1867] It apparently understood that principle as constituting a general principle of Union law, without explicitly stating that it was enshrined in either Article 49(1) CFR or Article 7(1) ECHR or that it formed part of the Member States' common constitutional traditions. In the later *Garenfeld* judgment, the ECJ explicitly recognized that the legality principle constitutes a general principle of Union law.[1868] The Court additionally acknowledged the relevance of Article 49(1) Charter, which, in the ECJ's view, is one of the legal bases of the legality principle in Union law.

The relevance of legality as a general principle of Union law was not indicated in *Caronna*.[1869] Instead of limiting the duty of consistent interpretation on the basis of common constitutional traditions or Article 7 ECHR as in pre-Lisbon judgments, the ECJ merely referred to Article 49(1) Charter.[1870] The Court's simultaneous reference to its earlier judgment in *X 2004* arguably indicated the substantive conformity of its approach in *Caronna* with its pre-Lisbon case-law.[1871] Given the apparent conformity with *X 2004* it is noteworthy that the ECJ only referred to the Charter's legality principle as the reason for limiting consistent interpretation in criminal matters. In *Caronna* the Charter reference thus replaced the earlier references to Article 7 ECHR and the common constitutional traditions of the Member States as the source of the EU legality principle.

In other judgments the CJEU acknowledged the *cumulative* relevance of Article 7 ECHR and Article 49 Charter. In *Italmoda*, for example, the ECJ rejected the applicability of Article 7 ECHR and, as an apparent consequence, the applicability of Article 49 Charter.[1872] The Court did not, however, refer to

---

1866 See *Jungbunzlauer*, para 81; Case T-69/04, Schunk GmbH and Schunk Kohlenstoff-Technik GmbH v Commission of the European Communities, EU:T:2008:415, para 34.

1867 See para 59. Another example is *Aurubis Balgaria*. On these judgments, see subsection 4.3.3.

1868 See para 48. On the judgment, see subsection 4.5.6.

1869 On the judgment, see subsection 4.2.3.

1870 See para 55.

1871 See paras 52, 55.

1872 See para 61. On this judgment, see subsection 4.5.3. This approach is also perceivable more generally, see the judgments in *Deutsche Bahn* and *WebMindLicenses* and further subsection 5.2.4.

ECtHR case-law to determine the scope of the Convention's legality principle. The ECJ's Grand Chamber judgment in *Taricco* also referred to Article 7 ECHR, yet not as the source of the EU legality principle.[1873] The Court deemed Article 7 ECHR relevant in order to cite several ECtHR judgments that, in the ECJ's view, supported its own interpretation of the Charter's legality principle.[1874] Strictly speaking, therefore, the ECJ only relied on Article 49 Charter as the source of the EU legality principle and used the Strasbourg Court's judgments on Article 7 ECHR merely as an afterthought.[1875]

More recently, in *Paoletti*, the Court explicitly considered that, regarding the EU legality principle, reference only needed to be made to Article 6 TEU and Article 49 Charter.[1876] Unlike the referring court, which had mentioned Article 7 ECHR first,[1877] the ECJ implied that the two EU sources that formally contain the Union legality principle should considered exclusively or, at least, primarily. The Court reiterated that, as long as the Union has not acceded to the ECHR, the Convention is not an instrument that is formally incorporated in EU law.[1878] *Paoletti* confirms that only two sources enshrine the EU legality principle: the general principles of EU law and Article 49 Charter.

The focus on the Charter's legality principle is also perceivable in *Rosneft*. In line with *Taricco*, the Court merely recognized the Charter as the formal source of the EU legality principle, while additionally referring to Article 7 ECHR and the Strasbourg Court's case-law.[1879] Unlike in *Taricco*, however, where the Court referred to the ECtHR's case-law as an afterthought, in *Rosneft* the ECJ deemed the Strasbourg case-law relevant as a result of Article 52(3) CFR. For that reason, the Luxembourg Court apparently employed the ECtHR's case-law as the basis for the interpretation of the Charter's legality principle.

While early post-Lisbon judgments recognized the relevance of the general principles of Union law,[1880] most recent judgments indicate that the CJEU considers Article 49 Charter as the primary source of the EU legality principle.[1881] *Paoletti* indicates that Article 7 ECHR is not, in any event, to be relied upon as a direct source. A less restrictive position was apparently taken in *Italmoda*, however, which made a cumulative reference to Article 7 ECHR

1873 On the judgment, see subsection 4.5.4. Cf Case C-42-17, *Criminal proceedings against M.A.S. and M.B. (Taricco II)*, EU:C:2017:936, paras 52–55.

1874 See para 57. Cf Case C-42/17, *Criminal proceedings against M.A.S. and M.B. (Taricco II)*, Opinion of AG Bot, EU:C:2017:564, paras 127–141.

1875 Cf Glas and Krommendijk 2017, p. 573–576. See further subsection 5.2.4.

1876 See para 22. On the judgment, see subsection 4.5.2.

1877 See para 11.

1878 See para 21. Cf *Åkerberg Fransson*, para 44; Case C-199/11, *Europese Gemeenschap v Otis NV and Others*, EU:C:2012:684, para 47.

1879 See paras 162, 164–167. On the judgment, see subsection 4.5.7.

1880 See *E and F*; *Garenfeld*.

1881 See *Caronna*; *Taricco*; *Paoletti*; *Rosneft*. See also *BB construct* as described in subsection 4.5.3 and, more recently, Case C-42–17, *Criminal proceedings against M.A.S. and M.B. (Taricco II)*, EU:C:2017:936, paras 52–55.

and Article 49 Charter. *Taricco* and *Rosneft* illustrate that the strict *Paoletti* approach would not, in any event, result in the irrelevance of Article 7 ECHR or the ECtHR's case-law for the interpretation of the Charter's legality principle. As a result of Article 52(3) Charter, the CJEU is still required to ensure its interpretation of the legality principle conforms with that of the Strasbourg Court.[1882] As *Taricco* and *Rosneft* exemplify, the CJEU will therefore be inclined to use the ECtHR's case-law, at least as an afterthought.

As in pre-Lisbon judgments, the CJEU has not used common constitutional traditions as an actual interpretive source for the EU legality principle. The designated relevance of the Member States' constitutional traditions for the interpretation of Charter rights[1883] has not been used to examine how the principle of legality – as influenced by Article 7 ECHR – is protected in EU law. This is clearly exemplified by the preliminary ruling in *Taricco*. As described in the preceding chapter, *Taricco* required the disapplication of national limitation periods in order to comply with the EU duty to provide effective and dissuasive criminal penalties for that conduct.[1884] The Court thereby essentially required the retroactive extension of domestic limitation periods. Such an extension would nevertheless have been contrary to the legality principle enshrined in the Italian Constitution.[1885]

In *Taricco*, the ECJ did not recognize the relevance of the Italian legality principle, however.[1886] Instead, when interpreting the EU legality principle, the Court simply referred to existing EU case-law and ECtHR judgments.[1887] In line with the above-mentioned *Melloni* judgment,[1888] the Court apparently required the primacy and effectiveness of EU law to be given precedence over the potentially higher protection provided by a constitutionally enshrined domestic fundamental right.[1889] In light of Articles 52(4) and 53 Charter, the Court could have examined whether EU law ought to provide greater protection of the legality principle than the ECHR in light of an existing common constitutional tradition.[1890] Had the ECJ taken common constitutional traditions seriously, its judgment would have reflected on how the Member States protect against retroactive extensions of

---

1882 See, recently, Case C-42–17, *Criminal proceedings against M.A.S. and M.B. (Taricco II)*, EU:C:2017:936, paras 54–55.

1883 See Article 52(4) Charter and further subsection 5.5.4.

1884 See paras 49, 52–53.

1885 See the order for a preliminary reference by the Italian Constitutional Court, see Corte costituzionale, Order no. 24 of 2017, paras 4–5 (English translation available at www.cortecostituzionale.it/documenti/download/doc/recent_judgments/O_24_2017.pdf) and Case C-42/17, *Criminal proceedings against M.A.S. and M.B. (Taricco II)*, Opinion of AG Bot, EU:C:2017:564, paras 5–8, 38–48. Cf Timmerman 2016, p. 793.

1886 It arguably did so implicitly in *Taricco II*, however, see Case C-42–17, *Criminal proceedings against M.A.S. and M.B. (Taricco II)*, EU:C:2017:936, paras 58–61.

1887 See paras 56–57. This exemplifies that Article 52(4) Charter does not take a maximalist approach, see above subsection 5.5.4.

1888 See subsection 5.5.4.

1889 See Timmerman 2016, p. 794.

1890 Cf De Boer 2013, p. 1100–1101; De Witte 2014, p. 1536–1537.

limitation periods under their respective legality principles. The absence of such an examination provides another indication of the apparent practical irrelevance of common constitutional traditions for the EU legality principle.[1891]

Post-Lisbon II: the EU legality principle in judgments concerning administrative sanctions imposed by EU institutions

The post-Lisbon approach in the above-mentioned judgments is also perceivable in judgments on asset freezing measures. In *Ezz and Others*, for example, the General Court first referred to Article 49(1) Charter as the source of the EU legality principle.[1892] Due to the requirement in Article 52(3) Charter to interpret corresponding Charter rights in accordance with the ECHR,[1893] the Court nevertheless acknowledged the relevance of Article 7 ECHR.[1894] The General Court did in fact underline the need to interpret Article 49(1) Charter in accordance with the Strasbourg Court's case-law on Article 7(1) ECHR.[1895] To determine the scope of the Charter's legality principle, the Court referred to ECtHR case-law and paraphrased the judicially established applicability criteria for Article 7 ECHR.[1896] In the subsequent judgment in *Al Matri*, however, the General Court merely referred to Article 49(1) Charter and the judgment in *Ezz and Others* to reject the applicability of the EU legality principle.[1897] This is perhaps explained by the fact that in *Al Matri*, unlike in *Ezz and Others*, the General Court was able to rely on existing EU case-law.

Judgments on administrative sanctions in EU competition law paint a more diverse picture, however. Essentially, four different approaches to the EU legality principle can be identified in the case-law. The first approach entails only a brief reference to Article 7 ECHR. This approach is basically in line with the pre-Lisbon judgments on administrative sanctions imposed by EU institutions. In several judgments the General Court indicated that common constitutional traditions and Article 7 ECHR are of equal importance for the EU legality principle.[1898] At times, the CJEU additionally referred to ECtHR case-law on the Convention's legality principle.[1899]

1891 Cf subsection 5.5.3. Arguably, in *Taricco II*, the ECJ implicitly considered relevant the Italian legality principle for its interpretation of EU law in the preliminary ruling, see Case C-42-17, *Criminal proceedings against M.A.S. and M.B. (Taricco II)*, EU:C:2017:936, paras 58–61.

1892 On the judgment, see subsection 4.6.4.

1893 On Article 52(3) Charter, see subsection 5.5.4.

1894 See para 75.

1895 See para 75.

1896 See paras 76–81.

1897 See para 85. On the judgment, see subsection 4.6.4.

1898 See Case T-446/05, *Amann & Söhne GmbH & Co. KG and Cousin Filterie SAS v European Commission*, EU:T:2010:165, para 125; Case T-83/08, *Denki Kagaku Kogyo Kabushiki Kaisha and Denka Chemicals GmbH v European Commission*, EU:T:2012:48, para 120.

1899 See Case T-446/05, *Amann & Söhne GmbH & Co. KG and Cousin Filterie SAS v European Commission*, EU:T:2010:165, paras 128–129; Case T-83/08; Case C-501/11 P, *Schindler Holding Ltd and Others v European Commission*, EU:C:2013:522, para 57.

The second approach entails a cumulative reference to both Article 7 ECHR and Article 49 Charter, which is in line with the above-mentioned approach in *Italmoda*. These cumulative references are only perceivable post-Lisbon. In six judgments, the General Court recognized Article 49 Charter and Article 7 ECHR as relevant sources for the EU legality principle or elements thereof.[1900] In *Saint-Gobain Glass* the Court additionally referred to ECtHR case-law extensively in order to establish the general requirements of the EU principle.[1901] In *Marine Harvest* the General Court relied upon just one recent ECtHR judgment to substantiate the dismissal of a specific element of the applicant's complaint.[1902]

The General Court's judgment in *Moreda-Riviere* is an interesting example of the second approach. In this judgment the Court determined that Article 53 Charter requires that the CFR's legality principle provides at least equivalent protection to that resulting from the ECtHR's interpretation of Article 7(1) of the Convention.[1903] The Court subsequently determined the requirements of the legality principle by mentioning the Strasbourg Court's case-law. The Court did not explicitly refer to ECtHR judgments, however. Instead it merely referred to earlier CJEU case-law interpreting the EU legality principle based on, inter alia, the Strasbourg Court's case-law.[1904]

The third approach entails an exclusive reference to Article 49 Charter as the source of the EU legality principle. The exclusive focus on the Charter's legality principle under this approach is underlined by the absence of any reference to the Strasbourg Court's interpretive case-law. This 'Charter-centrism', remarkably, is perceivable in two judgments, one judgment by the ECJ's Grand Chamber and one by the General Court.[1905]

The fourth and final approach to the EU legality principle entails the reference to existing EU case-law alone. In line with the approach in the above-mentioned post-Lisbon preliminary ruling in *E and F*, the Court has recently recognized the legality principle without explicitly stating the source of that Union principle.[1906] By exclusively pointing to its earlier case-law, the CJEU

1900 See Case T-386/10, *Aloys F. Dornbracht GmbH & Co. KG v European Commission*, EU:T:2013:450, para 60; Cases T-56/09 and T-73/09, *Saint-Gobain Glass France SA and Others v European Commission*, EU:T:2014:160, para 267; Case T-92/13, *Koninklijke Philips Electronics NV v European Commission*, EU:T:2015:605, para 136; Cases T-426/10 to T-429/10 and T-438/12 to T-441/12, *Moreda-Riviere Trefilerías, SA and Others v European Commission*, EU:T:2016:335, para 417; Case T-472/13, *H. Lundbeck A/S and Lundbeck Ltd v European Commission*, EU:T:2016:449, para 736; Case T-704/14, *Marine Harvest ASA v European Commission*, EU:T:2017:753, para 376.

1901 See paras 268–272.

1902 See para 390.

1903 See para 417.

1904 See paras 418–437.

1905 See C-352/09, *ThyssenKrupp Nirosta GmbH v European Commission*, EU:C:2011:191, para 80; Case T-541/08, *Sasol and Others v European Commission*, EU:T:2014:628, para 202.

1906 See Case C-625/13 P, *Villeroy & Boch AG v European Commission*, EU:C:2017:52, para 149; Case C-90/15 P, *Hansen & Rosenthal KG and H&R Wax Company Vertrieb GmbH v European Commission*, EU:C:2017:123, para 78–80.

arguably underlines that legality is still recognized as a judicially established general principle of Union law. The absence of a reference to either Article 49(1) CFR or Article 7(1) ECHR as the source of this principle could, in any event, help to avoid questions about the applicability of the criminal law principle to administrative sanctions in the field of competition law.

Post-Lisbon judgments on EU administrative sanctions thus clearly entail different approaches. In line with the pre-Lisbon approach, most judgments recognized the relevance of Article 7 ECHR. Several judgments have additionally referred to case-law by the Strasbourg Court.[1907] The CJEU's post-Lisbon 'Charter-centrism' is only perceivable in two judgments.

5.6 MULTILEVEL DEFINITIONS AND INTERPRETATIONS OF CRIMES AND PENALTIES

5.6.1 INTRODUCTION

Chapter 4 distinguished two situations in which the CJEU understood the EU legality principle as relevant. The first situation concerned EU legislation implemented via national criminal law or punitive provisions. The second situation concerned administrative sanctions imposed by EU institutions. The interplay between EU law and implementing provisions in the first situation warrants further examination. The present section will describe how EU criminal law is generally multilayered, as it mostly entails definitions and interpretations of crimes and penalties at both the EU level and at the level of the Member State.[1908]

5.6.2 EU DEFINITIONS AND INTERPRETATIONS: INDIRECT AND DIRECT INFLUENCES

As described in sections 4.2–4.5, many judgments gave rise to considerations on the EU legality principle due to the implementation of Union law via domestic criminal law or punitive sanctions. Most of these judgments concerned EU legislation that was deemed non-criminal from the Union perspective, but only acquired a criminal law character due to its implementation. This was not only the case with regard to non-criminal EU directives,[1909] non-criminal regulations were also 'implemented'

1907 See Case T-446/05, *Amann & Söhne GmbH & Co. KG and Cousin Filterie SAS v European Commission*, EU:T:2010:165; Case T-83/08; Case C-501/11 P, *Schindler Holding Ltd and Others v European Commission*, EU:C:2013:522; *Ezz and Others*; *Saint-Gobain Glass*.

1908 Cf Peristeridou 2015, p. 7–9, 30; Klip 2016, p. 1–2.

1909 See, eg, *Fedesa*, *Arcaro*, *X 1996*, *Berlusconi*, *Intertanko*, *Damgaard*, *Caronna*, *Italmoda*, *Taricco* as described in subsections 4.2.2; 4.2.3; 4.4.2; 4.4.3; 4.5.3; 4.5.4.

via national criminal law or punitive sanctions.[1910] As a result, definitions in non-criminal EU legislation obtained relevance for national criminal law due to how they were implemented. For that reason, the CJEU's interpretation of non-criminal EU definitions became pertinent for the interpretation of implementing criminal provisions. In this situation, non-criminal Union law became *indirectly* relevant for the definition and interpretation of criminal implementing law.

The same indirect influence of Union law on domestic criminal law occurs when EU legislation with a criminal law character defines crimes and prescribes penalties. As described in subsection 5.3.3, the pre-Lisbon approximation of Member State substantive criminal law took place within the Union's former third pillar. The EU was obliged to adopt framework decisions,[1911] which, like directives, necessarily require implementing provisions.[1912] The inevitability of the domestic implementation of crimes and penalties defined by EU criminal law is presently a result of Article 83 TFEU, which limits the approximation of substantive criminal law to the instrument of a directive. For that reason, the clearest competence to enact EU criminal law legislation will also result in multilevel definitions of crimes and penalties.

Things could, perhaps, be different if a regulation is used to define crimes and penalties. Unlike directives and framework decisions, a regulation does not necessarily require implementation.[1913] As described in subsection 5.4.2, there are currently TFEU provisions that imply a competence to approximate substantive criminal law via the instrument of a regulation. The use of a regulation to define crimes and penalties could therefore result in directly applicable EU criminal legislation. Directly applicable EU legislation would not mean its direct application by the CJEU, however. Since the Luxembourg Court is not a criminal court, it is not competent to apply EU law to the facts of the case in order to *directly* determine criminal liability and impose a penalty.

The definition of crimes and penalties via an EU regulation would be consequential nonetheless, as the usually indirect definition of crimes and penalties in EU law could then be replaced by direct definitions. National courts would, in that event, only need to apply and interpret EU legislation in order to determine the extent of criminal liability and impose a penalty for the prohibited conduct. If a regulation did indeed define the criminalized conduct and determine which penalty would apply for the infringement thereof, a national court could use it as a *direct* basis for the imposition of a criminal penalty.

Until now, however, regulations have not criminalized conduct directly or prescribed an applicable penalty for such conduct. Regulations have generally

1910 See, eg, *X 2004*; *E and F*; *Aurubis Balgaria*; *Garenfeld* as described in subsections 4.2.2; 4.3.3; 4.5.6. Cf Klip 2016, p. 53–54.

1911 See Article 34(2)(b) TEU 2002.

1912 Framework decisions were adopted on many areas of crime, see Peers 2016b, p. 164–165.

1913 See Article 288 TFEU and Case 34/73, *Fratelli Variola S.p.A. v Amministrazione italiana delle Finanze*, EU:C:1973:101, paras 9–11.

called for the effective (criminal) sanctioning of violations of that instrument. In that situation, the conduct prohibited by the regulation still requires the addition of a national provision.[1914] The national provision could refer to the regulation's definition, but it would still have to penalize the violation thereof and prescribe the applicable penalty. Like directives and framework decisions, this use of a regulation establishes a multilevel system of EU criminal law as it requires two norms, one at the Union level and one at the domestic level, to determine criminal responsibility under domestic law. Since the EU definition of prohibited conduct is then only relevant when national law penalizes the violation thereof, the regulation cannot, in itself, determine or aggravate criminal liability.

Since the aforementioned use of regulations to define prohibited behavior necessarily requires domestic provisions, it is not surprising that the Court has applied its case-law on the limits of the effects of directives in criminal matters to these types of regulations.[1915] That case-law is not necessarily applicable to all regulations, however.[1916] In fact, if a regulation defined and penalized certain conduct, there would be no need for implementing provisions. The regulation could then define the prohibited behavior and stipulate that such behavior constitutes a criminal offense under the domestic law of the Member States and carries a certain penalty in those legal systems. In that situation, the EU regulation could arguably be used directly by domestic criminal courts to determine criminal liability and the applicable penalty in the national legal system. Since the EU regulation could then be applied *directly*, the Union instrument could indeed determine or aggravate criminal liability itself and independent of national implementing provisions.

5.6.3 INDIRECT DEFINITIONS AND INTERPRETATIONS OF CRIMES AND PENALTIES AS AN EXPLANATORY FACTOR

As described in the preceding subsection, at present, EU law is only *indirectly* relevant for the definition and interpretation of crimes and penalties in national law.[1917] EU law has not yet defined directly applicable crimes and penalties,[1918] and even if it did, their interpretation by the CJEU would still only be relevant for the interpretation and application of the EU provisions by the national courts. In order to determine criminal liability and impose a penalty for conduct

1914 See Miettinen 2013, p. 85.

1915 See Case C-60/02, *Criminal proceedings against X*, EU:C:2004:10, para 62. See further subsection 4.2.3.

1916 See Miettinen 2013, p. 87; Altena-Davidsen 2016, p. 113–114; Mitsilegas 2016, p. 65–66. See, conversely, Peristeridou 2015, p. 301; Klip 2016, p. 197–198.

1917 Cf Asp 2012, p. 214.

1918 Cf Altena-Davidsen 2016, p. 108–116.

defined by EU law, national criminal courts are required.[1919] As a result, EU criminal law is inevitably multilevel, as it generally entails not only norms on the EU and national levels, but also, without exception, the participation of the national judiciary, perhaps aided by the CJEU's interpretation of Union law.

The indirect relevance of EU definitions and CJEU interpretations thereof has likely resulted in the apparently limited applicability of the EU legality principle to EU definitions and interpretations. The CJEU's approach in *Intertanko* could, for example, be explained by how the definitions in an EU directive lack direct relevance for national criminal responsibility.[1920] Since directive's definitions require implementation, the national courts will formally apply only the implementing provisions to determine criminal liability and impose a penalty. For that reason, the applicability of the EU legality principle can seemingly be limited to the definition, interpretation, and application of the implementing provision.

The indirect relevance of the interpretation of EU law for national criminal responsibility could, moreover, explain the *Grøngaard and Bang* judgment.[1921] Since the CJEU's interpretation of non-criminal Union law would only be indirectly relevant for the interpretation of implementing criminal law, the protection of the EU legality principle was exclusively deemed appropriate at the domestic level. The indirect relevance of EU law could also explain the lack of guidance from the CJEU in preliminary rulings.[1922] Since domestic provisions and their interpretation ultimately determine criminal responsibility, the CJEU apparently deemed it appropriate to completely defer the protection of the legality principle to the national level. Since the national courts determine criminal liability on the basis of domestic provisions, it is apparently for them to independently determine and apply the limits to the interpretation and application of the implementing provisions in light of the EU legality principle.

5.7 CONCLUDING REMARKS

5.7.1 HISTORICAL DEVELOPMENT OF EU CRIMINAL LAW

The historical development of EU criminal law could partly explain the development of the EU legality principle. In the pre-Maastricht era, the CJEU did not generally recognize legality as a general principle of Union law.[1923] The only exception related to the *lex praevia* element, which was recognized as a

1919 Cf Asp 2012, p. 50.
1920 See subsection 4.4.2.
1921 See subsection 4.5.5.
1922 See subsection 4.5.6.
1923 See subsection 5.2.3.

self-standing principle. The absence of a general recognition of the EU legality principle was most likely the result of the contested and controversial influence of (then) EC law on criminal matters.

As EU criminal law was explicitly developed in the post-Maastricht era, the CJEU became more willing and able to recognize an EU legality principle.[1924] Although the Court's approach has not been consistent, explicit considerations on the legality principle have emerged. Both the legality principle as a whole and elements thereof were recognized as principles of Union law in the post-Maastricht era. This occurred in judgments on first pillar and third pillar Union law.[1925] Paradoxically, however, judgments relating to the non-criminal first pillar continued to result in the largest number of relevant judgments.

The confirmation of the Union's criminal law competences by the Lisbon Treaty, alongside legality being enshrined as a Charter right, have enhanced the CJEU's explicit approach to legality. The Court has continued to explicitly recognize the EU legality principle as from towards the end of the pre-Lisbon era. The largest category of judgments relating to the legality principle still concern non-criminal EU law. Even post-Lisbon, the EU legality principle is therefore mostly developed within the framework of non-criminal EU legislation.

The increasing recognition of the Union legality principle is largely in line with the development of EU criminal law. The shift from there being no mention of or only an implicit recognition of the legality principle to explicit consideration of the applicability and scope of that principle in Union law is therefore explicable on the grounds of the confirmation and acceptance of the Union's growing impact on domestic criminal law. Although this characteristic could explain the CJEU's case-law, it cannot remedy the somewhat haphazard early development of the EU legality principle. As a result, it should be concluded that the Luxembourg Court's judgments have failed to consistently recognize and develop the EU legality principle.

5.7.2 HISTORICAL DEVELOPMENT OF EU FUNDAMENTAL RIGHTS AND ARTICLE 6 TEU

The historical development of EU fundamental rights protection, which is presently codified in Article 6 TEU, could additionally explain the lack of uniformity in the CJEU's approach to legality. The Court has referred to the Member States' common constitutional traditions, Article 7 ECHR, and Article 49 Charter as the source of the EU legality principle.[1926]

1924 See subsection 5.2.3.
1925 See subsection 5.4.4.
1926 See subsection 5.5.5.

In pre-Lisbon judgments the Court generally recognized Article 7 ECHR as a source of inspiration for the unwritten EU legality principle or specific elements thereof. The CJEU additionally reiterated several of the Strasbourg Court's considerations on the legality principle. Other international human rights treaties enshrining a principle of legality such as the International Covenant on Civil and Political Rights, for example, have not been referred to by the CJEU. Common constitutional traditions were not used substantively, but only symbolically as a source of inspiration for legality as a general Union principle. By and large, therefore, the CJEU's approach to legality as a general principle of Union law has been in line with the Court's recognition of fundamental rights as general principles.[1927]

Although the continued relevance of the unwritten EU legality principle was mentioned at the start of the post-Lisbon era, most judgments recognize legality as a Charter right. Although Article 7 ECHR does not constitute a formal source of the EU legality principle, it continues to be a source of inspiration for the interpretation of the Union principle. The case-law of the Strasbourg Court on the Convention's legality principle is also considered relevant for the interpretation of Article 49 CFR.

The CJEU's post-Lisbon approach has not been consistent, however. In addition to referring to the legality principle as a general principle and a Charter right, the Court has also continued to indicate the direct relevance of Article 7 ECHR. The Court has not, in any event, adopted a consistent approach towards the use of the ECtHR's case-law for the interpretation of legality as either a general EU principle or a Charter right.

The lack of a general CJEU approach to the Convention and to ECtHR case-law has evidently affected the Court's approach to legality. Although the Court generally deemed Article 7 ECHR relevant for the EU legality principle pre-Lisbon, it is unclear how this provision and the ECtHR's interpretive judgments will be used in the post-Lisbon era. Due to the different tendencies evident in post-Lisbon judgments, it is uncertain whether the CJEU will only use the Strasbourg system symbolically, after a superficial examination, as an afterthought, or substantively after an extensive examination of the Convention's legality principle. What has been consistent over time, however, is the irrelevance – in practice – of Member State common constitutional traditions for the EU legality principle. Those traditions had only symbolic relevance pre-Lisbon and this has not changed post-Lisbon despite the addition of Article 4(2) TEU and Articles 52(4) and 53 Charter.

The apparent inconsistencies in the CJEU's approach to legality could partly be explained by the historical development of EU fundamental rights protection which is presently codified in Article 6 TEU. Article 6 TEU recognizes two direct sources of EU fundamental rights: Charter rights and rights recognized

---

[1927] See subsections 5.5.2–5.5.3.

as general principles of EU law.[1928] Both these sources indicate the relevance of different external sources, particularly the ECHR and the common constitutional traditions of the Member States.[1929] The Convention and common constitutional traditions arguably constitute indirect sources of EU fundamental rights. Due to Article 6 TEU and the Charter, EU fundamental rights are derived from multiple direct and indirect sources. The multiple direct and indirect sources could have been used in a uniform way. The CJEU has not, however, approached the interpretation of EU fundamental rights consistently. This inconsistency has apparently affected the Luxembourg Court's approach to the EU legality principle.

5.7.3 INDIRECT DEFINITIONS AND INTERPRETATIONS OF CRIMES AND PENALTIES

The fact that EU law is presently only of indirect relevance for definitions and interpretations of crimes and penalties could explain several other characteristics of the EU approach to legality. It could, for example, explain the apparent inapplicability of the EU principle to definitions in non-criminal EU legislation.[1930] More recent case-law has deemed the Union's *lex certa* principle applicable to the EU definitions, however, which makes it hard to determine a consistent EU approach.[1931] The indirect impact of EU law could additionally explain both the inapplicability of the EU legality principle to the CJEU's interpretations of non-criminal EU legislation and the lack of guidance to the national courts.[1932] The next chapter will examine these characteristics of the EU approach to legality further in order to assess their desirability.

1928 See Articles 6(1) and 6(3) TEU.

1929 See Article 6(3) TEU and Articles 52(3), 52(4), 53 Charter.

1930 See subsection 5.6.3.

1931 See subsection 4.5.7.

1932 See subsection 5.6.3.

CHAPTER 6

THE EU LEGALITY PRINCIPLE: REFLECTIONS AND RECOMMENDATIONS

6.1 INTRODUCTION

In order to reflect on the EU legality principle's scope, substance, and purpose, the present chapter reviews the CJEU's interpretation of the legality principle in light of criminal law theory and the ECHR. The aim is to determine whether, and if so to what extent, the CJEU acknowledges the distinctions in criminal law theory (section 6.2) and to assess the conformity with the Strasbourg legality principle (section 6.3). Section 6.4 provides some thoughts on the desirable construction of the EU legality principle in the future. It argues, tentatively, that the EU standard should go beyond the minimum legal certainty that is protected under Article 7 ECHR. The focus on future construction by the CJEU is justified, because the judicially constructed EU principle sets limits to the activities of the legislature and the judiciary at the EU level and at the level of the Member States. The recommendations for the CJEU will therefore provide (indirect) guidelines for legislative definitions and judicial interpretations of crimes and penalties in the multilevel system of EU criminal law.[1933]

6.2 SITUATING THE EU LEGALITY PRINCIPLE IN THE CONTEXT OF CRIMINAL LAW THEORY

6.2.1 INTRODUCTION

Both the CJEU's early strands of case-law – which were later related to the EU legality principle[1934] – and the Luxembourg Court's explicit considerations relating to legality,[1935] have resulted in the rather imprecise and inconsistent

1933 On the role of national courts in reaction to CJEU judgments in the field of EU criminal law, see Van Kempen and Van Elst 2006.

1934 See subsection 4.7.1.

1935 See subsection 4.7.2.

development of the Union legality principle. The Court's approach has not clearly and consistently established the scope, substance, and rationale(s) of the EU principle. The lack of clarity and consistency is, moreover, illustrated by the formulations used to recognize the legality principle or elements thereof. The Luxembourg Court has, in fact, referred to the principle in the following different ways: 'the principle of legality of criminal offenses and penalties',[1936] 'the principle of legality in relation to crime and punishment',[1937] 'the principle of legality',[1938] 'the principle *nullum crimen, nulla poena sine lege*',[1939] 'the principle of *nulla poena sine lege certa*',[1940] 'the principle that penalties must have a proper legal basis',[1941] 'the principle that a provision of criminal law may not be applied extensively to the detriment of the defendant',[1942] 'the principle of non-retroactivity of criminal laws',[1943] 'the principle of non-retroactivity of penalties',[1944] 'the principle that penal provisions may not have retroactive effect',[1945] 'the principle of non-retroactivity of provisions which may form the basis for a criminal conviction'.[1946]

When these formulations are viewed cumulatively, they indicate the Court's recognition of the entire legality principle and the specific elements *lex certa*, *lex stricta*, and *lex praevia*. As described in chapter 4, however, the Court has not consistently developed the scope and substance of the EU legality principle. It should be concluded, therefore, that the CJEU's formulations and general considerations have not clearly and consistently recognized the EU legality principle as containing all or some of the elements *lex scripta*, *lex certa*, *lex stricta*, and *lex praevia*.

The absence of consistent and explicit considerations might very well be a symptom of a lack of conceptual clarity about the EU legality principle. As described in chapter 2, both the substance of, and rationales behind, the legality principle differ rather significantly in the civil law and common law conception of legality. As observed, these differences impact the level of legal certainty that is necessarily protected by the legality principle. The Luxembourg Court's legality considerations do, in fact, indicate that both diverging conceptions of legality have been adopted in EU law. This is especially true for the CJEU's indications regarding the potential protection of the legality principle's elements *lex scripta* and *lex stricta*.

1936 See *Advocaten voor de Wereld*, para 49; *Intertanko*, para 70; *Aurubis Balgaria*, para 42; *Sasol*, para 202; *Taricco*, para 54; *Moreda-Riviere*, para 417.

1937 See *X 1996*, para 25; *Ezz and Others*, para 70; *Al Matri*, para 85.

1938 See *Jungbunzlauer*, para 71.

1939 See *AC-Treuhand 2008*, para 113; Case C-604/13 P, *Aloys F. Dornbracht GmbH & Co. KG v European Commission*, EU:C:2017:45, para 23; Case C-625/13 P, *Villeroy & Boch AG v European Commission*, EU:C:2017:52, para 149.

1940 See *Rosneft*, para 162.

1941 See *Caronna*, para 55. For further references to this formulation, see section 4.3; subsection 4.6.3.

1942 See *X 1996*, para 25.

1943 See *Danske Rørindustri*, para 202; *Saint-Gobain Glass*, para 267.

1944 See *X 2004*, para 63.

1945 See *Kent Kirk*, para 22; *Gerekens*, para 35; *Denki*, para 120; Case T-92/13, *Koninklijke Philips Electronics NV v European Commission*, EU:T:2015:605, para 136.

1946 See *E and F*, para 59.

6.2.2 SCOPE OF APPLICATION

As a principle of criminal law, the legality principle is applicable to both criminal offenses and penalties. In EU law, however, the legality principle has been given a broader scope, although not explicitly and consistently. It is nevertheless evident that the legality principle applies to administrative sanctions imposed by EU institutions in the field of competition law. Substantively comparable protection is also provided beyond the criminal sphere by virtue of limits to the effects of EU law, the requirement of a proper legal basis for penalties, and the Union principle of legal certainty. Both the specific protection of the legality principle and substantively comparable protective principles are therefore applied beyond criminal law *sensu stricto*.

6.2.3 SUBSTANCE: INDICATIONS OF A CIVIL LAW CONCEPTION

There are several indications that the EU legality principle conforms to the civil law conception of legality. This is, firstly, because some of the judgments imply that the EU legality principle enshrines a *lex scripta* element.[1947] Several of the CJEU's formulations could in fact be perceived as establishing a requirement that statutory law forms the basis for offenses and penalties. In *Caronna*, for example, the Court required an express provision of domestic law to form the basis for criminal penalties.[1948] This implies that the Luxembourg Court requires a statutory basis as a condition for the determination of criminal liability and the imposition of a penalty. The absence of an express provision of domestic law was also considered as precluding a penalty in the earlier judgment in *Aurubis Balgaria*,[1949] as well as, *a contrario*, in the ruling in *Italmoda*.[1950] An express legal basis in domestic legislation was, moreover, required by virtue of the principle of legal certainty in *Karelia*.[1951]

The need for legislation as the basis for criminal law is arguably required by the Court's influential definition of the legality principle in *Advocaten voor de Wereld* as well. In that judgment, the CJEU considered that the legality principle required that legislation must clearly define offenses and the penalties they attract.[1952] The use of the term 'legislation' instead of the broader term 'law' provides an indication that the Luxembourg Court requires a statutory legal basis for criminal law under the EU legality principle.[1953] As described

---

1947 Cf Altena-Davidsen 2016, p. 123.

1948 See further subsection 4.2.3. Cf Altena-Davidsen 2016, p. 106–108; Klip 2016, p. 199.

1949 See subsection 4.3.3.

1950 See subsection 4.5.3.

1951 See subsection 4.4.2.

1952 See *Advocaten voor de Wereld*, para 50. See also, eg, *Evonik Degussa*, para 39; *Intertanko*, para 71; *Aurubis Balgaria*, para 42; *Garenfeld*, para 48; *Rosneft*, para 162.

1953 Other language versions indicate this as well, see, for example, *de wet* (Dutch), *das gesetz* (German), *la loi* (French), *la legge* (Italian).

in chapter 2, such a requirement is not always upheld in common law legal systems.

Standards of clarity imposed by the EU requirement that penalties have a proper legal basis and the principle of legal certainty indicate protection comparable to the civil law *lex certa* element. Under the principle that penalties require a proper legal basis, for example, the Court has demanded a clear and unambiguous legal basis.[1954] In particular, the need for an unambiguous legal basis implies that a rather high level of clarity is a precondition for the imposition of penalty. As under the civil law *lex certa* principle, this requirement could be viewed as requiring a level of clarity which goes beyond the mere general foreseeability of criminal liability and the applicable penalty. It arguably requires the maximum predictability of criminal law.

A seemingly comparable level of clarity has also been required by virtue of the Union principle of legal certainty. As *M and Others* and *Karelia* illustrate, the principle of legal certainty can demand a very high level of foreseeability from the law. It can, in fact, require that individuals know unambiguously and precisely the extent of the legal obligations imposed upon them.[1955] The need for the law to indicate the applicable obligations *unambiguously and precisely*, fits with the high level of predictability that is required from offenses and penalties under the civil law *lex certa* element.[1956]

In addition, the Court's case-law contains indications about a civil law interpretation of the *lex stricta* requirement. Although the CJEU has expressly recognized *lex stricta* only twice,[1957] the case-law on the limits to consistent interpretation could be viewed as an implicit acknowledgment of this principle. Ever since *Kolpinghuis* the CJEU has regularly prevented the consistent interpretation of national criminal law when this determined or aggravated domestic criminal responsibility.[1958] This implies that one limit to the duty to interpret national law expansively is when this is to the detriment of the accused because it enlarges criminal liability or it aggravates the potential penalties. In the context of limits to consistent interpretation the Court appears to provide a high level of protection of *lex stricta*. The Court's formulations in several judgments in fact imply that it absolutely precludes expansive interpretations of domestic offenses and penalties on the basis of EU law.[1959]

The General Court's approach in *Ezz and Others* confirms the above observations.[1960] In the context of asset freezing, the Court essentially allowed

1954 See section 4.3.
1955 See subsection 4.4.2. Cf *Rosneft*, para 161; Case C-574/15, *Proceedings against Mauro Scialdone*, Opinion of AG Bobek, EU:C:2017:553, para 161.
1956 Cf Altena-Davidsen 2016, p. 165–168.
1957 See *X 1996*, para 25; *Ezz and Others*, para 70.
1958 See subsection 4.2.3.
1959 See subsection 4.2.3.
1960 See subsection 4.6.4.

a broad interpretation of a provision because the legality principle did not apply.[1961] This reasoning implies that a broad interpretation would have been precluded had the legality principle applied. Since the legality principle's prohibition on extensive interpretation is apparently deemed to preclude all broad interpretation,[1962] the *lex stricta* requirements are again formulated rather absolutely. Instead of precluding *overly* extensive interpretations, the Court appears to require the strict interpretation of criminal law.[1963] By arguably precluding expansive interpretations *outright*, the CJEU appears to adopt an even stricter approach than what is required by the civil law conception of legality.

The apparent recognition of a *lex scripta* principle, the high level of predictability following from the *lex certa* principle, and the broad protection against extensive judicial interpretations indicate the primacy of the legislature over the judiciary.[1964] The Court's above considerations could therefore be viewed as protecting the values of democracy and a strict separation of powers. The CJEU has never recognized these values explicitly in its considerations on, or related to, the legality principle, however. As described throughout chapter 4, the only value that has been explicitly linked to the legality principle is legal certainty.[1965]

As observed in chapter 2, legal certainty is protected as an element of the rule of law by both the civil law and the common law conceptions of legality. The difference between both conceptions lies in *the level of* legal certainty that is protected *at a minimum*. The recognition of additional rationales such as democracy and a strict separation of powers indicate a potentially higher minimum level of certainty. The rule of law rationale itself does not necessarily demand a high level of legal certainty. The absence of any recognition of democracy and a strict separation of powers by the CJEU precludes the conclusion that the EU legality principle reflects the civil law conception. For that reason, the current construction of the EU legality principle cannot convincingly be viewed as fully conforming with the civil law approach to legality.

6.2.4 SUBSTANCE: INDICATIONS OF A COMMON LAW CONCEPTION

In contrast with the above observations, several aspects of CJEU case-law indicate that the EU legality principle reflects a common law conception. It could, first of all, be argued that the CJEU has never explicitly recognized the *lex scripta* principle. Although the formulation in *Advocaten voor de Wereld* implies this requirement, the Court has never unequivocally required a statutory

---

1961 See paras 73–74.
1962 See paras 69, 73.
1963 See para 73.
1964 Cf Peristeridou 2015, p. 303–304.
1965 See, eg, subsection 4.4.2.

legal basis for criminal law *on the basis of the EU legality principle*. The absence of an explicit recognition of the *lex scripta* principle is, of course, an important first indication of a common law approach.[1966] An additional indication is the relevance of the ECHR and the Strasbourg case-law for the interpretation of EU fundamental rights.[1967] As the Convention's legality principle evidently protects only the common law conception of legality,[1968] that approach has made its mark on how the CJEU construes the legality principle.[1969]

The influence of the Strasbourg approach to legality is most visible in the Luxembourg Court's adoption of the foreseeability requirement. Alongside the ECtHR, the CJEU has accepted, as a point of departure that legislative definitions do not have to be absolutely precise.[1970] In fact, the law can still be sufficiently foreseeable if a person has to take legal advice in order to assess the consequences of certain conduct. It is sufficient if the legislation, *together with interpretive case-law*, makes it possible to know which acts and omissions a person will be criminally liable for and which penalties will apply. For that reason, the CJEU apparently accepts that criminal law definitions can be clarified by interpretive case-law.[1971] The *lex certa* principle does not necessarily require clear *legislative* definitions, which reflects a common law approach to this element of the legality principle.

Since case-law is recognized as a relevant source of legal definitions, it could be argued that the Luxembourg Court would accept a legal basis as sufficiently clear on the basis of case-law alone. This could, moreover, be argued on the grounds that in *Danske Rørindustri* the CJEU essentially adopted the broad interpretation of the term 'law' developed by the Strasbourg Court, which implies that both law of legislative origin and case-law are considered relevant sources for definitions of offenses and penalties.[1972] The conformity of CJEU case-law with the ECtHR's interpretation of the foreseeability requirement could therefore indicate the absence of a *lex scripta* requirement and the adoption of a common law approach to the *lex certa* element.

A common law conception of legality in EU law could also be the result of how the CJEU has reiterated the ECtHR's case-law on the acceptability of judicial interpretations of criminal law.[1973] By apparently accepting judicial interpretations of crimes and penalties on the condition that they are reasonably foreseeable, the Luxembourg Court provisionally allows expansive judicial interpretations. Unlike the – theoretically – strict limits to expansive interpretation under the

1966 See subsection 2.3.6.
1967 See subsections 5.5.2; 5.5.4.
1968 See subsection 3.6.1.
1969 See subsection 5.5.5.
1970 See, eg, *Rosneft*, para 164.
1971 See *Advocaten voor de Wereld*, para 50; *Intertanko*, para 71; *Rosneft*, para 167 and the judgments described in subsection 4.6.6. Cf Frese 2014, p. 73; Altena-Davidsen 2016, p. 156.
1972 See *Danske Rørindustri*, paras 216, 223. Cf Peristeridou 2015, p. 185–186; Altena-Davidsen 2016, p. 102, 198.
1973 See, eg, *Danske Rørindustri*, para 218; *Rosneft*, para 167.

civil law conception, the use of the criterion of reasonable foreseeability under the *lex stricta* principle provides a more lenient standard. The Court apparently accepts uncertainty regarding the scope of EU law and implementing provisions as long as this does not amount to the imposition of criminal liability and of a penalty that is not reasonably foreseeable. The acceptance of uncertainty, and the room for expansive judicial interpretations under the *lex stricta* principle, fits well with the common law conception of legality.

The CJEU's reiteration of ECtHR's case-law on the legality principle indicates the adoption of the common law conception of legality under Union law. One could also argue the CJEU has adopted the common law conception on the basis of the rationales that the CJEU has recognized for the EU legality principle. As described above, the Luxembourg Court has not identified the relevance of democracy or the strict separation of powers. In line with the ECtHR, the CJEU has sometimes identified that the legality principle aims to ensure effective protection against arbitrary prosecution, convictions and penalties.[1974] It has also recognized that the foreseeability of criminal law is required in order to protect the value of the rule of law.[1975] Together with the general recognition of legality as a corollary of legal certainty,[1976] these considerations indicate that the EU legality principle reflects the rationale of the common law conception.[1977]

6.2.5 ASSESSMENT

The Luxembourg Court's case-law on legality supports the adoption of two diverging conceptions of legality. This indicates a lack of conceptual clarity, which has undoubtedly affected the CJEU's constructions of legality over the years. As a result of diverging indications in EU case-law, both the substance of and rationales for the EU legality principle remain underarticulated. While the Court's approach makes it difficult to draw clear conclusions about the EU approach to legality, it is possible to formulate a thesis about the conception that is most likely employed by the CJEU when constructing the EU principle.

To begin with, it is important to note that when the Luxembourg Court acknowledged requirements in accordance with the civil law conception, it did so implicitly and/or by referring to related principles such as limits to the effect of EU law, the requirement of a proper legal basis for penalties, or the EU principle of legal certainty. In the absence of explicit considerations that indicate that the EU legality principle enshrines the elements *lex scripta*, *lex certa*, and *lex*

1974 See subsection 4.6.7. Cf Schroeder 2016, p. 23.
1975 See subsection 4.6.7.
1976 See, eg, *X 1996*, para 25; *Degussa*, para 66; *Dornbracht*, para 60.
1977 Cf Case C-592/14, *European Federation for Cosmetic Ingredients v Secretary of State for Business, Innovation and Skills and Attorney General*, Opinion of AG Bobek, EU:C:2016:179, para 146.

stricta in their civil law interpretation, it is unclear that the CJEU has adopted a civil law approach to legality.

Doubts about the protection of a civil law conception of legality are reinforced by the mere recognition of the rule of law as the rationale for the EU legality principle. It has to be concluded, therefore, that even if high demands regarding legislative clarity and strict limits to judicial interpretation in EU (criminal) law are perceivable in some CJEU case-law, they are not explicitly established *on the basis* of the EU legality principle. As a result, the EU legality principle cannot be viewed as protecting a level of legal certainty that goes beyond the minimum required under the common law conception.

By contrast, the CJEU's considerations are much clearer on the relevance of the common law approach to legality for the EU principle. The Luxembourg Court's considerations do, in fact, contain explicit indications that support the adoption of a common law legality principle. These indications stem from the significance of Article 7 ECHR and the ECtHR's case-law for the interpretation of the EU legality principle. As described in chapters 4 and 5, when the CJEU explicitly considers the legality principle it relies heavily on the ECtHR's approach to legality. Since the ECtHR has mostly adopted a common law approach, the CJEU's considerations indicate that conception of legality is also being protected. The demands for legislative clarity and the limits to judicial interpretation can therefore be viewed as necessarily providing only the rather minimal legal certainty that is protected by the ECtHR's approach.

Although the system of EU law itself contains elements of a civil law legal system, there are no explicit statements of the CJEU to support the conclusion that the EU legality principle reflects the civil law conception. Instead, CJEU case-law indicates conformity with the more common law-oriented Strasbourg approach to legality.[1978] At this point, the most viable thesis is, therefore, that the EU legality principle mostly reflects the Strasbourg standard, at least with regard to the minimum level of legal certainty that is required.

6.3 CONFORMITY WITH ARTICLE 7 ECHR

6.3.1 INTRODUCTION

The thesis that the EU legality principle mostly reflects the common law approach of the Strasbourg standard requires further scrutiny. The present section examines whether the EU legality principle has been constructed to reflect at least the Strasbourg minimum standard. Subsection 6.3.2 focusses on the legality principle's scope of application. Subsection 6.3.3 compares the principle's substantive requirements with the demands recognized under

1978 Cf Altena-Davidsen 2016, p. 103, 386.

Article 7 ECHR. Finally, subsection 6.3.4 concludes that the current CJEU approach is not sufficiently similar to the Strasbourg approach which, at least, implies the risk of constructing an EU legality principle that falls short of the Strasbourg minimum.

6.3.2 SCOPE OF APPLICATION

Chapter 4 determined that the CJEU has not adopted a consistent approach to the applicability of the EU legality principle. The Court has, for example, avoided the applicability question altogether by merely referring to an element of the legality principle without a recognition of either Article 7 ECHR or Article 49 Charter.[1979] The Luxembourg Court has not, moreover, used either the term 'criminal offense' or the ECtHR's *Engel* criteria to determine the applicability of, for example, the legality principle in the Charter. The CJEU has nevertheless employed the *Engel* criteria to determine the applicability of other corresponding rights, which could indicate the possibility of a more Strasbourg-oriented approach to the applicability of the EU legality principle in the future.[1980]

The Luxembourg Court has not generally used the term 'penalty' either. In fact, in several judgments the CJEU relies solely on its own case-law on the concept of a penalty to determine the applicability of the legality principle.[1981] When the Court has employed the ECtHR's criteria to determine whether a measure constitutes a penalty, the CJEU's considerations have not necessarily been insightful. In fact, *Ezz and Others* and *Al Matri* highlight how references to the Strasbourg criteria could lead to confusion.[1982] This is especially the case when the CJEU does not explicitly and clearly employ the Strasbourg criteria. By using the ECtHR's criteria rather implicitly and selectively as it did in the aforementioned asset freezing judgments, it is hard to determine whether the Luxembourg Court approach was in conformity with the ECHR legality principle.[1983]

The conformity with the ECtHR's approach to the applicability of the legality principle is also questionable in another regard. It is currently unclear whether the CJEU fully adopts the ECtHR's distinction between substantive and procedural rules. This is mostly due to the Luxembourg Court's approach in *Taricco*, notwithstanding its determination that the ECtHR case-law on Article 7 ECHR supported its interpretation of the scope of the legality principle

[1979] See, eg, *E and F.*
[1980] See subsection 4.5.3.
[1981] See *Gerekens*; *Italmoda*.
[1982] See subsection 4.6.4.
[1983] The same approach is perceivable in the recent judgment *Finančné riaditeľstvo Slovenskej republiky v BB construct s. r. o.*, EU:C:2017:820, paras 31–33.

enshrined in the Charter. In *Taricco*, the Court referred to, inter alia, *Coëme*[1984] and *Scoppola*[1985] to conclude that the retroactive extension of limitation periods did not infringe Article 7(1) ECHR so long as the prosecution of the alleged acts was not already time-barred at the time the limitation period was extended.[1986]

The ECJ's reiteration of the Strasbourg case-law does not indicate whether it agrees with the Strasbourg interpretation of the scope of the legality principle. More specifically, *Taricco* raises doubts about the Luxembourg Court's acceptance of the conditions under which limitation periods are allowed to be retroactively extended. This is important, because the ECtHR has only allowed the retroactive extension of a limitation period *on the condition* that the period, as applicable at the time of the accused's acts, had never expired.

The considerations in *Taricco* on Article 49 CFR could be viewed as entailing an *absolute* exclusion of procedural rules from the scope of the legality principle. According to the Luxembourg Court, the Charter's legality principle merely protects against convictions for acts which did not constitute an offense at the time of commission, or against the application of a penalty which, at the time of the impugned action, was not laid down by law.[1987] By this consideration, the Court focused on the potential impact of the retroactive application of rules that determine criminal responsibility or impose a penalty. This focus on rules of *substantive* criminal law could be read as excluding all procedural rules from the scope of the legality principle.[1988]

An absolute exclusion of procedural rules from the scope of Article 49(1) Charter would preclude that provision's applicability to rules on statutory limitation. This is because, as mentioned above, the retroactive application of limitation periods by definition only retroactively expands the possibility for prosecuting offenses. The retroactive expansion of the *procedural* possibilities for conviction and punishment would not, therefore, require any retroactive application of previously inapplicable, or more severe, offenses and penalties. Such an absolute exclusion of the applicability of the legality principle could, however, diverge from the ECtHR's *conditional* acceptance of the retroactive extension of limitation periods. Despite the reference to ECtHR case-law, the

---

1984 ECtHR, *Coëme and Others v. Belgium*, CE:ECHR:2000:0622JUD003249296.

1985 ECtHR (GC), *Scoppola v. Italy (No. 2)*, CE:ECHR:2009:0917JUD001024903.

1986 See para 57 and cf *Criminal proceedings against M.A.S. and M.B. (Taricco II)*, EU:C:2017:936, para 42. The ECJ recently confirmed this in Case C-584/15, *Glencore Céréales France v Etablissement national des produits de l'agriculture et de la mer (FranceAgriMer)*, EU:C:2017:160, paras 69, 73. On the Strasbourg interpretation of the distinction between substantive and procedural rules, see subsection 3.4.2.

1987 See *Taricco*, para 56.

1988 The fact that rules on limitation form part of the substantive law of a Member State can result in an unforeseeable retroactive extension of limitation rules, which could run counter to the EU legality principle, see *Criminal proceedings against M.A.S. and M.B. (Taricco II)*, EU:C:2017:936, paras 29, 45, 58–61.

interpretation of the legality principle in *Taricco* could thus still be contrary to what is required by the Convention.[1989]

In order to avoid doubts about the use of the applicability criteria, the CJEU should follow the ECtHR's approach more closely and more explicitly. Another way of avoiding a potential divergence with the ECtHR's approach is to omit an examination on the basis of the ECtHR's case-law altogether. This latter approach is evident in the CJEU's case-law on the applicability of the legality principle to EU administrative sanctions imposed for violations of competition law. As described in subsections 4.6.2–4.6.3, the CJEU deemed the legality principle applicable to sanctions in the field of competition law without explicitly assessing whether these fines amount to a penalty according to the Strasbourg criteria.

The evasive approach to applicability should not be generally adopted, however. In light of the special significance of Article 7 ECHR for legality as an unwritten fundamental right, and the need to provide at least equivalent protection under Article 49 CFR, the CJEU should consistently rely on the ECtHR's well-established applicability criteria.[1990] A divergence from the ECtHR's approach to applicability by the Luxembourg Court should, in any event, be explicit and well-reasoned. Such a divergence should, moreover, indicate how the CJEU's approach to applicability respects the ECHR minimum standard.

6.3.3 SUBSTANCE

The CJEU's imprecise approach to legality could also diverge from the ECtHR's interpretation of the distinct substantive elements. Since the elements *lex certa*, *lex stricta*, and *lex praevia* have different requirements under Article 7 ECHR, and these elements are interpreted differently under the first and second sentence of Article 7(1) ECHR, conformity with the Strasbourg approach requires precision. The required precision is not only absent due to the CJEU's use of different formulations, but also because of an apparent lack of conceptual clarity about the legality principle's theoretical background and a comprehensive understanding of the distinctions used in the Strasbourg case-law. As a result, the CJEU risks departing from the ECtHR's well-established interpretation not just regarding the applicability of the legality principle, but also on its substance. This divergence could be problematic in light of, for example, Article 52(3) CFR, which only allows Charter rights to deviate from their ECHR counterparts when it adopts a more protective standard. While the lack of conformity with

[1989] In *Taricco II*, the ECJ's Grand Chamber formulated the legality principle with more nuance. It considered that the immediate application of an extended limitation period to alleged offenses that are not yet time-barred does not, *in principle*, infringe the legality principle, see *Criminal proceedings against M.A.S. and M.B. (Taricco II)*, EU:C:2017:936, para 42.

[1990] See further subsection 6.3.4.

the Strasbourg approach does not necessarily result in the recognition of a less protective standard in EU law, it does bring about that risk.

An example of case-law that diverges from the Strasbourg standard are judgments wherein the Luxembourg Court fails to recognize the distinction between the *nullum crimen* principle enshrined in the first sentence of Articles 7(1) ECHR and the *nulla poena* principle enshrined in the second sentence.[1991] This unsophisticated and inaccurate approach to legality jeopardizes conformity with the ECHR standard since the ECtHR has articulated distinct substantive requirements under both principles.[1992] There is a risk of falling short of the Strasbourg standard here because in the aforementioned case-law the CJEU fails to explain why its approach is at least as protective as the ECHR standard and, at the same time, (more) appropriate for EU law.

Substantive protection under the EU legality principle could additionally diverge from the Strasbourg standard as a result of the Court's protection of the legality principle in competition law. Although the CJEU generally deemed the legality principle applicable in competition proceedings, it has sometimes explicitly lowered the intensity of its protection. Unlike what the CJEU implies by its references to the case-law of the ECtHR, the Strasbourg Court has never expressly relaxed the requirements of the legality principle in the area of competition law.[1993] The CJEU's approach remains somewhat ambiguous and could, therefore, be regarded as falling short of the requirements of the Convention's legality principle.[1994]

The EU *lex certa* element has not been interpreted in full conformity with the ECHR standard either. This is apparent from the *Rosneft* judgment. Although the ECJ referred rather extensively to the ECtHR's case-law to determine the *lex certa* principle's substance, in *Rosneft* the Court recognized only the foreseeability requirement.[1995] The ECJ did not refer to the Strasbourg Court's criterion of accessibility. Regarding foreseeability, moreover, the Court merely defined that requirement negatively. Unlike the ECtHR, the Luxembourg Court did not underline the positive requirements following from foreseeability. Instead, the ECJ emphasized the legislature's leeway for defining crimes and penalties under Article 7 ECHR's foreseeability requirement. The Court, in fact, appeared to require a rather low level of foreseeability as it stated that legislation should not make it *impossible* for an individual to foresee criminal liability. This implies that only absolutely unclear terms would fail the ECJ's interpretation of the foreseeability requirement under the EU *lex certa* principle. The absence of a recognized accessibility requirement

1991 See *Danske Rørindustri* and the asset freezing cases as described in subsections 4.6.4–4.6.5.

1992 See chapter 3.

1993 Only the requirements of the right to a fair trial enshrined in Article 6 ECHR, see *Jussila v. Finland*, CE:ECHR:2006:1123JUD007305301, para 43; *A. Menarini Diagnostics S.R.L. v. Italy*, CE:ECHR:2011:0927JUD004350908, para 62.

1994 Cf Soltesz 2012, p. 243–244; Wils 2014, p. 14–17.

1995 In judgments on EU sanctions imposed for competition infringements, the CJEU has also focused on the foreseeability requirement, see subsections 4.6.5–4.6.7.

and the Court's interpretation of the foreseeability requirement both threaten the conformity of the EU *lex certa* principle with the ECHR minimum standard.

As with the approach to *lex certa*, the CJEU's use of the ECtHR's considerations on *lex stricta* has been imprecise and incomplete. In *Rosneft*, and earlier in judgments on sanctions imposed for competition infringements, the Luxembourg Court deemed judicial interpretations of offenses and penalties acceptable as long as they remain reasonably foreseeable. Although that is undoubtedly a central criterion under Article 7 ECHR, it is not the only one. Unlike the ECtHR, the CJEU has not additionally required that any new expansive interpretation remains consistent with the 'essence of the offense'.[1996] By not recognizing the essence of the offense requirement, the CJEU apparently grants more room for expansive judicial interpretations in EU law than the Strasbourg Court does under the Convention.

Although the above-mentioned case-law implies a lesser protection of the *lex stricta* element, in judgments on limits to the effect of EU law the CJEU implied a standard of protection going beyond Article 7 ECHR.[1997] As observed in subsection 6.2.3, the Luxembourg Court apparently precluded expansive judicial interpretations outright.[1998] This is not required by the Convention's legality principle, however, as that principle merely precludes interpretations that are not reasonably foreseeable and/or contrary to the essence of the offense. Since the *lex scripta* principle is not protected under the Convention, and *lex stricta* only protects against *overly* extensive judicial interpretations, the Luxembourg Court's approach in *X 1996* and *Caronna* appears to offer greater protection than the ECtHR.[1999]

A final ground for divergence from the ECHR standard is the CJEU's use of the reasonable foreseeability requirement in *Danske Rørindustri*. Unlike the Strasbourg Court, the ECJ has considered retroactive applications of harsher penalties possible as long as they are reasonably foreseeable. Since the effectiveness of EU competition law allows the Commission to raise the level of applicable penalties if necessary, the possibility of the imposition of harsher penalties is, in the Court's view, generally foreseeable.[2000] By linking the permissibility of the retroactive application of criminal law to reasonable foreseeability, the ECJ has conditionally allowed retroactivity.[2001] Both with regard to new offenses and harsher penalties, however, the Strasbourg Court

---

1996 The ECtHR merely employs the reasonable foreseeability requirement with regard to the *lex stricta* element of the *nulla poena* principle, see subsections 3.5.4, 3.5.7. Although the *lex stricta* element with regard to penalties was relevant in *Danske Rørindustri*, the ECJ explicitly considered the *lex stricta* element with regard to offenses. The Court's explicit wording thus indicates that it diverges from the Strasbourg interpretation of the *nullum crimen lex stricta* element by merely recognizing the reasonable foreseeability requirement.

1997 Cf Dougan 2012, p. 116–117.

1998 See also subsections 4.2.3–4.2.4.

1999 See subsection 4.2.3.

2000 Cf Frese 2014, p. 75.

2001 This is in line with the CJEU's approach that allows foreseeable retroactivity outside the criminal sphere, see *Gerekens*, paras 28–32 and cf Groussot 2006, p. 199–200.

has prohibited this absolutely.[2002] For penalties, the ECtHR has even precluded the mere 'real possibility' that the retroactive application of law results in the imposition of a harsher penalty.[2003] A violation of the Convention standard is even more likely since, with regard to *lex praevia* and penalties, the ECtHR appears to protect a high standard of legal certainty by requiring maximum predictability.[2004]

The protection against retroactivity of offenses and penalties is therefore lower in EU competition law than under Article 7 ECHR. This divergence is not substantiated by an explicit consideration that the legality protection will be lower in competition matters than in criminal law *sensu stricto*. It remains unclear, therefore, whether the CJEU would generally provide *lex praevia* protection in conformity with the Convention minimum standard, or would lower it when deemed necessary for the effectiveness of EU (competition) law. At the same time, however, the CJEU has also indicated that it provides *lex praevia* protection that could go beyond the Strasbourg minimum. In *E and F* the Court did not only preclude the retroactive application of crimes and penalties themselves, but also the retroactive use of EU rules when they were relevant for the determination of domestic criminal liability.[2005]

6.3.4 ASSESSMENT

CJEU case-law risks deviating from Article 7 ECHR in terms of both scope and substance. The scope of the EU legality principle has not been consistently determined on the basis of explicit applicability criteria. The absence of a clear and consistent assessment of applicability precludes a conclusion on the conformity of the EU principle with the Strasbourg standard. In light of the Luxembourg Court's references to the ECtHR's considerations, the CJEU should either adopt the Strasbourg approach to applicability or develop its own approach that respects the Convention standard. The absence of a consistent approach to applicability that respects Article 7 ECHR provides clear potential for a divergence from the minimum Convention standard. Such a divergence could still occur when the CJEU does consider the ECtHR's considerations on Article 7 ECHR's scope, however. As *Taricco* illustrates, the exclusive applicability of the EU legality principle to substantive criminal law could narrow the principle's scope from the viewpoint of the Convention standard.

While the Luxembourg Court has often referred to the ECtHR's substantive considerations on Article 7 ECHR, there is still potential for diverging

2002 See subsection 3.6.2. Only one ECtHR judgment indicates the relevance of foreseeability for retroactivity, see ECtHR, *Mihai Toma v. Romania*, CE:ECHR:2012:0124JUD000105106.

2003 See subsection 3.5.5.

2004 See subsection 3.6.2.

2005 See subsection 4.4.3.

protection. This is mostly the result of the Court's selective use of the ECtHR's general considerations on Article 7 ECHR. Due to this, the CJEU has arguably adopted a lower *lex certa*, *lex scripta*, and *lex praevia* standard in several judgments. At the very least, the Court's approach entails the risk that the EU's protection of the legality principle falls short of the Strasbourg minimum.

As mentioned, a diverging interpretation of the scope and substance of the EU legality principle becomes problematic if it results in a narrower scope, and/or less-protective substance, than required under the Convention. Providing equivalent substantive protection is not just required by Article 52(3) CFR. It could also lead to a violation of the ECHR by the Member States, because the Union system could not then be viewed as providing equivalent substantive protection for the Convention's legality principle.

As a point of departure, the ECtHR presumes that the Member States respect the ECHR when implementing legal obligations from the EU.[2006] This presumption, better known as the *Bosphorus* doctrine, is nevertheless refutable. By virtue of the *Bosphorus* doctrine, a failure to respect the Convention minimum standard when defining the scope and substance of the EU legality principle could result in a rebuttal of the presumption of respect for the ECHR by the Member States when implementing Union law.[2007] That would be the case if protection of the Convention's legality principle has been manifestly deficient in an individual case.[2008] Although the Strasbourg Court will be cautious in making that determination, it is important to note that EU law is susceptible to such an indirect review of conformity with the ECHR even while the Union has not acceded to the Convention.[2009] The presumption of equivalent protection should not, in any event, be taken as a given when Member States are implementing EU law.[2010]

Member States are not only able to violate the Convention's legality principle when they are implementing EU obligations without discretion. A violation is also possible when the Member States are granted implementing discretion, but choose to ensure conformity with the CJEU's considerations on the EU legality principle.[2011] It is not necessary to rebut the *Bosphorus* presumption of equivalent protection in that event, because the doctrine does not apply when the Member States have discretion over how to implement EU law.[2012] In

[2006] See *Bosphorus Hava Yolları Turizm ve Ticaret Anonim Şirketi v. Ireland*, CE:ECHR:2005:0630JUD004503698, paras 154–156, 159 and, recently, *Avotiņš v. Latvia*, CE:ECHR:2016:0523JUD001750207, paras 101–103.

[2007] See *Bosphorus*, para 156.

[2008] See, eg, *Avotiņš v. Latvia*, CE:ECHR:2016:0523JUD001750207, para 112.

[2009] Which it is required to do under Article 6(2) TEU. Cf *Opinion 2/13 on the Accession of the European Union to the European Convention for the Protection of Human Rights and Fundamental Freedoms*, EU:C:2014:2454.

[2010] See Glas and Krommendijk 2017, p. 586.

[2011] See *Bosphorus*, para 157.

[2012] Cf *Avotiņš v. Latvia*, CE:ECHR:2016:0523JUD001750207, para 105.

these circumstances, the Member States will be fully responsible for a possible violation of the Convention's legality principle even though they sought to adopt the protection provided by the EU legality principle. Although the EU does not always require the Member States to adopt the EU legality standard, it is reasonable for the Member States to take this standard into account when implementing Union law.

The best way to guarantee conformity with the Convention is for the CJEU to employ the Strasbourg requirements on scope and substance of Article 7 ECHR when they are incorporated for the interpretation of the EU legality principle. When a diverging interpretation is adopted, the CJEU should indicate why such an interpretation is appropriate for EU law and how it still abides by the Convention's minimum standard. Even though the CJEU does not consider itself legally bound by the ECHR or by ECtHR judgments as a matter of Union law,[2013] it would certainly be desirable from the perspective of demonstrating conformity with the ECHR and for the intelligibility of the EU legality principle if the Luxembourg Court consistently adopted the Strasbourg-oriented approach. That would, moreover, provide a clear signal to the Member State authorities regarding which standard to respect when implementing Union law. The risk that the Member States might violate the Convention by conforming to the EU's legality standard could then be minimized.

Since the ECHR constitutes the minimum standard, the EU legality principle could, of course, offer more protection. Such a divergence from the ECHR legality standard is unproblematic from the point of view of the ECHR and EU law.[2014] The seemingly more protective *lex stricta* approach in *X 1996* and *Caronna* is therefore clearly acceptable. In these judgments on the limits to consistent interpretation, the Luxembourg Court omitted any reference to ECtHR case-law. For that reason, it is not clear whether the CJEU consciously diverged from the ECHR in order to provide greater protection. Had the CJEU aimed to do so, the Court could have been expected to do so explicitly and well-reasoned. In the absence thereof, it cannot be firmly concluded that the EU standard is even partly more protective than the Strasbourg legality principle.[2015] A more explicit CJEU approach would have, once again, provided greater insight into the conformity of the EU legality principle with the Strasbourg minimum. In a more explicit approach, the CJEU should also indicate whether, and if so for what reasons, a lower level of legality protection is possible in the area of EU competition law. Such an approach would, in any event, prevent the danger of setting a precedent on the diminished requirements for the legality principle which could be regarded as applicable to Union law as a whole.

2013 See Krommendijk 2015, p. 814–816. See also subsections 5.5.2; 5.5.4.

2014 See Article 53 ECHR and 52(3) CFR.

2015 Cf Dougan 2012, p. 118.

6.4 IS THE STRASBOURG STANDARD APPROPRIATE FOR EU LAW?

6.4.1 INTRODUCTION

Sections 6.2 and 6.3 identify reasons for criticizing the present construction of the EU legality principle. Section 6.2 indicates the lack of a clear, explicit, and consistent conceptual view underlying the CJEU approach to legality. Section 6.3 ascertains the potential for the EU construction of legality to fall below the ECHR legality principle on both scope and substance. The present section moves beyond the aforementioned critique and assesses the, perhaps hypothetical, situation in which the CJEU would unequivocally, explicitly, and consistently adopt the Strasbourg approach to legality. As described in subsection 6.2.5, the adoption of the ECtHR's approach to legality, which mostly reflects a common law conception, is more likely at present than the adoption of a civil law legality principle. The issue to be examined then, is whether the adoption of the Strasbourg standard would be appropriate and desirable for EU law. This matter will be the subject of the present section.

6.4.2 DIFFERENCES BETWEEN ECHR AND EU LAW

The ECHR legality standard is not necessarily the most appropriate for EU law in light of the differences between both legal regimes. To begin with, the ECHR legality principle merely reflects a minimum standard.[2016] The same is not true for EU law. As described in section 5.5, the CFR in fact allows for the adoption of a more protective legality standard than Article 7 ECHR. As the judgment in *Melloni* illustrates, Union standards could replace domestic fundamental rights standards, even if the domestic standards offer greater protection than the EU standard.[2017] Instead of a mere minimum standard, the EU legality standard could therefore become a common standard in some situations. This characteristic warrants careful reflection on the desirability of adopting only the ECHR minimum standard, for example in light of the legality standards protected by the EU Member States' constitutional traditions.

In addition to providing a minimum standard, the ECHR system of fundamental rights protection occupies a subsidiary position. As described in section 3.5, the ECHR's subsidiarity principle might have impacted the recognition and formulation of Article 7 ECHR's substantive elements. The generally lowered intensity of the ECtHR's review of domestic definitions and interpretations of offenses and penalties could have provided an additional reason why the Convention's legality principle merely reflects a minimum standard. When considering whether the Convention's

[2016] See Article 53 ECHR.
[2017] See subsection 5.5.4.

legality principle provides a desirable standard of protection for EU law, this characteristic of the ECHR system should not be overlooked.

Like the fact that the Convention merely provides a minimum standard, the ECHR's subsidiarity principle is not necessarily relevant for the formulation of the EU legality principle. Although the EU system of fundamental rights protection is not necessarily subsidiary to that of the Member States,[2018] the CJEU case-law on the EU legality principle could have adopted a lowered standard of review akin to that under the ECHR due to the ECtHR's subsidiary position. The division of competences in preliminary rulings concerning a question on the conformity of implementing criminal law with the EU legality principle does, in fact, resemble the situation when the ECtHR assesses domestic formulations and interpretations of offenses and penalties. As described in subsection 4.5.6, however, the CJEU's distant approach is not dictated by the division of competences. For that reason, the Luxembourg Court could provide more guidance on the demands of the EU legality principle for implementing criminal law.

In addition to Article 53 ECHR and the Convention's subsidiary principle, there is another characteristic of the ECHR's legality principle that is not necessarily transferable to EU law. This is the fact that Article 7 ECHR's substantive protection has mostly resulted from judgments concerning definitions and interpretations of offenses and penalties within a single state context. Most ECtHR case-law concerned the review of domestic definitions and interpretations of crimes and penalties that were applied solely within the legal context of a single Convention state.[2019]

As described in section 5.6, EU criminal law generally concerns a different situation. Until now, EU law has only been indirectly relevant for the definitions of crimes and penalties in domestic law. Since the CJEU cannot, in any event, determine criminal liability and impose a penalty, EU criminal law is necessarily multilevel. It entails not only norms on the EU and national levels, but also the activity of the national judiciary, which is sometimes aided by the CJEU's interpretation of Union law. This hierarchical interaction between legal orders and their respective institutions is *sui generis*. Its impact on the definition and interpretation of offenses and penalties at the level of each individual state should therefore be considered when constructing the EU legality standard.

Even when the ECtHR exceptionally examined situations concerning multilevel definitions and interpretations of crimes and penalties, the Strasbourg Court's approach is not necessarily appropriate for EU law. This is because the aforementioned ECtHR case-law generally concerned the interplay between international definitions and interpretations of the gravest crimes and penalties that were incorporated under domestic law.[2020] With grave offenses such as

2018 Cf Van Kempen and Van Elst 2006, 245.
2019 Cf Altena-Davidsen 2016, p. 93.
2020 Cf Altena-Davidsen 2016, p. 93.

war crimes and genocide,[2021] the foreseeability requirement is more easily met than with regard to acts that are not as evidently reprehensible. In light of the evidently reprehensible character of the acts in question in the ECtHR judgments concerning multilevel crimes and penalties, the protection of a minimum legality standard could indeed be justifiable. As multilevel EU criminal law mostly concerns more market related prohibited conduct,[2022] the foreseeability of criminal liability is less obvious. In these circumstances, the adoption of the ECHR minimum standard of legality protection is not self-evident.

A fourth important difference between ECHR and EU law is the fact that the EU institutions are themselves involved, albeit indirectly, in the definition and interpretation of offenses and penalties. This means that EU interests play a role in determining the extent to which EU criminal law satisfies the EU legality principle. In other words, unlike the ECtHR, the CJEU and Member State courts have an interest, as a matter of EU law, to ensure the effectiveness of Union law through the use of domestic criminal law. As described in chapter 5, the need for effective enforcement of EU law has historically been an important factor in the development of EU criminal law.[2023]

Since the effectiveness of Union (criminal) law is a significant EU interest, the CJEU will generally be called upon to limit the most effective interpretation of EU law only when this would clearly violate an EU fundamental right.[2024] Since the Luxembourg Court has often emphasized the need for Union law to be effective, an incentive exists to sometimes protect only a minimum level of legality.[2025] As a result, the EU legality standard could be driven towards only adopting the most marginal interpretation of the minimum ECHR standard when, for example, the effective penalization of infringements of EU law would require the imposition of criminal penalties.[2026]

This possible tendency towards protecting only the most minimal interpretation of the Convention legality standard would nevertheless be

2021 See, eg, the ECtHR's judgments in *Kononov* and *Vasliauskas*, which are described in subsection 3.4.3.

2022 See chapter 4.

2023 See, eg, subsections 5.2.2; 5.4.2. Cf Altena-Davidsen 2016, p. 79–80. The potential negative effect of effective cooperation in the Union's Area of Freedom, Security and Justice is recognize by the ECtHR, see *Avotiņš v. Latvia*, CE:ECHR:2016:0523JUD001750207, paras 113–114.

2024 See the CJEU case-law on the limits to consistent interpretation in criminal matters as described in subsection 4.2.3. Another example is *Könecke*, where the requirement of a proper legal basis prevailed over the need to effectively counter EU fraud, see further subsection 4.3.2.

2025 See, eg, *SGS Belgium* as described in subsection 4.3.2, *Ezz and Others* as described in subsection 4.6.4, *Afrasiabi* as described in 4.5.5, and *Sasol* as described in 4.6.2. On the features of the general relationship between fundamental rights protection and effectiveness of Union law, see Bockel and Wattel 2014, p. 879; Gullikson 2015, p. 157–174; Lenaerts and Gutiérrez-Fons 2016, p. 25–26.

2026 See the CJEU's judgments in *SGS Belgium* and *Taricco* as, *inter alia*, described in subsections 4.3.2; 5.5.5.

problematic due to the fact that the ECHR standard has already recognized the interest of crime control. Since the ECtHR has sometimes employed the severe nature of the individual's crime as a reason to limit the protection provided under Article 7 ECHR,[2027] the incorporation of the most minimal interpretation of Article 7 in EU law may become overly accommodating towards effective enforcement of prohibitions and crime control.[2028] The EU legality standard would then not just acknowledge the interest in controlling crime by virtue of the incorporation of the ECtHR's approach to legality, but also due to the recognition of the need to effectively enforce violations of Union law.

6.4.3 THE NEED FOR A MORE PROTECTIVE STANDARD OF LEGAL CERTAINTY IN EU LAW

As described in subsection 3.8.3, the Convention's minimum standard provides only minimal protection of legal certainty. While the minimal protection of legal certainty could be justified by the above Convention characteristics, the same is not true for EU law. As described in the preceding subsection, the differences between the Convention system and EU law indicate the need for reflection on the appropriateness of incorporating the ECHR standard into Union law. The present subsection will indicate why the EU legality principle should protect a higher level of legal certainty than the Convention standard.

There are three reasons why the minimal level of legal certainty provided by Article 7 ECHR is not necessarily appropriate for EU law. The first is the fact that the multilevel nature of EU criminal law complicates the foreseeability of criminal liability and the applicable penalties. Since the definition and interpretation of offenses and penalties in EU criminal law involves the legislature and the courts at both the EU level and the national level, the demands placed on an individual in order to understand the applicable criminal law are increased. In order to foresee criminal liability and the applicable penalties, an individual is not just required to know and understand national criminal law and its interpretation by national courts, (s)he is also required to know and comprehend the relationship between national criminal law and EU law and the potential influence of the CJEU's interpretation of EU law for the interpretation of implementing law. These are reasonable requirements for specialists in national criminal law, not for average persons.

The second reason is the relevance of multilingualism in the definition and interpretation of offenses and penalties in EU criminal law. Multilingualism influences EU criminal law in at least two different ways. First, the initial definition of criminal conduct by an EU measure is enacted in 24 legal languages that all are intended to bear the same exact meaning and have equal authority.[2029] Second,

2027 See subsection 3.6.3.
2028 See, conversely, Altena-Davidsen 2016, p. 384–385.
2029 See Derlén 2014, p. 300. Cf Sharpston 2010, p. 411.

the CJEU's interpretations of EU measures are complicated by multilingualism, since the authoritative language of the judgments varies from case to case, while the deliberations on, and drafts of, these judgments are always in French.[2030]

The influence of multilingualism complicates the interpretation of EU law in two ways. Firstly, the interpretation of primary and secondary Union law is complicated by the fact that, in order to derive the precise meaning of certain provisions, 24 different language versions need to be consulted.[2031] Secondly, the authoritative interpretation of primary and secondary EU law by the CJEU is itself hard to understand as a result of multilingualism.[2032] As a consequence, the exact influence of Union law becomes harder to determine, even for specialists.

In a multilevel legal order, the actual interpretation of EU law's requirements is nevertheless essential for the implementation and interpretation of national law. The complication of multilingualism for the determination of EU law's requirements presents a pressing problem in EU criminal law: it further obscures the foreseeability of the content and interpretation of rules that directly affect the determination of national criminal responsibility. For this reason, multilingualism seems to constitute a relevant factor with regard to the legality principle.

Since secondary EU law actually defines criminal conduct and the CJEU actually interprets those provisions, the above-mentioned complications of multilingualism find their way into EU criminal law. In an area of law that has particularly high standards of legal certainty, the influence of multilingualism is potentially more problematic than with regard to EU law as a whole. Just as with regard to the multilevel definition and interpretation of criminal conduct in EU law, the effects of multilingualism could give rise to the need for the protection of a higher standard than the minimal legal certainty protected under Article 7 ECHR.

In addition to the multilevel nature of EU criminal law and the influence of multilingualism, a third reason exists for providing a higher level of legal certainty under the EU legality principle. This is the paradoxical situation that a higher level of legal certainty appears to be required under principles related to the legality principle. As described in subsection 6.2.3, EU law appears to protect more than the minimal level of legal certainty required by Article 7 ECHR by virtue of, inter alia, the limits to consistent interpretation, the principle that penalties require a proper legal basis, and the general principle of legal certainty. If the EU legality principle only respected the ECHR standard, this would have the paradoxical effect that a higher level of legal certainty would be protected outside the criminal sphere than in EU criminal law. This would disregard the whole essence of the legality principle, which, as a specific principle of criminal law, is historically and theoretically intended to provide greater protection for individuals in criminal matters than when less intrusive measures apply.

2030 See Sharpston 2010, p. 417; Derlén 2014, p. 300.
2031 Cf Langheld 2016, p. 122.
2032 Cf Sharpston 2010, p. 423.

6.4.4 THE POSSIBILITY OF A MORE PROTECTIVE STANDARD OF LEGAL CERTAINTY

Subsections 6.4.2–6.4.3 provide reasons why protecting a minimum level of legal certainty, although possibly justified under the ECHR, is not appropriate for EU law. The complexity of the multilevel and multilingual definition and interpretation of offenses and penalties in EU criminal law justifies departing from the minimum level of legal certainty provided under the ECHR standard. The EU general legal certainty standard provides the third reason. The present subsection will indicate how a more protective standard of legal certainty could be respected in the future under the EU legality principle.

Since EU crimes and penalties are actually defined, interpreted, and applied at the domestic level, the focus will be on the protection of a more demanding standard of legal certainty by the Member State authorities. The EU legality principle can, of course, set requirements for the legislative and judicial activities of the EU institutions as well. As a fundamental right applicable in the criminal sphere, however, the actual protection of the legality principle will mostly be provided by limiting the application of legislative definitions and judicial interpretations of crimes and penalties that fall short of the EU principle's standard. For that reason, the below recommendations for the EU legality principle will mostly concern the protection of a higher minimum level of legal certainty at the domestic level. My observations here are tentative and rather abstract. I intend to demonstrate their implications more specifically in subsection 6.4.5.

As described in chapter 2, an obvious way to provide more legal certainty under the legality principle would be to move beyond the mere rule of law rationale. If the value of democracy is additionally protected by the legality principle, a strict separation of powers between legislative and judicial activity could be the result. In that event, the foreseeability of criminal liability and the applicable penalties would necessarily be increased. That approach would essentially require the EU legality principle to move more towards the civil law approach to legality. That approach could indeed be appropriate for EU law given that, for example, a tendency to recognize a *lex scripta* principle is perceivable in some of the CJEU's case-law. Since even common law states are increasingly recognizing the need for legislative definitions in criminal law, this could provide a reason for EU law to move beyond the ECHR's more common law-oriented conception of legality.

At the same time, however, CJEU case-law has only identified the rule of law and legal certainty as the legality principle's rationales. The need for a strict separation of powers and the value of democracy have not been identified as relevant for the EU fundamental right.[2033] That is not just understandable because the ECtHR has merely viewed the legality principle as a prohibition of arbitrariness and an essential element of the rule of law. It is also because the

[2033] Cf subsections 6.2.3–6.2.4.

multilevel nature of EU (criminal) law would require a new conceptual model with regard to the separation of powers and the value of democracy. If the EU legality principle would be deemed to protect the separation of powers and democracy, it would be necessary to identify what these rationales entail in a multilevel setting. This would give rise to difficult questions, for example: what is to be protected exactly and at which level? More specific questions would then inevitably occur, such as: does the EU legality principle require substantive criminal law to be established by the European Parliament or are national parliaments the only source of democratic legitimation for criminal law? A challenging additional question would be: does the doctrine of separation of powers only establish a division of labor between the legislature and judiciary within a Member State or also between, for example, the EU judiciary and the national judiciary?

The aforementioned conceptual questions are outside the scope of the present research.[2034] They could, in any event, be avoided by not requiring the EU to fully adopt the civil law conception of legality. This could additionally acknowledge the critique that it is practically impossible to adopt the civil law legality principle in full.[2035] In order to avoid the above-mentioned difficulties, the EU legality principle could still only recognize the rule of law rationale. It could nevertheless provide a higher level of legal certainty than the mere prohibition of arbitrariness of Article 7 ECHR. This is possible because the level of legal certainty that is *at a minimum* provided under the rule of law rationale is the general certainty that criminal law is not applied arbitrarily.[2036] The general certainty provided by the standard of non-arbitrariness could nevertheless be raised more closely towards the civil law standard of maximum predictability. Under this approach, the EU legality principle would both fit closely with the conceptual common law-oriented model behind Article 7 ECHR, but it would also protect the level of legal certainty that the CJEU sometimes protects under related EU principles such as the requirement of a proper legal basis and the general principle of legal certainty. As mentioned, this higher level of legal certainty is appropriate due to the characteristics of Union criminal law.[2037]

In order to protect a level of certainty closer to maximum predictability, the EU legality principle could place higher demands on the clarity of the applicable *legislation*.[2038] Unlike under Article 7 ECHR, the Union principle should draw different conclusions from the viewpoint that the statutory wording of offenses and penalties can never be completely clear. Instead of only requiring clarity from a cumulative reading of legislation and case-law, the EU principle should

2034 On the meaning of the doctrine of the separation of powers in the EU, see, eg, Fernandez Esteban 1999, p. 156–159; Möllers 2013, p. 47, 169–195; Merli 2016, p. 42; Schroeder 2016, p. 10.

2035 On that critique, see subsection 2.4.5.

2036 See section 2.4.

2037 See subsections 6.4.2–6.4.3.

2038 Cf Altena-Davidsen 2016, p. 397.

place separate demands on the clarity of the legislative wording, particularly at the level of the implementing legislation.

Whereas interpretive case-law can be deemed to contribute fully to the foreseeability of criminal liability and applicable penalties within the context of a single state, this view is more difficult to defend in a multilevel context. Instead of taking as a point of departure that a *combination* of statutory provisions and case-law generally satisfies the *lex certa* principle, under EU law more clarity should be required from domestic legislation alone. This is because implementing legislation constitutes a second legislative act which is additional to the EU measure. Since EU definitions involve two legislative processes, the clarity demands on the newly enacted provisions can be higher than the ECHR standard which is also applicable to, for example, very old and very general legislation enacted in a single state context. Unlike Article 7 ECHR, the EU legality principle should therefore unequivocally protect the *lex scripta* element. This should require a domestic legislative basis as a precondition for the determination of criminal liability and the applicable penalties in the multilevel context of EU criminal law.

While implementing legislation actually defines crimes and penalties, in the field of EU criminal law, these definitions are obviously based on EU definitions. These EU definitions should be contained in sufficiently clear legislation as well.[2039] As with regard to implementing legislation, the EU legality principle should not generally allow the clarification of vague legislative EU definitions by interpretive EU case-law. As a first definition to be implemented by domestic legislatures, the clarity requirements need to be higher than the ECHR standard which allows the elucidation of vague terms by subsequent case-law. The EU legislature's first definition should be so clear and precise that domestic legislatures who merely incorporate the EU definition will not violate the *lex certa* requirement.[2040] As with the clarity demands placed on definitions in implementing legislation, the legislative wording of EU definitions needs to provide greater clarity than is generally required under the ECHR legality standard.

In addition to the aforementioned adaptations, the EU legality principle could also enshrine a more demanding *lex certa* element by changing the point of departure for the foreseeability assessment. Instead of adopting the ECtHR's assessment of foreseeability from the viewpoint of an individual *who took legal advice*, the EU principle could take the individual layperson as the benchmark. Although professionals can indeed be required to foresee legal consequences that emanate from even complex multilevel regulatory frameworks, the same cannot be true for the average person subject to multilevel EU criminal law. For that reason, criminal liability and applicable penalties as a result of EU criminal law should be more quickly deemed to have been unforeseeable than would be

---

2039 Cf Asp 2012, p. 171–178; Altena-Davidsen 2016, p. 157–159, 200–201; Sicurella 2016, p. 74.

2040 If EU legislation requires Member States to implement rules that violate an EU fundamental right, EU legislation itself will violate that Union right, cf Case C-293/12, *Digital Rights Ireland Ltd v Minister for Communications*, EU:C:2014:238, paras 32–27, 54.

the case under the Convention's legality principle. In other words, the ECtHR's thin ice principle should not be employed under the EU legality principle. Claims about the lack of foreseeability for laypersons in EU criminal law should therefore be treated more generously for non-professional individuals.

A comparably limited adaptation of the ECHR's *lex stricta* approach is also appropriate. The ECtHR's point of departure – that it is always necessary for the judiciary to progressively develop the existing law – should not be incorporated into the EU legality principle. Although judicial interpretation is indeed inevitable, the extent to which this is allowed and encouraged should be more limited. This could be accomplished by the rejection of the ECtHR's low standard of foreseeability which, as mentioned, includes the thin ice principle.

The Convention standard of foreseeability, which is arguably even lower with regard to *lex stricta* as only *reasonable* foreseeability is then required, is insufficiently demanding for EU law. This is especially the case when the domestic interpretation of offenses and penalties is influenced by definitions and interpretations at the EU level. In this situation, regular individuals cannot be expected to take account of the influence that EU law exerts on the possibilities for domestic judicial interpretation. More specifically, if EU law or its interpretation becomes the reason to expansively interpret domestic offenses and penalties, the immediate application of this expansive interpretation should not be allowed even if this would be reasonably foreseeable. It should only be allowed if it was foreseeable in light of the professional capacity of the suspect or when it is clear that he had actually foreseen criminal liability or the applicable penalties. In the event of multilevel interpretations of crimes and penalties, the EU legality principle should therefore ensure maximum predictability instead of reasonable foreseeability.[2041]

This demanding foreseeability standard should also apply to the interpretation of domestic implementing offenses and penalties when it is not EU law that provides the reason for expansive interpretations. Although it could be argued that the regular ECHR standard of reasonable foreseeability could then be applied, this would obviously complicate legality protection. In that event, the EU *lex stricta* principle would provide two distinct standards. Maximum predictability would be ensured when EU law expands the domestic possibilities for judicial interpretation, while it would only require reasonable foreseeability in other situations. This complicated result appears to exist in EU law at present; the limits to consistent interpretation aim to ensure a high level of foreseeability, while the EU legality principle itself only appears to protect the ECHR standard of reasonable foreseeability.

[2041] This appears to be the view of Advocate General Bobek as well, who suggests not to fully apply the maxim *ignorantia legis europae non excusat* in multilevel EU criminal law, see Case C-574/15, *Proceedings against Mauro Scialdone*, Opinion of AG Bobek, EU:C:2017:553, paras 165–166.

Instead of the apparently different standards of protection against the immediate application of expansive interpretations, the EU standard should protect only the maximum predictability. This is required in multilevel situations as the CJEU case-law on limits to consistent interpretation has acknowledged. It is also appropriate in more internal situations, however. Firstly because of the need to provide a consistent standard of *lex stricta* protection. Secondly because the ECHR standard is only a minimum standard. In order to consistently ensure protection against overly expansive interpretations in EU criminal law, the CJEU should aim to ensure a higher level of legal certainty than the Strasbourg Court. That would also align the level of legal certainty protected by the legality principle with that provided by the general Union principle of legal certainty outside the criminal sphere.

6.4.5 THE PROPOSED APPROACH TO LEGALITY: AN ILLUSTRATION

I will illustrate the implications of the proposed approach by constructing an example based on Framework Decision 2008/913/JHA on combatting racism and xenophobia via criminal law.[2042] Article 1(1)(a) of this framework decision requires the Member States to criminalize the intentional public incitement to violence or hatred directed against a group of persons or a member of such a group defined by reference to race, color, religion, descent or national or ethnic origin.

Let's assume that Member State X introduced the offense of public incitement to violence or hatred into its domestic law by copying the above definition. Both before and after the entry into force of this provision, the Member State's courts consistently interpreted the term 'religion' restrictively. According to consistent domestic case-law, incitement to hatred or violence on the basis of religion is only punishable when it is directed against a religion that is officially recognized. Framework Decision 2008/913/JHA does not indicate such a limited definition of the term 'religion', however. In fact, recital 8 of the framework decision's preamble states that "[r]eligion should be understood as broadly referring to persons defined by reference to their religious convictions or beliefs".

Let's further assume that, after a few years, the CJEU interpreted the term 'religion' and confirmed that it required a broad construction in accordance with the preamble of the framework decision. The definition of religion could not, for that reason, be restricted to officially recognized religions. The Member States are also obliged to criminalize hatred or violence against people on the basis of non-

[2042] Council Framework Decision 2008/913/JHA of 28 November 2008 on combatting certain forms and expressions of racism and xenophobia by means of criminal law [2008] OJ L 328/55.

officially recognized religious convictions or beliefs. After the CJEU judgment, suspect Q publicly incited violence against a person for being a member of the Church of Scientology, a non-officially recognized religion in Member State X. Q is brought before the domestic court for having incited violence or hatred on the basis of religion.

Since the domestic offense implements EU law, the domestic court has to ensure conformity with the EU legality principle. In the proposed approach to legality, the domestic court cannot focus only on the interpretive case-law. As a point of departure, the domestic court is obliged to assess whether the statutory wording of the offense is generally clear enough to make criminal liability foreseeable for most cases. Since the dispute evidently only concerns the meaning of the word 'religion', it is clear that intentionally inciting violence against a person for being a member of an officially recognized religion gives rise to criminal liability. For that reason, inciting violence against a person for being a member of a group certainly carries the risk of criminal liability, which makes the scope of the offense generally clear. It enables individuals to avoid certain behavior to be sure of falling outside the scope of the offense. By having determined that a domestic legislative provision with sufficiently clear general wording existed at the time of the individuals acts, the domestic court can then conclude that the elements *lex scripta* and *lex praevia* were satisfied.

The domestic court can subsequently assess conformity with the elements *lex certa* and *lex stricta*. Although the legislative definition is not unclear as it is generally able to guide conduct,[2043] the exact scope of the offense is not evident. In order to determine the exact extent of criminal liability the individual can be required to consult *domestic* interpretive case-law. The individual cannot, however, be required to consult either the EU directive or the CJEU's interpretation thereof. EU criminal law's characteristics of multilevel definitions and interpretations and multilingualism should not be used to the individual's detriment. With regard to the present example, this means that the domestic court's case-law on the interpretation of the term 'religion' is the only relevant source for assessing the clarity and meaning of the domestic offense incitement to violence. As a result, individuals in Member State X will be able to escape criminal liability for incitement to violence when this is directed at a person for being a member of a non-officially recognized religion. Until the domestic courts reverse their case-law, criminal liability for these acts will have to be excluded.

Although the domestic court would, as a matter of EU law, be required to interpret the domestic offense of incitement to violence in accordance with the CJEU interpretation of the framework decision, it cannot apply this

[2043] While the domestic court is only required to review the clarity of the implementing definition, an unclear first definition in the Framework Decision could be relevant as this could affect the validity of the EU definition, cf Case C-293/12, *Digital Rights Ireland Ltd v Minister for Communications*, EU:C:2014:238, paras 32–27, 54.

new interpretation immediately to the detriment of suspect Q. It can merely determine that from the moment of the domestic court's judgment in the case of Q the domestic offense of incitement to violence shall be interpreted in accordance with the CJEU's interpretation. The domestic court cannot, however, apply that interpretation to acts that occurred before it laid down its ruling in the Q case. Although it could be argued that Q treaded on thin ice with his reprehensible behavior, which was moreover foreseeably prohibited by EU law, the individual suspect should still be protected against the imposition of criminal liability. This is justified because EU criminal law's specific characteristics have a negative impact on legal certainty at the domestic level.

If the domestic court asked the CJEU for a preliminary ruling, the EU legality principle would have to be directly considered by the Luxembourg Court. Like the domestic court, the CJEU would need to safeguard the EU legality principle in accordance with the proposed approach. Since the EU framework decision provides the first definition of incitement to violence, and the CJEU interprets that definition in a preliminary ruling relevant for the judgment against Q, the Luxembourg Court becomes independently responsible for the full protection of the EU legality principle.

In order to bear that responsibility, the Court should assess the potential impact of the framework decision's prohibition and its interpretation for the main proceedings. On the basis of the information provided by the domestic court, the CJEU should determine that Member State X's legislation and case-law presently provides immunity for incitement to violence when directed against non-officially recognized religions. As a result of that determination, which obviously depends on the cooperation of the domestic court and the Member State's government for example,[2044] the Luxembourg Court should unequivocally determine that Q's conviction for incitement to violence would violate the EU legality principle. Instead of merely deferring the responsibility to respect the EU legality principle to the national level without guidance,[2045] the CJEU should play its part in ensuring that a higher level of legal certainty is protected in situations of multilevel and multilingual definitions and interpretations. The Court should therefore adapt its deferential approach in preliminary rulings.

6.5 CONCLUDING REMARKS

As presently construed, the EU legality principle leaves much to be desired. The CJEU's approach to legality has lacked both consistency and a clear conceptual

[2044] About cooperation in preliminary rulings, see, eg, *Criminal proceedings against M.A.S. and M.B. (Taricco II)*, EU:C:2017:936, paras 22–24.

[2045] See subsection 4.5.6.

background. It has also failed to construct a legality principle which undoubtedly conforms to the ECHR minimum standard.

Even if consistency and conformity with the ECHR would be present, the desirability of the EU legality is still questionable in light of EU criminal law's specific characteristics. Due to the multilevel nature of the definition and interpretation of offenses and penalties, the influence of multilingualism, and the general EU standard of legal certainty provided outside the criminal sphere, it is appropriate for the EU legality principle to move beyond the minimum ECHR standard. Instead of functioning as a prohibition on arbitrariness, the EU legality principle should ensure a level of legal certainty that is closer to the maximum predictability of consequences for certain acts.

A more demanding EU standard could be achieved by unequivocally acknowledging a *lex scripta* element, by lowering the benchmark figure to a layperson and thus requiring more foreseeability from existing legal bases, and by also requiring a higher foreseeability standard when assessing judicial interpretations within the scope of EU criminal law. The EU legality principle could then provide a level of legal certainty that is closer to the theoretical standard provided under the civil law conception of legality without having to explicitly adopt additional rationales such as the value of democracy and the ensuing strict separation of powers. Since it is questionable whether these values can practically be protected by the civil law conception of legality, the EU legality principle would not necessarily be subject to the criticism that it has adopted a practically unattainable legality standard.

BIBLIOGRAPHY

1. LITERATURE

Alldridge 2002
P. Alldridge 'Making Criminal Law Known', in: *Criminal Law Theory: Doctrines of the General Part*, A. Simester S. Shute (eds.), Oxford: Oxford University Press 2002.

Altena-Davidsen 2016
J.G.H. Altena-Davidsen, *Het legaliteitsbeginsel en de doorwerking van Europees recht in het Nederlandse materiële strafrecht*, Deventer: Kluwer 2016.

Antolisei and Conti 2003
F. Antolisei and L. Conti, *Manuale di diritto penale*, Milano: Giuffrè 2003.

Ashcraft 1994
R. Ashcraft, 'Locke's political philosophy', in: *The Cambridge Companion to Locke*, V. Chappell (ed.), Cambridge: Cambridge University Press 1994.

Ashworth and Horder 2013
A. Ashworth and J. Horder, *Principles of Criminal Law*, Oxford: Oxford University Press 2013.

Asp 2012
P. Asp, *The Substantive Criminal Law Competence of the EU, Stockholm: Jure 2012.*

Asp 2014
P. Asp, 'European Criminal Law – Challenges for the Future', in: *European Police and Criminal Law Co-operation*, M. Bergström and A.J. Cornell (eds.), Oxford, Portland: Hart Publishing 2014.

Atrill 2005
S. Atrill, 'Nulla Poena Sine Lege in comparative perspective: retrospectivity under the ECHR and US Constitution', *Public Law*, 2005.

Barnett 2014
R.E. Barnett, *The Structure of Liberty. Justice and The Rule of Law*, Oxford: Oxford University Press 2014.

Baumbach 2011
T. Baumbach, 'The Notion of Criminal Penalty and the Lex Mitior Principle in the Scoppola v. Italy Case', *Nordic Journal of International Law*, 2011.

Bazzocchi 2011
V. Bazzocchi, 'The European Charter of Fundamental Rights and the Area of Freedom, Security and Justice', in: *The EU Charter of Fundamental Rights*, G. Di Federico (ed.), Dordrecht, New York: Springer 2011.

Beccaria 1764
C. Beccaria, *On Crimes and Punishments and Other Writings*, Cambridge: Cambridge University Press 1764 (1995).

Beddard 1996
R. Beddard, 'The rights of the "criminal" under Article 7 ECHR', *European Law Review*, 1996.

Bemelmans 2018
J.H.B. Bemelmans, *Totdat het tegendeel is bewezen. De onschuldpresumptie in rechtshistorisch, theoretisch, internationaalrechtelijk en Nederlands strafprocesrechtelijk perspectief*, Deventer: Kluwer 2018.

Bernardini 2015
R. Bernardini, *Droit criminel. Éléments préliminaires*, Bruxelles: Larcier 2015.

Besselink 2014
L.F.M. Besselink, 'The parameters of constitutional conflict after Melloni', *European Law Review*, 2014.

Biondi and Mastroianni 2006
A. Biondi and R. Mastroianni, 'A very ambiguous judgment? Berlusconi and others', *Common Market Law Review*, 2006.

Bleichrodt 2006
E. Bleichrodt, 'Freedom From Retrospective Effect of Penal Legislation (Article 7)', in: *Theory and Practice of the European Convention on Human Rights*, P. van Dijk, F. van Hoof, A. van Rijn and L. Zwaak (eds.), Antwerpen, Oxford: Intersentia 2006.

Blomsma and Peristeridou 2013
J.H. Blomsma and C. Peristeridou, 'The way forward: A general part of European criminal law', in: *Approximation of substantive criminal law in the EU: The way forward*, A. Weyembergh F. Galli (eds.), Brussels: Iee 2013.

Boot 2002
M. Boot, *Genocide, Crimes Against Humanity, War Crimes. Nullum Crimen Sine Lege and the Subject Matter Jurisdiction of the International Criminal Court School of Human Rights Research*, Antwerpen, Oxford, New York: Intersentia 2002.

Borgers 2011
M.J. Borgers, 'De Communicatieve strafrechter', in: *Controverses rondom legaliteit en legitimatie*, Deventer: Kluwer 2011.

Brems 1996
E. Brems, 'The Margin of Appreciation Doctrine in the Case-law of the European Court of Human Rights', *Zeitschrift für ausländisches öffentliches recht und völkerrecht*, 1996.

Brink and Nelkin 2013
D.O. Brink and D.K. Nelkin, 'Fairness and the Architecture of Responsibility', in: *Oxford Studies in Agency and Responsibility*, D. Shoemaker (ed.), Oxford: Oxford University Press 2013.

Brkan 2013
M. Brkan, 'The Role of the European Court of Justice from Maastricht to Lisbon: Putting Together the Scattered Pieces of Patchwork', in: *The Treaty on European Union 1993–2013: Reflections from Maastricht*, M. de Visser and A. P. van der Mei (eds.), Cambridge, Antwerp, Portland: Intersentia 2013.

Broberg and Fenger 2014
M. Broberg and N. Fenger, *Preliminary References to the European Court of Justice*, Oxford: Oxford University Press 2014.

Cadoppi and Veneziani 2005
A. Cadoppi and P. Veneziani, *Manuale di diritto penale*, Padova: CEDAM 2005.

Cameron 2016
I. Cameron, 'EU anti-terrorist sanctions', in: *Research Handbook on EU Criminal Law*, V. Mitsilegas, M. Bergström and T. Konstadinides (eds.), Cheltenham, Northampton: Edward Elgar 2016.

Carrithers 2001
D.W. Carrithers, 'Montesquieu and the Liberal Philosophy of Jurisprudence', in: *Montesquieu's Science of Politics. Essays on The Spirit of Laws*, D.W. Caritthers, M.A. Mosher and P. A. Rahe (eds.), Lanham: Rowman & Littlefield Publishers 2001.

Celano 2013
B. Celano, 'Publicity and the Rule of Law', in: *Oxford Studies in Philosophy of Law: Volume 2*, B. Leiter L. Green (eds.), Oxford: Oxford University Press 2013.

Christ 2003
A.E. Christ, *Bürgerliche Freitheit und Strafrecht bei Montesquieu im Kontext seiner Gestezes- und Staatslehre*, Berlin: Grauer Verlag 2003.

Claes 2003
E. Claes, *Legaliteit en rechtsvinding in het strafrecht. Een grondslagentheoretische benadering*, Leuven: Universitaire Pers Leuven 2003.

Claes and Krolikowski 2009
E. Claes and M. Krolikowski, 'The Limits of Legality in the Criminal Law', in: *Facing the Limits of the Law*, W. Devroe E. Claes, B. Keisbilck (eds.), Berlin, Heidelberg: Springer 2009.

Claes 2011
E. Claes, 'Legality and lex certa in the Criminal Law. Reply to Christina Peristeridou', in: *Substantive Criminal Law of the European Union*, A. Klip (ed.), Antwerpen, Apeldoorn, Portland: Maklu 2011.

Claes 2015
M. Claes, 'The Primacy of EU Law in European and National Law', in: *The Oxford Handbook of European Law*, A. Arnull and D. Chalmers (eds.), Oxford: Oxford University Press 2015.

Corstens and Pradel 2002
G. Corstens and J. Pradel, *European Criminal Law*, The Hague, London, New York: Kluwer Law International 2002.

Corthaut and Lenaerts 2006
T. Corthaut and K. Lenaerts, 'Of birds and hedges: the role of primacy in invoking norms of EU law', *European Law Review*, 2006.

Christoffersen 2009
J. Christoffersen, *Fair Balance: Proportionality, Subsidiarity and Primarity in the European Convention on Human Rights*, Leiden, Boston: Martinus Nijhoff Publishers 2009.

Craig 2010
P. Craig, 'Rights, Legality, and Legitimacy', in: *The Lisbon Treaty: Law, Politics, and Treaty Reform*, P. Craig (ed.), Oxford: Oxford University Press 2010.

Craig and De Búrca 2015
P. Craig and G. de Búrca, *EU Law: Text, Cases and Materials*, Oxford: Oxford University Press 2015.

Cupido 2015
M. Cupido, *Facts Matter: A Study into the Casuistry of Substantive International Criminal Law*, The Hague: Eleven International Publishing 2015.

Dauses 2010
M.A. Dauses, The Protection of Fundamental Rights in the Legal Order of the European Union. With Emphasis on the Institutional Protection of those Rights, Frankfurt Am Main: Peter Lang 2010.

De Hullu 2015
J. De Hullu, *Materieel strafrecht. Over algemene leerstukken van strafrechtelijke aansprakelijkheid naar Nederlands recht*, Deventer: Wolters Kluwer 2015.

Deimling 1989
G. Deimling, 'Der gesellschaftskritische Ansatz des Präventionsgedankes im Werk Beccaria's', in: *Cesare Beccaria. Die Anfänge moderner Strafrechtsplege in Europa*, G. Deimling (ed.), Heidelberg: Kriminalistik Verlag 1989.

De Jong 1999
D.H. de Jong, 'Naar een common law-conceptie van legaliteit?', *Delikt & Delinkwent*, 1999.

De la Mare and Donelly 2011
T. de la Mare and C. Donelly, 'Preliminary rulings and EU legal integration: evolution and stasis', in: *The Evolution of European Union Law*, P. Craig and G. de Búrca (eds.), Oxford: Oxford University Press 2011.

De Boer 2013
N. De Boer, 'Addressing rights divergences under the Charter: Melloni', *Common Market Law Review*, 2013.

De Búrca 2011
G. de Búrca, 'The Evolution of EU Human Rights Law', in: *The Evolution of European Union Law*, P. Craig and G. de Búrca (eds.), Oxford: Oxford University Press 2011,.

De Búrca 2013
G. de Búrca, 'After the EU Charter of Fundamental Rights: The Court of Justice as a Human Rights Adjudicator?', *Maastricht Journal of European and Comparative Law*, 2013.

De Hert 2016
P. De Hert, 'EU criminal law and fundamental rights', in: *Research Handbook on EU Criminal Law, V. Mitsilegas*, M. Bergström and T. Konstadinides (eds.), Cheltenham, Northampton: Edward Elgar 2016.

Deportes and LeGunehec 2008
F. Desportes and F. LeGunehec, *Droit pénal général*, Paris: Economica 2008.

Dérlen 2014
M. Derlén, 'Multilingual interpretation of CJEU case law: rule and reality', *European Law Review*, 2014.

De Witte 1999
B. de Witte, 'The Past and Future Role of the European Court of Justice in the Protection of Human Rights', in: *The EU and Human Rights*, P. Alston (ed.), Oxford: Oxford University Press 1999.

De Witte 2011
B. de Witte, 'The use of the ECHR and Convention case law by the ECJ', in: *Human rights protection in the European legal order. The interaction between the European and the national courts*, Cambridge, Anwerp, Portland: Intersentia 2011.

De Witte 2014
B. de Witte, 'Article 53 – Level of Protection', in: *The EU Charter of Fundamental Rights*, T. Hervey S. Peers, J. Kenner, A. Ward (eds.), Oxford, Portland: Hart Publishing 2014.

Dhont and Cromheecke 2004
F. Dhont and M. Cromheecke, 'Artikel 7. Geen straf zonder wet', in: *Handboek EVRM. Deel 2. Artikelsgewijze Commentaar*, Y. Haeck J. Vande Lanotte (eds.), Antwerpen, Oxford: Intersentia 2004.

Di Federico 2011
G. Di Federico, 'Fundamental Rights in the EU', in: *The EU Charter of Fundamental Rights*, G. Di Federico (ed.): Dordrecht, New York: Springer 2011.

Di Punzio and Natalini 2006
I. Di Punzio and A. Natalini, *Manuale completo di diritto penale*, Santarcangelo di Romagna: Maggioli 2006.

Dougan 2007
M. Dougan, 'When Worlds Collide! Competing Visions of the Relationship Between Direct Effect and Supremacy', *Common Market Law Review*, 2007.

Dougan 2012
M. Dougan, 'From the Velvet Glove to the Iron Fist: Criminal Sanctions for the Enforcement of Union Law', in: *Compliance and the Enforcement of EU Law*, M. Cremona (ed.), Oxford: Oxford University Press 2012.

Dougan 2015
M. Dougan, 'Judicial Review of Member State Action Under the General Principles and the Charter: Defining the "Scope of Union Law"', *Common Market Law Review*, 2015.

Douglas-Scott 2011
S. Douglas-Scott, 'Freedom, Security, and Justice in the European Court of Justice: The Ambiguous Nature of Judicial Review', in: *The Legal Protection of Human Rights: Sceptical Essays*, K.D. Ewing T. Campbell, A. Tomkins (eds.), Oxford: Oxford University Press 2011.

Douglas-Scott 2013
S. Douglas-Scott, 'The ECJ and ECtHR after Lisbon', in: *The Protection of Fundamental Rights in the EU After Lisbon*, S. de Vries, U. Bernitz and S. Weatherill (eds.), Oxford and Portland: Hart Publishing 2013.

Dreyer 2012
E. Dreyer, *Droit pénal général*, Paris: LexisNexis 2012.

Dubber 2013
M.D. Dubber, 'The Legality Principle in American and German Criminal Law: An Essay in Comparative Legal History', in: *From the Judge's Arbitrium to the Legality Principle. Legislation as a Source of Law in Criminal Trials*, G. Martyn, A. Musson and H. Pihlajamäki (eds.), Berlin: Duncker & Humblot 2013.

Eser 2010
A. Eser, 'Charta Artikel 49 Grundsätze der Gesetzmäßigkeit und der Verhältnismäßigkeit im Zusammenhang mit Straftaten und Strafen', in: *Charta der Grundrechte der Europäischen Union*, Meyer (ed.), Baden-Baden: Nomos 2010.

Fenwick and Wrbka 2016
M. Fenwick and S. Wrbka, 'The Shifting Meaning of Legal Certainty', in: *Legal Certainty in a Contemporary Context. Private and Criminal Law Perspectives*, M. Fenwick and S. Wrbka (eds.), Singapore: Springer 2016.

Fernandez-Esteban 1999
M.L. Fernandez Esteban, *The Rule of Law in the European Constitution*, The Hague, London, Boston: Kluwer Law International 1999.

Foqué and 't Hart 1990
R. Foqué and A.C. 't Hart, *Instrumentaliteit en rechtsbescherming. Grondslagen van een strafrechtelijke waardendiscussie*, Arnhem: Gouda Quint 1990.

Forster 2008
S. Forster, 'Das Gesetzlichkeitsprinzip in England und Wales', in: *Nationales Strafrecht in rechtsvergleichender Darstellung. Allgemeiner Teil. Band 2: Gesetzlichkeitprinzip, Internationaler Geltungsbereich des Strafrechts, Begriff und Systematieserung der Straftat*, U. Sieber and K. Cornils (eds.), Berlin: Duncker & Humblot 2008.

Frese 2014
M.J. Frese, *Sanctions in EU Competition Law. Principles and Practice*, Oxford and Portland: Hart Publishing 2014.

Frowein 2009
J. Frowein, 'Artikel 7 (keine Strafe ohne Gesetz)', in: *Europäische MenschenRechtsKonvention. EMRK-Kommentar*, W. Peukert J. Frowein (eds.), Kehl am Rhein: N.P. Engel Verlag 2009.

Fuller 1969
L.L. Fuller, *The Morality of Law*, New Haven: Yale University Press 1969.

Gallant 2009
K.S. Galllant, *The Principle of Legality in International and Comparative Criminal Law*, Cambridge: Cambridge University Press 2009.

Gamper 2016
A. Gamper, 'Legal Certainty', in: *Strengthening the Rule of Law in Europe. From a Common Concept to Mechanisms of Implementation*, W. Schroeder (eds.), Oxford, Portland: Hart Publishing 2016.

Gerards 2011
J.H. Gerards, *EVRM – Algemene leerstukken*, Den Haag: Sdu Uitgevers 2011.

Gerards 2011a
J. Gerards, 'Pluralism, Deference and the Margin of Appreciation Doctrine', *European Law Journal*, 2011.

Giannakopoulos 2011
T. K. Giannakopoulos, *Safeguarding Companies' Rights in Competition and Anti-dumping/Anti-subsidies Proceedings*, Alphen aan den Rijn: Kluwer Law International 2011.

Glas and Krommendijk 2017
L.R. Glas and J. Krommendijk, 'From Opinion 2/13 to Avotiņš: Recent Developments in the Relationship between the Luxembourg and Strasbourg Court', *Human Rights Law Review*, 2017.

Gough 1973
J.W. Gough, *John Locke's Political Philosophy*, Oxford: Clarendon Press 1973.

Goyard-Fabre 1973
S. Goyard-Fabre, *La Philosophie du droit de Montesquieu*, Paris: Librairie C. Klincksieck 1973.

Grabenwarter 2014
C. Grabenwarter, *European Convention on Human Rights. Commentary*, München: C.H. Beck 2014.

Groenhuijsen 1987
M.S. Groenhuijsen, *Straf en wet. Beschouwingen over de betekenis van het legaliteitsbeginsel in het hedendaagse strafrecht tegen de achtergrond van actuele legitimatieproblemen*, Arnhem: Gouda Quint 1987.

Groussot 2006
X. Groussot, General Principles of Community Law, Groningen: Europa Law Publishing 2006.

Gulliksson 2015
M. Gulliksson, 'Effective Sanctions as the One-dimensional Limit to the Ne Bis in Idem Principle in EU law', in: *Human Rights in Contemporary European Law*, J. Nergelius and E. Kristoffersson (eds.), Oxford, Portland: Hart Publishing 2015.

Hall 1937
J. Hall, 'Nulla Poena Sine Lege', *The Yale Law Journal*, 1937.

Hallevy 2010
G. Hallevy, *A Modern Treatise on the Principle of Legality in Criminal Law*, Heidelberg, Dordrecht [etc.]: Springer 2010.

Hancox 2013
E. Hancox, 'The meaning of "implementing" EU law under Article 51(1) of the Charter: Åkerberg Fransson', *Common Market Law Review*, 2013.

Harding 2016
C. Harding, 'The relationship between EU criminal law and competition law', in: *Research Handbook on EU Criminal Law*, V. Mitsilegas, M. Bergström and T. Konstadinides (eds.), Cheltenham, Northampton: Edward Elgar 2016.

Hart 1982
H.L.A. Hart, *Essays on Bentham: Jurisprudence and Political Philosophy*, Oxford: Oxford University Press 1982.

Hayek 1945
F.A. Hayek, *The Road to Serfdom with The Intellectuals and Socialism*, London: The Institute of Economic Affairs 1945 (2005).

Heath 1963
J. Heath, *Eighteenth Century Penal Theory*, Oxford: Oxford University Press 1963.

Hecker 2015
B. Hecker, *Europäisches Strafrecht*, Berlin, Heidelberg: Springer 2015.

Herlin-Karnell 2012
E. Herlin-Karnell, *The Constitutional Dimension of European Criminal Law*, Oxford, Portland: Hart Publishing 2012.

Herlin-Karnell 2014
E. Herlin-Karnell, 'Recent Developments in the Field of Substantive and Procedural EU Criminal Law - Challenges and Opportunities', in: *European Police and Criminal Law Co-operation*, A.J. Cornell M. Bergström (eds.), Oxford, Portland: Hart Publishing 2014.

Herlin-Karnell 2016
E. Herlin-Karnell, 'Is administrative law still relevant? How the battle of sanctions has shaped EU criminal law', in: *Research Handbook on EU Criminal Law*, V. Mitsilegas, M. Bergström and T. Konstadinides (eds.), Cheltenham, Northampton: Edward Elgar 2016.

Hilgendorf 2012
E. Hilgendorf, 'Gesetzlichkeit als Instrument der Feiheitssicherung. Zur Grundlegung des Gesetzlichkeitsprinzips in der französischen Aufklärungsphilosophie und bei Beccaria', in: *Gesetzlichkeit und Strafrecht*, H. Kudlich, J.P. Montiel and J.C. Schuhr (eds.), Berlin: Duncker & Humblot 2012.

Himma 2014
K.E. Himma, 'What Exactly Is the Problem with Judicial Supremacy? The Rule of Law, Moral Legitimacy, and the Construction of Constitutional Law', in: *Courts, Interpretation, The Rule of Law*, M. Jovanović and K.E. Himma (eds.), The Hague: Eleven International Publishing 2014.

Hinarejos 2011
A. Hinarejos, 'Integration in criminal matters and the role of the Court of Justice', *European Law Review*, 2011.

Hobbes 1647
T. Hobbes, *On the Citizen*, R. Tuck and M. Silverthorne, Cambridge: Cambridge University Press 1647 (1998).

Hobbes 1651
T. Hobbes, *Leviathan*, C.B. Macpherson, Middlesex: Penguin Books 1651 (1968).

Hobbes 1681
T. Hobbes, *A Dialogue between a Philosopher and a Student of the Common Laws of England*, Chicago, London: The University of Chicago Press 1681 (1971).

Hüning 2007
D. Hüning, 'Hobbes on the Right to Punish', in: *The Cambridge Companion to Hobbes's Leviathan*, P. Springborg (ed.), Cambridge: Cambridge University Press 2007.

Jefferson 2015
M. Jefferson, *Criminal Law*, Harlow: Pearson 2015.

Juratowitch 2008
B. Juratowitch, *Retroactivity and the Common Law*, Oxford and Portland: Hart Publishing 2008.

Kadelbach 2006
S. Kadelbach, 'Keine Strafe ohne Gesetz', in: *EMRK/GG Konkordanzkommentar zum europäischen und deutschen Grundrechtsschutz,* R. Grote and T. Marauhn (eds.), Tübingen: Mohr Siebeck 2006.

Karvers 2008
K. Jarvers, 'Das Gesetzlichkeitsprinzip in Italien', in: *Nationales Strafrecht in rechtsvergleichender Darstellung. Allgemeiner Teil. Band 2: Gesetzlichkeitprinzip, Internationaler Geltungsbereich des Strafrechts, Begriff und Systematieserung der Straftat*, U. Sieber and K. Cornils (eds.), Berlin: Duncker & Humblot 2008.

Keiler and Klip 2013
J. Keiler and A. Klip, 'Substantive Criminal Law in the European Union', in: *The Treaty on European Union 1993–2013: Reflections from Maastricht*, M. de Visser and A. P. van der Mei (eds.), Cambridge, Antwerp, Portland: Intersentia 2013.

Kenny 2006
A. Kenny, *The Rise of Modern Philosophy. A New History of Western Philosophy. Volume 3*, Oxford: Oxford University Press 2006.

Klimchuk 2012
D. Klimchuk, 'Hobbes on Equity', in: *Hobbes and the Law*, D. Dyzenhaus and T.M. Poole (eds.), Cambridge: Cambridge University Press 2012.

Klip 2012
A. Klip, *European Criminal Law. An Integrative Approach*, Antwerp, Oxford, Portland: Intersentia 2012.

Klip 2016
A. Klip, *European Criminal Law. An Integrative Approach*, Cambridge, Antwerp, Portland: Intersentia 2016.

Kostakopoulou 2007
D. Kostakopoulou, 'The Area of Freedom, Security and Justice and the European Union's Constitutional Dialogue', in: *The Fundamentals of EU Law Revisited: Assessing the Impact of the Constitutional Debate*, C. Barnard (ed.), Oxford: Oxford University Press 2007.

Krausse 2001
S. Krausse, 'Despotism in the Spirit of Laws', in: *Montesquieu's Science of Politics. Essays on The Spirit of Laws*, D.W. Caritthers, M.A. Mosher and P. A. Rahe (eds.), Lanham: Rowman & Littlefield Publishers 2001.

Krey 1983
V. Krey, *Keine Strafe ohne Gesetz. Einführung in die Dogmengeschichte des Satzes "nullum crimen, nulla poena sine lege"*, Berlin, New York: Walter de Gruyter 1983.

Krommendijk 2015
J. Krommendijk, 'The use of ECtHR case law by the CJEU after Lisbon. The view of Luxembourg insiders', *Maastricht Journal of European and Comparative Law*, 2015.

Krommendijk 2016
J. Krommendijk, 'HvJ EU en EHRM: toenemende Alleingang?', *Asiel & Migratierecht*, 2016.

Langheld 2016
G.C. Langheld, 'Multilingual Norms in European Criminal Law', in: *Legal Certainty in a Contemporary Context. Private and Criminal Law Perspectives*, M. Fenwick and S. Wrbka (eds.), Signapore: Springer 2016.

Lautenbach 2013
G. Lautenbach, *The Concept of the Rule of Law and the European Court of Human Rights*, Oxford: Oxford University Press 2013.

Leanza 2014
P. Leanza, 'Article 6 ECHR', in: *The Right to a Fair Trial. Article 6 of the European Convention on Human Rights*, P. Leanza and O. Pridal (eds.), Alphen aan de Rijn: Wolters Kluwer 2014.

Lelieur, Pfützner and Volz 2008
J. Lelieur, P. Pfützner and S. Volz, 'Das Gesetzlichkeitsprinzip in Frankreich', in: *Nationales Strafrecht in rechtsvergleichender Darstellung. Allgemeiner Teil. Band 2: Gesetzlichkeitprinzip, Internationaler Geltungsbereich des Strafrechts, Begriff und Systematieserung der Straftat*, U. Sieber and K. Cornils (eds.), Berlin: Duncker & Humblot 2008.

Lenaerts, Arts, Maselis and Bray 2006
K. Lenaerts, D. Arts, I. Maselis and R. Bray, *Procedural Law of the European Union*, London: Sweet & Maxwell 2006.

Lenaerts and Gutiérrez-Fons 2016
K. Lenaerts and J.A. Gutiérrez-Fons, 'The European Court of Justice and fundamental rights in the field of criminal law', in: *Research Handbook on EU Criminal Law*, V. Mitsilegas, M. Bergström and T. Konstadinides (eds.), Cheltenham, Northampton: Edward Elgar 2016.

Letsas 2007
G. Letsas, *A Theory of Interpretation of the European Convention on Human Rights*, Oxford: Oxford University Press 2007.

Locke 1690
J. Locke, 'The Second Treatise of Government', in: *The Second Treatise of Government and A Letter Concerning Toleration*, T. Crawford (ed.), Mineola: Dover Publications 1690 (2002).

Loughlin 2012
M. Loughlin, 'The political jurisprudence of Thomas Hobbes', in: *Hobbes and the Law*, D. Dyzenhaus and T.M. Poole (eds.), Cambridge: Cambridge University Press 2012.

Luchtman 2013
M.J.J.P. Luchtman, 'Choice of forum and the prosecution of cross-border crime in the European Union – What role for the legality principle?', in: *Choice of forum in cooperation against EU financial crime – Freedom, security and justice and the protection of specific EU-interests*, M.J.J.P. Luchtman (ed.), The Hague: Eleven 2013.

MacCormick 2005
N. MacCormick, *Rhetoric and The Rule of Law: A Theory of Legal Reasoning*, Oxford: Oxford University Press 2005.

Maestro 1973
M. Maestro, *Cesare Beccaria and the Origins of Penal Reform*, Philadelphia: Temple University Press 1973.

Manes 2017
V. Manes, 'Common law-ization of criminal law'? The evolution of nullum crimen sine lege and the forthcoming challenges', *New Journal of European Criminal Law*, 2017.

Masferrer 2013
A. Masferrer, 'Principle of Legality and Codification in the Western Criminal Law Reform', in: *From the Judge's Arbitrium to the Legality Principle. Legislation as a Source of Law in Criminal Trials*, G. Martyn, A. Musson and H. Pihlajamäki (eds.), Berlin: Duncker & Humblot 2013.

Mayaud 2015
Y. Mayaud, *Droit pénal général*, Paris: Presses Universitaires de France 2015.

Merli 2016
F. Merli, 'Principle of Legality and the Hierarchy of Norms', in: *Strengthening the Rule of Law in Europe. From a Common Concept to Mechanisms of Implementation*, W. Schroeder (ed.), Oxford, Portland: Hart Publishing 2016.

Merry 1970
H.J. Merry, *Montesquieu's System of Natural Government*, West Lafayette: Purdue University Studies 1970.

Miettinen 2013
S. Miettinen, *Criminal Law and Policy in the European Union*, London, New York: Routledge 2013.

Miglietti 2014
M. Miglietti, 'The First Exercise of Article 83(2) TFEU Under Review: An Assessment of the Essential Need of Introducing Criminal Sanctions', *New Journal of European Criminal Law*, 2014.

Mitsilegas 2009
V. Mitsilegas, *EU Criminal Law*, Oxford, Portland: Hart Publishing 2009.

Mitsilegas 2014
V. Mitsilegas, 'EU Criminal Law Competence after Lisbon: From Securitised to Functional Criminalisation', in: *EU Security and Justice Law. After Lisbon and Stockholm*, C.C. Murphy D. Acosta Arcarazo (eds.), Oxford, Portland: Hart Publishing 2014.

Mitsilegas 2014a
V. Mitsilegas, 'Article 49 – Principles of Legality and Proportionality', in: *The EU Charter of Fundamental Rights*, T. Hervey S. Peers, J. Kenner, A. Ward (eds.), Oxford, Portland: Hart Publishing 2014.

Mitsilegas 2016
V. Mitsilegas, *EU Criminal Law After Lisbon. Rights, Trust and the Transformation of Justice in Europe*, Oxford, Portland: Hart Publishing 2016.

Möllers 2013
C. Möllers, *The Three Branches: A Comparative Model of Separation of Powers*, Oxford: Oxford University Press 2013.

Montesquieu 1748
Montesquieu, *The Spirit of the Laws*, Cambridge: Cambridge University Press 1748 (2011).

Morre 2015
H. Morre, 'Artikel 7. Geen straf zonder wet', in: *Sdu Commentaar EVRM. Deel 1 – Materiële bepalingen*, J.H. Gerards, Y. Haeck, P. de Hert, M.K.G. Tjepkema, J. van der Velde and A.J.TH. Woltjer (eds.), Den Haag: Sdu Uitgevers 2015.

Mowbray 2015
A. Mowbray, 'Subsidiarity and the European Convention on Human Rights', *Human Rights Law Review*, 2015.

Munday 2001
R. Munday, 'Le principe de la légalité en droit Anglais et dans les pays de Common Law', *Revue pénitentiaire et de droit pénal*, 2001.

Murphy 2010
C.C. Murphy, 'The principle of legality in criminal law under the European Convention on Human Rights', *European Human Rights Law Review*, 2010.

Nan 2011
J.S. Nan, *Het Lex certa-beginsel*, The Hague: Sdu Publishers 2011.

Naucke 1989
W. Naucke, 'Die Modernisierung des Strafrechts durch Beccaria', in: *Cesare Beccaria. Die Anfänge moderner Strafrechtsplege in Europa*, G. Deimling (ed.), Heidelberg: Kriminalistik Verlag 1989.

Norrie 2001
A. Norrie, *Crime, Reason and History. A Critical Introduction to Criminal Law*, London: Butterworths 2001.

O'Boyle, Harris, Bates and Buckley 2014
M. O'Boyle, D. Harris, E. Bates and C. Buckley, *Harris, O'Boyle & Warbrick: Law of the European Convention on Human Rights*, Oxford: Oxford University Press 2014.

Packer 1969
H.L. Packer, *The Limits of the Criminal Sanction*, Stanford: Stanford University Press 1969.

Pangle 1973
T.L. Pangle, *Montesquieu's Philosophy of Liberalism. A Commentary on The Spirit of the Laws*, Chicago, London: The University of Chicago Press 1973.

Panzavolta 2013
M. Panzavolta, 'Is the Glass Half Empty or Half Full? Twenty Years of EU Cooperation in Criminal Matters', in: *The Treaty on European Union 1993–2013: Reflections from Maastricht*, M. de Visser and A. P. van der Mei (eds.), Cambridge, Antwerp, Portland: Intersentia 2013.

Peers 2014
S. Peers, 'Justice and Home Affairs Law since the Treaty of Lisbon: A Fairy-Tale Ending?', in: *EU Security and Justice Law. After Lisbon and Stockholm*, C.C. Murphy D. Acosta Arcarazo (eds.), Oxford, Portland: Hart Publishing 2014.

Peers and Prechal 2014
S. Peers and S. Prechal, 'Article 52 – Scope of Guaranteed Rights', in: *The EU Charter of Fundamental Rights*, T. Hervey S. Peers, J. Kenner, A. Ward (eds.), Oxford, Portland: Hart Publishing 2014.

Peers 2016a
S. Peers, *EU Justice and Home Affairs Law: Volume I: EU Immigration and Asylum Law*, Oxford: Oxford University Press 2016.

Peers 2016b
S. Peers, EU Justice and Home Affairs Law: Volume II: EU Criminal Law, Policing, and Civil Law, fourth edition., Oxford: Oxford University Press 2016.

Peristeridou 2011
C. Peristeridou, 'The principle of lex certa in national law and European perspectives', in: *Substantive Criminal Law of the European Union*, A. Klip (ed.), Antwerpen [etc]: Maklu 2011.

Peristeridou 2015
C. Peristeridou, *The Principle of Legality in European Criminal Law*, Cambridge, Antwerp, Portland: Intersentia 2015.

Pin 2016
X. Pin, *Droit pénal général*, Paris: Dalloz 2016.

Popović 2014
D. Popović, 'Judicial Creativity', in: *Courts, Interpretation, The Rule of Law*, M. Jovanović and K.E. Himma (eds.), The Hague: Eleven International Publishing 2014.

Pradel 2014
J. Pradel, *Droit pénal général*, Paris: Éditions Cujas 2014.

Prechal 2005
S. Prechal, *Directives in EC Law*, Oxford: Oxford University Press 2005.

Rahe 2001
P.A. Rahe, 'Forms of Government: Structure, Principle, Object and Aim', in: *Montesquieu's Science of Politics. Essays on The Spirit of Laws*, D.W. Caritthers, M.A. Mosher and P.A. Rahe (eds.), Lanham: Rowman & Littlefield Publishers 2001.

Ramacci 2013
F. Ramacci, *Corso di diritto penale*, Torino: Giappichelli 2013.

Raulus 2011
H. Raulus, 'Fundamental Rights in the Area of Freedom, Security and Justice', in: *Freedom, Security and Justice after Lisbon and Stockholm*, F. Goudappel S. Wolff, J. de Zwaan (eds.), The Hague: T.M.C. Asser Press 2011.

Raz 1979
J. Raz, 'The Rule of Law and its Virtue', in: *The authority of law: Essays on law and morality*, Oxford: Oxford University Press 1979.

Rebut 2001
D. Rebut, 'Le principe de la légalité des délits et des peines', *Revue pénitentiaire et de droit pénal*, 2001.

Renout 2012
H. Renout, *Droit pénal général*, Bruxelles: Larcier 2012.

Reuter 1989
L. Reuter, 'Die Ansichten des Marchese von Beccaria zu den Strafgesetzen, Verbrechen und Strafen – Strafgesetze, Strafjustiz und strafrechtliches Denken im 18. Jahrhundert', in: *Cesare Beccaria. Die Anfänge moderner Strafrechtsplege in Europa*, G. Deimling (ed.), Heidelberg: Kriminalistik Verlag 1989.

Richter 1977
M. Richter, *The political theory of Montesquieu*, Cambridge: Cambridge University Press 1977.

Rijpma 2013
J.J. Rijpma, 'The Third Pillar of the Maastricht Treaty: The Coming Out of Justice and Home Affairs', in: *The Treaty on European Union 1993–2013: Reflections from Maastricht*, M. de Visser and A. P. van der Mei (eds.), Cambridge, Antwerp, Portland: Intersentia 2013.

Ristroph 2012
A. Ristroph, 'Criminal law for humans', in: *Hobbes and the Law*, D. Dyzenhaus and T.M. Poole (eds.), Cambridge: Cambridge University Press 2012.

Sanz-Caballero 2017
S. Sanz-Caballero, 'The Principle of Nulla Poena Sine Lege Revisited: The Retrospective Application of Criminal Law in the Eyes of the European Court of Human Rights', *The European Journal of International Law*, 2017.

Sarmiento 2013
D. Sarmiento, 'Who's afraid of the Charter? The Court of Justice, national courts and the new framework of fundamental rights protection in Europe', *Common Market Law Review*, 2013.

Satzger 2012
H. Satzger, *International and European Criminal Law*, München: C.H. Beck 2012.

Satzger 2012a
H. Satzger, 'Le Principe de Légalité', in: *Le droit pénal de l'Union européenne au lendemain du Traité de Lisbonne*, C. Lazerges G. Giudicelli-Delage (eds.), Paris: Société de législation comparée 2012.

Scalia 2012
D. Scalia, *Du principe de légalité des peines en droit international pénal*, Bruxelles: Bruylant 2012.

Schabas 2015
W.A. Schabas, *The European Convention on Human Rights. A Commentary*, Oxford: Oxford University Press 2015.

Schoep 2010
A. Schoep, 'The Judicial Branch: A Partner in the Business of Governing Security?', in: *Governing Security under the Rule of Law?*, J. Blad, M. Hildebrandt, K. Rozemond, M. Schuilenburg and P. Van Calster (eds.), The Hague: Eleven International Publishing 2010.

Schönfeld 1979
K.M. Schönfeld, *Montesquieu en 'La Bouche de la Loi'*, Leiden: New Rhine Publishers 1979.

Schreiber 1976
H.-L. Schreiber, *Gesetz und Richter. Zur geschichtlichen Entwicklung des Satzes nullum crimen, nulla poena sine lege*, Frankfurt am Main: Alfred Metzner Verlag 1976.

Schroeder 2016
W. Schroeder, 'The European Union and the Rule of Law – State of Affairs and Ways of Strengthening', in: *Strengthening the Rule of Law in Europe. From a Common Concept to Mechanisms of Implementation*, W. Schroeder (ed.), Oxford, Portland: Hart Publishing 2016.

Schünemann 1978
B. Schünemann, *Nulla poena sine lege? Rechtstheoretische und verfassungsrechtliche Implikationen der Rechtsgewinnung im Strafrecht*, Berlin, New York: Walter de Gruyter 1978.

Schuhr 2012
J.C. Schuhr, 'Der "Grundsatz der Gesetzmässigkeit der Strafen" im Recht der Europäischen Union', in: *Gesetzlichkeit und Strafrecht*, H. Kudlich, J.P. Montiel and J.C. Schuhr (eds.), Berlin: Duncker & Humblot 2012.

Senden 2011
H. Senden, *Interpretation of Fundamental Rights in a Multilevel Legal System. An analysis of the European Court of Human Rights and the Court of Justice of the European Union*, Cambridge, Antwerp, Portland: Intersentia 2011.

Sharpston 2010
E. Sharpston, 'Transparency and Clear Legal Language in the European Union: Ambiguous Legislative Texts, Laconic Pronouncements and the Credibility of the Judicial System', *Cambridge Yearbook of European Legal Studies*, 2010.

Sicurella 2016
R. Sicurella, 'EU competence in criminal matters', in: *Research Handbook on EU Criminal Law*, V. Mitsilegas, M. Bergström and T. Konstadinides (eds.), Cheltenham, Northampton: Edward Elgar 2016.

Silva Sánchez 2012
J.-M. Silva Sánchez, 'Gesetzeauslegung und strafrechtliche Interpretationskultur', in: *Gesetzlichkeit und Strafrecht*, H. Kudlich, J.P. Montiel and J.C. Schuhr (eds.), Berlin: Duncker & Humblot 2012.

Simester and Sullivan 2007
A.P. Simester and G.R. Sullivan, *Criminal Law Theory and Doctrine*, Oxford and Portland: Hart Publishing 2007.

Simmons 1992
A.J. Simmons, *The Lockean Theory of Rights*, Princeton: Princeton University Press 1992.

Soleil 2013
S. Soleil, '"Lex Imperat": Creation and Exportation of the French Model of the Legality Principle (18th-19th C.)', in: *From the Judge's Arbitrium to the Legality Principle. Legislation as a Source of Law in Criminal Trials*, G. Martyn, A. Musson and H. Pihlajamäki (eds.), Berlin: Duncker & Humblot 2013.

Soltetz 2012
U. Soltesz, 'Due process and judicial review – mixed signals from Luxembourg in cartel cases', *European Competition Law Review*, 2012.

Spano 2014
R. Spano, 'Universality or Diversity of Human Rights? Strasbourg in the Age of Subsidiarity', *Human Rights Law Review*, 2014.

Spaventa 2007
E. Spaventa, 'Opening Pandora's Box: Some Reflections on the Constitutional Effects of the Decision in Pupino', *European constitutional law review*, 2007.

Spencer 2014
J.R. Spencer, 'EU criminal law', in: *European Union Law*, C. Barnard and S. Peers (eds.), Oxford: Oxford University Press 2014.

Steiner 2016
E. Steiner, 'The Rule of Law in the Jurisprudence of the European Court of Human Rights', in: *Strengthening the Rule of Law in Europe. From a Common Concept to Mechanisms of Implementation*, W. Schroeder (ed.), Oxford, Portland: Hart Publishing 2016.

Stevenson and Harris 2010
K. Stevenson and C. Harris, 'Breaking the Thrall of Ambiguity: Simplification (of the Criminal Law) as an Emerging Human Rights Imperative', *The Journal of Criminal Law*, 2010.

Strauss 1953
L. Strauss, *Natural Right and History*, Chicago and London: The University of Chicago Press 1953 (1971).

Sudre 2001
F. Sudre, 'Le principe de la légalité et et la Jurisprudence de la Cour européenne des droits de l'homme', *Revue pénitentiaire et de droit pénal*, 2001.

Summers, Schwarzenegger, Ege and Young 2014
S. Summers, C. Schwarzenegger, G. Ege and F. Young, *The Emergence of EU Criminal Law. Cybercrime and the Regulation of the Information Society*, Oxford, Portland: Hart Publishing 2014.

Tamanaha 2004
B.Z. Tamanaha, *On the Rule of Law. History, Politics, Theory*, Cambridge: Cambridge University Press 2004.

The European Criminal Policy Initiative 2011
The European Criminal Policy Initiative, 'The Manifesto on European Criminal Policy in 2011', *European Criminal Law Review*, 2011.

Timmerman 2015
M.A.P. Timmerman, 'Case Note Rohlena v. Czech Republic', *European Human Rights Cases*, 2015.

Timmerman 2016
M. Timmerman, 'Balancing effective criminal sanctions with effective fundamental rights protection in cases of VAT fraud: Taricco', *Common Market Law Review*, 2016.

Timmerman 2016a
M.A.P. Timmerman, 'Case Note Dallas v. The United Kingdom', *European Human Rights Cases*, 2016.

Torres Pérez 2009
A. Torres Pérez, *Conflicts of Rights in the European Union: A Theory of Supranational Adjudication*, Oxford: Oxford University Press 2009.

Tridimas 2011
T. Tridimas, 'Constitutional review of member state action: the virtues and vices of an incomplete jurisdiction', *International Journal of Constitutional Law*, 2011.

Tridimas 2015
T. Tridimas, 'The ECJ and the national courts. Dialogue, cooperation and instability', in: *The Oxford Handbook of European Law*, A. Arnull and D. Chalmers (eds.), Oxford: Oxford University Press 2015.

Tully 1993
J. Tully, *An approach to political philosophy: Locke in contexts*, Cambridge: Cambridge University Press 1993.

Valentini 2011
V. Valentini, 'European Criminal Justice and Continental Criminal Law –A Critical Overview', *European Criminal Law Review*, 2011.

Van Bael 2011
I. Van Bael, *Due Process in EU Competition Proceedings*, Alphen aan den Rijn: Kluwer Law International 2011.

Van Bockel and Wattel 2014
B. van Bockel and P. Wattel, 'New wine into old wineskins: the scope of the Charter of Fundamental Rights of the EU after Akerberg Fransson', *European Law Review*, 2014.

Van de Heyning 2011
C. van de Heyning, *No place like home. Discretionary space for the domestic protection of fundamental rights', in: Human rights protection in the European legal order. The interaction between the European and the national* courts, Cambridge, Anwerp, Portland: Intersentia 2011.

Van Dijk and Viering 2006
P. van Dijk and M. Viering, 'Right to a Fair and Public Hearing (Article 6)', in: *Theory and Practice of the European Convention on Human Rights*, P. van Dijk, F. van Hoof, A. van Rijn and L. Zwaak (eds.), Antwerpen, Oxford: Intersentia 2006.

Van Kempen and Van Elst 2006
P.H.P.H.M.C. van Kempen and R. van Elst, 'Ongehoorzaamheid van de strafrechter aan het EHRM en HvJEG. Gemotiveerde afwijking van Europese rechtspraak en de noodzaak tot dialoog', in: *De ongehoorzame rechter. Rechters versus andere rechters, de wetgever, de bevolking en het Europees recht*, L.E. de Groot-van Leeuwen, A.M.A.P. van den Bossche and Y. Buruma (eds.), Deventer: Kluwer 2006.

Van Kempen and Fedorova 2015
P.H.P.H.M.C. van Kempen and M.I. Fedorova, *'Foreign terrorist fighters': strafbaarstelling van verblijf op een terroristisch grondgebied? Een toetsing aan materieel strafrechtelijke, mensenrechtelijke en volkenrechtelijke parameters*, Deventer: Kluwer 2015.

Venturi 1971
F. Venturi, *Utopia and Reform in the Enlightenment*, Cambridge: Cambridge University Press 1971.

Viljanen 2003
J. Viljanen, *The European Court of Human Rights as a Developer of the General Doctrines of Human Rights Law. A Study on the Limitation Clauses of the European Convention on Human Rights*, Tampere: Tampereen yliopisto 2003.

Von Bogdandy 2000
A. von Bogdandy, 'The European Union as a Human Rights Organization? Human Rights and the Core of the European Union', *Common Market Law Review*, 2000.

Von Feuerbach 1801
P.J.A. von Feuerbach, *Lehrbuch des gemeinen in Deutschland gültigen penlichen Rechts*, Giessen: Georg Friedrich Heyer 1801 (1836).

Von Hirsch and Husak 1993
A. Von Hirsch and D. Husak, 'Culpability and Mistake of Law', in: *Action and Value in Criminal Law*, J. Gardner S. Shute, J. Horder (eds.), Oxford: Oxford University Press 1993.

Walter 2007
C. Walter, 'History and Development of European Fundamental Rights and Fundamental Freedoms', in: *European Fundamental Rights and Freedoms*, Berlin: De Gruyter Recht 2007.

Ward 2014
A. Ward, 'Article 51 – Field of Application', in: *The EU Charter of Fundamental Rights*, T. Hervey S. Peers, J. Kenner, A. Ward (eds.), Oxford, Portland: Hart Publishing 2014.

Westen 2007
P. Westen, 'Two Rules of Legality in Criminal Law', *Law and Philosophy*, 2007.

Whelan 2012
P. Whelan, 'Legal Certainty and Cartel Criminalisation within the EU Member States', *The Cambridge Law Journal*, 2012.

Whelan 2014
P. Whelan, 'European Antitrust Criminalization and the Challenge of Legal Certainty', in: *The Criminalization of European Cartel* Enforcement, Oxford: Oxford University Press 2014.

White and Ovey 2017
B. Rainey, E. Wicks and C. Ovey, *Jacobs, White, and Ovey The European Convention on Human Rights*, Oxford: Oxford University Press 2017.

Williams 2015
A. Williams, 'Human Rights in the EU', in: *The Oxford Handbook of European Law*, A. Arnull and D. Chalmers (eds.), Oxford: Oxford University Press 2015.

Wils 2014
W.P.J. Wils, 'The Compatibility with Fundamental Rights of the EU Antitrust Enforcement System in Which the European Commission Acts Both as Investigator and as First-Instance Decision Maker', *World Competition*, 2014.

Wilson 1998
W. Wilson, *Criminal Law. Doctrine and Theory*, London and New York: Longman 1998.

Zetterquist 2011
O. Zetterquist, 'The Charter of Fundamental Rights and the European Res Publica', in: *The EU Charter of Fundamental Rights*, G. Di Frederico (ed.): Dordrecht, New York: Springer 2011.

Zwaak 2006
L. Zwaak, 'General Survey of the European Convention', in: *Theory and Practice of the European Convention on Human Rights*, P. van Dijk, F. van Hoof, A. van Rijn and L. Zwaak (eds.), Antwerpen, Oxford: Intersentia 2006.

2. CASE-LAW

COUNCIL OF EUROPE

EComHR

- 24 September 1963, Appl. no. 1169/61 (admissibility decision), *X. v. Germany*, CE:ECHR:1963:0924DEC000116961.
- 6 July 1976, Appl. no. 7512/76 (admissibility decision), *X. v. The Netherlands*, CE:ECHR:1976:0706DEC000751276.
- 7 May 1982, Appl. no. 8710/79 (admissibility decision), *X. Ltd and Y. v. United Kingdom*, CE:ECHR:1982:0507DEC000871079.
- 6 March 1989, Appl. no. 13079/87 (admissibility decision), *G. v. Germany*, CE:ECHR:1989:0306DEC001307987.
- 12 January 1995, Appl.no. 21915/93 (admissibility decision), *Lukanov v. Bulgaria*, CE:ECHR:1997:0320JUD002191593.
- 13 January 1997, Appl. no. 29420/95 (admissibility decision), *Touvier v. France*, CE:ECHR:1997:0113DEC002942095.
- 12 December 2001, Appl. no. 52207/99 (admissibility decision), *Banković and Others v. Belgium*, CE:ECHR:2001:1212DEC005220799.

ECtHR

- 1 July 1961, Appl. no. 332/57, *Lawless v. Ireland (No. 3)*, CE:ECHR:1960:1114JUD000033257.
- 8 June 1976, Appl. nos. 5100/71; 5101/71; 5102/71; 5354/72; 5370/72, *Engel and Others v. The Netherlands*, CE:ECHR:1976:0608JUD000510071.
- 7 December 1976, Appl. no. 5493/72, *Handyside v. The United Kingdom*, CE:ECHR:1976:1207JUD000549372.
- 26 April 1979, Appl. no. 6538/74, *Sunday Times v. The United Kingdom*, CE:ECHR:1979:0426JUD000653874.
- 24 October 1979, Appl. no. 6301/73, *Winterwerp v. The Netherlands*, CE:ECHR:1979:1024JUD000630173.
- 13 August 1981, Appl. nos. 7601/76; 7806/77, *Young, James and Webster v. The United Kingdom*, CE:ECHR:1981:0813JUD000760176.
- 21 February 1984, Appl. no. 8544/79, *Öztürk v. Germany*, CE:ECHR:1984:0221JUD000854479.
- 7 July 1989, Appl. no. 14038/88, *Soering v. The United Kingdom*, CE:ECHR:1989:0707JUD001403888.
- 28 March 1990, Appl. no. 10890/84, *Groppera Radio AG and others v. Switzerland*, CE:ECHR:1990:0328JUD001089084.
- 27 September 1990, Appl. no. 10843/84, *Cossey v. The United Kingdom*, CE:ECHR:1990:0927JUD001084384.
- 20 January 1992, Appl. no. 12963/87, *Margareta and Roger Andersson v. Sweden*, CE:ECHR:1992:0225JUD001296387.
- 25 May 1993, Appl. no. 14307/88, *Kokkinakis v. Greece*, CE:ECHR:1993:0525JUD001430788.

- 9 February 1995, Appl. no. 17440/90, *Welch v. The United Kingdom*, CE:ECHR:1995:0209JUD001744090.
- 23 March 1995, Appl. no. 15318/89, *Loizidou v. Turkey* (preliminary objections), CE:ECHR:1995:0323JUD001531889.
- 8 June 1995, Appl. no. 15917/89, *Jamil v. France*, CE:ECHR:1995:0608JUD001591789.
- 27 September 1995, Appl. no. 15312/89, *G. v. France*, CE:ECHR:1995:0927JUD001531289.
- 22 November 1995, Appl. no. 20190/92, *C.R. v. The United Kingdom*, CE:ECHR:1995:1122JUD002019092.
- 22 November 1995, Appl. no. 20166/92, *S.W. v. The United Kingdom*, CE:ECHR:1995:1122JUD002016692.
- 11 November 1996, Appl. no. 17862/91, *Cantoni v. France*, CE:ECHR:1996:1115JUD001786291.
- 25 November 1997, Appl. no. 24348/94, *Grigoriades v. Greece*, CE:ECHR:1997:1125JUD002434894.
- 24 February 1998, Appl. no. 23372/94, *Larissis and Others v. Greece*, CE:ECHR:1998:0224JUD002337294.
- 20 May 1999, Appl. no. 25390/94, *Rekvényi v. Hungary*, CE:ECHR:1999:0520JUD002539094.
- 8 July 1999, Appl. nos. 23536/94; 24408/94, *Başkaya and Okçuoğlu v. Turkey*, CE:ECHR:1999:0708JUD002353694.
- 8 July 1999, Appl. nos. 25067/94; 25068/94, *Erdoğdu and İnce v. Turkey*, CE:ECHR:1999:0708JUD002506794.
- 8 July 1999, Appl. no. 23500/94, *Polat v. Turkey*, CE:ECHR:1999:0708JUD002350094.
- 4 June 2000, Appl. no. 26629/95, *Witold Litwa v. Poland*, CE:ECHR:2000:0404JUD002662995.
- 22 June 2000, Appl. nos. 32492/96; 32547/96; 32548/96; 33209/96; 33210/96, *Coëme and Others v. Belgium*, CE:ECHR:2000:0622JUD003249296.
- 26 October 2000, Appl. no. 30210/96, *Kudła v. Poland*, CE:ECHR:2000:1026JUD003021096.
- 27 February 2001, Appl. nos. 29295/95; 29363/95, *Ecer and Zeyrek v. Turkey*, CE:ECHR:2001:0227JUD002929595.
- 22 March 2001, Appl. no. 37201/97, *K.-H. W. v. Germany*, CE:ECHR:2001:0322JUD003720197.
- 22 March 2001, Appl. nos. 34044/96; 35532/97;44801/98, *Streletz, Kessler and Krenz v. Germany*, CE:ECHR:2001:0322JUD003404496.
- 25 September 2001, Appl. no. 44787/98, *P.G. and J.H. v. The United Kingdom*, CE:ECHR:2001:0925JUD004478798.
- 11 December 2001, Appl. no. 53059/99 (admissibility decision), *Savvas Kyriakides v. Cyprus*, CE:ECHR:2001:1211DEC005305999.
- 29 April 2002, Appl. no. 2346/02, *Pretty v. The United Kingdom*, CE:ECHR:2002:0429JUD000234602.
- 11 July 2002, Appl. no. 28957/95, *Goodwin v. The United Kingdom*, CE:ECHR:2002:0711JUD002895795.
- 21 January 2003, Appl. no. 45771/99, *Veeber v. Estonia (No. 2)*, CE:ECHR:2003:0121JUD004577199.

- 10 July 2003, Appl. no. 43522/98, *Grava v. Italy*, CE:ECHR:2003:0710JUD004352298.
- 22 July 2003, Appl. no. 68066/01, *Gabarri Moreno v. Spain*, CE:ECHR:2003:0722JUD006806601.
- 9 October 2003, Appl. nos. 39665/98; 40086/98, *Ezeh and Connors v. The United Kingdom*, CE:ECHR:2003:1009JUD003966598.
- 10 February 2004, Appl. no. 55103/00, *Puhk v. Estonia*, CE:ECHR:2004:0210JUD005510300.
- 30 March 2004, Appl. no. 53984/00, *Radio France and Others v. France*, CE:ECHR:2004:0330JUD005398400.
- 20 April 2004, Appl. no. 60115/00, *Amihalachioaie v. Moldova*, CE:ECHR:2004:0420JUD006011500.
- 13 July 2004, Appl. no. 69498/01, *Pla and Puncernau v. Andorra*, CE:ECHR:2004:1110JUD003123696.
- 10 November 2004, Appl. no. 31236/96, *Kalin v. Turkey*, CE:ECHR:2004:1110JUD003123696.
- 17 February 2005, Appl. nos. 42758/98; 45558/99, *K.A. and A.D. v. Belgium*, CE:ECHR:2005:0217JUD004275898.
- 30 June 2005, Appl. no. 45036/98, *Bosphorus Hava Yolları Turizm ve Ticaret Anonim Şirketi v. Ireland*, CE:ECHR:2005:0630JUD004503698.
- 17 January 2006, Appl. nos. 23052/04; 24018/04 (admissibility decision), *Kolk and Kislyiy v. Estonia*, CE:ECHR:2006:0117DEC002305204.
- 29 March 2006, Appl. no. 67335/01, *Achour v. France*, CE:ECHR:2006:0329JUD006733501.
- 10 October 2006, Appl. no. 40403/02, *Pessino v. France*, CE:ECHR:2006:1010JUD004040302.
- 23 November 2006, Appl. no. 73053/01, *Jussila v. Finland*, CE:ECHR:2006:1123JUD007305301.
- 3 May 2007, Appl. nos. 11843/03; 11847/03; 11849/03, *Custers, Deveaux and Turk v. Denmark*, CE:ECHR:2007:0503JUD001184303.
- 24 May 2007, Appl. nos. 77193/01; 77196/01, *Dragotoniu and Militaru-Pidhorni v. Romania*, CE:ECHR:2007:0524JUD007719301.
- 12 July 2007, Appl. no. 74613/01, *Jorgic v. Germany*, CE:ECHR:2007:0712JUD007461301.
- 12 February 2008, Appl. no. 21906/04, *Kafkaris v. Cyprus*, CE:ECHR:2008:0212JUD002190604.
- 19 February 2008, Appl. nos. 74357/01; 26764/02; 27434/02, *Kuolelis, Bartoševičius and Burokevičius v. Lithuania*, CE:ECHR:2008:0219JUD007435701.
- 19 September 2008, Appl. no. 9174/02, *Korbely v. Hungary*, CE:ECHR:2008:0919JUD000917402.
- 9 October 2008, Appl. no. 62936/00, *Moiseyev v. Russia*, CE:ECHR:2008:1009JUD006293600.
- 20 January 2009, Appl. no. 75909/01, *Sud Fondi SRL and others v. Italy*, CE:ECHR:2009:0120JUD007590901.
- 17 March 2009, Appl. no. 13113/03 (admissibility decision), *Ould Dah v. France*, CE:ECHR:2009:0317DEC001311303.

- 25 June 2009, Appl. no. 12157/05, *Liivik v. Estonia*, CE:ECHR:2009:0625JUD001215705.
- 17 September 2009, Appl. no. 10249/03, *Scoppola v. Italy (No. 2)*, CE:ECHR:2012:0522JUD000012605.
- 15 December 2009, Appl. no. 16012/06, *Gurhuchiani v. Spain*, CE:ECHR:2009:1215JUD001601206.
- 17 December 2009, Appl. no. 16428/05, *Gardel v. France*, CE:ECHR:2009:1217JUD001642805.
- 17 December 2009, Appl. no. 19359/04, *M. v. Germany*, CE:ECHR:2009:1217JUD001935904.
- 12 January 2010, Appl. no. 4158/05, *Gillan and Quinton v. The United Kingdom*, CE:ECHR:2010:0112JUD000415805.
- 6 April 2010, Appl. no. 25576/04, *Flinkkilä and Others v. Finland*, CE:ECHR:2010:0406JUD002557604.
- 6 April 2010, Appl. no. 43349/05, *Jokitaipale and Others v. Finland*, CE:ECHR:2010:0406JUD004334905.
- 6 April 2010, Appl. no. 25711/04, *Tuomela and Others v. Finland*, CE:ECHR:2010:0406JUD002571104.
- 17 May 2010, Appl. no. 36376/04, *Kononov v. Latvia*, CE:ECHR:2010:0517JUD003637604.
- 10 June 2010, Appl. no. 302/02, *Jehovah's Witnesses of Moscow and Others v. Russia*, CE:ECHR:2010:0610JUD000030202.
- 6 January 2011, Appl. no. 34932/04, *Paksas v. Lithuania*, CE:ECHR:2011:0106JUD003493204.
- 25 January 2011, Appl. no. 30865/08, *Reinboth and Others v. Finland*, CE:ECHR:2011:0125JUD003086508.
- 14 April 2011, Appl. no. 30060/04, *Jendrowiak v. Germany*, CE:ECHR:2011:0414JUD003006004.
- 21 June 2011, Appl. no. 8014/07, *Fruni v. Slovakia*, CE:ECHR:2011:0621JUD000801407.
- 9 September 2011, Appl. no. 32820/08 (admissibility decision), *Boumaraf v. France*, CE:ECHR:2011:0830DEC003282008.
- 27 September 2011, Appl. no. 43509/08, *Menarini Diagnostics S.R.L. v. Italy*, CE:ECHR:2011:0927JUD004350908.
- 6 October 2011, Appl. no. 50425/06, *Soros v. France*, CE:ECHR:2011:1006JUD005042506.
- 24 January 2012, Appl. no. 1051/06, *Mihai Toma v. Romania*, CE:ECHR:2012:0124JUD000105106.
- 7 February 2012, Appl. no. 20134/05, *Alimuçaj v. Albania*, CE:ECHR:2012:0207JUD002013405.
- 6 March 2012, Appl. no. 54468/09, *Huhtamäki v. Finland*, CE:ECHR:2012:0306JUD005446809.
- 15 March 2012, Appl. nos. 39692/09; 40713/09; 41008/09, *Austin and Others v. The United Kingdom*, CE:ECHR:2012:0315JUD003969209.
- 22 January 2013, Appl. no. 42931/10, *Camilleri v. Malta*, CE:ECHR:2013:0122JUD004293110.

- 5 February 2013, Appl. no. 23341/06, *Martirosyan v. Armenia*, CE:ECHR: 2013:0205JUD002334106.
- 12 February 2013, Appl. no. 1845/08 (admissibility decision), *Previti v. Italy*, CE: ECHR:2013:0212DEC000184508.
- 14 March 2013, Appl. nos. 26261/05; 26377/06, *Kasymakhunov and Saybatalov v. Russia*, CE:ECHR:2013:0314JUD002626105.
- 11 April 2013, Appl. no. 20372/11, *Vyerentsov v. Ukraine*, CE:ECHR:2013:0411JUD 002037211.
- 18 July 2013, Appl. nos. 2312/08; 34179/08, *Maktouf and Damjanović v. Bosnia and Herzegovina*, CE:ECHR:2013:0718JUD000231208.
- 25 July 2013, Appl. nos. 11082/06; 13772/05, *Khodorkovskiy and Lebedev v. Russia*, CE:ECHR:2013:0725JUD001108206.
- 21 October 2013, Appl. no. 42750/09, *Del Río Prada v. Spain*, CE:ECHR:2013:1021 JUD004275009.
- 29 October 2013, Appl. no. 17475/09, *Varvara v. Italy*, CE:ECHR:2013:1029JUD 001747509.
- 28 November 2013, Appl. no. 7345/12, *Glien v. Germany*, CE:ECHR:2013:1128JUD 000734512.
- 15 July 2014, Appl. no. 45554/08, *Ashlarba v. Georgia*, CE:ECHR:2014:0715JUD 004555408.
- 16 September 2014, Appl. no. 1660/03, *Plechkov v. Romania*, CE:ECHR:2014: 0916JUD000166003.
- 27 January 2015, Appl. no. 59552/08, *Rohlena v. The Czech Republic*, CE:ECHR: 2015:0127JUD005955208.
- 14 April 2015, Appl. no. 66655/13, *Contrada v. Italy (No. 3)*, CE:ECHR:2015:0414 JUD006665513.
- 3 September 2015, Appl. no. 42875/10, *Berland v. France*, CE:ECHR:2015:0903JUD 004287510.
- 20 October 2015, Appl. no. 35343/05, *Vasiliauskas v. Lithuania*, CE:ECHR:2015: 1020JUD003534305.
- 7 January 2016, Appl. no. 23279/14, *Bergmann v. Germany*, CE:ECHR:2016:0107 JUD002327914.
- 11 February 2016, Appl. no. 38395/12, *Dallas v. The United Kingdom*, CE:ECHR:2016:0211JUD003839512.
- 12 May 2016, Appl. nos. 26711/07; 32786/10; 34278/10, *Poletan and Azirovik v. the former Yugoslav Republic of Macedonia*, CE:ECHR:2016:0512JUD002671107.
- 23 May 2016, Appl. no. 17502/07, *Avotiņš v. Latvia*, CE:ECHR:2016:0523JUD 001750207.
- 1 September 2016, Appl. no. 48158/11, *X and Y v. France*, CE:ECHR:2016:0901JUD 004815811.
- 4 October 2016, Appl. no. 37462/09, *Žaja v. Croatia*, CE:ECHR:2016:1004JUD 003746209.
- 6 October 2016, Appl. no. 55594/13, *W.P. v. Germany*, CE:ECHR:2016:1006JUD 005559413.
- 29 November 2016, Appl. no. 76943/11, *Lupeni Greek Catholic Parish and Others v. Romania*, CE:ECHR:2016:1129JUD007694311.

- 24 January 2017, Appl. no. 67503/13, *Koprivnikar v. Slovenia*, CE:ECHR:2017:0124 JUD006750313.
- 2 February 2017, Appl. nos. 10211/12; 27505/14, *Ilnseher v. Germany*, CE:ECHR: 2017:0202JUD001021112.

EUROPEAN UNION

CJEU

- 5 February 1963, Case 26/62, *NV Algemene Transport- en Expeditie Onderneming van Gend & Loos v Netherlands Inland Revenue Administration*, EU:C:1963:1.
- 12 November 1969, Case 29/69, *Erich Stauder v City of Ulm, Sozialamt*, EU:C:1969:57.
- 6 October 1970, Case 9/70, *Franz Grad v Finanzamt Traunstein*, EU:C:1970:78.
- 17 December 1970, Case 11/70, *Internationale Handelsgesellschaft mbH v Einfuhr- und Vorratsstelle für Getreide und Futtermittel*, EU:C:1970:114.
- 10 October 1973, Case 34/73, *Fratelli Variola S.p.A. v Amministrazione italiana delle Finanze*, EU:C:1973:101.
- 14 May 1974, Case 4/73, *J. Nold, Kohlen- und Baustoffgrosshandlung v Commission of the European Communities*, EU:C:1974:51.
- 4 December 1974, Case 41/74, *Yvonne van Duyn v Home Office*, EU:C:1974:133.
- 28 October 1975, Case 36/75, *Roland Rutili v Ministre de l'intérieur*, EU:C:1975:137.
- 2 February 1977, Case 50/76, *Amsterdam Bulb BV v Produktschap voor Siergewassen*, EU:C:1977:13.
- 14 July 1977, Case 8/77, *Criminal proceedings against Concetta Sagulo, Gennaro Brenca and Addelmadjid Bakhouche*, EU:C:1977:131.
- 13 February 1979, Case 85/76, *Hoffman-La Roche & Co. AG v Commission of the European Communities*, EU:C:1979:36.
- 5 April 1979, Case 148/78, *Criminal proceedings against Tullio Ratti*, EU:C:1979:110.
- 13 December 1979, Case 44/79, *Liselotte Hauer v Land Rheinland-Pfalz*, EU:C:1979:290.
- 11 November 1981, Case 203/80, *Criminal Proceedings against Guerrino Casati*, EU:C:1981:261.
- 28 March 1984, Case 8/83, *Officine Fratelli Bertoli SpA v Commission of the European Communities*, EU:C:1984:129.
- 10 April 1984, Case 14/83, *Sabine Von Colson and Elisabeth Kamann v Land Nordrhein-Westfalen*, EU:C:1984:153.
- 10 July 1984, Case 63/83, *Regina v Kent Kirk*, EU:C:1984:255.
- 25 September 1984, Case 117/83, *Karl Könecke GmbH & Co. KG, Fleischwarenfabrik v Bundesanstalt für landwirtschaftliche Marktordnung*, EU:C:1984:288.
- 26 February 1986, Case 152/84, *M.H. Marshall v Southampton and South-West Hampshire Area Health Authority (Teaching)*, EU:C:1986:84.
- 27 February 1986, Case 238/84, *Criminal proceedings against Hans Röser*, EU:C:1986:88.
- 15 May 1986, Case C-222/84, *Marguerite Johnston v Chief Constable of the Royal Ulster Constabulary*, EU:C:1986:206.
- 11 June 1987, Case 14/86, *Pretore di Salò v X*, EU:C:1987:275.

- 8 October 1987, Case 80/86, *Criminal proceedings against Kolpinghuis Nijmegen*, EU:C:1987:431.
- 2 February 1989, Case 186/87, *Ian William Cowan v Le Trésor public*, EU:C:1989:47.
- 13 July 1989, Case 5/88, *Hubert Wachauf v Bundesamt für Ernährung und Forstwirtschaft*, EU:C:1989:321.
- 21 September 1989, Case 68/88, *Commission of the European Communities v Hellenic Republic (Greek maize)*, EU:C:1989:339.
- 21 September 1989, Joined Cases 46/87 and 227/88, *Hoechst AG v Commission of the European Communities*, EU:C:1989:337.
- 13 November 1990, Case C-331/88, *The Queen v Minister of Agriculture, Fisheries and Food and Secretary of State for Health, ex parte: Fedesa and others*, EU:C:1990:391.
- 18 June 1991, Case C-260/89, *Elliniki Radiophonia Tiléorassi AE and Panellinia Omospondia Syllogon Prossopikou v Dimotiki Etairia Pliroforissis and Sotirios Kouvelas and Nicolaos Avdellas and others (ERT)*, EU:C:1991:254.
- 27 October 1992, Case C-240/90, *Federal Republic of Germany v Commission of the European Communities*, EU:C:1992:408.
- 14 July 1994, Case C-352/92, *Milchwerke Köln/Wuppertal eG v Hauptzollamt Köln-Rheinau*, EU:C:1994:294.
- 14 July 1994, Case C-91/92, *Paola Faccini Dori v Recreb Srl*, EU:C:1994:292.
- 30 April 1996, Case C-13/94, *P v S and Cornwall County Council*, EU:C:1996:170.
- 26 September 1996, Case C-168/95, *Criminal proceedings against Luciano Arcaro*, EU:C:1996:363.
- 12 December 1996, Joined Cases C-74/95 and C-129/95, *Criminal proceedings against X*, EU:C:1996:491.
- 25 June 1997, Joined Cases C-304/94, C-330/94, C-342/94 and C-224/95, *Criminal proceedings against Euro Tombesi and Others*, EU:C:1997:314.
- 8 July 1999, Case C-186/98, *Criminal Proceedings against Maria Amélia Nunes and Evangelina de Matos*, EU:C:1999:376.
- 14 December 2000, Case C-110/99, *Emsland-Stärke GmbH v Hauptzollamt Hamburg-Jonas*, EU:C:2000:695.
- 16 May 2002, Case C-63/00, *Land Baden-Württemberg v Günther Schilling and Bezirksregierung Lüneburg v Hans-Otto Nehring*, EU:C:2002:296.
- 17 September 2002, Case C-253/00, *Antonio Muñoz y Cia SA and Superior Fruiticola SA v Frumar Ltd and Redbridge Produce Marketing Ltd*, EU:C:2002:497.
- 26 September 2002, Case T-199/99, *Sgaravatti Mediterranea Srl v Commission of the European Communities*, EU:T:2002:228.
- 7 January 2004, Case C-60/02, *Criminal proceedings against X*, EU:C:2004:10.
- 15 January 2004, Case C-235/02, *Criminal proceedings against Marco Antonio Saetti and Andrea Frediani*, EU:C:2004:26.
- 25 March 2004, Joined Cases C-231/00, C-303/00 and C-451/00, *Cooperativa Lattepiù arl and Others*, EU:C:2004:178.
- 15 July 2004, Case C-459/02, *Willy Gerekens and Association agricole pour la promotion de la commercialisation laitière Procola v État du grand-duché de Luxembourg*, EU:C:2004:454.
- 11 November 2004, Case C-457/02, *Criminal proceedings against Antonio Niselli*, EU:C:2004:707.

- 3 May 2005, Joined Cases C-387/02, C-391/02 and C-403/02, *Criminal Proceedings against Silvio Berlusconi and Others*, EU:C:2005:270.
- 16 June 2005, Case C-105/03, *Criminal proceedings against Maria Pupino*, EU:C:2005:386.
- 28 June 2005, Joined Cases C-189/02 P, C-202/02 P, C-205/02 P TO C-208/02 P and C-213/02 P, *Danske Rørindustri and Others v Commission of the European Communities*, EU:C:2005:408.
- 13 September 2005, Case C-176/03, *Commission v Council*, EU:C:2005:542.
- 22 November 2005, Case C-384/02, *Criminal proceedings against Knud Grøngaard and Allan Bang*, EU:C:2005:708.
- 21 February 2006, Case C-255/02, *Halifax plc, Leeds Permanent Development Services Ltd and County Wide Property Investments Ltd v Commissioners of Customs & Excise*, EU:C:2006:121.
- 5 April 2006, Case T-279/02, *Degussa AG v Commission of the European Communities*, EU:T:2006:103.
- 18 May 2006, Case C-397/03 P, *Archer Daniels Midland Co. and Archer Daniels Midland Ingredients Ltd v Commission of the European Communities*, EU:C:2006:328.
- 27 September 2006, Case T-43/02, *Jungbunzlauer AG v Commission of the European Communities*, EU:T:2006:270.
- 8 February 2007, Case C-3/06 P, *Groupe Danone v Commission of the European Communities*, EU:C:2007:88.
- 13 March 2007, Case C-432/05, *Unibet (London) Ltd and Unibet (International) Ltd v Justitiekanslern*, EU:C:2007:163.
- 3 May 2007, Case C-303/05, *Advocaten voor de Wereld VZW v Leden van de Ministerraad*, EU:C:2007:261.
- 23 October 2007, Case C-440/05, *Commission v Council*, EU:C:2007:625.
- 22 May 2008, Case C-266/06 P, *Evonik Degussa GmbH v Commission of the European Communities*, EU:C:2008:295.
- 3 June 2008, Case C-308/06, *The Queen, on the application of International Association of Independent Tanker Owners (Intertanko) and Others v Secretary of State for Transport*, EU:C:2008:312.
- 8 July 2008, Case T-99/04, *AC-Treuhand AG v Commission of the European Communities*, EU:T:2008:256.
- 3 September 2008, Joined cases C-402/05 P and C-415/05 P, *Yassin Abdullah Kadi and Al Barakaat International Foundation v Council of the European Union and Commission of the European Communities*, EU:C:2008:461.
- 8 October 2008, Case T-69/04, *Schunk GmbH and Schunk Kohlenstoff-Technik GmbH v Commission of the European Communities*, EU:T:2008:415.
- 19 March 2009, Case C-510/06 P, *Archer Daniels Midland Co. v Commission of the European Communities*, EU:C:2009:166.
- 2 April 2009, Case C-421/07, *Criminal proceedings against Frede Damgaard*, EU:C:2009:222.
- 23 December 2009, Case C-45/08, *Spector Photo Group NV, Chris Van Raemdonck v Commissie voor het Bank-, Financie- en Assurantiewezen (CBFA)*, EU:C:2009:806.
- 28 April 2010, Case T-446/05, *Amann & Söhne GmbH & Co. KG and Cousin Filterie SAS v European Commission*, EU:T:2010:165.

- 29 April 2010, Case C-340/08, *The Queen, on the application of M and Others v Her Majesty's Treasury*, EU:C:2010:232.
- 29 June 2010, Case C-550/09, *Criminal proceedings against E and F*, EU:C:2010:382.
- 30 September 2010, Case T-85/09, *Yassin Abdullah Kadi v European Commission*, EU:T:2010:418.
- 7 October 2010, Case C-224/09, *Criminal proceedings against Martha Nussbaumer*, EU:C:2010:594.
- 28 October 2010, Case C-367/09, *Belgische Interventie- en Restitutiebureau v SGS Belgium NV and Others*, EU:C:2010:648.
- 29 March 2011, Case C-352/09, *ThyssenKrupp Nirosta GmbH v European Commission*, EU:C:2011:191.
- 31 March 2011, Case C-546/09, *Aurubis Balgaria AD v Nachalnik na Mitnitsa Stolichna*, EU:C:2011:199.
- 16 June 2011, Case T-240/07, *Heineken Nederland BV and Heineken NV v European Commission*, EU:T:2011:284.
- 10 November 2011, Case C-405/10, *Criminal proceedings against Özlem Garenfeld*, EU:C:2011:722.
- 8 December 2011, Case C-386/10 P, *Chalkor AE Epexergasias Metallon v European Commission*, EU:C:2011:815.
- 21 December 2011, Case C-72/11, *Criminal proceedings against Mohsen Afrasiabi and Others*, EU:C:2011:874.
- 2 February 2012, Case T-83/08, *Denki Kagaku Kogyo Kabushiki Kaisha and Denka Chemicals GmbH v European Commission*, EU:T:2012:48.
- 14 February 2012, Case C-17/10, *Toshiba Corporation and Others v Úřad pro ochranu hospodářské soutěže*, EU:C:2012:72.
- 5 June 2012, Case C-489/10, *Criminal proceedings against Łukasz Marcin Bonda*, EU:C:2012:319.
- 28 June 2012, Case C-7/11, *Criminal proceedings against Fabio Caronna*, EU:C:2012:396.
- 24 April 2012, Case C-571/10, *Servet Kamberaj v Istituto per l'Edilizia Sociale della Provincia autonoma di Bolzano (IPES) and Others*, EU:C:2012:233.
- 6 November 2012, Case C-199/11, *Europese Gemeenschap v Otis NV and Others*, EU:C:2012:684.
- 12 November 2012, Case T-76/11, *Kingdom of Spain v European Commission*, EU:T:2012:613.
- 26 February 2013, Case C-617/10, *Åklagaren v Hans Åkerberg Fransson*, EU:C:2013:105.
- 26 February 2013, Case C-399/11, *Stefano Melloni v Ministerio Fiscal*, EU:C:2013:107.
- 18 July 2013, Case C-501/11 P, *Schindler Holding Ltd and Others v European Commission*, EU:C:2013:522.
- 16 September 2013, Case T-386/10, *Aloys F. Dornbracht GmbH & Co. KG v European Commission*, EU:T:2013:450.
- 16 September 2013, Joined Cases T-373/10, T-374/10, T-382/10 and T-402/10, *Villeroy & Boch Austria GmbH and Villeroy & Boch AG v European Commission*, EU:T:2013:455.

- 6 February 2014, Case T-27/10, *AC-Treuhand AG v European Commission*, EU:T:2014:59.
- 27 February 2014, Case T-256/11, *Ahmed Abdelaziz Ezz and Others v Council of the European Union*, EU:T:2014:93.
- 6 March 2014, Case C-206/13, *Cruciano Siragusa v Regione Sicilia – Soprintendenza Beni Culturali e Ambientali di Palermo*, EU:C:2014:126.
- 27 March 2014, Cases T-56/09 and T-73/09, *Saint-Gobain Glass France SA and Others v European Commission*, EU:T:2014:160.
- 8 April 2014, Case C-293/12, *Digital Rights Ireland Ltd v Minister for Communications*, EU:C:2014:238.
- 30 April 2014, Case C-390/12, *Proceedings brought by Robert Pfleger and Others*, EU:C:2014:281.
- 12 June 2014, Case T-286/09, *Intel Corp. v European Commission*, EU:T:2014:547.
- 10 July 2014, Case C-198/13, *Víctor Manuel Julian Hernández and Others v Reino de España (Subdelegación del Gobierno de España en Alicante) and Others*, EU:C:2014:2055.
- 11 July 2014, Case T-541/08, *Sasol and Others v European Commission*, EU:T:2014:628.
- 18 December 2014, Joined Cases C-131/13, C-163/13 and C-164/13, *Staatssecretaris van Financiën v Schoenimport 'Italmoda' Mariano Previti vof*, EU:C:2014:2455.
- 18 December 2014, *Opinion 2/13*, EU:C:2014:2454.
- 5 March 2015, Case C-220/14 P, *Ahmed Abdelaziz Ezz and Others v Council of the European Union*, ECLI:EU:C:2015:147.
- 18 June 2015, Case C-583/13 P, *Deutsche Bahn AG and Others v European Commission*, EU:C:2015:404.
- 9 July 2015, Case C-607/13, *Ministero dell'Economia e delle Finanze and Others v Francesco Cimmino and Others*, EU:C:2015:448.
- 3 September 2015, Case C-398/13 P, *Inuit Tapiriit Kanatami and Others v European Commission*, EU:C:2015:535.
- 8 September 2015, Case C-105/14, *Criminal proceedings against Ivo Taricco and Others*, EU:C:2015:555.
- 9 September 2015, Case T-92/13, *Koninklijke Philips Electronics NV v European Commission*, EU:T:2015:605.
- 22 October 2015, Case C-194/14 P, *AC-Treuhand AG v European Commission*, EU:C:2015:717.
- 17 December 2015, Case C-419/14, *WebMindLicenses kft v Nemzeti Adó- és Vámhivatal Kiemelt Adó- és Vám Főigazgatóság*, EU:C:2015:832.
- 15 February 2016, Case C-601/15 PPU, *J. N. v Staatssecretaris van Veiligheid en Justitie*, EU:C:2016:84.
- 19 April 2016, Case C-441/14, *Dansk Industri (DI) v Estate of Karsten Eigil Rasmussen*, EU:C:2016:278.
- 2 June 2016, Cases T-426/10 to T-429/10 and T-438/12 to T-441/12, *Moreda-Riviere Trefilerías, SA and Others v European Commission*, EU:T:2016:335.
- 2 June 2016, Case C-81/15, *Kapnoviomichania Karelia AE v Ypourgos Oikonomikon*, EU:C:2016:398.
- 30 June 2016, Case T-545/13, *Fahed Mohamed Sakher Al Matri v Council of the European Union*, EU:T:2016:376.

- 8 September 2016, Case T-470/13, *Merck KGaA v European Commission*, EU:T:2016:452.
- 8 September 2016, Case T-467/13, *Arrow Group ApS and Arrow Generics Ltd v European Commission*, EU:T:2016:450
- 8 September 2016, Case T-460/13, *Sun Pharmaceutical Industries Ltd, formerly Ranbaxy Laboratories Ltd and Ranbaxy (UK) Ltd v European Commission*, EU:T:2016:453.
- 8 September 2016, Case T-472/13, *H. Lundbeck A/S and Lundbeck Ltd v European Commission*, EU:T:2016:449.
- 21 September 2016, Case C-592/14, *European Federation for Cosmetic Ingredients v Secretary of State for Business, Innovation and Skills and Attorney General*, EU:C:2016:703.
- 6 October 2016, Case C-218/15, *Criminal proceedings against Gianpaolo Paoletti and Others*, EU:C:2016:748.
- 8 November 2016, Case C-554/14, *Criminal proceedings against Atanas Ognyanov*, EU:C:2016:835.
- 8 November 2016, Case C-243/15, *Lesoochranárske zoskupenie VLK v Obvodný úrad Trenčín*, EU:C:2016:838.
- 8 December 2016, Case C-453/15, *Criminal proceedings against A and B*, EU:C:2016:933.
- 15 December 2016, Case T-758/14, *Infineon Technologies AG v European Commission*, EU:T:2016:737.
- 26 January 2017, Case C-604/13 P, *Aloys F. Dornbracht GmbH & Co. KG v European Commission*, EU:C:2017:45.
- 26 January 2017, Case C-625/13 P, *Villeroy & Boch AG v European Commission*, EU:C:2017:52.
- 16 February 2017, Case C-90/15 P, *Hansen & Rosenthal KG and H&R Wax Company Vertrieb GmbH v European Commission*, EU:C:2017:123.
- 2 March 2017, Case C-584/15, *Glencore Céréales France v Établissement national des produits de l'agriculture et de la mer (FranceAgriMer)*, EU:C:2017:160.
- 7 March 2017, Case C-638/16, *PPU, X and X v État belge*, EU:C:2017:173.
- 28 March 2017, Case C-72/15, *PJSC Rosneft Oil Company v Her Majesty's Treasury and Others*, EU:C:2017:236.
- 5 April 2017, Joined Cases C-217/15 and C-350/15, *Criminal proceedings against Massimo Orsi and Luciano Baldetti*, EU:C:2017:264.
- 26 October 2017, Case C-534/16, *Finančné riaditeľstvo Slovenskej republiky v BB construct s. r. o.*, EU:C:2017:820.
- 26 October 2017, Case T-704/14, *Marine Harvest ASA v European Commission*, EU:T:2017:753.
- 5 December 2017, Case C-42–17, *Criminal proceedings against M.A.S. and M.B. (Taricco II)*, EU:C:2017:936.

Opinions Advocates General CJEU

- Opinion of Advocate General Reischl in Case 85/76, *Hoffman-La Roche & Co. AG v Commission of the European Communities*, EU:C:1978:162.

- Opinion of Advocate General Jacobs in Joined Cases C-206/88 and C-207/88, *Criminal proceedings against G. Vessoso and G. Zanetti*, EUC:1989:644.
- Opinion of Advocate General Mischo in Case C-331/88, *The Queen v Minister of Agriculture, Fisheries and Food and Secretary of State for Health, ex parte: Fedesa and others*, EU:C:1990:109.
- Opinion of Advocate General Elmer in Case C-168/95, *Criminal proceedings against Luciano Arcaro*, EU:C:1996:107.
- Opinion of Advocate General Ruiz-Jarabo Colomer in Joined Cases C-74/95 and C-129/95, *Criminal proceedings against X*, EU:C:1996:239.
- Opinion of Advocate General Jacobs in Joined Cases C-304/94, C-330/94, C-342/94 and C-224/95, *Criminal proceedings against Euro Tombesi and Others*, EU:C:1996:399.
- Opinion of Advocate General Léger in Case C-63/00, *Land Baden-Württemberg v Günther Schilling and Bezirksregierung Lüneburg v Hans-Otto Nehring*, EU:C:2001:497.
- Opinion of Advocate General Jacobs in Case C-198/01, *Consorzio Industrie Fiammiferi (CIF) v Autorità Garante della Concorrenza e del Mercato*, EU:C:2003:58.
- Opinion of Advocate General Ruiz-Jarabo Colomer in Case C-60/02, *Criminal proceedings against X*, EU:C:2003:326.
- Opinion of Advocate General Kokott in Case C-457/02, *Criminal proceedings against Antonio Niselli*, EU:C:2004:365.
- Opinion of Advocate General Tizzano in Joined Cases C-189/02 P, C-202/02 P, C-205/02 P TO C-208/02 P and C-213/02 P, *Danske Rørindustri and Others v Commission of the European Communities*, EU:C:2004:415.
- Opinion of Advocate General Kokott in Joined Cases C-387/02, C-391/02 and C-403/02, *Criminal Proceedings against Silvio Berlusconi and Others*, EU:C:2004:624.
- Opinion of Advocate General Kokott in Case C-105/03, *Criminal proceedings against Maria Pupino*, EU:C:2005:386.
- Opinion of Advocate General Ruiz-Jarabo Colomer in Case C-303/05, *Advocaten voor de Wereld VZW v Leden van de Ministerraad*, EU:C:2006:552.
- Opinion of Advocate General Bot in Case C- 76/06 P, *Britannia Alloys & Chemicals Ltd v Commission of the European Communities*, EU:C:2007:128.
- Opinion of Advocate General Kokott in Case C-308/06, *The Queen, on the application of International Association of Independent Tanker Owners (Intertanko) and Others v Secretary of State for Transport*, EU:C:2007:689.
- Opinion of Advocate General Ruiz-Jarabo Colomer in Case C-297/07, *Criminal proceedings against Klaus Bourquain*, EU:C:2008:206.
- View of Advocate General Kokott in Case C-296/08 PPU, *Ignacio Pedro Santesteban Goicoechea*, EU:C:2008:455.
- Opinion of Advocate General Mengozzi in Case C-340/08, *The Queen, on the application of M and Others v Her Majesty's Treasury*, EU:C:2010:13.
- View of Advocate General Mengozzi in Case C-550/09, *Criminal proceedings against E and F*, EU:C:2010:272.
- Opinion of Advocate General Kokott in Case C-367/09, *Belgische Interventie- en Restitutiebureau v SGS Belgium and Others*, EU:C:2010:440.
- Opinion of Advocate General Bot in Case C-352/09, *ThyssenKrupp Nirosta GmbH v European Commission*, EU:C:2010:635.

- Opinion of Advocate General Kokott in Cases C-403/08 and C-429/08, *Football Association Premier League Ltd and Others v QC Leisure and Others and Karen Murphy v. Media Protection Services Ltd*, EU:C:2011:43.
- Opinion of Advocate General Bot in Case C- 72/11, *Criminal proceedings against Mohsen Afrasiabi and Others*, EU:C:2011:737.
- Opinion Advocate General Kokott in Case C-489/10, *Criminal proceedings against Łukasz Marcin Bonda*, EU:C:2011:845.
- Opinion of Advocate General Sharpston in Case C-79/11, *Criminal proceedings against Maurizio Giovanardi and Others*, EU:C:2012:297.
- Opinion of Advocate General Szpunar in Joined Cases C-131/13, C-163/13 and C-164/13, *Staatssecretaris van Financiën v Schoenimport 'Italmoda' Mariano Previti vof*, EU:C:2014:2217.
- Opinion of AG Kokott in Case C-105/14, *Criminal proceedings against Ivo Taricco and Others*, EU:C:2015:293.
- Opinion of Advocate General Wahl in Case C-194/14 P, *AC-Treuhand AG v European Commission*, EU:C:2015:350.
- Opinion of Advocate General Bot in Case C-81/15, *Kapnoviomichania Karelia AE v Ypourgos Oikonomikon*, EU:C:2016:66.
- Opinion of Advocate General Bobek in C-592/14, *European Federation for Cosmetic Ingredients v Secretary of State for Business, Innovation and Skills and Attorney General*, EU:C:2016:179.
- Opinion of AG Saugmandsgaard Øe in Case C-119/15, *Biuro podróży 'Partner' Sp. z o.o, Sp. komandytowa w Dąbrowie Górniczej v Prezes Urzędu Ochrony Konkurencji i Konsumentów*, EU:C:2016:387.
- Opinion of Advocate General Wathelet in Case C-453/15, *Criminal proceedings against A and B*, EU:C:2016:639.
- Opinion of Advocate General Tanchev in Case C-102/16, *Vaditrans BVBA v Belgische Staat*, EU:C:2017:82.
- Opinion of Advocate General Mengozzi in Case C-638/16 PPU, *X and X v État belge*, EU:C:2017:93.
- Opinion of Advocate General Bobek in Case C-111/16, *Criminal proceedings against Giorgio Fidenato and Others*, EU:C:2017:248.
- Opinion of Advocate General Bobek in Case C 574/15, *Proceedings against Mauro Scialdone*, EU:C:2017:553.
- Opinion of Advocate General Bot in Case C-42/17, *Criminal proceedings against M.A.S. and M.B. (Taricco II)*, EU:C:2017:564.

NATIONAL COURTS

England

House of Lords, R. v. R. [1992] 1 AC 599.

Italy

Corte costituzionale, Order no. 24 of 2017 (in English translation available at www.cortecostituzionale.it/documenti/download/doc/recent_judgments/O_24_2017.pdf).

The Netherlands
Hoge Raad, 7 January 1997, NL:HR:1997:ZD0608.

3. LEGISLATION AND POLICY DOCUMENTS

COUNCIL OF EUROPE

- High Level Conference on the Future of the European Court of Human Rights, Interlaken Declaration, 19 February 2010.
- Venice Commission, Report on the Rule of Law, CDL-AD(2011)003rev.
- Joint communication from ECtHR and ECJ Presidents Costa and Skouris of 17 January 2011.

EUROPEAN UNION

- Joint Declaration by the European Parliament, the Council and the Commission, [1977] OJ C103/1.
- Treaty on European Union (Maastricht Treaty), [1992] OJ C 191.
- Treaty of Amsterdam amending the Treaty on European Union, the Treaties establishing the European Communities and certain related acts, [1997] OJ C 340.
- Guidelines on the method of setting fines imposed pursuant to Article 15(2) of Regulation No 17 and Article 65(5) of the ECSC Treaty, [1998] OJ C 9.
- Treaty of Nice amending the Treaty on European Union, the Treaties establishing the European Communities and certain related acts, [2001] OJ C 80.
- Council Framework Decision 2001/220/JHA of 15 March 2001 on the standing of victims in criminal proceedings [2001] OJ 2001 L 82.
- Council Framework Decision 2002/584/JHA of 13 June 2002 on the European arrest warrant and the surrender procedures between Member States [2002] OJ L 190.
- Consolidated version of the Treaty on European union, [2002] OJ C 325
- Explanations relating to the Charter of Fundamental Rights, [2007] OJ C303/02.
- Treaty of Lisbon amending the Treaty on European Union and the Treaty establishing the European Community, [2007] OJ C 306.
- Council Framework Decision 2008/913/JHA of 28 November 2008 on combatting certain forms and expressions of racism and xenophobia by means of criminal law [2008] OJ L 328/55.
- Draft Council conclusions of 25 November 2009 on model provisions, guiding the Council's criminal law deliberations, Council doc 16542/1/0
- Joint communication from ECtHR and ECJ Presidents Costa and Skouris of 17 January 2011.
- Communication from the Commission to the European Parliament, the Council, the European Economic and Social Committee and the Committee of the Regions, Towards an EU Criminal Policy: Ensuring the effective implementation of EU policies through criminal law, COM(2011) 573 final.

- European Parliament Resolution of 22 May 2012 on an EU approach to criminal law, (2010/2310 (INI)).
- Consolidated version of the Treaty on European Union, [2012] OJ C 326.
- Proposal for a Directive of the European Parliament and of the Council on the fight against fraud to the Union's financial interest by means of criminal law, COM(2012) 363 final.
- Council Regulation (EU) No 833/2014 of 31 July 2014 concerning restrictive measures in view of Russia's actions destabilising the situation in Ukraine, [2014] OJ L 229.
- Report on the proposal for a Directive of the European Parliament and of the Council on the fight against fraud to the Union's financial interest by means of criminal law, A7–0251/2014.
- Opinion of the European Parliament's legal affairs committee on the legal basis for the proposal for a Directive of the European Parliament and of the Council on the fight against fraud to the Union's financial interests by means of criminal law (COM(2012)0363 – C7–0192/2012 – 2012/0193(COD))
- Position No 4/2017 of the Council at first reading with a view to the adoption of a Directive of the European Parliament and of the Council on the fight against fraud to the Union's financial interests by means of criminal law adopted by the Council on 25 April 2017, [2017] OJ C 184.

www.ingramcontent.com/pod-product-compliance
Ingram Content Group UK Ltd.
Pitfield, Milton Keynes, MK11 3LW, UK
UKHW051920100926
8556IPUK00021B/1280

9 781780 683041